UNIVERSITY OF Southampton
Series In Archaeology No.5

A Multidisciplinary Approach to Alexandria's Economic Past

The Lake Mareotis Research Project

Lucy Blue
Emad Khalil

Assisted by

Athena Trakadas

BAR International Series 2285
2011

Published in 2016 by
BAR Publishing, Oxford

BAR International Series 2285

University of Southampton Series in Archaeology Monographs 5
Series editor: S. Moser

A Multidisciplinary Approach to Alexandria's Economic Past

ISBN 978 1 4073 0862 3

COVER IMAGE *"Reflections on fieldwork in Mareotis" by Julian Whitewright and Darren Glazier.*

DTP by Athena Trakadas

BAR Publishing is the trading name of British Archaeological Reports (Oxford) Ltd. British Archaeological Reports was first incorporated in 1974 to publish the BAR Series, International and British. In 1992 Hadrian Books Ltd became part of the BAR group. This volume was originally published by Archaeopress in conjunction with British Archaeological Reports (Oxford) Ltd / Hadrian Books Ltd, the Series principal publisher, in 2011. This present volume is published by BAR Publishing, 2016.

Printed in England

BAR
PUBLISHING

BAR titles are available from:

BAR Publishing
122 Banbury Rd, Oxford, OX2 7BP, UK
EMAIL info@barpublishing.com
PHONE +44 (0)1865 310431
FAX +44 (0)1865 316916
www.barpublishing.com

Contents

List of Figures

List of Tables

List of Graphs

Foreword and Acknowledgements

Between 2004 and 2008 the Centre for Maritime Archaeology (CMA), University of Southampton and the Department of Underwater Antiquities of the Egyptian Supreme Council for Antiquities (SCA), in conjunction with the Centre for Maritime Archaeology and Underwater Cultural Heritage (CMAUCH), University of Alexandria, conducted five seasons of survey along the shores of the western arm of Lake Mareotis, Alexandria, Egypt. This was to be the first systematic, comprehensive survey of the region, the aim being to more fully appreciate the nature of Lake Mareotis and the role it played in the economy of ancient Alexandria.

An initial visit to the region in 2002 alerted the co-directors of the subsequent project, Lucy Blue (CMA) and Sameh Ramses (SCA), to the huge potential of the area, as well as the immediate threats that the archaeology of the region faced. In collaboration with Emad Khalil (CMAUCH), it was decided that funding to support a project should be sought. Initial help was provided by the British Academy in the form of a Small Grant that funded a pilot season in 2004. During this three-week period over 60 sites were identified along the shores of the western arm of the lake, the majority of which were new discoveries. The potential wealth of the region was thus realised and subsequently further funding was sought and awarded. The project is immensely grateful to the British Academy for both initial Small, and subsequent, Large, Grant support, and to the Leverhulme Trust for awarding a post-doctoral research fellowship to Emad Khalil to undertake more in depth research into the archaeology of the Lake Mareotis/Alexandria region. The Lake Mareotis Research Project (LMRP) as it became known, and this publication, would not have been possible without the generous support of both funding bodies and the permission to undertake the survey granted by the Egyptian Supreme Council of Antiquities. We are indebted to all and to our host institutions, for their support.

This volume is divided into seven chapters. All the chapters are written by the primary authors unless otherwise stated. The first three chapters outline the context of the research and the methodology adopted by the LMRP. Contributions have been made to Chapter 3 by members of the LMRP team, namely Julian Whitewright, Athena Trakadas, Ross Thomas and Darren Glazier. Chapter 4 comments on the results of the ceramic survey and we are very grateful to Roberta Tomber and Ross Thomas, with help from Mervat Yahya, for presenting an extremely comprehensive report. Ahmed Shokry Omar is also thanked for his help with the appendix to this chapter. The ceramic assemblage is critical for understanding both the chronological scope of the material recovered that broadly equates to the mid 4th century BC to the 7th century AD, and the nature of activities at the sites. Chapter 5 sets the physical context and is the partial product of doctoral research undertaken by Clement Flaux of the University of Aix, Marseille/Centre Europeìen de Recherches et d'Enseignement des Geìosciences de l'Environnement, UMR-CNRS/Centre d'Études Alexandrines. The geomorphological survey has provided invaluable new insight into the environmental context in which the archaeological sites should be viewed. Chapter 6 is essentially the meat of the volume. Extending to 177 pages in length, it outlines a catalogue of all the 73 sites recorded as part of the LMRP. Many people contributed to the collection of this material, which outlines and displays, amongst other things, the topographical and archaeological features visible at each site. Julian Whitewright should be particularly congratulated for his excellent work processing, collating and presenting the bulk of the data. Chapter 7 presents some concluding remarks and an attempt is made to reflect on and make sense of the mass of information collated. We are hugely indebted to Athena Trakadas who worked beyond the call of her editorial duties to compile all this work and ensure the high quality of this volume.

This volume represents an enormous amount of work conducted both in the field (over 350 hectares of topographical data has been gathered, and some 12,000 ceramic sherds collected), and in the library, by a large number of people. The team consists of members from all three institutions: Students and staff of the Faculty of Arts, University of Alexandria, with support from faculty members including Prof Mostaffa El Abbadi, Prof Mona Haggag and Prof Mohamed Abdel Ghani; colleagues from the SCA Department of Underwater Antiquities, lead by Sameh Ramses, co-director of the LMRP, whose field experience and keen archaeological eye were invaluable to the success of the project. He headed up a team of colleagues from the SCA including Ahmed Shokry Omar, Magdy Abdala Gazaba, Ibrahim Matwaly, Ehab Fahmy, Sahar el Sayed, Hani Ezz El-Din and Bassem Ibrahim. Finally, thanks to the Southampton crew including John Cooper, Katerina Cooper, Penny Copeland, Graeme Earl, Peter Girdwood, Ben Gummer, Darren Glazier, Dylan Hopkins, Alexander James, Arturo Rey da Silva, Kirsten Rothey, Lucy Semaan, Ross Thomas, Roberta Tomber, Athena Trakadas, Julian Whitewright & Rachel Varghese. None of this would have been possible without a great deal of hard work by all the team members. In addition, we are grateful to the Centre d'Études Alexandrines for logistical support, and of course to our car driver Samir Metwaly. Finally, we thank our anonymous referees who undertook an extremely thorough review of the volume. The reader will be grateful for their input which enabled us to eliminate certain errors and to make substantial improvements to this volume.

Drawing conclusions from the work was and still is, a daunting task and we appreciate that we do not by any means present the final word on Lake Mareotis and its role and its relationship to the great city of Alexandria in the Hellenistic and Roman eras. In fact, we hope that in future, scholars will use this volume as a first stop to explore further specific sites or particular aspects of the archaeology of the region. We intended a maritime, or rather, lacustrine, focus to our research, and thus have only touched on, for example, matters of comparative ceramic assemblages in the region and beyond, and the implications of trade or Romanisation in the region. In addition, we essentially conducted survey and thus our results have breadth but are limited in depth, hence some specific avenues of enquiry, for example the precise agricultural and industrial nature of the sites investigated, have only been hinted at. Importantly, we hope we have raised awareness of the significance of the archaeology of Lake Mareotis. We hope that this will encourage future, more nuanced investigation of the sites, that can really only be further appreciated through excavation. We also hope that this volume has highlighted the fact that archaeological sites around the shores of Lake Mareotis are being lost. It is our hope that the authorities will be altered to the very real threats that these sites face and that measures will be made to protect and preserve them for future investigation.

Lucy Blue
University of Southampton

Emad Khalil
University of Alexandria

Chapter 1. Lake Mareotis and Alexandria: a brief introduction

Alexandria was, by any standards, one of the great cities of the Mediterranean. Since its foundation in 331 BC and for almost a millennium to follow, it was the political, economic and cultural capital of Egypt, and one of the most significant emporia and complex ports in the Hellenistic and Roman world. As such, Greco-Roman Alexandria has been the subject of much historical and archaeological research (Fraser 1972; Haas 1997; Empereur 1998a; Goddio, *et al.* 1998) that has revealed the wealth of the city, much of which was generated by trade through its important and monumental harbour (Fig. 1.1). However, Alexandria had not only the harbours on the sea, but also on Lake Mareotis to the south and west of the city. Lake Mareotis was a vital maritime link between the Mediterranean Sea and the Nile River (Fig. 1.2). Moreover, it is known that the shores of Lake Mareotis supported various agricultural activities and embraced major production centres for different industries such as glass, textiles, pottery and wine, which contributed significantly to the economy of Alexandria and Egypt as a whole. Nevertheless, the role that Lake Mareotis played in the economy of ancient Alexandria has never been fully appreciated, substantial areas along the shores of Lake Mareotis remained unexplored, and the relationship between the Mareotic region and the Alexandrian harbour system has never been investigated in a comprehensive manner.

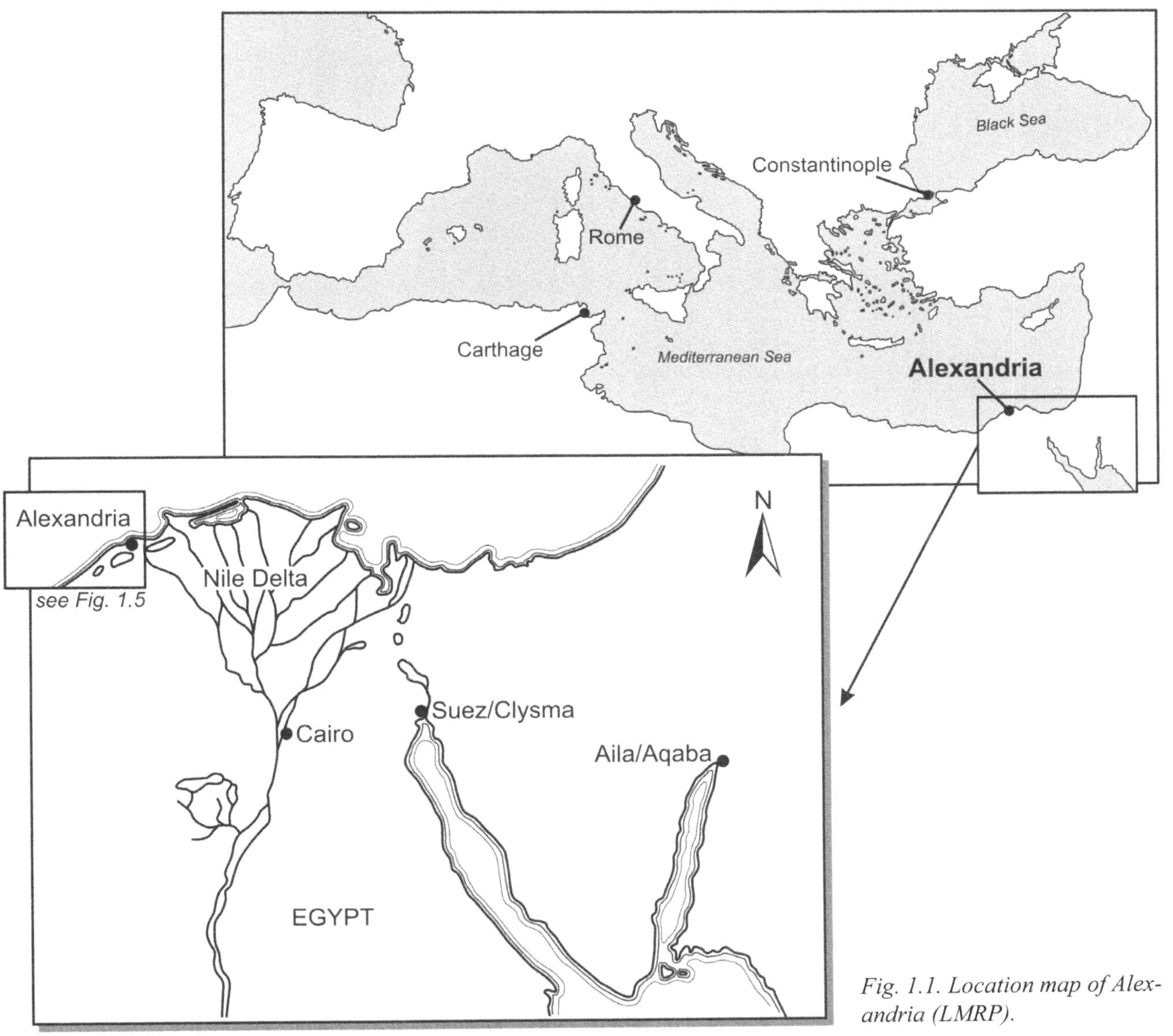

Fig. 1.1. Location map of Alexandria (LMRP).

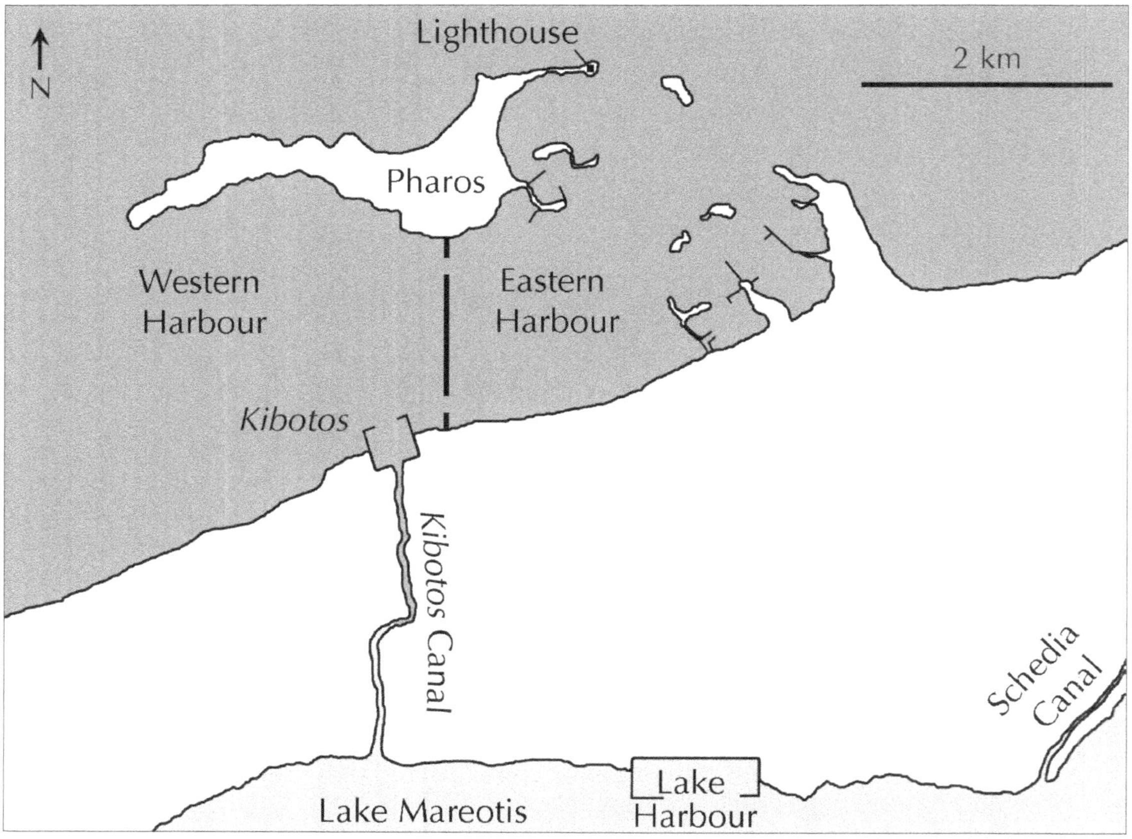

Fig. 1.2. Map of Alexandria in relation to the Mediterranean Sea and Lake Mareotis, also with the location of the maritime harbours and the Lake Harbour (E. Khalil).

Fig. 1.3. Empereur & Picon (1998: 76, fig. 1) amphorae production sites on the shores of Lake Mareotis (with kind permission from J.-Y. Empereur).

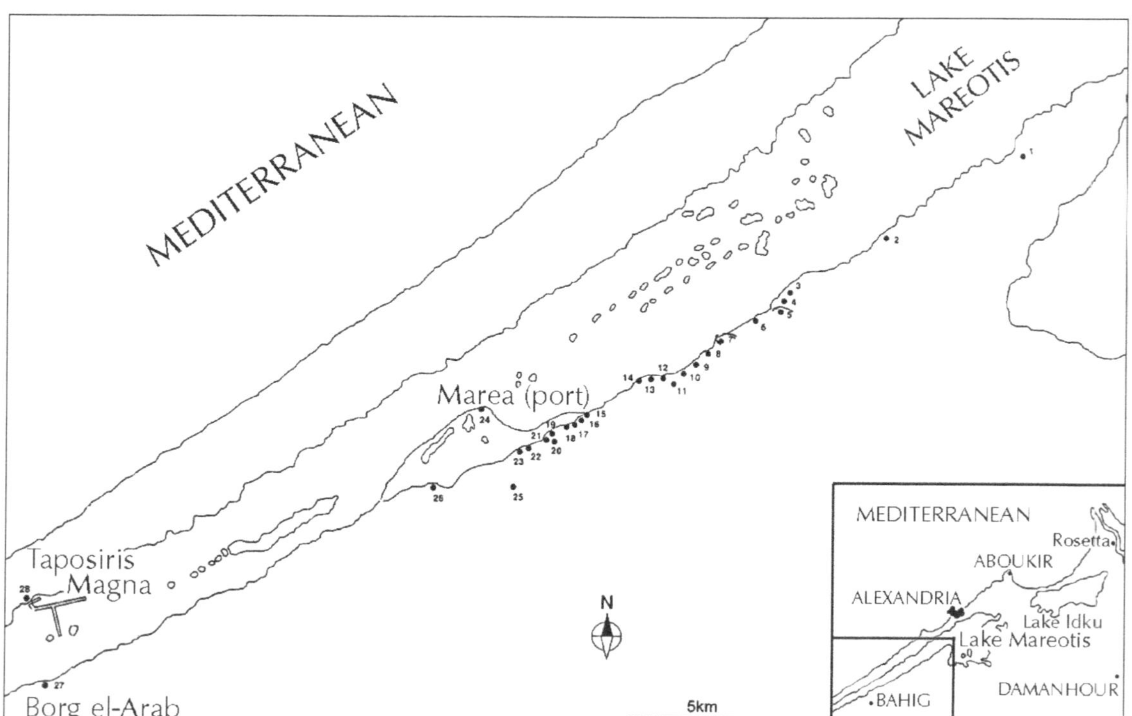

Previous archaeological research conducted along the shores of Lake Mareotis has been largely limited to specified areas and topics, such as the investigation of the sites of Marea and Taposiris Magna (El-Fakharani 1974, 1983; Petruso & Gabel 1982; Rodziewicz 1990, 1998a, 1998b, 2003, 2010; Haggag 2010a, 2010b; Babraj & Szymańska 2010; Pichot 2010; Boussac & El Amouri 2010) and studies carried out by Empereur & Picon (1986, 1992, 1998) of amphorae production in the Mareotis region (also see Dzierzbicka 2010) (Fig. 1.3). Additionally, rescue work has been undertaken by the Supreme Council of Antiquities (SCA) at a number of smaller sites around the shores of the lake largely in advance of development. Moreover, recent investigations conducted in the broader region have helped shed light on the nature of the harbours of Alexandria and aspects of the internal transport system in the Mareotis region. French teams have been investigating the submerged sea harbours of Alexandria, the submerged towns of Herakleion and Canopus at the mouth of the Canopic Branch northeast of the city, and are conducting further work on selected installations at Marea on the southern shores of the lake. A German/British team is conducting a geophysical survey at Schedia, the transhipment settlement at the junction of the Nile to the southeast of Alexandria (see Chapter 2). Thus, research conducted in the region during the past century has begun to highlight the archaeological potential of the area, with archaeological remains ranging in date from the pre-Hellenistic to the Late Antique periods, as well as evidence for large-scale wine and pottery industries, particularly from the Hellenistic and Roman times. However, as yet no comprehensive survey has been conducted, the role that the harbours and maritime installations of Lake Mareotis played in the internal transport system in Egypt has never been fully appreciated, and nor has the extent to which the production centres of the Mareotic region influenced the economy of Alexandria been thoroughly investigated. Thus, the Mareotic region has remained a much-underrated resource particularly with respect to its maritime significance and its economic relationship to Greco-Roman Alexandria and, in many cases, conclusions concerning the Mareotic region's maritime and economic potential have been based on supposition rather than concrete evidence.

Therefore, the principal objective of the Lake Mareotis Research Project (LMRP) is to investigate an important commercial and industrial area which played a significant role in the economy of Greco-Roman Alexandria, namely the Mareotic region, in order to redress this imbalance and acquire a comprehensive understanding of a vital part of Alexandria's hinterland, and its relation to the city's ancient economic systems. Since antiquity, the size and nature of Lake Mareotis has changed significantly, to the extent that at present most of the lake has dried out and became integrated into the western Deltaic region (Fig. 1.4) (see Chapter 2 for more detail). However, it is believed that the western extremities of Lake Mareotis do in fact reflect the extant remains of the original lake that have not been subject to dramatic change since antiquity, and that they support the largest and most extant settlements that have been

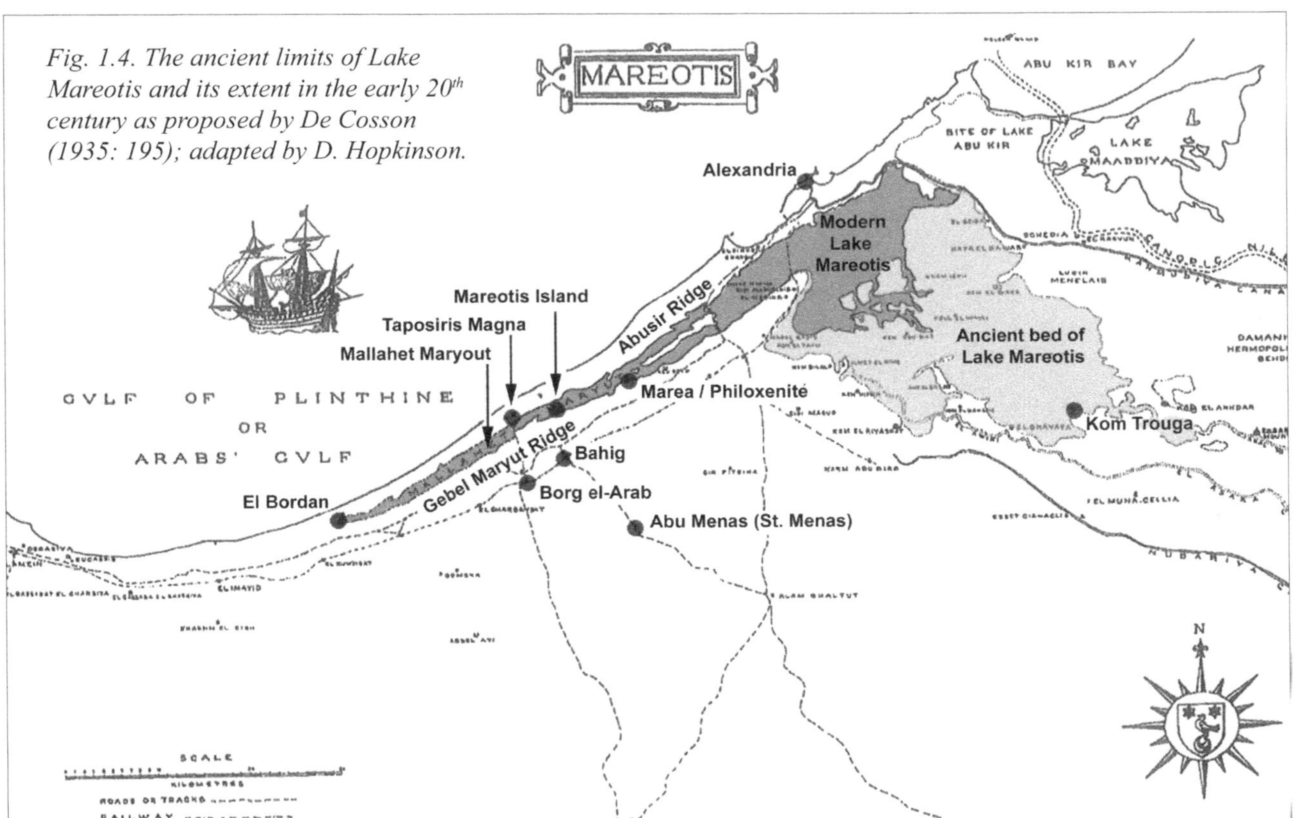

Fig. 1.4. The ancient limits of Lake Mareotis and its extent in the early 20th century as proposed by De Cosson (1935: 195); adapted by D. Hopkinson.

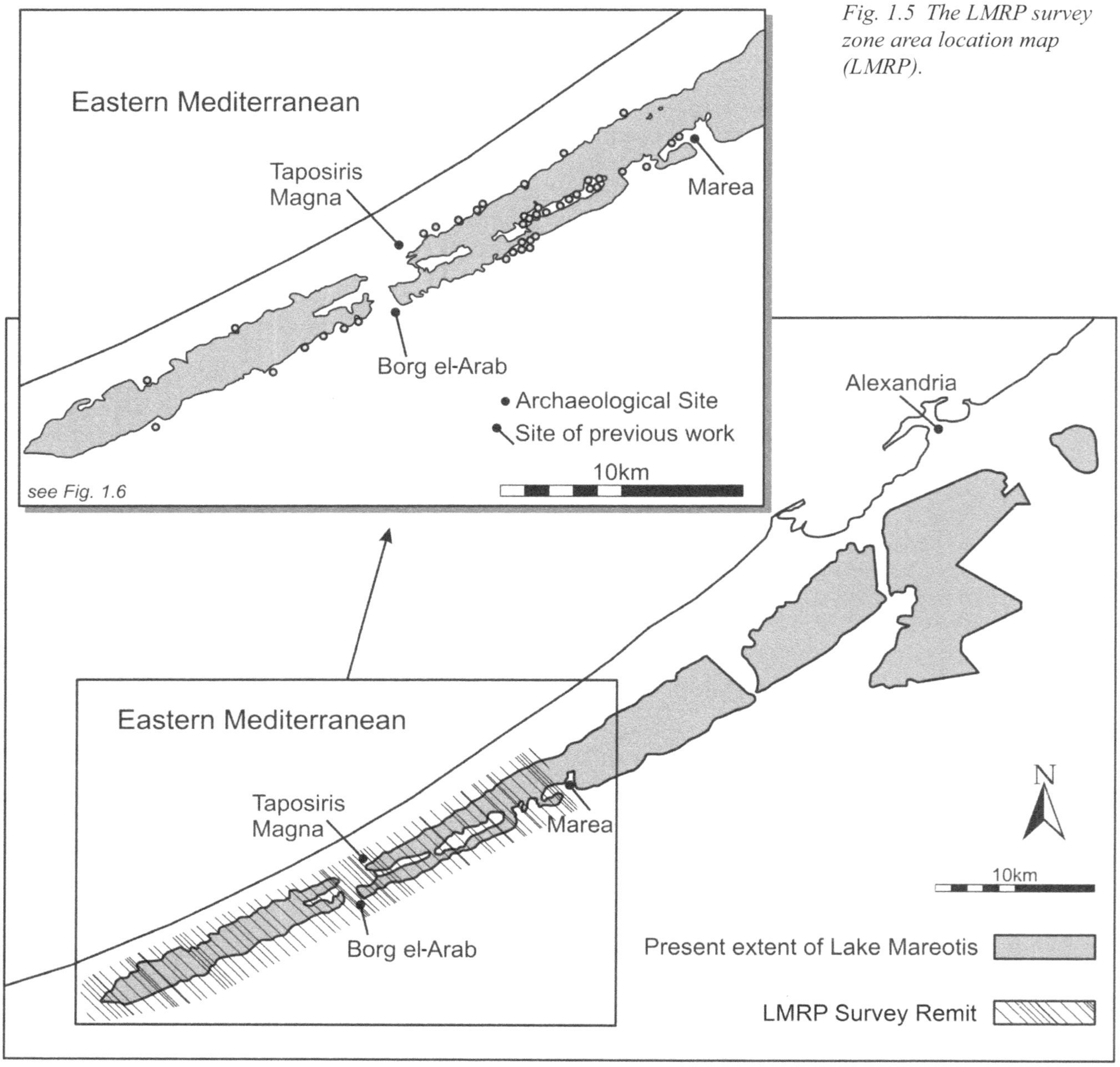

Fig. 1.5 The LMRP survey zone area location map (LMRP).

identified in the region to date (see above and Chapter 2 below). Thus, the western arm of Lake Mareotis became the area of focus of the Lake Mareotis Research Project.

The Lake Mareotis Research Project perfectly compliments previous research and enhances the broader picture. The objective of the project was to undertake a comprehensive systematic survey of the archaeological resource along the shores of the western extremities of Lake Mareotis in order to produce a coherent overview of activities in the region and their role in relation to the economy of Alexandria. By looking at all visible evidence for industry, trade and transport along the shores of the western arm of the lake, the project intended to quantify and assess the archaeological resource of the area in a comprehensive manner, in the context of its palaeogeographical history, its spatial and temporal distribution and its relation to the harbour of Alexandria. The main chronological focus was Greco-Roman times; a period when Alexandria was considered to be 'the greatest emporium in the inhabited world' (Strabo 17.1.13).

Unlike the traditional 'foreign mission' approach, the Lake Mareotis Research Project was directed through collaboration between the Centre for Maritime Archaeology at the University of Southampton and the Department of Underwater Antiquities of the Egyptian Supreme Council for Antiquities, in conjunction with the University of Alexandria. This represented a rare opportunity for British archaeologists to work with Egyptian institutions and to investigate a region significant for wider studies of ancient trade and economy throughout the Mediterranean region. The project started in 2004 when a British Academy Small Grant was awarded to support a pilot survey season of the lake shore. The survey covered an area of approximately 40km east to west by 3km wide along the shores of the western extension of Lake Mareotis, from Sidi Kerir to El-Hammam (Fig. 1.5). During that season over 60 sites were identified, many equating to new discoveries (Blue & Ramses 2005). The potential wealth of the sites in the area was thus realised and subsequently further funding was sought and awarded from both the British Academy and the Leverhulme Trust to conduct a more detailed survey on both shores of Lake Mareotis and Mareotis Island that is located in the eastern region of the survey area (Fig. 1.6).

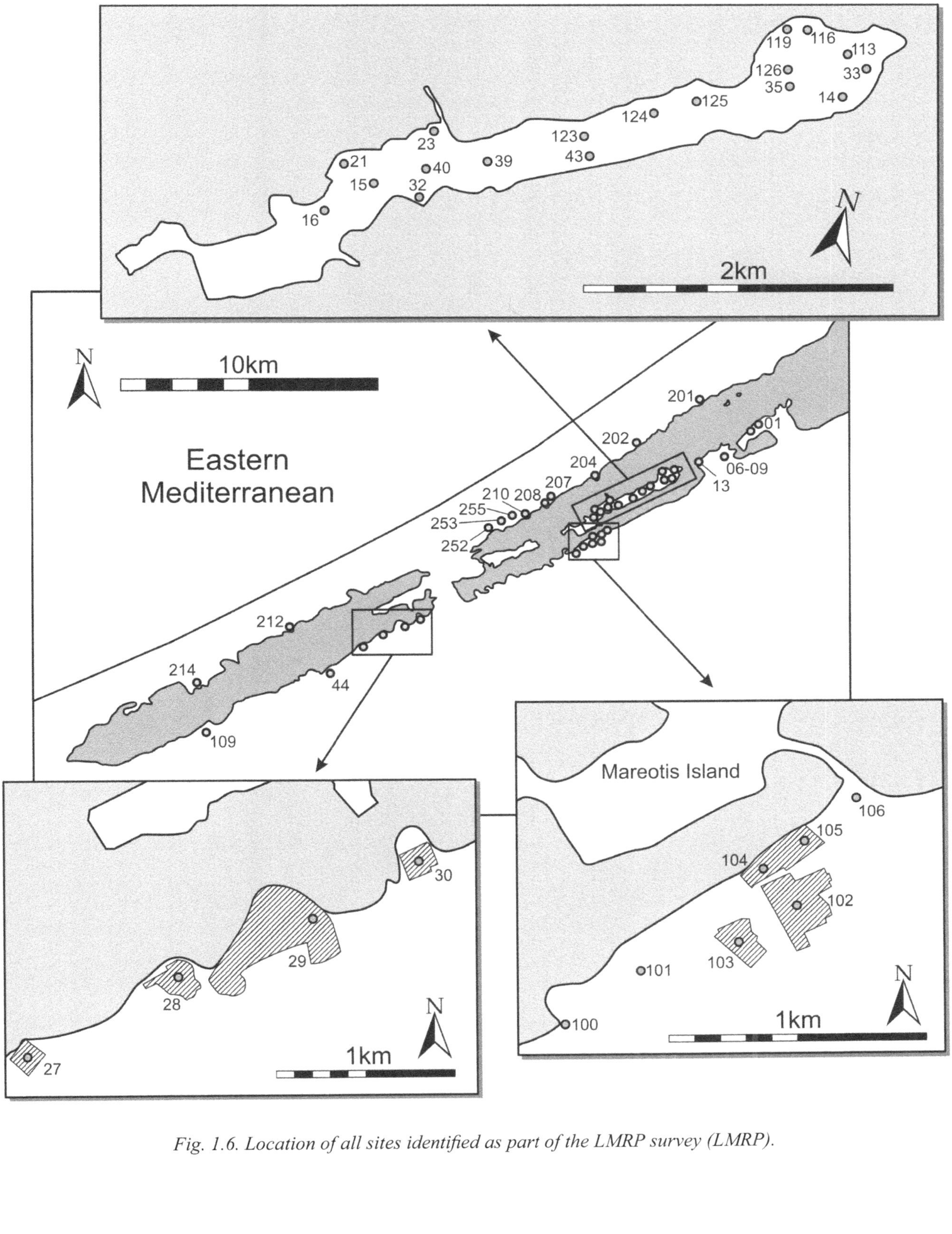

Fig. 1.6. Location of all sites identified as part of the LMRP survey (LMRP).

Chapter 2. The environmental and historical context of Lake Mareotis: the threats it faces and the previous work conducted in the region

2.1 Introduction

Lake Mareotis, precursor of the present Maryut Lake (henceforth referred to as Lake Mareotis), represented one of the most distinctive geomorphic features on the north-west coast of Egypt during the Holocene (Warne & Stanley 1993a). It was, and still is, quite unique compared to other lakes on the Egyptian north coast, which are from east to west: Al-Manzala, Al-Borolus, Idco and Maryut (Gouda 1994: 67) (Fig. 2.1). Lake Mareotis is the only one with no direct connection to the Mediterranean Sea; in fact, unlike the other three lakes, which were formed as a result of the sea inundating the north coast of the Nile Delta, Lake Mareotis was made solely by the Nile and thus had direct access to it and hence to the whole of Egypt. Therefore, it is believed that the location and characteristics of Lake Mareotis gave the city of Alexandria one of its major advantages (Strabo 17.1.7).

2.1.1 Geological and environmental context of Lake Mareotis

Lake Mareotis lies on the north-western edge of the Nile Delta. It occupies an area where the Nile Delta Plain meets chains of lithified carbonate ridges extending east parallel to the northern shore line. These ridges increase in elevation, from north to south, from about 10m above mean sea level near the coastline to more than 100m about 40km inland. The first three coastal ridges, which are 10m, 25m and 35m high from north to south, respectively, are bordered to the south by five inland ridges 60m, 80m, 85m, 90m and 110m high, respectively. These ridges are separated by silted longitudinal depressions of shallow lagoonal deposits and *sabkhas* (Said 1990: 499; Warne & Stanley 1993a; Frihy 1996: 282).

The lake consists primarily of two sections, which, although they originally formed one water body, differ significantly in their geomorphological nature. The first section is the lake's main body which currently extends south of Alexandria for about 12km and merges at its southern and eastern shores into the Western Deltaic region. The second part of the lake is its western extension, which is about 3km wide and extends west of Alexandria for about 40km. This western sub-basin is delimited from the south and north by two carbonate ridges, known as Abusir Ridge

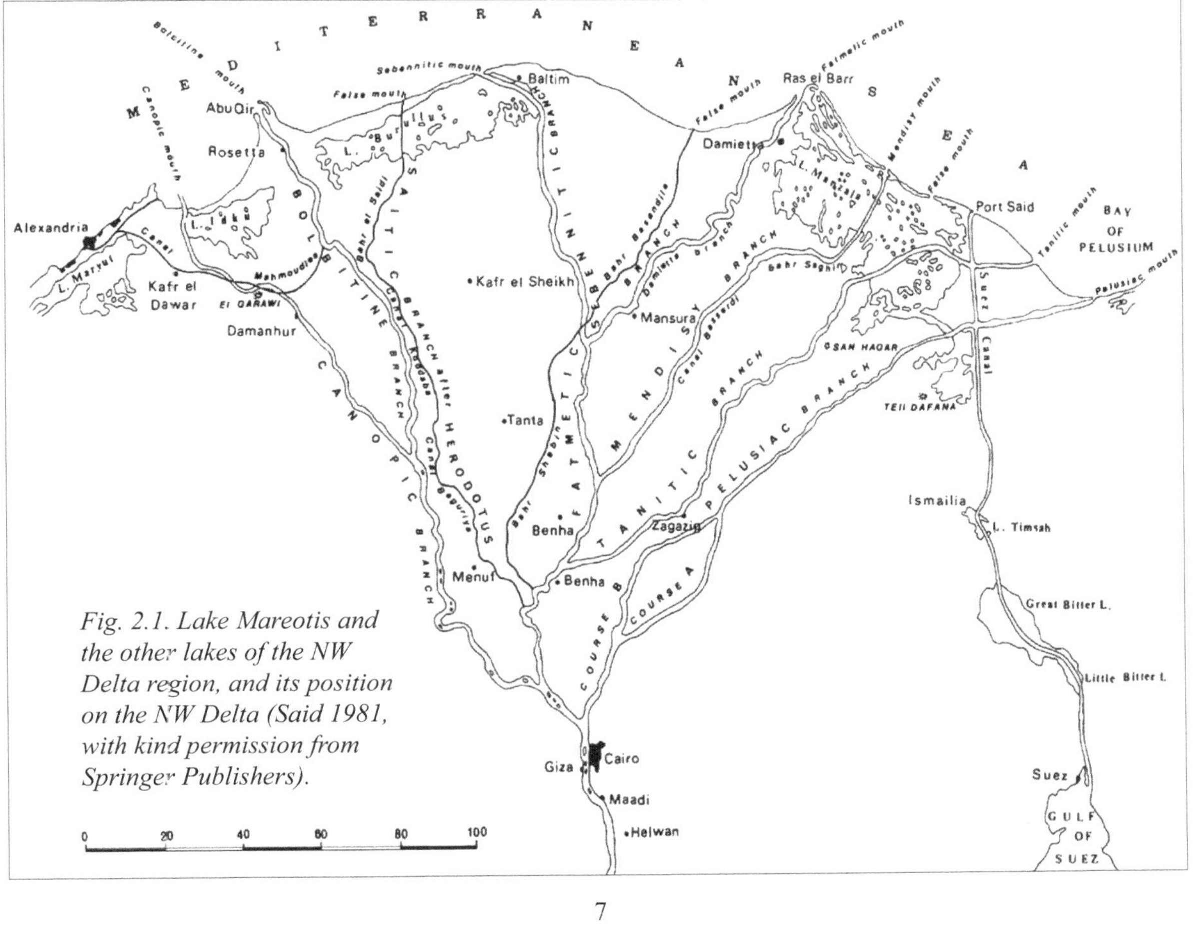

Fig. 2.1. Lake Mareotis and the other lakes of the NW Delta region, and its position on the NW Delta (Said 1981, with kind permission from Springer Publishers).

and Maryut Ridge. The Abusir Ridge stretches westward parallel to the coast from Aboukir east of Alexandria, to Al-Sallum on the Egyptian border with Libya, with an average elevation of about 25m, decreasing eastward to 6m at Aboukir, and an average width of between 200-400m (El-Zouka 1979: 86-7; Said 1990: 499; El-Sayed & Khadr 1999). To the south of the Abusir Ridge extends a longitudinal depression 3-4km wide known as the Al-Alamein-Maryut Depression or Mallahet Maryut (Maryut Salina) Depression (Said 1990: 499). The depression is generally about 3m below sea level; however, as it extends west towards Al-Hammam area, about 60km west of Alexandria, its level rises until it reaches 4m above sea level west and southwest of Al-Hammam (Hamdan 1980: 442). Part of this depression forms the some 30km long western arm of Lake Mareotis. At present, several parts of this depression have been artificially segmented into sub-basins by causeways and canals and roads. It has also been utilised for various agricultural and industrial purposes (Warne & Stanley 1993a: 34).

About 5-9km south of the Abusir Ridge extends the Gebel Maryut Ridge, which delimits the southern edge of the Al-Alamein-Maryut Depression. The ridge rises to about 35m above sea level with an average width of 300-400m. It extends westward for about 100km to just a few kilometres east of Al-Alamein (Shahin 1965; Warne & Stanley 1993a: 35; El-Sayed & Khadr 1999). Although this ridge forms the southern limit of the western arm of Maryut Lake, it is noticeable that the distance between the Gebel Maryut Ridge and the southern shore of the lake's western arm is almost twice the distance between the Abusir Ridge and the northern shore of the lake. This was to have implications for the way that the land adjacent to the northern and southern shores of the lake's western arm was utilised through different ages.

2.1.2 The lake in antiquity

In antiquity, as at present, there was a difference between the extent and limits of Lake Mareotis and those of the Mareotic region. The lake occupied part of the Mareotic region, which extended beyond the limits of the lake, particularly to the west and southwest. Moreover, literary, archaeological and historical evidence indicate that there is a great difference between the present size of Lake Mareotis and the size of its precursor (see Fig. 1.3, above).

Ancient texts and historical evidence are considered to be the main sources of information about the size and extent of Lake Mareotis in antiquity. For example, when Strabo (17.1.14) speaks of the size of Lake Mareotis, he states that "... it has a breadth of more than 150 *stadia* and a length of less than 300". He is speaking therefore of a water body that is rectangular in shape, with its length (presumably from north to south) almost twice its breadth. Assuming that the *stade* which was used by Strabo as a measurement unit was the Alexandrian *stade* (Al-Falaki 1966: 186; Empereur 1998: 57, 2002: 15), which is about 167m, the lake's dimensions would have been about 25km wide and 50km long.

Pliny (5.11.63) also speaks of the dimensions of Lake Mareotis and mentions that it was "... 30 miles across and 250 miles in circumference". Since Pliny expresses the distances in Roman miles – 1 Roman mile = 1.48km (Humphrey, *et al.* 1999: xxiv) – the lake would therefore have been about 45km across, presumably from north to south, which is not far off the figure Strabo gives as the length of the lake. Pliny also suggests that the lake is about 370km in circumference. Moreover, according to Warne and Stanley's (1993a) sedimentological and petrological study of the north-west Delta region, through which they attempted to define the extent of Lake Mareotis, the circumference of the lake, based on their estimation of its extent, is about 360km; very close to Pliny' suggestion.

By the early 5th century AD, St. Palladius, in his *Historia Lausiaca* (7.1), mentions that he sailed across Lake Mareotis, which extends between Alexandria and the monastic settlement of Mount Nitria (the present-day Al-Barnugi village south of Alexandria) (De Cosson 1935: 152-3; Bagnall 1993: 20-2) in a day and a half. This sailing trip would be from the northern-most limit of the lake, south of Alexandria, to its southern-most navigable limit. The direct distance between Alexandria and Mount Nitria (present Al-Barnugi) is about 55km. Therefore, it is quite possible that the navigable distance in Lake Mareotis at this time, from north to south, extended for about 50km.

Finally, the surveyors of the Napoleonic Campaign, which occupied Egypt from 1798-1801 published a map in the encyclopaedic *Description de l'Égypte* in 1809 (Néret 1997: 572-3), showing Lake Mareotis after it had been inundated by the sea in 1807 as a strategic action of the British army (Fig. 2.2). The map shows the lake extending from north to south for about 40km as far as north of Abu El-Matamir, and from east to west for about 55km as far as east of Taposiris Magna. On the other hand, Gratien Le Père, of the Napoleonic Campaign, gives an account of the lake after its first inundation in 1801. He states that the lake extended parallel to the coast from Alexandria to Borg el-Arab (southeast of Taposiris Magna) for about 40km and that, as a result of the inundation, it was filled with water so its depth ranged between 7m to 10m (Al-Shayeb 2002: 126). Since the lake was now connected to the sea its level could not exceed sea level, however, in antiquity when the shores of the lake had not been breached, the water levels were possibly higher (see Chapter 2.1.5 below).

It is also believed that in antiquity Lake Mareotis contained a number of islands. Strabo (17.1.14) for example mentions that "It contains eight islands", while Pliny (5.11.63) states that "It includes a considerable number of islands". However, the exact number, size and location of the islands in Lake Mareotis are currently unknown. The Napoleonic map of the Delta (Néret 1997: 572-3) shows a number of islands in the centre and to the southeast of the lake's main basin, as well as in the western sub-basin. By the mid 19th century Al-Falaki (1966: 187-8) mentions five islands that he believed were the remnants of the eight islands that Strabo mentions.

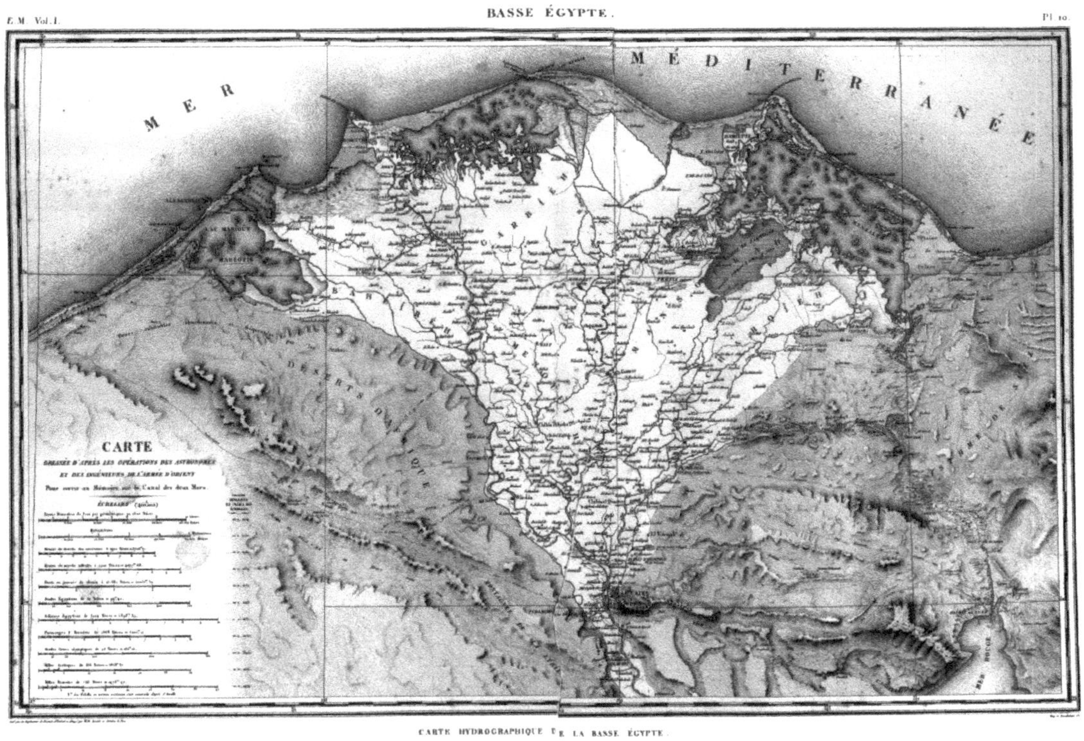

Fig. 2.2. Description de l'Égypte *map as described in the text (with kind permission from Centre d'Études Alexandrines).*

All the islands that Al-Falaki mentioned were located in the main body of the lake. However, four of those islands were, in fact, peninsulas projecting from the southern and south-eastern shores of the lake. He also suggested that the remaining three form a longitudinal mound that extended into the middle of the western sub-basin, west of Marea.

At present, due to the diminishing size of the lake's main basin, most of these islands have become unrecognisable as they are now well within the Delta (Fraser 1972: II.254 n.97). However, the western extension of the lake still contains at least two clearly identifiable islands. The main one is about 4km long from NE to SW and 500-800m wide, while the second is about 600m from NE to SW and about 400m wide and it is located to the east of the archaeological site of Marea.

2.1.3 Water supply

It is evident from historical sources that Lake Mareotis was fed through canals that indirectly connected the lake to the western-most Nile branch, the Canopic Branch. The now defunct branch actually bifurcated at Zawiyat al-Bahr although the ancient conception was that it began at the head of the Delta and debouched into the Bay of Canopus to the west of Alexandria (Hamdan 1980: 818-41; Said 1993: 69-77). The Canopic Branch started silting up during the 5th century AD and it became defunct by the 12th century AD.

In the 1st century BC, when Strabo (17.1.7) speaks of the water supply for the lake, he states that "...it is filled by many canals from the Nile, both from above and on the sides". And on another occasion (17.1.22) he speaks of "...several canals, which empty into Lake Mareotis". Accordingly, it is believed that the lake was fed by means of a number of canals, which branched off the Canopic Branch of the Nile and flowed into the south and east sides of the lake. Some of these canals were navigable (Strabo 17.1.22), which enabled merchandise to be transported to and from the hinterland. Although these canals were mentioned in a number of ancient sources, there is a considerable degree of uncertainty about their exact number, location and routes (Fig. 2.3).

Nonetheless, based on Strabo's description (17.1.22), it is believed that one of the main canals branched off the Canopic Branch close to the town of Naucratis (present Kom Geᶜeif), and entered the lake from the southeast at Kom Trouga (De Cosson 1935: 79; see Fig. 1.4). Another canal that was connected to the lake was the Schedia Canal. It branched off the Canopic Branch at Schedia, and debouched into the lake close to the eastern gate of Alexandria, the Canopic Gate (Strabo 17.1.16).

In fact, due to subsidence that occurred in the Western Delta, where the eastern and southern shores of the lake extended, and due to the existence of high coastal ridges to the west and southwest of the lake, it was only possible for the canals to approach the lake from the east and south. Petrological data analyses of core samples that date between 6000-800 years BP, taken from south, southeast and southwest of the main basin of the lake, confirm that the area contained fluvially-influenced lagoonal deposits

Fig. 2.3. Classic image of Alexandria and its ancient canals around the city plus the location of the Lake Harbour and Lake Mareotis (with kind permission from Centre d'Études Alexandrines).

with significant fluvial input from the southeast (Warne & Stanley 1993a: 54-5).

Since Lake Mareotis was indirectly connected to the Nile, its water level was governed by the Nile's level. Strabo (17.1.7) states that "... at the beginning of summer the Nile, being full, fills the lake". So, when the Nile flooded, the water level in the lake would rise and when the Nile's water level dropped, so did the lake's. In the flood season when the lake's level rose, it could have threatened to inundate the land around it (De Cosson 1935; El-Zouka 1979: 98, 101). Nevertheless, there is no reference in the ancient literature of such inundation events resulting from lake level rise. Therefore, it is possible that an overflow canal connected the lake and the sea to prevent Lake Mareotis from overfilling and endangering the Alexandria region during flooding (Warne & Stanley 1993a: 54).

A navigable canal that connected Alexandria's Western Harbour to the lake could have performed such a function (Fig. 2.3). The canal had its seaward outlet in the vicinity of an artificial basin, which Strabo (17.1.10) calls the "*kibotos*" (box-shaped), located inside the Western Harbour. However, Strabo did not give this canal a name, calling it only a navigable canal that carried traffic between the lake and the sea. Unfortunately, ancient documents are quite obscure about the location of the connection point between this canal and Lake Mareotis (Fraser 1972: II. 79-80 n.184). Nonetheless, Le Père (1809: 322) of the Napoleonic campaign investigated the remains of a tributary that could have linked the *kibotos* Canal and Lake Mareotis, southwest of the hill of the Serapeion of Alexandria (Kom Al-Shoqafa). This canal had a pre-Roman foundation, since a 3rd century BC document implies that merchandise was carried through it from the lake to the sea (Fraser 1972: I.144).

Since Lake Mareotis was indirectly connected to the Nile through canals that approached the lake from the south and the east, the main basin of the lake had the advantage of not being directly affected by large quantities of Nile sediments since these canals would have carried only a fraction of the sediment load of the Canopic Branch (Warne & Stanley 1993a: 53). As a result, the main body of Lake Mareotis remained deep enough to enable relatively large boats and barges to sail on it. The central area of the main basin as well as the western extension of the lake were the deepest parts, while its shores were subject to a number of factors that resulted in their instability.

Since the canals that supplied the lake with Nile water approached the lake from the south and east, Nile sediments that were carried by these canals, particularly during flood periods, were predominantly deposited on the eastern and southern shores of the lake; therefore, these areas were the most vulnerable to silting. Moreover, wind and wave action may have contributed to the deposition of sediments along the eastern and southern coasts of the lake. The lake's proximity to the seacoast made it subject to the prevailing north-western winds, which blew across the lake from the northwest to the southeast generating waves that travel in the same direction. Wave action in Lake Mareotis would have contributed to the build up of quantities of Nile silt carried by the canals against the southern and eastern shores of the lake.

The accumulation of sediments on the relatively shallow coasts of the lake resulted in reducing their depths gradually and eventually in their mergence with the Western Delta. Such a process would result in a gradual reduction in the size of the lake's main basin, as well as constant change in its coastline. Therefore, it is reasonable to suggest that the lake's eastern and southern shores were shallow and unstable, even in antiquity.

Accordingly, it is acceptable that the main basin of Lake Mareotis extended for 40-50km from north to south; however, determining the exact southern and south-eastern limits of the lake is quite problematic. De Cosson (1935: 151) suggests that the southern navigable limits of the main body of the lake in the Hellenistic and Roman times extended as far as Kom Trouga, once a lake harbour of ancient Mareotis, about 30km south of the southern limits of the present Lake Mareotis. In addition, as mentioned above, Lake Mareotis was fed from the Nile by a number of canals and waterways that approached the lake from the south and southeast (Strabo 17.1.7). The exact number and location of these canals is unknown; most likely it changed through time as a result of the continuous sediment deposition which led to the instability of the southern and eastern shores of the lake. However, maps of the 18th and 19th centuries clearly depict a number of canal beds that were still visible, although generally not functioning at that time (Jondet 1921). On the other hand, Pliny (5.11.63) states that "Lake Mareotis, which lies on the south side of the city, carries traffic from the interior by means of a canal from the Canopic mouth of the Nile". Therefore, it is evident that some of these canals were navigable in the Roman period.

2.1.4 The Lake Harbour

To the south of Alexandria, probably in the vicinity of present Gheit El-Enab south of the El-Mahmoudeyah Canal, existed the Lake Harbour which flourished during Hellenistic and Roman periods (Fig. 2.3). This area in the Alexandria region has never been subject to archaeological investigation and is now completely reclaimed. However, in the 18th century, the surveyors of the Napoleonic campaign noted the existence of some constructional remains and quays at the northern shore of the lake, to the south of the Alexandria Canal (Le Père 1809: 352), which could relate to the Lake Harbour.

Strabo (17.1.7) described the Lake Harbour as being "... richer than that on the sea", a statement which has been interpreted as describing the Lake Harbour as being busier than the seaports of Alexandria throughout the Hellenistic and Roman periods. In Strabo's time, the north-bound traffic passing through the Schedia Canal came out at the Lake Harbour. It also received Egyptian products, such as wine, papyrus and textiles, which were shipped to Alexandria from settlements around Lake Mareotis' western arm. On the other hand, the Lake Harbour would have been the departure point for river vessels on their south-bound journey from Alexandria through Lake Mareotis. Therefore, the size and facilities of the Lake Harbour must have been substantial to handle all this traffic; unfortunately, no traces of it have yet been identified.

2.1.5 The present lake

The lake's main body, which merges with the Delta Plain, has changed dramatically during the past millennia. By 12th century AD the relation between Lake Mareotis and the Nile started to terminate due to the silting of the Canopic Branch and all the canals and waterways that fed the lake (Said 2002). As a result, the level of Lake Mareotis fell so that the depression became a series of salty marshes and *sabkhas*. Mareotis became a closed lagoon without a constant supply of water, and due to increasing evaporation, the size of the lagoon decreased significantly and the once rich fertile regions to the south and west of Alexandria disappeared (Warne & Stanley 1993a: 58).

By the early 19th century Le Père (1809: 111-3) informs us that Lake Mareotis was nothing more than a sandy depression which caught rain water during the winter season. He also informs us that reports from the 15th, 16th and 17th centuries indicate that the canals were still carrying Nile water to the lake during the flood season. Accordingly, he infers that the drying out of the lake took place at the end of the 17th or the beginning of the 18th century.

By the end of the 18th century Mareotis was almost dry, except in the rainy seasons, to the extent that armies used to march across the depression (De Cosson 1935: 62; Al-Shayeb 2002: 111-3). Lake Mareotis remained dry for almost 700 years, between the 12th century and the early 19th century, until it was intentionally flooded with seawater twice, as a consequence of strategic actions.

The first inundation event occurred in April 1801, during the Napoleonic Campaign in Egypt, when the British army breached the dyke between the Maryut Depression and the former Aboukir Lagoon. This dyke carried the canal, which supplied Alexandria with Nile water prior to the construction of the Al-Mahmoudeyah Canal in 1820. Therefore, the dyke was breached to cut off the freshwater supply to the French garrison stationed in Alexandria and to prevent any reinforcements reaching them from the main French forces in Cairo (De Cosson 1935: 88; Warne & Stanley 1993a: 55). As a result, seawater from Aboukir Lagoon rushed into Lake Mareotis until its level reached sea level, which enabled English warships to sail from Aboukir through the lake to attack the rear of the French garrison in Alexandria. The saltwater lake extended west until Taposiris Magna, and south until north of Abu El-Matamir (Hamdan 1980: 220; Néret 1997: 572-3; Al-Shayeb 2002: 113). In 1804 the breach was repaired and the freshwater canal was reconnected to Alexandria (De Cosson 1935: 89).

In May 1807, the lake was flooded for a second time when the British garrison in Egypt, under Major-General Fraser, breached the dyke to prevent Egyptian forces moving from Cairo from attacking the British garrison at Rosetta.

Fig. 2.4. Refineries along the shores of Lake Mareotis (LMRP).

Accordingly, twelve British warships were able to sail into the lake and besiege Alexandria (El-Zouka 1979: 101-2; Warne & Stanley 1993a: 55). Subsequently, in February 1808 the dyke was rebuilt and the freshwater canal was reconnected again, and Lake Mareotis started drying up once more (De Cosson 1935: 90).

In 1820 the Al-Mahmoudeyah Canal was built by Mohamed Ali Pasha to supply Alexandria with fresh water, but more importantly it was to be the main waterway between the city and the Nile. Once again Alexandria became the principal harbour in Egypt. However, the lake's depression did not receive any water from the Al-Mahmoudeyah Canal (Warne & Stanley 1993a: 36), which largely took the course of the previous Alexandria Canal. Therefore, Mareotis remained a shallow salty lagoon. It was not until 1892 when major irrigation projects in the Western Delta were established, that the depression started receiving agricultural runoff and irrigation water carried by a number of canals and drains, filling the depression and creating the present Lake Mareotis (Frihy, *et al.* 1996: 291). The water level of the lake had to be kept relatively low for irrigation water to flow into its main basin, and also to avoid the threat of inundation. Therefore, to control inundation around the lake, its water level is constantly maintained at about 3m below sea level, by pumping water from the lake to the sea at El-Mex (El-Raey, *et al.* 1995: 192). As a result, the lake's maximum depth is less than 1.5m, although the level of its bottom is about 4.3m below sea level. Therefore, if the water level of the lake was allowed to reach sea level, its depth would be more than 4m, and its size would be more than six times than that at present (Warne & Stanley 1993a: 35-6).

Thus, at present, Lake Mareotis is a body of shallow brackish water that occupies about 13% of an extensive subsea-level depression that is also referred to as the Maryut Depression. The remaining 87% of the depression silted up or has been drained and is now used mainly for agriculture. The main body of the lake covers an area of about 90km^2 south and west of Alexandria, with no direct link to the sea (Warne & Stanley 1993a: 36; El-Raey, *et al.* 1995: 192). It is nearly rectangular in shape, with its northern shore extending for about 20km and its eastern shore for 12km long (El-Zouka 1979: 98; Hamdan 1980: 818-41; Frihy, *et al.* 1996: 291). The main body of the lake is heavily polluted by untreated sewage and industrial wastes. It has also been divided into sub-basins, which are used for industrial and agricultural purposes. Moreover, the shores of the lake are subject to continuous irrigation, drainage and reclamation projects as well as subdivision by causeways, which make it constantly changing and unstable (Warne & Stanley 1993a: 29-30; Frihy, *et al.* 1996: 282).

The western sub-basin is a closed water body with no constant supply of water. The average depth of this part of the lake is less than 1m. It receives its water from groundwater seepage, agriculture runoff and rainfall; therefore, its water level fluctuates widely according to the seasons. In the rainy winter season, agriculture runoff and rain water percolate through the ground and cause the water level of the sub-basin to rise, while in the dry summer season, the high rate of water evaporation from the surface as well as pumping ground water from wells for irrigation purposes, contribute to lowering the water level. The change in water level from summer to winter can be clearly seen in the remains of a number of ancient harbours around the lake's western arm. In summer, these sites become more exposed and mostly dry, while in winter they turn into marshes and wetland or become partially submerged. This section of the lake has also been subject to land reclamation as well as a number of agricultural and industrial projects (El-Sayed & Khadr 1999).

2.1.6 Threats

Despite the archaeological and cultural importance of the Mareotic region, Lake Mareotis and its shores have suffered from numerous environmental challenges. The lake is threatened by extensive urban development which not only has had a destructive effect on the archaeological sites along its shores but also on the lake itself. The threats that the Mareotic region faces can be summarised by two main themes, discussed below.

2.1.6.1 Reclamation, inundation and land use

The Mareotic region is the natural urban extension of Alexandria. Since the city is delimited by the sea to the north and the valuable arable land of the Delta to the east and southeast, the only possible direction for the city to develop is towards Lake Mareotis. Therefore, for the past two decades sections of the lake have been reclaimed and used for building highways, factories, refineries (see Fig. 2.4), houses, resorts and even used as arable land (Fig. 2.5). This problem is not only noticeable in the main body of the lake, close to Alexandria, but also in certain areas in the western Mareotic Arm, such as the area to the west of Mareotis Island and the area south of Taposiris Magna.

A combination of land reclamation and inundation is also extensively deployed along the shores of Lake Mareotis to create fish farms (Fig. 2.6). As mentioned earlier, Lake Mareotis receives it water supply from ground seepage, agricultural runoff and waster water, and due to the fact that the lake is divided into many sections by roads and viaducts, some sections of it have a water quality which is suitable for fish breeding. Accordingly, one of the major economic activities that has expanded along the shores of the Mareotic Arm is the creation of fish farms formed by dredging sections of the shore and constructing dykes and canals to develop large basins for breeding fish. Not only

Fig. 2.5. Modern walls built over archaeological sites (LMRP).

Fig. 2.6. Fish farming encroaching on Lake Mareotis (LMRP)

Fig. 2.7. A large mound of lime for use in the cement factory which operates on one of the archaeological sites (LMRP).

Fig. 2.8. Quarrying along the north shore (LMRP).

has this activity resulted in the destruction of numerous archaeological sites along the shores of the lake, but it also makes others inaccessible from the shore as many of the sites are completely surrounded by water.

Another major activity that impacts on sites in the region are large scale industries, namely, the cement and salt industries. Both industries occupy more than 50km^2 of the lake and its shores. Solar salt production results in the dredging, inundating and drying of sections of the lake, and cement production results in the destruction of the calcareous coastal ridge for the production of lime (Fig. 2.7). Further destruction is caused by quarrying for which there are extensive examples particularly on the Abusir Ridge that defines the northern shores of the lake (Fig. 2.8). As a result the archaeology is being destroyed, and the possibility of discovering more sites in the future is greatly reduced. For example, in an attempt to relocate the amphora production sites that were recorded east of Marea by Empereur and Picon in the 1970s and 1980s (Empereur & Picon 1989, 1992, 1998), it was realised that most of those sites were partially or completely destroyed as a result of urban development. As such, one of the major concerns relating to encroaching urbanisation upon archaeological sites along the shores of Lake Mareotis is the fact that many of the sites have not been recorded. Even those sites that are recoded and known tend to be relatively remote and therefore difficult for the authorities to monitor and protect from destruction.

2.1.6.2 Water quality and pollution

An extensive network of irrigation canals and drains extends across the lake, particularly in its eastern section (Warne & Stanley 1993a: 36). These carry to the lake in-

Fig. 2.9. The water in Lake Mareotis is polluted by industrial and domestic waste water as well as agricultural runoff (LMRP).

dustrial and domestic waste from the larger Alexandria region, as well as agricultural runoff from the cultivated lands east and south of the lake. The lake also receives groundwater seepage and rainfall (Frihy, *et al.* 1996: 291). More than 600,000m^3 of wastewater and 200,000m^3 of untreated industrial and domestic wastes are deposited daily into the lake (Warne & Stanley 1993a: 36; Frihy, *et al.* 1996: 291). As a result, the main body of Lake Mareotis is considered one of the most polluted areas in the Alexandria region (Fig. 2.9). The high level of pollution of the lake's waters hinders archaeological research of the lake itself; particularly the study of coastal or partially submerged sites.

In addition to water pollution, there is also land pollution since some areas long the southern and northern shores of the lake are used as the main waste dumps for the city of Alexandria. Again, amongst other things, these factors prevent access to archaeological sites.

2.2 Previous archaeological investigations conducted in the Mareotis region

2.2.1 Al-Falaki

For centuries, Lake Mareotis has attracted the attention of historians, geographers and explorers; however, it was not until the middle of the 19th century that the first well recorded archaeological exploration of the shores of Lake Mareotis was undertaken by Mahmoud Al-Falaki (1966: 172-89). During his extensive survey of Alexandria and its outskirts, Al-Falaki surveyed the shores of the Marotic Arm west of Alexandria producing a detailed map in 1866 (Fig. 2.10). The western limit of his survey was Taposiris Magna since, during this period, the lake's water did not extend beyond this area. However, within the area surveyed to the south of Alexandria, Al-Falaki speaks of the ruins of seven ancient settlements including the key sites of Marea and Taposiris Magna. However, it is noticeable that four of these ancient settlements were located on the southern shore east of Marea, an area which has since been subject to extensive urban development. The final site Al-Falaki mentions is located between Marea and Taposiris Magna and corresponds to what is presently referred to as Mareotis Island. It is evident from his map, however, that it was not an island at the time but in fact a headland that was connected to the mainland from the east (Fig. 2.10). Al-Falaki also, on more than one occasion, mentions the existence of a large number of ancient wineries, basins, wells and water-wheels (*sakkias*), and on his map he notes that there are more than three hundred wells and *sakkias* in the Mareotis region.

The two main sites that Al-Falaki discusses in more detail are Marea and Taposiris Magna. At Marea (Al-Falaki 1966: 180-1), he particularly mentions its harbour's quays and the extensive remains of buildings and basins (probably referring to the baths). Moreover, Al-Falaki also believes that Marea, an important harbour in antiquity, gave its name to the lake and the region as a whole, which suggests the site's ancient origin. With regard to Taposiris Magna, Al-Falaki only mentions its location as a key ancient site (see Chapter 2.3.3 below). In addition, it is worth mentioning that Al-Falaki believed that the extent of Lake Mareotis during the time of his survey, in the mid 19th century, was similar to its extent in antiquity, the only difference being that it was not as navigable because at the time the lake's depth was too shallow. In other words, Al-Falaki believed that Taposiris Magna marked the western end of Lake Mareotis and that the lake in antiquity did not extend beyond that point.

2.2.2 De Cosson

In 1935 Anthony De Cosson published the first comprehensive study of the Mareotic region (De Cosson

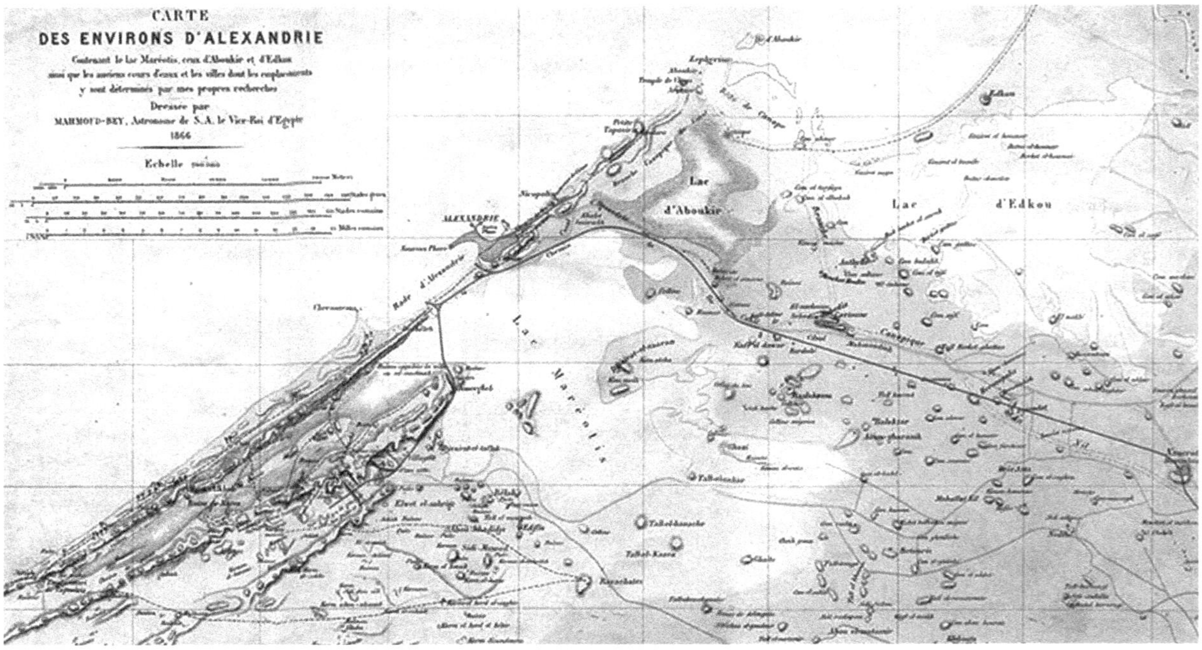

Fig. 2.10. Al-Falaki map of survey area and including Marea and Mareotis Island (after Jondet 1921: 105, XXXVIII, with kind permission from Centre d'Études Alexandrines).

1935). In his book he covered the history and archaeology of what he called the "Maryut District", which extended west beyond El-Hammam and south until Abu Menas. The study looked at the history, development and human activities in the Mareotic region from prehistoric times until the early 20th century, including the accounts of ancient authors as well as travellers of the 18th and 19th centuries.

Among the main subjects that were discussed by De Cosson were the lake's water supply and utilisation in different periods. Accordingly he studied the network of canals that connected the lake to the Nile in successive periods as well as those that possibly connected the lake to the sea near Alexandria. The study also commented, on more than one occasion, on the abundance of evidence for water management particularly relating to the Greco-Roman period, including rock-cut cisterns, wells, *karums* (artificial catchment areas), stone water channels and *sakkias*.

De Cosson also describes what he calls "Ancient Sites and Places of Interest", which were not necessarily archaeological sites, but sites of historical or cultural significance located from just west of Alexandria to west of Al-Hammam. Amongst the key archaeological sites he mentions was Taposiris Magna, which De Cosson (1935: 109) describes as the finest ancient monument still remaining north of the Pyramids. He also mentions Marea (De Cosson 1935: 131) the site he believed was the capital and the major port of the region from ancient Egyptian times until the 16th century. However, it seems that by the time De Cosson was writing, the only significant part of Marea was its harbour's jetties as extensive remains of the town were quite unrecognisable.

The other site he describes with admiration is Mareotis Island, which he associated with the inland town of Bahig. At his time it seems that the island was accessible via a track that led to it from the southern shore of the lake. De Cosson (1935: 130) describes it as a town site built on an island close to the south shore and states that it contains many buildings, cisterns and pottery kilns. It is worth mentioning his description of one particular area on Mareotis Island: he describes a circular stone platform of an ancient *sakkia* and a stone channel leading from the *sakkia* to a cistern, and to the south of that the remains of two pottery kilns and pottery wasters, while to the north of the *sakkia* there was a long jetty that extended into the lake. This description by De Cosson fits perfectly an area that was surveyed during the project (see Chapter 6 below): the *sakkia* and the cistern (Site 40), the pottery kiln to the south (Site 32), and the long jetty to the north (Site 23). However, De Cosson describes this area as being located at the eastern end of the island, while in fact it is located at the western end. One possible explanation is that at his time, the water level at this part of the lake was higher than today which resulted in the separation of the eastern and western ends of the island perhaps in the low marshy area just to the east of Site 40.

De Cosson describes other sites in the Mareotis region, however, they are mostly towns and settlements in the greater area, including sites such as Kom Trouga and El Barnugi, located in the Western Deltaic region (see below), which in antiquity would have been located on the eastern shore of the main body of Lake Mareotis.

De Cosson's study of the Mareotic region has remained for decades the only study of its kind, and for many years formed the basis of research.

2.2.3 El-Fakharani

Following De Cosson's study of Mareotis, archaeological research along the shoes of Lake Mareotis remained dormant until the early 1970s when some of the key sites of the region started to attract the attention of academics and archaeologists.

In 1974 Fawzy El-Fakharani published his paper on the Lighthouse of Abusir (Taposiris Magna), in which he discussed the nature and possible function of this monumental tower that stands on the top of the coastal ridge marking the site of Taposiris Magna at the northern shore of the lake. In his paper, El-Fakharani challenged previous ideas about the function and date of the tower of Taposiris and suggested that it is was actually a funerary monument centred over a Ptolemaic funerary hypogeum; a theory that has remained valid until today (El-Fakharani 1974). El-Fakharani published another paper in 1984 in which he looked at a type of harbour known as a *kibotos* or the box-shaped harbour (El-Fakharani 1984) which Strabo (17.1.10) mentioned existed in Alexandria. El-Fakharani came across two examples of this type of harbour in the Mareotic region, which he believed were pre-Hellenistic in date. One of them was constructed of limestone blocks and the other was rock-cut. During the project the first *kibotos* was relocated and surveyed on the southern shore of the lake about 3km west of Marea (Site 09) (see Chapter 6); but the second *kibotos* mentioned by El-Fakharani was not possible to relocate. Nevertheless, it is worth mentioning that at the time El-Fakharani was writing, the *kibotos* west of Marea was totally on dry land and the southern shore of the lake was several metres to the north. By contrast, during the LMRP survey, the harbour projected out into the water, an obvious indication of the rising level of the lake over only the past few decades.

El-Fakharani's main contribution to the archaeology of the Mareotic region was through the extensive excavations he carried out at the ancient town of Marea (El-Fakharani 1983). Not only did El-Fakharani excavate numerous buildings and structures in the Byzantine town of Marea, but he also extended his research to areas in the west, east and south of the Byzantine settlements. Accordingly he associated other buildings and remains in the region with Marea. This included the pre-Hellenistic *kibotos* to the west and another substantial pre-Hellenistic structure c. 700m west of the *kibotos* (Site 13 in the LMRP survey), which he believed to be an ancient Egyptian fortress, both of which he associated with Marea. He also recorded a cluster of tombs to the south of Marea which he believed to be of late Pharaonic date. Within the Byzantine settlements, El-Fakharani recorded baths, a winery, tombs, shops, a grain mill, residential areas, and a basilica, all of which date to a period between the 5th to the 7th centuries AD (Fig. 2.11).

El-Fakharani believed that the Marea he excavated was much greater in size and much older in date than Al-Falaki, De Cosson and others had believed it to be. He dated it from the late Pharaonic period to the Early Islamic period, and noted that it extended more than 2km to the south of the Byzantine coastal settlement. The work that was conducted by El-Fakharani in Marea revealed to the archaeological community the importance and potential of the site. Subsequently, other archaeologists started to show an interest in the area. Amongst them were Gabel and Petruso (1980) who joined El-Fakharani in his fieldwork as part of a field school from Boston University in 1979. Their publications broadly centre on the environment and history of Lake Mareotis and the Mareotic region, however, they mainly focus on Marea as a key archaeological site in the region (Petruso & Gabel 1982).

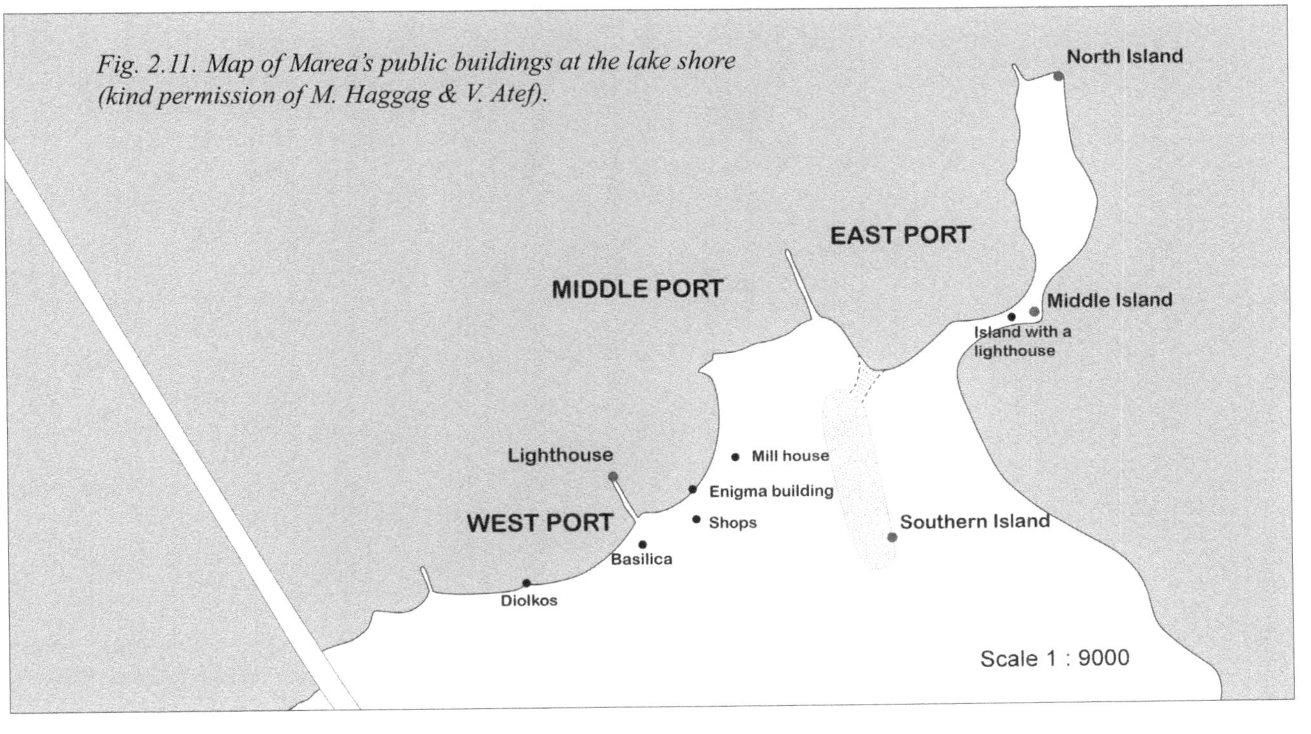

Fig. 2.11. Map of Marea's public buildings at the lake shore (kind permission of M. Haggag & V. Atef).

2.2.4 Rodziewicz

Mieczyslaw Rodziewicz started investigating the Mareotic region in the early 1970s; however, his publications about the archaeology of the region did not appear until the 1980s. In one of his earliest publications, Rodziewicz (1983) tries to shed light on the different types of harbours that exist along the shores of Lake Mareotis, noting that the archaeological potential of the area had yet to be explored. However, the paper focuses on the harbour of Marea which had been excavated by El-Fakharani between 1977-1981 (see above), presenting for the first time the idea that this site might not be Marea, the capital of the Mareotic nome since the pre-Hellenistic period, but the harbour town of Philoxenité established at the end of 5th century as a stopover between Lake Mareotis and the Christian monastic town of Abu Menas (Fig. 2.12). This is a controversial argument that has been strongly advocated by Rodziewicz since (Rodziewicz 1990, 2003). He also addresses the decline of the main towns and settlements in the Mareotic region and links this to the decline of the lake's water supply by the 7th century AD.

In another general paper about the archaeology of the Mareotic region Rodziewicz (1990) emphasises the potential of archaeological exploration along the shores of Lake Mareotis particularly the waterfront sites, such as jetties, quays and other harbour installations that were exposed as a result of the low water level in the lake at that time. The paper also warns that archaeological sites in the area were being destroyed as a result of urban development. However, the papers again focuses on the two main sites in the region: Marea and Taposiris Magna, stressing that there are still many questions to be answered about the nature, role and development of these two sites.

In 1998 a complete volume was published about Alexandria as part of the *Bulletin de Correspondance Hellénique* (Empereur 1998c). In that volume Rodziewicz published two further thematic papers about the Mareotic region. The first paper (Rodziewicz 1998a) looks briefly at the ancient land routes and waterways linking Alexandria with the north-west coast of Egypt. It outlines the main harbours and settlements that were located on the north coast between Alexandria and Sallum, as well as the main Mareotic harbours Taposiris Magna, Marea, and Portus Mareoticus, the ancient lake harbour of Alexandria to the south of the city for which, as yet, no trace has been identified. The paper also classifies the Mareotic harbours into three types: a harbour surrounded with artificial jetties forming a closed basin with one or two entries; an open harbour with constructed quays extending into the lake, and a small structured boxed-shaped harbour (Rodziewicz 1998a: 101). However, again, the paper focuses mainly on the harbours of Taposiris Magna and Marea describing their structures and possible maritime function. This was the first attempt to look at the Mareotic harbours in a more structured way. In a later publication Rodziewicz (2002) addresses this issue from a slightly different perspective.

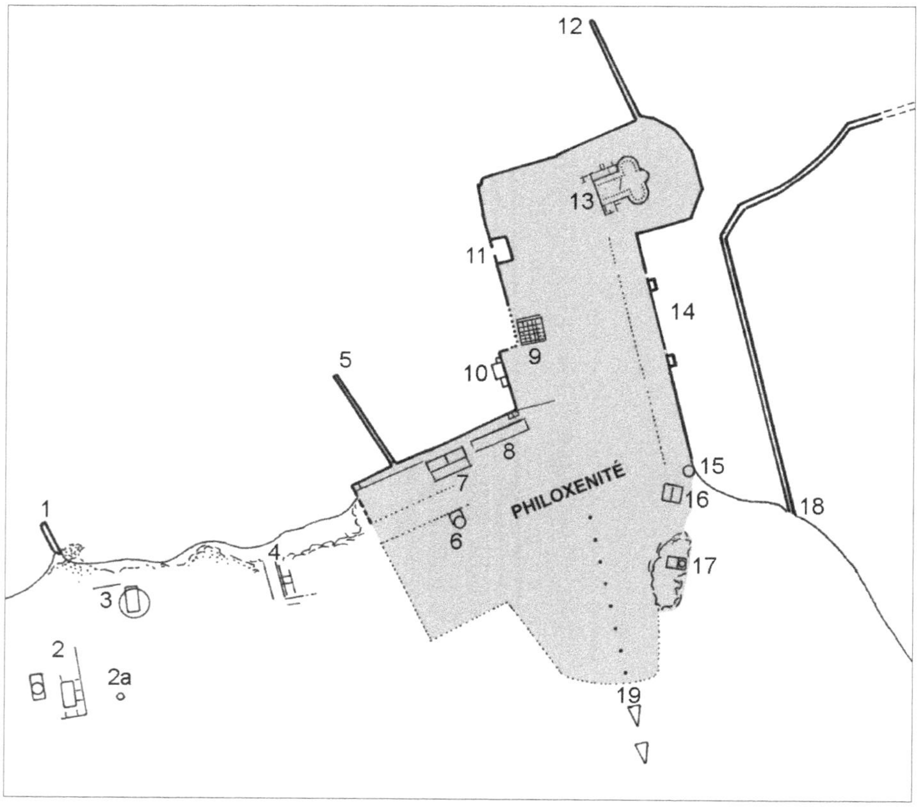

KEY:
1 – Jetty of pre-Byzantine date
2 – Rural estate with large water-wheel
2a – Small kiln
3 – Unidentified structure of rural character
4 – Structures with moorings
5 – Pier
6 – Water-wheel (sakkia)
7 – Public double bath
8 – Insula with shops
9 – Public building
10 – Public lavatory
11 – Kibotos*?*
12 – Pier
13 – Transept Basilica
14 – Eastern harbour
15 – Water-wheel (sakkia)
16 – Public bath
17 – Rock-hewn tomb/ hypogeum
18 – Causeway leading to the island
19 – Pilgrimage track to Abu Menas

Fig. 2.12. Interpretation of the Byzantine pilgramage harbour/Philoxenité (Nos. 5-17) and western/coastal rural remains (Nos. 1-4). On the eastern side, structured causeway (No. 18) (drawn by M. Rodziewicz, used with kind permission).

He attempts to establish the possible link between the Mareotic harbour landscape and artistic representations of Nilotic scenes believed to have been set in Alexandria, such as the glass mosaic of Kenchreai, the eastern port of ancient Corinth. In doing so, the paper examines the main two harbours in the region, Taposiris Magna and Marea, or Philoxenité as it is referred to by Rodziewicz, suggesting that the glass mosaic from Kenchreai, which depicts a marshy maritime landscape and its associated harbours, was probably executed in Alexandria and was influenced by the harbours of Lake Mareotis.

A further paper that Rodziewicz (2003) published about Mareotic harbours was dedicated to the argument he presented earlier (Rodziewicz 1983) about the identification of the Byzantine settlement of Marea. He advocates the idea that the site known as Marea is in fact the city of Philoxenité, which was built by the Praefect Philoxenus upon orders of the Emperor Anastasius (AD 491 – 518). Philoxenité was to function as a landing place and pilgrimage station on the way from Lake Mareotis to the shrine of Abu Menas. The main argument Rodziewicz presents to support this hypothesis is his belief that the archaeological remains in the area date no earlier than the 5th century, and no later than the 7th century, while the city of Marea, the capital of the Mareotic region, should date much earlier. Thus, he proposes that the settlement only qualifies as a port to access Abu Menas. This argument, however, has been questioned since the recent discoveries of an Early Roman kiln underneath the Byzantine basilica in Marea (Babraj & Szymańska 2010), and a Hellenistic and Roman metal workshop on Marea's eastern peninsula (Pichot 2010). Rodziewicz suggests that the kiln and other associated pre-Byzantine installations belong to an earlier Roman rural estate, one of many in the region, and has nothing to do with the city of Marea (Rodziewicz 2010; Fig. 2.12).

Finally, another paper of Rodziewicz's should be noted (Rodziewicz 1998b); here, he looks at a completely different aspect of the region. It addresses regional wine production, which was one of the main activities for which the area was famous for in antiquity. The study explores some of the literary and archaeological evidence of wine production in the Mareotic region, and offers, for the first time, an introductory classification of the wineries discovered. It lists the fourteen Greco-Roman wineries that were recorded in the region, including those in Abu Menas 20km south of Marea, into eight categories based on their structure, components and design. There have been other studies that looked at individual wineries in the Mareotic region, such as the study of El-Ashmawi (1998) on the winery south of Taposiris Magna, and of El-Fakharani (1983) on the winery south of Marea. Subsequently, there have been more general studies of the wineries and of wine production in Egypt (Dzierzbicka 2005). However, Rodziewicz's introductory classification facilitated the study of wineries in the region and provides a basis for a more comprehensive classification.

2.2.5 Empereur and Picon

Probably the most important aspect of the Mareotic region that has been studied so far is the role it played in the production of amphora in the Hellenistic and Roman periods. Pottery wasters and amphora kilns were noted by many researchers, however, the most extensive study of Mareotic amphora production was carried out by Empereur and Picon from the late 1970s (Empereur & Picon 1986, 1989, 1992, 1998; Empereur 1993, 1998). The importance of amphora production in this region, and hence their study, cannot be over emphasised. As containers of wine and other commodities, they provide a proxy indicator of economic production and trade in the region and beyond.

One of the best examples for large-scale production of amphorae in Egypt comes from the Mareotic region, where Empereur and Picon (1986: 103-9, 1992, 1998) identified a series of 28 amphora production sites. Almost all of them were located along the southern shore of the western Mareotic Arm in an area about 30km long, from Al-Amreya, c. 20km southwest of Alexandria, to Taposiris Magna. Most of the sites were located east of Marea while only three sites were reported in the area from Marea to Taposiris Magna (see Fig. 1.3). The recorded sites were in the form of mounds comprised mainly of layers of broken amphorae, in some cases as large as 50m across and 20m high, in addition to extensive traces of burning associated with amphorae kiln sites. The sites range in date from the 2nd century BC to the 6th century AD, however, the majority of them, about 17 out of the 28 sites, were producing amphorae between the 1st and 3rd centuries AD (Empereur & Picon 1998). Moreover, the actual remains of two amphorae kilns were also discovered, associated with large amounts of refuse. The first one was excavated at Al-Amreya and it dates to the 2nd – 3rd centuries AD (Abd El-Fattah 1998), while the other one was excavated at Taposiris Magna and dates to the 1st – 3rd centuries AD (El-Ashmawi 1998). Unfortunately, none of these sites were accurately mapped by their initial discoverers. Only their approximate locations were marked on maps of the Mareotic Arm. Recent attempts by E. Khalil to re-examine the sites mentioned by Empereur and Picon (1986: 106-9, 1992, 1998) resulted in only 12 of the 28 sites being relocated. Unfortunately, the rest of the sites mentioned by Empereur and Picon (1992, 1998), including the kiln in Al-Amreya, have been destroyed as a result of urban development.

The study carried out by Empereur and Picon for the amphora production sites resulted in the creation of a typology for Mareotic amphorae and hence allows for a better appreciation of the distribution of such amphorae within and outside Egypt. The only limitation of Empereur and Picon's study is their focus mainly on the area east of Marea, while little information is provided about the area from Taposiris Magna to Marea, and no information is provided either Mareotis Island or about the area west of Taposiris Magna.

2.3 Recent work in the Mareotic region

During the past few years a number of archaeological projects were undertaken in the Mareotic region. Some of these focused on the main two sites along the shores of the western Mareotic Arm, Marea and Taposiris Magna, while others looked at more distant areas, yet still related to the Mareotis region and the activities around the ancient lake.

These recent projects include the excavations carried out by the Polish archaeological mission at Marea and those of the French archaeological missions at Marea and Taposiris Magna. Also included is the Western Delta Regional Survey conducted by the Egypt Exploration Society and the University of Durham, and survey as well as the excavation carried out by the German archaeological mission at the Hellenistic Nile harbour of Schedia southeast of Alexandria. These two last projects, although not directly related to the western arm of Lake Mareotis, however, have contributed significantly to our understanding of the role that Lake Mareotis played in antiquity.

2.3.1 The Polish excavation: Marea

Between 2000 and 2008 a team from the Polish Centre for Mediterranean Archaeology of Warsaw University and the Archaeological Museum in Cracow excavated two sites in the Byzantine town of Marea: a bath complex with a *sakkia*-well and a funerary chapel. The site explored by the Polish team covers c. 19ha and is located in the north-eastern part of the Marea Peninsula.

As mentioned earlier, El-Fakharani (1983) identified this area and its associated harbour as the town of Marea, the capital of the Mareotic region, which was the main town and military base in the region since the time of King Psammetichus of the 26th Dynasty (Herodotus II.2.31; Rodziewicz 2003: 27). In Marea, El- Fakharani excavated a double bath complex, the waterfront street and shops, grain storage facilities and harbour installations. The remains of the harbour of Marea indicate that it was the largest lake harbour on the Mareotic Arm. It contained four quays which divided the 1.5km-long shoreline into eastern, central and western basins. The dimensions of the quays from west to east (length and breadth) are: 41m x 6.5m, 111m x 5m, 125m x 7m and 35m x 4m, respectively (Szymańska & Babraj 2008: 11-15). However, until recently, all archaeological investigation carried out in the area revealed no evidence earlier than the 5th century AD.

During eight campaigns the mission excavated a large Byzantine bath dating to the 6th – 8th centuries connected to a *sakkia*, which is located about 5m to the north of the Byzantine baths, together with a well that supplied it with water. A funerary chapel of the same date was also uncovered and the excavation of a Christian basilica is still ongoing. The ceramics studied indicate that the complex functioned between the first half of the 6th century and early 8th century. Arab coins found during the excavation that date from the late 7th until mid 8th centuries, confirm the continued operation of the baths after the Arab conquest.

However, in recent years, in addition to the Byzantine remains, the Polish mission's excavations have revealed earlier structures that indicate that a large pre-Byzantine settlement once flourished at the site. Specifically the excavation revealed the remains of Early Roman pottery, and more importantly a 2nd – 3rd centuries AD amphora kiln underneath the apse of the basilica. The size of the

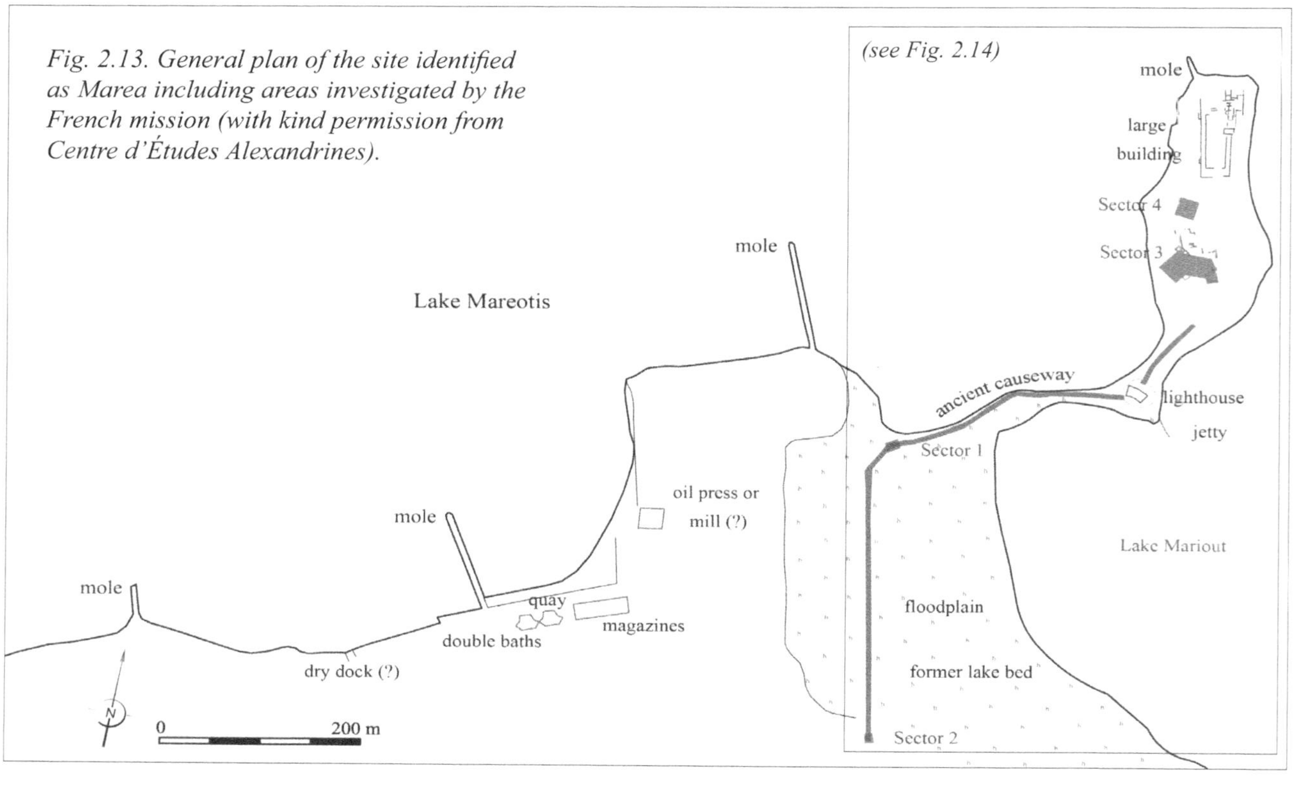

Fig. 2.13. General plan of the site identified as Marea including areas investigated by the French mission (with kind permission from Centre d'Études Alexandrines).

kiln, c. 8m in diameter, is unmistakable proof that a flourishing amphora production centre existed here prior to the Byzantine period.

Judging by the accumulation of coin finds, the town had its heyday in the 7th century and was abandoned by the first quarter of the 8th century. Therefore, it is evident that Marea never lost its importance as a commercial harbour despite the founding of Alexandria, and that the Mareotis region remained the most important agricultural and industrial producer in north-west Egypt until after the Arab conquest (Szymańska & Babraj 2008: 11).

Fig. 2.14. The peninsula of Marea (with kind permission from Centre d'Études Alexandrines).

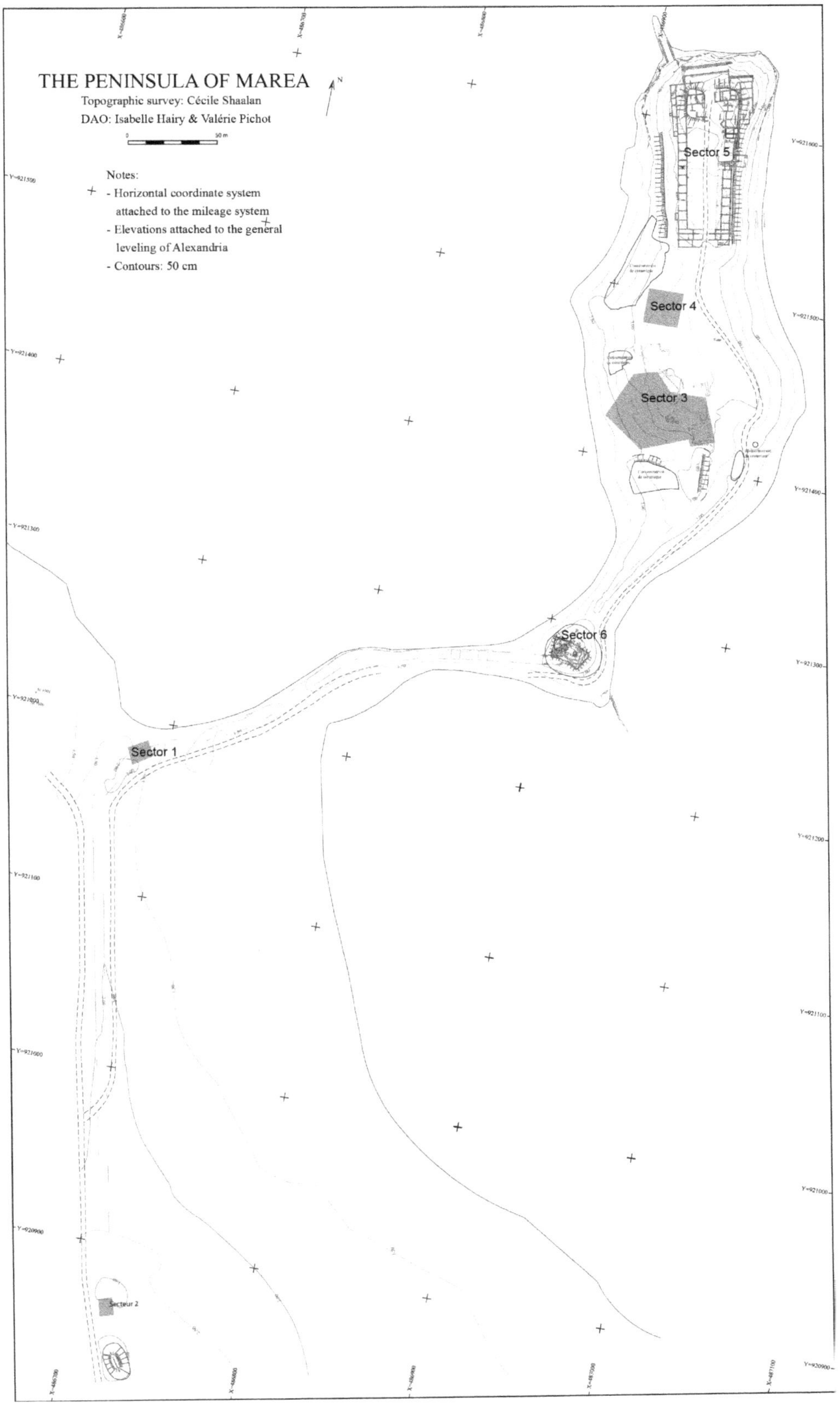

2.3.2 The French excavation: Hellenistic Marea

Another project has been ongoing in Marea since 2003 (Pichot 2010). It is an excavation directed by the Centre d'Études Alexandrines that focuses on the eastern peninsula (Figs. 2.13 & 2.14). Discoveries in this area of the site have made a significant contribution to our understanding of Marea and have finally settled the argument regarding its dating. With the exception of the Early Roman amphora kiln discovered by the Polish mission (discussed above), all other major archaeological remains in Marea suggest a somewhat later occupation. However, excavations on the eastern peninsula have also started revealing evidence from Hellenistic and Early Roman times.

The eastern peninsula is connected to the mainland by a causeway more than 600m long. Archaeological material in this area dates the causeway to between the 1st and 3rd centuries AD. Moreover, excavation revealed the existence of a number of buildings of commercial and industrial nature. At the very northern part of the peninsula, the foundations of a building more than 100m long built of large limestone blocks and hydraulic mortar similar to the causeway leading to the peninsula, were discovered. The building consisted of a large courtyard surrounded by numerous rooms of relatively similar size. The building is also connected to a quay to the north, through a system of terraces and stairways cut into the bedrock. It has been suggested that the building could have been used for storage and trade (Pichot 2010) (see Fig. 2.14).

In the central section of the Marea Peninsula, another complex of buildings was excavated. The excavation revealed the remains of slag, furnace walls, charcoal and fragments of iron, in addition to ceramics, bones and fragments of faience. The remains indicated that the buildings were used as workshops, mainly for processing metals, from the 1st century BC to the 1st century AD, however, the ceramics indicated activities as early as the 3rd century BC (Pichot 2010).

Recent archaeological research undertaken at Marea is thus beginning to indicate that the area was thriving before the 5th century AD and as early as the Hellenistic period. It is also quite likely that further investigation in the region has the potential to reveal more evidence for pre-Byzantine occupation of Marea.

2.3.3 The French excavation: Taposiris Magna

Another ongoing project that is taking place in the Mareotic Arm is the excavation of the Hellenistic and Roman town of Taposiris Magna about 15km west of Marea and 45km west of Alexandria on the northern shore of the lake. Previous archaeological investigation at Taposiris Magna

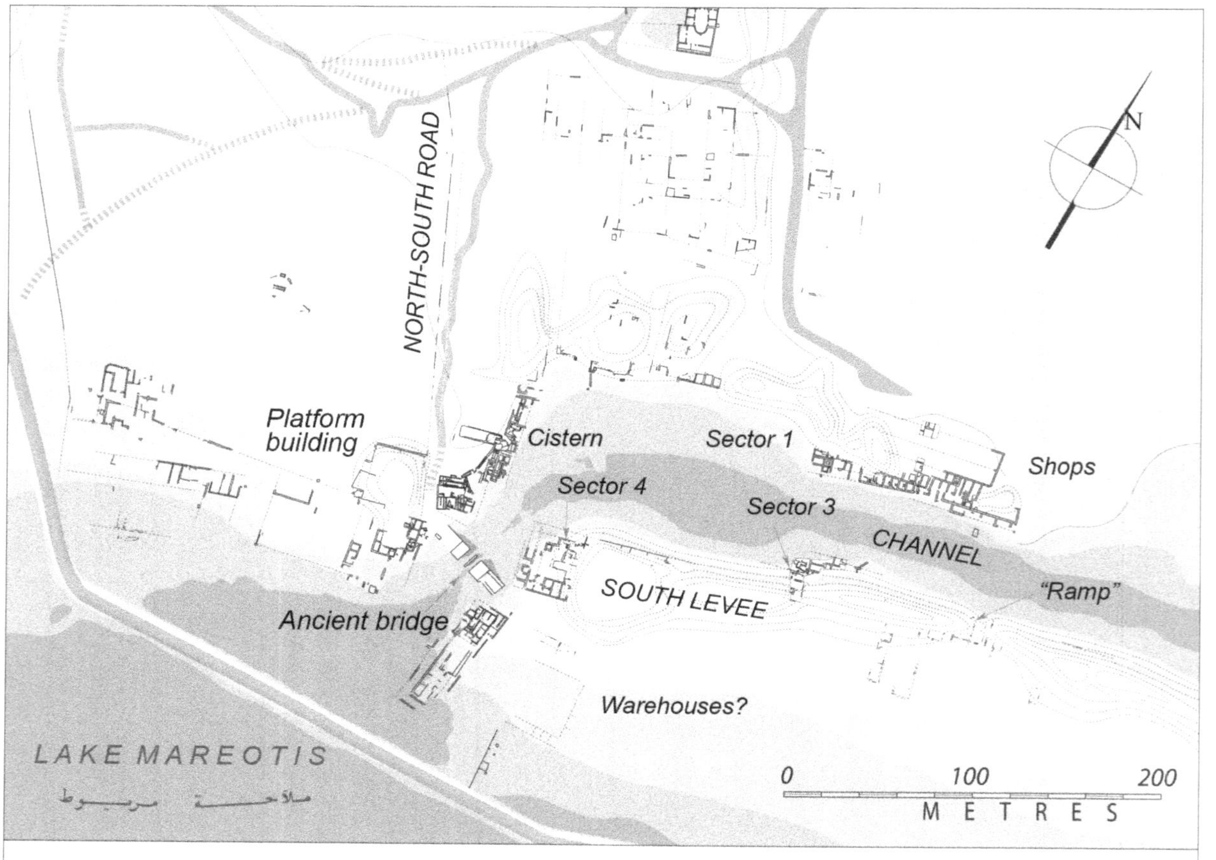

Fig. 2.15. Plan of Taposiris Magna and harbour (with kind permission from MAFTM – Mission archéologique française à Taposiris Magna).

has focused mainly on its monumental sites, namely the Hellenistic Temple and the tower-like funerary monument which represented a 1:4 or 1:5 replica of the Pharos lighthouse of Alexandria (El-Fakharani 1974; Kadous 2001: 457-60; Vörös 2001: 37) (Fig. 2.15).

The site has extensive archaeological remains that date from the early Hellenistic period to about the 7th century AD, including evidence for thriving maritime and commercial activities, such as the remains of one of the best-preserved harbours in Lake Mareotis (Empereur 1998a: 225-7; Rodziewicz 1998a, 1998b).

Since 1998, the archaeological mission of the Maison de l'Orient la Méditerranée of the University of Lyon has been conducting excavations at the town and harbour of Taposiris Magna, as well as the town and necropolis of Plinthene, 2km east of Taposiris Magna.

Commercial activities in Taposiris Magna were mainly focused on handling products transported across the lake as well as receiving goods arriving from the west through overland routes and shipping them to Alexandria (Empereur 1998a: 225). Under the Ptolemies and the Romans, Taposiris Magna was a customs station where dues were levied on products coming from the Mareotic region and from Cyrenaica heading east towards Alexandria or to the Nile Delta and vice-versa (Empereur 1998a: 225-7; Vörös 2001: 15-6). On the other hand, river vessels heading west could have travelled on the lake through the harbour of Taposiris Magna to the west as far as the lake extended.

The harbour of Taposiris Magna was thus structured to control the movement of vessels travelling through it. This was achieved by digging a channel c. 1600m long and 50m wide parallel to the northern shore of the lake. The spoil resulting from the digging was piled to form an artificial ridge which delimits the channel to the south. At the western end of the channel stood a limestone structure that took the form of a double-opening gate or bridge through which all boats wishing to pass through Taposiris Magna had to pass (Empereur 1998a: 225-7; Rodziewicz 1998a: 102, n. 32; Vörös 2001: 15-6). The total width of the gate is 8.3m, but, it is divided by a 1.2m-thick wall into two openings; one is 4.10m wide and the other one is 3m wide, thus indicating the maximum possible width of the vessels that were passing through it (Fig. 2.16). The eastern entrance of the channel is partially blocked by a jetty which is c. 230m long extending from north to south perpendicular to the shoreline. The distance between the southern end of the jetty and the eastern end of the artificial ridge, c. 100m, forms the eastern entrance of this semi-closed harbour basin of Taposiris Magna. The eastern jetty of the harbour includes at least two openings to allow water to flush away the silt and sediments that might have accumulated in the harbour basin.

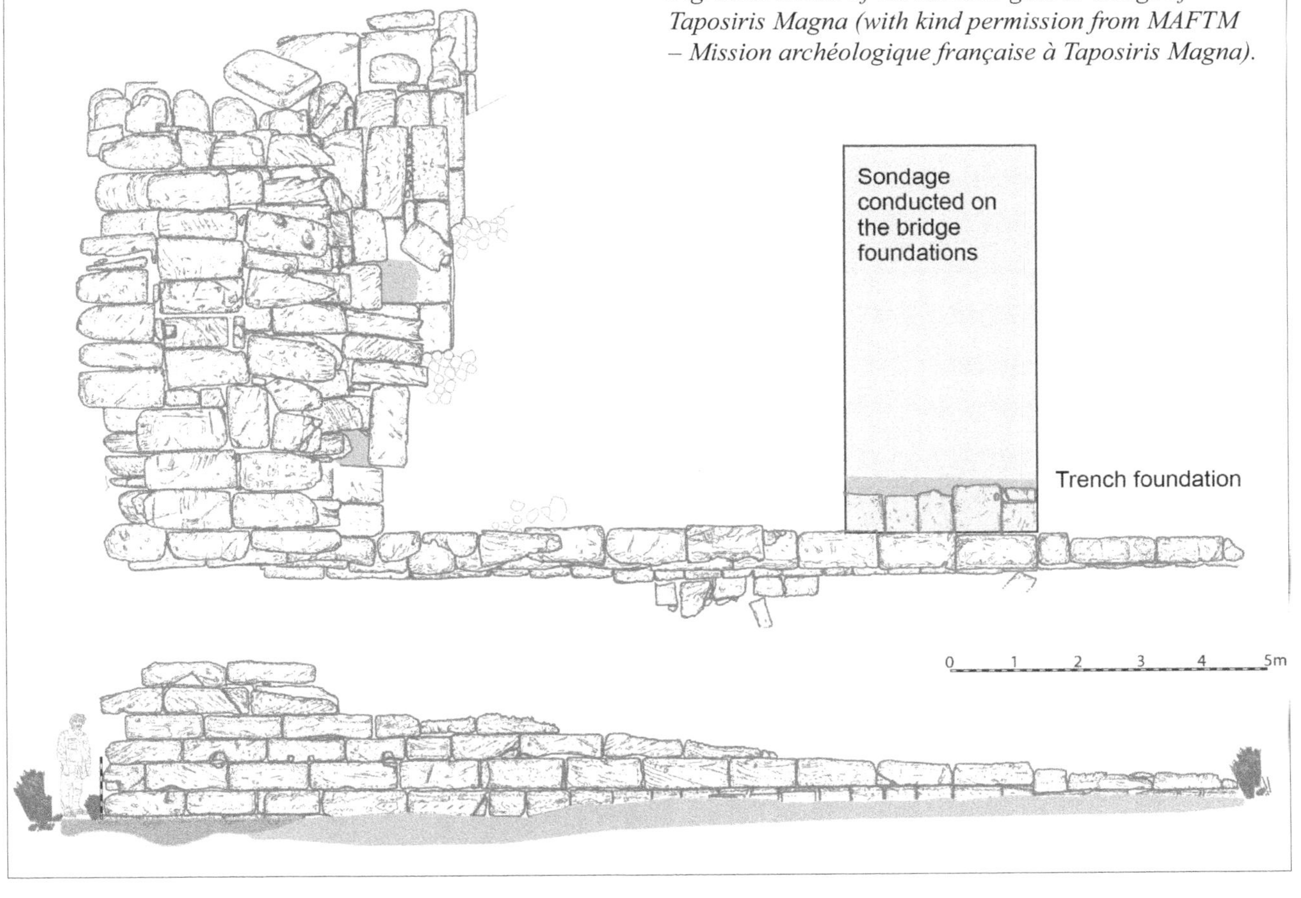

Fig. 2.16. Detail of the harbour gate or bridge of Taposiris Magna (with kind permission from MAFTM – Mission archéologique française à Taposiris Magna).

The arrangement to control the harbour was supplemented by a solid limestone wall known as "the wall of the Barbarians" which extended from the northern shores of the lake to the seashore across the coastal ridge. This regulated the passage of land caravans and ensured that caravans travelling in both directions had to go through the town of Taposiris Magna (De Cosson 1935: 111; Rodziewicz 1990: 72-4). It was also supplemented by the construction of a 1700m-long causeway that extends southwards from the northern ridge to the southern shore of the lake. As a result of recent excavations, it is now believed that the digging of the channel and the construction of this harbour system took place during the Early Roman period rather than during the Hellenistic period as was previously believed (El-Fakharani 1974; Boussac & El Amouri 2010). Although the northern shoreline was occupied during the Hellenistic period, as indicated by the remains of houses and shops from the 2nd and 1st centuries BC, it seems that it was abandoned by the end of the Hellenistic period as a result of a rise in the lake level. The channel was then excavated in the Roman period to create the closed harbour (Boussac & El Amouri 2010).

In addition to the harbour system, the mission also excavated various other remains in the towns of Taposiris Magna and Plinthene including the remains of a rock-cut Hellenistic *tholoi* baths, a necropolis of sacred animals (EA33), a chapel and a peristyle house. These discoveries have allowed further clarification of the date of the occupation of Taposiris Magna which extended from the Early Hellenistic period until the early 7th century AD (Boussac & El Amouri 2010).

2.3.4 The Western Delta Survey

As mentioned earlier in this chapter, in antiquity Lake Mareotis was much larger than its present size as its main body extended for about 50km south of Alexandria. De Cosson (1935: 151) suggests that the southern navigable limits of the main body of the lake in the Hellenistic and Roman times extended as far as Kom Trouga, about 30km south of the southern limits of the present Lake Mareotis. Along the shores of the lake's main body were many towns and settlements which are now completely land-locked and are located within the cultivated areas of the Western Delta (De Cosson 1935; Al-Falaki 1966). It is evident that those towns and settlements, once located along canals and distributaries connected to the lake's main body, were significantly affected by the silting of the Canopic Branch and hence the diminishing of the canal network that used to supply Lake Mareotis with Nile water. With the reduction of the lake's size, these settlements lost their importance as well as their connection to Alexandria, and with time, they became part of the agriculture land of the Delta, forming the basis for modern towns and villages (Wilson 2007; Wilson & Grigoropolous 2009).

The investigation of these sites was part of an extensive survey project, known as the "Sais and its Hinterland" Project, conducted in the Western Nile Delta by the Egypt Exploration Society and Durham University since 1997 (Wilson 2007). The survey revealed the sites that have been the focus of human activity along the eastern, southern and western shores of the main body of Lake Mareotis in antiquity. In addition to recording some key archaeological sites in the Western Delta region such as Sais (Sa el-Hagar) and Buto (Tell Farain), the project also recorded tell sites and settlements such as El-Barnugi, Kom Trugi (Kom Trouga), Kom el-Mahar, Kom el-Hagg and Kom el-Qadi, which could have been located at or near the southern and eastern shores of Lake Mareotis in antiquity (Wilson 2007; Fig. 2.17). Based mainly upon the study of ceramic collections, it was realised that the sites range in date from the Ptolemaic to the Late Roman period; the period during which maritime traffic was most active on Lake Mareotis. In addition to pottery of local production, the ceramic collections also included imported pottery from North Africa, Italy, Greece, Cyprus and the Syro-Palestinian coast (Wilson 2007).

The survey revealed that many of the sites investigated have been subject to modern urban development which resulted in the sites being built over or levelled to be used for agriculture. However, the study of ceramics and other archaeological material revealed that some sites were more extensive and probably more significant than others in terms of their role as economic and maritime centres in the past. For example, it has been suggested by Wilson (2010) that some of these sites, such as Kom el-Hagg and Kom Ishu, which were situated close to the western shores of ancient Lake Mareotis, could have had strategic value as stopping off places or in guarding the lake shores and watching over the desert areas to the west, the river to the south and marshes or fields on all sides.

Both of these sites mentioned above are small rocky outcrops about 4m high located on the edge of a limestone rock formation. They are within signalling distance (less than 2km apart) and they are surrounded by villages and fields. The study of ceramic samples from the sites showed that the site of Kom el-Hagg was mostly active during the Ptolemaic and Early Roman periods, while most of the pottery samples from Kom Ishu dates to the Later Roman period. Most of the pottery was Egyptian in origin, and was probably produced locally (Wilson 2007, 2010).

Other sites which have been studied during the Western Delta Survey included Kom Trouga, Kom el-Mahar and Kom el-Qadi and are located on the south-eastern shores of Lake Mareotis.

At present, the archaeological site at Kom Trouga covers an area of about 350m from north to south and 300m from east to west. It consists of an elevated sandy area with several excavated red brick structures. Other archaeological remains on the site include a number of red brick and plastered tanks, which probably belonged to wineries. They also include several red granite grindstones and the remains of limestone walls and a paved floor. To the north of this area lies a modern village which may have been built upon part of the original site. However, it is believed that in antiquity this was an extensive site and a key harbour town on the lake. It was used by travellers going from Alexandria to the Wadi el-Natrun and for receiving and dispatching commodities transported between Alexandria and the Delta (De Cosson 1935: 79, 151; Wilson 2007). The study of ceramic collections from Kom Trouga revealed that the site was used from the Ptolemaic through to the medieval period; however, its heyday was probably during the Early Roman period (Wilson 2010).

Kom el-Mahar (the mound of shells) is located 13km northwest of Kom Trouga. The main part of the site consists of a 10-12m-high mound of sandy deposits which contains seashells from degraded local oolitic limestone. As with most archaeological sites in the Delta region, the original site at Kom el-Mahar was probably larger than its present size since parts of the site has been used for agriculture purposes. Currently the archaeological remains include ashlar limestone blocks, a wall made of sandy and shell-filled mudbricks, fragments of red granite and glass fragments, as well as pottery sherds which include imported

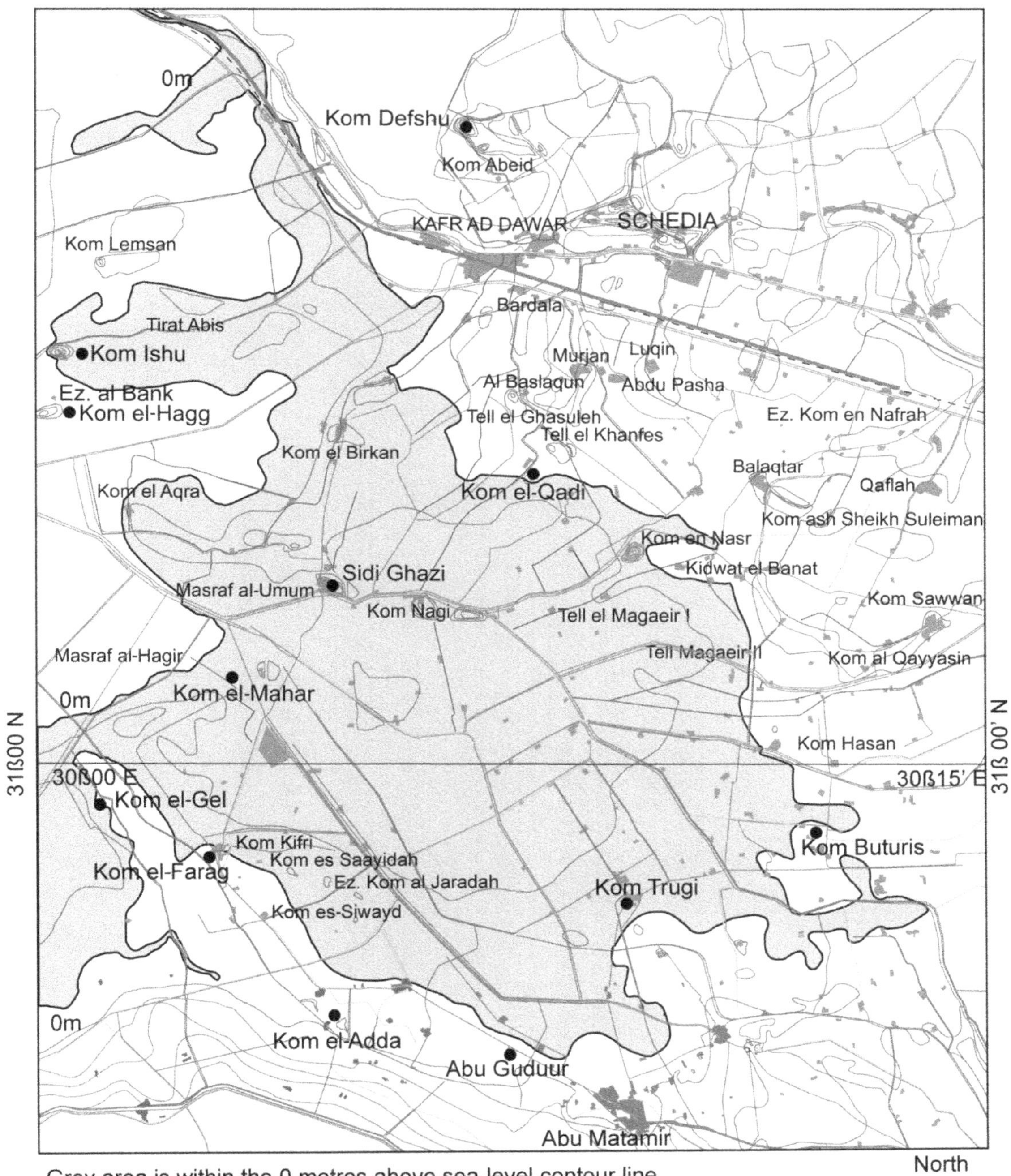

Fig. 2.17. Map of sites in the Western Delta Survey region (by kind permission of P. Wilson).

table wares and imported finewares. The study of ceramic samples suggested a date for the site from the Late Ptolemaic to the Early Roman period, however, it seems that it was abandoned around the 2nd century (Wilson 2007, 2010).

Kom el-Qadi lies 10km northeast of Kom el-Mahar and it extends for about 370m east to west and 170m north to south. The main archaeological area is a mound about 8m high with its southern and northern faces cut away to form sheer sections. The mound contains sandbrick and mudbrick walls, pottery deposits and human burials. Within the village, there are the remains of a Roman bath-house including a section of concrete floor of a *tholos*, as well as the remains of furnaces and tanks. To the east of the village brick chambers and fragments of limestone were noted. The ceramic collections from the site date mostly to the Early Roman period and include some imported fine wares, local cooking pots and some Egyptian amphora. The material seems to indicate the domestic nature of the site in the Roman period (Wilson 2007, 2010).

These sites constitute what were probably the main settlements along the southern shore of Lake Mareotis in antquity. They would have functioned as key agricultural and production sites in the service of Alexandria as well as internal trans-shipping stations and points of control around the lake during the Ptolemaic and Roman eras (Wilson 2010).

2.3.5 The Schedia Project

Most modern authors agree that the Canopic Branch of the Nile bifurcated at Zawiyat al-Bahr and subsequently took a north-westerly route until it reached the town and harbour of Schedia, originally a Hellenistic foundation southeast of Alexandria that was later known as Chaereu (Strabo 17.1.23; El-Zouka 1979: 75).

Strabo (17.1.16) described Schedia as "...the station for paying duty on the goods brought down from above it and brought up from below it; and for this purpose, also, a *schedia* (float) has been laid across the river, from which the place has its name". Schedia also contained a station of "*thalamegoi*" (cabin-boats; Strabo 17.1.16), which were used by the *potamophylacia*, the Roman service which exercised fiscal and police supervision over the river (Starr 1941: 112).

At Schedia the Canopic Branch splits into two routes. The main branch continued to the Bay of Canopus (present-day Aboukir Bay) east of Alexandria, while the second branch formed what was then known as the Schedia Canal, which flowed to the northwest towards Alexandria, following a course close to that of the present Al-Mahmoudeyah Canal, finally to debouch into Lake Mareotis, close to the eastern gate of Alexandria, the Canopic Gate (Strabo 17.1.16). This canal played a key role in internal transport to and from the city during the Hellenistic and Roman periods (Fig. 2.18).

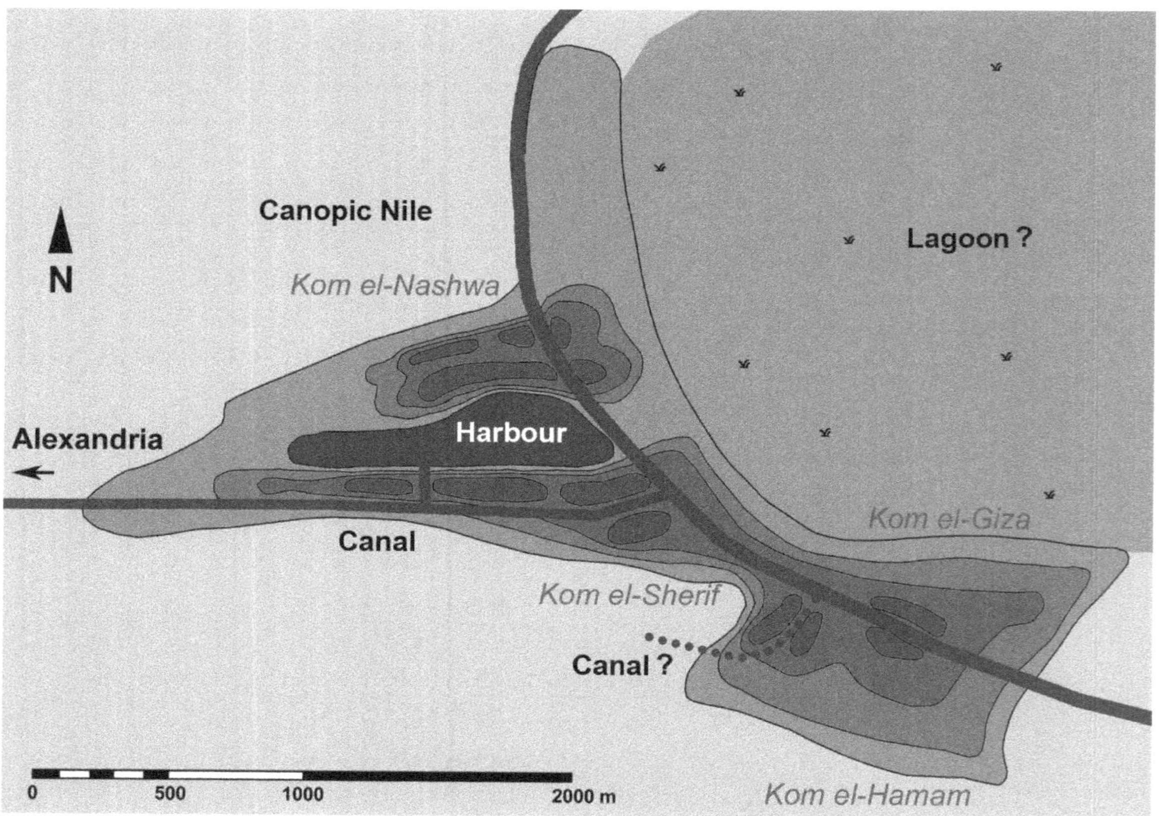

Fig. 2.18. Map to locate Schedia, the canal and the links with surrounding river/water systems (with kind permission Heinzelman & Bergmann).

Besides its navigational aspect, the Schedia Canal played a major role in supplying the city of Alexandria with drinking water, which flowed during the Nile flood to fill the numerous cisterns of the city (Empereur 1998a: 126-43). The Schedia Canal remained functioning until the early medieval period; however, after the silting of the Canopic Branch, the canal was extended to take its water supply from the Rosetta Branch (El-Zouka 1979: 98), and it was then known as the Alexandria Canal (Weheba 1989: 259-62; Haas 1997: 348).

Schedia was the main Nile emporium, customs harbour and checkpoint east of Alexandria in the Hellenistic and Roman period, where custom duties were imposed on imported and exported goods (Empereur 1998a: 225). Moreover, it seems that the Canopic Branch at Schedia, which was about 250m wide (Heinzelmann 2005), was obstructed by some kind of a pontoon that prevented boats from sailing past it until duties were paid on merchandise travelling in both directions. Additionally, it was at Schedia where commodities for export brought from upriver were transferred from large Nile boats to smaller boats that could travel easily through the canals to Alexandria (Procopius 6.1.3; Haas 1997: 365 n. 13).

The site of Schedia currently extends through the villages of Kom El-Giza, Kom El-Nashw and Kom El-Hamam, some 30km southeast of Alexandria (Bergmann & Heinzelmann 2003). Since 2003 an archaeological project in Schedia has made much progress in revealing its extent, nature, role and its functional and spatial relationship with the Canopic branch of the Nile (Bergmann & Heinzelmann 2003, 2004, 2005, 2010). The excavations revealed much evidence which confirms that Schedia was a prosperous and flourishing emporium during the Hellenistic and Roman periods. Of particular interest was a large building measuring 70m x 40m constructed around AD 100 above earlier mudbrick structures. This structure shows two main phases of use. In the Early Roman period it appeared to have been used as a residential area while by the late 4th or early 5th centuries AD the area was abandoned and levelled in order to install a granary which was in use until the late 5th or 6th centuries AD, when it was destroyed by fire (Bergmann & Heinzelmann 2003, 2005, 2010). Moreover, a number of inscriptions found in Schedia indicated there was a large garrison stationed in the area that under Roman administration (Bergmann & Heinzelmann 2003).

Based on the archaeological investigation of the area it has been suggested that the foundation of Schedia took place in the Ptolemaic period around an artificial harbour basin following the construction of the Canopic Canal, later the Schedia Canal, and hence it developed on both sides of the Canopic Branch. The town reached its maximum extension in the 2nd and 3rd centuries AD, and in the Late Roman period it seems that various areas were transformed from residential and urban districts to economic and agricultural areas.

Schedia was affected by the gradual silting of the Canopic Branch; however, it was still active until the beginning of the 7th century, when it was then completely abandoned at the time of the Arab conquest (Bergmann & Heinzelmann 2003, 2005).

Chapter 3. Methodology

3.1 Objectives of the Lake Mareotis Research Project

The objectives of the collaborative Lake Mareotis Research Project were to undertake a detailed systematic survey of the western extension of the lake in order to record, quantify and assess the archaeological resources of the area in a comprehensive manner. The aim was to acquire a better understanding of the nature and extent of economic and maritime activities in the Mareotic region and to explore the relationship between the component parts of this complex system and how they developed and changed over time, in order to determine a more comprehensive understanding of the economic functions of ancient Alexandria.

The specific objectives of the collaborative Lake Mareotis Research Project were to:

• Systematically survey the shores of the western arm of Lake Mareotis that extends some 40km in length and is a maximum 3km wide. This includes Mareotis Island located towards the southeast of the survey area that is some 3.7km in length and up to 680m wide (see Fig. 1.6). This survey was undertaken within the context of the complex palaeogeographical history of the lake.

• Record, quantify and assess the archaeological resource.

• Determine the extent, chronology and, where possible, function, of each site.

• Determine the nature and the extent of the economic and maritime activities of the Mareotic region.

• Determine the significance of the Mareotic region in relation to Alexandria, particularly during the Hellenistic, Roman and Byzantine periods when the lake was most active.

• Identify the degree of threat to the archaeological resources in the Mareotic region in relation from development and pollution.

3.2 Methodology

The pilot survey conducted in 2004 identified over 60 sites. Some of these sites were already documented in the archaeological record, some having been partially excavated by the Western Nile Delta section of the Supreme Council for Antiquities (SCA) and foreign missions, or noted but not recorded in detail in previous publications. However, at least half of the sites identified were believed to be new discoveries. The sites were prioritised on the basis of their maritime significance, particularly where maritime installations such as moles, jetties, quays, mooring rings, etc., had been identified. GPS coordinates were taken to fix the position of each site located and each site was photographed and basic data pertaining to its nature were recorded on site record sheets. Since 2004 four further seasons of survey have been conducted between autumn 2006 and summer 2008, and the following methodology implemented:

• A desk-based assessment of the region was undertaken with the aid of high-resolution Quickbird Satellite Imagery (Egypt 28th June 2004 & 16th July 2004. NPA 2007 Published by NPA Group www.npagroup.com), to establish the nature and extent of the sites already identified (Fig. 3.1). This information, along with all the data acquired as part of the Lake Mareotis Research Project, is archived in a GIS-based database.

• Each site was surveyed using a GPS-based Real Time Kinematic (RTK) satellite navigation system to produce detailed topographic maps of each site.

• Specific buildings and/or features were planned using a Leica TCR705 Total Station, and the data were downloaded in the field into AutoCAD via TheoLt software.

• Ceramic survey was undertaken to determine the chronology, nature and function of each site (for further details, see Chapter 4).

• A Fluxgate Radiometer Magnetometer geophysical survey was conducted at specific sites to establish the layout of structures beneath the surface.

• Sedimentological survey to determine the changing lake levels and identify geomorphological changes was conducted at selected sites (for further details, see Chapter 5).

• Limited site-clearing and excavation to articulate walls and identify more detailed building phases was undertaken at selected sites.

• A photographic archive was compiled of each site and features within the site.

The three main survey seasons conducted between 2007 and 2008 focused on the principal geographical areas in the survey region, the northern and southern lake shores and the shores of Mareotis Island. Each site was surveyed as comprehensively as possible although constantly increasing water levels over the four-year survey period did restrict the recording of some sites whose waterfront installations became submerged and thus they were out of reach of terrestrial survey. Another challenge that also influenced the survey rationale was the potential threat to particular sites (see Chapter 2). Those sites that were obviously facing immediate risk were prioritised for recording. Regrettably, at times recording was not possible prior to destruction, as was the case at Site 202 where a bulldozer was encountered destroying the site and specifically a Hellenistic tomb. In other parts of the survey region, it was not possible due to the limitations of time, to record in detail all visible building remains. This was a particular

Fig. 3.1. Quickbird Satellite Imagery (Egypt 28th June 2004 & 16th July 2004. NPA 2007) of the western extent of Lake Mareotis.

challenge along the ridge at both the western and eastern ends of Mareotis Island where the extant remains were extensive and substantial in nature. However, the full extent of every site identified was topographically surveyed as indicated.

3.3 Survey

3.3.1 Topographic and building feature survey

(with assistance from J. Whitewright & A. Trakadas)

The basis of any comprehensive archaeological survey is a detailed topographic survey of the site or area under investigation. Such a survey allows subsequent surveys using specific sampling techniques (such as ceramic sampling or building survey) to be located accurately within the boundaries of the site. A detailed topographic survey may also highlight underlying features of the terrain which may otherwise go unnoticed. Likewise the characteristics of certain features (e.g. relative height) can be accurately compared and contrasted. Large-scale topographic surveys have been carried out using a variety of equipment. Traditionally, tools such as Theodolites or Total Stations have been used. In the last few years the advent of widely available Global Positioning System (GPS) technology has provided advantages when compared to more traditional techniques, namely the opportunity to record accurately the global position of a site as well as the topographical features. This attribute is particularly advantageous when a regional survey incorporating a number of sites is being conducted so that it is also possible to position accurately-all sites relative to one another.

The Lake Mareotis Research Project utilised a GPS based survey system to undertake the topographical recording. A Leica GPS500 unit was used as the reference station while a Leica GPS1200 unit was used as the mobile data recorder (Fig. 3.2). Such equipment allowed a relative accuracy within the survey of a single site of up to 0.01m. The GPS1200 is a backpack-mounted unit with the option of deploying a detail pole for surveying specific features. For the Mareotis survey the unit was preconfigured to take a reading when changes occurred to its horizontal or vertical position of 1m and 0.1m, respectively. The standard transect used on all sites was at 5m intervals, except on particularly flat areas or where the density of the archaeological remains was thin; a 10m transect width was then chosen. The large size of Mareotis Island required that two GPS1200 units were used in tandem by a pair of surveyors. Data were processed using Leica Geo Office and ArcMap software (Fig. 3.3). Height data across all sites, where presented, remain relative to the Helmert 1906 Ellipsoid that was applied during processing.

In addition to the topographic survey, detailed feature surveys were conducted at a number of different sites utilising TheoLt. TheoLt is a survey program developed by Latimer

Fig. 3.2. (right) RTK GPS data survey kit (LMRP).

Fig. 3.3. (below) Site survey methodology demonstrated through the sequential examination of one site, Site 39 indicated by '39' on all four images of this figure.
A: Desk-based assessment and location of site on satellite photographs combined with field observation and handheld GPS coordinates taken during the pilot survey.
B: Detailed inspection of site during full field season, site extent established and topographical survey undertaken using RTK equipment.
C: Topographical data collected at the site are processed and superimposed over the satellite imagery.
D: Extant archaeological remains are recorded and ceramic survey is conducted, and placed on the topographical map of the site.

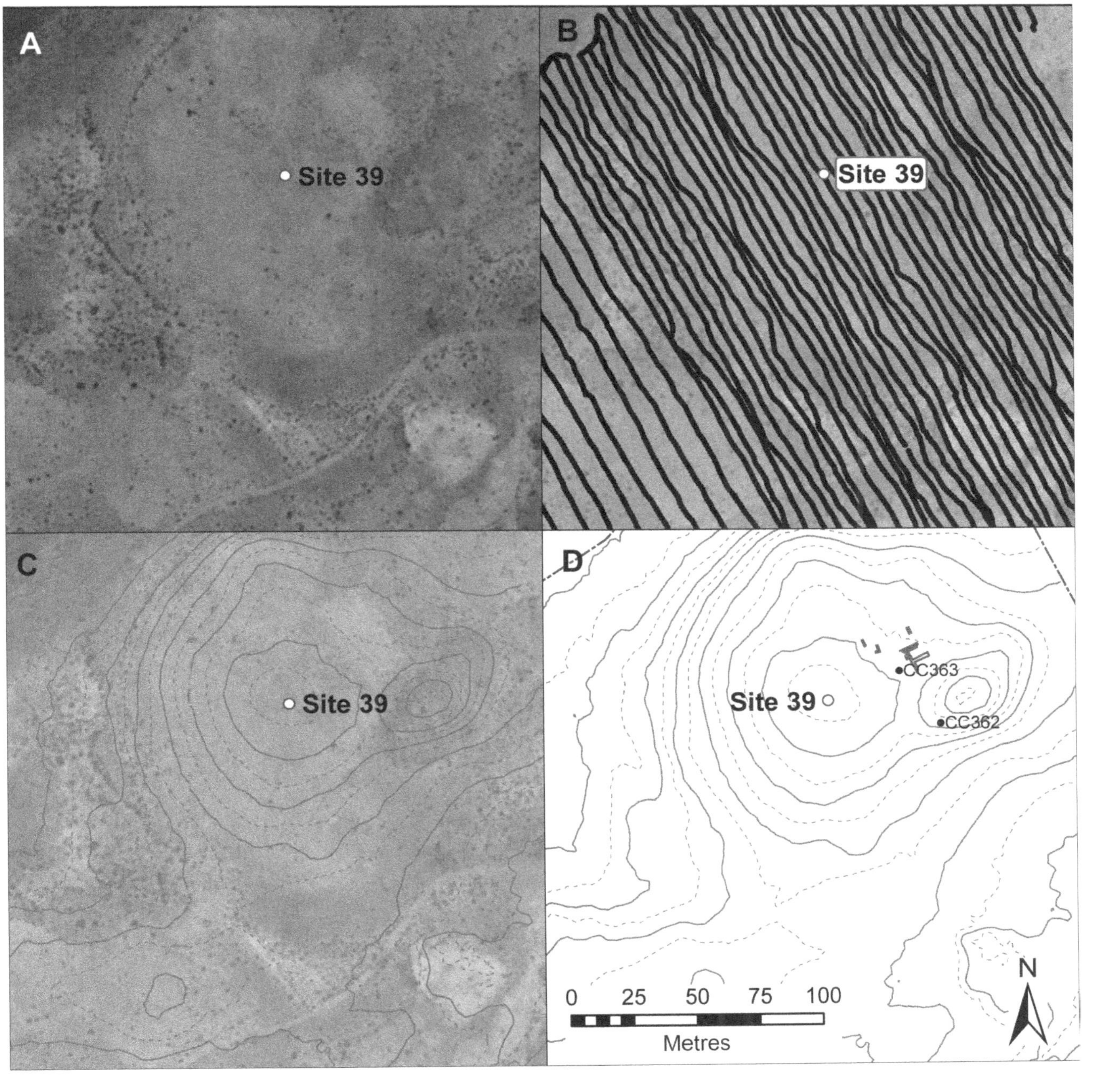

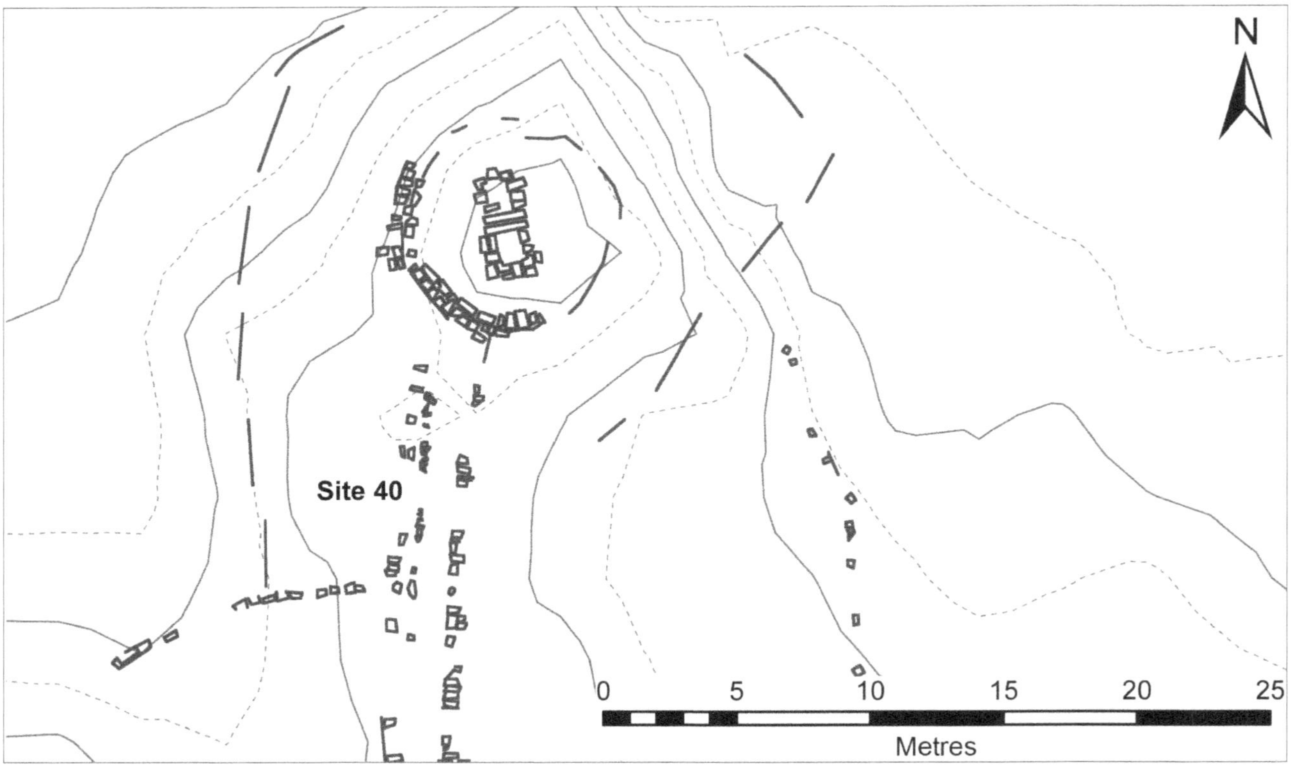

Fig. 3.4. A detailed example of CAD planning results e.g. Site 40 (LMRP).

CAD that allows the user to record information directly into AutoCAD, thus negating the requirement to transfer data from surveying software and enabling the surveyor to check the accuracy of the data during acquisition. The surveys were conducted using a Leica Total Station TCR307, recording straight into AutoCAD 2007 via TheoLt. This allowed the specific features of exposed buildings to be accurately recorded, thus providing more data to support interpretations of site function (Fig. 3.4).

3.3.2 Ceramic survey

(with assistance from R.Thomas)

Ceramic survey was attempted at every site, producing data for most sites. The principal methodology employed was the collection of surface ceramics from a series of designated "ceramic circles". Areas of higher density ceramic remains were targeted across the full extent of each site. The number of circles varied from one site to another depending on the site area and density of ceramic remains. Each circle had a diameter of 10m and all diagnostic sherds (rims, bases, handles, decorated sherds) were collected. The object of this approach was to get an insight into the range of ceramic type, function and date across the full extent of each site. In some cases, where the density of the ceramic remains was intense, a grid was laid across the site and ceramics were systematically collected from a series of 20m x 20m squares that made up each grid (Fig. 3.5). This methodology was employed at three sites (Site 40, Site 113 and Site 126) and the number of squares varied according to the nature and extent of each site selected. In addition, any sherds thought by the field walker to be distinctive or different in any way were collected, although many of these body sherds were not used in the statistical analysis (see Chapters 4 and 6). Finally, ceramics were also collected from stratigraphic contexts as part of the limited cleaning and excavation that was undertaken at Sites 118, 119, and 123.

All ceramics collected were bagged and made ready for sorting and analysis. On collection, each bag of ceramics was individually labelled with a unique bag number that referenced the site number and the individual bag number. A GPS co-ordinate was taken either at the centre of each ceramic circle or the location of the grid was mapped and the individual squares numbered. In this way the location of all ceramics collected was noted to within 10m.

The pottery from survey and excavations was processed in the same manner. A pottery processing form was created based on early observations to accelerate processing. Every sherd was sorted, counted and entered onto the processing forms. Where possible, published parallels were noted on all forms. Subsequently the data were entered into an Excel database. Recurring and exceptional types (including stamps) were drawn and photographed. All drawn examples were catalogued, Munsell color numbers noted, and fabric descriptions based on observations were made with a hand lens and entered into a database. Rubbings were also made of all stamps.

Reference to ceramics throughout this volume considers the site from which the sherds were collected and a unique

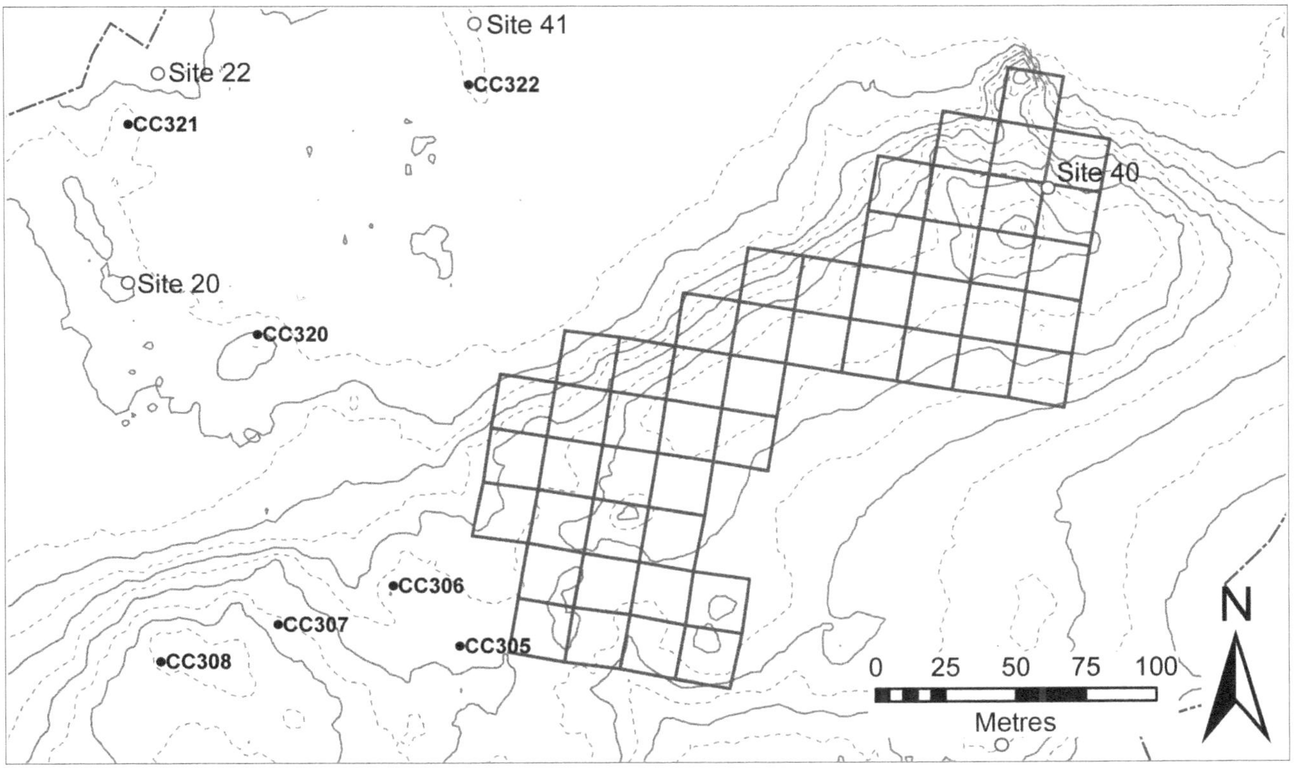

Fig. 3.5. Ceramic survey around the central ridge of western Mareotis Island; both ceramic grids and ceramic circles were used as sampling techniques in this area (LMRP).

number in square brackets after the site number that refers to the specific context: either the ceramic circle number, a specific square within in a grid, or an excavation context. In some cases, sherds were collected as general indicators from the site and are thus labeled as such by the letter 'G'.

3.3.3 Geophysical survey

(with assistance from J. Whitewright & D. Glazier)
Geophysical (magnetometer) investigation was conducted at selected sites on Mareotis Island and the southern shore. Magnetometry is widely employed by archaeologists to record differing magnetic gradients beneath the surface. Human actions affect the magnetic profile of the soil and thus allow the surveyor to infer human interventions across a site. It was specifically employed as part of the Lake Mareotis Research Project in the hope that the results would provide an insight into both the function of particular buildings and thus the sites of which they were a part. This would also serve to highlight areas of sedimentation and hence landscape changes since antiquity which may be further investigated as part of the sedimentological survey (see Chapter 5).

In 2007 a total of three areas were subject to geophysical (magnetometer) survey: an area across Site 126, an area around Site 118 incorporating several waterfront structures, and an area around Site 40. The survey was conducted with the use of a GeoScan Research Fluxgate Gradiometer FM36 instrument, within a series of 20m x 20m grids, with the instrument recording a sample every 0.5m. The success of the survey was limited by the topography of the sites and the vegetation, although sub-surface structures were identified at all three sites. However, in 2008 as the previous results had not proven to be as insightful, geophysical survey was conducted with a Bartington Instruments Grad 601-2 dual sensor fluxgate gradiometer. The dual sensors survey at twice the rate of a single sensored instrument such as the FM36, and produce more refined results. In total six sites were surveyed using the Bartington Instrument Grad 601-2 dual sensor fluxgate gradiometer (Fig. 3.6). Each survey grid was 30m x 30m and was set out using the Leica TCR 307 Total Station and processed in Geoplot software in the Digital Archaeology Computing Laboratory at the University of Southampton, and placed onto the topographic survey of the region. The results contributed towards a more informed interpretation of the sites surveyed.

The six sites that were chosen for geophysical prospection in 2008 included Sites 21, 44, 109, 119, 123, and 126 (Fig. 3.7). These sites were selected for two primary reasons – all were thought to have possessed substantial waterside features, and all consisted of terrain conducive to systematic geophysical survey. Examples of the results of the geophysical survey are discussed in more detail from Site 21 and Site 126 (all results are discussed in Chapter 6). Site 21 is located on the west of the island and the area of this site covered by geophysical survey was 300m x 210m. Results clearly show a number of linear features that may

Fig. 3.6. *Deployment of Bartington Instrument Grad 601-2 dual sensor fluxgate gradiometer (LMRP).*

Fig. 3.7. *Example of geophysical survey results from the western end of Mareotis Island, Site 21 (LMRP).*

be interpreted as architectural remains. These are oriented NW-SE and are roughly perpendicular to the present lakeshore (see Figs 6.182, 6.183 & 6.184). The geophysical survey of Site 126 covered 270m x 120m. The remains of a substantial rectangular structure c. 30m in length by c. 20m wide are visible in the NW corner of the survey (see Fig. 3.7). Given the proximity to the waterfront it is feasible that such anomalies may represent warehouses; however, any further interpretation is dependent on groundtruthing through excavation.

3.3.4 Sedimentological survey

(with assistance from C. Flaux)

The sedimentological survey was essentially based on field observations. Six sites were studied (Fig. 3.8). Preliminary sedimentary interpretations compared present-day depositional processes with fossil sediments facies (buried surfaces). Surface descriptions derive from geomorphological surveys, surface sediment analysis and topographical surveys, complimented by satellite images from Egypt Quickbird Imagery (28th June 2004). This primary assessment of the sedimentary facies and dynamics of the study area helps to identify and understand the palaeotopography through stratigraphic observations. The available chronostratigraphy is only relative. In some cases, archaeological artefacts have allowed preliminary relative dating of palaeosurfaces.

Drilling was undertaken using a manual auger (Fig. 3.9). This allowed a rapid assessment of stratigraphy down to a depth of 7m, with a resolution <0.2m. The advantage is that it allows the boring of several points in one day (up to four drillings, 3m deep). However, the turning auger head can destroy sedimentary structures and interface features.

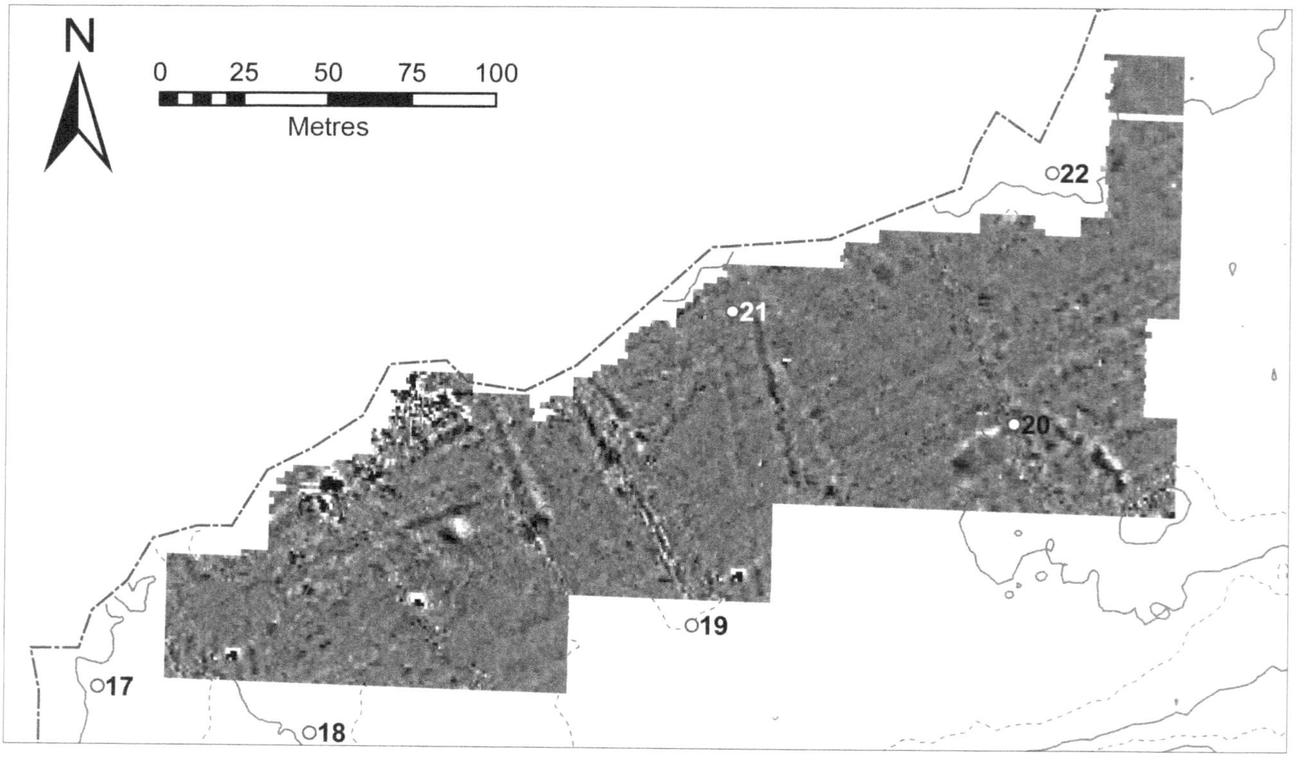

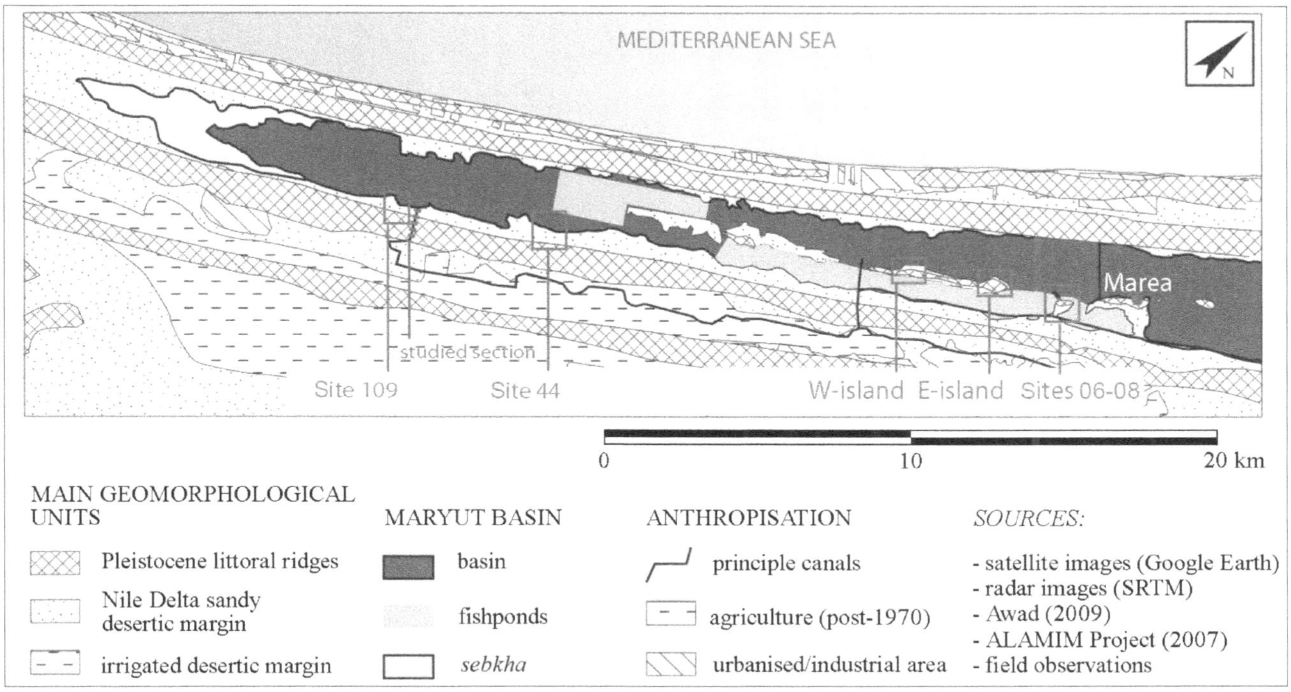

Fig. 3.8. Topographical scheme of the study area with the location of the sedimentological cores extracted (C. Flaux).

Fig. 3.9. Coring with a manual auger (LMRP).

Forty cores were extracted, representing in total around 90m of stratigraphy, and 450 sediment samples were extracted.

In conjunction with the topographical survey (see above), auger GPS points were presented according to the WGS84 system. Altitudes are thus elliptical heights. This reference level has been converted to mean sea level in Alexandria, using data from the Centre d'Études Alexandrines (CEAlex) topographic service (C. Shaalan). Thirty-four benchmarks in Alexandria, leveled in relation to mean sea level (calculated with a maregraph situated inside the western harbor of Alexandria; Administration égyptienne de topographie 1931) have been measured by a differential GPS (Meulien 1999: 84). The mean difference was calculated between elliptical altitudes and altitudes in relation to mean sea level in Alexandria to be 14.61 ± 0.03m. The error margin is probably due to the field leveling procedure (Meulien 1999: 84). It was therefore possible to convert all auger points into altitudes, benchmarked relative to mean sea level in Alexandria. This calculation was important, as the connection of Lake Mareotis to the sea is a key area of investigation in our study. The results of this work are presented in Chapter 5.

3.4 Conclusion

The five survey seasons conducted in the western arm of Lake Mareotis between 2004 and 2008 as part of the Lake Mareotis Research Project resulted in the identification of a total of 73 sites, dating from the Hellenistic period to the 7th century. These results are outlined below (see Chapter 6) and serve to add to our knowledge of this important region and its contribution to the great city of Alexandria in antiquity.

Chapter 4. Pottery from the Lake Mareotis Research Project

R. Tomber & R. Thomas[1]

4.1 Introduction

The main objectives of the pottery analysis were 1) to date the sites, 2) to examine whether there was chronological or functional variation within a site, 3) to compare the individual sites and the main areas with each other, and 4) to provide a quantitative overview of the different source regions involved in pottery supply.

4.1.1 Method and layout of the report

Pottery collection from all sites of the Lake Mareotis Research Project followed the procedure described in Chapter 3. As noted, this emphasised the recovery of rim, base and handle sherds, together with others that the collector considered different or diagnostic in some way. As a result some body sherds, particularly finewares or decorated pieces, were retained. All the collected sherds have been catalogued by count, although body sherds are not used in the statistics compiled from this data. Over the course of the project c. 12,000 sherds were collected for analysis, c. 11,400 of which were indicator sherds, namely bases, rims and handles. The remainder were body sherds, sometimes decorated and representing fabrics not otherwise present in the assemblage, but more often duplicating information from diagnostic sherds. In addition, excavation was carried out at Sites 118, 119 and 123 and the pottery from those excavations is incorporated here.

The pottery was classified according to three main variables: ware type (amphorae, coarse wares – including vessels for the table, storage and cooking – finewares, lamps), fabric type (clay body) and form type (shape variants within ware), all of which inform on each other. All fabric and form combinations were isolated, and significant or recurring types were illustrated unless too fragmentary. From this an overall type series was constructed, against which unillustrated pottery was compared.

The complete type series is described and illustrated in the catalogue that follows. It is presented in three sections, with Mareotic amphorae treated separately since they are represented from the kiln sites recorded during the project. While other products may be Mareotic, they are grouped with other Egyptian wares due to lack of kiln evidence.

The four main sections in this report are:

- 4.2 Overview
- 4.3 Mareotic kiln products (amphorae and pot stands)
- 4.4 Other Egyptian wares
- 4.5 Imported wares

4.1.2 Fabric and form catalogue

Each main section presents fabrics and a form typology in differing formats suitable to the level of knowledge of those types and the contribution made by this survey. Well-known fabrics and forms are not described in detail but a citation is provided. Munsell Color values are cited only for the Mareotic kiln products. This is an area where we could make a particular contribution, although it must be remembered that kiln products can be discoloured and their clays over fired. The forms are ordered from closed to open and where possible are presented chronologically. For each type an indication of quantity is given, based on the following parameters:

- Single vessel
- Rare: 10 or less sherds
- Sparse: 11-50 sherds
- Moderate: 51-100 sherds
- Common: 101-499 sherds
- Abundant: 500+ sherds

Further quantification, by site, is found in Chapter 6.

4.2 Overview

Of the indicators the majority (75%) were datable to a specific phase of occupation: Ptolemaic (mid 4th to mid 1st

Fig. 4.1. Pie graph of all indicator pottery sherds by period based on count data.

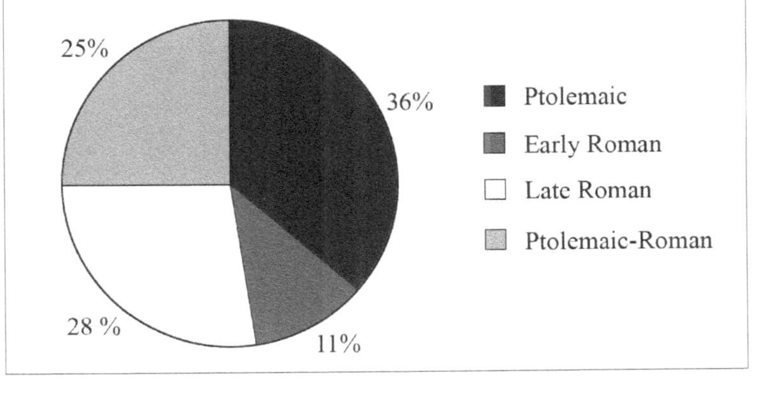

1. We are very grateful to Mervat Yehya from the National Museum Alexandria for her help with identifying the Hellenistic material.

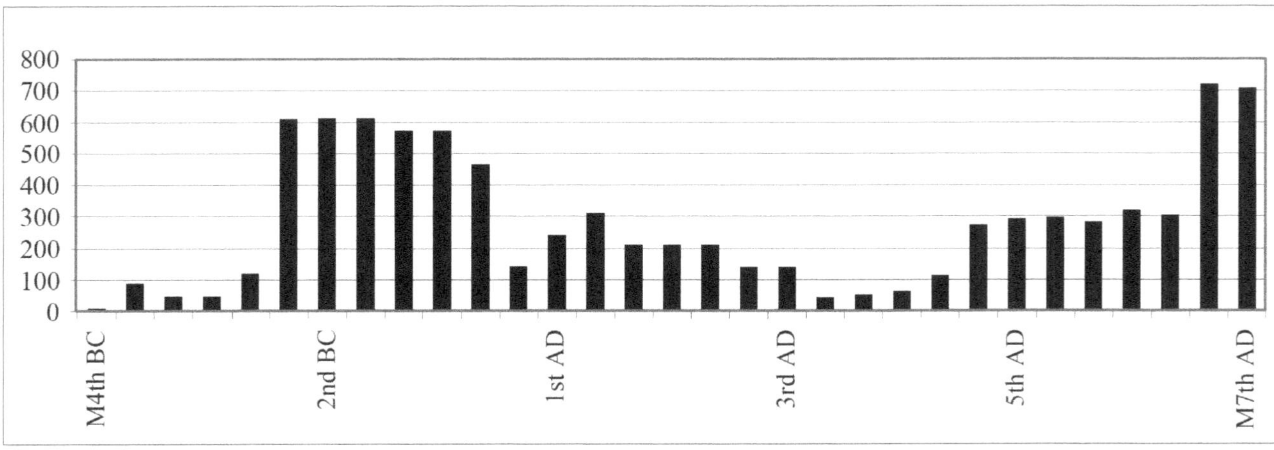

Fig. 4.2. Histogram of pottery dates based on an equal distribution over time for each securely dated ceramic form by count data. This may have an averaging effect.

centuries BC), Early Roman (late 1st century BC to 3rd century AD) and Late Roman (4th through 7th centuries AD). The remaining 25% of all sherds, mostly local or Nile silt coarse wares, fitted a general Ptolemaic or Roman date, but could not be more precisely dated. It is possible that some LR Amphora 5 and LR Amphora 7 vessels are 8th century AD in date, but as this is not supported by other wares securely dated later than the Arab conquest of AD 641-3, they are considered Late Roman in date here. It is likely that the area was abandoned around or shortly after the Arab conquest. The term Hellenistic is reserved for imported wares and Ptolemaic is used in the Egyptian context. A general and more detailed breakdown of the chronological distribution of the pottery is found in Figs 4.1 & 4.2.

Fig. 4.3 shows the heavy reliance on Mareotic products during the Ptolemaic and Early Roman periods, and their disappearance during the Late Roman to be replaced by Abu Mena ware. Fig. 4.4 illustrates trends in imported amphorae with the Ptolemaic period dominated by Aegean amphorae, especially Rhodian and Knidian products. There is a dramatic lessening of imports during the Early Roman period, but those from the eastern Mediterranean are most common. Finally, the Late Roman period sees a boost in imports, particularly from Cilicia/Cyprus represented by LR Amphora 1 and Cypriot Red Slip ware.

4.3 Mareotis

4.3.1 Fabric

Ceramic production around the shores of Lake Mareotis has been documented since the 1980s (e.g. El-Fakharani 1983; Empereur 1986). In a 1998 summary, Empereur and Picon itemised 28 workshops (see Chapter 2.2.5). Kilns were also identified within our study area, one each at four

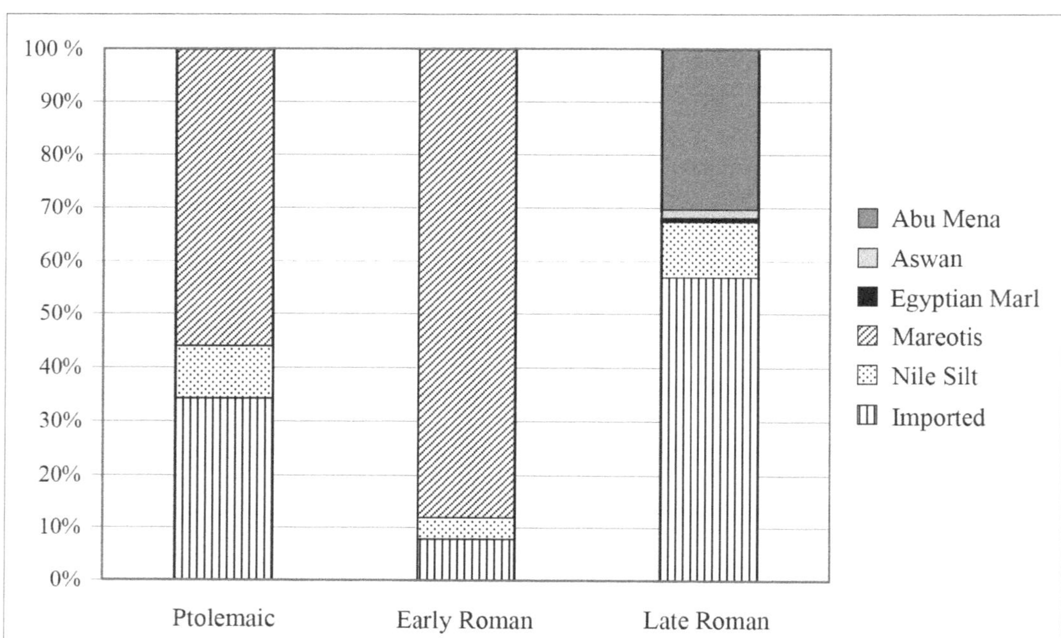

Fig. 4.3. Chronological breakdown of ceramic provenance by count data.

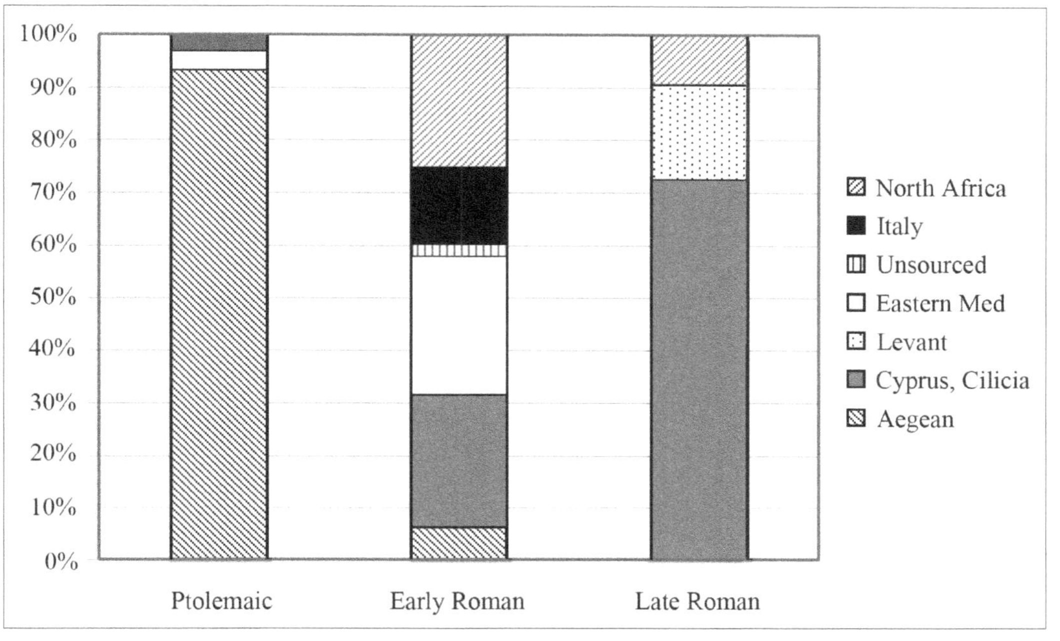

Fig. 4.4. Chronological distribution of imported ceramics by provenance based on count data.

of our Mareotis Island sites (Sites 32, 39, 124, 125). Sites 39 and 125 date to the Ptolemaic period, Sites 32 and 124 to the Early Roman. Production was limited to amphorae and pot stands. Site 37 also had a high proportion of locally made Ptolemaic and some Early Roman amphorae, suggesting that a kiln may have been originally located there despite the lack of a structure. Locally produced amphorae were common on all Ptolemaic and Early Roman sites, accounting for 28% of all pottery and 43% of all amphorae.

The Mareotic fabric is represented by wasters at the kiln sites. On the whole, across all sites, there was a consistent distinction in appearance between Ptolemaic and Early Roman fabrics despite the underlying similarities in the range of inclusions between kilns and across the entire survey area.

The Ptolemaic fabric is generally red or brown with yellow to pale green surfaces and abundant limestone inclusions (<1.0mm), particularly visible as reaction rims on the surface. Finer fragments (<0.5mm) of quartz, ironstone, voids and mica are also visible. In contrast, the Early Roman fabric is red-brown, macroscopically similar in appearance to a Nile silt with less common limestone, but more frequent and coarser quartz, ironstone, voids (<1.0mm) and mica. Varying quantities of shell are present in most samples.

The visual characteristics associated with each kiln most likely relate to their individual firing conditions. Products from the Ptolemaic Kiln Site 39 are brown (7.5YR 6/4), orange-brown (5YR 6/6) or pale yellow (2.5Y 7/3); brown variants often have pale yellow (2.5Y 7/3) surfaces. Those from Ptolemaic Kiln Site 125 are orange-red (2.5YR 5/8), crimson (2.5YR 3/3) or dark red-brown (5YR 4/2), often with yellow-green (2.5Y 6/3; 2.5Y 8/2) surfaces and common reaction rims. Products of Early Roman Kiln Site 32 are an orange-red (2.5YR 5/8), crimson (2.5YR 3/3) or dark red-brown (5YR 4/2), often with yellow-green (2.5Y 6/3; 2.5Y 8/2) surfaces and common reaction rims. Finally, sherds from Early Roman Kiln Site 124 are red-brown (2.5YR 5/6; 5YR 5/6) with pale brown (7.5YR 7/6) surfaces, possibly caused by salt (see also Rodziewicz 1998c).

4.3.2 Vessel types

The conventional typology for Mareotic amphorae was established by Empereur as Amphore Egyptienne 1-4, with AE1-2 the Ptolemaic forms, and 3-4 the Roman ones (Empereur & Picon 1998).

4.3.2.1 Ptolemaic (Fig. 4.5)

Empereur dated AE1 to the 3rd century BC on the basis of the form that copied the handles of amphorae from Rhodes and Knidos (Empereur & Picon 1998: 75). It has a bead rim and sharp spike with a long neck and body and particularly long, straight handles joined to the neck and the top of a low, carinated shoulder. From the 2nd century BC, vessels copied the Knidian style and became squatter with rounder bodies, shorter and more rounded handles and a tall collared rim, as exemplified by the AE2.

Only this grooved, collared rim type of the AE2 was found at the kiln sites in association with either long or short handles (present together in most assemblages) and the single base type (Fig. 4.5, No. 7). The rim was most common at kiln Sites 39 and 125. A more intact example from Tell al-Haraby (Majcherek 1992: 134, no. 4) shows the rim joined to the long handle, another is found at Pelusium (Ballet 1997: 118, pl. II, no. 29). Outside Mareotis the type has been variously dated between the 2nd and 1st centuries BC. Here we suggest that the form may be intermediary between AE1 and AE2, yet due to the nature of the sites with exclusively amphora sherds, an absolute date could not be assigned. From the handles alone it is not possible to tell whether AE1 is present but the absence of any classic AE1 rims would suggest not. For this reason in the histograms the Mareotic Ptolemaic amphorae have been dated to the 2nd and 1st centuries BC.

Pot stands were also produced in these kilns and are contemporary with the amphorae. The height as illustrated by Fig. 4.5, No. 8, is typical of the Ptolemaic kiln assemblages. They appear to be wheelmade.

AE1/2 grooved, collared rim. Probably 2nd or 1st century BC (see above). Abundant.

1. Upright rim with handle attached. Long voids (4.0mm) from chaff temper with fine (<1.0mm) angular limestone, quartz and black inclusions. Red (10YR 5/4) with black core. Site 113 [14].
2. Tall collar with slightly flared rim and handle scar. Common limestone and voids (<3.0mm) with some fine quartz and rare red and brown inclusions. Red-orange (2.5YR 5/8) with brown (7.5YR 6/4) core and cream (2.5Y 7/3) outside surface. Site 113 [16].
3. Short collar. Very common sub-rounded limestone up to 1.0mm with reaction rims on the surface; fine quartz and mica and rare sub-rounded dark ironstone inclusions up to 0.5mm. Red (2.5YR 5/8) with yellow-green (2.5Y 6/3) surfaces. Site 113 [3].

Long handles belonging to AE1 or AE1/2 variant. Dated as above. Moderate.

4. Long neck and handle. Hard fired with common limestone inclusions and reaction rims on the surfaces. Red-brown (5YR 4/2). Site 125 [357].
5. Long handle. Long chaff voids (4.0mm) with fine (<1.0mm) angular limestone, quartz and black inclusions. Red (10YR 5/4) with black core. Site 113 [14].

Short handles belonging to AE2 or AE1/2 variant. Dated as above. Common.

6. Common ill-sorted inclusions visible in the break and common reaction rims on surfaces. Brown (7.5YR 6/4). Site 125 [357].

Tapering, solid base belonging to vessel AE1/2. Dated as above. Abundant.

7. Concreted all over. Common limestone and numerous reaction rims on the surfaces. Orange-red (2.5YR 5/8). Site 125 [357].

Tall, wheelmade pot stand. Sparse.

8. Complete profile. Common limestone and vesicules, <3.0mm, with some fine quartz and rare red and brown inclusions. Purple (2.5YR 3/3) with cream-green (2.5Y 6/3) slip outside and on the rim top. Site 125 [357].

4.3.2.2 Early Roman (Fig. 4.5)

Empereur's typology for the Early Roman period comprises AE3 and AE4 (Empereur & Picon 1998). AE3 is a biconical amphora with a variety of rim forms and either a plain or ribbed body. Recently this type has been subdivided by Tomber (2007) into a series spanning from the late Augustan period through the 3rd century. However, the Mareotic products are distinct from the standard AE3 vessels made in workshops along the Nile. Generally speaking the Mareotic vessels are chunkier and poorly finished, especially the handle (Fig. 4.5, No. 11). Many of the vessels, including those illustrated as Fig. 4.5, Nos 9-10, belong to a variant of AE3 identified at Mons Claudianus as Amphora Types 22-3 where they were dated to the Trajanic and Antonine periods (Tomber 2006: 151, fig. 1.59, nos 882-4). This form, with a thick grooved rim, sometimes beveled, and rounded handles joined to the rim, is represented at our kiln Sites 32 and 124.

AE4 refers to vessels copying the imported Dressel 2-4 wine amphorae, originally produced at Kos and subsequently widely throughout the Empire. Their Egyptian production was first recognised at Mareotis and while this may be the major centre their occurrence in the classic silt fabric shows they were produced elsewhere as well. Empereur dates them from the 1st to the end of the 3rd centuries AD, the latest date derived from Meroé (Empereur & Picon 1998: 77), but a date into approximately the early or mid 3rd century seems more likely in the Egyptian context (Tomber 2006: 53).

Mons Claudianus Amphora Type 22/3, grooved rim, sometimes dropped internally with thick, sub-rounded handle. Trajanic and Antonine (Tomber 2006: 151, fig. 1.59, nos 882-4). Common.

9. Rim dropped internally. Common, fine sub-angular to sub-rounded (<1.0mm) quartz, black ironstone and limestone with reaction rims, very fine mica and common voids. Red-brown (2.5YR 5/6) with pale brown or yellow (2.5Y 6/3) surfaces. Site 40 [202].
10. Variant with flatly oriented rim. Fine matrix with common sub-angular to sub-rounded (<1.0mm) quartz, black ironstone and limestone with reaction rims, very fine mica and common voids. Red-brown (5YR 5/6) with pale brown (7.5YR 7/6) surfaces. Site 40 [202].
11. Handle belonging to Mons Claudianus Type 22/3 or similar. Fine matrix with dark inclusions and large voids. Orange-brown (5YR 6/6) core with greenish-yellow (2.5Y 6/3) surfaces. Site 113 [8].
12. Moderately tall base with ribbing on the lower wall. Its co-occurrence at the kiln sites with Nos 9-11 above suggests it belongs to Mons Claudianus Amphora Type 22/3 with a similar date. Elsewhere tall amphora bases of this form seem to belong to the second half of the 2nd or 3rd centuries AD (Tomber 2007: 530, fig. 3, no. 1). Limestone rich. Red-brown (2.5YR 5/6). Site 32 [325].

AE4 bead rim amphora with double-rod handle and peg base. Mid-1st into the early or mid 3rd century AD. Abundant.

13. Poorly made rim. Common large limestone with reaction rims (<3.0mm) and clay pellets (<2.0mm). Red-brown (5YR 5/6) with buff (7.5YR 7/6) surfaces. Site 124 [358].
14. Bead rim, slightly tooled. Surfaces with limestone reaction rims up to 2.0mm. Red-brown (2.5YR 5/6) with green-yellow (2.5Y 8/2) surfaces. Site 32 [324].

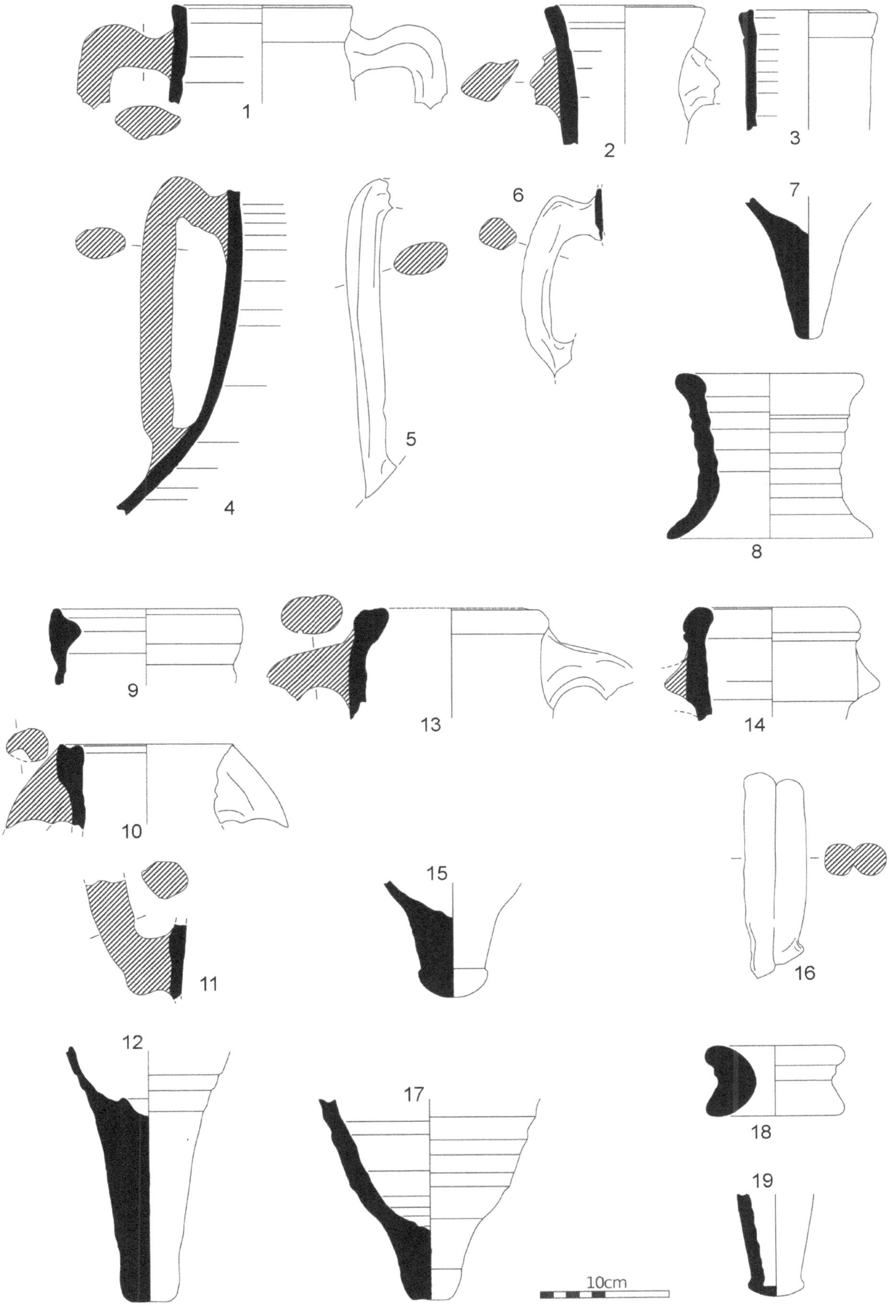

Fig. 4.5. Mareotic amphorae and pot stands: Ptolemaic (1-8); Early Roman (9-19) (J. Whitewright).

15. Base. Large limestone, including reaction rims, and red-brown clay pellets up to 3.0mm, sparse mica and quartz. Red-brown (2.5YR 5/6) with buff (7.5YR 7/6) surfaces. Site 202 [404].
16. Double-rod handle. Over-fired. Abundant ill-sorted limestone and quartz inclusions to c. 1.0mm. Pale orange (7.5YR7/6) with cream-yellow (2.5Y 8/2) surfaces. Site 124 [358].
17. Unusual variant base: fairly short spike with ribbed lower walls and depressed underside. A depression on the underside of the toe has been associated with the Late Augustan through Tiberian AE3 vessels in the Eastern Desert (Tomber 2007: 528, fig. 1, nos 4-10), although the overall shape and ribbing differs and is more like an AE4 variant illustrated by Hayes and Harlaut (2002: 112, fig. 67) and dated to around AD 100. Silty fine fabric with quartz and limestone inclusions <0.5mm. Red-brown (2.5YR 5/6). Site 32 [324].

Pot stand, with short profile in contrast to the taller Ptolemaic ones (No. 8, above). Although represented by only a small sample, in contrast to the Ptolemaic pot stands these are handmade. Their small height may suggest they were used as kiln spacers. They only occurred at the Early Roman kiln Site 32 where they were associated with pottery dating from the mid 1st to early or mid 3rd centuries AD. Rare.
18. Complete profile. Heavily salt encrusted. Common limestone and vesicules (<2.0mm) with some fine quartz and rare red, brown and dark inclusions. Purple (5YR 4/2) with slightly green (2.5Y 6/3) surfaces. Site 32 [325].

Tubular, hollow base. This particular vessel was not found at the kiln sites but it appears to be a Mareotic production, in the general style of African types of the Early Roman period (cf. Bonifay 2004: 105). Single vessel.
19. Very common sub-rounded limestone up to 1.0mm with reaction rims on the surfaces; fine quartz and mica, and rare sub-rounded dark ironstone inclusions up to 0.5mm. Red with yellow-green surfaces. Site 113 [3].

4.4 Other Egyptian wares

4.4.1 Fabrics

The well-known Egyptian fabric types are described here; others which may be Egyptian also occur in the catalogue.

4.4.1.1 Abu Mena fabric

Pottery production at Abu Menas has been documented by Engemann (1992) and Neutron Activation Analaysis grouped together pitchers and amphorae as being produced at this source (Ballet & Picon 1987: 33-5; Empereur & Picon 1992: 150-2). The fabric is orange-brown or dull orange, occasionally with a core but more frequently the same colour throughout with cream-yellow or pale orange-buff surfaces. Occasionally sherds are overfired to green. The clay is sandy marl with some larger inclusions, usually <0.5mm rarely to 1.0mm, and occasionally visible on the surface. It was common, constituting 8.5% of all pottery and 10.6% of all amphorae.

In our assemblage the most common form is an imitation of LR Amphora 5/Kellia 186 where it was dated from the mid 7th to the beginning of the 8th centuries AD (Egloff 1977: 117-18) with slight modifications suggested elsewhere. At present the general consensus is that they were current from the second quarter of the 7th to the early 8th century AD (Ballet 2003: 141-3; see also Majcherek 1992; Reynolds 2003: 731). The type was most likely produced at other centres west of Alexandria, with Mareotis a potential but unconfirmed additional source (Ballet 2003). A second form, a delicate basin or open jar with carinated walls (Fig. 4.9, Nos 79-80), also recurs.

4.4.1.2 Marl

The clay is calcareous, sometimes with sand-sized inclusions. Marl fabrics frequently have a pale brown to reddish-yellow core with cream-yellow surfaces. The fabric was used for the production of table ware and storage vessel forms. Those that can be dated are Ptolemaic to Late Roman; others remain undated. Overall the fabric accounts for <0.5% of the total pottery. Abu Menas is a probable but unconfirmed source for some vessels.

4.4.1.3 Nile silt

This is the best-known Egyptian fabric, comprising fine, micaceous, alluvial clay, orange-brown to dark chocolate brown in colour. It varies greatly in texture depending upon the temper added, or the range of naturally occurring impurities.

Vessels used for cooking, in particular, have added sand. A slipped version of this fabric is designated Egyptian Red Slip ware B (ERSB). Nile silt products account for 32% of all pottery; ERSB accounts for 0.6% of all pottery and 26% of all Egyptian Red Slip wares.

4.4.1.4 Egyptian Red Slip ware C (ERSC)

ERSC is less micaceous and coarser than ERSB, it is orange or red-brown with limestone and quartz inclusions. Hayes (1972: 399) suggested it might be a desert ware, as it resembles Abu Mena fabrics, but Engemann rejected this on the basis of scientific analysis and thought it to be from elsewhere on the coast (1992: 156). ERSC accounts for 0.5% of all pottery and 35% of all Egyptian Red Slip wares.

4.4.1.5 Aswan

Aswan table wares exploiting the pink kaolin clay are a relatively rare import to Mareotis, accounting for a little over 0.3% of all pottery and restricted to Late Roman forms. They all are at least partially slipped and belong to Egyptian Red Slip ware A (ERSA). ERSA accounts for 24% of all Egyptian Red Slip wares, slightly less than ERSB and ERSC.

4.4.1.6 Faience

This refers to white or off-white quartz-frit, normally with blue or blue-green glaze, that was produced during the Ptolemaic and Roman periods (Nenna & Seif el-Din 2000).

4.4.2 Vessel types

4.4.2.1 Juglets and unguentaria (Fig. 4.6)
Juglets are normally restricted to vessels with one handle, although the size of some of our double-handled vessels means they fit comfortably into this class.

Juglet with out-turned lid-seat rim; a single ovoid handle is joined to the neck and arches up under the rim. Possibly Ptolemaic. Single vessel.
20. Fabric with fine limestone, some black and red inclusions and voids, possibly local. Orange-pink with matt, dark red slip outside. Site 210 [446].

Juglet with slightly everted, plain rim; an ovoid handle is joined to the neck. Similar to Mons Claudianus Flagon Type 25, 2nd century AD (Tomber 2006: 56, fig. 1.20). Rare.
21. Marl. Reddish-yellow with white outside surface. Site 113 [49].

Jug with out-turned rim, long neck with broad cordon and broad girth; flattened double handles are joined to the neck cordon and upper girth. Similar to Mons Claudianus Flagon Type 37, early 2nd century AD (Tomber 2006: 58, fig. 1.21). Single vessel.
22. Abundant limestone both in the break and as surface reaction rims, similar to Mareotic products. Red-brown. Site 113 [48].

Jug with small lipped rim, long neck and wide girth; grooved ?double handles are joined to the base of the neck. Similar but not identical to Mons Claudianus Flagon Types 38-41, 1st and 2nd centuries AD (Tomber 2006: 58-60, fig. 1.21). Single vessel.
23. Thin black paint on shoulder. Marl with occasional quartz inclusions <0.5mm. Pale pink with cream-yellow margins and surfaces. Site 40 [220].

Juglet with upright, slightly beaded rim; flattened ?double handles are joined to the rim. Undated. Sparse.
24. Marl with fine quartz and angular white inclusions. Yellow throughout. Site 123 [953].

Juglet or unguentarium with long neck and out-turned bead rim. Undated. Single vessel.
25. Sandy silt. Brown-red. Site 118 [G].

Jug or juglet with out-turned, collared rim; no visible handle. Undated. Single vessel.
26. Poorly made and tooled inside. Very fine silt with occasional limestone impurities to c. 1.0mm on the surface. Orange-brown throughout with brown-grey rim top, red-brown matt slip on the outside and rim top. Site 103 [613].

Twisted handle from a jug or jar. Ptolemaic or Roman (for other twisted handles see Fig. 4.7, No. 47). Sparse.
27. Silt. Brown throughout. Site 113 [42].

Small juglet or unguentarium bases.
In total 14 small bases belonging to juglets or unguentaria were collected, each somewhat different in form and of no clear chronological period. Four are illustrated below.
28. Solid, flat base with out-splayed walls. Marl. Orange-brown with cream-yellow surfaces. Site 113 [41].
29. Flat base, similar to No. 28, but hollow. Marl with fine sand and limestone inclusions. Soft, pale orange throughout with patches of cream on the outside surface. Site 118 [G].
30. Thick, solid base with out-splayed walls, from a juglet or unguentarium. Marl with fine white inclusions and fine voids. Orange-yellow with white-yellow outside surface. Site 40 [244].
31. Lower half of juglet with flat base, globular walls and single handle scar on the shoulder. Dense, hard-fired silt. Pale brown with red-brown outside surface, partially covered with cream-pink slip, elsewhere discoloured. Site 118 [G].

4.4.2.2 Strainers (Fig. 4.6)
In addition to those illustrated below, fragments of spouts were sparse.

Neck with only single hole of strainer still visible; flattened, ?double handles are joined to the neck and upper shoulder. Painted strainers in Aswan fabric tend to be Late Roman in date (e.g. Gempeler 1992: 185-6). Rare.
32. Red paint, now badly abraded, is applied in bands to the shoulder. Marl or Aswan fine fabric with voids and white inclusions (<0.2mm). Pale buff. Site 40 [215].

Neck of narrow-necked funnel strainer; strainer with three holes reworked to one large hole; ?double handles are joined to the neck. Strainers with a narrow neck tend to be Late Roman in date (e.g. Egloff 1977: 127, pl. 9; pl. 67, no. 1, Kellia 210). Sparse.
33. Silt with occasional larger quartz up to c. 5.0mm and some voids. Orange-red with duller outside surface. Site 40 [203].

Strainer spout and shoulder decorated with black paint; two concentric semi-circles outline the base of the spout; elsewhere decorated by short lines perpendicular to the spout; swathes of fringed lines are repeated on the girth. While there are no exact parallels from Kellia, the overall form and decoration is similar to Kellia 202 and 204 that are dated to AD 390-500 (Egloff 1977: 124-6, pl. 63, nos 6, 9; pls. 64-5; pl. 66, nos 1-4). Late Roman. Rare.
34. Marl. Pale-buff with slightly pinker margins; the inside surface is discoloured by salt, outside the surface is cream coloured, but peeling. Site 18 [G].

4.4.2.3 *Sakkia* and other jars (Fig. 4.6)
In the Eastern Desert these jars are first present during the Trajanic period, but more typical of the Antonine and Severan periods (Tomber 2006: 95). They also flourish into the Late Roman period (Bailey 1998: 75-6) with no clear

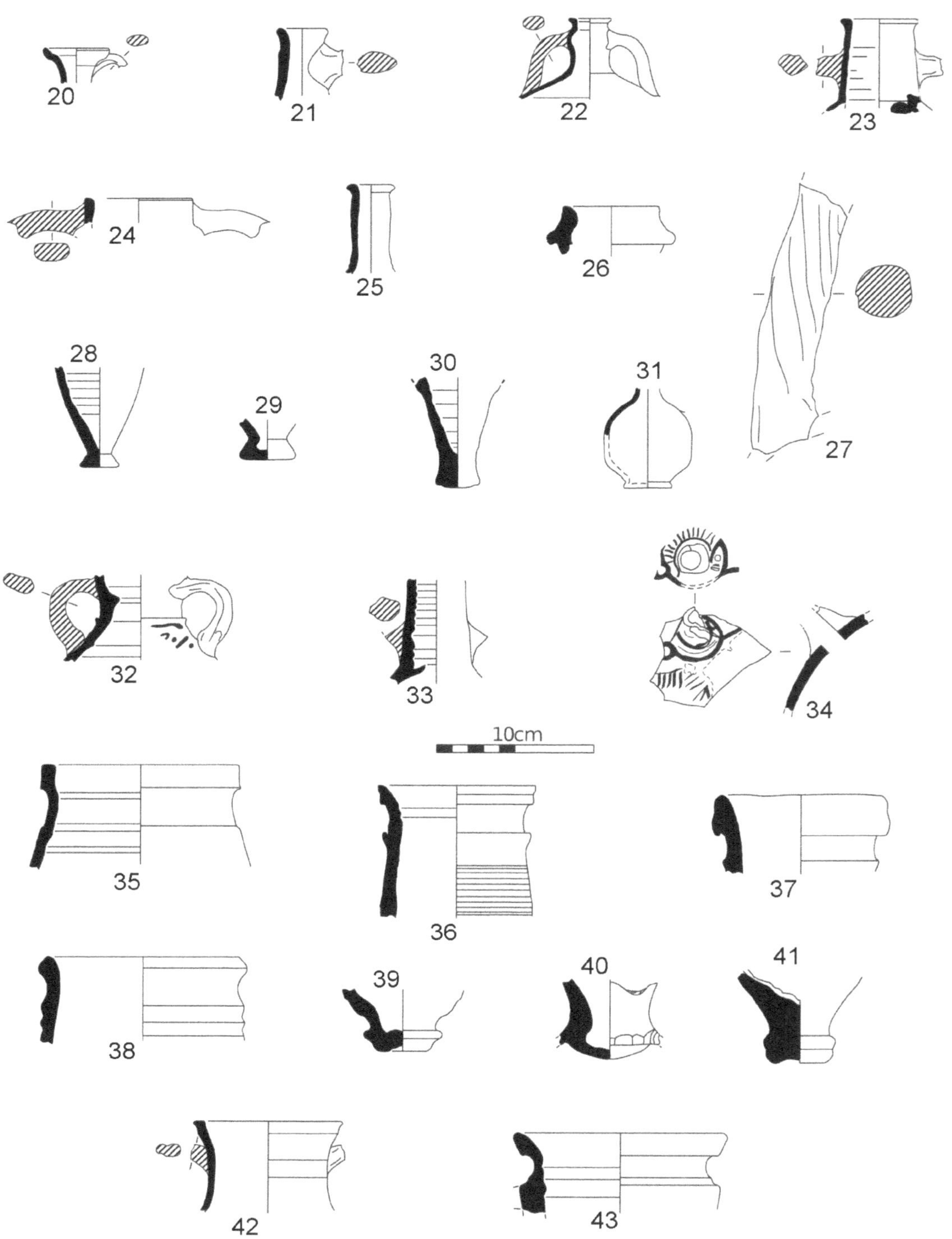

Fig. 4.6. Egyptian coarse wares: Juglets, Jugs and Unguentaria (20-31); Strainers (32-4); Sakkia *(35-41); Jars (42-3) (J. Whitewright).*

typological development. Here most are grouped together as Early to Late Roman, though an Early Islamic date cannot be excluded. The exception to this are those in the Abu Mena fabric which are Late Roman in date. Silt examples are more numerous (Common) than those in a marl (Sparse) fabric; cumulatively Common.

Rim flat on top with slightly grooved face, somewhat uneven inside on the rim; long neck, well-defined shoulder and plain walls. This is the most common shape in the marl fabric. Marl: Rare; ?Abu Mena: Rare; cumulatively Sparse.

35. Marl with moderate sand and large limestone inclusions to 4.0mm. Pale brown-orange with greenish core, yellow outside surface and rim top. Site 204 [417].

Double-lip rim, pronounced upturned shoulder cordon and shallowly ribbed lower walls. Rare.

36. Marl. Cream-yellow throughout with some dark discolouration and concretion on the outside. Site 40 [200].

Double-lip rim with short neck and pronounced shoulder; unevenly finished on the rim top. Rare.
37. Silt. Red-brown throughout. Site 40 [473].

Enlarged, triangular-shaped rim, short neck and fairly straight, ribbed walls. Similar to Claudianus Jar Type 94 (Tomber 2006: fig. 1.36, no. 486). This is the most typical vessel shape in a silt fabric. Common.
38. Fine silt, slightly vesicular. Red-brown with orange-brown sandwich. Same vessel as No. 39 below. Site 01 [473].

Crudely made, uneven base with a broken or abraded bottom and ridge around the widest point. Rare.
39. Hard-fired silt. Red-brown, concreted on the outside. Same vessel as No. 38 above. Site 01 [473].

Base with broken, downward turned flange or lip. Rare.
40. Silt with occasional limestone and dark iron impurities <1.0mm. Orange-brown with the outside surface discoloured; concreted outside and inside. Site 119 [910].

Base with double-lip foot; a clay disc is wedged in the inside. Rare.
41. Marl. Very hard-fired, dense matrix with moderate coarse sand and flat red pellets to c. <0.5mm. Orange with pale brown inner margin, yellow on the outside surface. Site 113 [48].

Cooking pot or jar with out-turned, flattened rim; grooved, ?double handles are joined below the rim. Undated. Single vessel.
42. Sandy silt with fine sub-angular quartz, black and white inclusions. Red; the outside surface is smoothed or possibly slipped with a red-brown wash. Site 113 [49].

Jar with out-turned rim with flattened bead on the underside, short neck and pronounced shoulder with handle scar. Undated. Single vessel.
43. Silt with some limestone, mica and voids. Red-brown with black-purple core. Site 210 [G].

4.4.2.4 Cooking pots (Fig. 4.7)
Cooking pot with cup-shaped, lipped rim; grooved ?double handles are joined to the rim. Probably Ptolemaic or Early Roman. Rare.
44. Coarse, sandy silt with occasional limestone up to 1.5mm on the surfaces. Red-brown with grey surfaces. Site 204 [416].

Cooking pot with sharply enlarged, flattened rim, grooved on the inside for a lid seat; irregular, flattened ?double handles are joined to the rim and shoulder, c. 120 BC (Hayes & Harlaut 2002: 106, fig. 32). Moderate.
45. Micaceous, sandy silt with quartz and limestone and voids up to 2.0mm. Brick orange-red with matt dark red slip outside. Site 113 [47].

Cooking pot with a bowed, upright rim, grooved on the outside lip; narrow ribbing on the shoulder. Similar to Kellia 138 where it is dated to the 7th century AD (Egloff 1977: 103, pl. 52, no. 2). Single vessel.
46. Silt with moderate sand and rare limestone <0.5mm. Orange-red with grey-brown outside surface; discoloured, especially inside. Site 202 [481].

Cooking pot with upright rim, recessed inside for lid; ?double rounded, twisted handles are joined to the rim. Similar to Kellia 128 where it is dated to the 7th century AD (Egloff 1977: 102, pl. 50, no. 1). Rare.
47. Silt. Brown throughout. Site 15 [302].

4.4.2.5 Cooking casseroles and lids (Fig. 4.7)
Lid-seat casserole with broad out-turned rim, external rounded, bead lip and internal, sharpened bead; applied intermittent horizontal handles. c. 120 BC (Hayes & Harlaut 2002: fig. 30); elsewhere it is present into the Early Roman period (Ballet 1997: 117). Common.
48. One intermittent handle visible. Silt with some limestone impurities <0.5mm. Orange-brown core, dark margins and red-brown surfaces, slightly abraded. Site 113 [48].

Carinated, handled casserole with flattened rim and groove for lid seat (cf. No. 45), c. 120 BC (Hayes & Harlaut 2002: 106, fig. 29). Sparse.
Not illustrated.

Casserole with dropped, reeded rim, similar to Hayes & Harlaut (2002: 110) fig. 55, c. AD 100; Tomber (2006: 113, fig. 1.43), Mons Claudianus Casserole Type 50, 2nd century AD. Sparse.
Not illustrated.

Casseroles with slightly rounded walls, flat rims, internally beveled, frequently with horizontal handles and ribbed walls. Similar to Kellia 110-16 where they are dated between the late 4th and 7th centuries AD, although mostly 5th (Egloff 1977: 100, pl. 47). Common.
49. Handled casserole with plain walls. Coarse, sandy silt with occasional organic inclusions, especially the handle. Grey to black break and inside surface and rim top; outside surface red-brown. Site 204 [412].
50. Handled casserole with ribbed walls. Sandy silt. Red-brown. Site 204 [414].
51. Handled casserole with ribbed walls. Sandy silt with frequent sub-rounded quartz <0.5mm. Heavily burnt to black throughout. Site 204 [419].

Hollow, tubular handle from skillet with internally folded spout rim. Similar to Snape (1997: 104, fig. 4, S1), 4th to 6th centuries AD. Rare.
52. Probably Egyptian. Fine sandy matrix with moderate coarse sand and limestone inclusions to c. 1.5mm. Grey to orange-brown with grey surfaces. Site 15 [G].

Domed casserole lid with thin, gently ribbed walls and flattened, lipped rim, belonging to Fig. 4.7, Nos 49-51. Kellia 347-50 where their dating conforms with casseroles Nos 50-1, with most of 5th century date but some variants continuing to the 8th century AD (Egloff 1977: 179-80, pl. 55). Sparse.

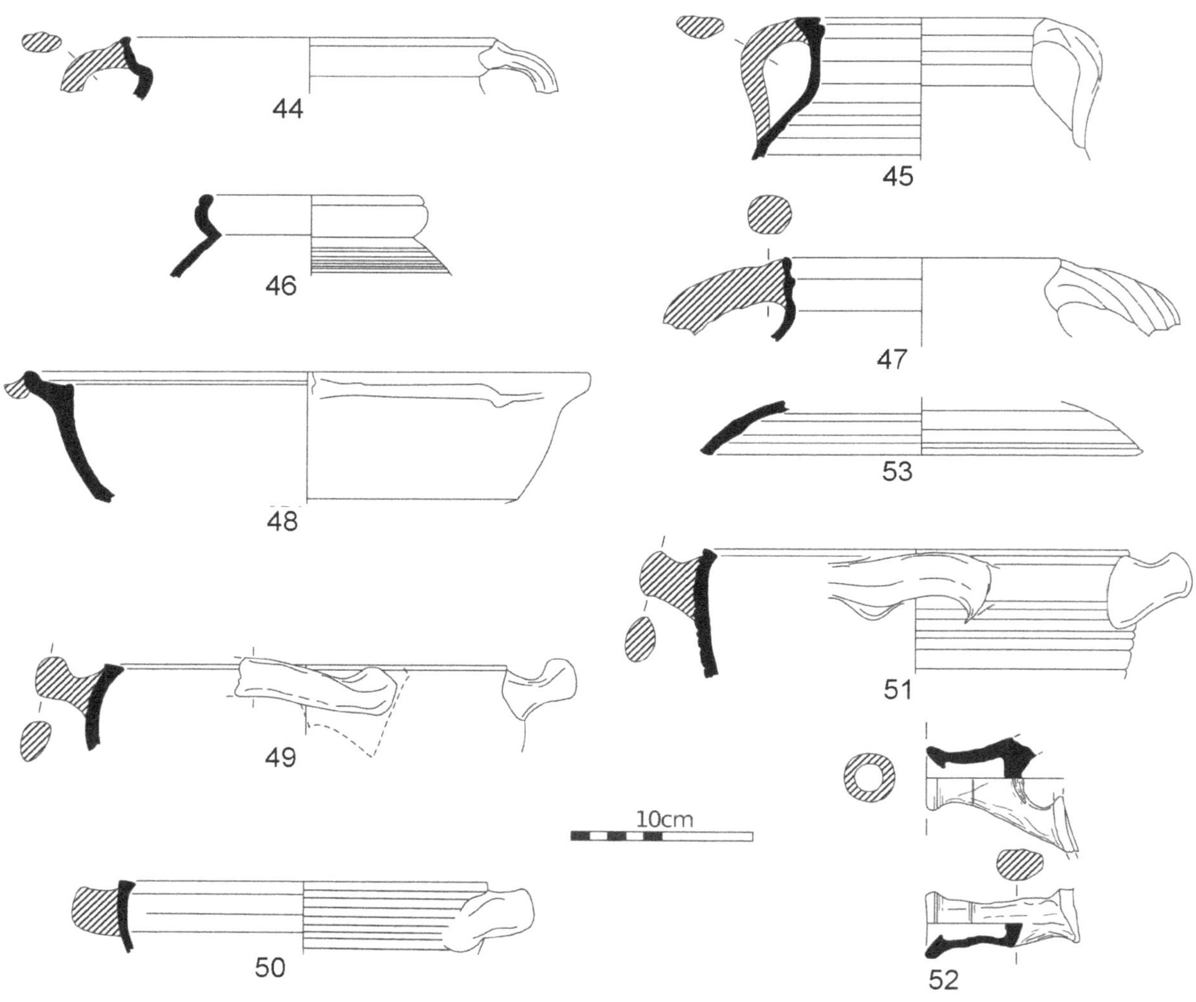

Fig. 4.7. Egyptian cooking wares: Cooking pots (44-7); Casseroles (48-52); Lid (53) (J. Whitewright).

53. Very coarse sandy silt with occasional limestone impurities <1.0mm. Red-brown, somewhat discoloured to brown in part. Site 204 [413].

4.4.2.6 Ptolemaic and Early Roman table wares (Fig. 4.8)
Dishes with out-splayed walls and internal bead rim, frequently described as fish dishes or plates. The type was produced at Tell al-Haraby, west of Alexandria, which was active during approximately the 2nd – 1st centuries BC (Majcherek & el-Shennawi 1992: 136, fig. 4c), although elsewhere these dishes may have a broader production period into the Early Roman period. Other examples include Hayes & Harlaut (2002: 105, fig. 23, c. 120 BC); Élaigne (2000a: 19, fig. 1, no. 6 from a late Ptolemaic/Augustan deposit, 50 BC-AD 50); Élaigne (1998: 81, figs 15-16), Ptolemaic to Early Roman. Red slip: Moderate; Black slip: Sparse; cumulatively Moderate.
54. Squared-off bead rim, grooved internally. Sandy silt with mica inclusions, fine voids and sand <0.5mm. Brown-purple sandwich with orange slip in patches on the inside. Site 201 [G].
55. Internally flattened bead rim. Micaceous silt with sub-rounded quartz <0.5mm. Brown with red core and patches of red-brown slip on the inside. Site 100 [610].

Carinated platter with overhanging, angled collared rim, squared-off on the top. The form is similar to an imported vessel from Alexandria dated to the 2nd to 1st centuries BC (Élaigne 1998: 78, fig. 5). Single vessel.
56. Sandy, granular Egyptian fabric with occasional angular milky quartz to 1.0mm, especially visible on the surfaces. Light brown throughout; abraded brown-black slip inside, brown outside. Site 204 [414].

Small, rounded bowl with in-turned rim and low footring base. The type was produced at Tell al-Haraby, west of Alexandria, which was active during approximately the 2nd – 1st centuries BC (Majcherek & el-Shennawi 1992: 136, fig. 4b), although elsewhere these dishes continue into the early 1st century AD (Élaigne 2000a: fig. 1, no. 8; see also Hayes & Harlaut 2002: 104, figs 16-18, c. 120 BC; Élaigne 2000b: fig. 2, Ptolemaic/Early Roman). Sparse; Footring bases of this and similar bowls: Moderate.
57. Very fine silt with some sand and sub-rounded limestone (<0.5mm) erupting near the surface. Buff with glossy red-brown slip on the outside and matt black slip inside. Site 201 [G].
58. Slight internal lip on the rim and flattened footring. Two rims, joining. Fine, sandy silt. Grey throughout with

abraded outside surface; the inside surface has some staining, possibly vestiges of matt black slip. Site 113 [48].
59. Slightly in-turned lip. Silt. Burnt surfaces. Site 113 [41].

Bowl with slightly in-turned plain rim, similar to above but slightly larger and unslipped (cf. Hayes & Harlaut 2002: 108, fig, 45, c. AD 100). Common.
60. Sandy silt with moderately well-sorted sub-rounded quartz, limestone, voids and red inclusions (<0.5mm), possibly Mareotis. Orange-red with grey core; orange-red slip or wash that is just darker than the fabric. Site 113 [2].

Egyptian imitation of Cypriot Sigillata (CS) P40/1 bowl with moulded rim and rouletting on the girth. The CS vessels are most common during the second half of the 2nd century, but present by c. AD 100 or earlier (Hayes 1985: 88). Rare.
61. Silt with poorly sorted limestone, quartz and voids (<1.0mm). Red-brown; originally slipped all over but now remnants of badly abraded dark red slip. Site 33 [327].

Jug rim, club-shaped and slightly dropped on the outside. Undated. Single vessel.
62. Sandy Egyptian fabric with abundant, well-sorted inclusions of moderate sized sand and rare red and black iron-rich inclusions with occasional voids. Cream-yellow with matt brown-red slip, originally all over, but now mostly abraded. Site 28 [703].

Body sherd from a bowl, with parallel incised lines outside. No exact parallel is available, but a large open vessel with similar incised lines occurs on Type 2.3.C dated to the 2nd century BC (Nenna & Seif el-Din 2000: 200, pl. 4, no. 151). Single vessel.
63. Probably faience. Sandy matrix. Off-white to slightly yellowed; off-white outside (possibly decayed glaze); remnants of pale-green glaze on the inside. Site 100 [608].

4.4.2.7 Egyptian Late Roman Red Slip bowls and dishes (Fig. 4.8)
Included here are vessels, in decreasing order of quantity, produced from ERSB, ERSC and ERSA. Forms generally copy those produced in ARS or CRS and therefore their dating is related to their prototypes, although sometimes the Elephantine dates for ERSA diverge.

Copy of ARS 67 dish, mid 4th to early 5th centuries AD (Hayes 1972: 116). At Aswan they are dated from the mid 4th through 5th centuries AD (Gempeler 1992: 67, Abb. 10, nos 10-12, Abb. 11, nos 1-4, T211a). ERSB: Rare.
Not illustrated, for form see No. 99 below.

Copy of ARS 75 dish, c. 420-50 (Hayes 1972: 124). Rare.
64. ERSA sandy fabric. Buff with matt red-brown slip originally all over but now abraded. Site 204 [414].

Copy of ARS 84 dish, early to late 5th century AD (Hayes 1972: 133). At Aswan the form is dated between the last quarter of 5th through the third quarter of the 6th centuries AD or somewhat later (Gempeler 1992: 73, Abb. 18, nos 1-4, T228). ERSA: Rare; ERSB: Sparse, ERSB/C: Rare; cumulatively Sparse.
65. ERSB with sub-rounded quartz, black inclusions and fine voids, some large ones <6.0mm. Red-brown with black core and thick red-brown slip. Site 40 [230].
66. ERSB with fine mica, organic and rare white inclusions. Red-brown with layers of crimson and red; thick dark red-brown slip, missing where organic voids appear near the surface. Site 208 [G].

Copy of ARS 91A bowl, mid-late 5th century AD (Hayes 1972: 144). At Aswan they may continue through the third quarter of the 6th century (Gempeler 1992: 94, Abb. 36, nos 12-15, T319). ERSA: Rare; ERSB: Rare; cumulatively Rare.
67. ERSA. Pale orange with pale greenish core; pale orange semi-glossy slip originally all over, now abraded. Site 123 [955].

Copy of ARS 91D bowl, c. 600-650 (Hayes 1972: 144). Single vessel.
68. ERSA with sparse sand inclusions. Buff with matt slip, red-brown inside and brown-red on the outside of the rim; the outside wall may originally have had a thin wash. Site 204 [414].

Copy of ARS 96 bowl, c. AD 490-540 (Hayes 1972: 150). At Aswan the type dates between the first quarter/mid 5th through the 7th century AD (Gempeler 1992: 96, Abb. 36, nos 7-17, T324). ERSB: Rare.
Not illustrated.

Copy of ARS 99 bowl, late 5th to early 7th centuries AD (Hayes 1972: 155). ERSA: Rare; ERSB: Rare; cumulatively Rare.
Not illustrated.

Copy of ARS 104B dish, c. 570-600+ (Hayes 1972: 166). Rare.
69. ERSB/C with common limestone (1.0mm), rare red and black inclusions and common voids up to 5.0mm long. Light red-brown with thick red-brown slip eroded due to limestone inclusions and voids on the surface. Site 208 [438].

Copy of ARS 104C dish, c. AD 550-625 (Hayes 1972: 166). ERSB/C: Rare; ERSB: Rare; cumulatively Rare.
70. ERSB/C with abundant quartz, sparse white inclusions, mica and voids <0.5mm. Red-brown with dark brown slip burnt black and heavily pitted in places. Site 212 [455]
71. ERSB with moderate, rounded voids and rare limestone <0.5mm; unusually hard-fired. Red-brown; thick semi-glossy red slip. Site 204 [416].

Low footring base, possibly copying ARS 104. Rare.
72. ERSB/C with common mica, limestone and rare black inclusions <0.5mm. Red-brown with purple core; abraded red slip. Site 208 [G].

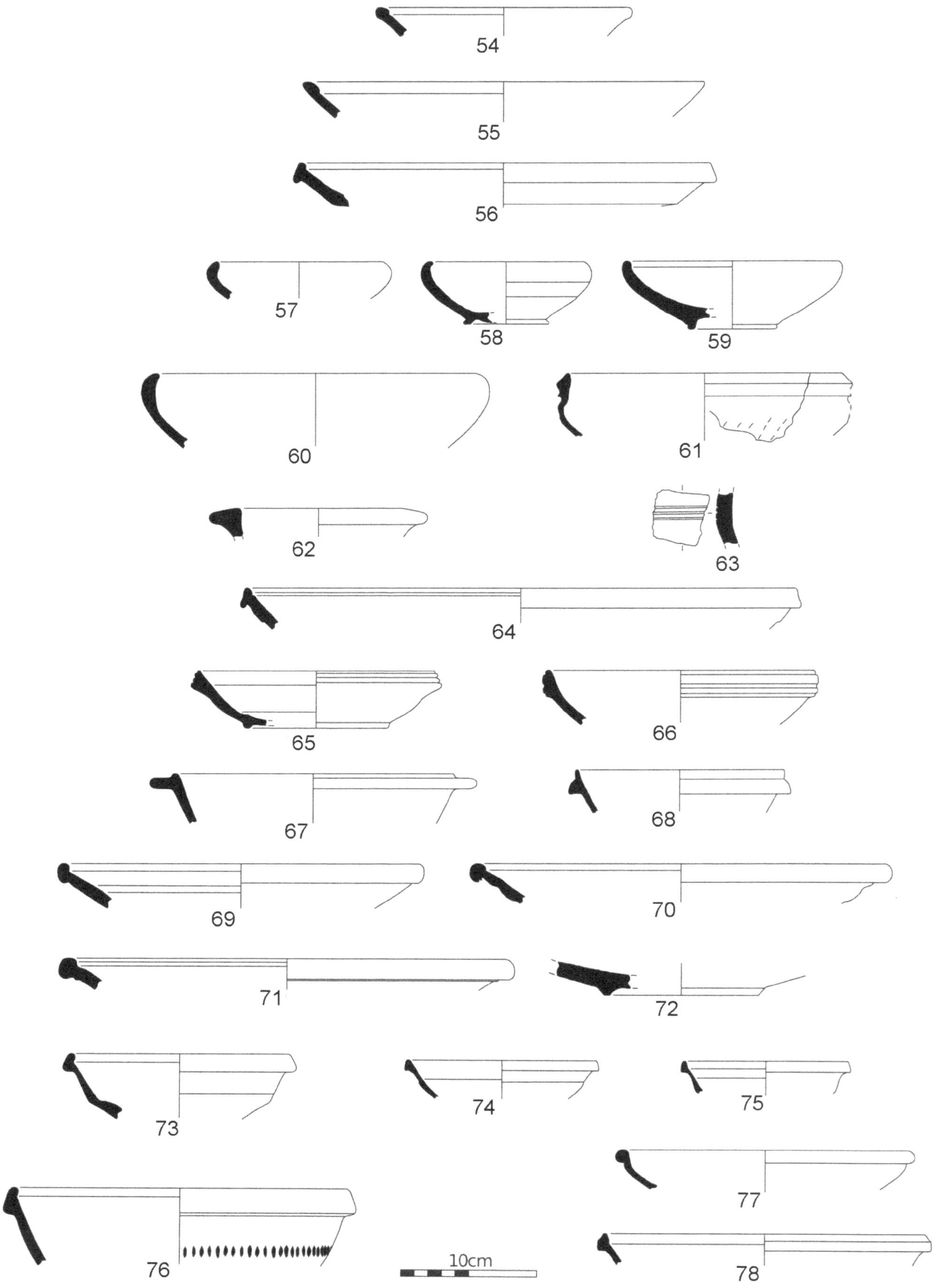

Fig. 4.8. Egyptian finewares: Ptolemaic and Early Roman Slip wares (54-62); Faience (63); Late Roman Red Slip wares (64-78) (J. Whitewright).

Small carinated bowl with angled, triangular-shaped rim projecting inside. Late Roman. Rare.
73. ERSA sandy fabric. Pale buff-orange with red-brown matt slip all over; rim outside darkened brown-grey. Site 204 [414].

Small carinated bowl with triangular shaped, overhanging rim, second quarter 5th to early 7th century AD or later (Gempeler 1992: 70, Abb. 14, nos 5-7, T220c). Rare.
74. Aswan sandy fabric. Pale orange with thin matt orange wash on the outside, brown wash on the rim and rim top. Site 204 [414].
75. Rim depressed internally. ERSA very fine fabric. Pink with matt yellow slip and a dark brown band on the rim. Site 202 [481].

Copy of CRS 9B or C, c. 580 through the end of the 7th century AD (Hayes 1972: 382) although Meyza (2007: 67-70) puts its end date at around AD 660/65. At Aswan the type occurs during the 6th century AD, although its dating may not be reliable (Gempeler 1992: 105-6, Abb. 50, nos 6-10, T 356a-b). ERSA: Rare; ERSB: Rare; ERSC: Rare; cumulatively Sparse.
76. Rouletted decoration on the lower wall. ERSA. Pink with matt orange-red slip and a reddish-brown band on rim. Site 201 [G].

Shallow bowl with prominent bead rim. Similar to Rodziewicz (1976, pl. 21, K30), Late Roman. Single vessel.
77. ERSB/C sandy fabric with occasional black impurities up to 2.0mm and small white impurities, possibly limestone <0.5mm. Orange throughout with outside abraded; slightly smoothed inside surface. Site 123 [905].

Large bowl or dish with chunky rim. Late Roman. Single vessel.
78. ERSA sandy fabric. Buff with thin orange wash inside and outside; brown wash on the rim and rim top. Site 202 [407].

4.4.2.8 Basins (Fig. 4.9)
Carinated basin with flange and dropped bead rim and footring base. The most common variant is that represented by No. 80. AD 650-730 (Egloff 1977: 151-2, pl. 80, no. 9, Kellia 284). Common.
79. Rim and base, non-joining. Probably Abu Mena fabric. Pale brown with slightly more orange margins and yellow-cream surfaces. Site 202 [407].
80. Similar to No. 79 but with a more delicate rim, without bead and beveled inside. Probably Abu Mena fabric with a mixture of coarse sand, limestone <0.5mm, and occasional dark iron-rich fragments; limestone eruptions on the surface, up to 3.0mm, are fairly common. Brown-orange with the inside surface and rim top cream-green; the outside surface may be abraded. Site 204 [412].

Basin with flat rim, grooved on the top, and wide girth walls with v-shaped vertical applied thumbed strips, one visible and the start of a second one; two round scars suggest a vertical handle and incised decoration between the applied strips. Decoration but not form is similar to Rodziewicz's (1986) Mareotic Incised Ware. Late Roman. Single vessel.
81. Fabric containing common coarse sand <0.5mm, sub-angular in shape and moderately to poorly sorted. Handmade. Red-brown with grey core and brown surfaces. Site 204 [412].

Basin with broad, sloping rim, flattened on the top. Similar to Bailey (1998: 103, pl. no. 64, N 173), at least Late Roman. Single vessel.
82. Silt with occasional larger quartz and limestone to c. 1.0mm, including eruptions on the surfaces. Grey core and margins with outside surface and inside of the rim brown; red-brown inside and on the rim top. Site 253 [472].

4.4.2.9 Miscellaneous types (Fig. 4.9)
Vessel with flat base, poorly made, and ribbed, upright walls, thought to be a bread mould. In the Roman context they start by at least the 2nd century AD (Tomber 2006: 139) and continue through the Late Roman period (Bailey 1998: 72-3). Rare.
83. Silt or silt and marl mix. Fairly fine fabric with small ill-sorted inclusions. Brown with cream-green surfaces, apart from the underside. Site 33 [32].

Possibly a brazier with club rim; at least one irregular vertical handle is joined outside to the rim and wall, and another horizontal handle to the inside. The rim is thumbed on the top and incised on the outside; there are also vertical incisions on the outside wall in a near herringbone shape. Decoration but not form is similar to Rodziewicz's (1986) Mareotic Incised Ware. Late Roman. Single vessel.
84. ?Abu Mena or Mareotis. Marl with poorly mixed quartz and limestone impurities, regularly up to 1.0mm in a sandy matrix. Pale brown with slightly darker margins and cream-yellow surfaces. Site 15 [G].

Pedestal base with flat, up-turned footring and splayed walls; string or wire cutting marks on the underside of the base. Undated. Single vessel.
85. Silt with some limestone and quartz visible. Red-brown with dark brown surfaces and black to crimson-brown core. Site 113 [11].

4.4.2.10 Amphorae (Fig. 4.9)
The Egyptian silt amphorae were represented by small fragments, mostly from handles. Only one rim sherd, No. 86, could be illustrated. An attempt was made to assign handles and bases to the Early versus Late Roman forms, but this could be done for only a small percentage.

Mons Claudianus Type 1 biconical amphora with almond-shaped rim. Late 1st century BC into at least the early 3rd century AD (Tomber 2006: 143; Tomber 2007). Rare.
Not illustrated.

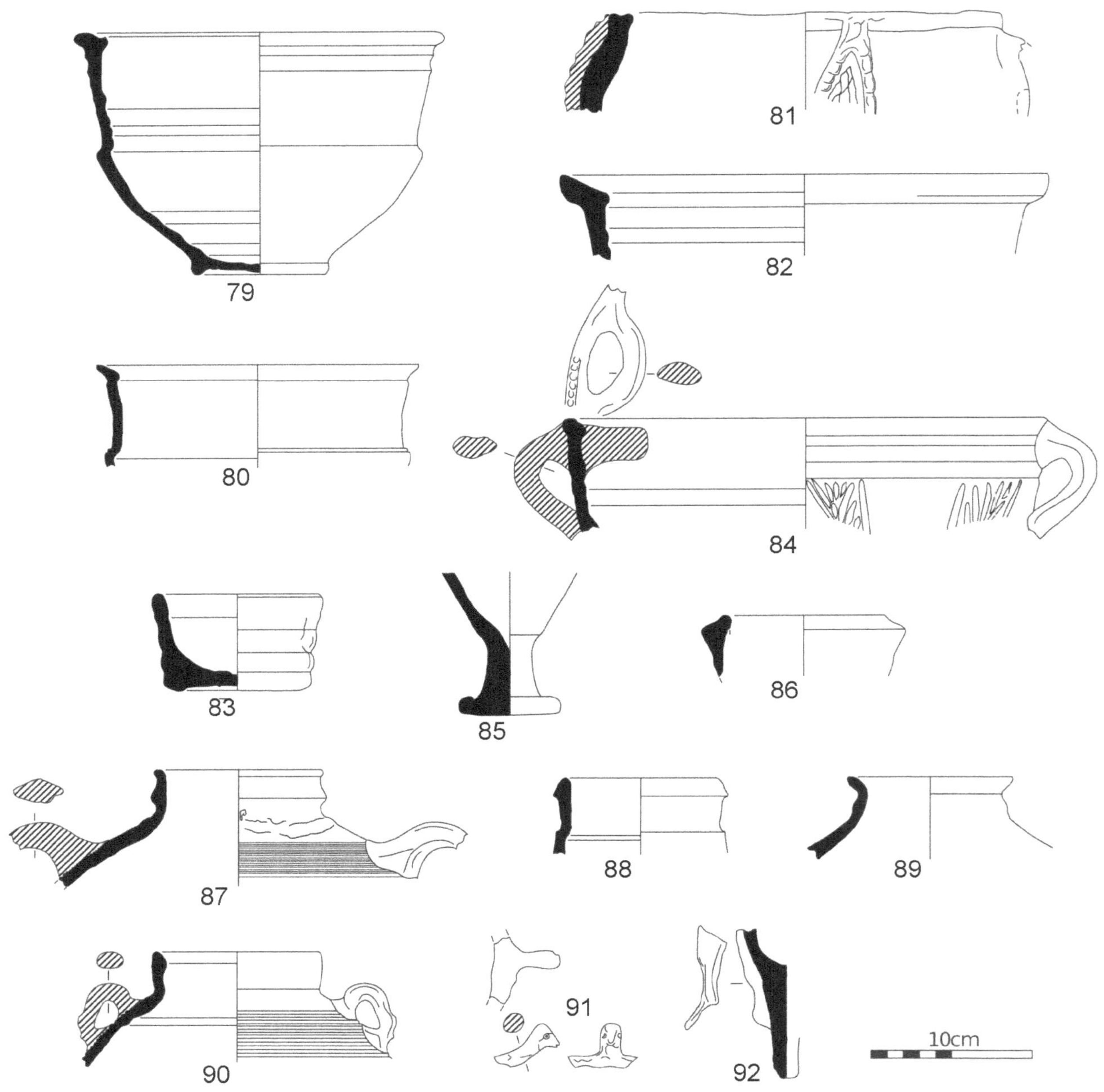

Fig. 4.9. Egyptian wares: Basins (79-82); Miscellaneous (83-5); Amphorae (86-90); Lamp (91); Figurine (92) (J. Whitewright).

Mons Claudianus Type 2 or 12, biconical amphora with dropped, slightly depressed rim, mid 1st through early 3rd centuries AD (Tomber 2006: 145, 148). Rare.
86. Badly eroded on the inside. Silt with poorly sorted quartz and black inclusions up to 2.0mm. Brown throughout. Site 08 [629].

LR Amphora 7, Kellia 172-4 (Egloff 1977: 114-15, pl. 58, nos 5-7, pl. 59, nos 1-2;), late 4th through 7th centuries AD. Rims: Rare; total Sparse.
Not illustrated.

Copy of LR Amphora 5 from Abu Menas, second quarter of the 7th to the early 8th centuries AD (see Section 4.4.1.1 for discussion of Abu Mena fabric). Abundant.

87. Rim and handle with combed shoulder; clay accretions on neck. Of the Abu Mena LR Amphora 5 this is the most common variant. Sandy fabric with some limestone <0.5mm; on handle some grey inclusions of ?shell similar to those seen on LR Amphora 4. Dull orange with outer pale buff-orange margin and inside surface. Site 202 [G].
88. Over-hanging, triangular-shaped rim, poorly made with clay concretions on the rim top and to a lesser degree inside and on the shoulder (not shown on the illustrations). Fine sandy fabric with occasional limestone <0.5mm. Dull orange with paler surfaces. Site 204 [417].
89. Out-turned rim and neck bulge; rare variant. Sandy matrix with some voids and less large limestone up to 2.0mm. Orange-brown with cream-yellow outside surface and halfway down the neck on the inside. Site 204 [416].

Copy of LR Amphora 5 from Kom Abou Billou / Térénouthis in the Delta with bowed neck, internally beveled rim and broad grooved girth; double sub-rounded, looped double handles are joined to the upper and lower shoulder. Kellia 187 and 190, dated AD 650-730 (Egloff 1977: 118). The fabric is the same as that described by Ballet for the products of Kom Abou Billou dated from the mid 7th to the end of 8th century AD at Kellia; at Fustat it continued until the end of the 9th century AD (Ballet 2007: 158; for another example see Majcherek 1992: 110, AD 650-750). There is no evidence that the Mareotic examples extend into the 9th or even 8th century AD. Rare.
90. Silt with organic temper. Grey with orange-brown margins and surfaces orange-brown to brown, discoloured in part. Site 40 [249].

4.4.2.11 Lamps and figurines (Fig. 4.9)
Lamp handle modeled as a bird. No exact parallel could be found, although Ptolemaic and Roman bird lamps have been found in Egypt and other Roman provinces. Ptolemaic lamps from Egypt occasionally had bird heads as features on the body or side lug (Bailey 1975: 242). Italian plastic bird lamps, dated from 1st and 2nd centuries AD, used the bird head as a handle (Bailey 1980: 254, 259, pl. 48 Q1144-5, Type L). These may have copied Roman bronze lamps that used swan heads for part of their handle (Szentléleky 1969: pl. 1, no. 28, pl. 6, no. 96, pl. 13, no. 433). 1st-2nd centuries AD. Single vessel.
91. Fine marl with occasional large quartz, some red and black iron-rich inclusions. Buff with buff-pink margins and cream-yellow surfaces. Site 15 [300].

Fragment of a handmade figurine. Undated. Single vessel.
92. Marl, fairly fine and hard-fired with occasional voids seen in the fresh break and quartz to c. 1.0mm on the surface, creating a granular texture. Buff-brown throughout. Site 08 [623].

4.5 Imported wares

4.5.1 Imported finewares

4.5.1.1 Imported Red Slip wares (Fig. 4.10)
Both Early and Late Roman finewares are present. Many of the established dates for these finewares have been recently or are in the process of being reassessed (e.g. Meyza 2007). Here we primarily rely on established dates, for the nature of our surface sherds make any refinement in dating difficult. Fabric and form typologies follow the standard references which are cited below.

The early period is represented by the late Hellenistic to Early Roman Syrian Eastern Sigillata A (ESA, Hayes 1985: 9-48) and rare Italian sigillata (Ettlinger, *et al.* 1990) body sherds that were not assignable to form. ESA accounts for only 0.2% of all pottery.

The Late Roman types are more common and include Tunisian African Red Slip ware (ARS), Cypriot Red Slipware (CRS) and Phocaean Red Slip ware (PRS) (Hayes 1972).ARS accounts for 12% of all Late Roman Red Slipware and 0.5% of all pottery. CRS was much more common, accounting for 54% of all Late Roman Red Slipware and 2% of all pottery. PRS was rare accounting for just 4% of Late Roman Red Slip ware or 0.2% of all pottery.

?Crater with in-turned bead rim. Excavated Early Ptolemaic context, c. 2nd century BC. Single vessel.
93. Imported Red Slip ware. Fine matrix with well-sorted rare quartz <0.5mm and voids <0.1mm. Orange with orange slip. Site 119 [918].

Squared-off footring base, slightly splayed, from an open vessel, such as illustrated in Fig. 4.8, Nos 57-9 above. Similar to Élaigne (2000b: 100, fig. 1.10), 2nd – 1st centuries BC. Rare.
94. Probably imported. Hard-fired, fine silt or marl clay with some fine limestone inclusions and elongated voids. Buff with dark red outside margin and surface; slightly metallic brown-black slip all over. Site 30 [709].

Low footring base, grooved on the underside from ESA Form 22 bowl, late 2nd century BC to AD 10 (Hayes 1985: 23, tav. 3, nos 10-13). Single vessel.
95. Yellow with semi-glossy to glossy red-orange slip, only extant in patches, originally slipped on the foot and underside. Site 113 [13].

ESA Form 45 bowl, c. AD 1/10-50/60 (Hayes 1985: 33). Single vessel.
96. Buff-cream; originally slipped all over, now patchy semi-glossy red slip on the outside, underside and in patches on the inside. Site 210 [451].

Dish or shallow bowl with plain, out-splayed rim, belonging to a range of ESA forms, including Form 4, late 2nd century BC to Augustan (Hayes 1985: 16, tav. 1, nos 9-23); Form 14, early 1st century AD (Hayes 1985: 20, tav. 2, no. 13); Form 38, mid 1st century AD (Hayes 1985: 32, tav. 5, nos 14-15). Single vessel.
97. Warm buff with glossy red-brown slip all over. Site 28 [703].

Base with small out-turned and tapered foot, most similar to ESA bowl Forms 42 and 45 dating between the late 1st century BC and mid 1st century AD (Hayes 1985: 33-4, tav. 7, nos 4, 11-12). Single vessel.
98. Badly pitted. Warm buff with patchy, matt orange-red slip all over. Site 44 [602].

ARS 32/58 dish, late 3rd to early 4th centuries AD (Hayes 1972: 96, fig. 14, no. 22). Single vessel.
Not illustrated.

ARS 67 dish, mid 4th to early 5th centuries AD (Hayes 1972: 116). Rare.
99. Fine sandy fabric with occasional small limestone impurities <0.5mm. Orange with abraded semi-glossy orange slip on the rim and rim top. Site 40 [248].

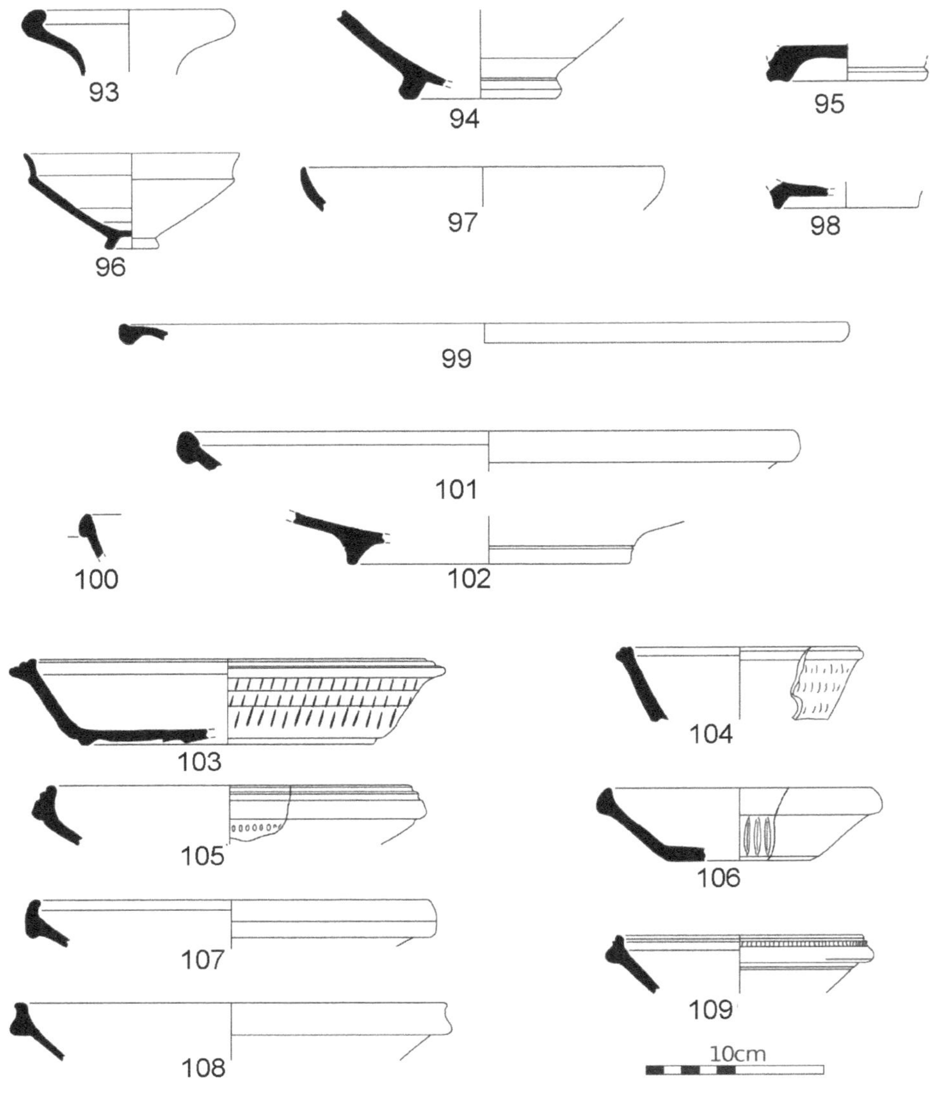

Fig. 4.10. Imported finewares: Ptolemaic/Early Roman Slip wares (93-4); Eastern Sigillata A (95-8); African Red Slip ware (99-102); Cypriot Red Slip ware (103-6); Phocaean Red Slip ware (107-9) (J. Whitewright).

ARS 99 bowl, late 5th to early 7th centuries AD (Hayes 1972: 155). Rare.
100. Fine sandy fabric with rare limestone inclusions. Orange throughout with glossy orange slip all over, slightly abraded. Site 123 [955].

ARS 103 dish, late 5th to third-quarter of the 6th century AD (Hayes 1972: 160, fig. 29). Rare.
Not illustrated.

ARS 104B dish, c. AD 570-600/625+ (Hayes 1972: 166). Cumulatively with ARS 104A-B (c. AD 530-600/625+, Hayes 1972: 166). Sparse.
101. Sandy, granular fabric. Orange with abraded red slip. Site 109 [810].

Low, flared footring base, probably from ARS late dish series, ARS 104-106, c. mid 6th to mid 7th centuries AD (Hayes 1972: 166-71). Rare.
102. Sandy fabric with some limestone inclusions <0.5mm. Brown-orange with orange margins and surfaces; semi-glossy, thin red slip all over. Site 204 [G].

ARS 105 dish, c. AD 580/600-660+ (Hayes 1972: 169, fig. 32). Rare.
Not illustrated.

ARS 107 dish, c. AD 600-660+ (Hayes 1972: 171, fig. 33). Rare.
Not illustrated.

ARS 108 dish, early 7th century AD (Hayes 1972: 171, fig. 33). Single vessel.
Not illustrated.

CRS 2 dish with rouletted decoration, c. mid 5th to mid 6th centuries AD (Hayes 1972: 375); Meyza (2007: 53) places its end date at either the mid- or third quarter of the 6th

century AD. Moderate.
103. Orange fabric with red slip. Heavily concreted. Site 202 [G].
104. Orange fabric with patchy orange-brown slip that is glossy on the inside and matt and browner on the outside. Site 252 [G].

CRS 5 dish, conventionally dated mid-late 6th century AD (Hayes 1972: 377, fig. 81); a date between the early 6th and early 7th centuries AD is proposed by Meyza (2007: 56). Single vessel.
Not illustrated.

CRS 7 dish, mostly mid 6th to early 7th centuries AD (Hayes 1972: 379, fig. 81). According to Meyza (2007: 58) the form started shortly before AD 450 and continued until the late 6th or early 7th century AD. Single vessel.
Not illustrated.

CRS 8 dish, conventionally dated to the 6th century AD (Hayes 1972: 379, fig. 81). Meyza (2007: 60-1) charts an evolution starting in the 5th through the early 7th century AD. Rare.
Not illustrated.

CRS 9 dish, conventionally dated mid 6th to late 7th centuries AD (Hayes 1972: 382), although Meyza (2007: 64-8) starts the form slightly earlier, around 530. Common.
105. Rouletted decoration below the rim. Similar to Meyza (2007: 70) Type K4B, last quarter of the 6th through the 7th centuries AD. Pale red with matt red-brown slip, originally all over, now slightly worn on the rim. Site 204 [G].
106. Rouletted decoration on the outside wall. Buff-pink with splotchy red-brown matt slip outside; inside slipped halfway down the wall with slip colour redder than outside. Site 204 [G].

Copy of CRS 9 dish, mid 6th to late 7th centuries AD (Hayes 1972: 382). Single vessel.
107. PRS? Very hard-fired clay, dense with abundant small limestone impurities. Red with matt brown-red slip all over; the outside of the rim is pitted. Site 202 [411].

PRS 3 dish, mostly mid 5th to mid 6th centuries AD (Hayes 1972: 336-8). Sparse.
108. Form 3C. Fine fabric with some mica and common fine limestone inclusions with reaction rims, some voids. Red-brown; pitted red slip with a black band on the outside of the rim. Site 210 [G].
109. Form 3D with rouletting on the rim. Fine fabric, rich in limestone. Red-brown with matt slip of the same colour on the rim and inside. Site 202 [409].

4.5.2 Imported amphorae

Stamps from imported amphorae are catalogued in Appendix 1. Rare sherds that occur both here and in Appendix 1 have been assigned two separate catalogue numbers but they are cross-referenced. One amphora type, from Chios, is represented only by a stamped sherd, Appendix 1, No. 211, and does not occur in the catalogue below.

4.5.2.1 Aegean

4.5.2.1.1 Knidian amphorae (Fig. 4.11)

The dating framework here follows Monachov's summary article on Knidian amphorae (Monachov 1999). These amphorae were produced from the 4th – 1st centuries BC (Monachov 1999: 161; Grace 1949: 1985) and are well represented in the survey, accounting for 3% of all pottery and 4.9% of all amphorae, and cumulatively are Common. They provide an important indicator for Ptolemaic occupation at many sites. Out of over 350 sherds, mostly unassigned handles, only 12 indicator sherds belong to types that began in the mid-late 4th century BC, while over 50 are at least late 4th century in date. Therefore, when used for dating in Chapter 6 (see below) the presence of unassigned Knidian handles is taken to be from the late 4th BC, and only from the mid 4th century if Knidian type I is present.

The vessel has a bead rim, with the neck lengthening and the body becoming less rounded and more elongate through time; long ovoid to flattened handles are joined to below the rim and upper shoulder; frequently they are stamped on the outside surface (for stamps see Appendix 1, Nos 175-82). The base developed from a mushroom to a pointed one with a ridge (Monachov 1999: figs 7-12).

In thin section the main fabric summarised by Whitbread contains a range of metamorphic, sedimentary and volcanic inclusions, particularly phyllite, quartz, chert, limestone, sandstone and mica (Whitbread 1995: 73). Hand specimens from the survey are pale brown to red-brown throughout, often with light red surfaces. It is usually a very hard-fired, coarse, sandy fabric. Poorly sorted inclusions vary greatly in size between 1.0 and 3.0mm and include pale grey, dark grey and red-brown fragments, quartz, limestone (occasionally shelly or with microfossils) and some voids.

Monachov rim and handle fragment Type IIB, late 4th to early 3rd centuries BC (Monachov 1999: 166, 168, figs 7-8, 11). Sparse.
110. Sandy, hard-fired fabric with sub-angular quartz, limestone, rock fragments (pale and dark grey, red-brown) and voids (<0.1-3.0mm). Pale red-brown. Site 118 [G].

Monachov base Type I, mid-late 4th century BC (Monachov 1999: 162-3, figs 1-4). Rare.
111. Reworked by being rounded and pierced through the middle. Frequent large quartz (2.0mm), shelly limestone with microfossils, black and red rock fragments and voids. Brown. Site 119 [910].

Monachov base Type ID, mid-late 4th century BC (Monachov 1999: 163, fig. 4). Rare
112. Fine sandy, hard-fired fabric with frequent dark inclusions. Red-brown. Site 42 [G].

Monachov base Types IIB or IIC, late 4th to early 3rd centuries BC (Monachov 1999: 166-7, figs 6-9). Rare.

113. Fine sandy, hard-fired fabric. Pale red-brown. Site 113 [47].
114. Fairly fine fabric with some visible quartz. Orange. Site 118 [G].
115. Sandy, hard-fired fabric. Pale red-brown. Site 113 [47].
116. Sandy, hard-fired fabric. Pale red-brown. Site 113 [47].
117. Very hard-fired sandy fabric with pale rock fragments c. 1.0mm, and limestone. Pale brown. Site 252 [G].
118. Sandy, hard-fired fabric with sub-angular limestone and dark grey rock fragments and voids (c.1.0mm). Red-brown. Site 113 [48].

Monachov base Type IIG, late 3rd to mid 1st centuries BC (Monachov 1999: 168, figs 11.2 and 12). Sparse.
119. Sandy with quartz, limestone, red-brown and black inclusions (0.5-2.0mm) and some voids. Red-yellow with light red surfaces. Site 113 [14].

4.5.2.1.2 Rhodian amphorae (Fig. 4.12)
Rhodian amphora imports, dating from the ancient Rhodian forms of the 3rd century BC to Early Roman forms of the 2nd century AD are present. However, only one sherd belonged to the Early Roman series with peaked handles, from Site 44, and it is not illustrated. Rhodian amphorae are well represented, accounting for 3.5% of all pottery found and 5.7% of all amphorae. Cumulatively they are Common. Of the 27 Rhodian stamps (four are from two amphorae), the majority dated to the 2nd century BC, only one to the 3rd century BC and 13 undated, but Hellenistic in form. Stamps and their details are found in Appendix 1, Nos 183-208.

The most common Rhodian fabric is described in thin section by Whitbread as a yellowish groundmass with common serpentinite and less pyroxene, olivine and quartz (Whitbread 1995: 60). Hand specimens from the survey can be separated into two groups. Those of the 3rd century BC date are in a fine white to yellow-buff fabric, with white-cream outside surface and very fine red inclusions and voids. More common is a dark red to salmon-coloured fabric with a cream-yellow or white outside surface, normally without visible inclusions but occasionally with voids, clay pellets, white, black and red rock fragments (<0.5mm). This was used for the production of forms dating between the late 3rd – 1st centuries BC.

Monachov Type IB with overhanging rim, second quarter of the 3rd century BC (Monachov 2005: 88, fig. 1.5). Rare.
120. Fine matrix with very fine red inclusions and voids. Yellow-buff with yellow-cream surfaces. Site 118 [G].

Monachove Type IE2 and IF with arched handles and conical base, late 3rd and 2nd centuries BC (IE2) and second half of the 2nd – 1st century BC (IF) (Monachov 2005: 88, figs 4-8). Common.
121. Stamped on both handles (Appendix 1, No. 183). Very fine fabric without any visible inclusions. Salmon-red with a cream-yellow outside surface. Site 113 [934].
122. Stamped handle (Appendix 1, No. 185). Very fine fabric without any visible inclusions. Salmon-red with a cream-yellow outside surface. Site 115 [G].
123. Stamped handle (Appendix 1, No. 186). Very fine fabric without any visible inclusions. Salmon-red with a cream-yellow outside surface. Site 113 [9].
124. Very fine matrix with small voids and white inclusions (<0.2mm). Orange with cream-yellow outside surface. Site 113 [11].
125. Very fine fabric without visible inclusions. Salmon-red with a cream-yellow outside surface. Site 119 [924].

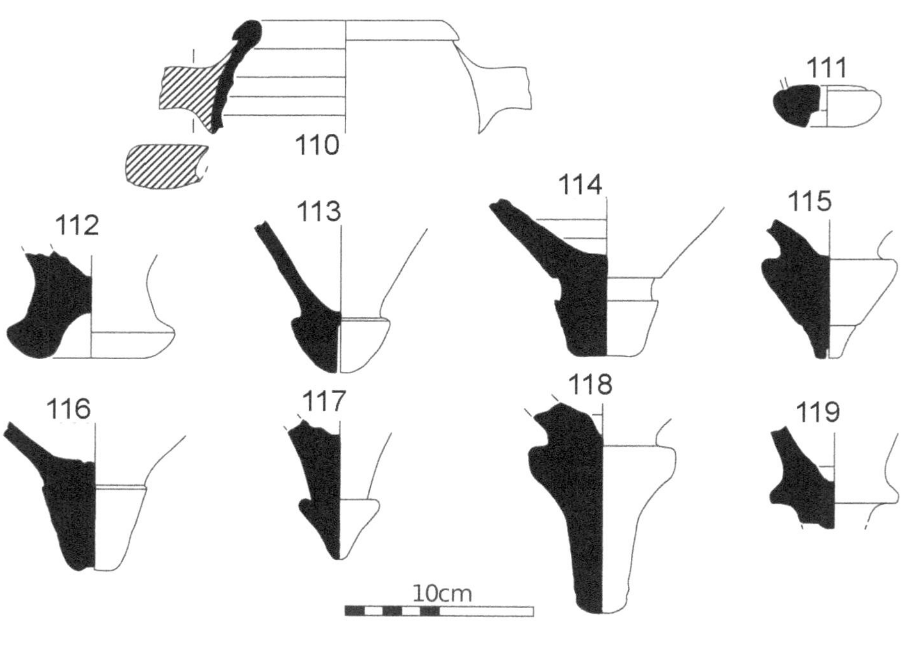

Fig. 4.11. Imported amphorae: Knidian (110-19) (J. Whitewright).

4.5.2.1.3 Koan amphorae (Fig. 4.12, for other Dressel 2-4 amphorae see sections on Italian and Cilician/Cypriot industries below).

This category refers to amphorae with the distinct bifid or double-rod handles whose body shape developed substantially through time, acquiring a carinated shoulder and elongate body. Produced on the island of Kos, it was later copied in many Roman provinces when it is normally referred to as a Dressel 2-4. The Koan differs from those made elsewhere in the Empire by having a button base rather than the peg base found on the Dressel 2-4.

Koan amphorae were produced between the 4th century BC and at least the 1st century AD (Hein, *et al.* 2008; Nicolaou & Empereur 1986). From the evidence of the bases, the most sensitive dating indicator we have at Mareotis for the Koan amphorae, ours date between the 2nd century BC and the 1st century BC, or possibly even into the 1st century AD (apart from No. 131). Koan amphorae are common at Mareotis, where they account for 1.5% of all the pottery and 2.5% of all amphorae. Cumulatively they are Abundant.

Whitbread describes the Koan amphora as being made in a variety of petro-fabrics resulting from the varied geology of the island, diverse production centres and long production period (Whitbread 1995: 83-96). The classic Koan fabric is a fine, micaceous reddish-yellow to pale brown one with a white slip (Hein, *et al.* 2008). At Mareotis four variants of Koan fabrics were identified; here they are combined into two groups, a fine, micaceous one (Variant A) and a coarser one, also micaceous, with notable white and red pellets between 0.5-4.0mm that comprise limestone and phyllites (Variant B).

Two stamped Koan handles are catalogued in Appendix 1, Nos 209-10.

Double-rod handles. Abundant.
126. Variant A with some larger inclusions of quartz, limestone and shell up to c. 1.0mm. Pale orange-pink with cream-yellow to green surfaces. Site 113 [13].

Button base with ridge and splayed walls. Rare.
127. Secondary burning on the outside. Fine sandy clay with moderate rounded dark iron-rich inclusions <0.5mm. Overfired calcareous fabric, probably Koan. Pale brown with cream-brown surface outside and brown-grey inside. Site 202 [G].

*Button base with splayed walls.*Sparse.
128. Variant B. Pale-orange/pink with cream-yellow outside surface. Site 113 [41].
129. Variant B with some possible volcanic fragments, 0.5-2.0mm, mostly less than <1.0mm. Dull orange-brown with cream-yellow surfaces. Site 214 [466].
130. Variant with underside pierced. Variant B with inclusions up to 4.0mm. Brown with yellow-grey outside surface. Site 113 [48].

Abraded base with apparently rounded toe. The type is similar to Koan bases present in late Augustan deposits from Berenike (Tomber personal inspection). Single vessel.
131.Variant B. Pale orange-pink with cream-yellow outside surface. Site 113 [13].

4.5.2.1.4 Thasian amphorae (Fig. 4.12)
Amphora with out-turned rim, long neck and flattened handles, at least where they join below the rim; the broad peg base has a concave underside. Two Mareotic sherds appear to be Thasian, dated between the late 3rd– 2nd centuries BC (Whitbread 1995: 165-6). They have a micaceous sandy fabric with limestone inclusions and are red in colour. Rare, possibly single vessel.
132. Site 113 [45].
133. Site 113 [11].

4.5.2.1.5 LR Amphora 2
5th – 7th centuries AD (Karagiorgou 2001). Sparse.
Not illustrated.

4.5.2.2 Italian amphorae (Fig. 4.13)
Italian amphorae from the Campanian region are distinctive in an orange-red black sand fabric. They were not particularly common, accounting for 0.4% of all pottery and 0.6% of amphorae, but they were imported over a long period of time, from the Ptolemaic period to the 3rd century AD.

Greco-Italic amphora with mushroom rim and handle scars below the rim, late 4th to mid-2nd centuries BC (Will 1987: 178). Sparse.
134. Common volcanic fragments (<0.5mm) and rare fine white inclusions. Orange-red. Site 113 [13].

Dressel 1A, triangular-shaped, overhanging rim, mid 2nd to mid 1st centuries BC (Keay & Williams 2005). Rare.
135. Fine (<1.0mm) black volcanic inclusions, quartz and rare mica. Red. Site 113 [49].

Small peg base, concave on the underside, from a Dressel 2-4, late 1st century BC to late 1st century AD (Peacock & Williams 1986: 105-6, Class 10). Rare.
136. Orange-red with cream-grey outside surface. Slightly concreted on the outside surface. Site 210 [452].

Grooved handle belonging to a vessel with an almond-shaped rim, 3rd century AD (Arthur & Williams 1992). Rare.
137. Orange. Site 40 [249].

4.5.2.3 Cilician/Cypriot amphorae (Fig. 4.13)
This category includes amphorae with a potential source in both these areas, since their fabrics cannot be separated macroscopically. Overall the fabric comprises 11.4% of all pottery and 18.3% of all amphorae. The Early Roman types are quite rare, but include a number of double-rod handle types (Agora M54, Dressel 2-4) as well as two flat-bottomed vessels (Pompeii V, Dressel 30) and a pinched-

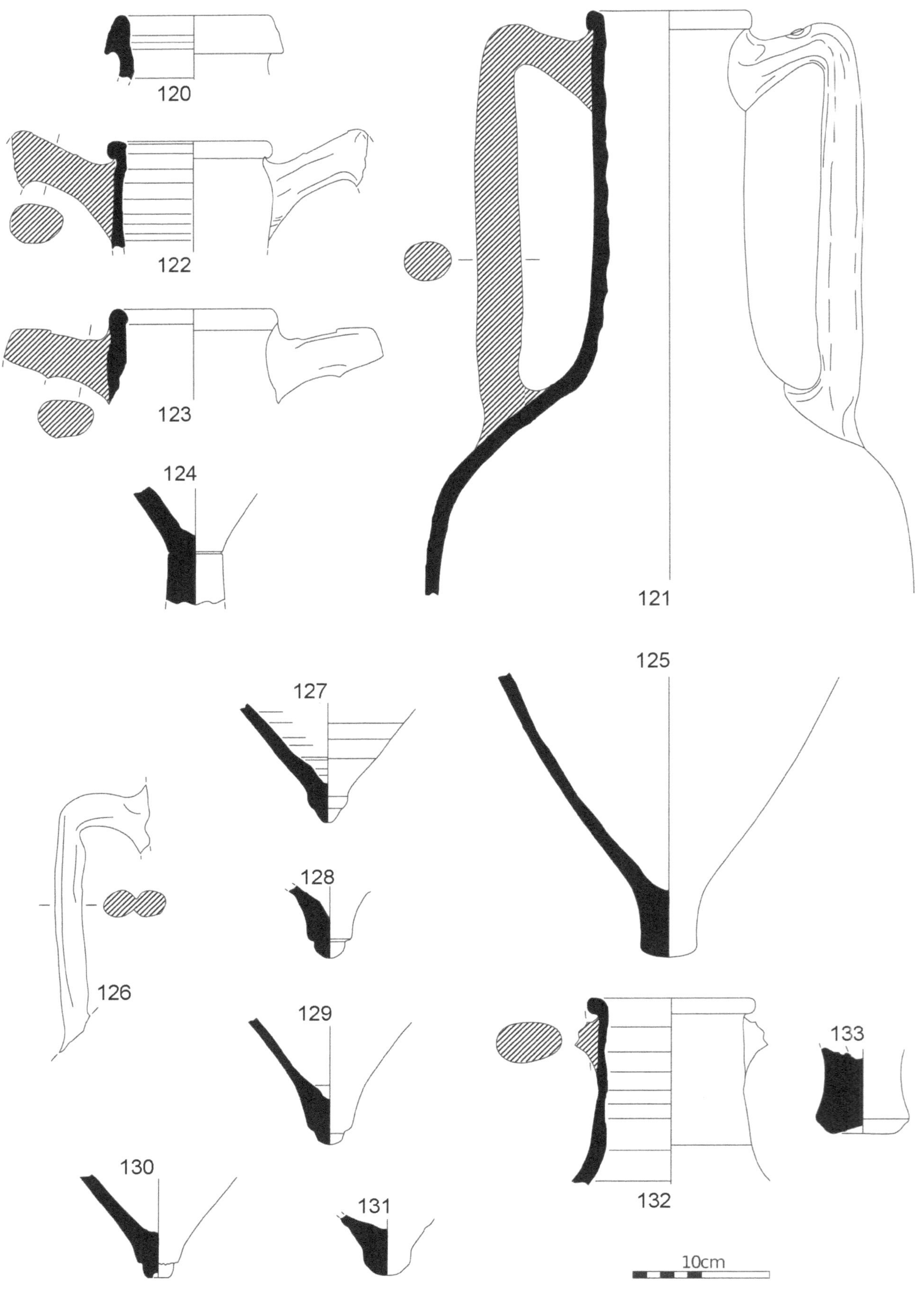

Fig. 4.12. Imported amphorae: Rhodian (120-25); Koan (126-31); Thasian (132-33) (J. Whitewright).

handle one (Agora G199). Of the early types, Empereur and Picon identified Dressel 2-4, Agora M54 and Pompeii V from their surveys at Yumurtalik (Empereur & Picon 1989: 228, 230-2). From the late 4th century onwards the LRA 1 becomes the most popular imported type at Mareotis, accounting for 17.9% of all amphorae. Late Roman amphora kilns are known from Ayas in the west to Seleucie de Pierie in the east (Empereur & Picon 1989: fig. 8); equally if indeed some of the LRA 1 are from Cyprus, this would correspond with the predominance of Cypriot Red Slip ware. Unlike the earlier types, kilns for LRA 1 have been identified in Cyprus (Demesticha & Michaelides 2001). The evolution and dating of these Cilician/Cypriot types has been discussed by Reynolds (2005: 564-7), who provides full citations for the summaries found below.

Fabrics vary between types but are centred around an ultrabasic suite comprising quartz, limestone, chert, some basalt and ferro-magnesian minerals including pyroxene and serpentine (Williams 2005). The overall effect is of a generally well-sorted, sandy fabric with clear, grey, white and black inclusions (<1.0mm) in a dense matrix.

Dressel 2-4 barrel-shaped amphora with carinated shoulder, double-rod handle and peg base. They began in the 1st century AD but are common in this fabric at Mons Claudianus, particularly during the 2nd and early 3rd centuries AD (Tomber 2006: 168-9, table 1.17), but they might be residual in the 3rd century AD. Illustrated sherds only.
138. Elongated, flattened bead rim and flattened handle scar, suggestive of Dressel 2-4. Pale red-brown. Site 113 [51].
139. Arched fragment of a double-rod handle. Buff-tan to orange-brown fabric with cream-yellow surfaces. Site 210 [451].

Agora M54 barrel-shaped amphora with carinated neck and shoulder, peaked-double-barrel handles and a solid, plain base with a rounded point. Usually considered to be mid 1st to late 2nd century AD in date, although Reynolds isolates a variant that may continue into the 3rd century AD (Reynolds 2005: 264, fig. 6). Rare.
140. Peaked-handle fragment. Pale brown fabric with cream-yellow outside surface, pale brown on the inside. Site 253 [G].

Pompeii V amphora with a footring base, stepped rim and long grooved handles, arched at the top, 1st to mid 2nd centuries AD (Reynolds 2005: figs 13-18). Rare.
141. Fragment of flat, grooved handle. Poorly sorted with some inclusions up to 3.0mm visible on the surface. Orange with cream-yellow surfaces. Site 44 [602].

Agora G199 barrel-shaped amphora with pinched handles and mushroom base. 1st to 4th centuries AD; in Beirut the Cilician version is common between the 2nd and 4th centuries AD (Reynolds 2005: 564, fig. 1). Rare.
142. Fragment of pinched handle. Pink with cream surfaces. Site 210 [445].

Copies of Dressel 30 or Gauloise 4 flat-bottomed amphora with footring base, and curved, grooved handles. Dating primarily to the 3rd century AD, although some variants continue into the 4th (Tomber 2009). Sparse.
143. Enlarged, elongate rim, slightly undercut. Orange-brown with yellow-buff outside surface. Site 210 [G]
144. Grooved handle with slightly abraded surface. Orange-brown throughout. Site 44 [601].

LR Amphora 1
This category includes a range of vessels that developed between the 4th and the 7th centuries AD. They are characterised by rounded and folded or grooved handles, and ribbed bodies (Reynolds 2005: 565-7, figs 24-34).

Small variant, similar to Egloff 169 (Egloff 1977: 113, fig. 58.2), late 4th /early 5th centuries AD. Sparse.
145. Pyroxene-rich fabric. Cream-yellow. Site 09 [622].

Standard LR Amphora 1 rims and handles, 5th to 7th centuries AD (Reynolds 2005: 565). Abundant.
146. Cream-yellow to pale brown with orange or orange-brown surfaces. Site 40 [228].
147. Cream-yellow to pale brown with orange or orange-brown surfaces. Site 40 [228].
148. Variant with flattened cup-mouth rim; handle projecting straight from neck. Heavy and burnt. Common coarse quartz and black ferromagnesian minerals. Orange with grey inside margin and handle core, and cream-green slip on the outside surface. Site 201 [G].
149. Variant with handle scar obscuring enlarged rim. Yellow-buff with orange-brown surfaces. Site 40 [226].

4.5.2.4 North African amphorae (Fig. 4.13)
North African amphorae of the 1st to 5th centuries AD account for just 0.6% of all pottery, slightly more prevalent than ARS finewares from the same region, and 1% of all amphorae.

Tripolitanian II amphora, 1st to 4th centuries AD (Bonifay 2004: 92). Rare; thicker examples, possibly Tripolitanian I: Rare; cumulatively Sparse.
150. Fabric, burnt and discoloured, with vestiges of red-brown lenses. Site 44 [601].

Africana III (Keay 1984: XXVP), late 3rd to the first quarter of the 5th century AD (Bonifay 2004: 122). Sparse.
151. Abundant well-sorted, coarse quartz and voids <0.5mm with common limestone inclusions up to 3.0mm and reaction rims on the surface. Red-orange with sandwich of grey-brown on the outer margin and some cream outside surface. Site 204 [412].

Africana IID (Grande, Keay 1984: VII), mostly 3rd and 4th centuries AD (Bonifay 2004: 117). Rare.
152. Brick red clay with unmixed lenses of white; sub-rounded quartz, black, red and sparse white inclusions <2.0mm. Thick cream outside surface. Site 202 [G].

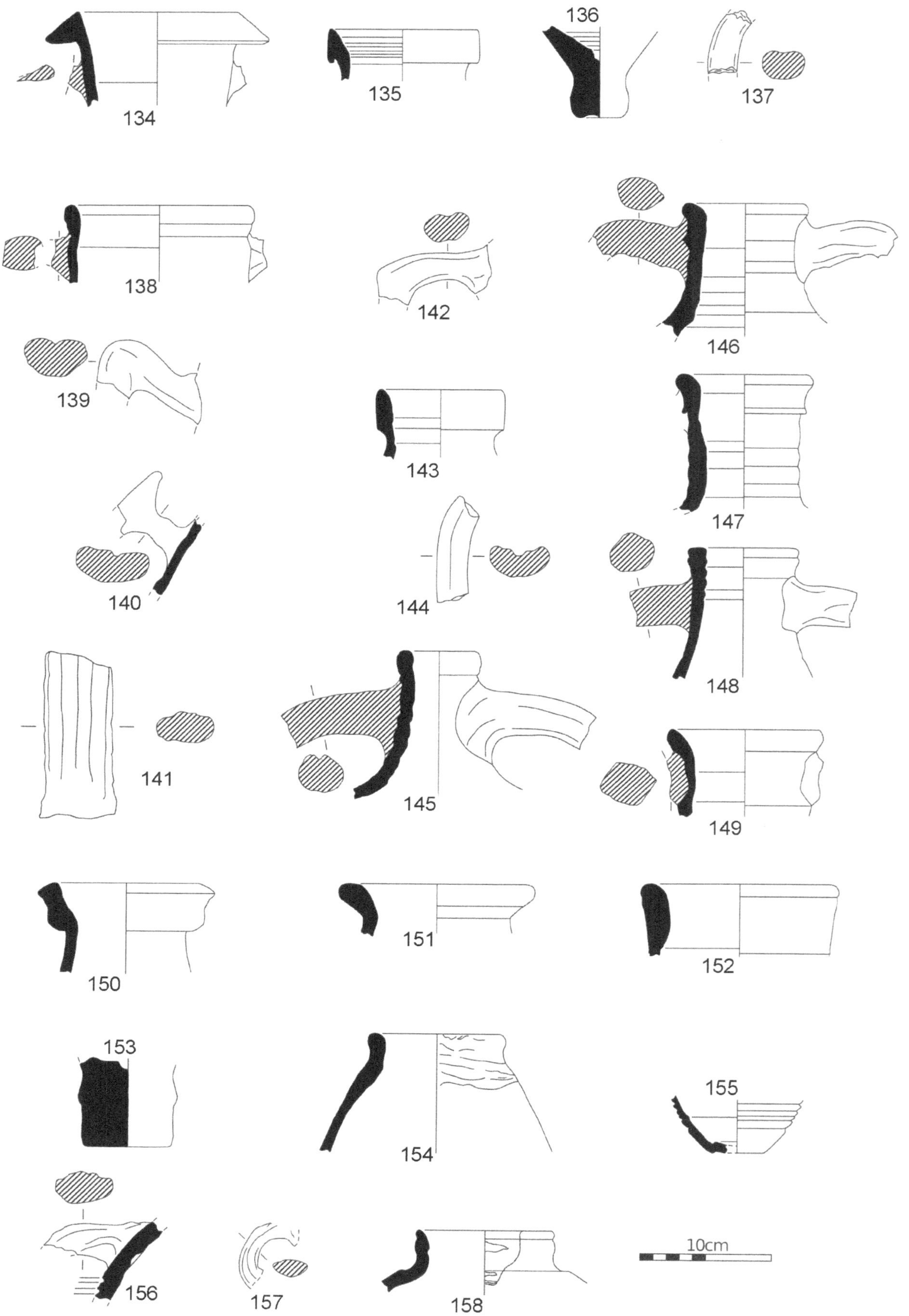

Fig. 4.13. Imported amphorae: Italian (134-37); Early Roman Cilician/Cypriot (138-44); LR Amphora 1 (145-49); North African (150-53); LR Amphora 4 (154-57); LR Amphora 5 (158) (J. Whitewright).

Base from Africana II (Keay 1984: XXV variant 1), late 2nd to 4th centuries AD (Bonifay 2004: 107-19). Single vessel.
153. Sandy with rare larger quartz and limestone inclusions up to 1.0mm. Red-brown with brown and grey-brown lenses sandwiched between and patches of cream slip on the outside surface. Site 30 [709].

4.5.2.5 Levantine amphorae (Fig. 4.13)
The group comprises LR Amphora 4 from Gaza, and LR Amphora 5 from Palestine. LRA 4 was relatively common, accounting for 1.9% of all pottery and 3.1% of all amphorae, with LRA 5 comprising only 0.6% of amphorae since the majority of vessels in this shape were produced at Abu Menas (see Fig. 4.9, Nos 87-9).

4.5.2.5.1 LR Amphora 4
Bag-shaped amphora characterised by clay accretions on the neck and shoulder and loop handles. Based on an earlier prototype, between the 4th and mid 7th centuries AD the body and base gradually became narrower and combing moves from the shoulder to the body (Majcherek 1995: Forms 2-4). There are united by a brown fabric with occasional sand, limestone and grey inclusions <2.0mm. Common.

Rim with accretions, wiped after their application. The narrow girth of the vessel is suggestive of Majcherek Form 4, dated from the late 6th to 7th century AD (Majcherek 1995: 169).
154. Red-brown with duller surfaces. Site 18 [G].

Broad base belonging to Majcherek Forms 3-4, late 5th to 7th century AD (Majcherek 1995: 168-9).
155. Pale brown to brown-red. Site 204 [418].

Handle positioned above combing and therefore belonging to Majcherek Form 2, late 5th through AD 535 (Majcherek 1995: 168).
156. Occasional limestone eruptions on the surface up to 5.0mm. Red-brown with tan outside surface. Site 44 [601].

Small, loop handle.
157. Two sherds, joining. Abraded. Some limestone eruptions <5.0mm on the surface. Pale brown. Site 204 [418].

4.5.2.5.2 LR Amphora 5
Bag-shaped amphora with upright rim, ribbed body with looped handles and broad base, probably late 5th to 7th centuries AD (Reynolds 2005: 574). Sparse.
158. Tooled rim, unevenly manufactured. Sandy with frequent sub-angular quartz (<0.5mm) and flat voids. Red-brown. Site 202 [407].

4.5.2.6 Other Eastern Mediterranean amphorae

4.5.2.6.1 Hollow-foot amphora or Peacock & Williams Class 47
2nd to 4th centuries AD (Peacock & Williams 1986: 193-5). Rare.
Not illustrated.

4.5.2.6.2 LR Amphora 3
1st to 6th centuries AD (Bezecky 2005: 203-5). Sparse.
Not illustrated.

4.5.2.7 Unsourced amphorae (Fig. 4.14)
This section includes a small number of amphorae that cannot be assigned to source. Together they constitute 0.22% of all amphorae and are cumulatively Sparse.

Whole-mouth amphora with flattened bead rim and broad shoulder. Source unknown but it resembles Tyrian and Palestinian jars of the 5th to 3rd centuries BC (Reynolds 2005: fig. 84). Ptolemaic. Sparse.
159. Fine sandy marl with abundant limestone <1.0mm. Pale red with grey core and brownish surfaces; cream-yellow-green slip on the rim, matt grey-brown on the body. Site 118 [1].

Wide-mouthed amphora or jar with out-turned rim and well-defined shoulder, probably imported. Ptolemaic. Single vessel.
160. Very hard-fired, fine fabric. Red with grey-brown margins; abraded red-brown matt slip on the outside and outer edge of the rim top (left of groove); matt black-brown slip inside the rim and on the rim top, somewhat discoloured. Site 202 [404].

Amphora with elongate, flattened bead rim with ovoid handle-scar directly below the rim and the handles appearing to arch upwards. Similar to a Corinthian type of the 3rd century BC illustrated by Koehler (1979: 88, pl. 18). Single vessel.
161. Fabric with large white limestone, black minerals and red pellets up to 4.0mm; small voids are also common. Beige-pink with grey bands in section. Site 113 [51].

Jar or amphora with overhanging rim, similar to Greco-Italic, however, the fabric suggests it may be a coarse ware jar. Undated. Rare.
162. Soft with moderate to sparse quartz and multi-coloured inclusions; common organic voids. Pale brown. Site 201 [G].

Amphora with well-rounded bead rim and round handle scar, possibly Brindisi, and if so dated between the late 2nd and late 1st centuries BC (Buchi 1973; Manacorda 2001). Single vessel.
163. Very fine matrix with moderate multi-coloured white, red and clear inclusions <0.5mm and possibly rare mica. Pale brown-red with cream-buff outside surface. Site 44 [601].

Amphora with large, slightly squared-off bead rim, long neck and flattened handles joined below the rim. Possibly in a Rhodian fabric and if so Monachov Type I (2005). Ptolemaic. Single vessel.
164. Fine, white-yellow with white surfaces. Site 113 [11].

Amphora with tall, collared rim, flattened on top, and ovoid handles joining at the rim. Possibly a Mareotic product, an

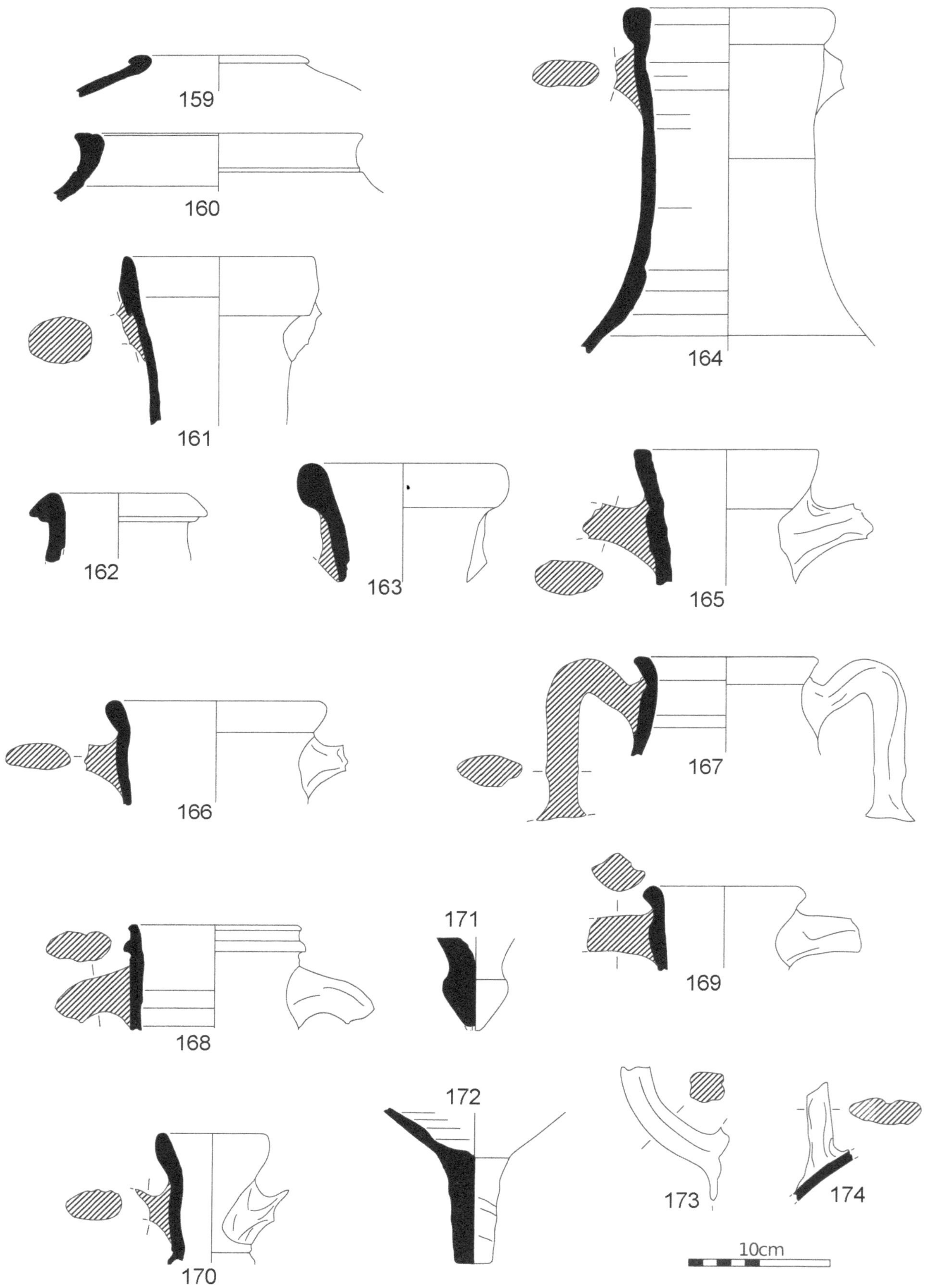

Fig. 4.14. Unsourced imported amphorae (159-74) (J. Whitewright).

AE1/2 variant with collared rim (cf. Fig. 4.5, Nos 1-3). Probably Ptolemaic. Single vessel.
165. Crudely made with visible wiping marks. Marl with rare sand <0.5mm and rare limestone to 1.0mm. Cream-green, slightly concreted on the outside. A pale green fabric also occurs at the Mareotic kilns. Site 113 [37].

Amphora with ovoid rim, out-turned, bowed neck, possibly caused by joining of the strap handles. Undated. Single vessel.
166. Fabric with fine white inclusions <0.4mm. Dark red-brown. Site 113 [51].

Amphora with short, out-turned rim and arched strap handles. Undated. Single vessel.
167. Sandy with small, frequent limestone and rounded quartz inclusions up to 1.0mm. Surface laminating. Red with grey core. Site 113 [76].

Amphora with double-lip rim and grooved handle joined to a straight neck. Undated. Single vessel.
168. Dense clay, possibly micaceous, with common well-sorted quartz <0.5mm; some larger inclusions especially red iron-rich fragments and limestone between 1.0 and 2.0mm. Orange with pitted and patchy yellow-brown surfaces. Site 113 [48].

Amphora with small, out-turned rim and thick handle joined below the rim and grooved on one face. Undated. Single vessel.
169. Very fine quartz, white and dark inclusions <0.25mm. Red with orange and yellow surfaces. Site 208 [444].

Small amphora with cup-like rim; flattened grooved handle scars project from the neck. Undated. Single vessel.
170. Fine, dense fabric with occasional very fine red and limestone impurities. Slightly burnt on rim and discoloured to brown with pale brown outside surface, mottled to orange-brown. Site 09 [622].

Solid amphora base with defined, tapered toe. Hellenistic. Single vessel.
171. Fine micaceous fabric with occasional inclusions <0.5mm, mostly white but some dark inclusions visible on the surfaces similar to the Koan fabric. Pale orange with pale brown-buff inside surface. Site 113 [53].

Amphora base with tall, thin solid spike and flared walls. Undated. Single vessel.
172. Imported fabric, silty with fine mica and sandy surfaces comprising black, white and quartz inclusions up to 2.0mm. Pale brown with surfaces smoothed or washed pale buff-brown. Site 39 [G].

Riley MR Amphora 1 with fluted handle, 1st to 4th centuries AD (Riley 1979: 177-9, figs 81-2, nos 215-21). A Tripolitanian or Byzacena source has been proposed, although our vessel with micaceous clay may come from kilns at Naxos, Sicily (Wilson 1990: 24). Single vessel.
173. Surface abraded. Micaceous, silty matrix with moderate, angular pale rock fragments, occasionally dark <1.0mm. Pale brown with cream surfaces. Site 100 [609].

Strap amphora handle grooved on the inside. No parallels are known but the form type is present at Quseir al-Qadim (Tomber personal inspection) and therefore suggests the Early Roman period. Single vessel.
174. Micaceous clay with sub-rounded white, black, red and dark brown inclusions <1.0mm. Red-brown with paler surfaces. Site 124 [358].

Appendix 1. Stamped amphora handles

A. Omar & R. Thomas

All stamps are from amphorae described in the ceramics Chapter 4 this volume and include Knidian, Rhodian, Koan and Chian forms. This is not an exhaustive specialist study, but a preliminary presentation and discussion of the material found during the Lake Mareotis Research Project. Readings were undertaken by Ahmed Omar, with rubbings and photography undertaken by Ross Thomas and Ahmed Omar. We would like to thank Fani Seroglou for her feedback and suggestions. Tentative or uncertain readings have been omitted. Parallels were subsequently researched with the aid of the rubbings, photographs and readings. Where precise parallels were not found, dating was based on amphora form (Grace 1985: 18; Monakhov 2004: 88).

All stamp parallels date from the late 4th to early 1st centuries BC. One Rhodian example is dated to the late 4th to early 3rd century BC, from Site 117. One example from Site 113 was dated to the late 2nd to early 1st century BC. The only 3rd century BC stamp came from Site 201 found in conjunction with 2nd century BC stamps. The 2nd-century BC stamps were by far the most common. Koan examples may date as late as the 1st century BC/AD where much broader dates are based on amphora form (Grace 1985: 18; Monakhov 2004: 88).

Analysis of the distribution of stamps was limited with such a small sample. Sites 33, 37 and 117 had one Rhodian, Site 119 had two Rhodian and Site 201 three Rhodian stamps. Site 100 had one Knidian and Site 24 had one possible Chian stamp. Site 113 had the largest collection including four Knidian, 15 Rhodian and two Koan stamps. Site 115 had the next largest sample of five Rhodian and three Knidian stamps. Stamps from excavated areas within Sites 113 and 115 dated to the 2nd century BC.

Knidian amphorae (Fig. 4.15)

175. Stamped handle. Reddish yellow core with light red surfaces. Hard fired, sandy texture with variable fine to coarse (<0.1-3.0mm) sub-angular inclusions of quartz, white limestone, pale grey, dark grey and red-brown rock fragments and some voids. Pale red-brown. Eponym (date) stamp. Rectangular, broken left x 11mm, with an anchor to the left and three poorly preserved lines, the top two can be read:

[...]Ẹ[.]ΜỌΚ̣Ρ̣Α   [...]‘Ẹ[.]μο̣κ̣ϱ̣α
[........]Π̣ΠΟΛΟ   [........]π̣πολο

No parallel found. Site 113 [1]. From the late 3rd to the (and most likely) 2nd century BC (Grace 1985: 18).

176. Stamped handle. Pale red-brown, sandy, hard-fired fabric. Reddish yellow core with light red surfaces. Sub-angular quartz, limestone, pale grey, dark grey and red-brown rock fragments and voids (<0.1-3.0mm). Fabricant (makers) stamp with a trident, on the bottom right. Rectangular, c. 32 x 11mm, one line reads:

Α̣[...]ΛΟΥ   ’Α̣[...]λου

Site 115 [G]. From the late 3rd to the (and most likely) 2nd century BC (Grace 1985: 18).

177. Stamped handle. Pale red-brown, sandy, hard-fired fabric. Reddish yellow core with light red surfaces. Sub-angular quartz, limestone, pale grey, dark grey and red-brown rock fragments and voids (<0.1-3.0mm). Eponym (date) stamp. Rectangular, c. 51 x 19mm, with an anchor facing left and three lines of text:

ΕΠΙΕ̣Π̣Ι̣ΦΑΝΙ̣ΥC   ’Επὶ ’Επιφάνιυς
ΑΡΙCΤΑ̣ΓΟ̣Ρ̣Α   ’Αϱιστά̣γο̣ϱ̣α
ΚΝΙΔΙ   Κνίδι

Note the Knidian ethnic is only present after 188 BC (Grace 1985: 18). The eponym Επιφανης is dated to 220-146 BC (Grace 1985: 33), placing this stamp in the range 188-146 BC. Site 115 [G].

178. Stamped handle. Pale red-brown, sandy, hard-fired fabric. Reddish yellow core with light red surfaces. Sub-angular quartz, limestone, pale grey, dark grey and red-brown rock fragments and voids (<0.1-3.0mm). Rectangular stamp c. 17mm (broken left). Three lines read:

[...]Α̣[...]   [...]α̣[...]
Ε̣[...]ΘΕ̣[Υ]   Ε̣[...]Θε̣[υ]
ΔΟΤΟΥ̣[...]   Δοτου̣[...]

No parallel found. Site 115 [G]. From the late 3rd to the (and most likely) 2nd century BC (Grace 1985: 18).

179. Stamped handle. Pale red-brown sandy, hard-fired fabric. Reddish yellow core with light red surfaces. Sub-angular quartz, limestone, pale grey, dark grey and red-brown rock fragments and voids (<0.1-3.0mm). Circular stamp c. 32mm diameter with either a bull head or a Rhodian rose stamp in the centre, with illegible text except for a single:

κ

Site 100 [608]. From the late 3rd to the (and most likely) 2nd century BC (Grace 1985: 18).

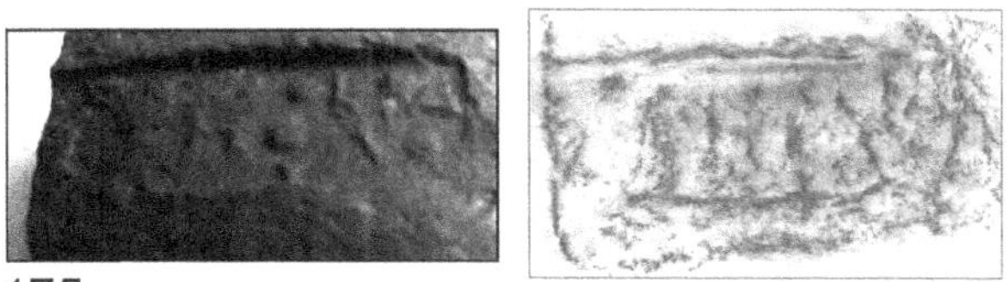
175

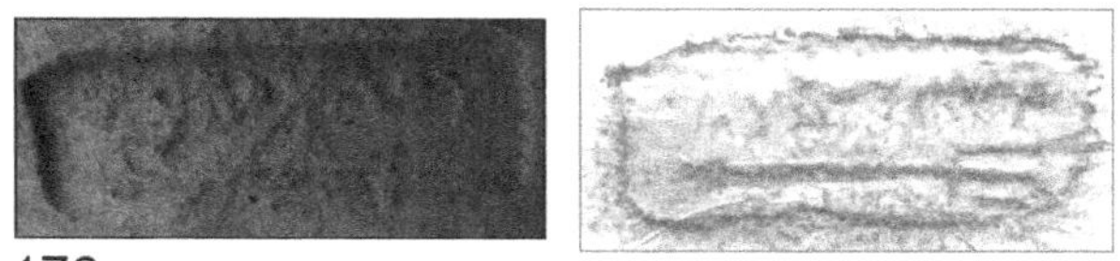
176

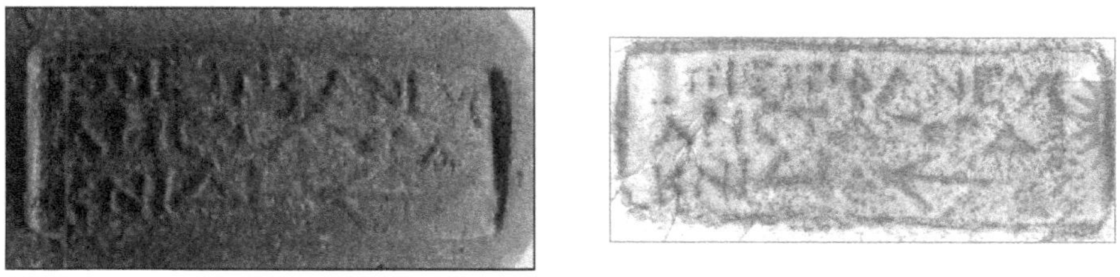
177

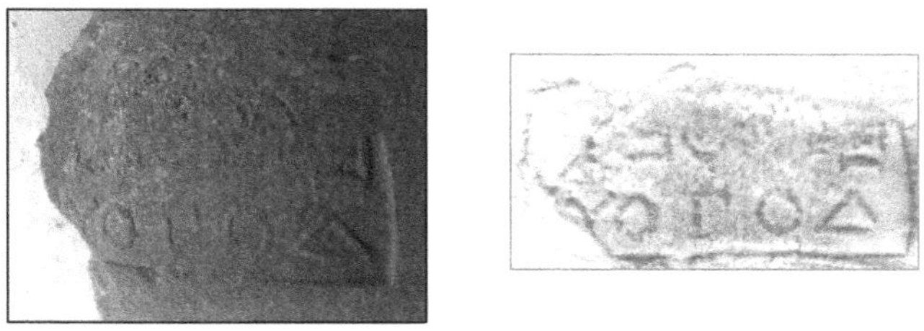
178

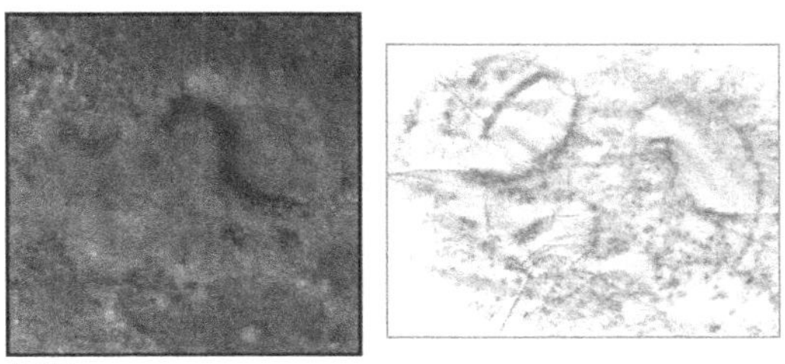
179

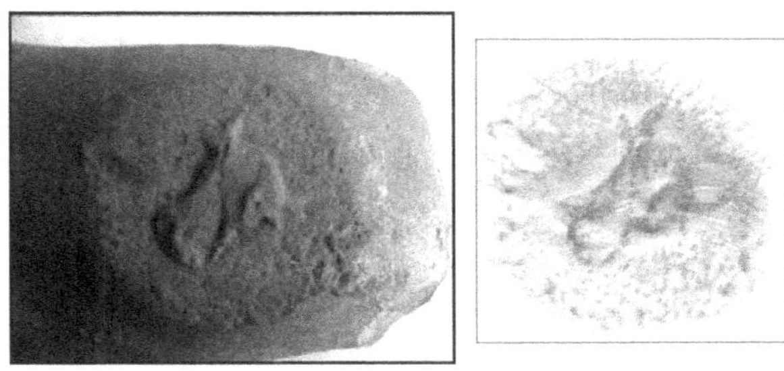
180

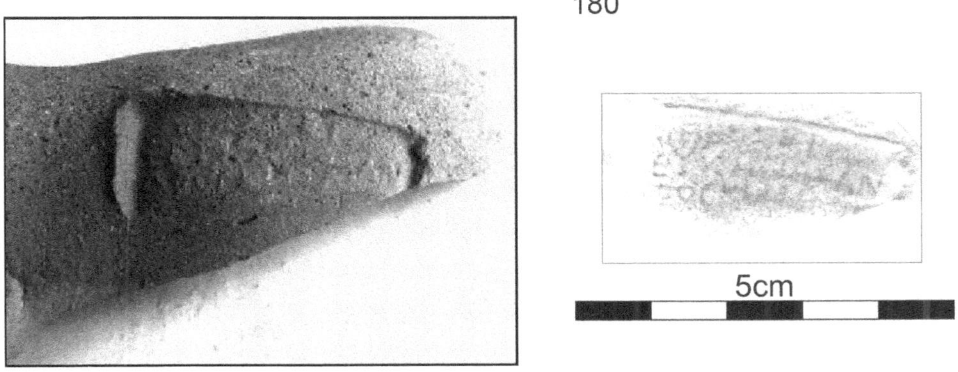

181

182

Fig. 4.15. Stamped amphora handles: Knidian (175-82) (R. Thomas & J. Cooper).

180. Stamped handle. Pale red-brown, sandy hard-fired fabric. Reddish yellow core with light red surfaces. Subangular quartz, limestone, pale grey, dark grey and red-brown rock fragments and voids (<0.1-3.0mm). Circular stamp c. 28mm diameter, with bull head, or *boukranion*, in centre and illegible text. Site 113 [13]. From the late 3rd to the (and most likely) 2nd century BC (Grace 1985: 18).

181. Stamped handle. Pale red-brown, sandy hard-fired fabric. Reddish yellow core with light red surfaces. Subangular quartz, limestone, pale grey, dark grey and red-brown rock fragments and voids (<0.1-3.0mm). Eponym (date) stamp. Rectangular, broken on right side, c. 40 x 14mm, with three lines, badly preserved. Stamp tentatively reads τευ...αν δοου.ν, no comparison found.

Ε̣Π̣[...]	'Ε̣π̣[...]
ΤΟ̣Υ[...]ΑΝ	του[.......]αν
ΔΡΟΥΚ̣Ν̣Ι̣Δ[...]	δρου Κ̣ν̣ι̣δ[...]

No parallel found. Site 113 [10]. From the late 3rd to the (and most likely) 2nd century BC (Grace 1985: 18).

182. Stamped, flat handle. Fine light red fabric with cream surface, no visible inclusions, unlike other Knidian fabric examples, possibly only Knidian in form. Rectangular stamp broken on the left x 16mm, with two lines of text:

[...]Δ̣Α[...]	[...]δ̣α[...]
[...]Δ̣Ι̣[...]	[...]δ̣ι̣[...]

No parallel found. Site 113 [72]. From the late 3rd to the (and most likely) 2nd century BC (Grace 1985: 18).

Rhodian amphorae (Figs 4.16-4.19)

183. (Chapter 4, No. 121) Squared-off bead rim, long neck and fairly narrow girth with stamped, rounded handles joined below the rim and to the shoulder. Stamped on both handles. Salmon-red fabric with a cream-yellow outer surface. Very fine fabric without clearly visible inclusions. Two Rhodian rose stamps. Eponym (date) stamp. Circular, c. 29mm diameter with Rhodian rose in centre:

Ε̣Π̣Ι̣[...]Ν̣[..]Ο̣[...Π]Α̣Ν̣Α̣Μ̣Ο̣[.]
'Επί [...]ν̣[..]ο̣[...Π]α̣ν̣α̣μ̣ο̣[.]

Year is missing, only the month (Παναμου) is known. The fabricant (potter's) stamp is circular, c. 31mm diameter with Rhodian rose in centre:

Β̣ΑΚΧ̣Ι̣ΟΥ	Β̣άκχ̣ι̣ου

The stamps resemble rose stamps dating to 145-108 BC, which also fits with potter Βάκχιος II who is dated to the same period and found on circular rose stamps (Finkielsztejn 2001: 143-5, 165, plate XXI.16). Site 113 [934].

184. Found with No. 183 above, stamped on both handles. Salmon-red fabric with a cream-yellow outer surface. Very fine fabric without clearly visible inclusions. Eponym (date) stamp. Rectangular, c. 40 x 15mm, with three lines of text:

[ΕΠΙ]Α̣ΡΙΣΤΡΑ̣	['Επὶ] 'Αριστρά̣
ΤΟ̣Υ	το̣ῦ
Υ̣ΑΚΙΝ̣[ΘΙΟΥ]	'Υ̣ακιν̣[θίου]

The fabricant (potter's) stamp is rectangular, c. 49 x 7mm, with a *cluster of grapes or caduceus to the right and* one line of text:

Μ̣Ι̣Δ̣Α̣	Μ̣ι̣δ̣α̣

Dated to the month of *Hyakinthios* 125-121 BC (Finkielsztejn 2001: 195). Μιδας is a known potter dated from c. 145-c. 108 BC (Finkielsztejn 2001: 131). Site 113 [934].

185. (Chapter 4, No. 122) Squared-off bead rim, stamped, peaked, flattish handle joined below the rim. Salmon-red fabric with a cream-yellow outer surface. Very fine fabric without clearly visible inclusions. Rectangular eponym (date) stamp, c 34 x 11mm with Helios head on left and two lines of text:

ΕΠΙ ΑΡΙΣ	Επι Αρισ
[...]ΜΟΥ	[οδα]μου

Dated to c. 166/164 BC (Finkielsztejn 2001: 109, stamp 132). Site 115 [G].

186. (Chapter 4, No. 123) Rounded, bead rim with stamped handle. Salmon-red fabric with a cream-yellow outer surface. Very fine fabric without clearly visible inclusions. Circular stamp, c. 29mm in diameter. Eroded with Rhodian rose or Helios bust in centre surrounded by illegible text. Site 113 [9]. Late 3rd to 1st century BC (Monakhov 2004: 88).

187. Stamped, flattish amphora handle, oval in section. Salmon-red fabric with a cream-yellow outer surface. Very fine fabric without clearly visible inclusions. Fragmentary rectangular eponym (date) stamp, with three legible lines reading right to left, broken on the left:

ΙΕΡΕ[...]	'Ιερε[...]
Αρι[......]	Αρι[....]
Δ[..........]	δ[......]

No parallel found. Site 119 [G]. Late 3rd to 1st century BC (Monakhov 2004: 88).

188. Stamped, rounded handle fragment. Salmon-red fabric with a cream-yellow outer surface. Very fine fabric without clearly visible inclusions. Rectangular eponym (date) stamp, broken on top and left. Bottom two of three lines are legible:

ΜΕΝΕΥ[Σ]	μενέυ[ς]
Δ̣ΑΛ̣[Ι]ΟΥ	Δ̣αλ̣[ί]ου

No parallel found. Site 113 [83]. Late 3rd to 1st century BC (Monakhov 2004: 88).

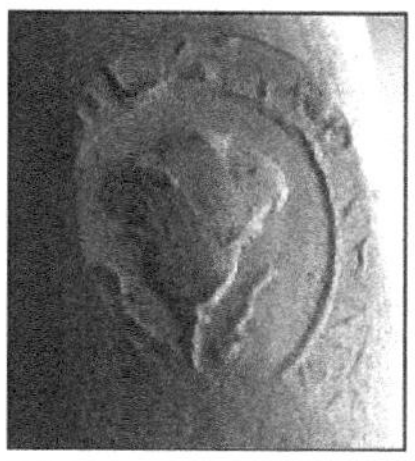
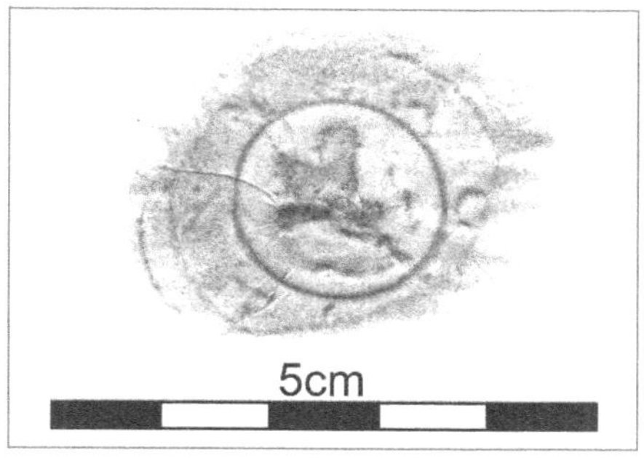

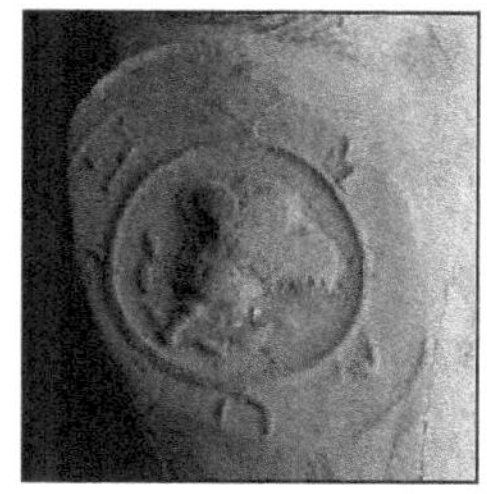

183

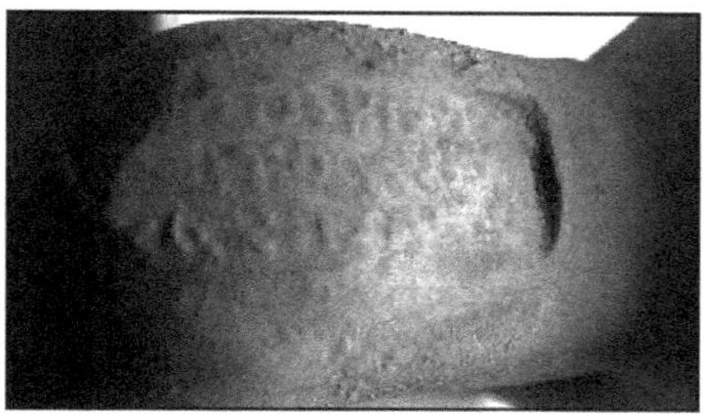
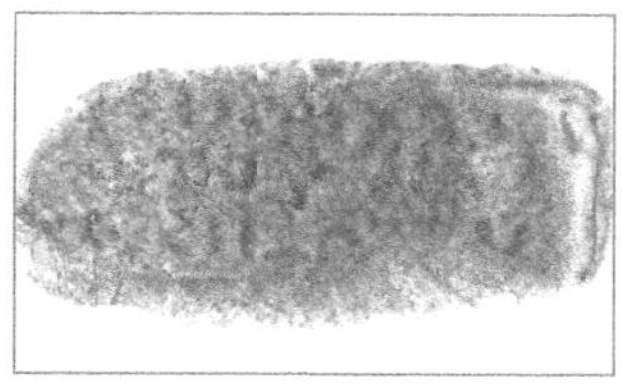
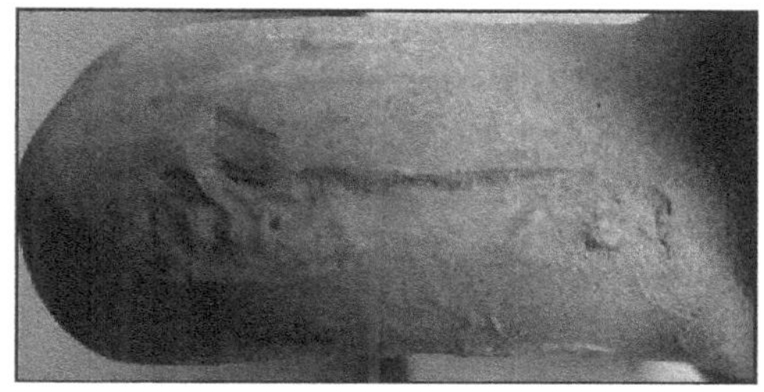

184

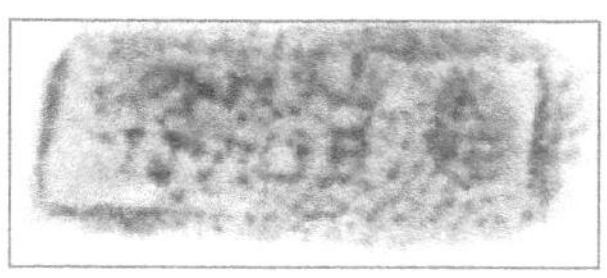

185

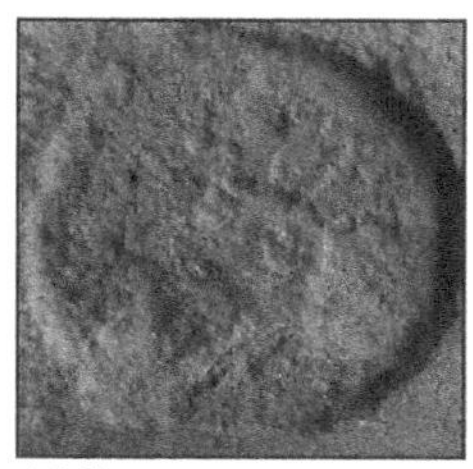
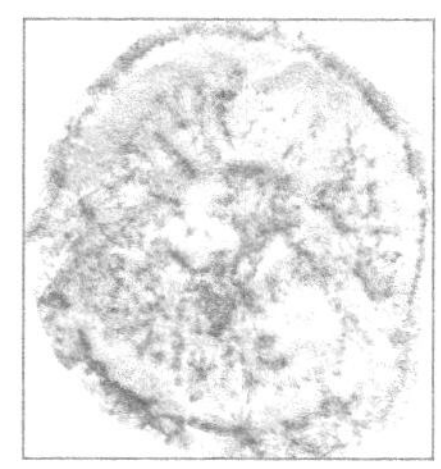

186

187

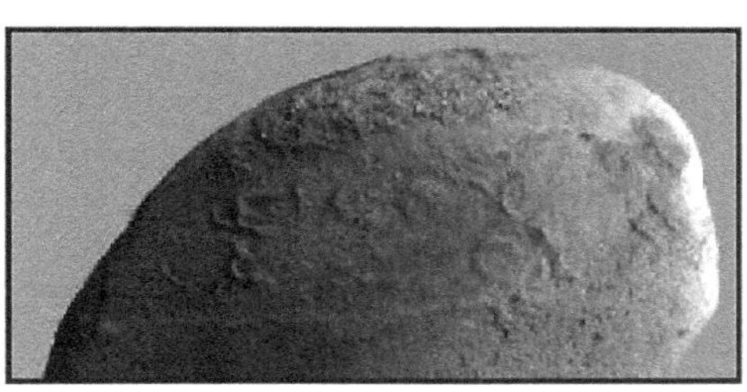
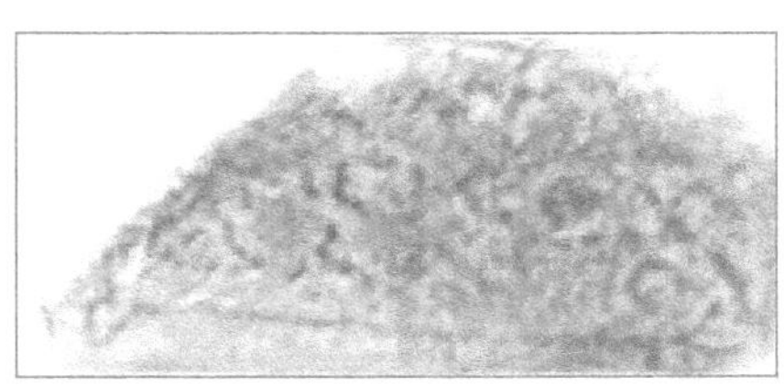

188

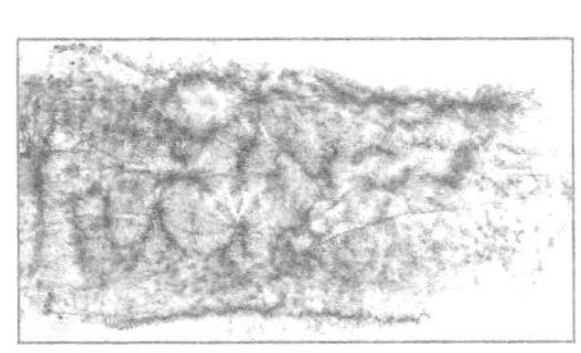

189

Fig. 4.16. Stamped amphora handles: Rhodian (183-89) (R. Thomas & J. Cooper).

189. Stamped, sub-rounded handle. Salmon-red fabric with a cream-yellow outer surface. Very fine without clearly visible inclusions. Badly eroded rectangular eponym (date) stamp c. 40 x 18mm. Bottom two of three lines legible, with *caduceus* on the right:

ΞΙΝΟΥ	ξίνου
Β̣Α̣Δ̣Ρ̣Ο̣Μ̣[ΙΟΥ]	Β̣α̣δ̣ϱ̣ο̣μ̣[ίου]

The most likely eponym is Καλλίξεινος, here in incorrect form with the ε omitted. If so this would be dated to c. 107-86 BC (Finkielsztejn 2001: 161; Nilsson 1909: 442-443 nos 267 and 268, 530 no. 9; Fani Seroglou pers. com.). Alternatively Alexinos (Αλεξίνος) is another possibility (Nilsson 1909: 87). Site 113 [48].

190. Stamped, round handle. Very fine salmon-red fabric with a cream-yellow outer surface. Rectangular fabricant (potter's) stamp, c. 42 x 17mm, one line, with *caduceus* underneath.

ΙΜΑΣ	'Ιμας

Fabricant 'Ιμας stamps with *caduceus* are dated to c. 159/158 to c. 146 BC. (Finkielsztejn 2001: 131). Site 113 [1].

191. Stamped, round handle. Very fine salmon-red fabric with a cream-yellow outer surface. Rectangular eponym (date) stamp, c. 41 x 19mm with three lines:

ΕΠ[ΙΕΡΕΩ]Σ	'Επ'[ιεϱέω]ς
ΤΙΜΟΘ[ΕΟ]Υ	Τιμόθ[εο]υ
ΔΑΛΙΟΥ	Δαλίου

The month of *Dalios* c. 128 BC (Finkielsztejn 2001: 195). Site 113 [46].

192. Stamped, round handle. Very fine salmon-red fabric with a cream-yellow outer surface. Eroded rectangular eponym (date) stamp, two lines visible, broken top and right, first line is unclear.

Ε̣Π̣Ι̣[...]	'Ε̣π̣ι̣
Δ̣Α̣ΛΙ̣Ο̣Υ̣	δ̣αλί̣ο̣υ̣

Possibly same stamp as 37 above, if so dated c. 128 BC (Finkielsztejn 2001: 195). Site 113 [52].

193. Stamped, round handle. Very fine salmon-red fabric with a cream-yellow outer surface. Rectangular eponym (date) stamp, c. 45 x 19mm, three lines:

Ε̣ΠΙΑΡΙΣ	'Ε̣πὶ 'Αϱισ
ΤΡΑ̣ΤΟΥ	τϱα̣τόυ
ΔΑΛ̣ΙΟΥ	Δαλ̣ίου

Dated to the month of *Dalios* c. 125-121 BC (Finkielsztejn 2001: 195). Site 33 [359].

194. Stamped, round handle. Very fine salmon-red fabric with a cream-yellow outer surface. Rectangular stamp c. 38 x 15mm with illegible text. Late 3rd to 1st century BC (Monakhov 2004: 88). Site 37 [360].

195. Stamped, round handle. Very fine salmon-red fabric with a cream-yellow outer surface. Rectangular fabricant (potter's) stamp, c. 48 x 11mm with two illegible lines of text. Late 3rd to 1st century BC (Monakhov 2004: 88). Site 113 [83].

196. Stamped, round handle. Very fine salmon-red fabric with a cream-yellow outer surface. Partial rectangular fabricant (?) stamp, c 44 x 15mm, two lines, with cluster of grapes at both sides:

[ΘΕ]Μ[Ι]	[Θε]μ[ι]
[ΣΩ]ΝΟ̣Σ	[σω]ν̣ος

Late 3rd to 1st century BC (Monakhov 2004: 88). Putative reading is of fabricant Θεμίσων (Themison), who is dated to c. 145-108 BC (Nilsson 1909: 429 no. 230; Jöhrens 2001: 419 no. 203; Sztetyllo 1991: 71 no. 122; Fani Seroglou pers. com.). Site 113 [83].

197. Stamped, round handle. Very fine salmon-red fabric with a cream-yellow outer surface. Rectangular fabricant (potter's) stamp, c. 46 x 10mm, one line of text with *caduceus* to the right:

Ι̣Ε̣Ρ̣Ω̣Ν̣ΟΣ	'Ι̣ε̣ϱ̣ῶ̣ν̣ος

Possible parallel dated to c. 150 BC (Nicolaou & Empereur 1986: 524-5). The fabricant Ιέϱων is dated to c. 205-146 BC, but this stamp is very common for a long period (Jöhrens 2001: 420 no. 207; Jöhrens 1998; Akamatis 2000: 78 no. P56; Fani Seroglou pers. com.). Site 113 [83].

198. Stamped, round handle. Very fine salmon-red fabric with a cream-yellow outer surface. Rectangular fabricant (potter's) stamp c. 44 x 16mm, with one line of unclear text and *caduceus* to the right.

[ΓΑ]Λ̣Ε̣Σ̣Τ̣[Η]Σ̣	[Γα]λ̣ε̣σ̣τ̣[η]ς̣

The name Γαλεστης c. is dated to 117-109 BC (Finkielsztejn 2001: 135, Plate XVIII, 47; Akamatis 2000: 91). Site 115 [G].

199. Stamped, round handle. Very fine salmon-red fabric with a cream-yellow outer surface. Rectangular eponym (date) stamp, c. 39 x 15mm, with three lines:

ΕΠΙΠΕΙΣΙ	ἐπὶ Πείσι
ΣΤΡΑ̣ΤΟΥ	στϱά̣του
ΒΑΔΡΟΜΙΟΥ	Βάδϱομιοῦ

Dated to the month of *Badromios* c. 160 BC (Finkielsztejn 2001: 193). Site 115 [G].

200. Stamped, round handle. Very fine salmon-red fabric with a cream-yellow outer surface. Rectangular fabricant (potter's) stamp, c. 39 x 15mm (incomplete) one line:

ΦΑΝ[Ι̣Α̣]	Φαν[ι̣α̣]

No parallel found. Late 3rd to 1st century BC (Monakhov 2004: 88; Akamatis 2000: 70 No. P37; Börker & Burow 1998, 52 no. 516). Site 115 [G].

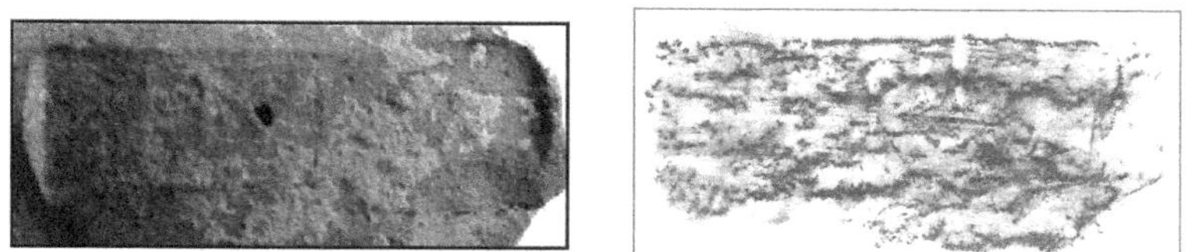

190

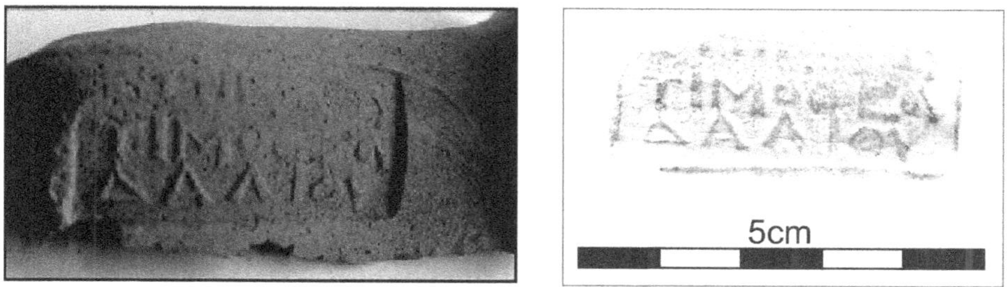

191

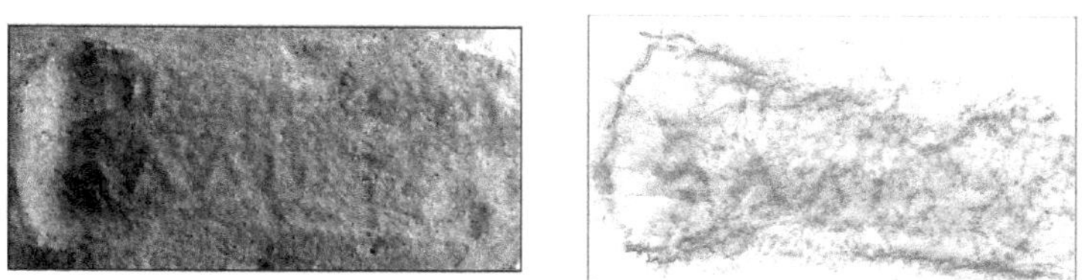

192

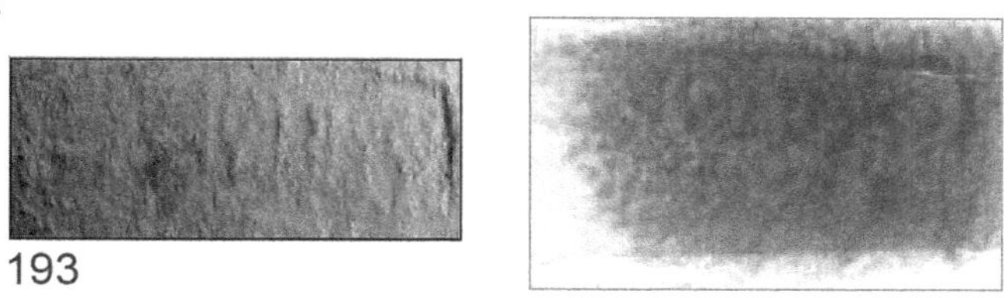

193

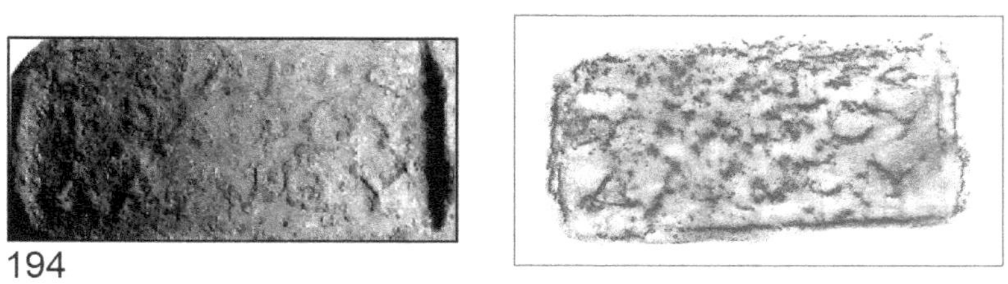

194

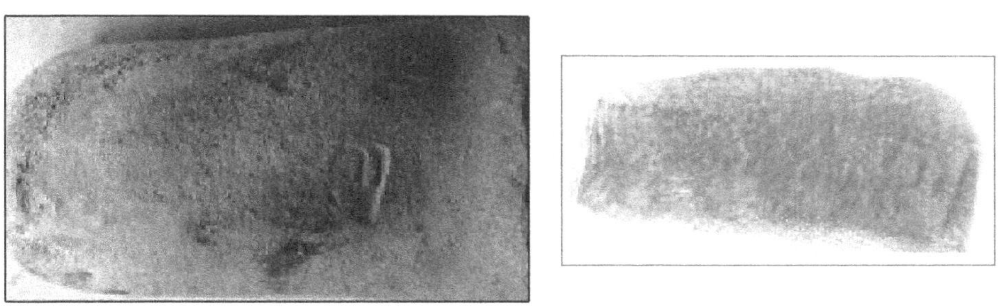

195

196

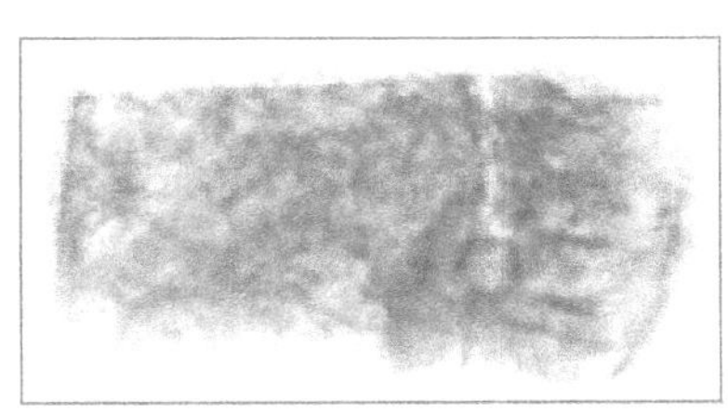

Fig. 4.17. Stamped amphora handles: Rhodian (190-96) (R. Thomas & J. Cooper).

201. Stamped, round handle. Very fine salmon-red fabric with a cream-yellow outer surface. Illegible rectangular stamp, c. 35 x 11mm. Late 3rd to 1st century BC (Monakhov 2004: 88). Site 115 [G].

202. Stamped, round handle. Very fine salmon-red fabric with a cream-yellow outer surface. Square, fabricant stamp, c. 14 x 15mm, two lines of text:

ΑΓ[Ε̣]	Αγ[ε]
Λ[Ο̣]	λ[ο̣]

The eponym Αγέλοχος is very early, dated to the end of the 4th century BC to c. 280 BC (Finkielsztejn 2001: 55; Fani Seroglou pers. com.). Site 117 [G].

203. Stamped, round handle. Very fine salmon-red fabric with a cream-yellow outer surface. Illegible circular stamp, c. 28mm diameter, with Rhodian rose in centre. Resemble rose stamps dating to 145-108 BC, (Finkielsztejn 2001: Plate XXI.16). Late 3rd to 1st century BC (Monakhov 2004: 88). Site 201 [403].

204. Stamped, round handle. Very fine salmon-red fabric with a cream-yellow outer surface. Rectangular eponym (date), stamp, c. 37 x 12mm, with three lines of text:

ΕΠΙΣΩΣΙ̣[	'Επὶ Σώσι̣[
ΚΛΕΥ̣Σ	Κλευ̣ς
Π̣Α̣Ν̣ΑΜΟΥ	Πανάμου

Eponym Σωσικλῆς is dated to 159-153 BC, the month of *Panamos* (Finkielsztejn 2001: 193; Grace 1953: 123, no. 150). Site 201 [403].

205. Stamped, round handle. Very fine salmon-red fabric with a cream-yellow outer surface. Rectangular eponym (date) stamp, c. 32 x 11mm, two lines of text:

ΕΠΙΣΩ	'Επὶ Σω
ΧΑΡΕΥΣ	χαρέυς

Eponym Σωχαρης, is dated to c. 219-210 BC, no month given (Finkielsztejn 2001: 191; Grace 1953: 123, no. 153). Site 201 [401].

206. Stamped, round handle. Very fine salmon-red fabric with a cream-yellow outer surface. Rectangular (date?) stamp c. 39 x 18mm with three illegible lines of text. Late 3rd to 1st century BC (Monakhov 2004: 88). Site 113 [60].

207. Stamped, round handle. Very fine salmon-red fabric with a cream-yellow outer surface. Rectangular stamp, c. 36 x 18mm, with illegible text. Late 3rd to 1st century BC (Monakhov 2004: 88). Site 119 [935].

208. Stamped, round handle. Very fine salmon-red fabric with a cream-yellow outer surface. Rectangular fabricant (potter's) stamp, with single line, broken at left and bottom. Reads:

ΔΩΡΟΥ	Δ̣ώρ̣ου̣

The potter Δώρος II was known to be operating in c. 117 BC, though may have operated over the broader period of 145-108 BC (Finkielsztejn 2001: 152-3). Site 113 [12].

Koan amphorae (Fig. 4.19)

209. Bifid, stamped on one half of double handle. Very fine, micaceous reddish-yellow fabric with a white slip. Clear rectangular fabricant (potter's) stamp with one line of text:

ΑΦΡΟΔΙC	'Αφρόδις

No parallel found. 2nd century BC to 1st century BC/AD. Site 113 [83].

210. Bifid, stamped on one half of double handle. Very fine, micaceous reddish-yellow fabric with a white slip. Fragmentary rectangular fabricant (potter's) stamp with *Trident* and one line of text:

Π̣Α̣Ρ̣	Π̣α̣ρ̣

No parallel found. 2nd century BC to 1st century BC/AD. Site 113 [47].

Unsourced Greek amphora (Fig. 4.19)

211. Small, stamped handle. Possibly of Chian design. Fine red fabric, reminiscent of Rhodian fabric. Rectangular, broken c. 33 x 7mm fabricant (potter's) stamp:

ΗΓΗΣΙΟΥ	'Ηγησίου

No parallel found. Probably 2nd to 1st century BC date. Site 24 [341].

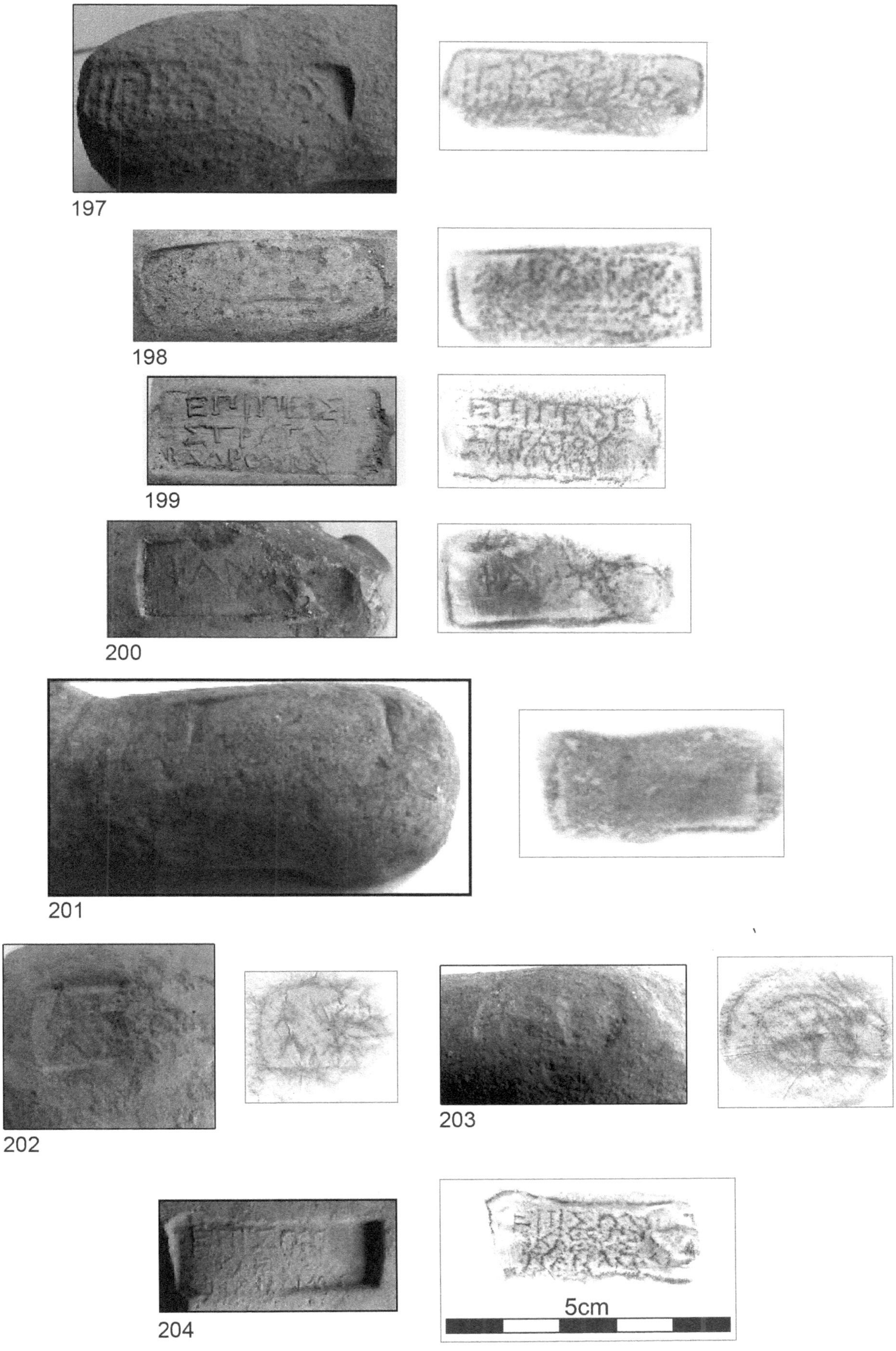

Fig. 4.18. Stamped amphora handles: Rhodian (197-204) (R. Thomas & J. Cooper).

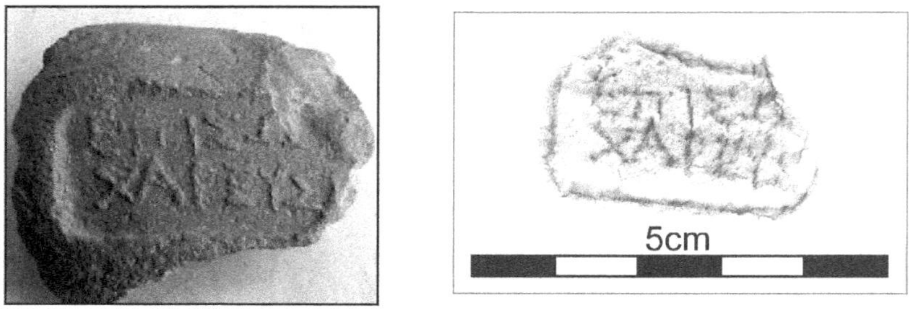

205

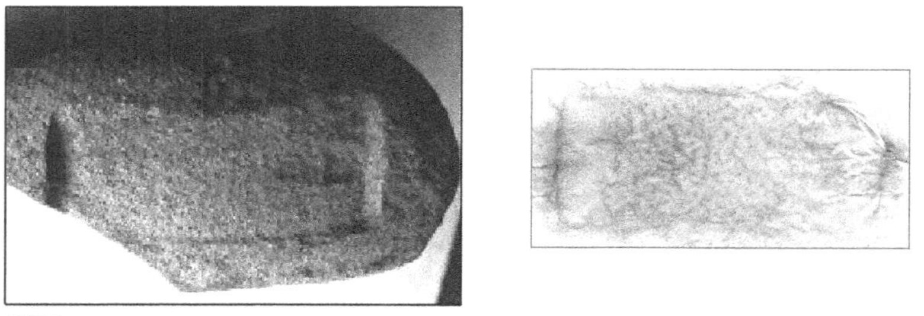

206

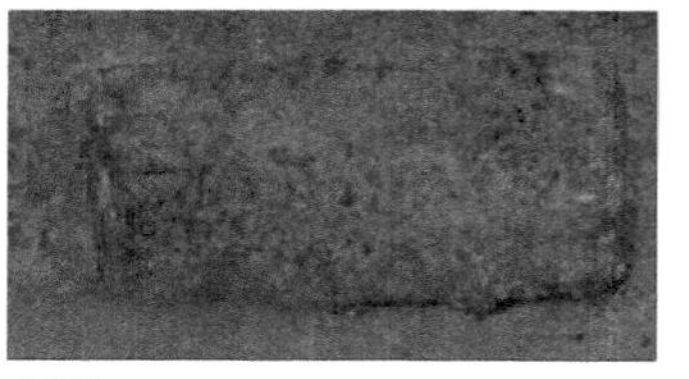

207

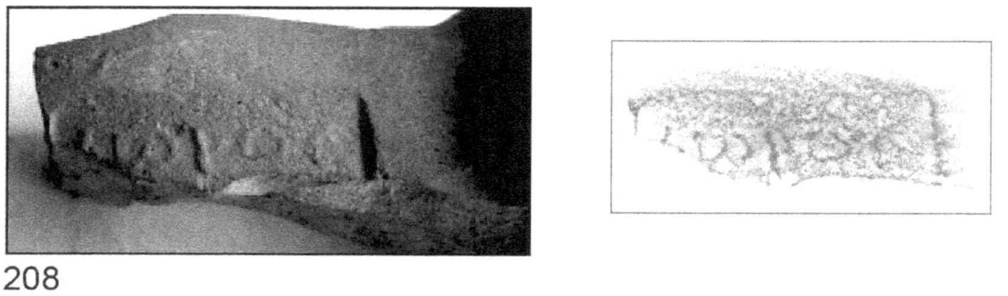

208

209

210

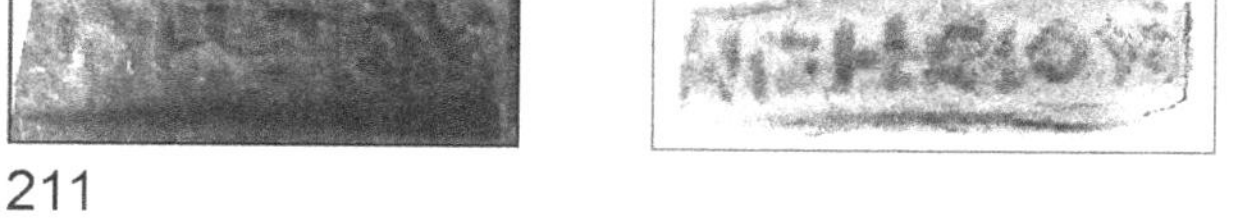

211

Fig. 4.19. Stamped amphora handles: Rhodian (205-06); Koan (209-10); Unsourced Greek amphora (211) (R. Thomas & J. Cooper).

Chapter 5. Geomorphological survey of the south-west shores of Lake Mareotis

C. Flaux

5.1 Introduction

This chapter presents the geomorphological field prospection in the Lake Mareotis area conducted during August 2008 (Fig. 5.1). Forty auger cores were taken, distributed over seven sites. Each core position and altitude was recorded using the RTK GPS

Lake Mareotis is known to have had an important role in the economy and communication of the region during antiquity (Empereur 1998a; see Chapter 2). This is attested by past and recent archaeological surveys undertaken along its shores (De Cosson 1935; Khalil 2005). Numerous archaeological structures located near the present lake shore have been unearthed, submerged or now stand in an elevated position relative to the present lake level. The latter fluctuates on an annual cycle, linked to meteorology, ir-

Fig. 5.1. Geomorphological setting of study area, NW Nile Delta, Egypt (based on data from Warne & Stanley 1993; Chen, et al. 1992; Empereur 1998a; Wilson 2010).

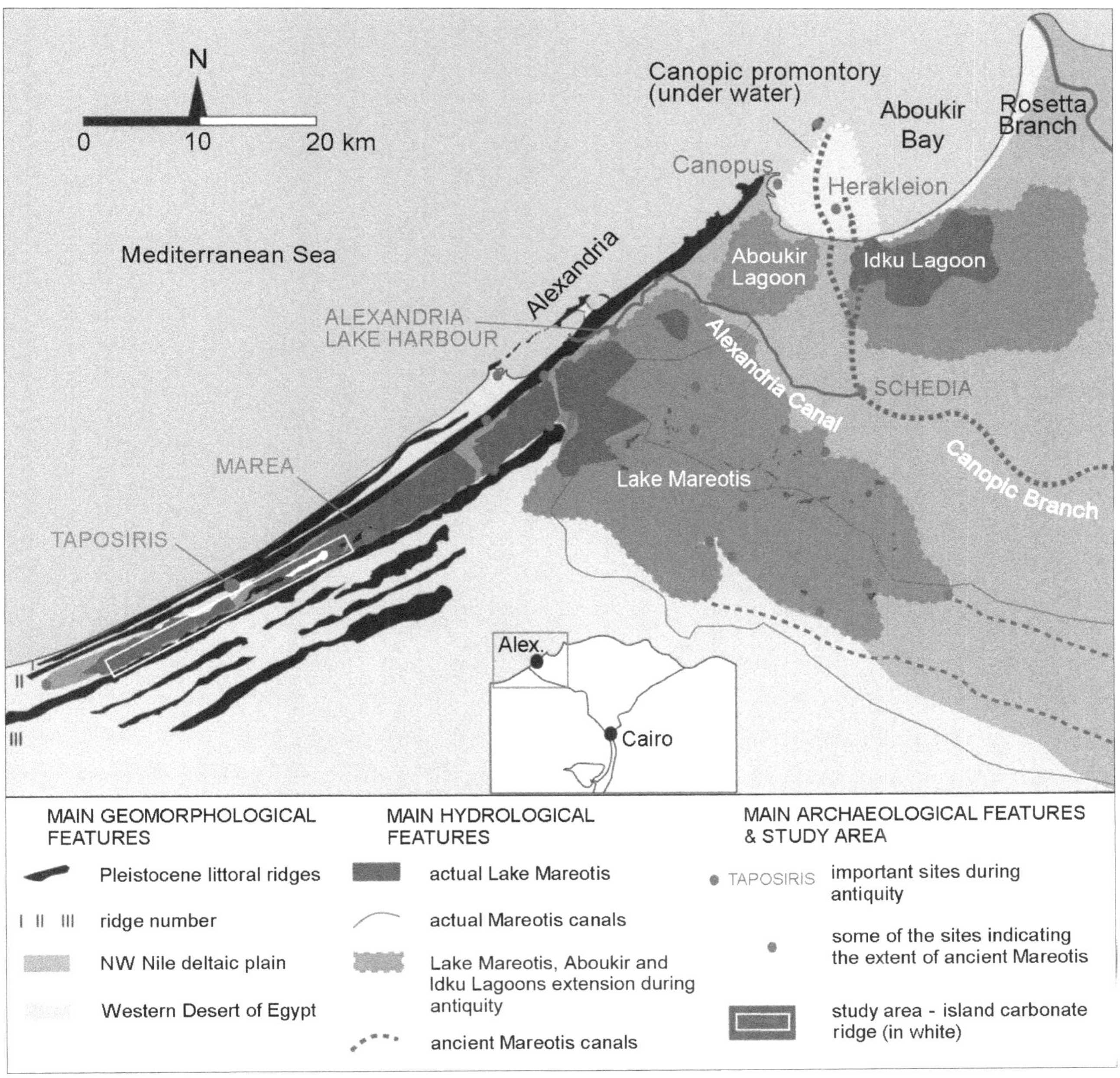

Fig. 5.2. Partial view of the island, within Lake Mareotis. Photograph taken from Ridge III looking towards the north. Ridge II is in the background (LMRP).

rigation discharge into the lake and relative sea level. The function of these archaeological structures is difficult to assess because no palaeo-topographical scheme exists. The establishment of the relationship between the archaeological sites' relative water levels, with the aim of providing further context for their function, was the main objective of the geomorphological investigation. Results show that an important progradation of the shoreline, linked to colluviation since antiquity, has disassociated the basin from structures that were originally constructed in direct relation to the ancient lake/coastal morphology; bathymetry at the time of occupation could not be inferred because no chrono-stratigraphy has been established.

This report deals only with field data. The general geomorphological context of the NW Nile Delta is first presented with reference to Chapter 2 of this volume, followed by field data acquisition and methods. Current sedimentary

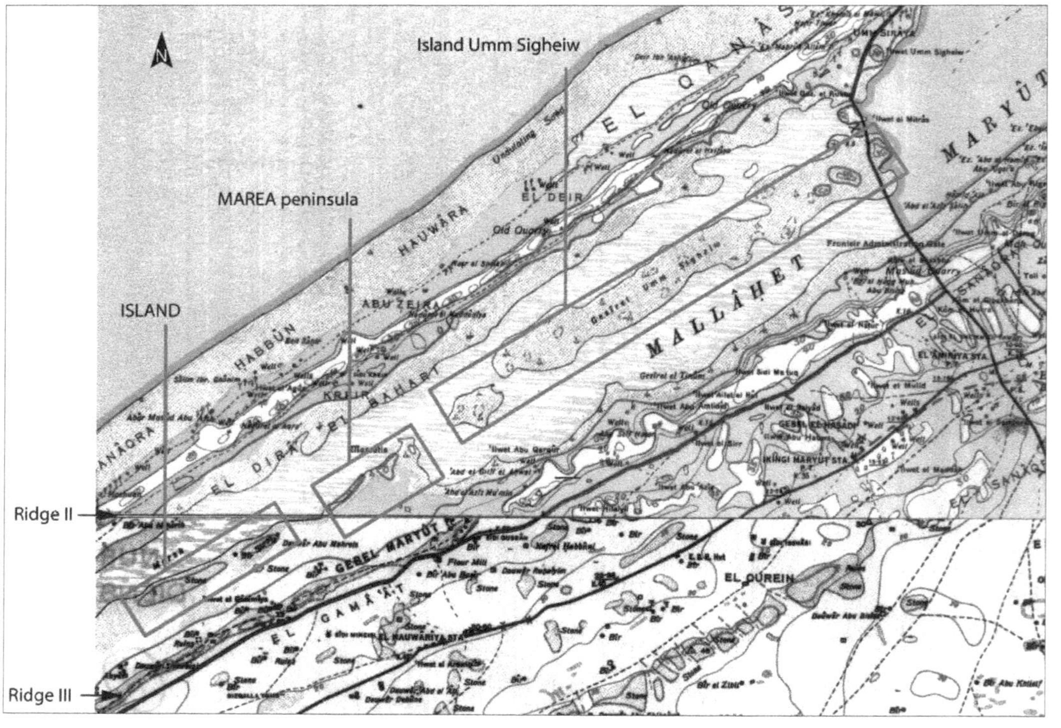

Fig. 5.3. Topography of the study area: 1/100,000 map of Egypt, assembling of sheet 88-48 al-Ghayata (1927) and sheet 92-48 Alexandria (1930). Drawn by the Generalstab des Heeres Abteilung für Kriegskunde und Vermessungswesen (Abteilung IV Mil. Geo.). Published by the Survey of Egypt © archives Jana Helmbold. On this extract, the island, Marea Peninsula and Umm Sigheiw Island constitute discontinuous parts of a carbonate ridge, parallel to the actual shoreline, within the basin of Lake Mareotis. It is an ancient littoral dune consolidated of a similar origin to Abusir Ridge (II) and Gebel Maryut Ridge (III). On this map dated from 1927, the lake level is at 2m below mean sea level and the island is connected to the mainland (see Figs 5.2, 5.6).

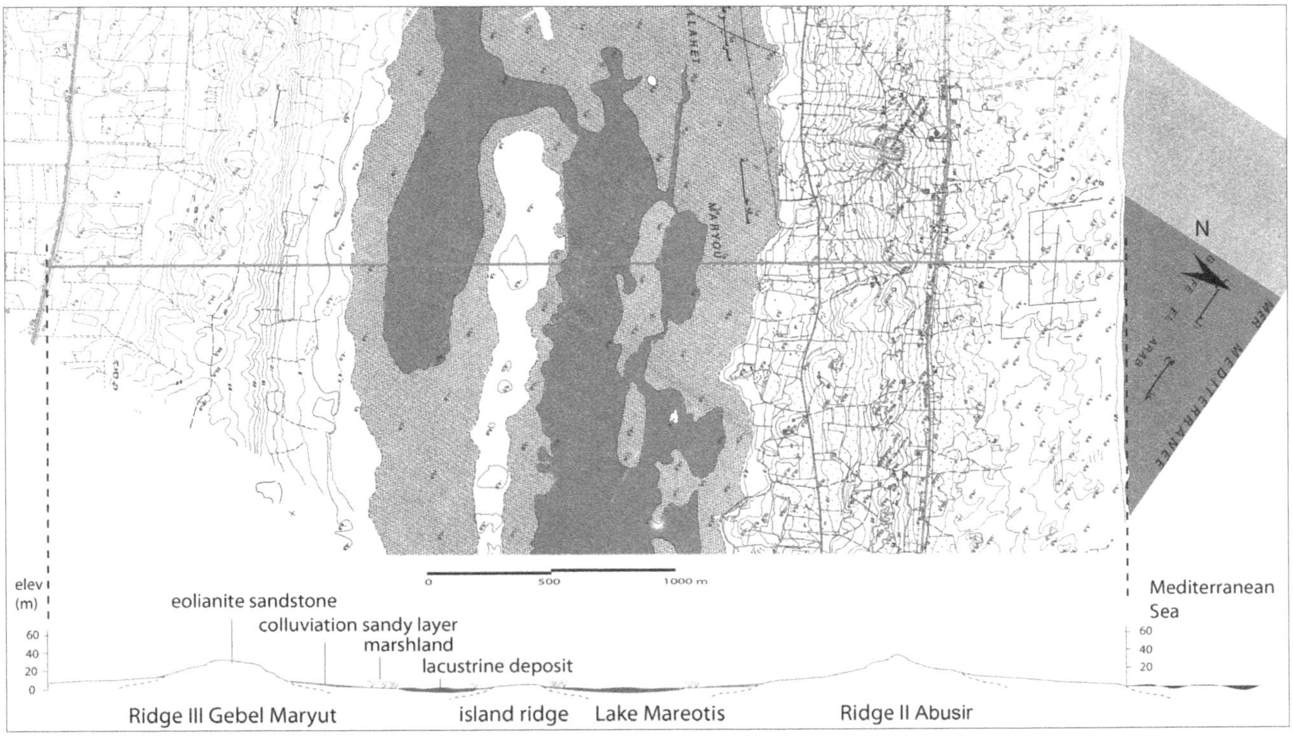

Fig. 5.4. SE-NW topographic profile across Lake Mareotis and its western watershed. Carbonate ridges bordering the lake and making up the island also constitute an ancient littoral ridge, also extending parallel to the Mediterranean coast (see also Fig. 5.2). Extract of the 1/10,000 maps series "El Hammam", assemblage of sheets K2, K3, J2 and J3, realised by the consortium of SFS-IGN FRANCE, 1978. © archives CEAlex.

processes and environments observed around the shores of Lake Mareotis are also described. This report presents 40 stratigraphic logs and preliminary interpretations for each site studied, mainly in an archaeological context. Finally, as a synthesis of all the acquired results, lake shoreline evolution is evaluated. Laboratory investigations are proposed in order to provide further detailed understanding of the stratigraphy of the area.

5.2 North-west Nile Delta: geomorphological context description

5.2.1 Lake Mareotis: basin topography

Lake Mareotis lies on the north-western edge of the Nile Delta. It marks the limit between the Holocene Deltaic Plain and a late Pleistocene littoral dune system (Stanley 2005a; Butzer 1962). The Maryut Depression morphology can be divided into two sub-basins, the western arm and the main eastern body (see Fig. 5.1). The origin of the eastern depression, bordered by the Nile Delta and the Western Egyptian Desert is still not thoroughly understood. Lake Mareotis' western watershed is structured by three ancient aeolianite coastal ridges all trending in a SW-NE direction (Figs 5.1 & 5.2), parallel to the present coastline. Previous geomorphological studies have described the Abusir and Gebel Maryut Ridges II and III, respectively, but authors have omitted another smaller ridge that is located between them. The irregular topography of this ridge forms a series of islands inside Lake Mareotis (Fig. 5.3). Despite its irregularity, the smaller ridge can be followed southwest to northeast from Taposiris, crossing Marea and up to near Chersonesos (see Fig. 5.3).

The topography of the western Mareotis Arm is thus structured by Pleistocene aeolianite ridges, trending in a SW-NE direction (see Fig. 5.1). Both Ridges II and III present an asymmetrical profile, with a gentler south-eastern slope and a steeper north-western scarp (Fig. 5.4). A cross-section studied by El-Asmar and Wood (2000) shows that this topography is mainly inherited from a fossilised dune system and further shaped by subsequent erosion. The ridge rises from 1.5m (present lake level) up to 35m above mean sea level (amsl). The hillside is not covered by vegetation and is intersected by perpendicular talwegs (trough or valley eroded by water run off; Fig. 5.5), a few of which have an incised concave slope morphology. The lower gentle slopes of the hillside are covered by sand, a product of colluviation. The sand is covered by halophyte and low vegetation that relates to brackish groundwater in a semi-arid climate. The Lake Mareotis shoreline comprises a saltmarsh whose width varies according to the lake level. The water is brackish and lake levels vary seasonally, controlled by irrigation, precipitation, evaporation, groundwater input (discharge) and output (recharge) (ALAMIN Project 2007).

These ridges were originally sedimentary deposits formed as shallow marine bars, mixed beach and aeolian ridges (El-Asmar & Wood 2000). The ridges experienced cemen-

Fig. 5.5. Sediment transportation along the flanks of the carbonate ridges (north hillside, Ridge III, Site 44). (A) Wadis network. The distribution is restricted between the upper outcropping ridge and the lowest sandy plain (in black, situation of the section studied in Fig. 5.6). (B) Detail of a small recent wadi. Pebbles and stones accumulate, though fine grains are rain-washed. (C) Down the slopes of Ridge III (Site 44). From south to north we observe a transition between the sand layer and the flat marshland. The sandy layer is irregular, with microdunes transported by the wind and fixed by vegetation. This sediment is orange in colour, likely induced by oxidation. Further up the hillside, carbonate ridge outcrops and erosion produces a white oolithic sand. It is believed that a palaeo-soil has been eroded and redeposited lower down the hill (see also Section 5.4.1.1) (C. Flaux).

tation and have since been intensively exploited (De Cosson 1935: 219). The present seashore is delimited by a coastal ridge (Ridge I). It is a recent dune system (3,400 – 1,350 BP; El-Asmar & Wood 2000), now destroyed by urbanisation. Ridge I disappears near Al-Agami (Chersonesos), then emerges in the form of reefs in El-Mex Bay and finally constitutes Pharos Island (Alexandria). Ridge II was formed between 90,000 ± 15,000 and 110,000 ± 5,000 BP while the most recent dating obtained for Ridge III places its formation at least 191,000 ± 42,000 BP. Stanley (2005a) describes the irregular topography and fractures of Ridge II and the abrupt contact between these Pleistocene carbonate ridges and the silicicalstic Nile Deltaic Plain deposit. He associates this well-defined boundary with vertical land motion which affected the northwestern Nile Delta. As a result, ridge formation has been identified under the Holocene deltaic sequence, notably in Aboukir Bay, east of Alexandria. This geological setting is supposed to be due to geological fault growth affecting the region, a readjustment at depth of the thick Mesozoïc to Quaternary sedimentary pile, that lies beneath the NW Nile Delta (Stanley 2005a). Recent subsidence has affected Aboukir Bay and ancient Alexandria harbour (Stanley & Toscano 2009) and it is likely that such subsidence also affected Lake Mareotis during its history. Such processes could also have controlled Mareotis' eastern depression and the western Nile Delta limit. But these processes are at the moment only marginally understood and hence these theories are mere speculation.

5.2.2 Lake Mareotis: hydrological system

According to previous work in the area, lake sedimentation began between 6,000 and 4,000 BP (Warne & Stanley 1993; Goodfriend & Stanley 1996). Recent work has established that Lake Mareotis was a lagoon linked to the sea in c. 7,500 BP (Flaux, *et al.*, in press). The lagoon was

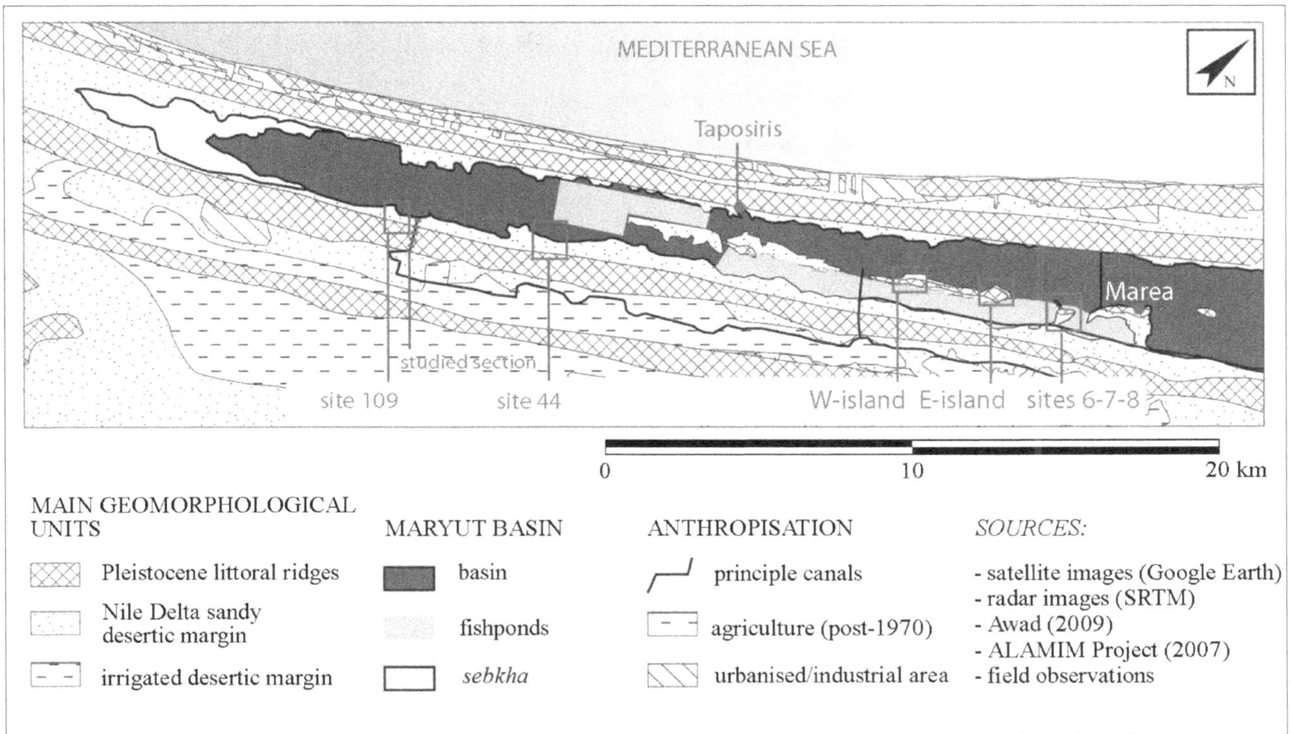

Fig. 5.6. Topographical scheme of the study area (C. Flaux).

subsequently shut off due to deltaic progradation and was supplied with fresh water from the Canopic Branch of the Nile (Fig. 5.1). Then, from c. 5,000 to 3,000 BP the lagoon sedimentary record once again indicates a phase of marine influence. These results indicate that the Nile and marine influence altered over time. The so-called lake was probably originally connected to the sea via Aboukir Lagoon, until the establishment of the Alexandria Canal, between the 4th century BC and the 1st century AD (Hairy & Sennoune 2006) (see Fig. 5.1).

Historical sources indicate that Lake Mareotis was much larger during antiquity (Yoyotte, *et al.* 1997). Contour line "0" refers to the present sea level used by Warne & Stanley (1993) to infer the ancient lake surface. They calculate that the present surface is only 13% that of the former one. Lake Mareotis was transformed into a *sebkha* during the 17th and 18th centuries. Phases of aridity are generally attributed to Canopic Branch infilling and drainage system abandonment during the Arabic and Ottoman periods, but these phases are not clear and historical maps testify that Lake Mareotis remained a large and perennial water body up until the 17th century (Awad 2009).

Thus, Lake Mareotis, which lies at the interface between the Nile's deltaic plain, the Mediterranean Sea and the Western Egyptian Desert, is a complex unit whose hydrological system is controlled by Nile flooding, its connection with the sea, groundwater intrusion (both marine intrusion and Nile Delta aquifers), precipitation (175mm/year) and evaporation in a semi-arid climate (*Meteorological Atlas of Egypt* 1931).

5.3 Fieldwork: data and methodology

5.3.1 Field data observations and drilling strategy

This report deals essentially with field observations. Seven sites were studied (Fig. 5.6). Preliminary sedimentary interpretations rely on the concept of actualism, comparing present-day deposition processes with fossil sediments facies (buried surfaces). Surface descriptions derive from geomorphological surveys, surface sediment analysis and topographical surveys, complimented by satellite images from Egypt Quickbird Imagery (28th June 2004). This primary assessment of the sedimentary facies and dynamics of the study area helps both to identify and understand the palaeo-topography through stratigraphic observations. It must be noted that the available chronostratigraphy is only relative. In some cases, archaeological artefacts have allowed preliminary relative datings of palaeo-surfaces.

Corings were undertaken using a manual auger (Fig. 5.7). Forty cores were extracted, representing in total around 90m of stratigraphy. More than 450 sediment samples have been archived for further analyses. Future research avenues are presented at the end of this chapter.

5.4 Topography and sedimentary processes of Lake Mareotis' western arm

5.4.1 Present sedimentary facies and processes

The sedimentary facies of each depositional environment was studied. They were observed at different sites in the study area. Table 5.1 summarises the sedimentary features,

Fig. 5.7. Photograph of auger in use and resulting core sample (in insert). Penetration is allowed by both turning and pushing the auger into the soil. Even if it obliterated sedimentary structures, stratigraphy is well preserved. The flexibility and ease of use of the Edelman auger allows multiple points to be studied in the same day (LMRP/C. Flaux).

subdivided into physical features (texture, colour, structure, deposit geometry and thickness), coarse sand composition (sediment, fossil and organic components) and pedogenic processes.

5.4.1.1 Hillside processes and sedimentary features

Ridge III and the island are late Pleistocene coastal ridges, mainly formed by sand dune accumulation. The sediment comprises fine white carbonate to coarse oolithic sands which are cross-laminated. These deposits have been lightly lithified; they are crumbly and sensitive to erosion.

Facies A: Colluvial sand layer

Ridge III's topographic profile (see Fig. 5.4) is characterised by a steep slope from the top that softens downslope. Respectively, up and down this slope, we observe ridge outcropping and a fine sand layer deposit. Some portions of a section cut into this deposit near Bahig (see Figs 5.5 & 5.6) have been observed (Fig. 5.8). Oolithic sand composition and its topographic position indicate that sediments are eroded from the ridge and accumulate downslope, a product of colluviation. The orange colour and carbonate precipitation is the result of remobilisation of iron oxide and calcium in the soil profile (see Fig. 5.8). Terrestrial gastropod colonisation, pedogenic processes and small tree trunks unearthed beneath the sand accumulations imply the existence of vegetation cover and pedogenesis. This facies was previously described by El-Asmar (1994), Hassouba (1995) and El-Asmar & Wood (2000) as a red-brown silty-sand carbonate soil, formed during wet climatic conditions like today. El-Asmar & Wood (2000) date this carbonate soil surface to 65,000 ± 31,000 BP (OSL technology). However, this method needs a high proportion of quartz to give an accurate age and thus may not be entirely accurate.

Downhill, sediments change to a reddish sand and silt (see Fig. 5.8). Due to the presence of groundwater, a sparse halophytic vegetation favours the trapping of fine sand in the form of micro-dunes (see Fig. 5.5). This leads to an irregular sand surface, indicating an aeolian deposit, sparsely colonised by terrestrial gastropods. In sum, this sandy to silty facies is characteristic of a colluviosoil potentially remobilised by wind and rainwater (see Fig. 5.5). Its general surface is concave from the lowest part of the hillside to the lake shore. These sedimentary inputs raise the question of both lake shore basin infilling, shoreline progradation and the burial of archaeological structures.

Facies B: Brown soil

Down the slopes of the island ridge we observed a spatially localised facies, covered by grass and some mud. In light of the homogeneous sand sheet all around, its dark brown colour and lumpy structure, this facies is thought to be a soil, an *in situ* neo-formation deriving from the association between organic matter and fine sediment. This localised facies could derive from some agricultural and/or pastoral practices (Fig. 5.9).

5.4.1.2 Present shoreline

Facies C: Beach deposits

At some sites, shells and "sea grass" have accumulated to form fixed linear shorelines or large surfaces. This bio-detritic component has accumulated on the shore by swell and current processes, controlled by the dominant north-west wind direction. Thus, this deposit is observed only on the north shore of the island and the southern lake shore, facing the prevailing wind direction (see Fig. 5.11). Beach deposits show the influence of swell and present aeolian processes on sedimentation. Shores facing the main north-west wind direction are subject to sedimentary inputs, potentially from the lake, transported in suspension and deposited in sheltered areas.

Facies D & E: Saltmarsh

The groundwater level ranges between 0.3 and 0m below the marshland surface. Brackish groundwater rises up to the surface by capillary action. Salt precipitates by water evaporation. It forms a fine salt film over the present marshland. The saltmarsh is covered by halophytic vegetation (Fig. 5.10) which provides organic material and traps

Sedimentary facies	***Physical features***				***coarse sand fraction composition***			***Pedogenic process***	***Deposits environment interpretation***	
	Texture	*Colour*	*Structure*	*Deposit geometry*	*Sedimentary component*	*Fossil component*	*Organic component*			
A	silty fine sand to coarse sand	reddish to orange	laminations observed in a few case	piedmont	oolithic sand, matt, some are white, others yellowish-orange, few quartz	lake shells fragments - terrestrial gastropod (*Eremina desertorum* and *Helix sp*)	-	?	colluvial sand layer	HILLSIDE FACIES
B	silty sand	dark brown	lumpy	localised surface	?	-	roots and grass not decomposed, excrements	organic matter and sediment association	soil pasture / cult	HILLSIDE FACIES
C	coarse	translucent shells – black/ dark green seagrass	-	lineation or surface	-	*Cerastoderma glaucum* (connected valves)	lacustrine seagrass	-	beach deposit	SHORELINE FACIES
D	silty clay	black	spongy	flat deposit	silt and clay trapped by plants	-	organic matter (halophile plants)	-	marshland	SHORELINE FACIES
E	sandy	white with bright facet	encrusting	fine film above marsh surface	-	-	-	salt precipitation	saltmarsh	SHORELINE FACIES
F	silty clay to coarse sand	mid grey	lightly spongy	-	oolithic sand	-	roots/organic inclusions	organic decomposition	"marsh-like" facies	SHORELINE FACIES
G	silty clay	dark grey	-	-	-	*Cerastoderma glaucum* *Hydrobia ventrosa* *Melanoides sp* *Cyprideis sp* *Ammonia beccarii* *Neritidae, Vermetus sp*	organic fragments "sea grass"	-	Lake Mareotis deposits	LAKE
H	silty clay	dark grey	-	-	-	*Hydrobia ventrosa Melanoides sp, Cyprideis sp* *Ammonia beccarii*	abundant organic fragments	-	Idku Lagoon deposits	LAKE

Table 5.1. Present sedimentary facies description.

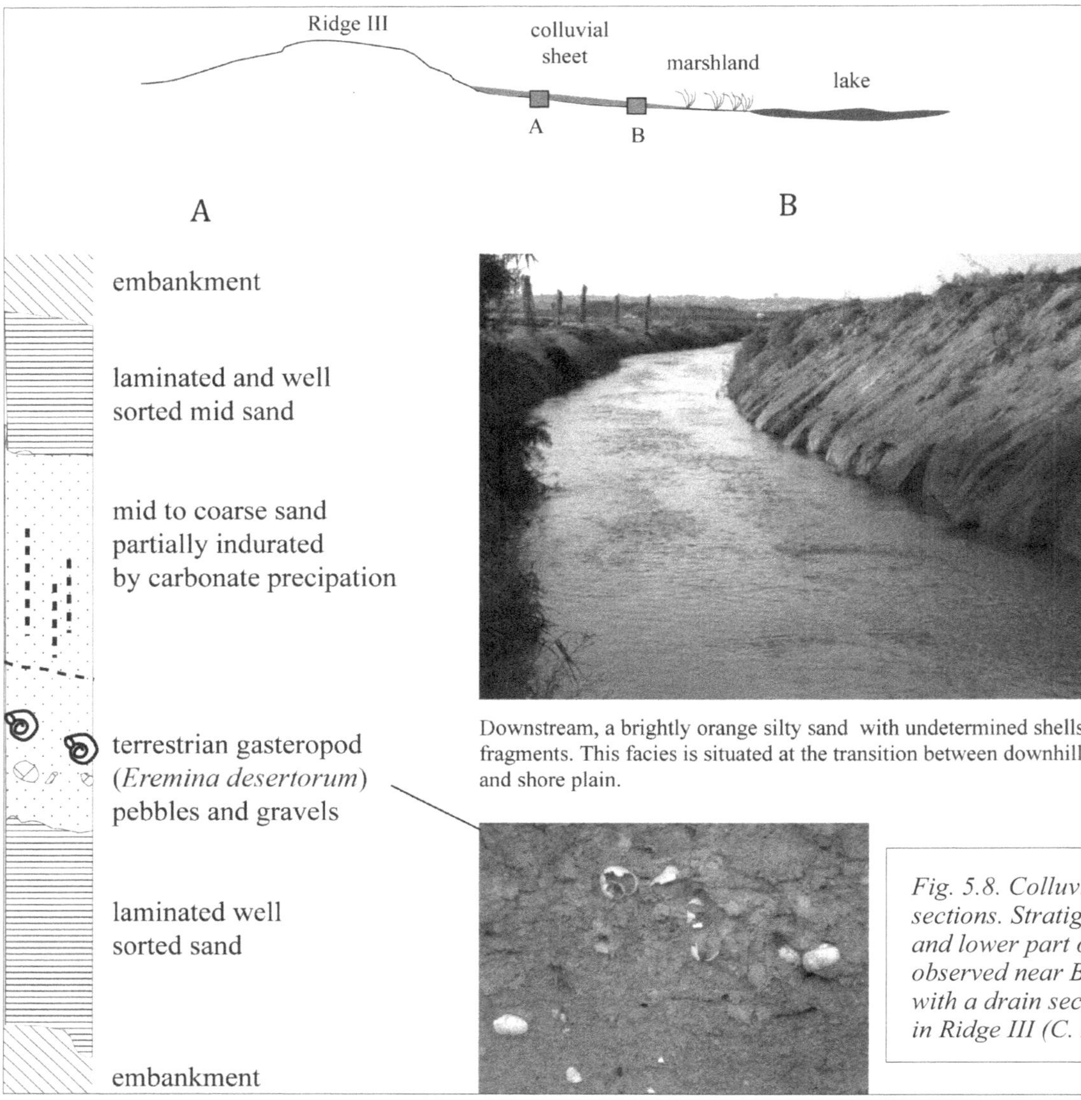

Fig. 5.8. Colluvial sandy layer, sections. Stratigraphic log (A) and lower part of the deposit (B), observed near Bahig, associated with a drain section cut out within Ridge III (C. Flaux).

Fig. 5.9. Actual land management: Site 21 located on the island ridges (the photographic arrangement has slightly deformed the real topography). Microtopography shows some small elongated ridges that delimitate the grassland areas (dry in August 2008) (C. Flaux).

a fine grain inorganic component. In the case of borehole M37, for instance, marshland presents an irregular microtopography with small humps and depressions. Marshland deposits only accumulate in the depressions, while the mounds comprise sand. This indicates that marsh develops on an irregular sand layer, a product of colluviation. Moreover, the depth of the marsh deposits never exceeds 0.05m except in one case (M34). Thus, this marshland is inferred

Fig. 5.10. An example of one of the saltmarshes present throughout the Lake Mareotris area, at Site 44. The saltmarsh is covered by halophytic vegetation and the white colour corresponds to salt precipitation on the surface of the marshland (C. Flaux).

Fig. 5.11. Actual shoreline facies. Lake Mareotis' currents and waves transport "sea grass" in the form of linear or larger deposits, similar to a tidal marine area. Here it indicates a seasonal lake level change, mainly in relation to wind conditions, irrigation water inputs, groundwater inputs and outputs and variable evaporation rates (C. Flaux).

to be very recent, linked to the high lake level. It develops on an inherited topography; its altitude and extension are directly linked to the present lake level, rather than typical infilled basins.

Facies F: Marsh-like facies

All marsh deposits exceed 0.2 to 0.4m and comprise sandy silt. A grey to dark grey colour and a slight spongy structure indicates organic matter supply. Organic inclusions (partially decomposed roots) were occasionally observed but most were decomposed and the main component is inorganic sediment. This facies could result from organic decomposition of the present upper marshland. However, usually a mean grain size, finer than the colluvial sand layer, was observed. This could result from sediment trapping by marsh vegetation. This facies is not totally understood, but in general it translates as a shore context with both organic and inorganic supply from marsh formation and hillside sediments transit, respectively. As such, marsh organic deposits are best preserved when a fine layer of water covers them as the oxidation of organic matter is avoided. In turn, when deposits emerge, they are subject to air oxidation. Thus, the decomposition of organic matter is favoured in case of lake level variations because they do not allow the formation of a permanent marsh.

5.4.1.3 Lake level

A topographical map of the area, drawn in 1978, shows a very large marshland today covered by Lake Mareotis water in most areas. Archaeologists who for many years have worked along the shores of Lake Mareotis have never seen a lake level higher than today. Moreover, beach deposits indicate that the lake level has risen above that observed in August 2008 (Fig. 5.11). However, the range of lake level variations is unknown. Lake Mareotis' water budget comes from precipitation, evaporation and is artificial for the large part (irrigation, pumping, etc.). This implies that the present Mareotis water level cannot be considered as a reference altitude. Reconstructing lake level variations, in relation with the Nile flood and a potential connection to the sea, is fundamental to understanding the distribution of archaeological structures lying near the shoreline.

5.4.1.4 Lake deposits and ecology

Facies G and H: Lake Mareotis and Idku Lagoon deposits

Two surface samples were studied by granulometry and sand fraction binocular microscope observations. Present lake sediments show a high silt and clay fraction, which derives from Nile sedimentary inputs.

The fauna described is typically lagoonal, eurytherm and euryhaline (see Table 5.1), which means that is has adapted to an unstable environment, notably in terms of salinity and temperature (Guelorget & Perthuisot 1983). Lagoon environments are subject to both marine and continental influences, varying seasonally, mainly according to climate and meteo-marine conditions. Salinity, measured in April and August 2008 in the Marea Basin, ranges respectively from 10.8 to 18%. The sub-basin lying near the island is not connected to the sea but inherited ground salt water; which explains the present brackishness of Mareotis water. In the case of Idku Lagoon, the basin is directly connected to the sea via the El Maadieh outlet. However, the fauna represented there is very similar to that associated with Lake Mareotis. This infers that the type of connection to the sea is not a decisive factor in controlling lagoon ecology but rather the degree of instability is significant, as is the case of both Mareotis and Idku Lakes which are controlled seasonally by varying rates of evaporation, irrigation freshwater inputs and marine intrusion (directly or indirectly via groundwater).

5.4.2 South-west shores of Lake Mareotis: fossil sedimentary facies synthesis

Despite the same geomorphological context (interface between aeolianite Pleistocene and the modern Lake Mareotis) for the 40 cores drilled at each site studied, a large number of sedimentary facies have been observed. This diversity will be discussed in Section 5.5 with regards to the local topographical context and archaeological hypotheses. Here a systematic description of each facies observed during fieldwork is presented (Table 5.2A-B). Archaeological components are not presented in Table 5.2 because they are not specific to a sedimentary facies but rather a sedimentary context. Sedimentary facies have been identified by sedimentological observations and stratigraphical correlation. Specific sedimentary features will be discussed in Section 5.5. Our objective here is to propose a synthetic table of sedimentary facies observed along the south-western shore of the lake.

The facies were divided into three depositional contexts: lacustrine, shoreline and hillside. Interpretation comes from the concept of actualism: we assume that sedimentary composition, textures, structures and colours observed in the fossil facies and associated fauna have the same origin as present facies. The study area's geomorphological context is inherited from the late Pleistocene ridges, the late Pleistocene red soil formation and subsequent colluviation and aeolian redeposition on the hillsides of the ridges (El-Asmar & Wood 2000), the regular Nile regime in the Delta that was initiated around 6,000 BP (De Wit 1993), and a series of lake sediments that were first deposited around 7,500 BP (Warne & Stanley 1993; Flaux, *et al,*, in press). Therefore the general geomorphological context of the study area has been the same since the mid-Holocene.

5.4.2.1 Lake facies (I to N)

Six lake facies were sampled. All lake facies are characterised by a silty clay sedimentary matrix. Such fine components indicate a very low energy depositional environment, interpreted as Lake Mareotis. A few shell components, represented by *Cerastoderma glaucum* and *Melanoides sp.* support a lagoonal environment, characterised by changing environmental conditions (salinity, temperature, etc.). This fauna is typically present in Nile Delta lagoon environments (Bernasconi 1991; Reinhardt 2001).

Laminated facies

Lake facies I, J, K and M are characterised by a very compact millimetric laminated structure, very difficult to penetrate (Fig. 5.12). This structure indicates that no disturbance has reworked the deposits (such as waves and currents or bioturbation; besides, very few shells were observed in this facies). This facies could correspond to lake varves, indicating a seasonal sedimentation (Touchard 2000). Here, lamination was observable thanks to their colour: orange, blue, brown, white and sometimes dark grey. No specific alternation was observed and sometimes the facies were multi-coloured rather than laminated. Typically, orange and blue colours in sediment translate as oxidation and reduction processes. Indeed, this alternation could derive from different seasonal conditions, linked to the hydric balance (because of summer evaporation and/or Nile flooding). However, we must keep in mind that the orange colour is also typical of the colluvial sand layer (see Figs 5.5, 5.8). This means that colour is not necessarily linked to lake deposits but also to sedimentary sources. *Facies K,* only observed in borehole M47, is characterised by a clear alternation of black and white millimetric laminations.

In some cases (notably *facies M*), fine shell fragments constitute a single layer. This could indicate a depositional process as the origin of laminations, with a sorting of sedimentary components. Moreover, laminations were not observed systematically in *facies I* and *J*, and occasionally instead of a very compact sediment, a soft and fluid sediment was observed.

After these diverse observations, more studies are necessary to understand the origin of this laminated sedimentation in the study area, at a millimetric scale, using a non-destructive sampling method.

Others lake facies

Lake facies L was also observed at different sites. Its main property is a blue-greenish colour, usually indicating a confined environment associated with reduction processes. These could derive from post-depositional processes, such as an anoxic groundwater aquifer.

An important observation is that lake deposits have recorded contributions from oolithic sand ridge erosion, dispersed inside a silty-clay matrix or in the form of very fine deposits. This indicates a more or less continuous rain-washed hillside sediment flux.

Lake facies N was only observed on the shore of Ridge III. It is characterised by an orange-reddish silty clay sediment rich in *Cerastoderma glaucum*. This reddish fine matrix is very similar to the fine colluvial sediments described below (*facies R*, see Fig. 5.8). In the case of borehole M21, a coarse sand matrix was sampled. The presence of shells, with some connected valves, suggests a lake depositional environment. Shell connection is maintained by organic ligaments easily decomposed when the organism died. This means that shells with connected valves were deposited alive and subsequently remained *in situ*.

Other facies are greatly enriched by archaeological artefacts. These are described below (see Section 5.5.3.2.2.1) within their archaeological context.

Conclusion

None of these facies present similar sedimentological features to the present Mareotis or Idku Lagoons. In the latter we observe a dark grey homogeneous mud. Nevertheless, the present fauna of Mareotis and Idku is characterised by lagoonal species. *Cerastoderma glaucum* and *Melanoides sp.* have both been observed in present and fossil facies,

Sedimentary facies - Cores		Physical features				Coarse sand fraction composition			** Chemical processes	Deposits' environment interpretation	
		Texture	Dominant colour	*Structure	Thickness range (cm)	Sediments	Fossils	Organic matter			
24, 25, 26, 27, 28, 29, 30, 32, 33, 34, 35, 37, 39, 47, 50, 51, 55, 56	I	silty clay	orange to bluish gray	laminations (infra-millimetric to pluri-millimetric) compact	40 to 250	oolithic sand supply (fine to coarse) in form of laminations or dispersed in the matrix others?	sparse shell fragments, rare *Cerastoderma glaucum*	in form of laminations	oxido-reduction processes at the lamine scale (alternation orange – blue) ??	lake	LACUSTRIAN FACIES
24, 25, 26, 29, 30, 33, 35, 37, 54, 56	J	silty clay	brown	laminations (infra-millimetric) very compact	30 to 90	oolithic sand supply (fine to coarse) in form of laminations or dispersed in the matrix others?	sparse shell fragments, rare *Cerastoderma glaucum* rare *Melanoïdes sp.*	in form of laminations or inclusion	lamines oxido-reduction (blue to yellowish orange) ??	lake	
47	K	silty clay	black and white	laminations (infra-millimetric) very compact	20	-	-	in form of laminations	?	lake	
34, 37, 56	L	silty clay	dark brown to turquoise blue	isotropic and compact	50 to 70	oolithic sand supply (fine to coarse) in form of laminations or dispersed in the matrix – some sparse dark orange to red laminations	sparse shell fragments	?	rare oxidation trace dark blue colour attributed to reduction processes	lake	
34	M	silty clay	light brown to light grey	laminations (millimetric)	70 to ?? (M34 unfinished)	oolithic sand supply (fine to coarse) in form of laminations or dispersed in the matrix	shells fragments, sometimes very fines and accumulated in form of laminations	?	?	lake	
20, 21, 22, 23	N	silty clay	orange reddish	isotropic	20 to 25	-	abundant *Cerastoderma glaucum*, connected valves	?	-	lake	

*Table 5.2A. Sedimentary fossil facies. *Structure includes sedimentary processes (aeolian lamination, lake varves, ...) and physical processes (desiccation, pedogenesis, ...). **Chemical processes include oxidation, reduction and precipitation.* *(continued on next page.)*

Sedimentary facies - Cores		Physical features				Coarse sand fraction composition			** Chemical processes	Deposits' environment hypothesis	
		Texture	*Colour*	*Structure*	*Thickness range (cm)*	*Sediments*	*Fossils*	*Organic matter*			
20, 21, 22	O	silty clay	orange grayish to dark grey	isotropic	60 to 80	oolithic sand and ridge gravels dispersed	sparse shell fragments	organic matter partially decomposed ??	abundant gypsum precipitation, notably rose des sables, oxidation traces and partial organic matter decomposition	marsh / confined environment	SHORELINE FACIES
43, 46, 51,	P	silty fine sand	mid grey	lightly spongy	5 to 25	-	-	organic matter??	partial organic matter decomposition	marsh / confined environment	SHORELINE FACIES
20, 22, 24, 25, 26, 27, 30, 31, 35, 36, 37, 38, 39, 40 41, 42, 43, 44, 45, 46, 48, 49, 50, 51, 52, 52bis 53, 54, 54bis, 54ter, 55, 56	Q	fine sand to coarse sand	reddish to orange	isotropic	30 to 180	oolithic carbonate sand very rounded, matt, yellowish to orange rare quartz	shells fragments observed in a few cases - entire terrestrial gastropods shell *Eremina desertorum* (observed in core 27 only)	-	?	colluvial sand layer	HILLSIDE FACIES
20, 21, 22, 27, 28, 39, 40, 42	R	clayey silt	reddish to orange	isotropic	10 to 140	-	-	-	?	colluvial and/ or aeolian silt layer	HILLSIDE FACIES
39, 43, 44, 45, 46, 55	S	silty sand	dark brown	lumpy	30 to 80	-	-	roots and grass not decomposed	?	brown soil	HILLSIDE FACIES
20, 21, 22	T	silty clay/ sand mix	brown to yellowish brown	very fluid	40 to 30 downstream	oolithic sand and sandstone (ridge) gravels	-	-	?	mud flow ???	HILLSIDE FACIES
24, 25, 26, 29, 30, 32, 33, 35, 36, 37, 43, 46, 47, 50, 51, 54, 56	U	coarse sand	white to bluish white (M35 only)	isotropic	impassable surface, except M35: 50 cm observed	oolithic sand embankment	-	-	reduction (M35) ?	ridge oolithic sand disaggregation	HILLSIDE FACIES

*Table 5.2B. Sedimentary fossil facies. *Structure includes sedimentary processes (aeolian lamination, lake varves, ...) and physical processes (desiccation, pedogenesis, ...). **Chemical processes include oxidation, reduction and precipitation.*

indicating that the so-called "Lake" Mareotis has always been a lagoon with unstable physical conditions. This instability is assumed to be linked to variable freshwater inputs. Today, freshwater input balances are linked to irrigation practices. In the past, this balance regime was maintained by Nile flooding. In both case, a low freshwater flow is offset by marine intrusion. Even if no direct connection exists between the lake and the sea, marine intrusion can occur via groundwater inflow. At present, such marine intrusion is observed in the northern Nile Delta, south of the lagoon belt (Kotb, *et al.* 1999).

These numerous lake facies point to diverse environmental conditions in time and space. Even if it is mis-understood, laminated facies derive from short-term environmental changes, probably linked to annual Nile flooding.

5.4.2.2 Shoreline facies (O and P)

Marshland fossil facies have been interpreted by comparison with present ones. Grey colour, a slight spongy structure and the presence of partially decomposed organic matter indicate an important organic supply. In the case of *facies P*, some gypsum flowers suggest a confined environment that means a short water column.

5.4.2.3 Hillside facies (Q and U)

Facies Q

The same sedimentological features (orange oolithic sand) as the surface colluvial sandy layer were observed in *facies Q*. Its thickness ranges from 0.3 to 1.8m. In borehole M27 we observed some terrestrial gastropods (similar to those found on the present sand surface, known as *Eremina desertorum,* very common in the area), that suggest a terrestrial environment.

Facies R

This facies was distinguished from previous *facies Q* on the basis of a very fine sedimentary component. However, as shown in Figs 5.5 and 5.8, it was observed in the same sedimentary context, down the slope from Ridge III, in front of the colluvial sandy layer. Fine sediment colluvial layers mark the transition between ridge hillside and lake shores. Hume and Hughes (1921) observed a similar granulometric profile along the hillside ridge, from the top to the lake shore. Aeolian transportation could cause the accumulation this fine sedimentary product.

Facies S

This facies is the brown soil already described in Section 5.4.1.1 (*facies B*). Its depth ranges from 0.30 to 0.80m from the surface. This facies is interpreted as a soil with an organic component closely linked to the sedimentary matrix (brown colour and lumpy structure). If this interpretation is correct, the facies thickness (up to 0.8m) indicates either deep pedogenic processes, or contemporaneous pedogenic processes with sedimentary accretion.

Facies T

In cores M21, M22 and M23, we observed a brown to yellowish sediment, comprising clay, sand and gravels. This

Fig. 5.12. Varved sedimentation? Lake facies I, characterised by orange, white and bluish laminations (borehole M25) (C. Flaux).

facies could correspond to a mud flow. However, without any modern analogue, this is purely hypothetical and requires more investigation.

Facies U

Finally, at the base of the core a coarse white oolithic sand was observed. With the exception of M35, we were not able to go through this facies with the manual auger. We assume that a hard rock surface was encountered. All cores were drilled near the lake shore, which might explain the proximity of the bedrock. A coarse white oolithic sand was sampled, probably originally part of the aeolianite bedrock. The isolated case of M35, where 0.5m of bluish white oolithic sand was encountered, is not understood.

5.5 South-west shores of Lake Mareotis: palaeo-topography and geomorphological processes

Seven sites were studied, presented here in three parts: (1) Ridge III shores, (2) the depression between Ridge III and the island and (3) the island itself (Table 5.3; see Fig. 5.3). Altitudes are given above/below present mean sea level (amsl/bmsl). Each stratigraphic log is described from the bottom to the top of the sequence. A single legend is common to each figure dealing with geomorphological prospection (Fig. 5.13).

5.5.1 Ridge III shores

Two sites were studied along the shoreline of Ridge III in the extreme west of the present Lake Mareotis (see Fig. 5.6, Table 5.3). The two sites (Sites 44 and 109) present a large sandy shore with a gentle slope, marking the transition between the hillside and the shoreline. These two sites were selected as they provided an opportunity to explore two of the key sedimentological objectives of this research. Firstly, the geomorphology of these sites offers the opportunity to compare sedimentary features between the island and Ridge III shorelines. Secondly, the geomorphology helps to understand the origin of the small sandy ridges that have

Location		*Archaeological sites*	*Auger points*
Ridge III shore	Mareotis west	109	M26, M27, M28
	central Mareotis (cement fatory)	44	M20, M21, M22, M23
between Marea and the island		6-7-8	M32, M33, M34 M47 to M51
Island	west island	21	M37 to M46
	east island – inlet	126	M24, M25, M29, M30, M31, M35, M36
	east island	114 to 118	M52 to M56

Table 5.3. (above) Site location (see Fig. 5.6), corresponding archaeological sites and boreholes.

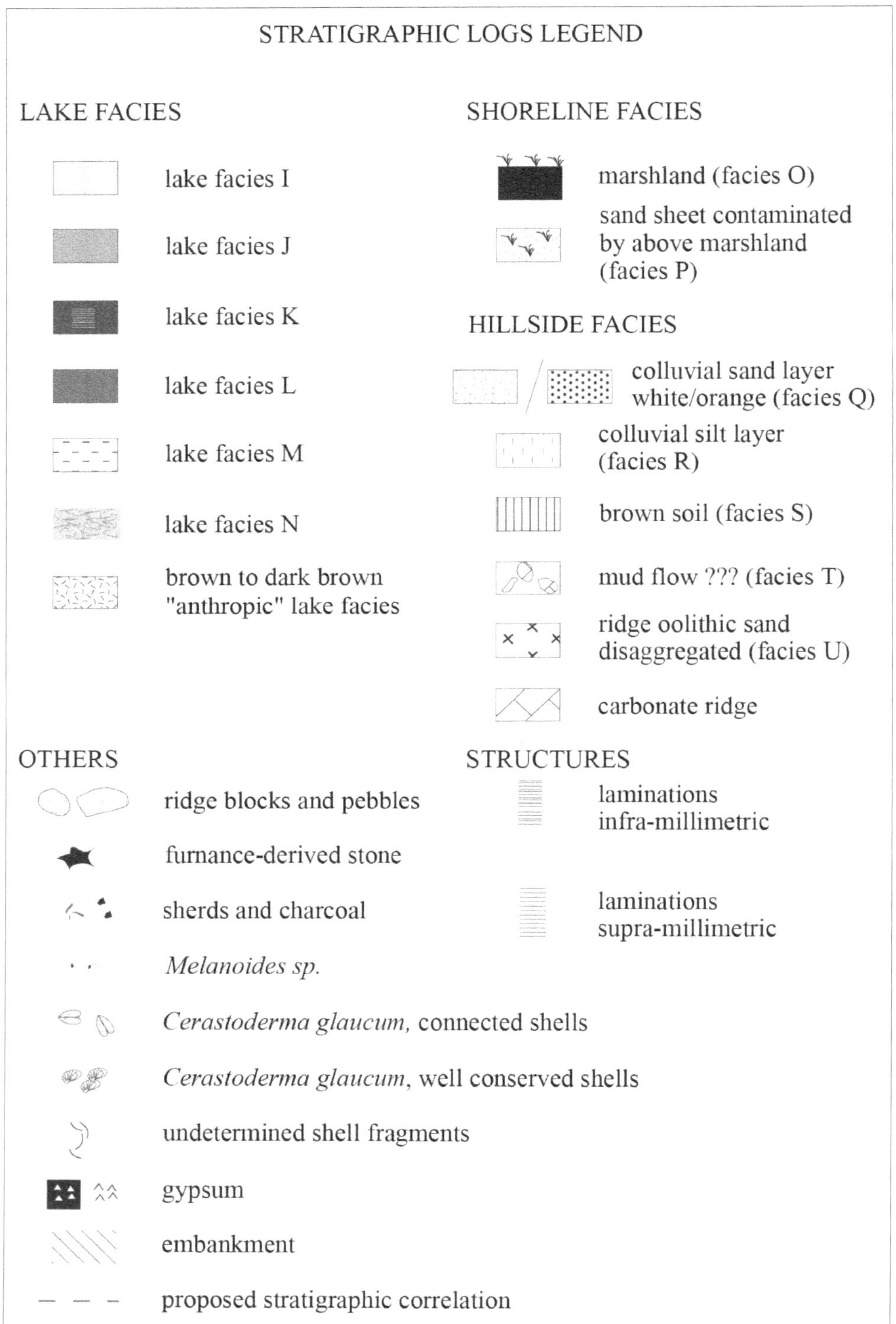

Fig. 5.13. (left) Stratigraphic logs legend (C. Flaux).

been identified as clear features pertaining to these sites. The main questions arising are whether these ridges anthropogenic features and what is their function?

5.5.1.1 Site 44

Presentation (Fig. 5.14)

Across a shore plain around 270m in length, three sandy ridges extend parallel to the shoreline (see Chapter 6). A wall was observed perpendicular to the sandy ridges (Fig. 5.14B). Another extends parallel to the ridge lying near the shoreline (Fig. 5.14A). Some stone blocks were also observed on top of the ridges. Such configurations are inferred to be man-made. Between the parallel ridges, two large saltmarshes were observed covered by halophytic plants. A third smaller marsh constitutes the present shoreline of the site. The marsh in the middle presents a slightly drowned depression. It is elongated in a direction parallel to the ridges. This linear direction, perpendicular to the slope, suggests the presence of an artificial channel, perhaps for drainage purposes.

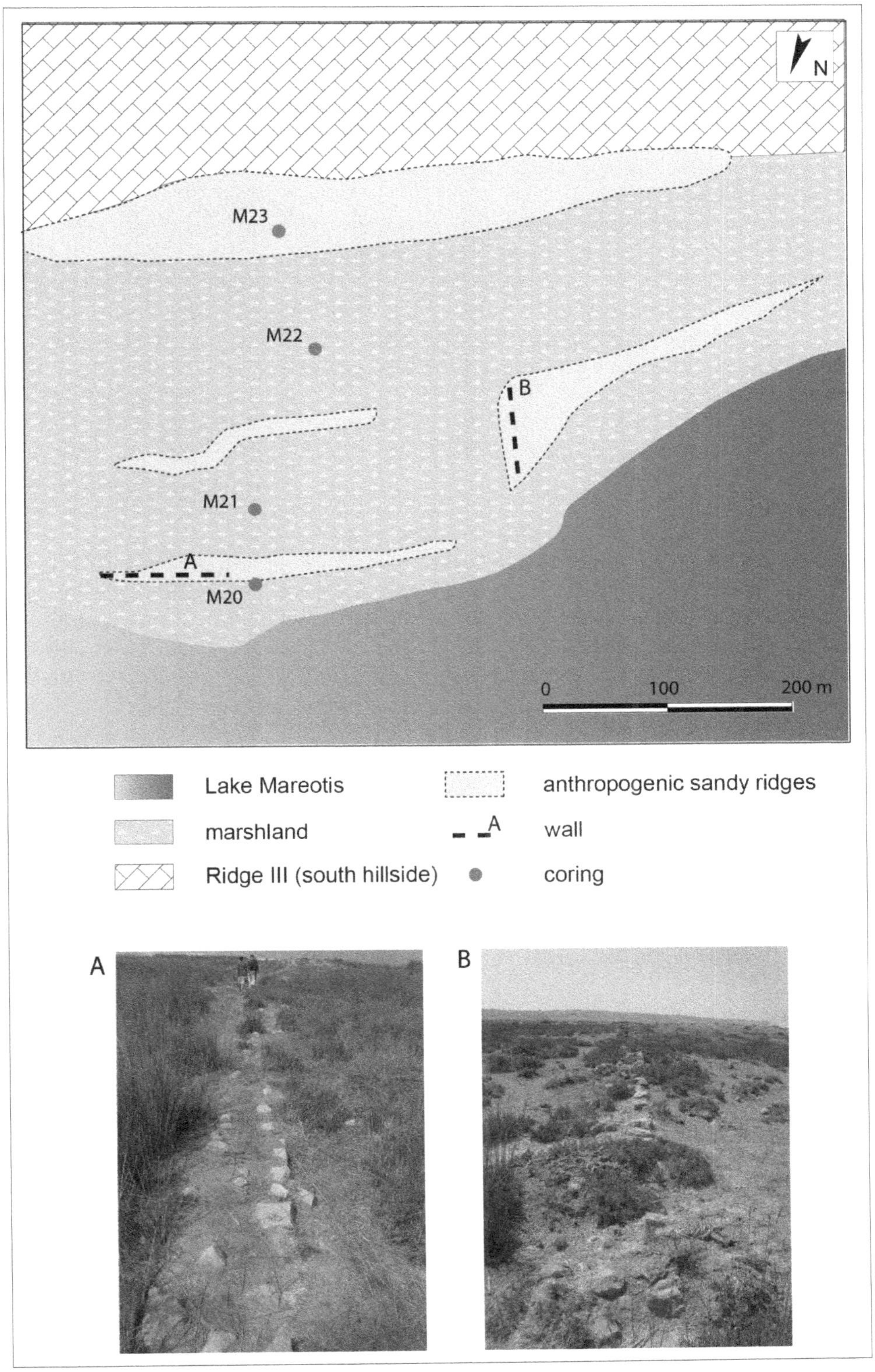

Fig. 5.14. Situation map of boreholes, Site 44 (C. Flaux).

Four boreholes were made, one in each marsh and a final one on the first ridge closest to the landward slope. There were two main objectives: (1) to assess the local environment on which these small ridges had been established; and (2) to identify the sedimentary impact of ridges blocking sediment transfers from the hillside.

Results (Fig. 5.15)
1. On the bedrock the lowest deposit occurred in three boreholes, but its depositional process is misunderstood (see Section 5.4.2.3, sedimentary *facies T*).
2. A confined and/or marsh-like deposit, between +0.20 and +0.65m amsl, was observed in three boreholes at the same level, which confirms a marsh environment. This indicates a maximum lake level around +0.2m amsl at the time of deposition.
3. The following lake deposits indicates a lake level rise of at least up to +1.5m amsl (lowest limit), or probably more, but this is difficult to estimate.
4. Finally, the ancient lake bottom surface was covered by colluvial deposits. Inside the latter were found some shells and gypsum. Shells are likely reworked from the lake bottom or from a previous lake deposit. Gypsum in borehole M22 until +2m amsl indicate that the water table was at least at this level at the time of formation, but once again it could have been reworked.
5. The present lake level is measured at +2m amsl and a marsh deposit has developed on the colluvial sand sheet.

Discussion
An ancient maximum lake level range is assumed at around +0.2m amsl. This phase is followed by a lake transgression the limit of which was not investigated. The analysis determines a progradation of the shoreline by hillside sedimentary supply. Lake sediments are unearthed below 1 to 1.5m of silt and sand, a product of colluviation. Present marshes develop upon the latter sandy layer, meaning that at present the marshland does not retrace the ancient lake basin or its shoreline.

Stratigraphic log correlation does not show a lateral sedimentary discontinuity due to the small transversal ridges. Moreover, borehole M23 demonstrates that ridges are formed of the same sediments as the sandy layer. It denotes that these ridges have been set up above the sandy colluvial layer or during its formation.

A marsh deposit was not observed below the ridge bored at point M23. This indicates that marsh formation post-dates the formation of the ridges and could be a consequence of them. The presence of sandy ridges elongated perpendicular to the slope stops the surface water runoff as it travels down the hills. The aquifer is thus mostly supplied by precipitation waters. In the sector of boreholes M20, M21 and M22, groundwater lies at or near the surface, and forms a marshland with a fine salt crust. The surface level from M20 to M22 was measured from +3 to +2m amsl, indicating that a marsh environment can develop, here up to 1m above lake level. Marsh vegetation is presently used for pasture. Thus, it is assumed that these small ridges derive from irrigation practices in a semi-arid climate, in order to increase soil humidity.

5.5.1.2 Site 109

Presentation (Fig. 5.16)
This site presents a similar geomorphological context to the previous one: a large sandy plain (around 250m long) with a gentle slope that forms a topographic transition between the hillside and the shore (see Chapter 6). A large and high sand ridge, parallel to the shoreline, breaks the regular topography. It appears to have been recently man-made (Fig. 5.17). To the northeast of the ridge in front of the shoreline and parallel to it, a wall outcrops just above the ground. It forms an embankment, 0.6m high, between a narrow saltmarsh and the sandy plain. To qualify the function of this so-called "lake wall", two boreholes were made on either side of it. A third core was made inland to confirm the sedimentary impact of the wall.

Results (Fig. 5.18)
1. Lake deposit. At the top of this lower lake deposit, a layer rich in shell fragments was observed. A black sandstone pebble was also found at the top of this layer.
2. The ancient surface of the lake bottom was covered by colluvial deposits. In borehole M27, two terrestrial gastropods (*Eremina desertorum*) confirm this interpretation. In boreholes M27 and M28, colluvial deposits comprise a fine sand to silt layer.
3. A +1.90m amsl, current lake level forms a thin marshland above the sand layer.

Discussion
The sedimentary sequence observed again indicates an infilled lake basin overlain by colluviums. The upper lacustrian layer is rich in shell fragments. At the top of the lake deposits, the black sandstone pebble is assumed to derive from an ancient burning activity. It is a weak indication that the upper sand layer could have been deposited since antiquity.

Between boreholes M26 and M27, the "lake wall" forms an embankment, meaning that it blocked the sedimentary transit from the hillside. Just behind the wall, a finer sedimentary component was deposited (comparing M27 to M26 colluvial layers). Such a prompt lateral change at the base of the break of the hillside is not believed to be natural and would rather derive from the wall construction. It implies that the wall reaches at least 1m below the surface, at which point the sedimentary facies change is observed. Surface M28 is almost 1m above the present lake level but a high groundwater level allows marsh conditions and a fine salt crust to form. The function of the wall running parallel to the shoreline and perpendicular to the hill slope may be to favour sedimentary accumulation that increases the soil water stockage capacity. This hypothesis is supported by current and traditional practices in the Mareotis region (Figs 5.17, 5.19; Hume & Hugues 1921). No sedimentary impact is observed in lake facies from either side of the wall, as would be expected if the wall had been set up during lake sedimentation. Thus, it is assumed that the

Fig. 5.15. Stratigraphic logs correlation (M20, M21, M22, M23), central Lake Mareotis, archaeological Site 44 (cement factory). NB: Vertical scale bar exaggerated around 25 times (C. Flaux).

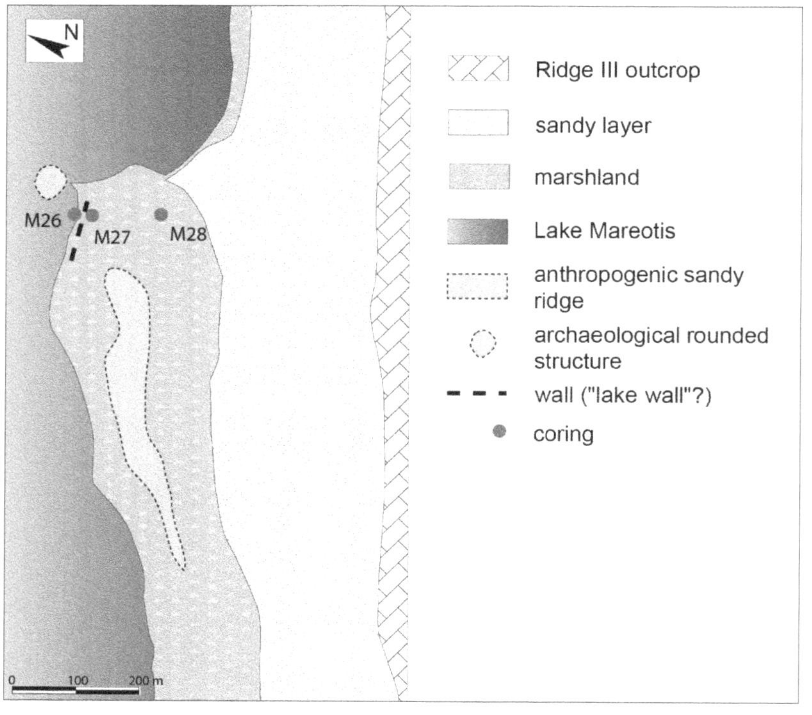

Fig. 5.16. Location of boreholes, Site 109, west of survey area (C. Flaux).

Fig. 5.17. Vegetation base cover of Ridge III at Site 109, view toward the lake. According to local people, the sandy ridge lying downhill and parallel to the lake (dashed line) was constructed only a few decades ago in order to retain rainwater streaming from the hillside. This would raise soil moisture and allow the development of a relatively dense vegetation cover, supporting pasturage activity (C. Flaux).

wall is contemporary with the accumulation of the sandy colluvium. This indicates that no lake front function can be associated with the wall, in spite of its position so close to the shore. It is proposed that this man-made feature is connected to irrigation practice rather than lake-front activity.

5.5.2 The depression between Ridge III and the island

Presentation

Archaeological structures are not evenly distributed along the north and south side of Mareotis Island. Most of the structures situated along the northern island shoreline are thought to have a waterfront function (harbour, jetty, etc.; see Chapter 6). There is a relative absence of archaeological sites along the shores of both the south side of the island and Ridge III (Fig. 5.20), even though it provides shelter from the main north-west wind, and raises the question of the area's palaeo-topography in antiquity: was the present depression between the island and Ridge III part of Lake Mareotis or not during antiquity? A topographic map drawn in 1927 shows that the area between Ridge III and the south side of the island was a dry area as Mareotis' lake level was around 2m bmsl at this time (see Fig. 5.3).

Three areas were investigated (Auger M32, M33, M34). Fig. 5.20 shows an alignment between the island and the Marea Peninsula, flanked to the east by an islet and another elongated island presently covered by fishing installations, but visible on ancient topographic maps (see Fig. 5.3). This linear topographic feature is an ancient carbonate ridge. Aeolianite outcrops have been observed on the island and on the Marea Peninsula (Fig. 5.21). Lying in the bed of Lake Mareotis, with an irregular topography, it appears like a discontinuous island belt. Three corings (M32, M33, M34; Fig. 5.22) were drilled between the island, Marea and Ridge III, in order to characterise the palaeo-topography. A transect (M51 to M47; Figs 5.20, 5.23) was also taken in front of un-

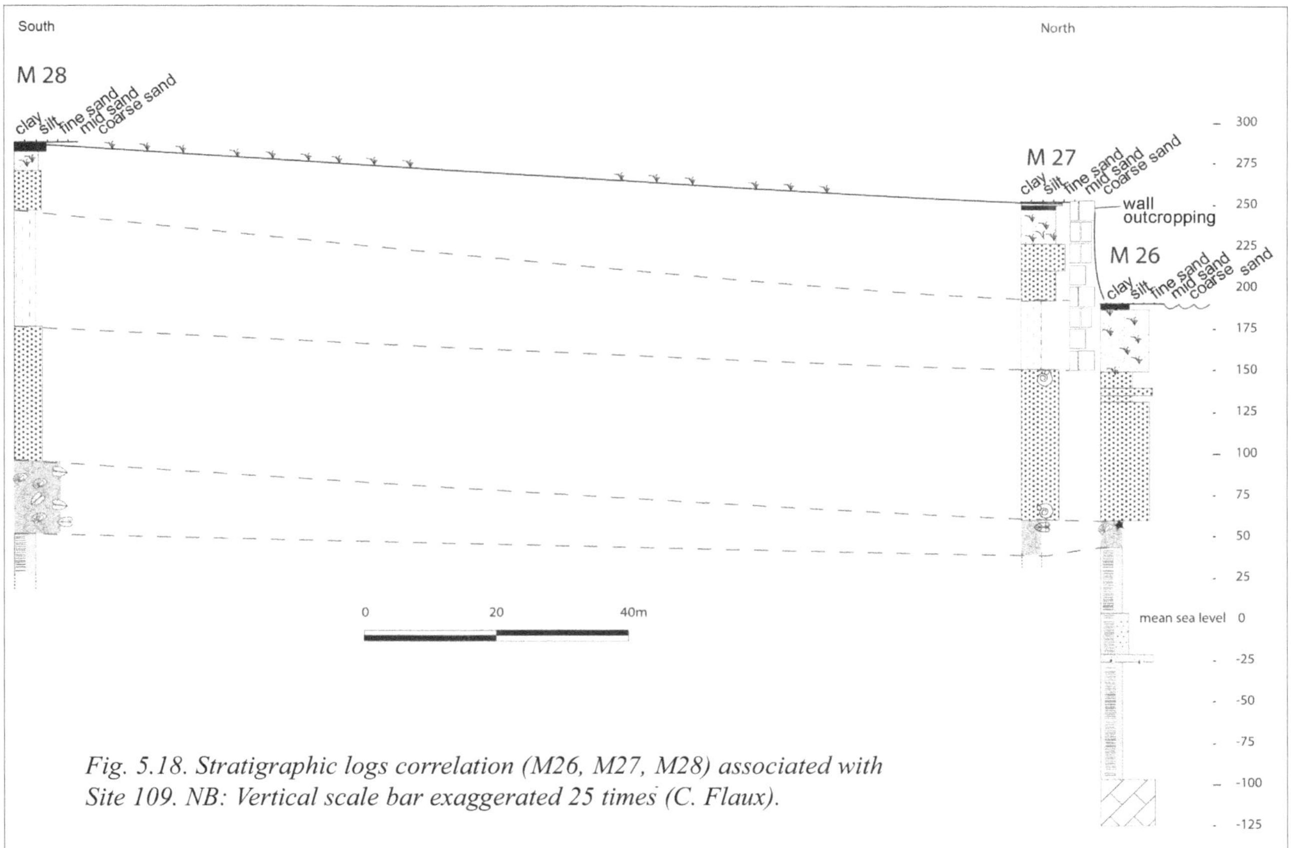

Fig. 5.18. Stratigraphic logs correlation (M26, M27, M28) associated with Site 109. NB: Vertical scale bar exaggerated 25 times (C. Flaux).

Fig. 5.19. Map showing the density of rectangular kurum (thick dotted lines), in the region of Abu Menas, south of Lake Mareotis. Extract of the 1/100,000 map of Egypt, sheet 88/48 al-Ghayata, (1927). Drawn by the Generalstab des Heeres Abteilung für Kriegskunde und Vermessungswesen (Abteilung IV Mil. Geo.). Published by the Survey of Egypt. © archives Jana Helmbold. Hume and Hughes studied soil and water supply in the district of Lake Mareotis in 1921. They described rectangular mounds 3-4m high, used to collect rainwater in the central area. In one case, they observed the cultivation of fig trees inside a rectangular area called "a karm, entirely dependent on water brought to it by runnels from the flanks of a neighbouring karm" (Hume & Hughes 1921: 5). The authors attribute these structures to ancient Roman irrigation schemes in the area, situated 21km west of Alexandria, near Ikinj Maryut, southeast of Ridge III. However, they did not provide any dating evidence to support this hypothesis and thus the karums could also be relatively modern constructions.

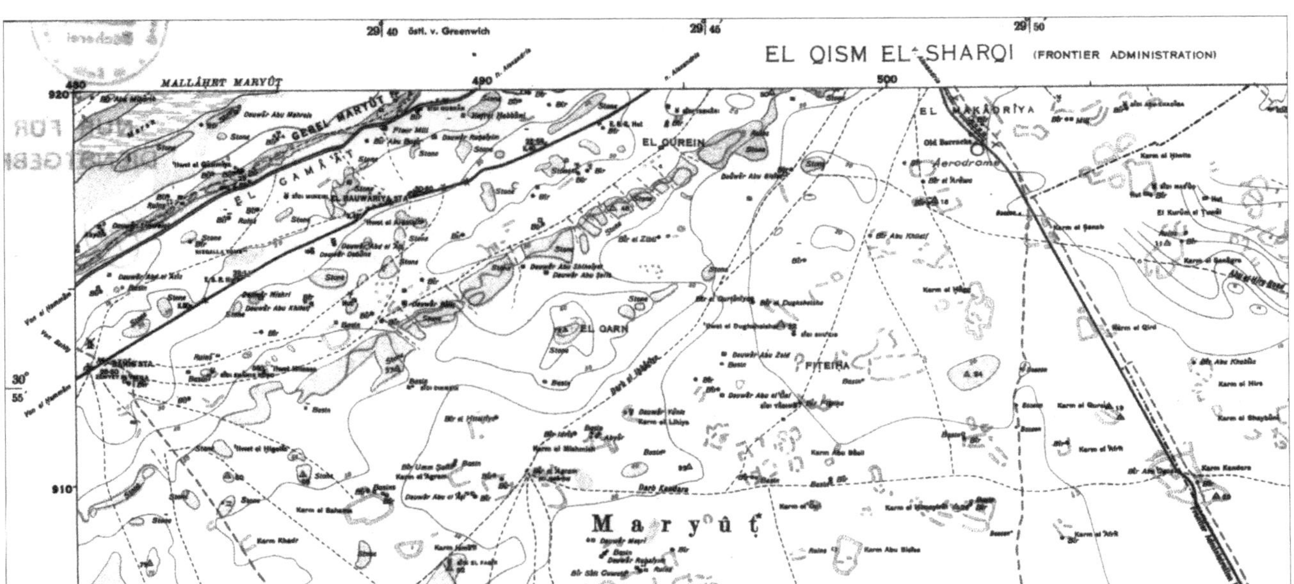

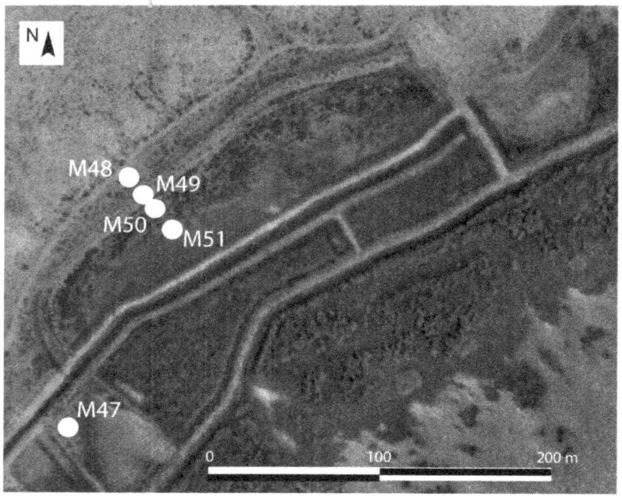

Fig. 5.20. (above and left) Location of boreholes between Ridge III, the island and Marea Peninsula. Archeological structures are densely represented on the northern shores of the island (hatched area). It raises the question: was the depression present between the island and Ridge III part of Lake Mareotis or not during antiquity? (C. Flaux).

Fig. 5.21. (below, left and right) Carbonate sandstone outcrops on the island (A) and the Marea Peninsula (B). This bedrock has the same nature as Ridges II and III that surround the western arm of Lake Mareotis. It is also an ancient littoral ridge that extends parallel to the others, inside Lake Mareotis' basin. In photograph (A) we can see a caliche, carbonate cementation covering the altered sandstone (Hassouba & Shaw 1980) (C. Flaux).

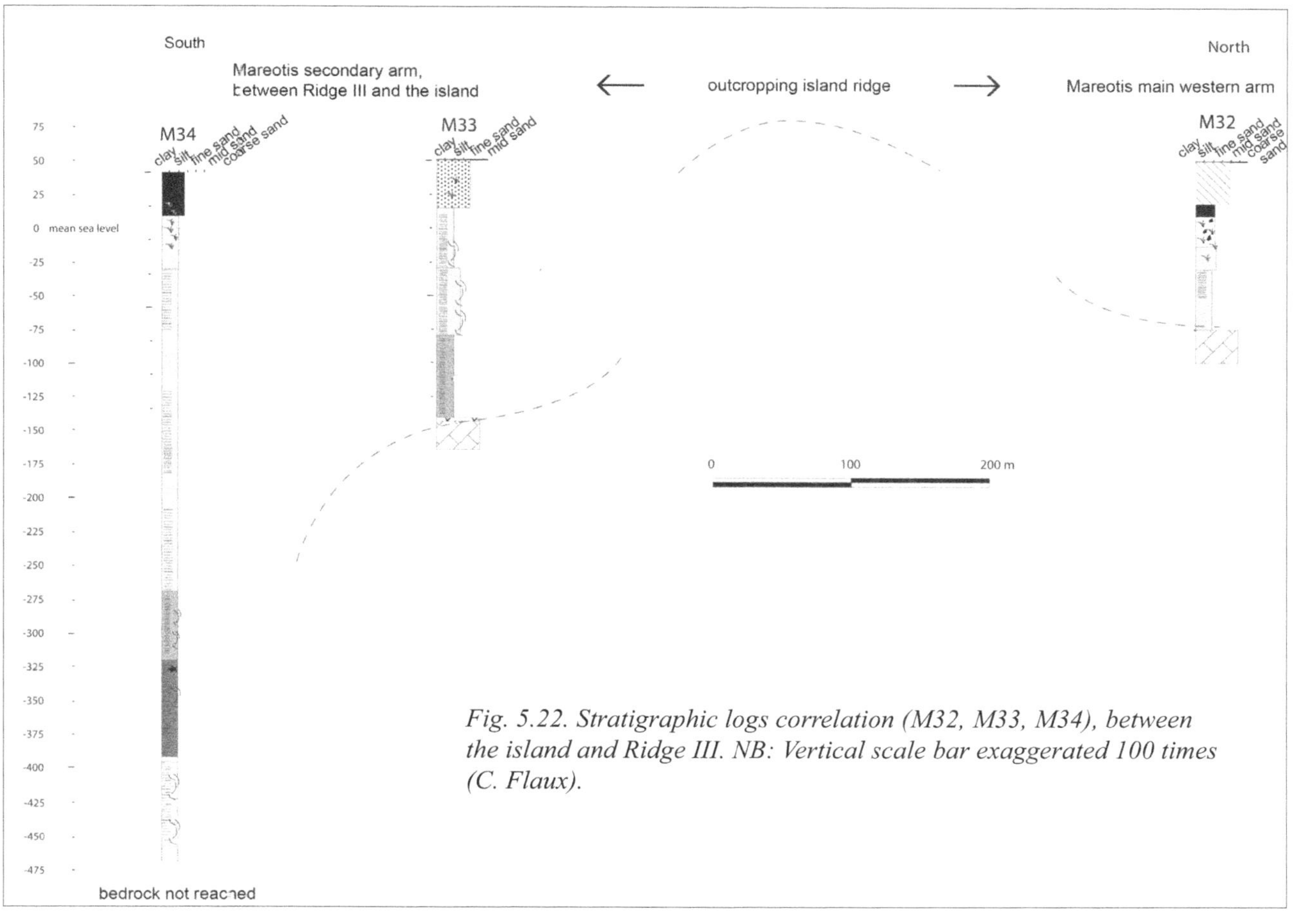

Fig. 5.22. Stratigraphic logs correlation (M32, M33, M34), between the island and Ridge III. NB: Vertical scale bar exaggerated 100 times (C. Flaux).

determined archaeological structures to understand the palaeo-morphology of the southern shorelines of Mareotis Island.

Results (1) (see Fig. 5.22: M32, M33, M34)
1. Lake sedimentary infilling.
2. Thin colluvial deposits (M33) or marshland deposits (M32, M34).

Analysis
Borehole M32 was stopped at -0.75m bmsl by bedrock. This core is located close to the island ridge, which extends towards Marea Peninsula and Umm Sigheiw Island (see Fig. 5.3). This indicates that the core struck this irregular but persistent lineation of the carbonate ridge lying inside Lake Mareotis. On the contrary, core M34 was uninterrupted until 4.5m bmsl (due to time, it was not possible to complete the stratigraphy). Thus, a depression between Ridge III and the island ridge was identified, which is confirmed by core M47 (see Figs 5.20, 5.23), drilled more than 5km westward, inside the same depression.

The presence of a lake shoreline south of the island is thus determined. Relative absence of human occupation along this sheltered shoreline can be explained by the continuity of the island carbonate ridge. Even if it has been immersed in some parts, a shallow water column made it difficult to access the southern part of Lake Mareotis. However, a well assessed and dated lake level is still required to emphasise this hypothesis.

Results (2) (see Fig. 5.23)
1. Lake sedimentary infilling.
2. A buried "marsh-like" deposit was assessed in core M51.
3. Sandy colluvial deposits on the hillside.

Discussion
From cores M48 to M51, the transect studied presents a well-defined shore sedimentation processes. It shows the progradation of the shoreline, supplied by colluviums that bury the lake sediments. A marsh deposit has been preserved in core M51. It indicates a lake level lying below 1.5m amsl. Fortunately, we found in this deposit burnt sandstone typical of the Mareotis region, covering the period from Hellenistic to Roman times (see Chapter 6). In both cores M48 and M49, drilling was stopped by an indeterminant rocky surface. Either bedrock or archaeological structures can be inferred. However, the typical facies always encountered at the base of the core, as a coarse and white oolithic sand (see Section 5.4.2.3) was absent here. The archaeological context of these cores suggests some archaeological structures buried 1 to 1.5m below the present soil surface. In core M49, at the interface between blocks and colluviums, there was a ceramic sherd common in the Mareotis region, imported from Gaza between the 4th and 7th centuries AD (see Chapter 6).

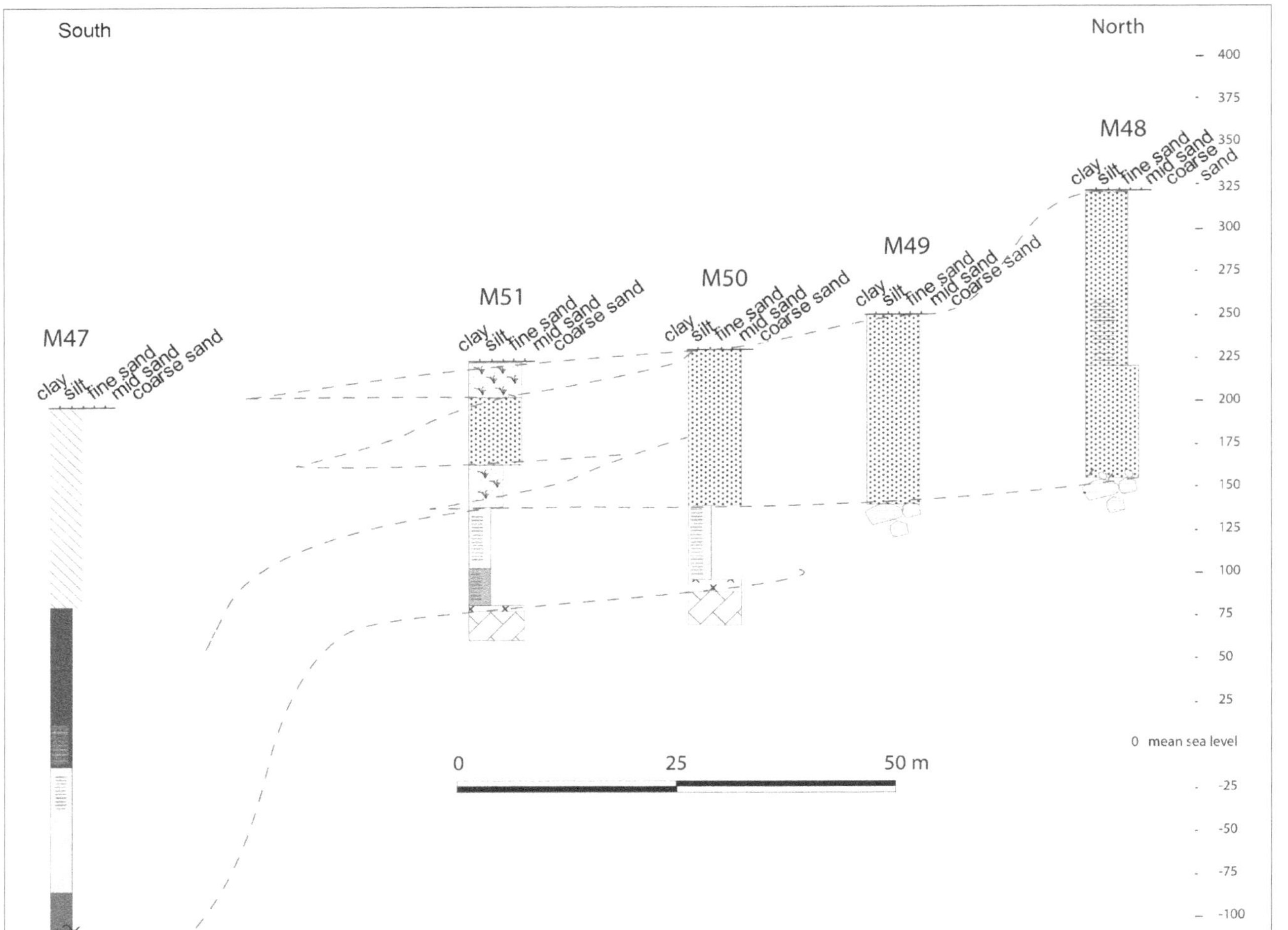

Fig. 5.23. Stratigraphic logs correlation (M47, M48, M49, M50, M51), west island, southern shore. NB: Vertical scale bar exaggerated 20 times (C. Flaux).

Both marsh deposits and the buried archaeological surface are situated at the same level. We assume that this translates to the altitude of an ancient shoreline, at around 1.5m amsl. The age of this surface is poorly understood. Marsh deposits occur during or after the Hellenistic period, since a sherd potentially used at this time was integrated into the deposit. In a similar fashion, this surface was covered by colluviums after the 4th century.

With a lake level at 1.5m amsl for an undetermined time during antiquity, the depression between Ridge III and the island should have been an arm of Lake Mareotis, considering that the lake bottom does not occur above 0.5m amsl. At point M32, the immerged part of the island carbonate ridge, a minimum water column of 1.25m can be inferred, the difference between the palaeo-lake level and the upper sedimentary deposit.

5.5.3 Island's northern shore

The island has yielded the most archaeological structures in the study area. Sedimentological studies undertaken in the area between the island and Ridge III have shown that a lake depression isolates this emergent ridge of land from the ridge shore. Thus, the island was an island in antiquity and ancient settlement is likely linked to its lake-front position. Archaeological structures are only visible just at the surface thus their function without excavations, remains hypothetical (see Chapter 6). The objective of the sedimentological prospection is to reconstruct, as best as possible, the ancient palaeo-topography, in order to help to understand the function of the archaeological structures.

5.5.3.1 Island's north-western shore

Presentation

The western part of the island, on the north lake shore, presents a complex geomorphological setting (Fig. 5.24). The highest point is a large ridge, densely occupied by archaeological structures (Sites 40 & 15). This ridge, oriented SW-NE, is inherited from a Pleistocene coastal ridge (see Section 5.2.1; see Fig. 5.3). It should be noted however, that no bedrock outcrops were observed during field survey, no doubt covered by archaeological remains.

From this ridge to the lake, the plain is divided into a western part covered by a sandy layer (see Fig. 5.24) and an eastern part occupied by a saltmarsh. This large shore plain is a singular feature of the northern shore of the island.

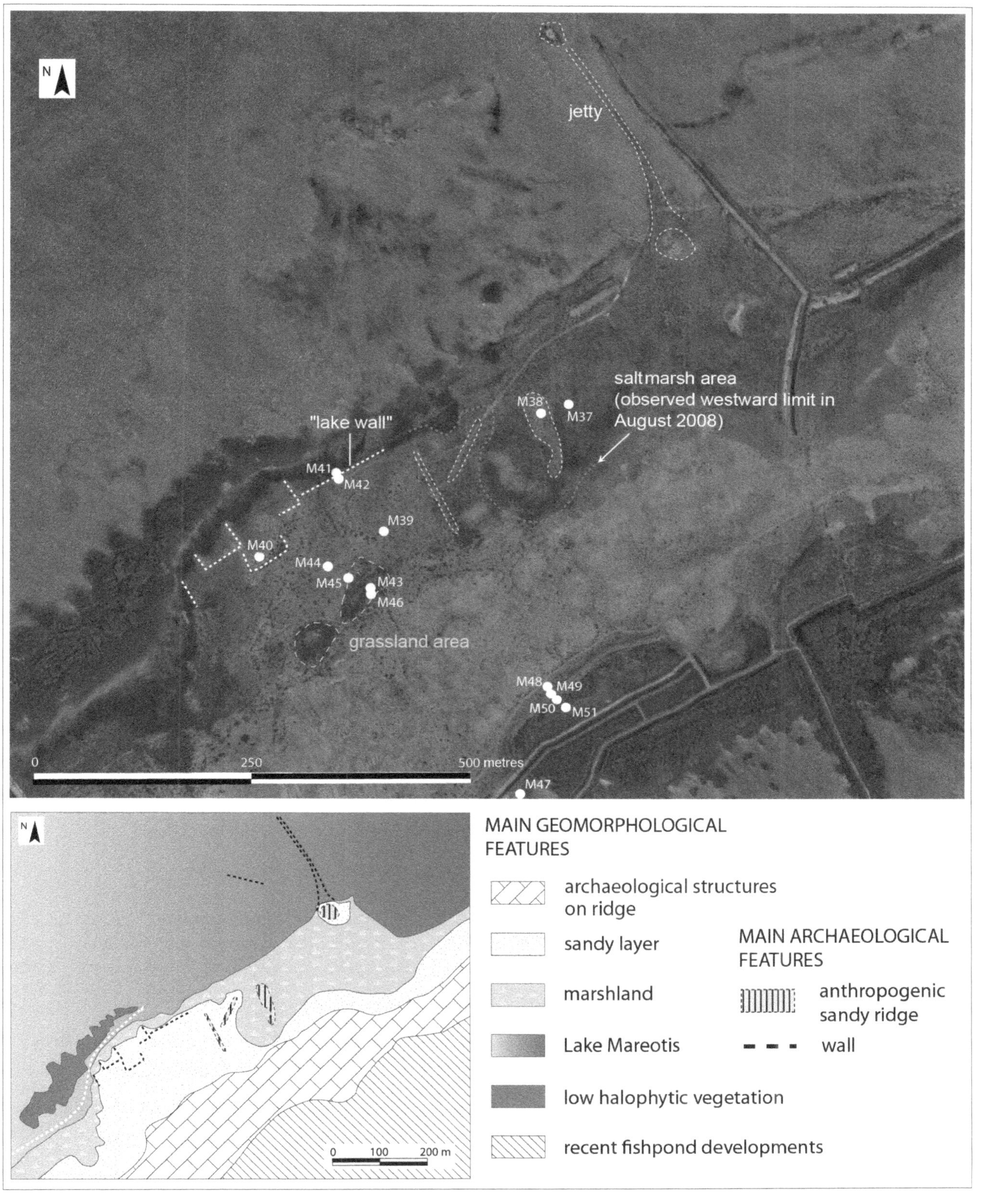

Fig. 5.24. Location of boreholes, west island, northern shore (C. Flaux).

Thus, the origin of this sedimentary accumulation constitutes the main research question at the site.

At the northern corner of the saltmarsh, a small sandy mound (around 40m wide) emerges above the marsh (Site 23) (Figs 5.24 & 5.25). A linear feature some 250m long and perpendicular to the shoreline can been observed, extending from this mound northwards into the lake to a second mound that emerges above the lake (see Fig. 5.24). This structure has been interpreted as a jetty. West of the second hillock lying above the present lake level, some other mounds emerge (see also Chapter 6).

Fig. 5.25. View of the small mound above the saltmarsh, Site 23 (photograph taken toward the north from M37) (C. Flaux).

In the western part of the marsh area, a small sand ridge was observed some 0.7m above the marsh and extending perpendicular to the shoreline (Site 41). Westward, another sand ridge constitutes a small embankment between the sandy plain and the flat marsh area (Site 20; see Fig. 6.158 in Chapter 6). A third sandy ridge, between the latter and oblique to them, is observed (Site 22). These straight sandy ridges, sometimes with stony blocks on the top of them, are probably man-made and limit the extension of the marsh to the west. Facing the lake and extending parallel to the lake edge, a "lake wall" (Site 21), outcropping just above the soil, limits the northern part of the sandy plain as do other archaeological features (see Chapter 6). These linear features appear to have outlined a sedimentary trap.

Archaeological structures are distributed on the highest part of the area (carbonate sandstone ridge) and near the present shoreline. Thus, two main questions arise regarding the intermediate area: what could its function be and is the present geomorphology as a result of human activities?

The entire width of the sandy plain has been investigated by coring (boreholes M39 to M46), from the shoreline to the carbonate ridge (see Fig. 5.24). In most cases, coring stopped at the lake facies, because we were most interested in understanding the formation of the complex topography of the site.

Two other boreholes were made, one on the marshland (M37) and another above the sandy ridge lying above the marsh (M38), in order to establish the natural depositional environment on which this sandy ridge was established.

Synthetic stratigraphy (Figs 5.24, 5.26, 5.27 & 5.28)
Three sedimentary transects are presented. Two of them cross the sandy plain from the island ridge to the shoreline whilst the other is perpendicular, from the sand to the marsh area. The stratigraphy can be summarised thus:
1. Upper lake deposits (M37 to M42, M44 and M45).
2. "Marsh-like" facies deposits against the island ridge (M43 and M46).
3. Sandy colluvium layers (all boreholes).
   a. A fine grain deposit occurs within coarse colluviums in boreholes M42, M40 and M39.
   b. A soil formation was observed at the surface of a restricted area including boreholes M43, M44, M45 and M46.

Discussion
Lake extension and level (see Figs 5.24, 5.26, 5.27 & 5.28)
The whole shore plain was investigated. A lacustrine environment has been elucidated in all cores except M43 and M46. The latter constitutes the geographical limit of the lake in the area. The altitude of the upper lake deposit decreases from 0.8m amsl (M45) to 0.3m bmsl (M41). It retraces the regular topographical profile of the lake bottom, going progressively deeper from the island ridge towards Lake Mareotis (see Figs 5.27 & 5.28). In boreholes M43 and M46, deposited upon the bedrock, a "marsh-like" sedimentary facies was recorded, measured at 1.5m amsl. It could represent an ancient lake level. A sherd was found in this deposit, a well-preserved Hellenistic handle, of local origin (R. Thomas, pers. comm.). Thus, assuming the handle was accurately identified and deposited *in situ*, a lake level at 1.5m amsl occurred during or after the Hellenistic period. A lake level of a similar date was also observed on the southern shore of the island (see Section 5.5.2 and Fig. 5.23).

Like the small mound (Site 23) described in Fig. 5.25 that emerged above the saltmarsh which lay at around 1m amsl, this circular feature could have been an islet with 1.5m amsl lake level conditions. The dating of this area (Site 23) would indicate activity in the region from the late 1st to 6th or 7th centuries AD. However, an exact interpretation of the palaeo-topography of the area during antiquity has yet to be determined.

5.5.3.1.1 Shore plain morphology

5.5.3.1.1.1 Colluvial deposits (see Figs 5.26, 5.27 & 5.28)
Colluvial deposits were observed in all boreholes. A 200m sandy shore plain covering the lake bottom is still visible. Such a width was not observed elsewhere along the northern part of the island. Along a transect parallel to the island ridge, 350m long (see Fig. 5.26), its thickness above the upper lake deposit is higher across the sandy plain than across the marsh area, ranging respectively from 2.2m (M44) to 0.8m (M37) high. Numerous linear topographic features (ridge, wall) on the sandy plain surface probably formed a sedimentary trap and favoured the present emergence of the plain in spite of the high lake level.

5.5.3.1.1.2 Sandy ridge (M38, see Fig. 5.26)
The presence of blocks above the sandy ridge suggests an anthropogenic origin. No marsh deposit was observed beneath the sandy ridge, indicating that the present marshland post-dates the ridge. Upper lake deposits in cores M37 and M38 lie at the same altitude. If the ridge was established during lacustrian sedimentation (i.e. during the lake presence in this area), lake sediments should have continued

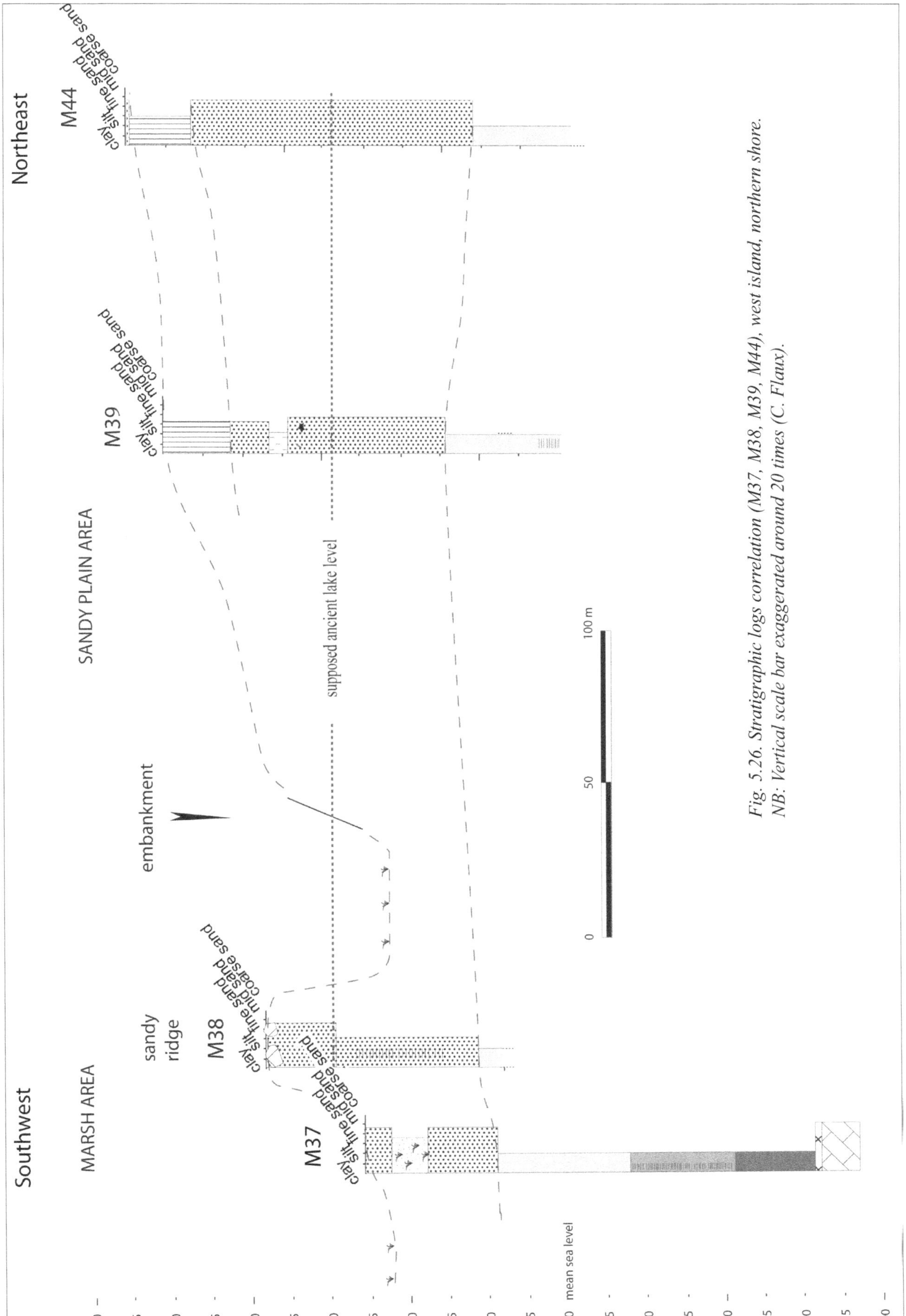

Fig. 5.26. Stratigraphic logs correlation (M37, M38, M39, M44), west island, northern shore. NB: Vertical scale bar exaggerated around 20 times (C. Flaux).

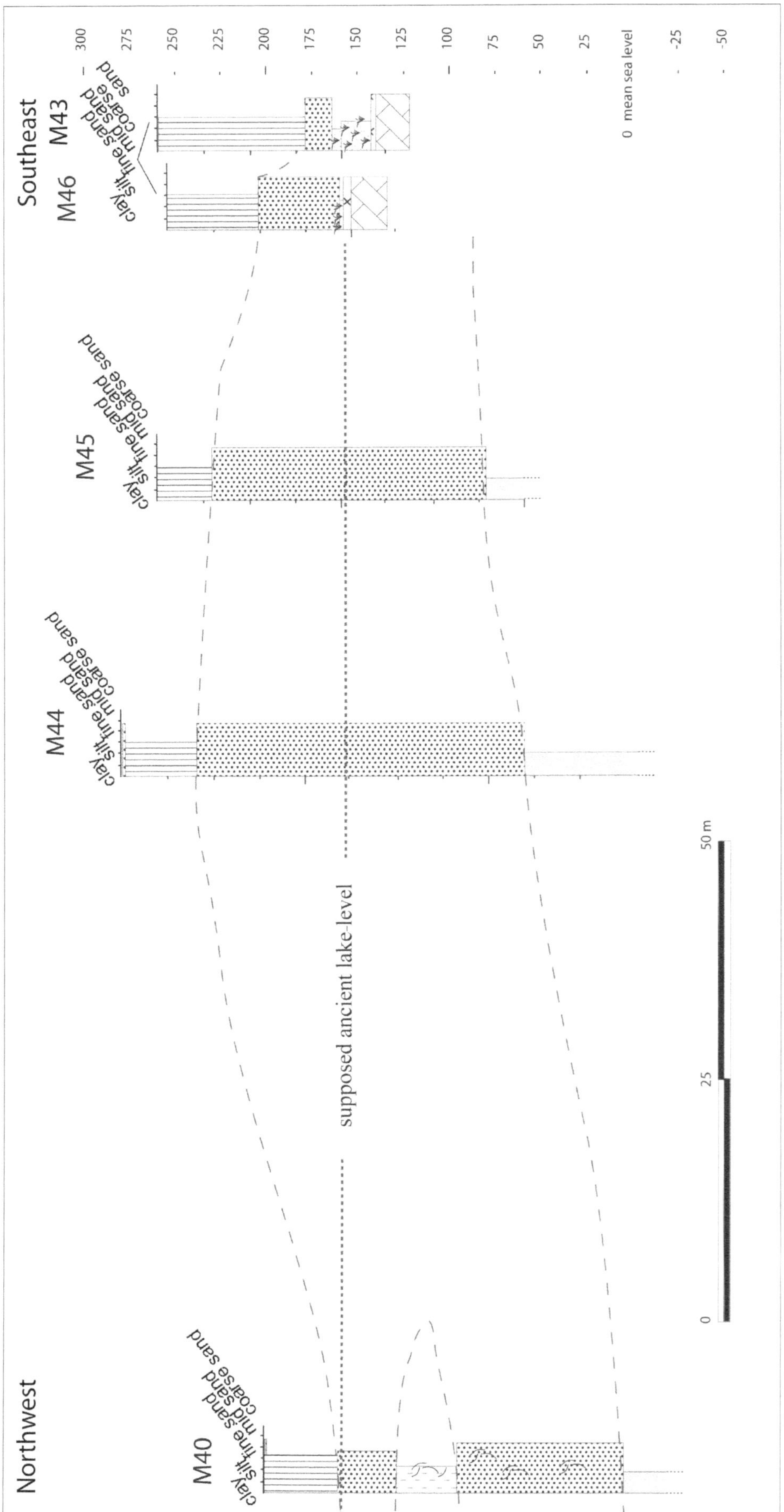

Fig. 5.27. Stratigraphic logs correlation (M40, M44, M45, M46, M43), west island, northern shore. NB: Vertical scale bar exaggerated around 20 times (C. Flaux).

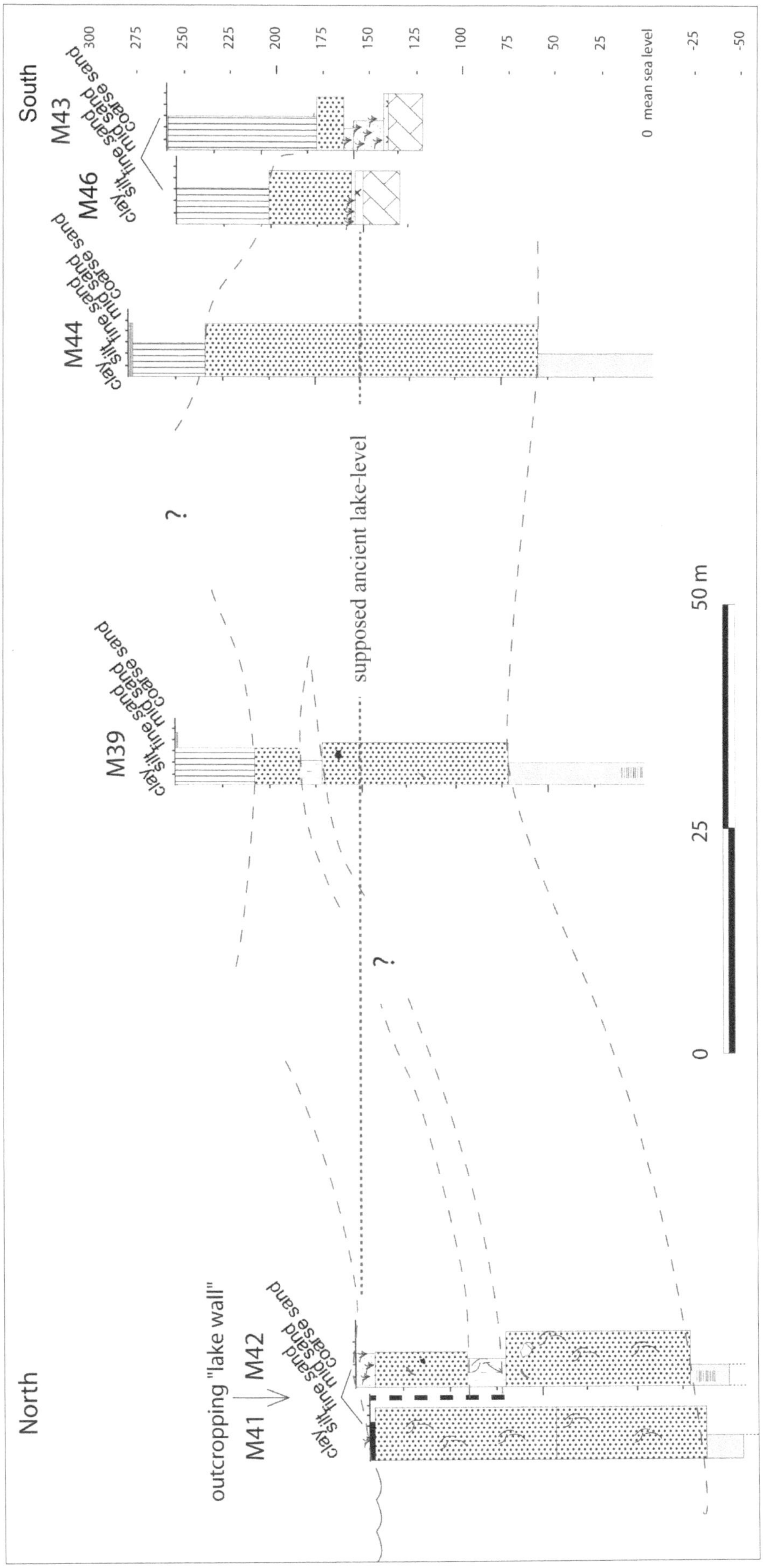

Fig. 5.28. Stratigraphic logs correlation (M41, M42, M39, M44, M46, M43), west island, northern shore. NB: Vertical scale bar exaggerated 20 times (C. Flaux).

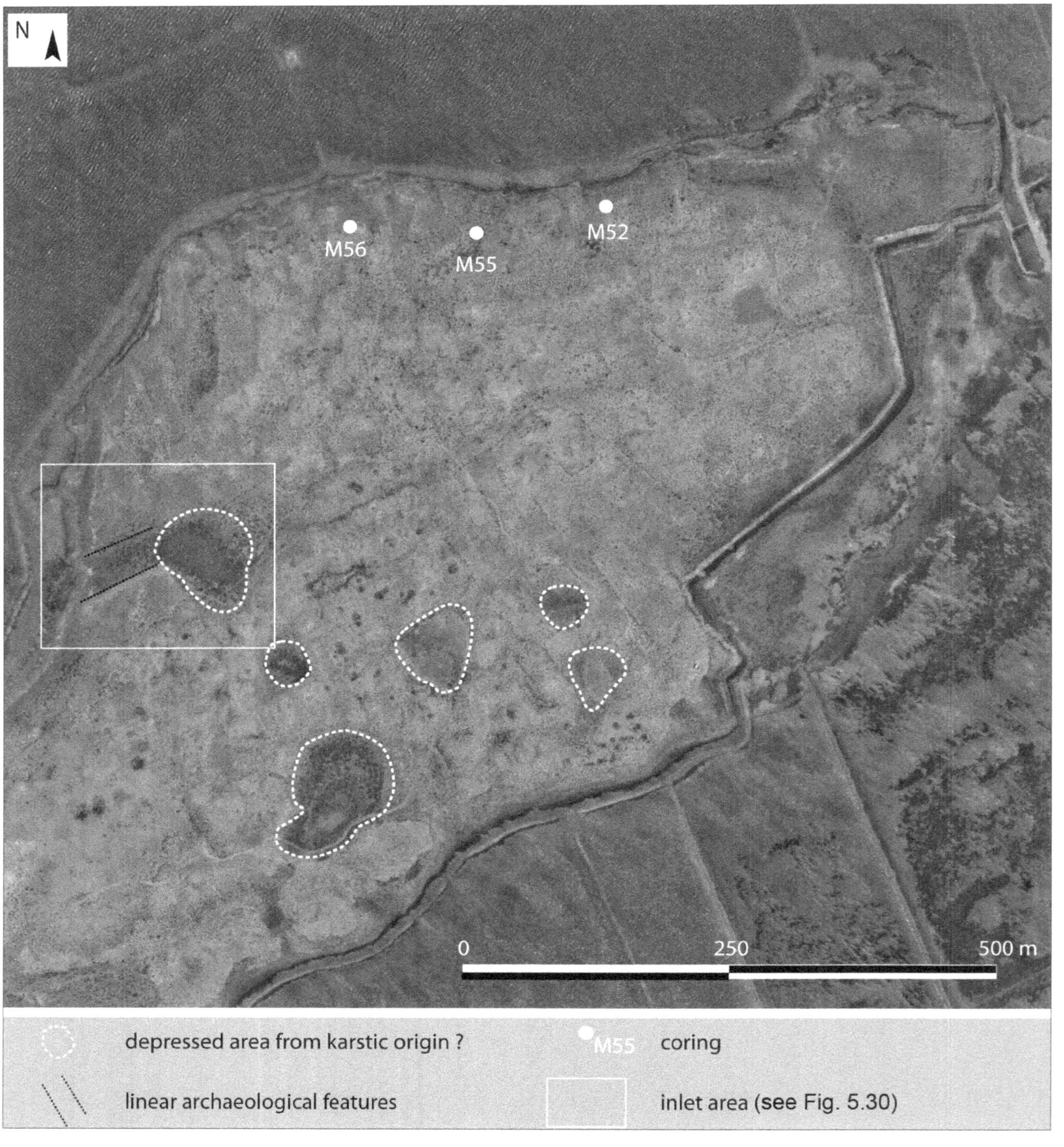

Fig. 5.29. North-eastern island, location of Site 29 (C. Flaux).

to be deposited in the M37 borehole. As no lateral change to the sedimentary facies was observed from core M37 to core M38, we assume that the ridge is contemporaneous with the colluviation phase, which covered lake deposits in both M37 and M38 at the same time. Thus, this sandy ridge is not expected to have a waterfront function.

5.5.3.1.1.3 Sedimentary impacts of the wall (see Fig. 5.28) A distance of 2.5m separates boreholes M41 and M42 which were taken either side of the so called "lake wall". The altitude of the top of the wall is 1.5m amsl, as indicated by the lake level from the marsh deposits in boreholes M43 and M46. The sedimentary sequence represented in both boreholes are very similar, however, borehole M41 registered on the water side of the wall, 1.75m of coarse sand. Such a facies does not indicate a lake environment. The upper level of the lake deposit is 0.25m bmsl in both boreholes. A wall set up inside the lake should have modified the lake deposit facies and the sedimentation rate from lakeside to hillside. Thus, the wall is assumed to have been established during the colluvial sedimentary phase. We assume it is not associated with a lake-front function.

A grain size change, from coarse sand to silt, is observed from M41 (lakeside) to M42 (hillside) within the sand deposits. A silty-clay texture was also observed in boreholes M39 and M40. The latter was drilled inside a rectangular structure. In cores M26 and M27 (Site 109), drilled from one side to the other of a similar wall that was located parallel to the shoreline on the south-western shore of the lake (see Figs 5.16, 5.18), a similar reduction in grain size was observed against and at the back of the "lake wall". However, this fine sedimentary facies is not observed up to the surface, neither in M42 nor M39 or M40. Thus, the outcropping wall cannot be associated with certainty with this buried sedimentary sequence and its function remains unclear. A late Roman body sherd tentatively dated to the 6th and 7th centuries AD (see Chapters 4 and 6) was found just below the fine grain deposit in core M42 between 0.5 – 0.75m below the surface. Thus, assuming this sherd was deposited *in situ*, the grain size reduction observed against the wall occurred at the earliest after the 6th century AD.

5.5.3.1.1.4 Brown soil facies (see Figs 5.27 & 5.28)
Transition between the fine grain soil facies and coarse colluviums indicates that this soil has been deposited and is not the result of pedogenic processes on the colluviums. The surface area of the soil facies can be observed from satellite images because it comprises a flat grassland within the sandy surface (see Fig. 5.24). From M44 to M43, soil thickness of the facies increases and then decreases in front of the island ridge. This profile forms a small basin within the colluvial layer. This topography could derive from land use, in order to collect rain water and develop grazing, as already discussed above in Sections 5.5.1.1 & 5.5.1.2 (see Fig. 5.17). M40 soil facies is found inside a rectangular archaeological structure. Use of this topographical feature as a small depression (as observed in Fig. 5.9) could post-date the primary function of the structure.

Uniquely in boreholes M44, M39 and M40, a fine sandy layer has covered the soil facies. This suggests some recent colluvial processes, wind- and rain-driven. However, the soil facies constitutes the upper part of the sedimentary sequence and is expected to be recent. In borehole M46, a sherd indicates that the lower marsh deposit is contemporaneous with or post-dates the Hellenistic period. Soil deposition occurs after this time. The lateral extension of this facies across the site was not investigated.

5.5.3.1.2 Summary
A shoreline is assumed to have been present at 1.5m amsl just in front of the carbonate ridge, at the same time or after the Hellenistic period. Later, shoreline progradation resulted from hillside sediment colluviation and aeolian transportation. The "lake wall" and sandy ridges described upon the sandy plain do not seem to have any lake function. They would appear to be contemporaneous with the colluviation phase. A sherd was found within sandy deposits, just below the grain size reduction observed at the back of the "lake wall". It is dated to the 6th century AD suggesting that at the earliest, the 1m sand accumulation below the sherd would have been deposited before this date (see Fig. 5.28), or possibly later if the sherd was not *in situ*. As the hillside is relatively small, such a depth of sand accumulation (around 2m thick) is surprising. As this accumulation is localised to the sandy plain, between numerous linear features (sand ridge and walls) we assume that it could have an anthropogenic origin, such as a polder. There is no pottery later than the 7th century anywhere in the area which would indicate that these linear remains are associated with activity in antiquity. As a shoreline has been inferred just beside the limestone ridge and dated at or after Hellenistic time, it would indicate that the shoreline has experienced progradation during antiquity. The jetty (Site 23) that extends for c. 300m into the lake, seems not to be connected to the limestone ridge but rather to the sandy plain. The jetty is thought to have been in use from the 1st to the 7th centuries AD (see also Chapter 6). It would indicate that the sandy plain was at least partially developed during this period and has effectively an anthropogenic origin. The shoreline was extended into the water maybe in order to enlarge the area of this narrow shore plain. However, the function of these sedimentary archaeological structures remains ambiguous, although animal grazing activity can be proposed. Sandy ridges and wall networks could derive from an irrigation system, aimed at maintaining soil humidity, vegetation cover and pasture activity. This hypothesis should be compared with data from the complete archaeological survey and the micro-topography of the area. The main difficulty is to determinate the contemporaneousness of all structures noted.

5.5.3.2 North-eastern island shore

5.5.3.2.1 "Inlet" (Site 126)
Presentation
Site 126 is characterised by an oval-shaped marshland completely surrounded by archaeological structures (Figs 5.29 & 5.30; see also Chapter 6). A channel provides access to the lake, the entrance to which is currently delimited by two walls outcropped just above the surface. This very sheltered area may have provided protection during antiquity, facing the lake on the north shore of the island. A series of seven boreholes were made in order to test the basin hypothesis, and to check its perimeter and channel width.

Synthetic stratigraphy (Figs 5.31 & 5.32)
1. Lake sedimentation above an irregular hard surface (0.65 to 1.5m bmsl).
2. From the inlet to the waters edges.
   a. Lake sedimentation inside the present inlet perimeter.
   b. Sandy colluvial deposits with two traits:
      i. A marsh-like deposit was observed in cores M30 and M31, between 0.55 and 1.05m amsl.
      ii. In cores M35 and M36, a brown to dark-grey fine sand was observed. It is assumed that the proximity of archaeological structures infers anthropogenic sediment source.
3. The present lake level at 1.25m amsl is characterised by a marsh deposit.

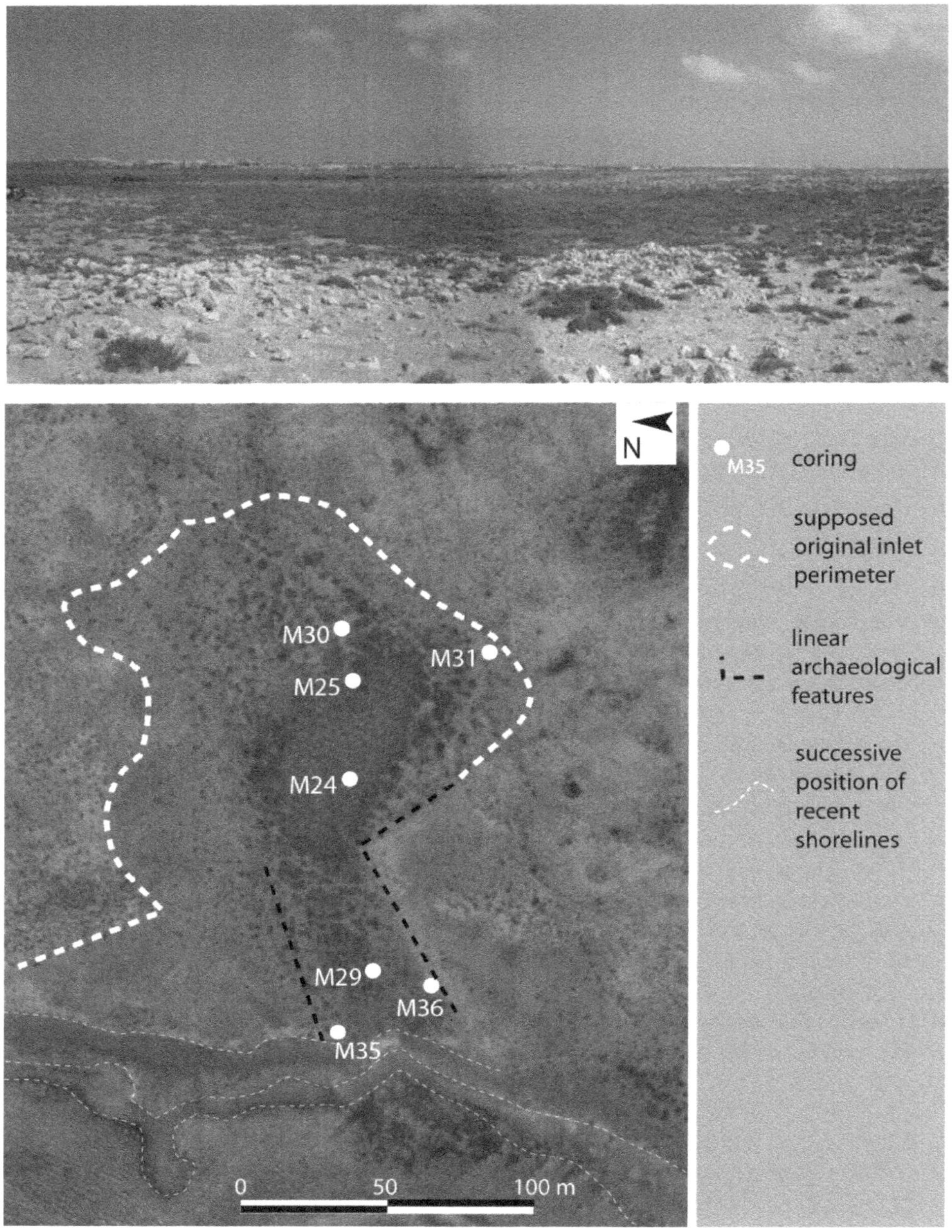

Fig. 5.30. Photographs and location of boreholes associated with the inlet Site 126. Lower lake level witnessed at the time the satellite image was taken provides insight into ancient shorelines. Shoreline progradation at Site 126 does not necessarily reflect that observed in the immediate area. Indeed, during fieldwork (August 2008), lake levels were higher than those depicted on the satellite image, extending almost to auger M29. Thus, shoreline position is controlled by both lake level variations and shore sedimentary budget (C. Flaux).

Discussion

Two perpendicular transects were examined. In both, the stratigraphy reveals a lateral sedimentation change from the inlet to the waters edge. This raises the following question: are these sedimentary lateral changes that occurred within the inlet contemporary?

The W-E transect follows the longitudinal axis of the inlet (see Fig. 5.31). Over the irregular bedrock topography, lake sediments regularise the lake bottom, as the sedimentation rate is higher in areas of greater accommodation space. Sedimentary deposits change laterally. Lake sediment deposition continues at the centre of the inlet, whereas along the edges deposition is covered by sandy layers, a product of colluviation from hinterland watersheds. A marsh-like deposit was observed in core M30, inside colluvial deposits. This facies is a product of both preserved organic matter and colluvial supplies (see Section 5.4.1.2) and indicates a maximum lake level range between 0.55 and 1.05m amsl at the time of deposition. This undated palaeo-lake level is then observed below colluvial sediments, indicating the progradation of the shoreline. This lateral dynamic reaches point M25 whilst lake sedimentation continues to be registered in M24 and M29. As a result, the inlet basin infilled and its extent decreased. Current marsh environment register current lake levels, higher than that fossilised in M30. Therefore, this stratigraphy may describe lake level rise, basin infilling and shoreline progradation.

A NNW-SSE transect was made to understand the origin of the channel linking the inlet to the lake (see Fig. 5.32). From south to north, the first lake deposit lies upon a slope of the bedrock. Lake *facies J* and *I* thickened according to this slope gradient (highest space accommodation). Then sedimentary deposits change laterally. Boreholes M35 and

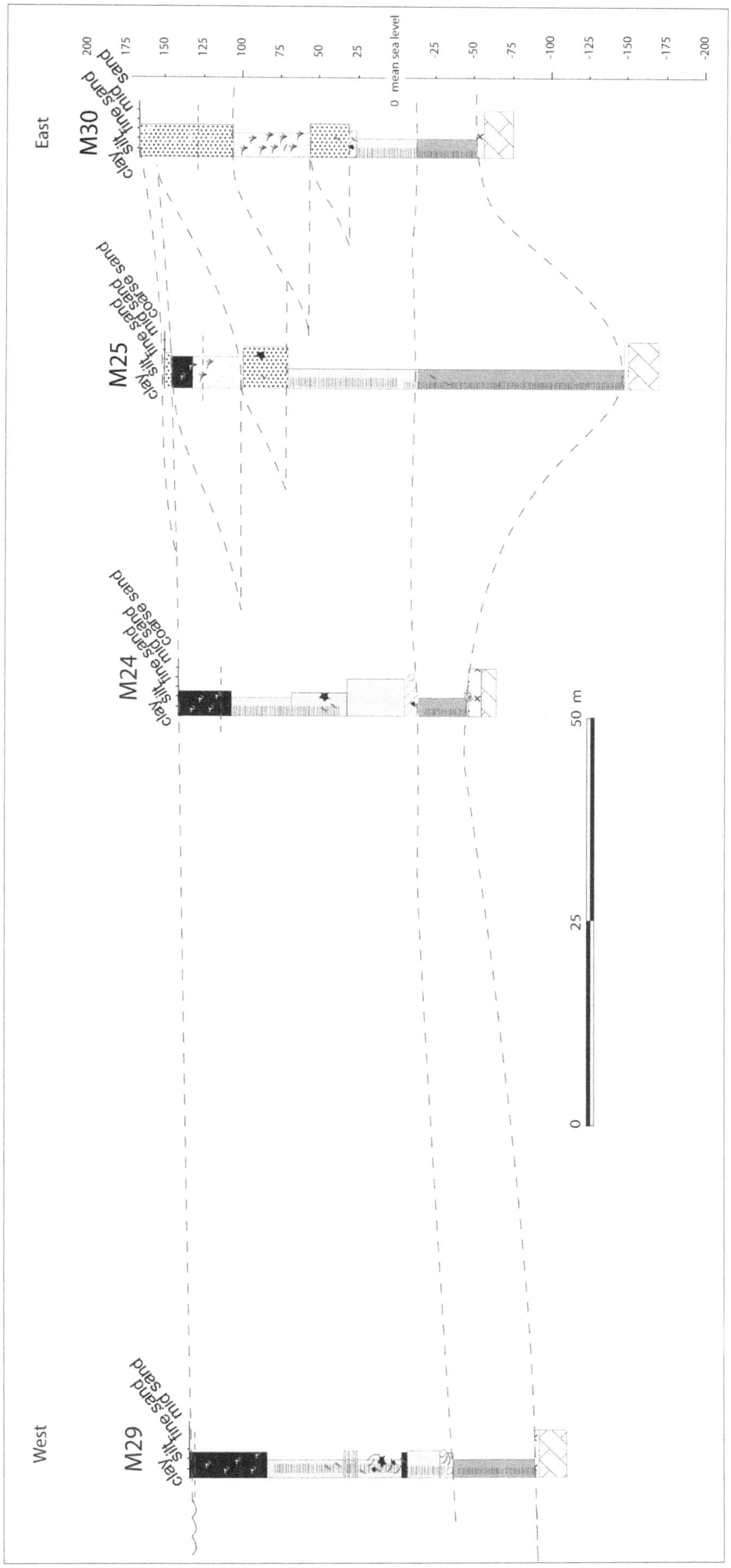

Fig. 5.31. Stratigraphic logs correlation (M29, M24, M25, M30), inlet, W-E longitudinal transect. NB: Vertical scale bar exaggerated around 20 times (C. Flaux).

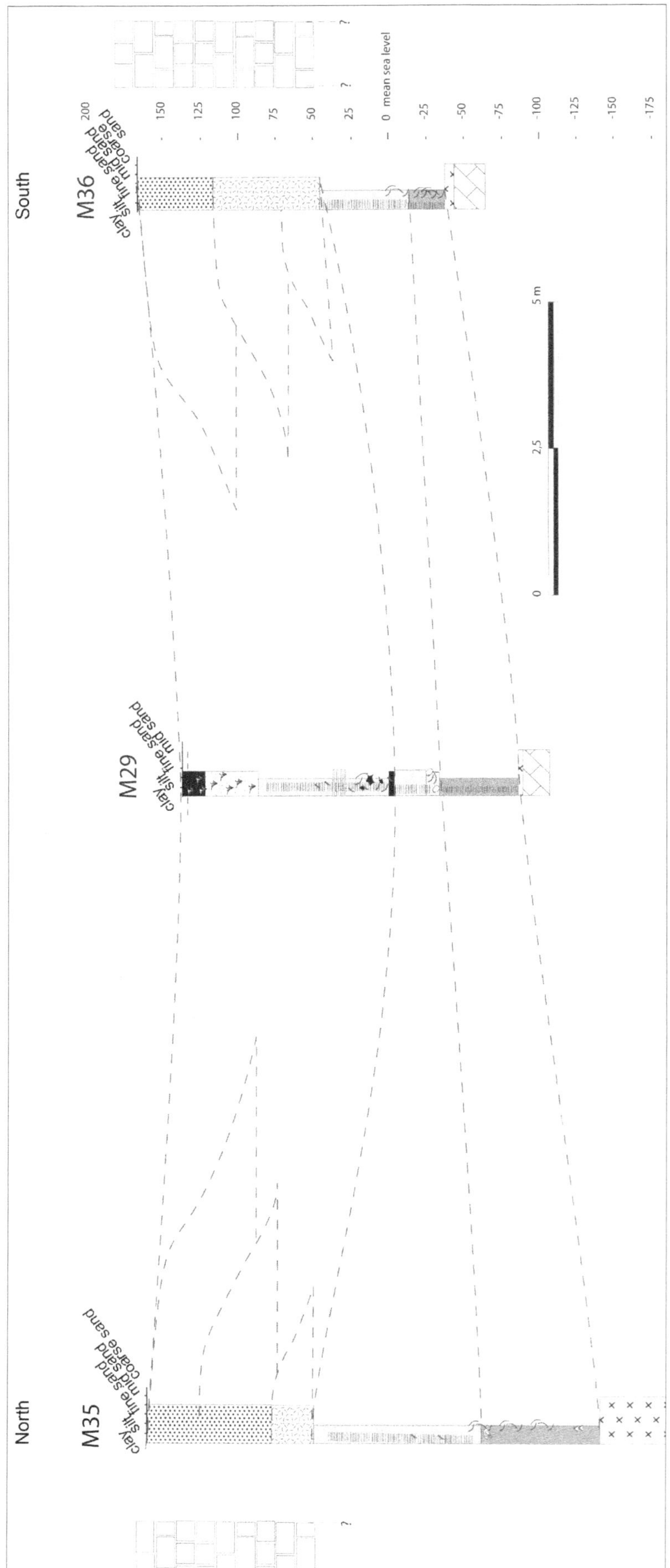

Fig. 5.32. Stratigraphic logs correlation (M35, M29, M26), inlet, N-S channel transect. NB: Vertical scale bar exaggerated 5 times (C. Flaux).

M36 were both located at the flank of two linear archaeological structures that delimit the current channel, between the inlet and the lake. A fine, dark-grey sand was observed in both of these cores, while M29 simply registered lake deposits. A similar dark colour was observed in cores M54, M55 and M56 and during the excavation of Site 119, and was probably at least in part, a product of human activity (i.e. an organic or kiln area; see below Section 5.5.3.2.2.1). This facies can be correlated with a rich organic layer and is associated with the appearance of numerous archaeological artefacts in cores M29 (three sherds and a fragment of black sandstone, associated with burning activity). If so, the lake sedimentation in M29 at the centre of the channel may be contemporary with the rich organic sands deposition in M35 and M36. This lateral change of sedimentation is probably contemporaneous with the use of the channel walls.

Ancient inlet morphology
Linear archaeological structures convey the present straight channel (around 20m in length) that forms an angle with the oval part of the inlet (see Fig. 5.30). We have not observed another case of such morphology along the island or Ridge III shorelines. Neither bedrock topography reached in the cores nor lake sedimentation geometry describe a natural depression in place of the present channel (see Fig. 5.32). Moreover, the interruption of lake sedimentation in boreholes M35 and M36 (replaced by a fine, dark-grey sand) translates as a sudden change of the shoreline in the area. Thus, the present channel morphology appears inherited from the structure of archaeological remains, rather than from the natural coastal geomorphology.

Lake sediments were observed inside boreholes M30 and M31. These corings were done at the back of the current extent of the marsh area in front of a mound covered by numerous archaeological structures. Lake deposits have been covered by sandy sediments probably eroded from the mound at the back of the inlet. This can be interpreted as progradation of the shoreline in the form of a short sandy plain between the marsh and the highest altitude of the mound. Such a sandy plain can be seen from the satellite image around the marsh area and probably equates to the ancient extension of the inlet (see Fig. 5.30). Shoreline morphology has been reshaped in this restricted area by the anthropogenic channel arrangement and its associated walls.

Dating
Unfortunately, no sherds were recovered to provide a precise date. In M29, sherds were found in a laminated matrix, meaning that no reworking has disturbed deposition. There are no reasons to explain why lake sedimentation has stopped, so we can suggest that the sherds were not deposited long after their use. As the ceramics found in the coring derived from the Hellenistic to Byzantine period (R. Thomas, pers. comm.), we can only assume that the inlet was functional during antiquity. Marsh-like deposits were observed both in M31, M30 and M25, between 0.55 and 1.25m amsl. As no dating is available for this imprecise lake level, we can not assess the water depth during the inlet's use.

Fig. 5.33. Photograph and location of borehole M56 (white point), Site 118. View westward. Between two linear archaeological structures that extend perpendicular to the shoreline that are interpreted as walls, a small rectangular depression is delimited. Dense cover of halophile plants equate to an actual marsh deposit environment. White colour at the shoreline corresponds to "sea grass" accumulation, dried by the sun (C. Flaux).

Archaeological artefacts found in M29 have been associated with "channel" walls and dark sands accumulated in the M35 area. However, below these sands, i.e. before occupation, within the lake sediments were found two ancient coarseware sherds (see Chapter 6). Thus, if the dark sands are contemporary with "channel" walls as proposed, it is suggested that some ancient occupation may have preceded the establishment of the channel.

5.5.3.2.2 Eastern end of the island
The north-east island is densely covered by archaeological structures outcropping just above the soil surface, from the top of the carbonate ridge to the present lake shoreline. Perpendicular to the shoreline some walls dissect the shore plain in a series of slightly depressed units (M56; Fig. 5.33) and sand plain units (M55; Fig. 5.34). The function of these archaeological structures is unknown, although considering their waterfront position they could be linked to lake activities. The main aim of geomorphological surveys was to determine the location of the ancient shoreline, although time did not permit a thorough investigation. Three main cores were made (see Fig. 5.29), which are described in Fig. 5.35. Cores M54, M55 and M56 are all underlined by a new lake facies which is associated with this rich archaeological context.

5.5.3.2.2.1 "Anthropogenic" lake facies (see Figs 5.29, 5.35)
This is a brown to dark-brown clayey-silt which is very rich in archaeological artefacts such as sherds, charcoal and a few black, sandstone pebbles, particularly when compared to all others facies described above. It is also often associated with coarse sedimentary material (coarse sand, oolithic gravels and a few pebbles), as a "waste" facies. Some lagoon fauna identified as *Melanoides sp.*, together

Fig. 5.34. Photographs and location of borehole M55 (white point). View northward. Borehole M55 is located between two walls (Sites 116 and 117) that extend perpendicular to the shoreline. The walls actually contain a curved shoreline. Towards the back of the photograph, a wall parallel to the shoreline outcrops just above the soil (C. Flaux).

Fig. 5.35. Stratigraphic logs correlation (M56, M55, M54), east end of the island (C. Flaux).

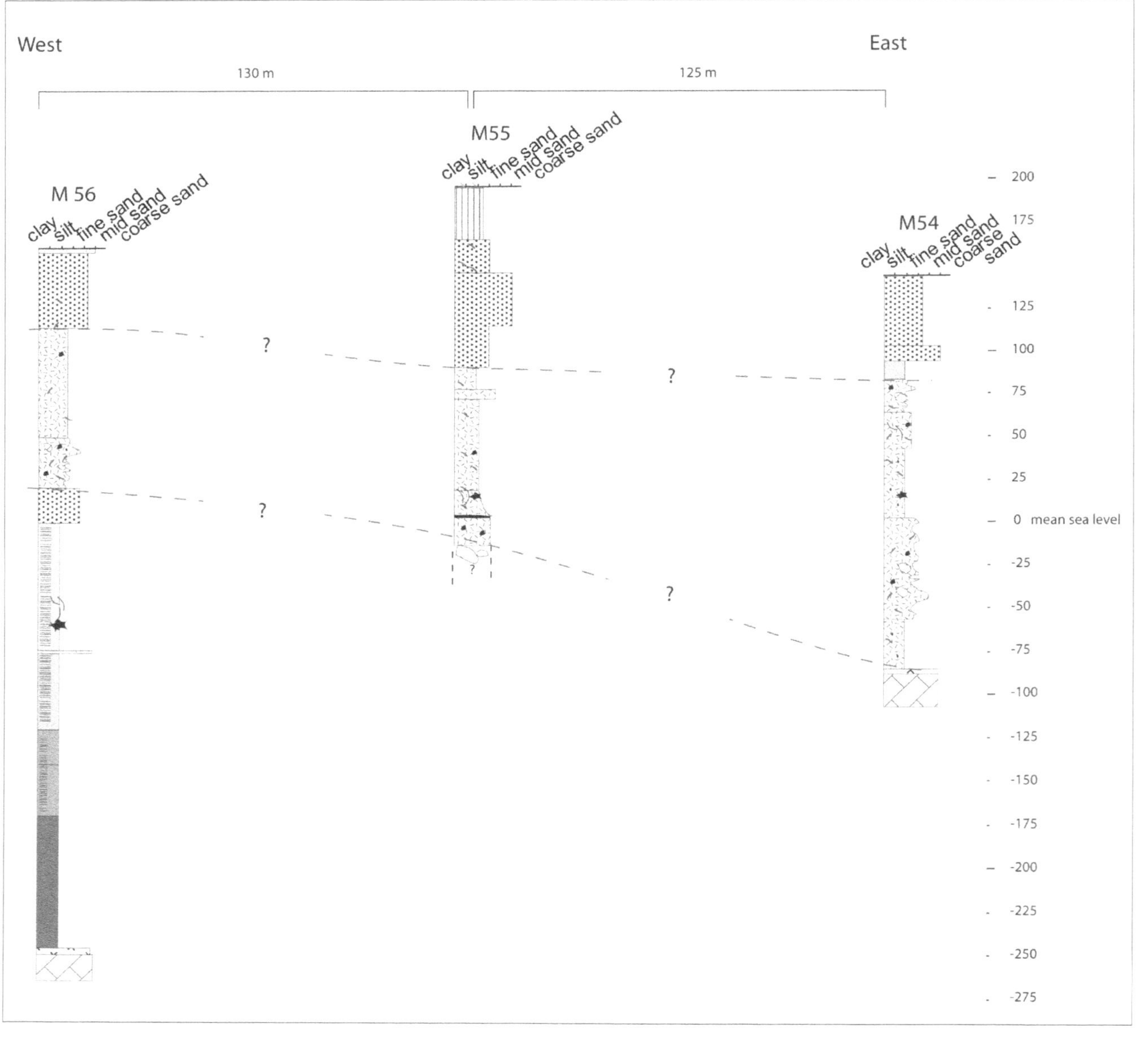

with settling mud, helped determine this as a water basin deposit environment. Ostracods were also observed in one sample of this facies, from borehole M56. Dark colour, heterometric sediments and numerous sherds present throughout the accumulation of this facies are linked to the rich archaeological context where the boreholes were made. This facies describes both the deposition of lake sediments and archaeological artefacts. Thus, it is assumed that it was deposited during occupation characterised by archeological structures of the north-eastern island area.

5.5.3.2.2.2 M54, M53, M52 (Site 114-115)

This site is characterised by a square area, 60 x 60m, delimited on three sides by archaeological structures and to the north by the lake (Fig. 5.36). Six boreholes were made in order to identify depositional milieu inside this area. In four of them, hard rock probably deriving from archaeological structures was encountered at a shallow depth preventing deeper coring. However, in cores M54 and M54bis sediments that had been deposited in a water-logged environment were identified. Archaeological blocks have been found between 1 to 1.6m amsl (respectively from M53 to M52, see Fig. 5.36). This range of depths comprises a potential maximum lake level range at the time of land use. However, four boreholes (namely M52, M52bis, M53 and M54ter) are not enough to assess if these rocks are *in situ* or whether they have been removed after land use. Sherds found within the basin sediments did not yield a precise date but all correspond to ancient land use, namely from Hellenistic to Late Roman times (see also Chapter 6). Between the bottom of the "anthropogenic" lake facies and the altitude of archaeological blocks interpreted as a possible maximum lake level, the water column reaches a maximum of 2m depth

In each borehole a sand layer, a product of colluviation, covers either the basin infilling or archaeological structures. This sedimentary dynamic probably post-dates land use in ancient times and could be a consequence of land abandonment.

5.5.3.2.2.3 M56 (Sites 117 and 118)

M56 borehole was made between two walls just in front of a small marshland set in a low depression. It presents a dense halophile vegetation cover, closely linked to groundwater (see Figs 5.29, 5.33, 5.35).

Drilling was stopped at 4m below soil surface, at 2.5m bmsl (see Fig. 5.35). In borehole M54 only 250m east of M56, bedrock was reached at 0.9m bmsl, indicating the irregularity of the bedrock surface.

Then, lake *facies L*, *J* and *I* (see Table 5.2, Section 5.4.2.1) were sampled, a stratigraphy already described in the two deepest boreholes, M34 (5m, see Fig. 5.22) and M37 (3m, see Fig. 5.26), was again realised. "Anthropogenic" lake facies overlies this sedimentation. It indicates that Lake Mareotis existed before the occupation of the sites around the shores of ancient Mareotis. M56 was drilled between two walls placed 10m apart and perpendicular to the shoreline. Even if the bedrock is irregular, there is no reason to think that these walls were set upon an inherited topography. We assume that they constitute an artificial shoreline bordering a small rectangular basin.

Later, the basin was covered by a sand layer, a product of colluviation. As in site M54, this indicates that colluviation is later than the ancient land occupation, associated with its abandonment.

5.5.3.2.2.4 M55

Borehole M55 was placed between two walls associated with Sites 116 and 117 (see Figs 5.29, 5.34 & 5.35). Behind the borehole, a wall parallel to the shoreline outcrops just above the soil. Drilling was stopped when hard rock was hit but no white coarse oolithic sand was observed as described in the majority of cores that reached bedrock (see Table 5.2). Here a stone could have blocked the drilling. The deposit above the rock has been correlated to the "anthropogenic" lake facies because of its colour, the presence of archaeological artefacts and stratigraphical position. However, it should be noted that no shells were observed to confirm that this facies was deposited in a basin water environment. It was subsequently covered by sandy colluviation products as in the previous stratigraphy studied (M54 and M56). Here, a brown soil sedimentary facies is observed above a sand layer. Colluviation processes are expected to have occurred since antiquity (see M54 and M56). As a consequence, this soil management should not be associated with land use in antiquity. It has to be noted that again, soil facies are observed in a restricted area (M55), relatively devoid of archaeological structures (see Fig. 5.34). Comparison can be made between the upper soil facies of core M55 and those described in Fig. 5.29. This can only equate to soil management, in a zone densely covered by archaeology.

5.6 Synthesis and future areas of research

5.6.1 Lake facies

5.6.1.1 Variability of facies

Numerous different lake facies were observed, both within the stratigraphic sequence and along the shores of Lake Mareotis within the study area. This equates to both changes in time and space of sedimentary sources and perhaps sedimentary conditions. More investigation is necessary to understand the origin of these changes, so far assessed only from sediment structure and colour. Sedimentary sources, depositional modes and post-depositionnal processes could be investigated by mineralogy, micromorphology and geochemistry. Such a study would be underpinned by the specific conditions of the study area, that is the extreme margin of the Nile Delta and Maryut Basin watershed (carbonate ridges). Land use could be a third specificity of the study area.

5.6.1.2 Fauna

Molluscan fauna recovered in drill cores were very sparse. We only found a few well preserved samples of *Cerasto-*

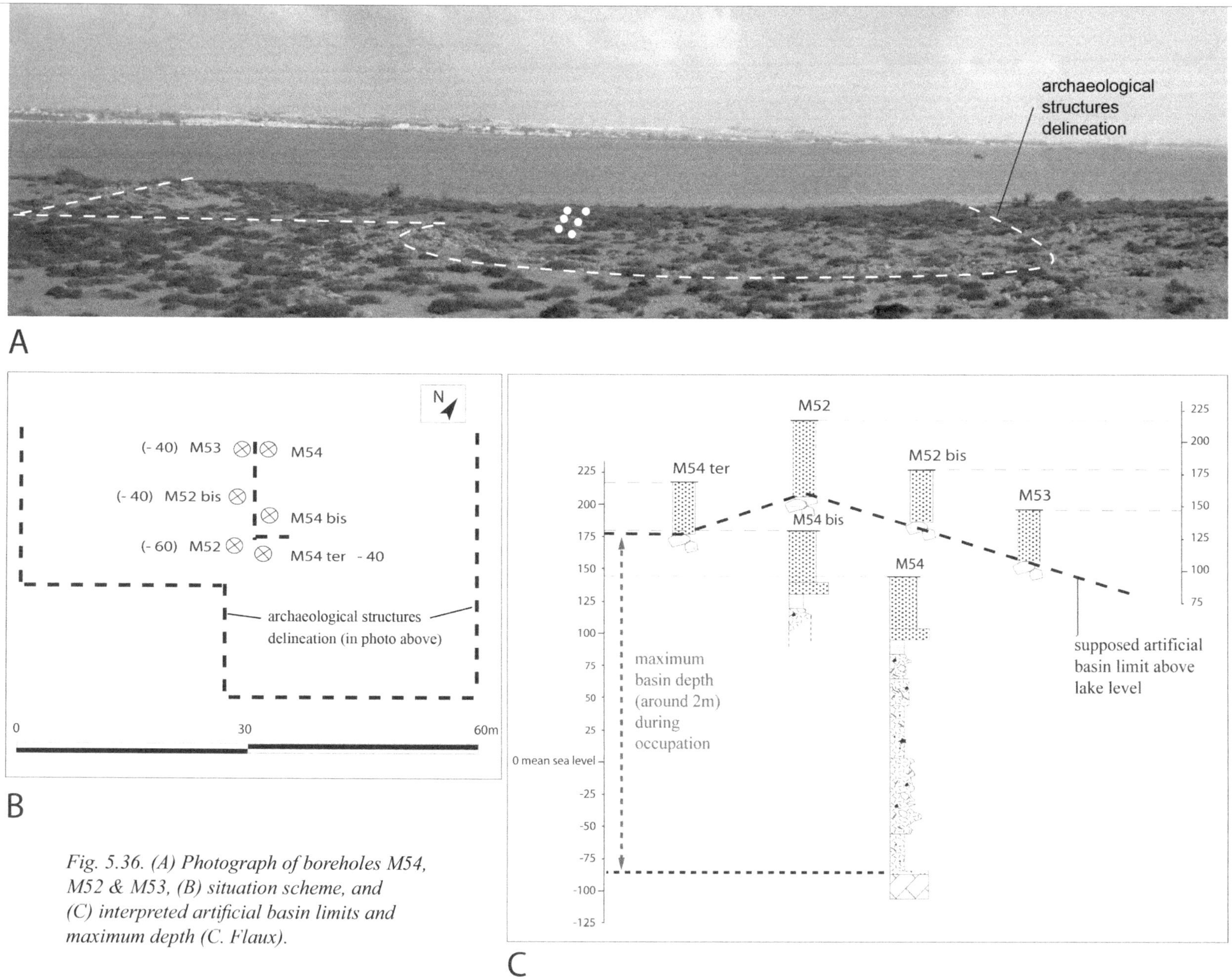

Fig. 5.36. (A) Photograph of boreholes M54, M52 & M53, (B) situation scheme, and (C) interpreted artificial basin limits and maximum depth (C. Flaux).

derma glaucum and *Melanoïdes tuberculata*. In one lake sediment sample observed under the microscope, the ostracod *Cyprideis torosa* was found. These species are presently found in the northern lagoonal belt of the Nile Delta (Bernasconi, *et al.* 1991). *Cerastoderma g.* and *Cyprideis t.* are euryhaline, which means they are very tolerant to salinity changes (Bernasconi, *et al.* 1991). *Melanoïdes t.* indicate low brackish conditions (Plaziat & Younis 2005). Although weakly represented, this fauna describes a lagoon environment with unstable physical conditions and brackish lake water. Though these preliminary results require more study, notably regarding the microfauna, it is likely that such instability derives from Lake Mareotis being at the interface between marine and Nilotic water supply.

5.6.1.3 Laminated facies

The most interesting observation is the fine laminated structure in most of the lacustrine facies. It implies the absence of bioturbation, a sheltered coastal context and probably a cyclic sedimentation mode. Millimetric to infra-millimetric laminations may be linked to annual Nile floods and could constitute a sedimentary record at the annual scale, both the dry season and the flooding season. In the future, it is proposed to use an XRF core scanner. In order to determine the chemical composition of sediments at an infra-millimetric scale. The XRF core scanner should provide a good understanding of various water conditions and sedimentary sources between high and low lake levels. XRF core scanning necessitates a non-destructive sampling method, such as vibracore technology. This study should enable us to assess whether Nile floods reached Lake Mareotis.

5.6.2 Lake level

The present lake level does not constitute a reference point. Indeed, Lake Mareotis is no longer a single body. It has been divided into several basins and its water budget is controlled by human action, mainly by the irrigation systems. In fact, very different lake levels were measured at each site, differences ranging between 0.4 and 2m amsl (Fig. 5.37).

5.6.2.1 Historical lake level

In the 1930s, the lake level was 2m bmsl in the study area (see Fig. 5.3). Low lake levels are described in ancient maps and historical sources from the 17th century: "On peut tirer aussi du sel du Lac Sebaca, [...] mais son eau est salée, & son sel est amer" (Johann Michael Varleb, stayed in Alexandria from the 15th to the 29th of June 1672; Senoune 2008). Earlier, some authors described a connection between Lake Mareotis and the sea: "Le 25 octobre [1588] au matin, nous aperçumes de loin Alexandrie. Vers huit heures, nous laîssames à notre droite le débouché du lac Maréotis" (Reinhold Lubeneau, stayed in Alexandria from the 25th to the 28th of October 1588; Senoune 2006). Much earlier, Strabo in the 1st century AD also described a connection between Lake Mareotis and the western maritime harbour of Alexandria: "Immédiatement après l'Heptastade vient le port d'Eunostos, et, au delà, le port artificiel, dit le Kibôtos, possédant lui aussi ses arsenaux. Plus loin, à l'intérieur de ce port, débouche un canal navigable allant jusqu'au lac Maréôtis" (Charvet 1997). These comments could signify that lake levels at these times were stabilised at sea level. Today, such a connection exists at El-Mex, 7km west of Alexandria. This connection was also described by Gratien le Père (*La Description de l'Égypte*, Empereur 2006). However, even if a connection between Mareotis and the sea did exist during antiquity, there is no evidence about its annual durability. Indeed, as proposed by Gratien le Père (*La Description de l'Égypte*, Empereur 2006), such a connection could have been used only in the case of high Nile levels, to prevent the flooding of Lake Mareotis shores.

5.6.2.2 Lake level geomorphological data

During antiquity, sea level ranged between 0.5 and 1m bmsl (Stanley 2005b; Goiran, *et al.* 2005; Sivan, *et al.* 2004; Morhange, *et al.* 2001). Yet the mean upper lake deposit investigated in this study lies between 0.20 and 1.35m amsl (see Fig. 5.37). Thus, the lake level must have been higher than this latter level in antiquity. Two buried marsh-like deposits were observed on both sides of the island, lying at around 1.5m amsl (see Figs 5.23, 5.27). Sherds found in this deposit give a relative date contemporary to or post-dating the Hellenistic era, since these sherds were potentially used at this time (Section 5.5.2). In borehole M22, some gypsum crystals precipitated inside colluvium deposits between 1.25 and 1.5m amsl (see Fig. 5.15), indicating close proximity of groundwater levels. Moreover, some archaeological structures, probably relating to the lake, also lay at or around 1.5m amsl. These data are summarised in Fig. 5.37, probably indicating an upper lake level at 1.5m amsl during antiquity.

More investigation will be needed to emphasise these preliminary results. Especially, marsh-like facies should be better characterised, thanks to comparison between current and palaeo-facies. Microfauna and organic matter percent will be analysed.

5.6.2.3 A lake level range?

The main difficulty in assessing the lake level during antiquity relates to the potential variability of this level at the annual scale, according to Nile flooding. This variability was described by Strabo: "Á Alexandrie, juste quand l'été commence, les eaux débordées du Nil remplissent le lac [Mariout] et ne laissent subsister sur ses bords aucuns dépôts vaseux de nature à produire des miasmes délétères" (Strabo, XVII I, 7: Charvet 1997), and later by Prosper Alpin, who stayed in Alexandria from March to July 1581: "À côté de la ville se trouve le lac nommé «Maréotis», formé par de l'eau dérivée du Nil mêlée à de l'eau de mer. Ce lac, en effet, lorsqu'il est à son niveau le plus haut, se mêle à la mer au point de sembler lui-même en faire partie" (in Sennoune 2006). As a result, we should search for a lake level range. Sedimentary evidence does not provide a definitive tool to assess such a range because the sediment deposit relative to high lake level can be eroded during the following water retreat. On the other hand, numerous archaeological structures with a lake function should provide a relevant data set. For example, during August

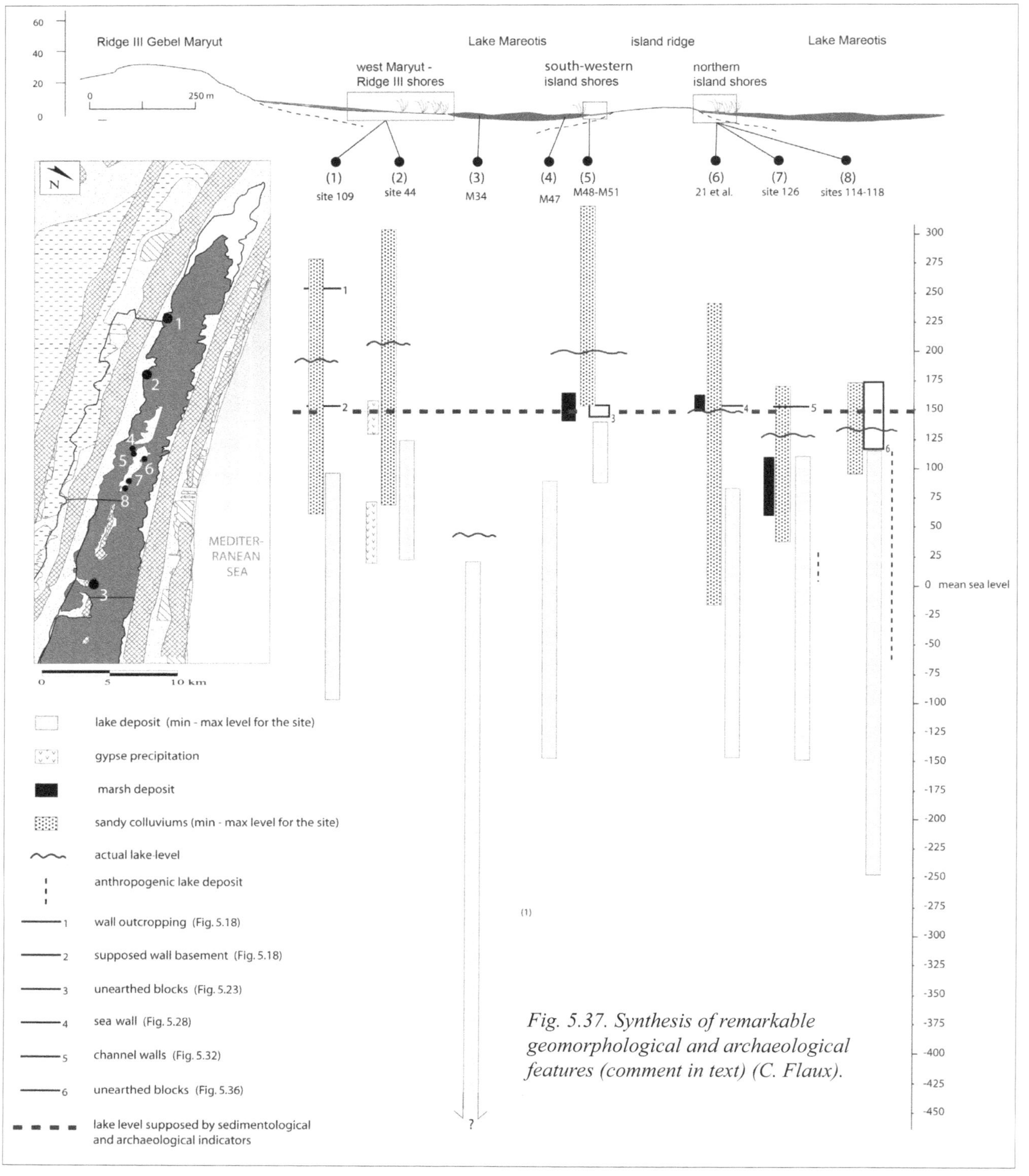

Fig. 5.37. Synthesis of remarkable geomorphological and archaeological features (comment in text) (C. Flaux).

2008, the so-called Mareotis *kibotos* harbour (Site 09) structure was largely submerged. To the west the large kiln site of Taposiris was excavated near the southern shores of Lake Mareotis (Fig. 5.38; El-Ashmawi 1998). In April 2008, the firing chamber of the Taposiris kiln was observed under water. Obviously, the lake level would have been lower during the use of this kiln. As a last example, numerous long jetties have been described along the shores of Lake Mareotis. On Mareotis Island, one of the jetties extends for 250m in length (Site 23; see Chapter 6,). Such a length could derive from an adaptation to annual lake level variation. At low water level stages, the lake experiences a retreat of water, the effects of which on the lake morphology would be noticeable both vertically and horizontally. As such, little as 1m of lake level lowering would result in a large lateral retreat of the shoreline. Thus, during the dry season, the ends of the jetties could still remain in the water and thus, despite the reduced lake water, may still have functioned in the service of vessels (Hopkinson 2007).

5.6.3 Ancient shoreline: lakefront structures hypothesis

5.6.3.1 Mareotis Island used to be an island

Archaeological features with a function related to the lake (jetty, inlet) are mainly situated along the northern coast of the island. As a result it was assumed that the southern shores of the island were thought to be connected to the mainland in antiquity. However, boreholes M34, M47 and M37 (see Figs 5.22, 5.23 & 5.26) have shown continuous lake sedimentation between the island and Ridge III to the south, conferring that the island was an island in antiquity.

As in the case of the latter and the Abusir Ridge II, the island is an ancient coastal ridge that extends parallel to and in between them. The island ridge topography is irregular and emerges as a discontinuous islet belt within Lake Mareotis (see Fig. 5.3). To confirm this hypothesis, a submerged point of this island ridge was assessed in borehole M32 at 0.75m bmsl (see Fig. 5.22), which suggested amongst other things, that from north to south the island ridge presented a barrier to vessels navigating within Lake Mareotis. More study is required to determine the palaeobathymetry of this linear feature and to compare it with contemporary lake levels: this will also provide further insight as to how much the island ridge was an obstacle to lake movement. As such the island ridge, as either an emerged or submerged linear rock feature, divides the western arm of Mareotis into two elongated basins. The north one, as the largest, was used preferentially for navigation. This could partially explain why a higher density of archaeological features was found along the northern shore of the island. One should also note that the city of Marea was also founded upon the same ridge.

5.6.3.2 North-east island: probable small harbour basin

The inlet (Site 126) was investigated to test the hypothesis of a harbour function. It is supported by continuous lake sedimentation inside this basin. A channel delimited by linear archaeological features connects this basin to the main body of Lake Mareotis (see Figs 5.30, 5.32). In the eastern end of the island (Site 114 to Site 118; see Fig. 5.29), lake sediments were also deposited within a small basin delimited by linear structures perpendicular to the present coastline. Archaeological artefacts found inside the upper sequence of lake sedimentation indicate the contemporaneity of basin infilling and land use. This assessment suggests an irregularly shaped shoreline likely determined by archaeological structures latterly regularised by colluviation processes. As the current high water renders excavations difficult in these areas, a dense grid of boreholes to complement the geophysical prospection already conducted in this area, is required to assess the exact nature of this dissected coastline during ancient times.

5.6.4 Shoreline progradation

The western arm of Lake Mareotis (also called Wadi Maryut) is confined within two carbonate ridges, a topographic heritage from ancient littoral ridges formed during the late Pleistocene (El-Asmar & Wood 2000). Oolithic sands, as a main component of these ridges, have been eroded and deposited lower on the hillside. Such colluvial layers can be observed along the hillside of Ridge III (see Figs 5.5, 5.8). These hillside deposits have experienced some pedogenic processes, assessed from carbonate and iron remobilisation. A carbonated red soil has formed, described in this study (see Fig. 5.8) and previously by El-Asmar (1994), Hassouba (1995) and El-Asmar & Wood (2000). Initiation of this process is probably very ancient, as El-Asmar & Wood (2000) have dated this red soil to 65,000 ± 31,000 BP. It seems likely that this formation constitutes the source of sedimentary colluviation products and aeolian transportation observed in this study, covering lake sediments and bringing about the progradation of the shoreline.

Fig. 5.38. Vestige of a Roman kiln, relative indicator of lake level, located near Borg el-Arab. In April 2008, the firing chamber (accessible via a trap-door, at right) was submerged under lake water. This indicated lower lake levels at the time of use of the kiln (C. Flaux).

The stratigraphic position of this formation and other indicators allow a relative dating of the progradation process:

- In cores M49 (see Fig. 5.23) and M46 (see Fig. 5.27), at the base of the colluvial layers, were found sherds common in Mareotis – imported from Gaza between the 4th and 7th century AD and a Hellenistic handle of local production, respectively.
- In cores M48 and M49 (see Fig. 5.23), M52, M52bis, M53 and M54ter (see Fig. 5.36) and also at the back of the inlet (Site 126), archaeological structures were found to be buried by colluvial deposits.
- At the north-western island shore site (see Fig. 5.24), at least part of the colluviation phase was contemporary with land occupation between the 1st and 7th centuries AD. Anthropogenic processes are eventually thought to be responsible. It would explain at least partially the 2m thickness of this deposit at this site, similar to the site lying at the piedmont of Ridge III although the latter has a much more extended watershed (see Figs 5.14, 5.16).
- In cores M54, M55 and M56 (see Fig. 5.35), lake deposits are contemporary with land use (see Section 5.5.3.2.2.1).

• Cores extracted to the east of the survey area as part of a large sedimentological investigation of Lake Mareotis (Flaux, forthcoming) were radiocarbon dated and attest to a drying up phase of the lake after the 9th century AD. Similar sedimentary phases were not identified in the sedimentary facies recorded in the present study area. Here, in almost every case, a sharp contact between sandy plain deposits and lake infilling is attested. It is postulated, therefore, that the sandy colluvial layer deposit above the lake sediments began deposition before the 9th century drying-up phase.

Thus, the colluviation and aeolian transportation processes probably occurred during or after late antiquity. However, within lake sediments we observed a sparse but continuous oolithic sand supply. The burial of lake sediments and of some archaeological structures implies that the highest sediment supply was derived from the hillside. Land abandonment and/or a drier climate could be inferred to explain the higher denudation rate of the hillside. However, the current topography could also be a product of recent land use, as a man-made landscape, as discussed below.

5.6.5 Recent land use

5.6.5.1 *Jessour* or harvesting techniques

Archaeological Sites 44 (see Fig. 5.14), 109 (see Fig. 5.16), and 21 (see Fig. 5.24) support sandy ridges, probably man-made, as indicated by the identification of walls associated with these ridges (see also Chapter 6). At Sites 44 and 21 no impact upon lake sedimentation was observed either side of the ridge (see respectively, Sections 5.5.1.1 & 5.5.3.1.1.3). It has been deduced therefore that these ridges do not have a function that relates directly to the lake, unless perhaps pertaining to the management of flood water from the lake. Rather, their function appears more likely to be linked to an irrigation system, perhaps to restrain the stream of rainwater downhill, which would thus maintain a higher soil moisture content.

Colluvial layers extend up to a depth of 2.50m at Sites 21, 44 and 109 (see Fig. 5.37). It is surprising to find a piedmont accumulation of similar depths at sites with such distinctively different sediment supplies. Site 21 is essentially located on the plain below the island ridge which has a maximum altitude of 5-7m high amsl, whereas Sites 109 and 44 are located at the base of Ridge III (that culminates at 35m high amsl). These two watersheds are very different in size and should not have produced a similar sedimentation rate. Thus, we propose two hypotheses to explain this great sedimentation supply:

• Sediments could derive from land abandonment post-antiquity, with archaeological structures being washed by the rain.

• Anthropogenic action has complemented natural colluviation processes. The implication is that the man-made sand ridges would constitute the topographic remainder of artificial sediment supply in order to reclaim land at the expense of the lake, similar to polder practices. In other words, such sand ridges identified at Sites 21, 109 and 44 would block the sedimentary transit along the hillside and thus allow a greater sedimentation rate in a localised area. At Site 21 (see Figs 5.24, 5.26), the sandy plain lies 0.7m above the closed marsh area. There is no evidence to indicate that this sandy plain could have received a greater sediment supply than the closed marsh area. Moreover, an embankment was observed between the two superficial formations. Thus, it has been proposed that these numerous linear man-made features (sand ridges and walls) operated as sedimentary traps. Such practices are currently known in arid and semi-arid climatic areas. In Tunisia for example, in the region of Medinine, some man-made sedimentary dykes called *jessour* or *tabias*, perpendicular to the slopes of the hillside, i.e. parallel to the ridge, allow sedimentary accumulation behind the dyke, which facilitated soil thickening and a greater groundwater volume after rainfall (Bonvallot 1986; Schiettecatte, *et al.* 2005). These harvesting techniques result from centuries-old experience.

This hypothesis necessitates bibliographical research and investigations into current agricultural operations practiced in semi-arid environment, and particularly in the Mareotis area.

5.6.5.2 Soil management?

Brown soil described at Site 21 and at borehole M55 (see Figs 5.28, 5.35) was found in the upper part of the sedimentary sequence. It has been proposed that this facies found in restricted areas relatively devoid of archaeological structures and usually associated with depressed topography (see Sections 5.5.3.1 & 5.5.3.2.2.3) may derive from grazing practices. Nevertheless, more study is required to better characterise the origin and formation of this facies. Micromorphology and mineralogy would emphasise the analysis of soil structure and composition.

As colluviation processes are expected to have been initiated after antiquity, it is thus proposed that both sandy ridges and brown soil may be related to pastoral land use since ancient times. Furthermore, the present sandy layer that covers almost all sites investigated is very mobile because it is not fixed by vegetation. As a consequence, abandoned brown soil may be rapidly covered by this sand. Such a process was observed in boreholes M44 and M39 where a fine sandy layer 0.03m thick covers the soil. Thus, outcropping soil facies suggests very recent use.

5.7 Conclusion

Forty boreholes were made along the south-western shores of Lake Mareotis. A hypothetic sedimentary sequence can be summarised as follows, based on fieldwork prospections and sedimentary facies descriptions:

• Lake sedimentation occurs above the irregular bedrock topography. A frequent laminated sedimentation may suggest a cyclic sedimentary supply, probably associated with Nile flooding.

• At the top of the sequence, in boreholes realised within archaeological structures at the eastern part of the island, an anthropogenic lake facies has been elucidated. It attests to the lake front function of these ancient remains.

• A lake level was inferred at 1.5m above mean sea-level. It may have been at this level during antiquity.

• A colluviation phase and aeolian transportation has covered lake sediments and induced the progradation of the shoreline. It is believed to have happened after antiquity and may be due to land abandonment.

• Later grazing activities are presumed as a result of a brown soil facies found at the top of the sedimentary sequence. Man-made sandy ridges desiccated the superficial topography and could be related to harvesting practices.

Radiocarbon dating, sedimentological study and geo-chemical analysis are required to ascertain the chronology, and refine and examine sedimentary facies interpretation.

Acknowledgements
Great appreciation is expressed to Dr. Lucy Blue for inviting me to join the Lake Mareotis Research Project and for subsequently reviewing this manuscript. C. Morhange and N. Marriner reviewed the first draft of this manuscript and are thanked for their constructive suggestions. I also thank CEAlex (CNRS, USR 3134) for giving access to topographical maps. Partial funding for the study was obtained from the ANR PALEOMED (dir. C. Morhange) and IMHOTEP Franco-Egyptian project.

Chapter 6. The sites

6.1 Introduction

This chapter addresses each of the sites that were surveyed and examined as part of the Lake Mareotis Research Project.[1] A total of 73 sites are discussed, each site has a unique site number, co-ordinates in latitude and longitude and a general description including detail of specific visible or prominent features (Fig. 6.1). The sites on the southern shore are first addressed from east to west, then those located on the north shore, from east to west, and finally sites located on the island are described, again considered from east to west.

Fig. 6.1. Site numbers and locations of the main sites surveyed during the Lake Mareotis Research Project.

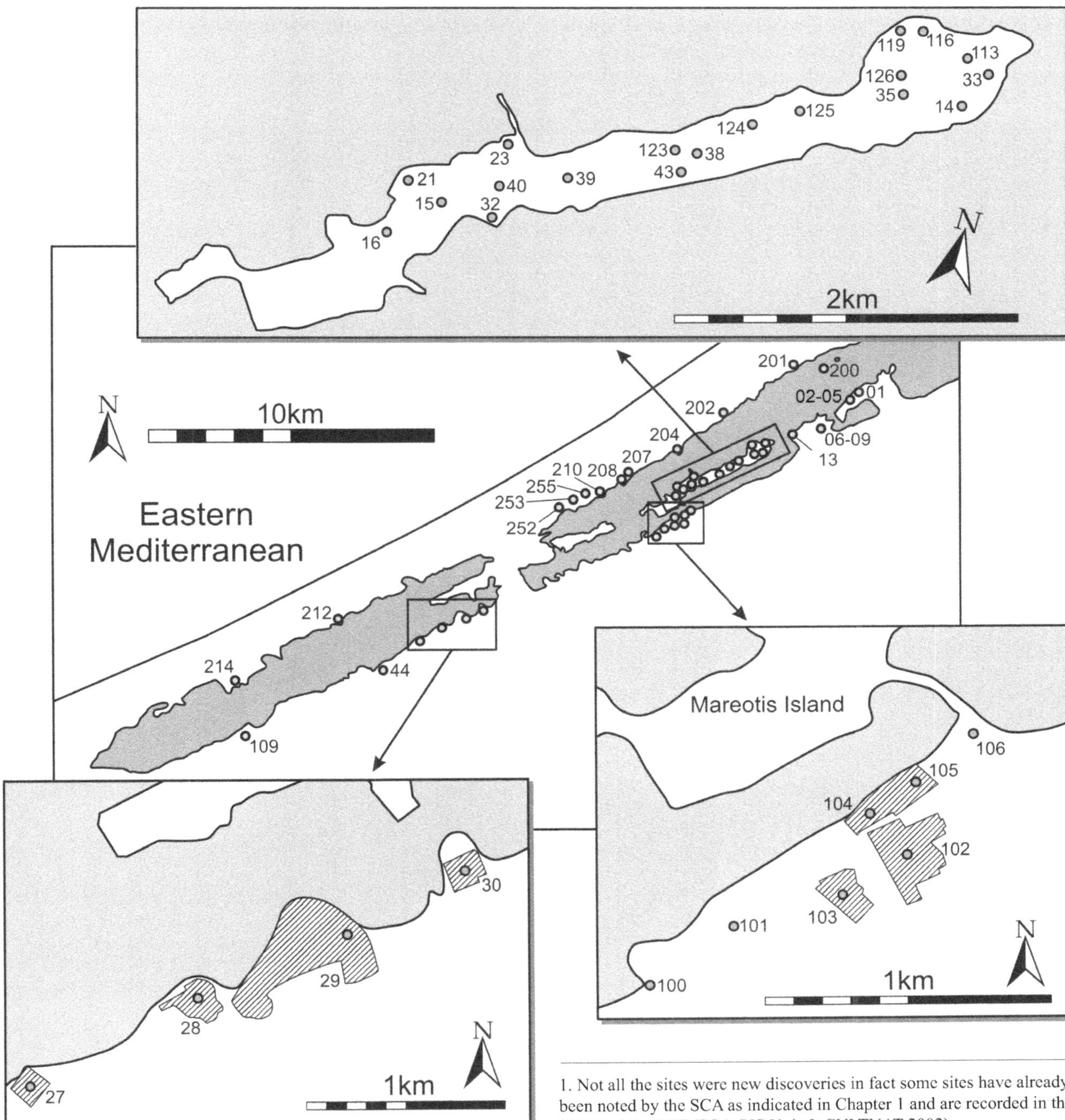

1. Not all the sites were new discoveries in fact some sites have already been noted by the SCA as indicated in Chapter 1 and are recorded in the SCA register REF (SCA GIS Unit & CULTNAT 2002).

At every site where ceramics were collected, a table indicates the quantity of pottery types recovered. These tables essentially consider indicator sherds (rims, bases and handles), with body sherds included only if they provide the sole evidence for particular types, not if they duplicate sherds represented by indicators. Body sherds were not used in the calculation of relative percentages and are enclosed within brackets on the tables. After the pottery type an internal reference to the drawn examples is given to the figure numbers from Chapter 4 (as e.g. no. 1) for every type that is illustrated. The main distinguishable Egyptian fabrics are described in Chapter 4 and rigorously applied to all the illustrated material. The remainder, when it was difficult to distinguish between classic Nile-silt alluvial fabrics and those produced more locally, are simply noted as "Egyptian".

For each site where 20 or more sherds were collected, the relative percentage of different ceramic types are represented in the table and a pie graph displays the chronological distribution, broken down as Ptolemaic (late 4th to mid 1st centuries BC), Early Roman (late 1st century BC to 3rd century AD) and Late Roman (4th through 7th centuries AD). Ptolemaic-Roman is used for pottery that is essentially undated within these periods.[2] Because of the overlap between Late Ptolemaic and Early Roman pottery types, the Early Roman period may sometimes be slightly over-represented on the pie graphs and this should be taken into consideration. Similarly, sherds dated Early/Late Roman overlap between the two periods on the pie graphs.

For the six sites where more than 300 sherds were collected (Sites 15, 35, 40, 113, 207-8, 204-5), further interrogation was conducted on the data based on form criteria, represented as bar graphs in the text. Types that straddle more than one period e.g. belonging to both the Early and Late Roman periods, appear only on the total bar.[3]

Fig. 6.2. Location of Sites 01-05.

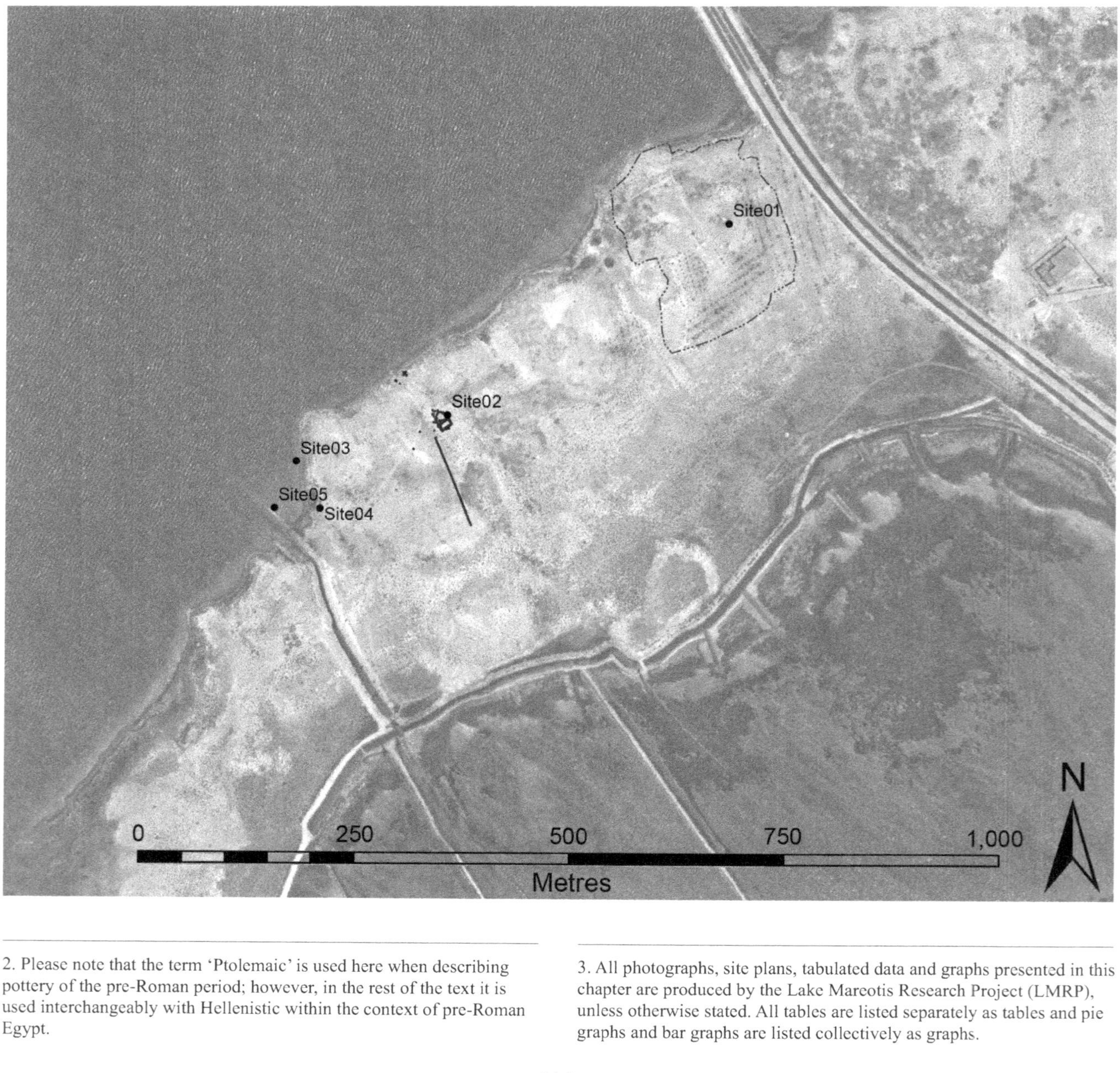

2. Please note that the term 'Ptolemaic' is used here when describing pottery of the pre-Roman period; however, in the rest of the text it is used interchangeably with Hellenistic within the context of pre-Roman Egypt.

3. All photographs, site plans, tabulated data and graphs presented in this chapter are produced by the Lake Mareotis Research Project (LMRP), unless otherwise stated. All tables are listed separately as tables and pie graphs and bar graphs are listed collectively as graphs.

6.2 Sites located along the southern shore of the lake

Sites 01-05 (Fig. 6.2)
Sites 01-05 are located along the shoreline to the west of the Marea Peninsula and west of the Sidi Kerir-Borg el-Arab road. The shoreline of this peninsula is 2.6km long and the Sidi Kerir road divides it into two halves. The site of Marea is located towards the east and Sites 01-05 are located to the west of the road along the western half of the same peninsula. However, in antiquity, Sites 01-05 could have been part of the Marea area and thus will be considered as a group. The south-western part of the peninsula has been artificially dredged to create modern fish farms; therefore, the area between the southern shore of the peninsula and the main southern shoreline is completely inundated. Recent increase in lake water levels has caused a number of the waterline structures identified in 2004 to become submerged. Limited excavation has been conducted in the area specifically in relation to Site 02.

Site 01(Fig. 6.3; Graph 6.1; Table 6.1)
Location: 30 59 18N 29 38 44E
Description: Site 01 is located about 700m west of Marea on the west side of the Sidi Kerir road. It is a coastal tell that is approximately 5m high.[4] The site contains several archaeological features that were partially excavated as part of previous Supreme Council of Antiquities (SCA) investigations.

To the east of the survey area, a tell site was identified some 190m E-W and 230m N-S, which was partially bulldozed. The tell contains scattered limestone blocks and pottery sherds.

Site 01 has a sample of 77 indicator sherds, primarily 2nd to 1st centuries BC in date, although a second smaller assemblage belongs to the 5th to 7th centuries AD. Exclusively Early Roman types were rare; those dating the Ptolemaic/Early Roman or Early/Late Roman more common. Six

Fig. 6.3. Site 01.

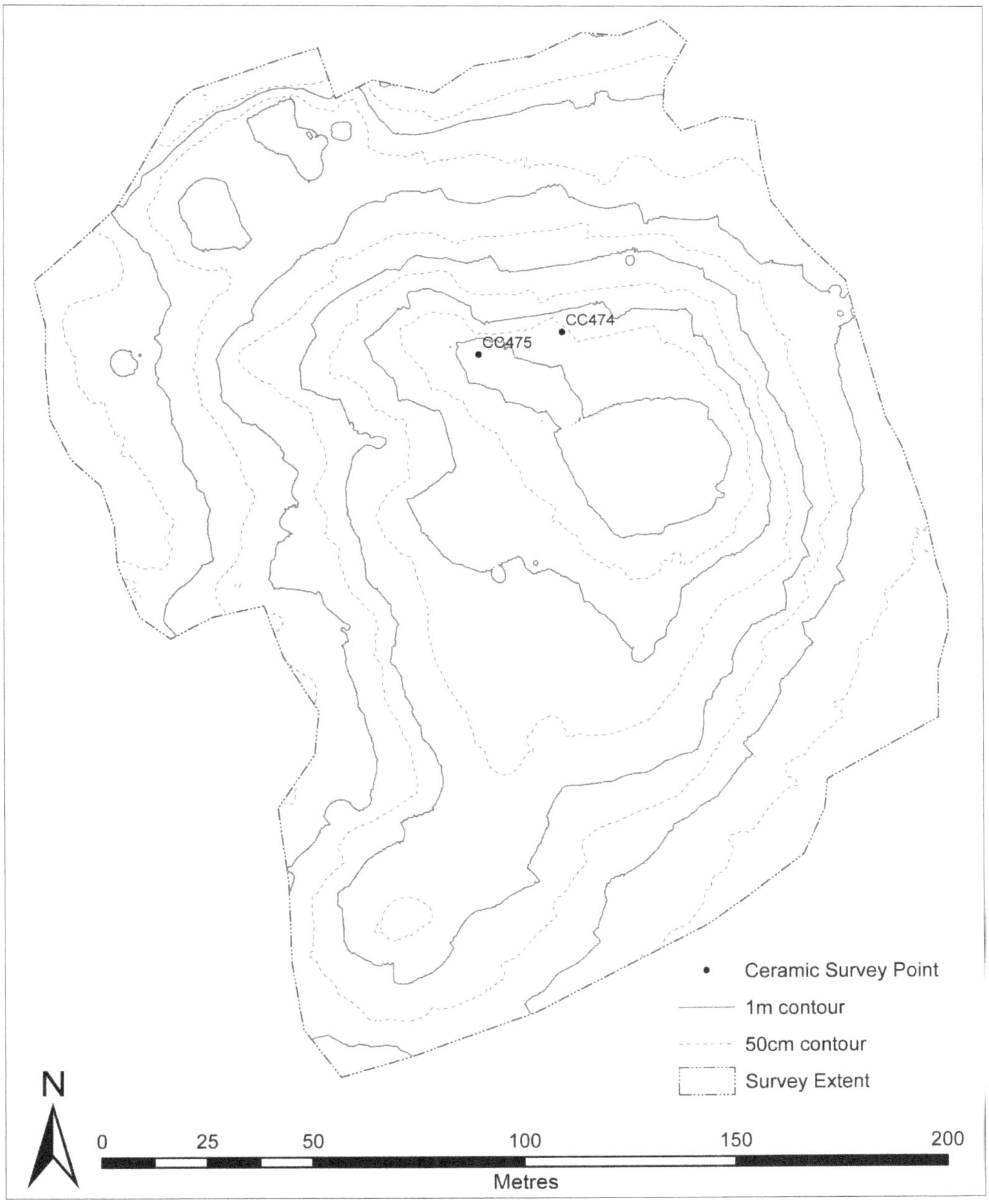

4. The word 'tell' is used here to reference the local term for a site that may, or more likely, may not, have formed as the result of accumulated archaeological material over time. Most commonly in this context, the mounds or low hills equate to ancient settlements located on top of natural limestone outcrops.

Fig. 6.4. Possible lake wall associated with Site 01.

sakkia pot sherds were found together in ceramic circle CC473 which may indicate a *sakkia* (water-wheel) was used in the vicinity.

To the north of the tell, less than 10m from the lake's shoreline, there is another site which was partially excavated by the SCA, revealing a wall that is aligned parallel to the shore. The wall is made of regular limestone blocks (c. 0.25m x 0.25m x 0.25m) secured with thick red mortar. The thick red mortar indicates that the structure was originally built to be exposed to the water, therefore it could be a lake wall built to protect the shoreline from the accumulation of sediments (Fig. 6.4).

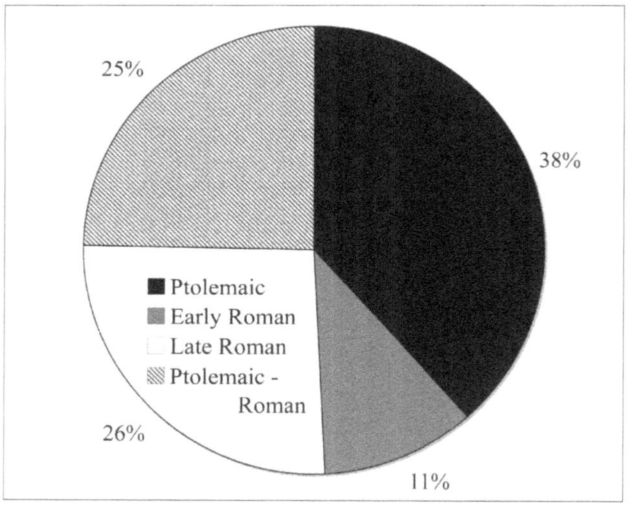

Type	No.	%
Finewares		
African Red Slip ware (ARS) 105	1	1.3
African Red Slip ware (ARS) 99 (no. 100)	1	1.3
Cypriot Red Slip ware (CRS) 9 (nos 105-6)	4	5.2
Egyptian red slip bowl	2	2.6
Egyptian Red Slip ware B (ERSB)	2	2.6
Egyptian silt red slip fish dish (nos 54-5)	2	2.6
?Imported black slip footring base (no. 94)	1	1.3
Coarse wares		
Egyptian basin	2	2.6
Egyptian silt casserole (nos 49-51)	1	1.3
Egyptian silt cup	1	1.3
Egyptian silt dolium	2	2.6
Egyptian silt funnel strainer (no. 33)	3	4.0
Egyptian silt handle	1	1.3
Egyptian silt jug	4	5.2
Egyptian silt lid	1	1.3
Egyptian silt *sakkia* pot (nos 35-41)	6	7.8
Mareotic jug	1	1.3
Amphorae		
Abu Mena LR Amphora 5 (nos 87-9)	1	1.3
Cilician/Cypriot LR Amphora 1 (nos 146-9)	3	3.9
Egyptian LR Amphora 7	3	3.9
Imported unidentified type	3	3.9
Knidian handle	2	2.6
Koan (nos 126-30)	7	9.1
Mareotic AE1/2 (nos 1-3)	9	11.7
Mareotic AE1/2 long handle (nos 4-5)	8	10.4
Mareotic AE1/2 short handle (no. 6)	2	2.6
Mareotic AE4 (nos 13-17)	1	1.3
Mareotic unidentified type	1	1.3
Rhodian IE2/IF (nos 121-6)	2	2.6
Total	77	100%

Table 6.1. (above) Quantity of pottery types for Site 01.

Graph 6.1. Pie graph showing the chronological breakdown of pottery from Site 01.

Site 02 (Figs 6.5 & 6.6)
Location: 30 59 18N 29 38 44E
Description: To the west of the tell Site 01 a number of remains were identified, subsequently identified as Site 02. About 70m south of the shoreline there is a 12.1m x 6.7m basin made of limestone and red brick, lined with red plaster (*opus signinum*), which indicates that is was made to contain liquid (Fig. 6.6). Considering its size and nature, the basin was probably a *natatio* (pool) that belonged to a bath complex. The entrance to the basin was from the north-east corner where the remains of steps made of limestone blocks still exist. Attached to the northern side of the basin are the remains of a round structure; probably a *sakkia* (water-wheel) which was used for lifting water from a well into the basin. The diameter of the *sakkia* is about 9m, which makes it comparable to other similar structures found during the survey (see below).

To the southwest of the basin and *sakkia* complex a channel was recorded clearly associated with the basin and visible on the surface. The channel extended some 40m to the south/southeast and appears to be connected to another building located to the south (see Fig. 6.2).

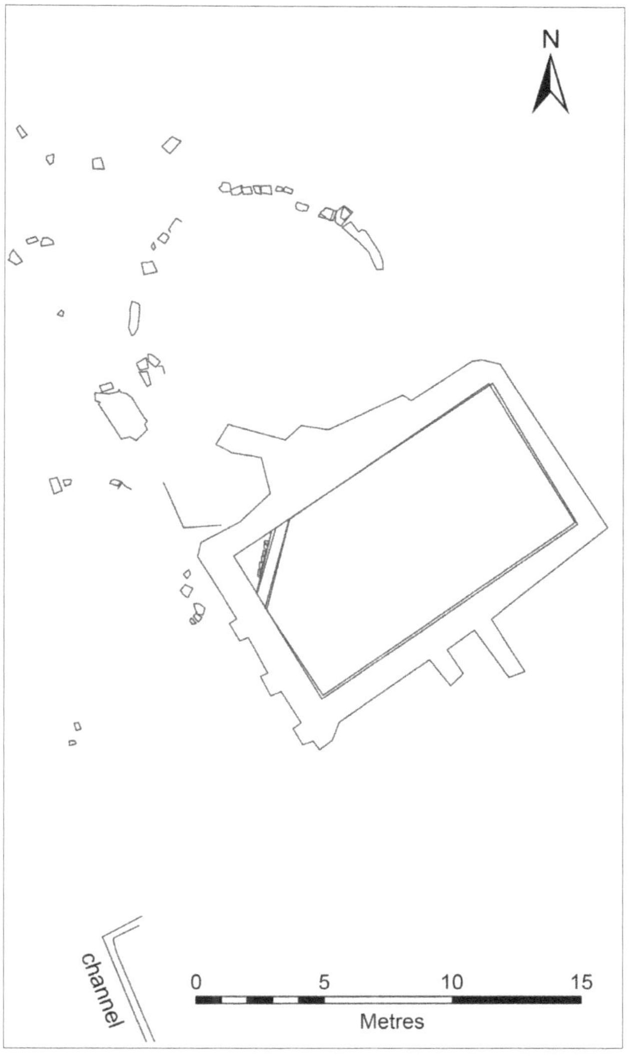

Fig. 6.5. (right) Site 02.

Fig. 6.6. (below) Limestone and brick-lined basin associated with Site 02.

Site 03 (Fig. 6.2)
Location: 30 59 17N 29 38 38E
Description: This site contains two small, semi-circular structures made of red bricks lined with red plaster. The first structure is 4m x 1.8m and the second is 2.2m x 1.7m. This site was first identified in 2004 when the structures were located some 2m from the waterline. However, in 2007 they were completely submerged, and in 2008 they were not possible to relocate due to the rise in water level. The exact use of these structures is unclear; however, their nature and location could suggest that they might have been used as fish tanks or for storing shellfish.

Site 04 (Fig. 6.2)
Location: 30 59 15N 29 38 38E
Description: This is a pile of black stones about 4m in diameter, which does not appear to be associated with any other remains. Therefore, it is possible that this pile of stones could be ballast dumped by a merchant vessel that was operating on Lake Mareotis. In 2004 this pile of stones was less than 2m from the waterline while in 2007 it was under water.

Site 05 (Fig. 6.7)
Location: 30 59 15N 29 38 36E
Description: This is a possible mole made of piled irregular limestone blocks without any evidence for the use of mortar. The mole is about 40m long and 4m wide. This site is about 30m west of the ballast pile associated with Site 04. It is also located directly opposite Site 200 on the northern shore of the lake. The distance between Site 05 and Site 200 is less than 1.5km. At present, due to the rise of water level, this mole is almost entirely submerged.

Fig. 6.7. Site 05 general view.

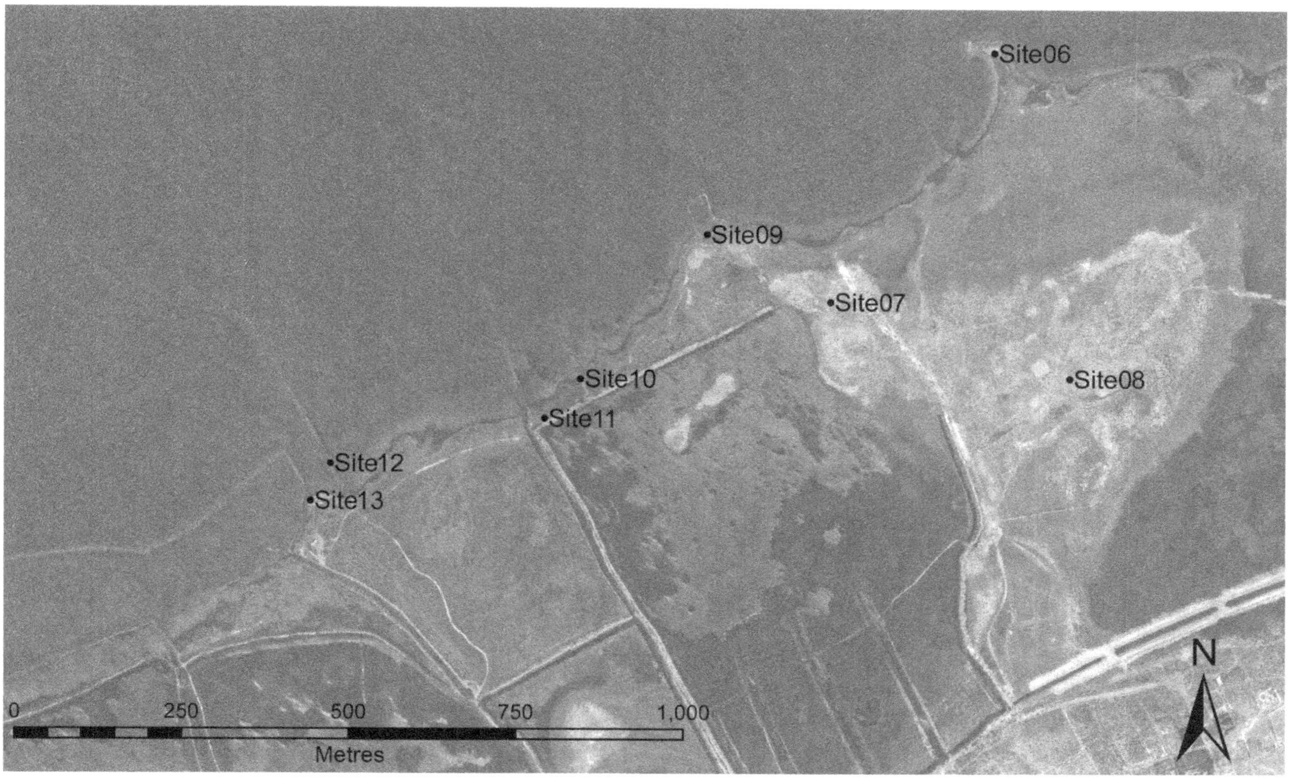

Fig, 6.8. Location of Sites 06-13.

Sites 06-13
Sites 06-13 extend along the southern shore for a distance of approximately 1.5km. They are located in an unstable area of the lake's southern shore, which has been subject to a change of water level as well as sedimentation. This area is backed from the south by fish farms, therefore it is constantly changing as a result of inundation and reclamation of land. A number of archaeological sites that were identified during the 2004 survey are currently completely inaccessible as a result of canals being dug around them for the use of the fish farms. However, in antiquity, it is possible that these sites were also part of the larger Marea Peninsula, although currently it is not possible to study them in detail.

Sites 06-09 (Fig. 6.8)
Sites 06-09 are located around an embayment some 450m across.

Site 06
Location: 30 58 59N 29 38 08E
Description: This site is a small natural rocky headland about 25m x 25m in size that appears to have been extended to the northwest in antiquity connected by limestone blocks to create a sheltered embayment (Fig. 6.9).

The headland is joined to the mainland to the south by a narrow causeway that creates a promontory c. 100m in length. About 150m south of the promontory, a number of previously excavated trenches were identified exposing a great deal of ceramic sherds. About 160m southwest of the shoreline end of the promontory there is a limestone mole which extends for about 60m into the water. At the time of survey, the southern end of the mole was submerged due to the high water level and as a result we were unable to record this feature.

To the southeast of the promontory there is a small tell site about 100m x 50m, which contains scattered pottery sherds and limited building stones. The promontory at Site 06 forms the eastern side of a bay about 450m wide. The box-shaped harbour Site 09 is located on the western site of the bay.

Fig. 6.9. Site 06 general view of headland (now largely submerged).

Site 07 (Fig. 6.8; Graph 6.2; Table 6.2)
Location: 30 58 47N 29 37 53E
Description: This site is located about 200m southeast of Site 09. It is a 30m long line of individual large limestone blocks about 0.8m x 1.5m x 0.6m. The blocks are not *in situ* but had been moved from another location, probably from Site 09 as they display similar characteristics.

Site 07 has a sample of 75 indicator sherds. While there is a Knidian handle that could date to the late 4th century BC, the assemblage is more likely to date from the 2nd century BC. The bulk of the assemblage belongs to the 5th to 7th centuries AD with LR Amphora 1 being the most common type.

Table 6.2. (right) Quantity of pottery types for Site 07.

Graph 6.2. (below) Pie graph showing the chronological breakdown of pottery from Site 07.

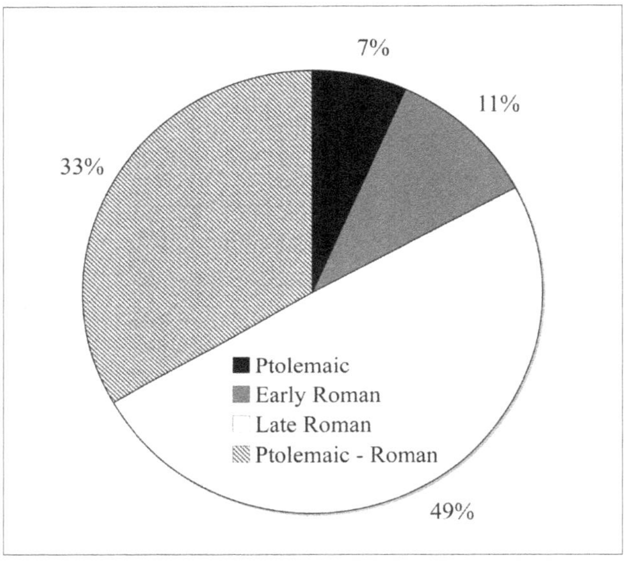

Type	**No.**	**%**
Finewares		
Egyptian red slip bowl	3	4.0
Cypriot Red Slip ware (CRS)	2	2.7
Cypriot Red Slip ware (CRS) 9 (nos 105-6)	1	1.3
Egyptian Red Slip ware C (ERSC) copy of ARS104	2	2.7
Coarse wares		
Egyptian basin	4	5.3
Egyptian bowl	1	1.3
Egyptian silt cooking pot	4	5.3
Egyptian silt dolium	2	2.7
Egyptian silt jug	6	8.0
Egyptian silt lid	3	4.0
Egyptian silt miscellaneous coarse ware	1	1.3
Egyptian small coarse ware handle	1	1.3
Amphorae		
Abu Mena LR Amphora 5 (nos 87-9)	9	12.0
Cilician/Cypriot LR Amphora 1 (nos 146-9)	18	24.0
Egyptian LR Amphora 7	5	6.7
Knidian handle	1	1.3
Koan (nos 126-30)	1	1.3
Mareotic AE1/2 short handle (no. 6)	1	1.3
Mareotic AE4 (nos 13-17)	3	4.0
Mareotic Mons Claudianus Type 22/3 (nos 9-12)	3	4.0
Mareotic unidentified type	1	1.3
Rhodian IE2/IF (nos 121-6)	2	2.7
Unidentified	1	1.3
Total	75	100%

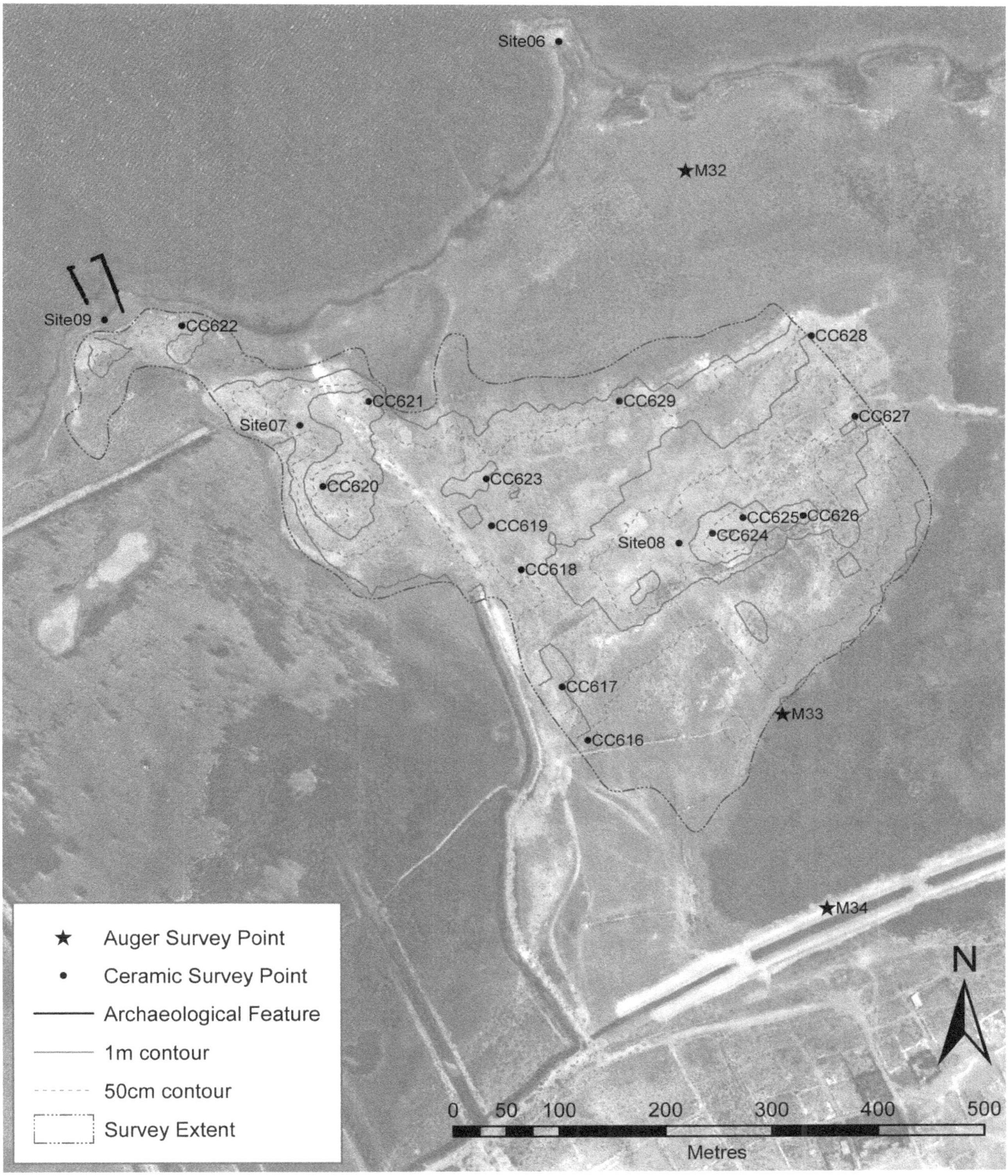

Fig. 6.10. Site 08.

Site 08 (Fig. 6.10; Graph 6.3; Table 6.3)
Location: 30 58 47N 29 37 52E
Description: Site 08 extends over the whole promontory south of Sites 06, 07 and 09. The area is about 600m E-W and 250m N-S. The site contains a number of SCA test trenches that revealed some walls made of irregular limestone imbedded in lime mortar. To the west it also displays a round opening (c. 1m in diameter) which leads to a cistern (Fig. 6.11). From the opening water can still be seen; however, the cistern is full of debris.

Site 08 has a sample of 182 indicator sherds. The pottery represents activity potentially as early as the late 3rd century BC but more likely the 2nd, continuing into the 7th century AD. Material of the late 4th and especially 5th to 7th centuries dominates, amphorae being most common. As is frequently seen LR Amphora 1 was the most common Late Roman type, but LR Amphora 4 was also notable in quantity.

Fig. 6.11. Site 08: opening of cistern.

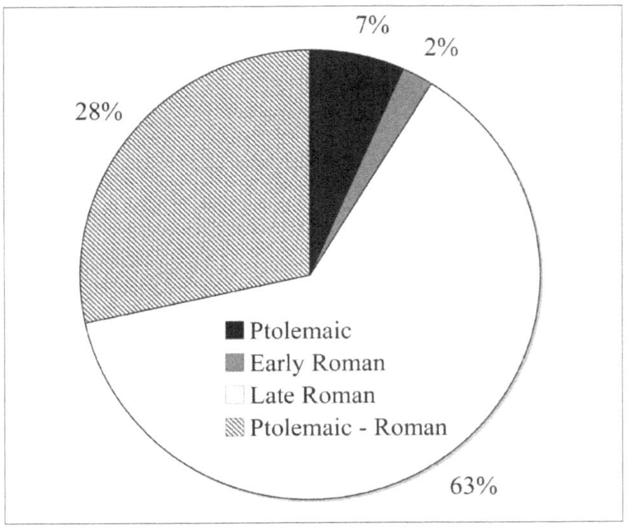

Graph 6.3. Pie graph showing the chronological breakdown of pottery from Site 08.

Table 6.3. Quantity of pottery types for Site 08.

Type	No.	%
Finewares		
African Red Slip ware (ARS)	1	0.5
Cypriot Red Slip ware (CRS)	4	2.2
Cypriot Red Slip ware (CRS) 2 (nos 103-4)	3	1.6
Cypriot Red Slip ware (CRS) 9 (nos 105-6)	3	1.6
Egyptian Red Slip ware A (ERSA) copy of CRS 9 (no. 76)	1	0.5
Phocaean Red Slip ware (PRS) 3 (nos 108-9)	2	1.1
Coarse wares		
Egyptian basin	7	3.8
Egyptian bowl	1	0.5
Egyptian miscellaneous coarse ware	3	1.6
Egyptian silt casserole	1	0.5
Egyptian silt casserole (nos 49-51)	2	1.1
Egyptian silt cooking pot	10	5.5
Egyptian silt cooking pot (no. 45)	2	1.1
Egyptian silt jug	12	6.6
Egyptian silt lid	3	1.6
Egyptian silt *sakkia* pot (nos 35-41)	2	1.1
Egyptian silt strainer (no. 32)	6	3.3
Mareotic jug	8	4.4
Amphorae		
Abu Mena LR Amphora 5 (nos 87-9)	5	2.7
Cilician/Cypriot Egloff 169 (no. 145)	4	2.2
Cilician/Cypriot LR Amphora 1 (nos 146-9)	69	37.9
Egyptian LR Amphora 7	1	0.5
Egyptian silt Mons Claudianus Type 2/12 (no. 86)	(1)	0.0
Gaza LR Amphora 4 Majcherek Forms 2-4 (nos 154-7)	12	6.6
Imported unidentified type	1	0.5
Koan (nos 126-30)	4	2.2
Mareotic AE1/2 (nos 1-3)	2	1.1
Mareotic AE1/2 long handle (nos 4-5)	2	1.1
Mareotic AE1/2 short handle (no. 6)	1	0.5
Mareotic AE4 (nos 13-17)	2	1.1
Mareotic unidentified type	3	1.6
Rhodian IE2/IF (nos 121-6)	3	1.6
Tunisian Africana III (no. 151)	2	1.1
Other		
Egyptian marl figurine (no. 92)	(1)	0.0
Total	182 (2)	100%

Site 09 (Figs 6.12 & 6.13; Graph 6.4; Table 6.4)
Location: 30 58 51N 29 37 47E
Description: This site includes one of the most substantial maritime structures along the southern shore of Lake Mareotis. It is a harbour built of large undressed limestone blocks and due to its box shape it is referred to as the "*kibotos*". The harbour consists of a series of moles which enclose an area c. 60m long N-S and 36m wide E-W. The eastern mole, which is the most complete, is 60m long and is constructed of a single line of blocks at its south-

Fig. 6.12. Detailed plan of kibotos, *Site 09.*

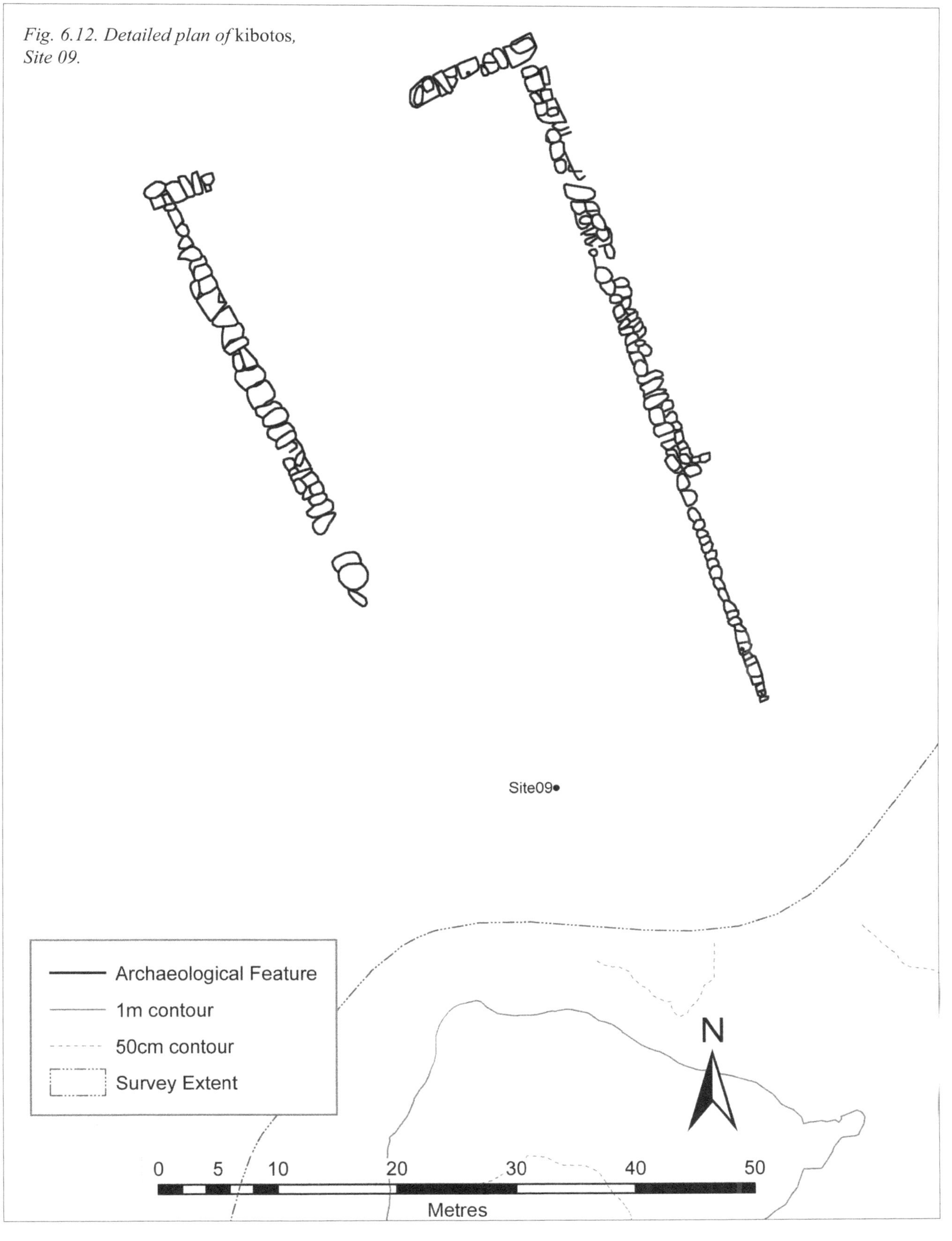

Fig. 6.13. (above) General shot of harbour Site 09.

Fig. 6.14. (below) Site 09: eastern mole.

ern end. This doubles in breadth along the length of the mole. At its northern extremity the mole returns to the west for a distance of 12m (Figs 6.14 & 6.15). The western mole, some 40m extant in length, is partially damaged at its southern end and returns to the east at the northern end for a distance of some 6m. A gap of 18m between the ends of the two moles represents the entrance of the harbour. The moles of the harbour are c. 2m wide and consist of at least three courses of large limestone blocks (c. 1.1m x 0.7m x 0.5m). The remains of thick red mortar can be seen between and beneath some of the stones of the upper course. Amongst the distinctive features of this harbour structure is a mooring ring carved in a limestone block of the upper course of the mole which interest-

Fig. 6.15. Site 09: eastern mole.

ingly, would have facilitated the mooring of vessels to the outside rather than the inside of the harbour (Fig. 6.16). The harbour is oriented SE-NW with the entrance facing NW.

The size of the building blocks, the method by which they were arranged, and the shape of the harbour, suggests that it could be of an early Hellenistic or even pre-Hellenistic date. Box-shaped harbours were quite common in the Pharaonic period particularly on the Nile. Moreover, Strabo (17.1.10) mentions a *kibotos "Κιβωτός"* (box-shaped) harbour inside the Western Harbour of Alexandria.

On the other hand, the use of coarse red mortar probably means that the harbour was in use at least until the Late Roman period.

Being located at the head of a peninsula, this harbour was significantly affected by the changes in the lake's water level. When El-Fakharani (1983) studied some of the Mareotic harbours in the late seventies, this harbour was completely land-locked, and the shore of the lake was several metres north of the harbour. However, at present, this harbour is almost completely submerged under the lake's surface.

Fig. 6.16. Mooring block associated with Site 09.

Site 09 has a sample of 33 indicator sherds although the majority of these were collected to the east of the harbour structure, along the shore, and thus may actually date general activity in the area rather than necessarily the harbour itself. All the dateable sherds, apart from one handle from a Knidian amphora, are Roman in date. Mareotic amphorae of the mid 1st to mid 3rd centuries AD and imported Late Roman amphorae (LR Amphorae 1, 2 and 4) from the 5th century AD, are also present. The lack of pre-Hellenic material is interesting considering previous claims that the *kibotos* type harbours may be Pharaonic in date (El-Fakharani 1983). Similarly, the lack of Abu Mena amphorae may indicate an absence of occupation during the 7th century, although both may be the result of a small assemblage size.

Type	No.	%
Coarse wares		
Egyptian bowl	1	3.0
Egyptian small coarse ware handle	2	6.1
Amphorae		
Aegean LR Amphora 2	8	24.2
Cilician/Cypriot Egloff 169 (no. 145)	1	3.0
Cilician/Cypriot LR Amphora 1 (nos 146-9)	4	12.2
Gaza LR Amphora 4 Majcherek Forms 2-4 (nos 154-7)	2	6.1
Imported unidentified type (no. 170)	1	3.0
Knidian handle	1	3.0
Mareotic AE4 (nos 13-17)	13	39.4
Total	33	100%

Table 6.4. Quantity of pottery types for Site 09.

Graph 6.4. Pie graph showing the chronological breakdown of pottery from Site 09.

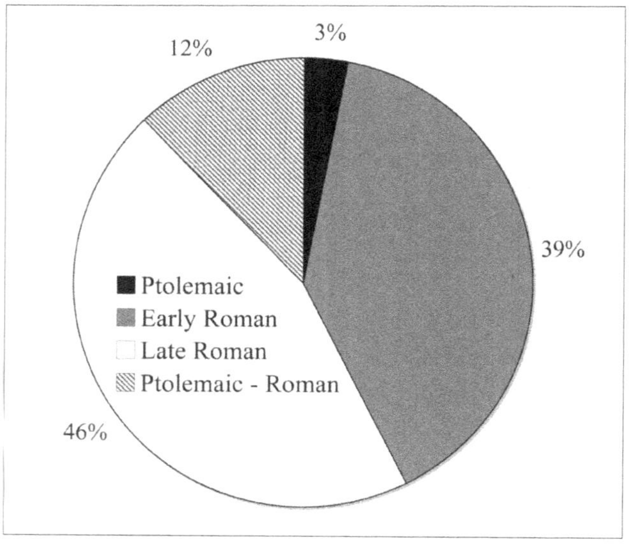

Site 10 (Fig. 6.8)
Location: 30 58 43N 29 37 39E
Description: This site is located c. 300m west of Site 09. It contains the remains of a badly preserved mole made of piled limestone extending into the lake. The remaining part of the mole is c. 10m long, but some limestone blocks could be seen aligned in the water which suggests that the mole may have previously been longer.

Site 11 (Fig. 6.8)
Location: 30 58 41N 29 37 37E
Description: This site is located c. 90m west of Site 10. It consists of the remains of a badly preserved mole made of piled limestone extending into the lake for a length of c. 20m.

Site 12 (Fig. 6.8)
Location: 30 58 37N 29 37 27E
Description: About 300m west of Site 11 and immediately east of and associated with Site 13, a mole was identified. The mole extended into the lake for c. 70m and is 3m wide. It is badly preserved and made of irregular piles of limestone.

The similarities between Sites 10, 11 and 12 are noticeable. All three moles are poorly constructed. The structures also appear to have been built in an area that has been subject to high levels of sedimentation that has resulted in the moles being largely buried and thus difficult to study without excavation. These moles were first recorded in 2004; however, in the 2008 survey they were mostly under water and hence very difficult to relocate.

Site 13 (Figs 6.8, 6.17 & 6.18)
Location: 30 58 37N 29 37 25E
Description: This is probably the most controversial structure in the Mareotic region. The shape and structure of this building are quite complex and unique, therefore it was referred to during the survey project as the "complex building". The building is located c. 700m west of Site 09. It is aligned E-W along the shore and is based upon a monolithic platform and is entirely contained within a continuous wall (some 3.5m wide) constructed

Fig. 6.17. Plan and elevation of Site 13.

of huge blocks, some as large as 2m in length and 1m wide (although usually c. 0.6m) and c. 1m high, substantially larger than any others recorded around the lake. The outer casing blocks of the wall are shaped to give the effect of a continuous smooth outside surface sloping up and inward at an angle of roughly 40 degrees from the foot of the building (Figs 6.19-6.21). The maximum dimensions of the building are 40m in length E-W and 19m wide N-S. From the east, the building is approached by an E-W orientated extension 'arm' that is c. 2.5m wide in the east, enlarging to a maximum width of 8m in the west where it merges with the main section of the extant building (Figs 6.22 & 6.23). The main section of the building is some 22m E-W and 19m N-S and is preserved to a maximum height of 3m.

Haggag (2010b: 49) describes the building as follows: "The blocks of the outer casing are carefully cut and fitted together in oblique joints without using any mortar except for a foliage layer of non reddish mortar used in some of the courses to facilitate the sliding of such gigantic sized blocks. These external walls are slanting inward at an angle of about 40 degrees, and are based on larger foundation blocks with squared edges. The building is entered from the south by means of a ramp of dressed and carefully fitted stone blocks (Haggag 1984: 277-80). The use of rough masonry for the core while the huge blocks of the facing are very carefully polished, the oblique joints of the blocks, the use of such a thin layer of mortar, the inward slanting of the outer walls as well as the general plan of the building, are clear indications to a Late Pharaonic date". El-Fakharani (1984: 25) also supported a Pharaonic date for this building, he believed that it was a fort that was erected by Psammeticus of the 26th Dynasty. Yet he provides no evidence to support this suggestion.

However, the exact nature, date and function of this building remain unknown, partially due to the fact that an associated ceramic assemblage was absent on the surface in the vicinity of the site. Therefore, when the site was first surveyed by the Lake Mareotis Research Project in 2006, future excavation was planned to answer some of these critical questions. However, when the site was re-visited in 2008 it was unfortunately inaccessible due to the rise of water level. Moreover, a small tell was identified some 500m to the north of the site, but it too was inaccessible.

Fig. 6.18. General view of Site 13.

Fig. 6.19. Block detail of Site 13.

Fig. 6.20. Block detail of Site 13.

In sum, Sites 06 to 13 (Fig. 6.8) appear to have all been situated along the northern shoreline of a promontory that extends west from Marea. The shores of this promontory have recently been subject to dredging in some locations such as the area south of Sites 10 and 11, in order to accommodate fish farms. This has resulted in the creation on an artificial basin about 740m x 490m in the middle of the promontory. The low-lying nature of the promontory has meant that it is particularly susceptible to sedimentation as well as changes in water level. It is possible that this promontory equates to an extension of the site of Marea in antiquity.

Fig. 6.21. Block detail of Site 13.

Fig. 6.22. General view of Site 13 from the east.

Fig. 6.23. General view of Site 13 from the east.

Sites 100-106 (Fig. 6.1)

Site 106 (Figs 6.24 & 6.25)
Location: 30 57 06N 29 35 15E
Description: This site is located on the shoreline opposite the western end of Mareotis Island. The main archaeological feature of the site is a section of a circular building made of limestone blocks previously exposed by the SCA. The feature was identified as the outer wall of a *sakkia* (water-wheel). Based on the dimensions of the remaining section it is believed that the *sakkia* was c.7.3m in diameter (Fig. 6. 24). The blocks were mostly arranged in headers and their dimensions 0.5m x 0.35m x 0.2m. In association with the *sakkia* structure there are the remains of a network of stone water channels for transporting the water that was lifted by the *sakkia* for irrigation purposes. Site 106 has a sample of only two Late Roman sherds (4th to 7th centuries AD), comprising an Egyptian Red Slip ware A (ERSA) copy of ARS 91A (no. 161) and a Late Roman silt strainer.

Fig. 6.24. General view of Site 106 and sakkia *structure.*

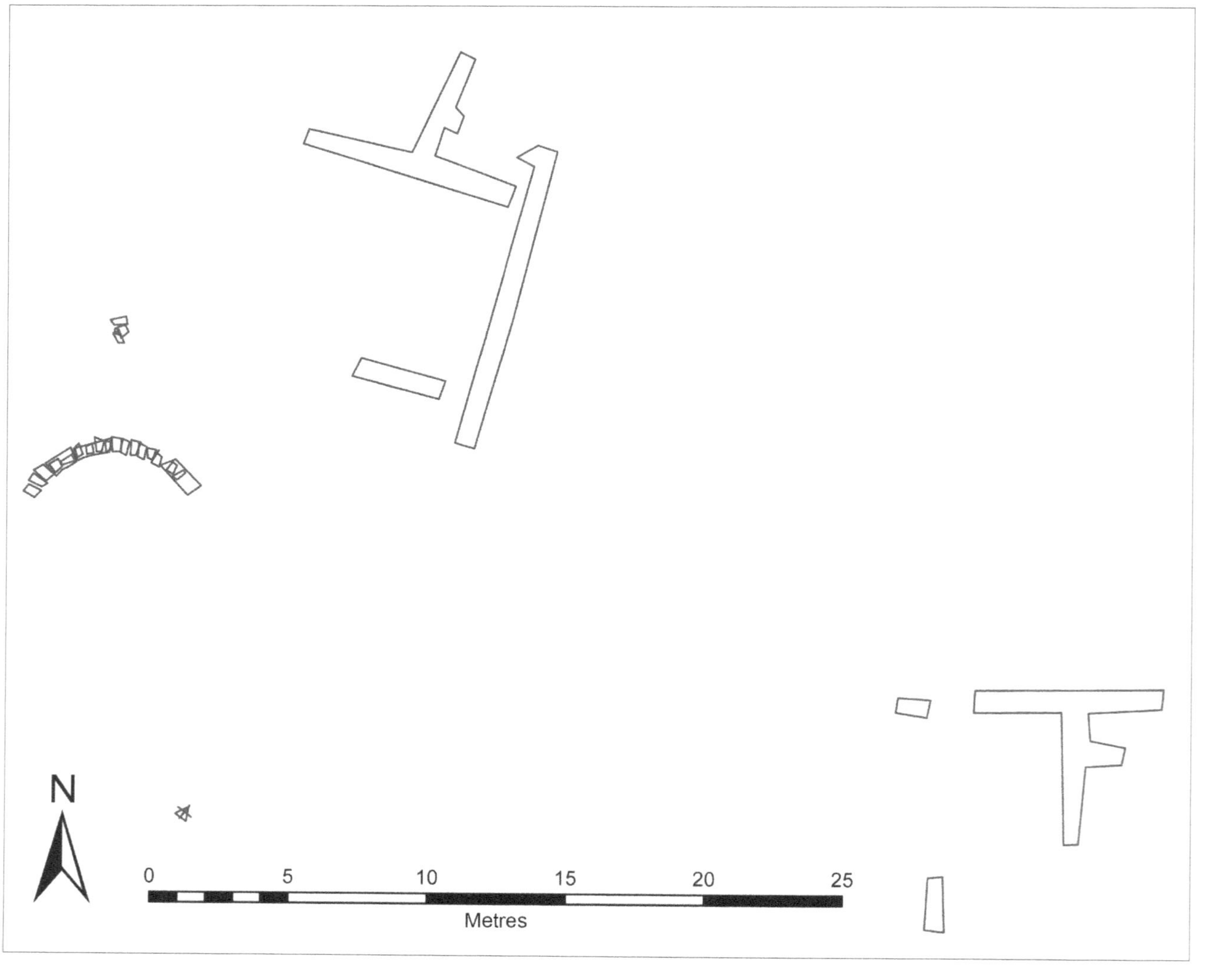

Fig. 6.25. Plan of Site 106.

Site 104-105 (Fig. 6.26; Table 6.5)
Location: 30 57 00N 29 35 07E to 30 56 55N 29 35 00E
Description: This site is located at a distance of 80-100m back from the lake's southern shoreline. Site 105 contains an extremely fragmentary wall which extends for c. 60m in a E-W direction parallel to the shoreline on top of a small ridge c. 2m high. Another wall extends for c. 4m in a N-S direction also parallel to the shore. There is a gap between the two walls of c. 30m where the ground is c. 1m lower than the surrounding mounds.

At a distance of c. 180m west of Site 105, Site 104 was noted (Fig. 6.27). This site contains a circular building of very sparse remains consisting of several limestone

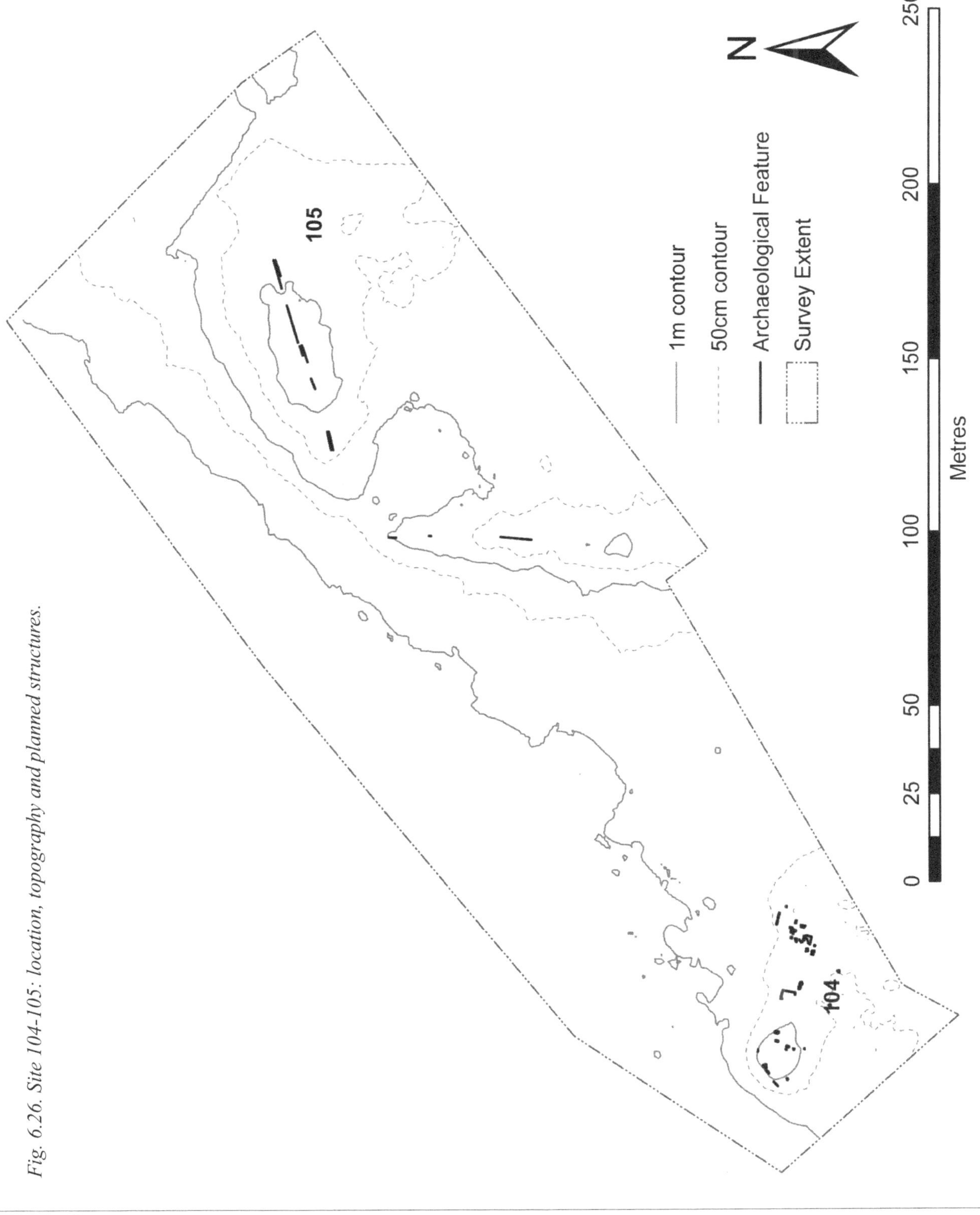

Fig. 6.26. Site 104-105: location, topography and planned structures.

Fig. 6.27. Plan of Site 104.

blocks aligned in headers. From the existing remains it was possible to calculate that the diameter of the building would have been c. 9m. About 10m southeast of the round structure, the remains of a partially excavated square vat (c. 2m x 3.5m) were located. The vat was constructed of limestone and fired bricks that were visible on the floor of the vat.

Considering its location and in comparison with other similar sites, the round structure could be a *sakkia* and the vat could be a tank for collecting water lifted by the *sakkia*.

Additional building blocks and a 3m long wall were recorded some 15m south of the vat, which could have been part of a network of channels used to transport water. Fourteen indicator sherds from Site 104-105, of which 12 belonged to amphorae, represent activity in this area from the Ptolemaic era c. 2nd/1st century BC, with Mareotic AE4 amphorae of the mid 1st through mid 3rd centuries being the most common.

Table 6.5. Quantity of pottery types for Site 104.

Type	No.
Egyptian silt dolium	1
Egyptian silt miscellaneous coarse ware	1
Koan (nos 126-30)	1
Mareotic AE1/2 short handle (no. 6)	1
Mareotic AE4 (nos 13-17)	8
Mareotic Mons Claudianus Amphora Type 22/3 (nos 9-12)	2
Total	14

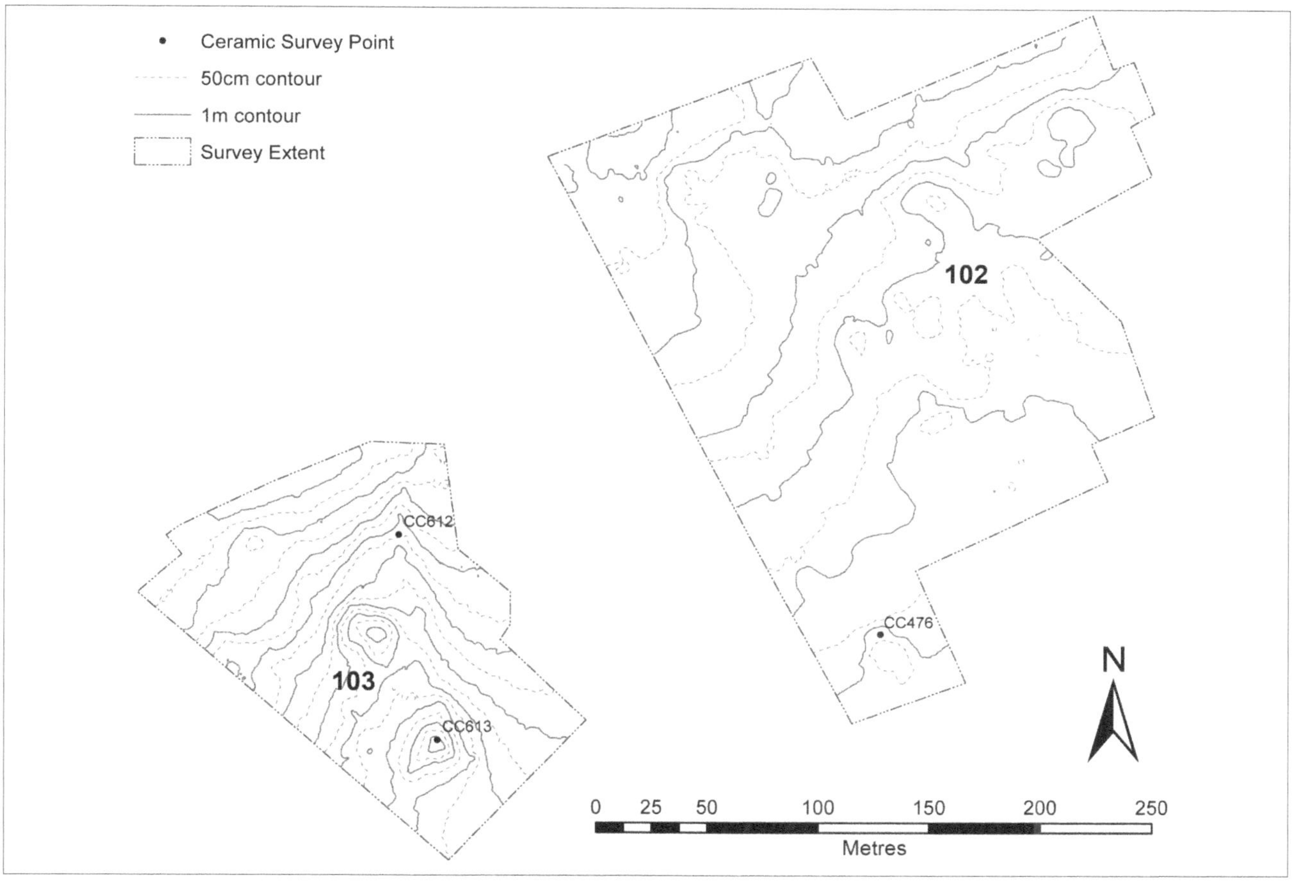

Fig. 6.28. Site 102-103.

Fig. 6.29. Site 102-103 Soliman El-Tayer tomb.

Site 102-103 (Soliman El-Tayer) (Fig. 6.28; Graph 6.5; Table 6.6)

Location: 30 56 47N 29 34 56E to 30 56 45N 29 35 00E

Description: Site 102-103 is located c. 300m southeast of Site 101 and it extends to the foot of a tell c. 8m in height for c. 200m N-S and 200m E-W. This is probably the main site associated with the coastal remains of Site 101 and is distinguished by the tomb of Soliman El-Tayer that can be seen located on the slopes of the hill (Fig. 6.29). The site is generally undisturbed and in a good state of preservation although very little of the site is exposed above ground level. It contains the remains of a number of walls made of limestone blocks. One of the main walls is located at the foot of the tell parallel to the shoreline, while another one extends between the tell and the shoreline perpendicular to the shore. Among the significant remains are parts of a 1m thick wall and plastered water channels, in addition to patches of burning, fired bricks and remains of vats or cisterns.

The exact function of the buildings is not possible to determine; however, the archaeological remains and the topographic nature of the site suggest agricultural and economic activities. A sample of 152 indicator sherds was collected. The balance of the assemblage dates to between the 5th to 7th centuries AD. Sherds potentially as early as the late 4th century BC are present, but occupation more likely begins during the late 3rd or 2nd century BC and continues throughout the sequence. Amphorae dominate at c. 84% of the assemblage, with LR Amphora 1 being the most common.

Graph 6.5. Pie graph showing the chronological breakdown of pottery from Site 102-103.

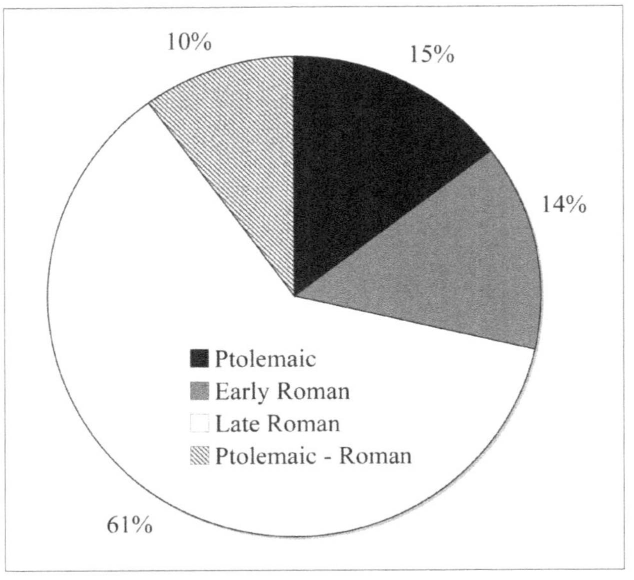

Table 6.6. (below) Quantity of pottery types for Site 102-103.

Type	No.	%
Finewares		
Cypriot Red Slip ware (CRS)	1	0.7
Cypriot Red Slip ware (CRS) 2 (nos 103-4)	1	0.7
Cypriot Red Slip ware (CRS) 9 (nos 105-6)	1	0.7
Egyptian Red Slip ware B/C (ERSB/C)	1	0.7
Egyptian silt red slip fish dish (nos 54-5)	1	0.7
Coarsewares		
Egyptian basin	2	1.3
Egyptian silt casserole (nos 49-51)	2	1.3
Egyptian silt cooking pot	2	1.3
Egyptian silt cooking pot (no. 45)	3	2.0
Egyptian silt jug	2	1.3
Egyptian silt juglet (no. 26)	3	2.0
Egyptian silt lid	1	0.7
Egyptian silt miscellaneous coarse ware	2	1.3
Egyptian silt *sakkia* pot (nos 35-41)	2	1.3
Amphorae		
Abu Mena LR Amphora 5 (nos 87-9)	24	15.8
Cilician Agora M54 (no. 140)	1	0.7
Cilician/Cypriot LR Amphora 1 (nos 146-9)	47	30.9
Gaza LR Amphora 4 Majcherek Forms 2-4 (nos 154-7)	6	3.9
Imported unidentified type	1	0.7
Koan (nos 126-30)	5	3.3
Mareotic AE1/2 base (no. 7)	7	4.6
Mareotic AE1/2 long handle (nos 4-5)	2	1.3
Mareotic AE1/2 short handle (no. 6)	1	0.7
Mareotic AE4 (nos 13-17)	10	6.6
Rhodian IE2/IF (nos 121-6)	4	2.6
Tunisian Africana III (no. 151)	4	2.6
Aegean hollow foot	1	0.7
Aegean LR Amphora 2	4	2.6
Egyptian LR Amphora 7	1	0.7
Knidian handle	2	1.3
Mareotic Mons Claudianus Type 22/3 (nos 9-12)	5	3.3
Palestine LR Amphora 5 (no. 158)	1	0.7
Tunisian unidentified type	2	1.3
Total	152	100%

Site 101
Location: 30 56 48N 29 34 48E
Description: This relatively flat site is located c. 380m west of Site 104. The area extends from the shore for c. 100m inland and it is generally in a poor state of preservation. Site 101 is located at the south side of a modern irrigation canal that runs parallel to the lake's southern shoreline. The site is very disturbed as a result of recent bulldozing. As a result plenty of limestone blocks are scattered haphazardly across the site. Site 101 has only a single indicator sherd from a Dressel 2-4 amphora, in an unidentified imported marl fabric, and is Late Ptolemaic or Early Roman in date.

Site 100 (Taher El Masry, SCA No. 110339) (Figs 6.30 & 6.31; Graph 6.6; Table 6.7)
Location: 30 56 35N 29 34 35E
Description: This site is located c. 600m west of Sites 101-103 and c. 200m south of the southern shore of the lake. The main archaeological feature of this site is a partially excavated wine production complex that consists of a winery and the remains of several associated buildings (SCA ref. 110339, SCA GIS Unit & CULTNAT 2002). The winery measures 9.5m x 4.5m and consists of a treading vat that measures c. 3.5m x 3.5m x 0.5m (LWD) and is connected to a collection tank that measures c. 2m x 1.8m x 1.2m. To the west of the collection tank there are the remains of a wine press tank that measures 1.5m x 1m. The winery is made of limestone blocks as well as smaller stones and the tanks are covered with several thick layers of *opus signinum*. The remains of a number of other walls were recorded north of the winery, which could have belonged to storage facilities associated with the winery complex. Unfortunately, large areas of the site have been subject to extensive bulldozer disturbance.

Fig. 6.30. Plan of Site 100.

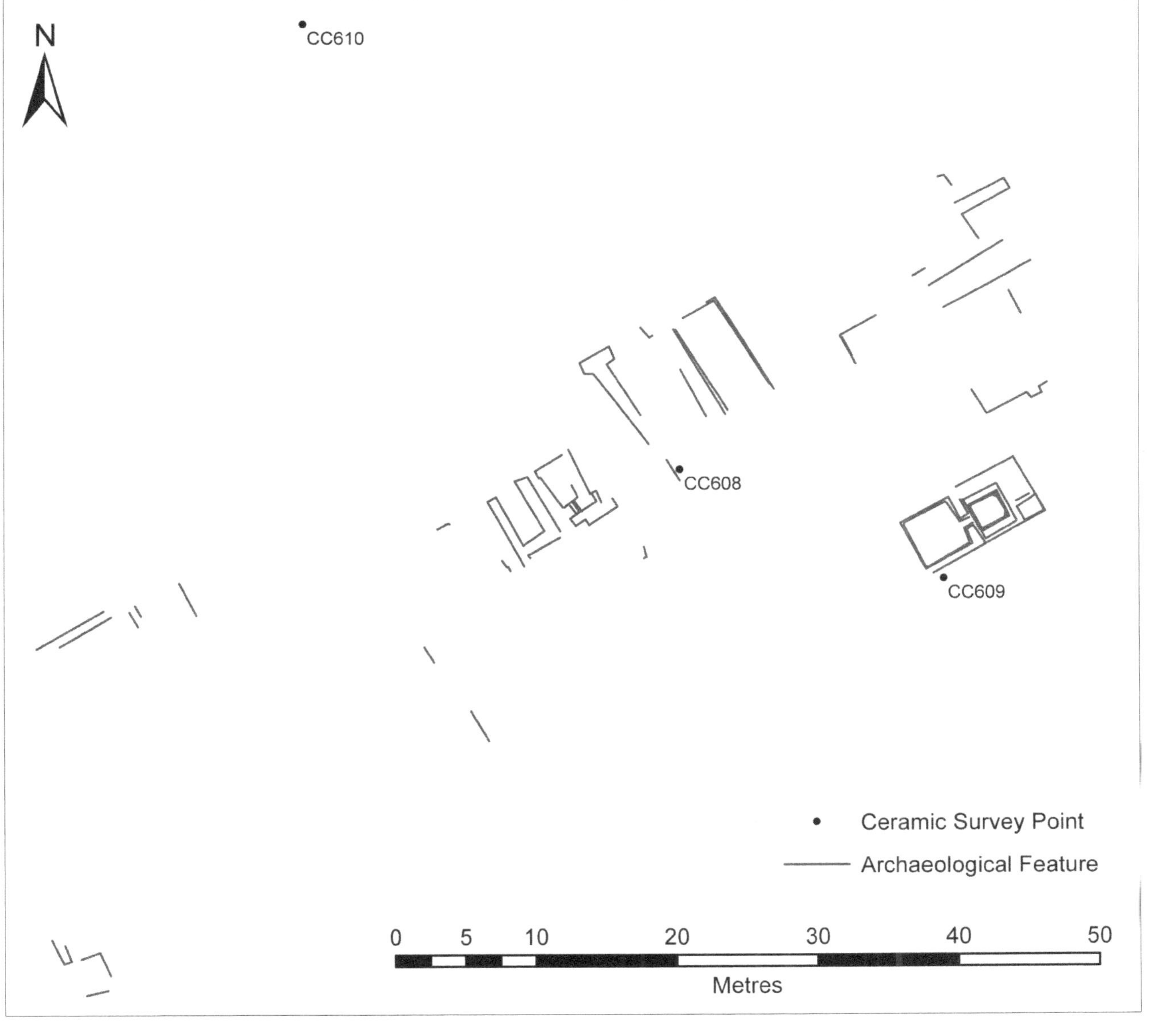

Site 100 has a sample of 71 indicator sherds dating potentially between the late 4th or late 3rd century BC through the 7th century AD. In comparison with other sites, the Early Roman period is well represented (especially by Mareotic AE4). Amphorae (59) dominated.

It is worth mentioning that this is just one of many wineries that have been recorded along the southern shore of the lake, most of which are outside of our survey area (Rodziewicz 1998a). As mentioned earlier, it would appear that wineries in our survey area are located exclusively on the southern shore with the exception of Site 215 that is located on the north shore of the lake.

Fig. 6.31. General view of Site 100.

Graph 6.6. Pie graph showing the chronological breakdown of pottery from Site 100.

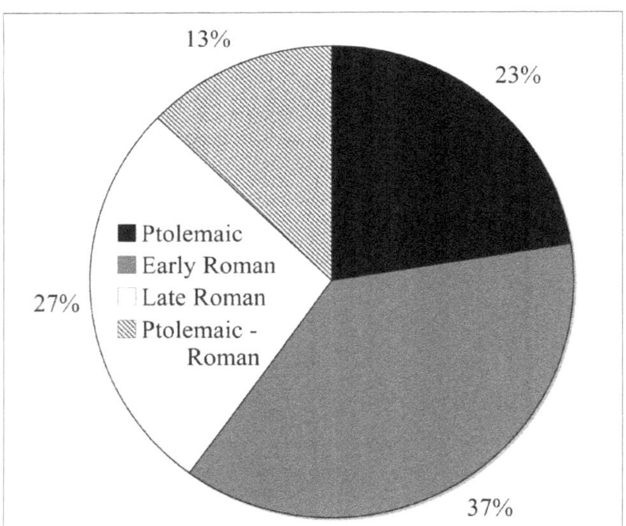

Table 6.7. Quantity of pottery types for Site 100.

Type	**No.**	**%**
Finewares		
Egyptian faience (no. 63)	1	1.4
Egyptian Red Slip ware B/C (ERSB/C)	1	1.4
Egyptian Red Slip ware C (ERSC) copy of CRS 9 (no. 76)	1	1.4
Egyptian silt red slip fish dish (nos 54-5)	2	2.8
Coarse wares		
Egyptian basin	1	1.4
Egyptian bowl	1	1.4
Egyptian silt casserole (no. 48)	3	4.2
Egyptian silt lid	1	1.4
Egyptian silt *sakkia* pot (nos 35-41)	1	1.4
Amphorae		
Abu Mena LR Amphora 5 (nos 87-9)	2	2.8
Aegean LR Amphora 2	1	1.4
Campanian Dressel 1A (no. 135)	1	1.4
Cilician Dressel 2-4 (nos 138-9)	1	1.4
Cilician/Cypriot LR Amphora 1 (nos 146-9)	6	8.5
Egyptian LR Amphora 7	2	2.8
Gaza LR Amphora 4 Majcherek Forms 2-4 (nos 154-7)	4	5.6
Imported unidentified type	4	5.6
Imported unidentified type (no. 173)	1	1.4
Knidian handle	6	8.5
Knidian IIG (no. 119)	1	1.4
Koan (nos 126-30)	7	9.9
Mareotic AE1/2 base (no. 7)	1	1.4
Mareotic AE4 (nos 13-17)	13	18.3
Mareotic Mons Claudianus Type 22/3 (nos 9-12)	4	5.6
Tunisian Africana III (no. 151)	1	1.4
Tunisian unidentified type	4	5.6
Total	71	100%

Sites 30-27 (Fig. 6.1)

Site 30 (Fig. 6.32; Table 6.8)
Location: 30 55 05N 29 30 48E
Description: Site 30 is a tell site that measures c. 160m E-W and 120m N-S and is 3m in height. The distance from the foot of the tell to the waterline is c. 150m, which is covered by accumulating sediments. Archaeological remains at this site are in a poor state of preservation. They include the lower course of a wall from a building c. 6m x 5m in dimension. The wall is made of irregular blocks and mortar. The foundations of a circular building c. 6.2m in diameter were also recorded.

The function of these buildings is unclear; however, the study of 14 indicator sherds collected at the site suggest that the site was active during the Ptolemaic (2nd to 1st centuries BC), Early Roman (3rd century AD) and Late Roman (late 4th to 7th centuries AD).

Type	No.
Abu Mena LR Amphora 5 (nos 87-9)	1
Campanian 3rd century amphora (no. 137)	1
Cilician/Cypriot Egloff 169 (no. 145)	1
Cilician/Cypriot LR Amphora 1 (nos 146-9)	1
Egyptian bowl	1
?Imported black slip footring base (no. 94)	1
Mareotic AE1/2 base (no. 7)	5
Mareotic unidentified amphora	2
Tunisian Africana II (no. 153)	1
Total	14

Table 6.8. Quantity of pottery types for Site 30.

Fig. 6.32. Site 30.

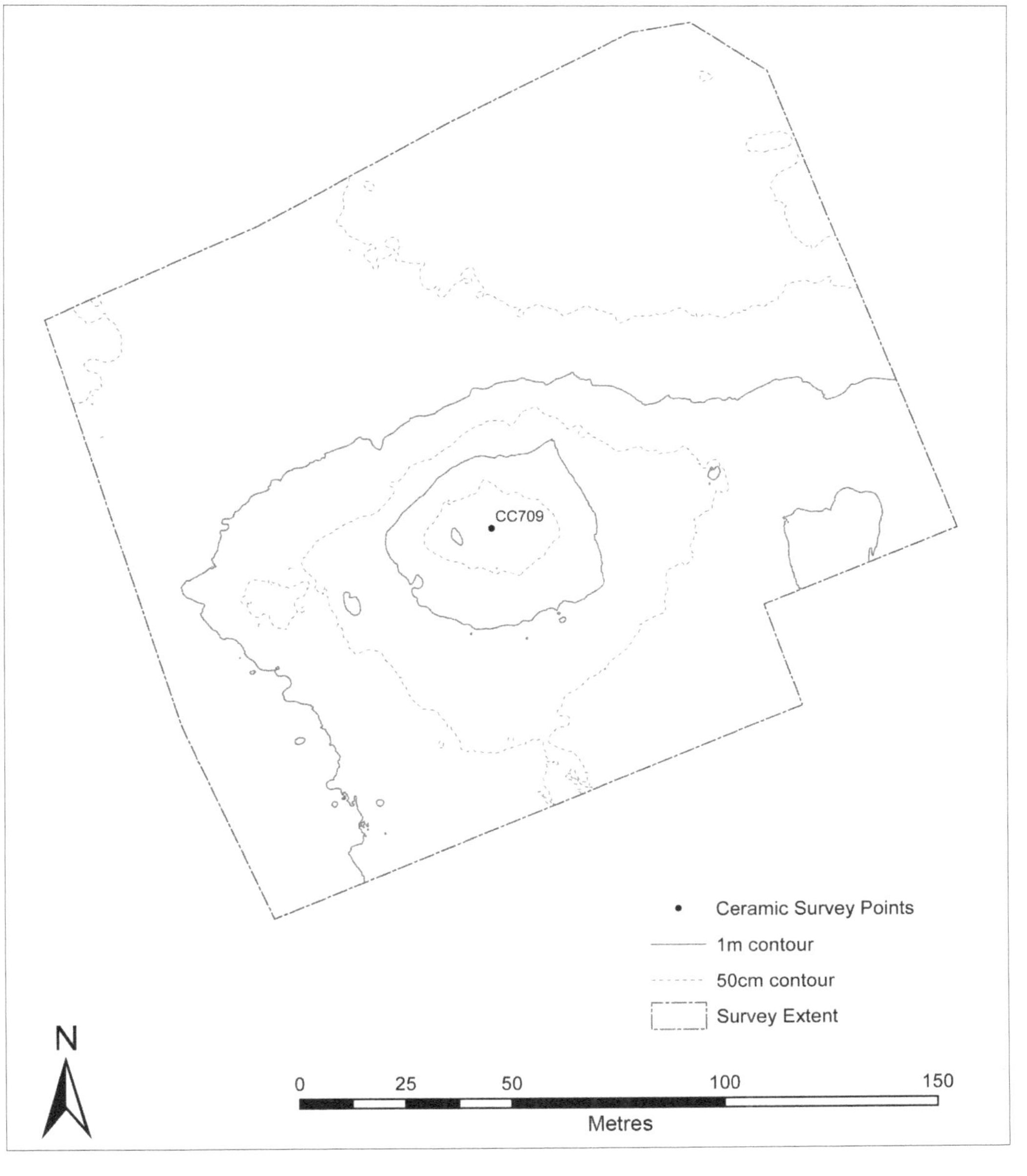

Site 29 (Figs 6.33 & 6.34; Graph 6.7; Table 6.9)
Location: 30 54 54N 29 30 16E to 30 54 48N 29 30 27E
Description: This site is located c. 800m west of Site 30, extending from the lake's shoreline to a tell c. 500m inland.

The first feature that was noticed at this site was a number of large limestone blocks (c. 1m x 0.4m x 0.40m) that were found on the side of a new road that extends parallel to the lake through the site as far as Site 28. The blocks were probably located there in a secondary, reused context.

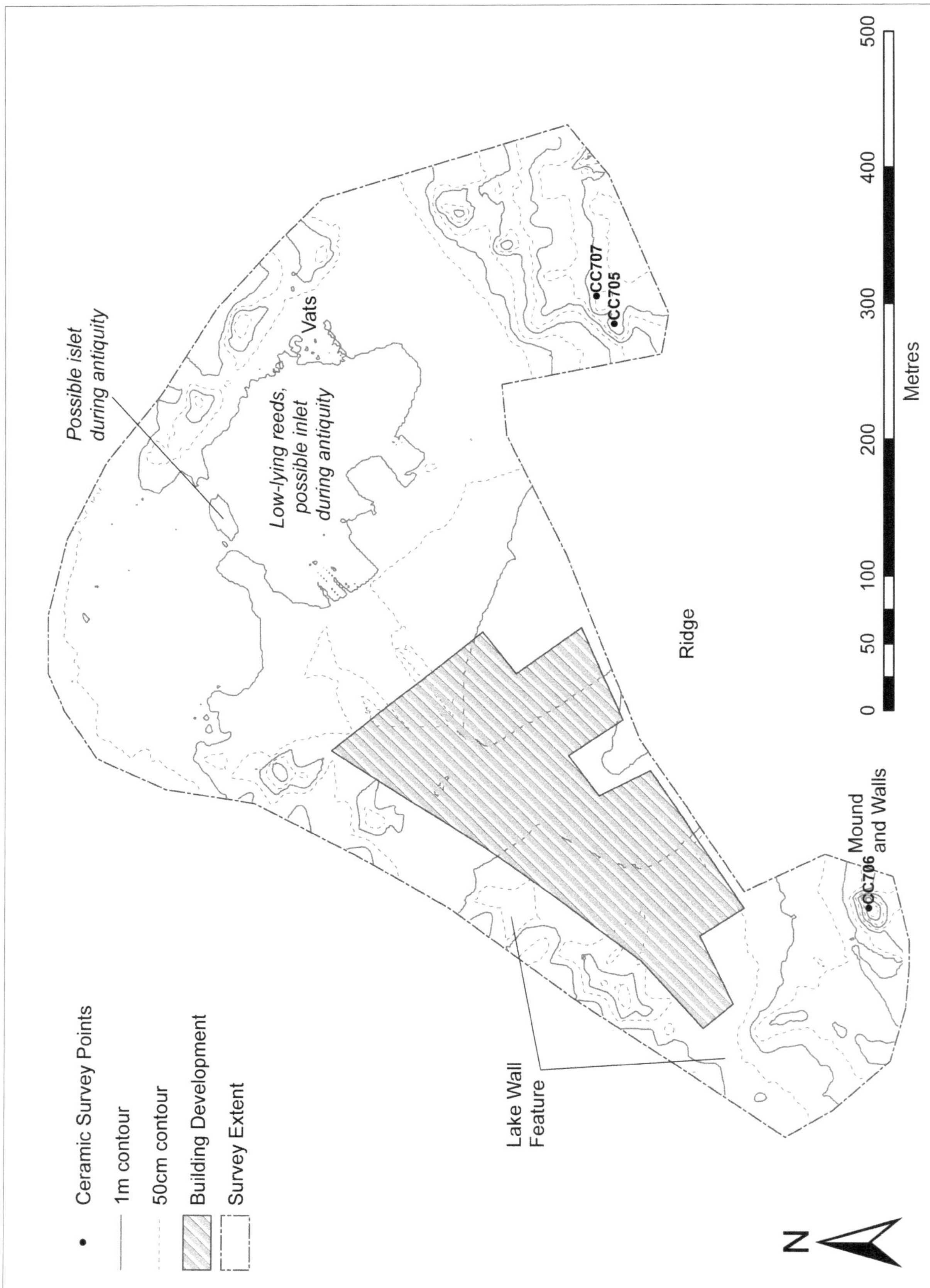

Fig. 6.33. Site 29.

Fig. 6.34. General view of Site 29 from the south.

Table 6.9. Quantity of pottery types for Site 29.

Type	**No.**	**%**
Finewares		
Cypriot Red Slip ware (CRS) 2 (nos 103-4)	1	3.6
Coarse wares		
Abu Mena basin (nos 79-80)	2	7.1
Egyptian silt cooking pot	2	7.1
Egyptian silt cooking pot (no. 45)	1	3.6
Egyptian silt dolium	1	3.6
Egyptian silt lid	1	3.6
Amphorae		
Abu Mena LR Amphora 5 (nos 87-9)	3	10.7
Cilician/Cypriot LR Amphora 1 (nos 146-9)	12	42.9
Knidian IIB (no. 110)	1	3.6
Mareotic AE1/2 base (no. 7)	1	3.6
Mareotic AE1/2 long handle (nos 4-5)	2	7.1
Mareotic unidentified type	(2)	0.0
Palestine LR Amphora 5 (no. 158)	1	3.6
Total	28 (2)	100%

About 300m south of the road there is a tell c. 5m high, with extensive evidence for building remains including scattered building blocks and smaller stones, as well as a badly damaged wall that extends westward along the foot of the tell. In front of the ridge extends a silted plain with more scattered remains. Accordingly, it is quite possible that the shoreline was closer to the ridge in antiquity before the accumulation of silt and sediments. To the north of and parallel to the ridge, a wall extends across the front of the site, perhaps similar in nature to the lake wall features noted at other sites (see Sites 44 and 109 below).

An area of c. 300m x 150m at the eastern part of the site has been subject to destruction by bulldozer activities, however, scattered limestone building blocks can be seen in the debris. This area also encloses low-lying marshy ground that could have contained a small inlet in antiquity. Further investigation of this site is needed to verify these interpretations.

The tell at Site 29 extends west towards Site 28. Accordingly it is possible that Site 29 and Site 28 were part of the same site. A small tell with a number of scattered sherds and building stones defines the western extent of the site.

Site 29 has 28 indicator sherds, primarily of Late Roman date (5th to 7th centuries AD) with Ptolematic sherds of the late 4th or 3rd through 1st centuries BC. Most of the sherds were amphorae (20).

Graph 6.7. Pie graph showing the chronological breakdown of pottery from Site 29.

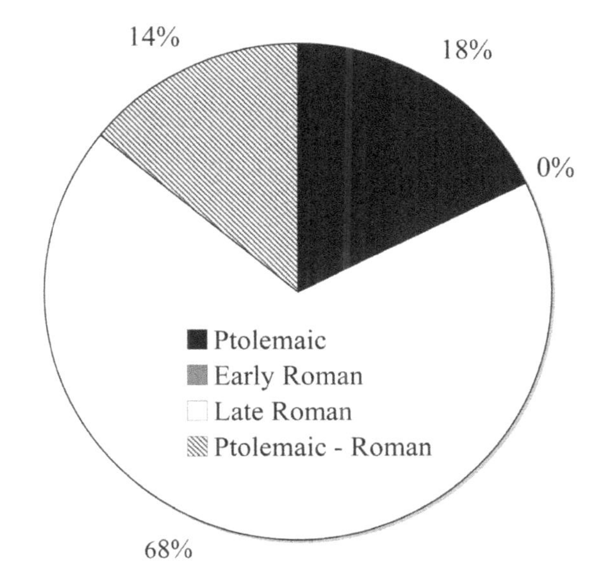

Site 28 (Fig. 6.35; Graph 6.8; Table 6.10)
Location: 30 54 45N 29 29 57E
Description: This site can be considered as an extension of Site 29. It is located c. 800m to the west of Site 29, and is an elongated rocky tell that appears to be part of a ridge that extends from Site 29 westwards. The tell at Site 28 is less than 200m from the current lake shoreline and it is 7m at its highest. The site extends for 200m N-S and 100m E-W. The main archaeological feature at this site is a possible rock-cut tomb located at the northern end of the tell (Fig. 6.36). The tomb consists of one burial chamber and its entrance is c. 1m x 0.8m. Site 28 has a sample of 71 indicator sherds dating potentially from the late 4th or 3rd century BC, but mostly 2nd/1st century BC, continuing into the 2nd century AD with rare Late Roman material into 7th century. All wares were represented with amphorae (37) being the most common.

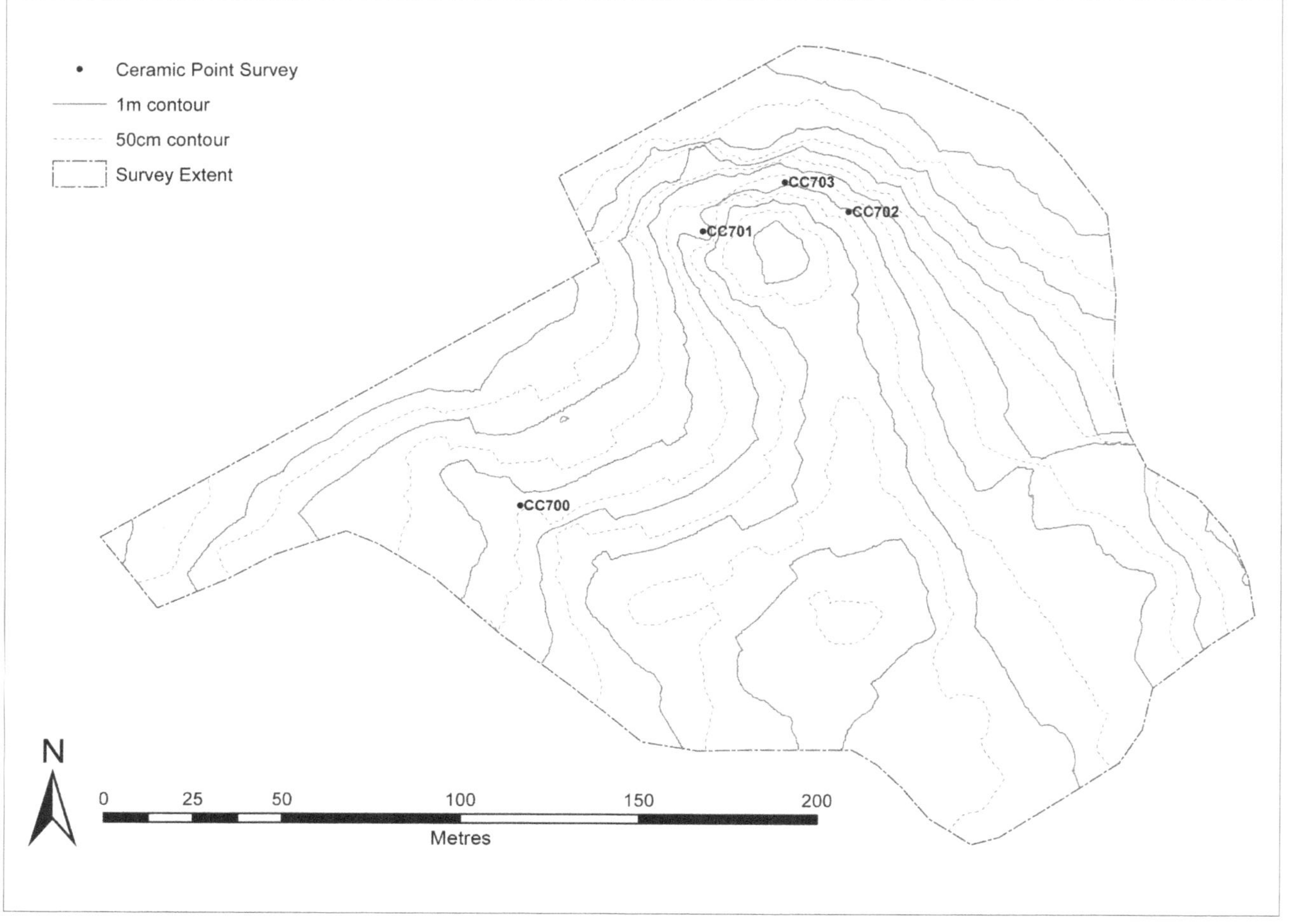

Fig. 6.35. (above) Site 28.

Fig. 6.36. Rock-cut tomb at Site 28.

Graph 6.8. Pie graph showing the chronological breakdown of pottery from Site 28.

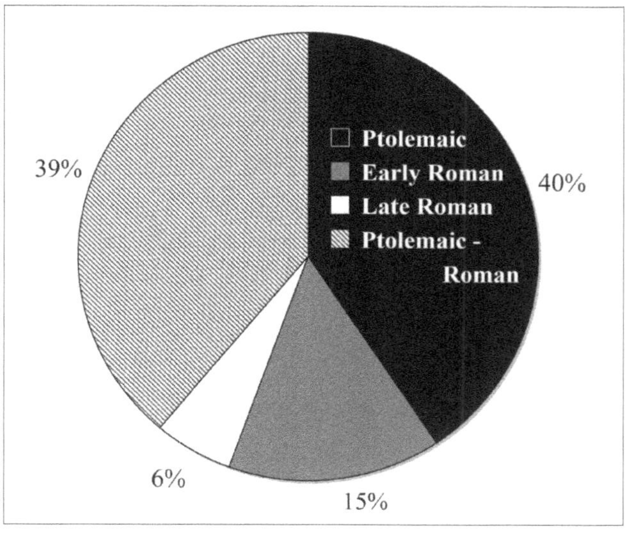

Table 6.10. Quantity of pottery types for Site 28.

Type	No.	%
Finewares		
Eastern Sigillata A (ESA) (no. 97)	1	1.4
Eastern Sigillata A (ESA) bowl/dish	5	7.0
Egyptian Ptolemaic/Early Roman red slip bowl/dish	7	9.9
Egyptian Red Slip ware B (ERSB)	1	1.4
Egyptian silt red slip fish dish (nos 54-5)	1	1.4
Coarse wares		
Abu Mena basin (nos 79-80)	1	1.4
Egyptian bowl	1	1.4
Egyptian jug (no. 62)	1	1.4
Egyptian marl *sakkia* pot (nos 35-41)	1	1.4
Egyptian silt casserole	5	7.0
Egyptian silt jar/jug with twisted handle (no. 27)	1	1.4
Egyptian silt lid	3	4.2
Egyptian silt miscellaneous coarse ware	3	4.2
Egyptian small coarse ware handle	3	4.2
Amphorae		
Abu Mena LR Amphora 5 (nos 87-9)	4	5.6
Cilician/Cypriot LR Amphora 1 (nos 146-9)	(1)	0.0
Egyptian silt AE3	1	1.4
Egyptian silt Mons Claudianus Type 1	1	1.4
Imported unidentified type	1	1.4
Knidian handle	5	7.0
Koan (nos 126-30)	7	9.9
Mareotic AE1/2 short handle (no. 6)	7	10.0
Mareotic AE3	1	1.4
Mareotic Mons Claudianus Type 22/3 (nos 9-12)	1	1.4
Mareotic unidentified type	2	2.8
Rhodian IE2/IF (nos 121-6)	7	9.9
Tunisian unidentified type	(1)	0.0
Total	71 (2)	100%

Site 27 (Table 6.11)
Location: 30 54 25N 29 29 25E
Description: This is a natural rock outcrop near the shore which is located c. 1km west of Site 28. The site measures c. 80m N-S, 70m E-W and is c. 5m in height. It is surrounded by marshes to the north, east and west, suggesting that if the water level was higher, this may have been a headland.

Limited archaeological remains were recorded on this site, which includes scattered irregular building blocks and limited pottery sherds concentrated on the top of the tell. Moreover, just north of the outcrop, a small tell at the water's edge appears to contain more building remains. On this tell very wind eroded remains of a wall extended parallel to the shore. Site 27 has a sample of nine indicator sherds dating between the 2nd and 1st centuries BC and the late 6th and 7th centuries AD.

Type	**No.**
Egyptian silt cooking pot	2
Egyptian small handle from coarse ware	1
Gaza LR Amphora 4 Majcherek Form 4 (no. 154)	1
Mareotic AE1/2 base (no. 7)	3
Mareotic AE4 (nos 13-17)	2
Total	9

Table 6.11. Quantity of pottery types for Site 27.

Site 44 (Abu Unis) (Figs 6.1, 6.37 & 6.38; Graph 6.9; Table 6.12)
Location: 30 53 52N 29 28 43E
Description: This site is located c. 1.5km west of Site 27 and opposite Site 212 on the northern shore of the lake. It is located next to the Amreya Cement Factory, and as a result parts of the site have been destroyed by bulldozers operating in the area to produce limestone for cement production, and a considerable area of the site is buried under a huge mound of limestone waste (Fig. 6.39).

Fig. 6.37. Site 44.

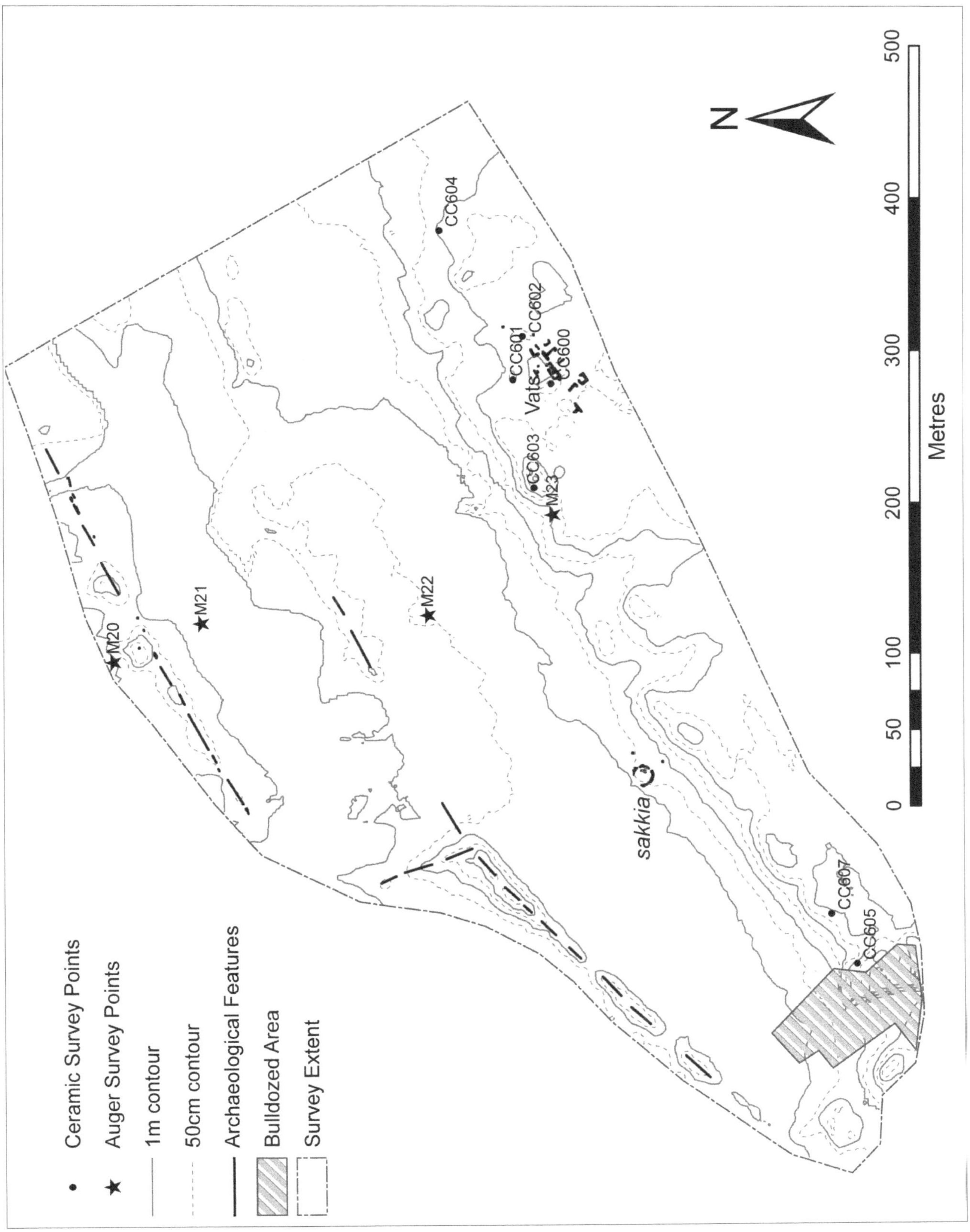

Fig. 6.38. General shot from the south of Site 44.

Fig. 6.39. Huge mound of limestone waste covering the western end of Site 44.

The geomorphology of this site is different from other sites in the region. The site consists of three sandy ridges that run parallel to the shoreline. The most southerly ridge furthest from the current shoreline, extends some 500m or so NE-SW and is c. 60m wide. About 100m or so to the north of the southern ridge exists a second ridge which extends for 250m NE-SW and is 13m wide. This second ridge is more intermittent and sections of its easterly extension can be identified at the very eastern extent of the site. The area between the two ridges is occupied by extensive marshland and vegetation. Some 100m northeast of the second ridge, a third ridge is located that extends parallel to and alongside the current shoreline. The marshy area between the second and third ridge merges with the present shoreline in the central section of the site.

Archaeological features in the area include the remains of a series of walls that extend for c. 270m E-W along the northerly ridge. A second wall stretches along the western extent of the central ridge for 250m before it turns to the north at its easterly end and continues towards the lake for a further 60m, where a circular building was identified at the water's edge. The walls are 0.8-1m wide and are made of small irregular limestone blocks arranged in two rows with a rubble fill in between (Fig. 6.40). The second ridge supports a series of buildings located towards the eastern end of the ridge at the very eastern extent of the site. The most southerly ridge supports the remains of a series of buildings, including evidence for cisterns and basins lined with mortar probably vats (partially excavated; Fig. 6.37). The western part of the ridge supports a circular wall c. 12m in diameter, which is believed to be the remains a *sakkia* (Fig. 6.37). To the west of the site at the base of the cement mound, a badly disturbed tell was noted with wall outlines partially exposed.

The geomorphological study of this site (see Chapter 5 above) indicate that the lake level in antiquity was c. 1.8m lower than present. Accordingly, the marshy area between the ridges could have been dry fertile land. Therefore, the walls that were constructed parallel and perpendicular to the shore could have been made to retain rainwater streaming from the hillside or lake water during high lake levels, to be used for agricultural purposes. A similar arrangement is believed to have taken place at Site 109 (see below).

To the south of the site, there is a rocky hill which contains evidence for quarrying activities. This could have been the source of limestone blocks that were used in buildings on the site. Cuttings were also noted in the hill that accommodated rock-cut tombs (Fig. 6.41).

Site 44 has a sample of 44 indicator sherds dating between the 2nd century BC and the 7th century AD, with a notable peak between the 1st and mid 3rd centuries AD. The assemblage was dominated by transport amphorae, although all ware types were represented.

Fig. 6.40. Close-up of lake walls at Site 44.

Fig. 6.41. Tombs associated with Site 44.

Graph 6.9. Pie graph showing the chronological breakdown of pottery from Site 44.

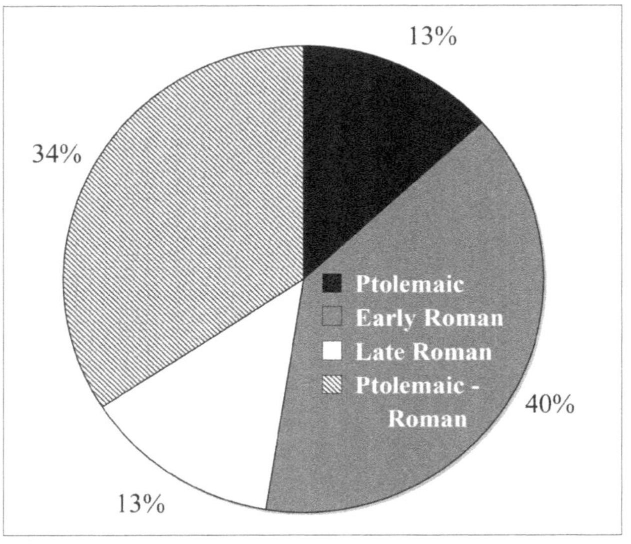

Table 6.12. Quantity of pottery types for Site 44.

Type	No.	%
Finewares		
Eastern Sigillata A (ESA) 42/45 (no. 98)	1	2.3
Egyptian silt copy of Cypriot Sigillata P40/1 (no. 61)	1	2.3
Coarse wares		
Egyptian bowl	3	6.8
Egyptian marl juglet (no. 24)	1	2.3
Egyptian silt cooking pot	5	11.4
Egyptian silt jar/jug with twisted handle (no. 27)	1	2.3
Amphorae		
Abu Mena LR Amphora 5 (nos 87-9)	2	4.5
Cilician Pompeii V (no. 141)	2	4.5
Cilician/Cypriot Agora G199 (no. 142)	1	2.3
Cilician Dressel 30 (nos 143-4)	2	4.5
Cilician/Cypriot Egloff 169 (no. 145)	1	2.3
Cilician/Cypriot LR Amphora 1 (nos 146-9)	2	4.5
Gaza LR Amphora 4 Majcherek Form 2 (no. 156)	1	2.3
Koan (nos 126-30)	9	20.5
Mareotic AE4 (nos 13-17)	4	9.1
Mareotic unidentified type	4	9.1
Mareotic Mons Claudianus Type 22/3 (nos 9-12)	1	2.3
Rhodian Early Roman handle	1	2.3
Tripolitanian II (no. 150)	1	2.3
Unsourced amphora, ?Brindisi (no. 163)	1	2.3
Total	44	100%

Site 109 (including 107 & 108) (Naga El Mawalek)
(Figs 6.42 & 6.43; Graph 6.10; Table 6.13)
Location: 30 52 26N 29 25 27E to 30 52 43N 29 25 43E
Description: This site is located c. 5km west of Site 44 and opposite Site 214-215 on the north shore of the lake. The site's general layout is quite similar to Site 44 in many aspects. It consists of a large plain that slopes northwards down towards the shore of the lake. A large sand ridge c. 350m E-W and 40m N-S extends parallel to the shore and at a distance of c. 120m from it. This distance is occupied by marshes and heavy vegetation. However, according to the local people, the sandy ridge was constructed a few decades ago in order to trap rainwater flowing down the hill so that is could be used for irrigation purposes and to encourage vegetation growth in the area. Sedimentological investigation of the area supports this hypothesis (see Chapter 5) and suggests that that the function of the wall may be to contain rainwater and hence increase soil humidity when lake levels were lower in antiquity.

Fig. 6.42. Site 109.

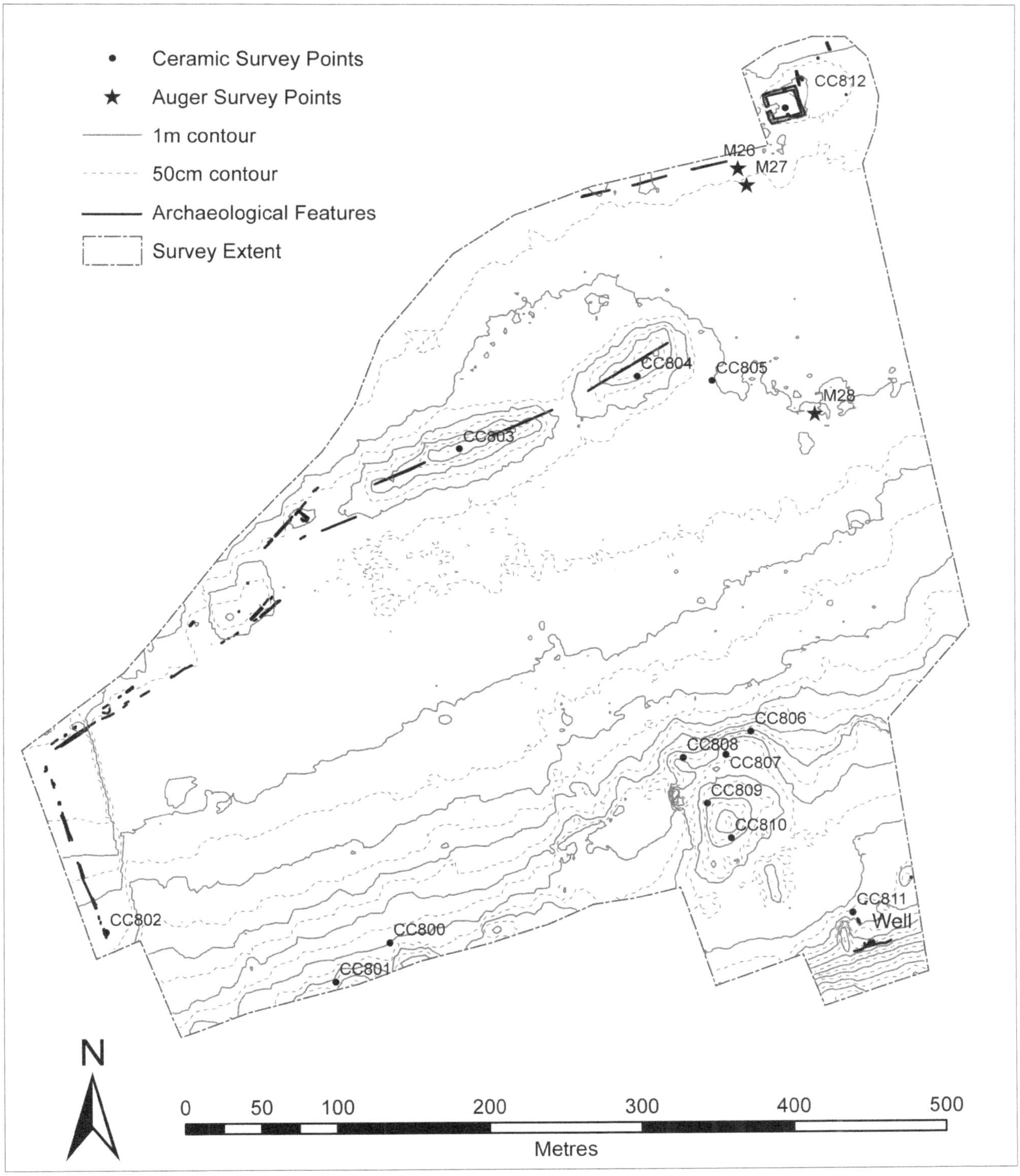

Fig. 6.43. (above) General view of Site 109.

Fig. 6.44. Shoreline lake walls at Site 109.

The large sandy ridge to the north supported at its southwestern end a wall that extends along the shoreline for 250m in an approximate E-W direction. At its western end it turns south at a right angle perpendicular to the shore for c. 130m (Fig. 6.44). The wall is c. 0.8m wide and c. 0.6m high. Parts of the wall are made of limestone blocks aligned in two rows and filled with smaller stones, while other sections are made of small irregular limestone blocks. The walls and the sandy ridge form a huge enclosure c. 140m N-S x 400m E-W, that it is open to the east.

Another distinctive archaeological feature was recorded on a small tell c. 60m E-W and 40m N-S, located northeast of the sandy ridge surrounded by marshlands. The tell contains the remains of a large rectangular building c. 22m x 20m. The walls of the buildings are c. 2.5m thick and are made of small irregular limestone blocks; however, cleaning some sections of the wall revealed evidence for larger regular blocks used in the building foundations. Parts of two more walls were recorded some 5m and 30m northeast of the building, that may have been associated with the building in antiquity. The walls are 10m and 6m long aligned in a N-S direction and some 25m apart. The 6m long wall extends along the edge of waterline perhaps indicating its maritime nature.

A third distinctive archaeological feature is an ancient well and a number of associated canals located at the foot of the limestone coastal ridge c. 500m south of the present shoreline. The well is still in use by the locals to obtain drinking water. About 100m north of the well there is another tell which measures c 70m N-S, 80m E-W and is 8-10m high. It is the main ancient settlement in the area. The tell contains evidence of occupation and activities in antiquity including building blocks and pottery sherds. Moreover, large areas at the eastern and southern sides of the tell have been flattened for agriculture purposes, but are still covered with ceramic sherds which could indicate that the flattened areas were originally part of the tell (Fig. 6.45).

Fig. 6.45. Site 109 disturbance to tell.

Site 109 has a sample of 160 indicator sherds representing activity potentially from the late 4th or 3rd centuries BC to the 7th century AD, dominated by the Late Roman period. All ware groups were represented, particularly amphorae (118), with the most common for the succeeding periods being Knidian (Ptolemaic), Mareotic AE4 (Early Roman) and Late Roman Amphora 1 (Late Roman).

Table 6.13. Quantity of pottery types for Site 109.

Type	**No.**	**%**
Finewares		
African Red Slip ware (ARS) 104B (no. 101)	1	0.6
Cypriot Red Slip ware (CRS)	1	0.6
Cypriot Red Slip ware (CRS) 2 (nos 103-4)	2	1.3
Egyptian Red Slip ware B (ERSB)	1	0.6
Coarse wares		
Abu Mena basin (nos 79-80)	6	3.8
Egyptian basin	1	0.6
Egyptian marl juglet (no. 21)	2	1.3
Egyptian Ptolemaic/Early Roman red slip bowl/dish	1	0.6
Egyptian silt bowl/dish	4	2.5
Egyptian silt casserole	1	0.6
Egyptian silt casserole (cf. Hayes & Harlaut 2002: fig. 55)	2	1.3
Egyptian silt cooking pot	6	3.8
Egyptian silt cup	1	0.6
Egyptian silt dolium	5	3.1
Egyptian silt jug	1	0.6
Egyptian small coarse ware handle	1	0.6
Amphorae		
Abu Mena LR Amphora 5 (nos 87-9)	14	8.8
Cilician Dressel 30 (nos 143-4)	2	1.3
Cilician/Cypriot Egloff 169 (no. 145)	3	1.9
Cilician/Cypriot LR Amphora 1 (nos 146-9)	45	28.1
Knidian handle	10	6.3
Koan (nos 126-30)	4	2.5
Mareotic AE1/2 base (no. 7)	3	1.9
Mareotic AE4 (nos 13-17)	25	15.5
Mareotic Mons Claudianus Type 22/3 (nos 9-12)	4	2.5
Mareotic unidentified type	5	3.1
Palestine LR Amphora 5 (no. 158)	1	0.6
Rhodian IE2/IF (nos 121-6)	8	5.0
Total	160	100%

Graph 6.10. Pie graph showing the chronological breakdown of pottery from Site 109.

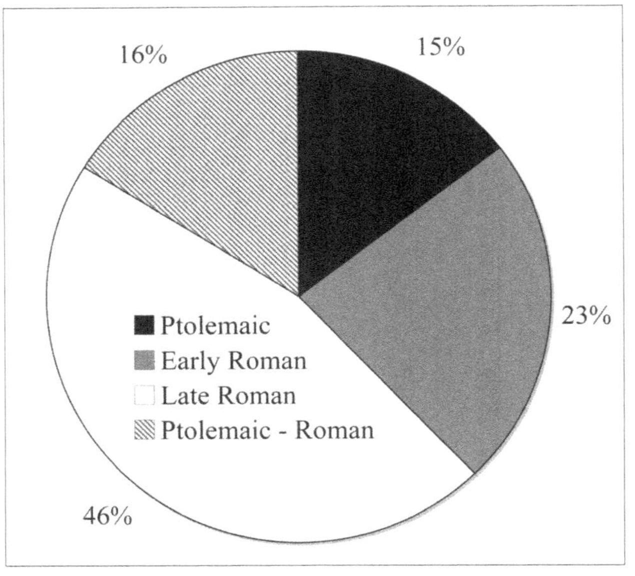

An assessment of the archaeological sites recorded along the southern shore of the lake reveals that Sites 30–27 have certain features in common, as do Sites 44 and 109. Sites 30-27 all take the form of relatively small coastal tells surrounded by marshes and flat extents of land. The archaeological remains at these sites are very limited. In contrast, Sites 44 and 109 are quite extensive in size. They both contain evidence for water management (*sakkia*, cisterns and wells) and were densely occupied. Both are associated with fertile areas that can be used for agricultural purposes. Sites 44 and 109 are also located opposite two large sites on the northern shore of the lake (Sites 212 and 214) (see below), whereas no recorded sites have been identified on the northern shore of the lake opposite Sites 30-27.

6.3 Sites located along the northern shore of the lake

Sites 200-211, 254-250, 212-215 (Fig. 6.1)
The size and nature of sites located on the north shore vary greatly; however, they can generally be divided according to their topographic nature into two groups: sites located east of Taposiris Magna and those located west of Taposiris Magna. A common feature relating to sites east of Taposiris Magna is that they tend to be focused around and defined by a hill or series of hills on the water's edge so that they resemble 'tell sites' up to 12m in height, containing evidence for occupation and domestic activities broadly from the Hellenistic to the Late Roman periods. These sites are also often associated with waterfront maritime installations. In contrast, sites which are located to the west of Taposiris Magna are topographically much flatter and the remains of ancient structures are located close to the waterline. Also some of these sites contain evidence for industrial activities.

Site 200 (Fig. 6.1)
Location: 30 59 51N 29 38 10E
Description: Site 200 is a small offshore island (c. 220m x 120m) aligned NE-SW at a distance of c. 400m south of the north shore of the lake, and 600m west of the Sidi Kerir road. The island was connected to the main road by a modern artificial dyke. Two smaller islands (60m x 50m & 120m x 80m) exist between the site and the road. As mentioned earlier (see Chapter 2), both Strabo (17.1.14) and Pliny (5.11.63) recall that Lake Mareotis contained a number of islands; this group of small islands is probably among those mentioned by the ancient authors.

Site 200 contains plenty of evidence for industrial activities in antiquity including fired bricks, pottery wasters, slag and the remains of a small furnace. However, at present the site is privately owned and it has been completely bulldozed; therefore further studies could not be carried out.

Site 201 (Figs 6.46 & 6.47; Graph 6.11; Table 6.14)
Location: 30 59 54N 29 37 30E
Description: Site 201 is located on the northern shore of the lake about 1km northwest of Site 200. It is a tell site c. 200m x 120m and c. 9m high. It is situated about 50m from the current water's edge. Limited wall remains were visible at this site, although it does contain plenty of ceramics and pottery wasters. A substantial part of the tell has been bulldozed and flattened to facilitate construction. The bulldozer dumps contain many pottery sherds. Moreover, spoil heaps at the water's edge also reveal evidence for pottery production. The shoreline here has been heavily distrubed and as a result it was not possible to determine any waterfront installations. North of the site a well was identified, which, although still in use, appears to have ancient foundations (Fig. 6.48).

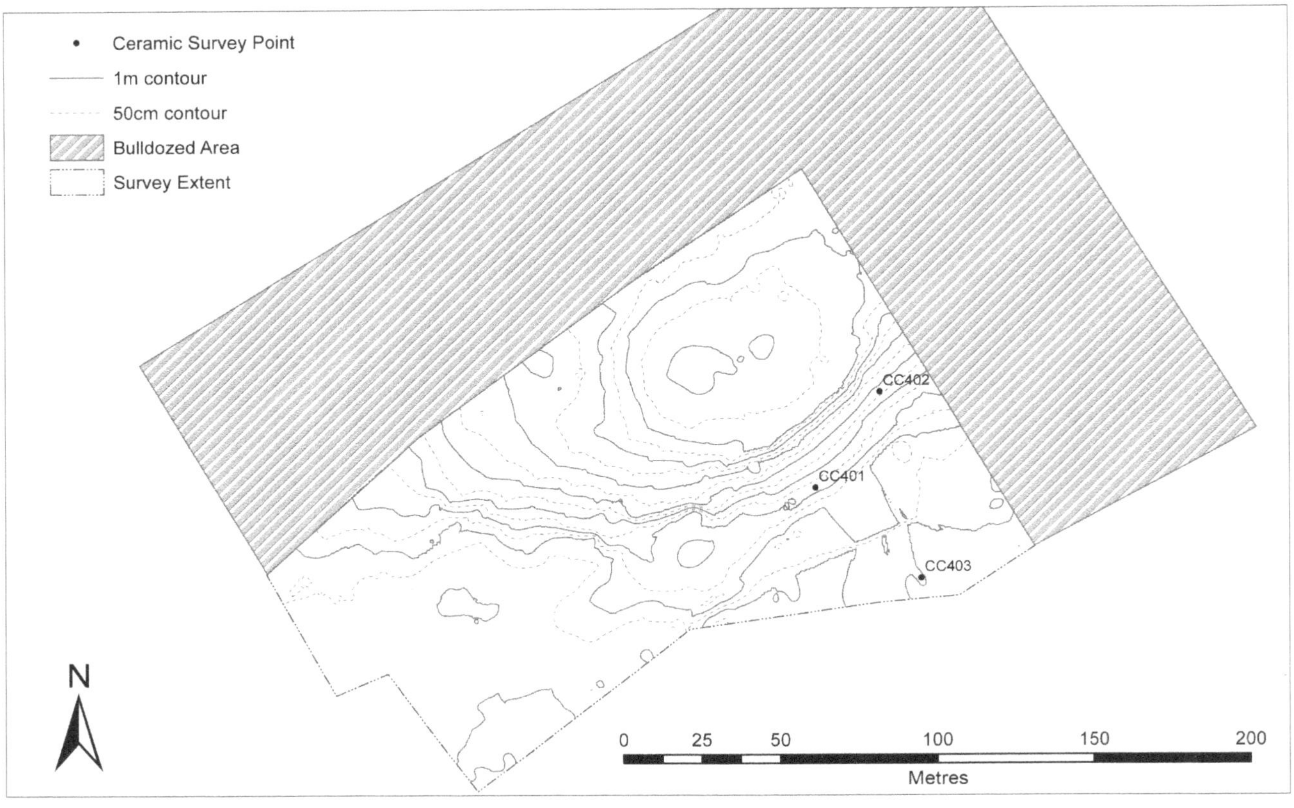

Fig. 6.46. (above) Site 201.

Fig. 6.47. (below) General view of Site 201 from the south.

Site 201 has a sample of 93 indicator sherds potentially spanning from as early as the late 4th century BC through the 7th century AD. Within this sample, the late 3rd through 1st centuries BC are the best represented. Over half the pottery was amphorae (69) with Rhodian and Knidian imports most prominent. Ceramic circle CC401 had a concentration of Ptolemaic domestic wares rather than amphorae.

Fig. 6.48. Possible ancient well at Site 201.

Graph 6.11. Pie graph showing the chronological breakdown of pottery from Site 201.

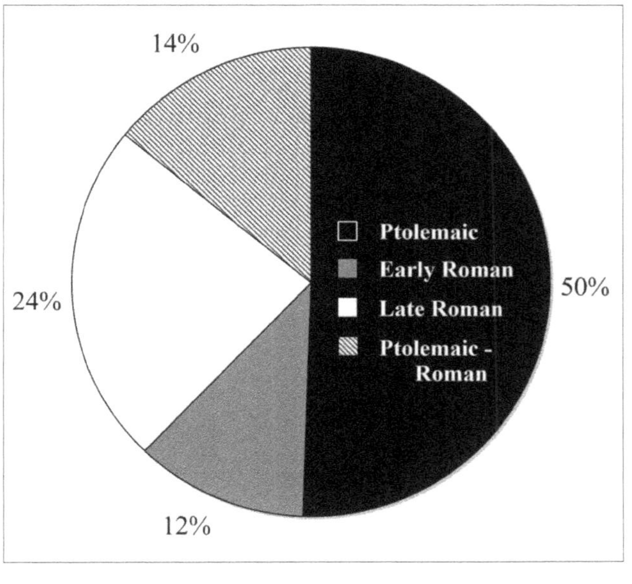

Table 6.14. Quantity of pottery types for Site 201.

Type	No.	%
Finewares		
Egyptian black slip slip bowl (nos 57-9)	1	1.1
Egyptian red slip bowl (no. 60)	1	1.1
Egyptian Red Slip ware A (ERSA) copy of CRS 9B or 9C (no. 76)	2	2.2
Egyptian silt red slip fish dish (nos 54-5)	4	4.3
Coarse wares		
Egyptian bowl	2	2.2
Egyptian miscellaneous coarse ware	5	5.4
Egyptian silt casserole (no. 48)	3	3.3
Egyptian silt casserole (nos 49-51)	1	1.1
Egyptian silt cooking pot	2	2.2
Egyptian silt cooking pot (no. 45)	1	1.1
Egyptian silt lid	1	1.1
Egyptian small coarse ware handle	1	1.1
Amphorae		
Abu Mena LR Amphora 5 (nos 87-9)	3	3.3
Aegean LR Amphora 2	5	5.4
Campanian Greco-Italic (no. 134)	6	6.5
Cilician Dressel 30 (nos 143-4)	3	3.2
Cilician/Cypriot Egloff 169 (no. 145)	2	2.2
Cilician/Cypriot LR Amphora 1 (nos 146-9)	5	5.4
Egyptian LR Amphora 7	3	3.2
Gaza LR Amphora 4 Majcherek Forms 2-4 (nos 154-7)	1	1.1
Imported unidentified type	2	2.2
Imported unsourced whole-mouth amphora (no. 159)	2	2.2
Knidian handle	11	11.8
Knidian IIB (no. 110)	1	1.1
Koan (nos 126-30)	4	4.3
Mareotic AE1/2 (nos 1-3)	2	2.2
Mareotic AE1/2 base (no. 7)	2	2.2
Mareotic AE4 (nos 13-17)	1	1.1
Rhodian IE2/IF (nos 121-6)	14	15.1
Unsourced amphora (no. 162)	1	1.1
Western Asia Minor LR Amphora 3	1	1.1
Total	93	100%

Site 202-203 (Naga El-Zohrat) (Figs 6.49 & 6.50; Graph 6.12; Table 6.15)
Location: 30 58 57N 29 35 58E
Description: The site extends c. 300m NE-SW along the shore and is c. 100m wide. It contains two tells with numerous archaeological remains.

The eastern tell is c. 170m in diameter, 10m in height and is situated c. 70m north of the present lake shoreline. The remains of a building made of limestone blocks and lime mortar were also visible, although during the period of the survey it was bulldozed flat.

Located on the eastern tell, at least four basins (c. 2m x 1m x 1m) lined with red plaster (*opus signinum*) and made of red bricks were identified which indicate that they were built to contain a liquid, probably water, and could have been part of a bath complex, probably Late Roman in date (Fig. 6.51). The basins were first seen and recorded in 2006. However, when the site was re-visited in 2007 the basins had been destroyed.

The waterfront area is also badly disturbed due to the construction of large electricity pylons. Several sections of the shoreline have been bulldozed. However, the spoil heaps at the shoreline include plenty of substantial building remains, particularly blocks which were attached using *opus signinum* and a limestone block that had a mooring hole carved in it, indicative of a maritime installation, probably a quay, which once existed at the foot of the hill. Less than 5m from the present waterline there is a rectangular basin (2m x 1m) made of limestone blocks that is presently filled with groundwater. This basin probably relates to the bath complex that existed in this area. To the north of the basin a linear feature extended to the foot of the tell.

The western extent of the tell is less than 50m from the eastern tell. It is about 130m in diameter and 12m in height. The tell was covered with ancient building material and ceramics much of which was badly disturbed by bulldozing. The most significant archaeological remains on the site were those of a Hellenistic building, dated by the building style, that was possibly a tomb made of large limestone blocks containing a niche and an arch set against natural bedrock. The tomb was photographed in 2004; however, when the site was visited in 2007 it had been completely destroyed by bulldozers (Figs 6.52 & 6.53).

To the southwest of the site continuing along the shore, numerous concentrations of building material are visible on the water's edge. To the west a small embayment c. 300m long and c. 100m wide, marks the continuation of the site that has been badly bulldozed to support a levelled field to

Fig. 6.49. Site 202-203.

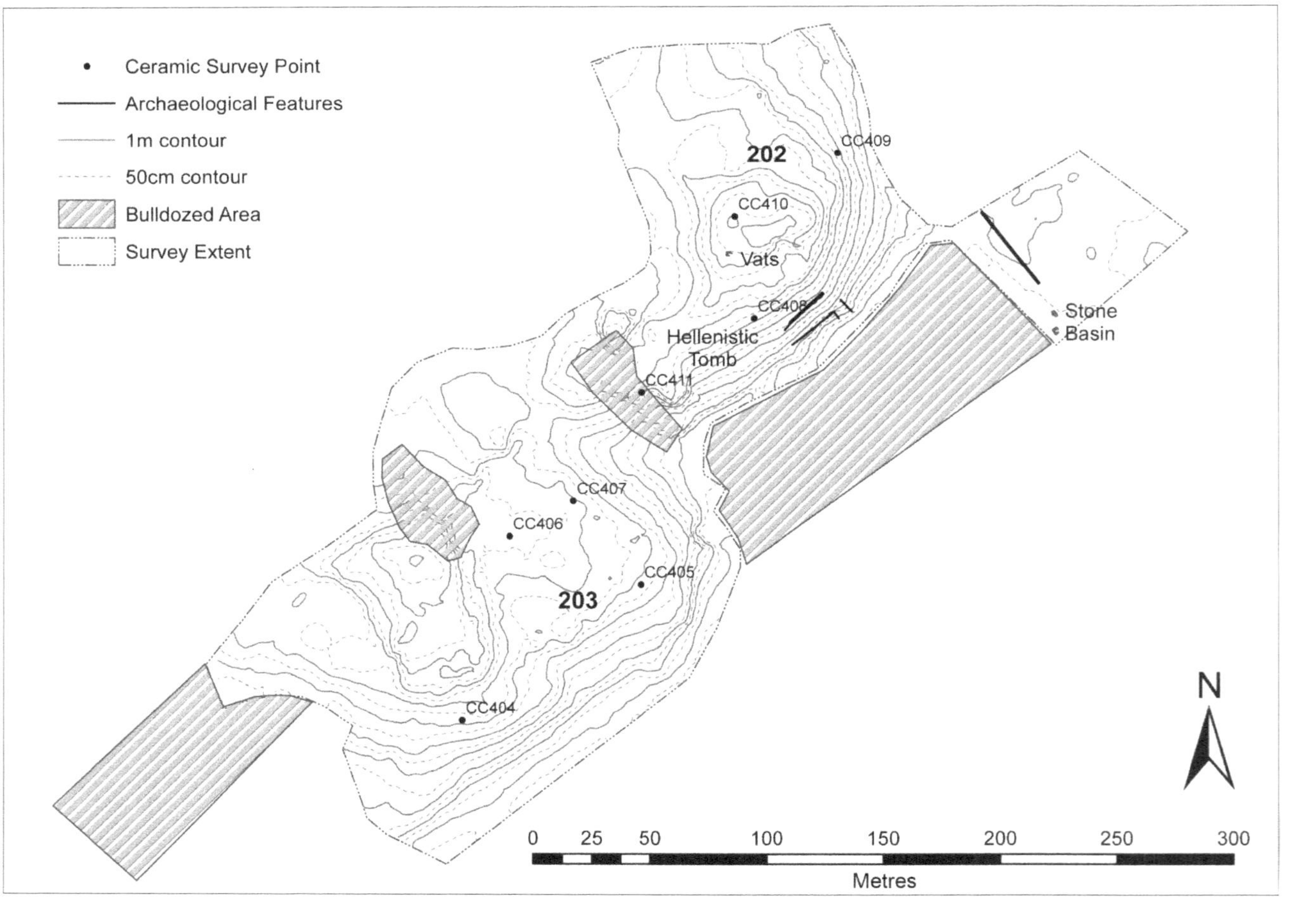

Fig. 6.50. (above) General view of Site 202-203.

Fig. 6.51. (right) Basin lined with plaster at Site 202-203.

the north. Trees define the boundary and break of slope between the bulldozed fields and further ancient and also disturbed building material that was identified along the shore. This material extends into the lake to the south as a small platform.

Site 202-203 has a sample of 271 indicator sherds. The sequence potentially begins as early as the 3rd century BC but is dominated by Late Roman material with the 7th century marked in particular. In addition to the standard repertoire of imported Late Roman amphorae, all imported finewares of this period are also represented. There was a concentration of *sakkia* pot sherds in near isolation from other ceramics at the edge of the steep terraced limestone ridge (CC410), with further sherds in nearby locations (CC408 and CC409), suggesting there was a *sakkia* (water-wheel) nearby. The rest of the areas were primarily domestic in nature, with Ptolemaic and Early Roman types concentrated in the west of the site (CC404), and entirely Late Roman to the east (CC405 and CC406).

The site has clearly gone through different phases of occupation. The Hellenistic tomb belonged to the earliest phase of occupation, while the main period of activity at the site dates to the Late Roman period and included a large building, possibly a bath complex. The site also appears to have had a maritime installation such as a jetty. It is noticeable that Site 202-203 is located opposite a cluster of sites on the eastern end of the island (Sites 114-126), perhaps accessed by boats from the former jetty at Site 202-203. No sites were recorded along the c. 2km stretch of shoreline between Site 202-203 and Site 204-205 on the north coast, but it is interesting to note that Site 204-205 is also located opposite sites at the western end of the island (Sites 15-40).

Fig. 6.52. Site 202-203: destruction of Hellenistic tomb (before).

Fig. 6.53. Site 202-203: destruction of Hellenistic tomb (after).

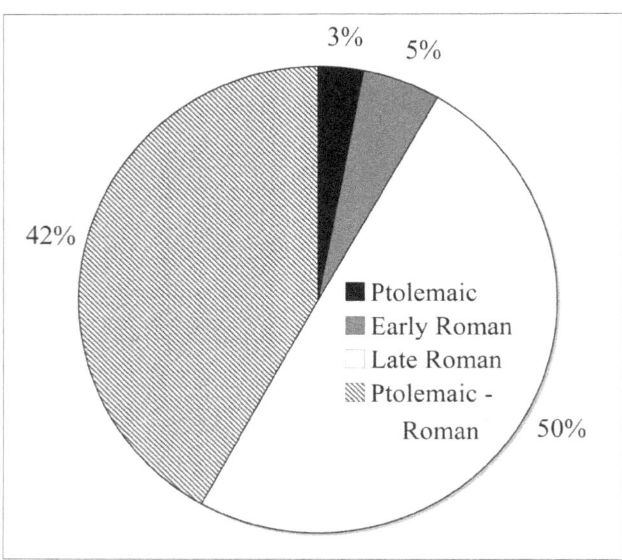

Graph 6.12. Pie graph showing the chronological breakdown of pottery from Site 202-203.

Table 6.15. Quantity of pottery types for Site 202-203.

Type	No.	%
Finewares		
African Red Slip ware (ARS)	(2)	0.0
African Red Slip ware (ARS) 99 (no. 100)	1	0.4
Cypriot Red Slip ware (CRS) 2 (nos 103-4)	6	2.2
Cypriot Red Slip ware (CRS) 9 (nos 105-6)	1	0.4
Eastern Sigillata A (ESA)	(1)	0.0
Egyptian Ptolemaic/Early Roman red slip bowl/dish	4	1.4
Egyptian Red Slip ware A (ERSA)	1	0.4
Egyptian Red Slip ware A (ERSA) bowl (no. 73)	2	0.7
Egyptian Red Slip ware A (ERSA) bowl (no. 78)	1	0.4
Egyptian Red Slip ware A (ERSA) bowl (nos 74-5)	2	0.7
Egyptian Red Slip ware A (ERSA) copy of ARS 75 (no. 64)	1	0.4
Egyptian Red Slip ware B (ERSB) copy of ARS 104C (nos 70-1)	1	0.4
Egyptian Red Slip ware B (ERSB) copy of ARS 67	1	0.4
Egyptian Red Slip ware B (ERSB) copy of ARS 96	1	0.4
Egyptian Red Slip ware B/C (ERSB/C) bowl	5	1.8
Egyptian silt red slip fish dish (nos 54-5)	2	0.7
Painted unidentified	(3)	0.0
Phocaean Red Slip ware (PRS) 3D (no. 109)	1	0.4
? Phocaean Red Slip ware copy of CRS 2 (no. 107)	1	0.4
Coarse wares		
Abu Mena basin (nos 79-80)	8	3.0
Egyptian basin	12	4.4
Egyptian bowl	6	2.2
Egyptian casserole	5	1.8
Egyptian marl jug	4	1.5
Egyptian marl juglet/unguentarim	1	0.4
Egyptian marl *sakkia* pot (nos 35-41)	1	0.4
Egyptian miscellaneous coarse ware	10	3.7
Egyptian silt bowl/dish	4	1.5
Egyptian silt casserole (no. 48)	2	0.7
Egyptian silt casserole (nos 49-51)	5	1.8
Egyptian silt casserole lid (no. 53)	4	1.5
Egyptian silt cooking pot	18	6.6
Egyptian silt cooking pot (no. 44)	1	0.4
Egyptian silt cooking pot (no. 45)	1	0.4
Egyptian silt cooking pot (no. 46)	1	0.4
Egyptian silt funnel strainer (no. 33)	1	0.4
Egyptian silt jar	2	0.7
Egyptian silt jug	19	7.0
Egyptian silt lid	2	0.7
Egyptian silt *sakkia* pot (nos 35-41)	14	5.2
Egyptian small coarse ware handle	8	3.0
Amphorae		
Abu Mena LR Amphora 5 (nos 87-9)	57	21.0
Aegean hollow foot	2	0.7
Aegean LR Amphora 2	(2)	0.0
Cilician/Cypriot Egloff 169 (no. 145)	2	0.7
Cilician/Cypriot LR Amphora 1 (nos 146-9)	3	1.1
Egyptian silt AE3	1	0.4
Gaza LR Amphora 4 Majcherek Forms 2-4 (nos 154-7)	24	8.9
Imported unidentified type	2	0.7
?Imported jar (no. 160)	1	0.4
Koan (nos 126-30)	2	0.7
Mareotic AE1/2 base (no. 7)	1	0.4
Mareotic AE4 (nos 13-17)	5	1.8
Mareotic Mons Claudianus Type 22/3 (nos 9-12)	2	0.7
Mareotic unidentified type	(1)	0.0
Palestine LR Amphora 5 (no. 158)	5	1.8
Rhodian IE2/IF (nos 121-6)	2	0.7
Tripolitanian II (no. 150)	1	0.4
Tunisian Africana IID (no. 152)	1	0.4
Total	271 (9)	100%

Site 204-205 (Al-Gamal, SCA No. 110304) (Figs 6.54 & 6.55; Graphs 6.13 & 6.14; Table 6.16)
Location: 30 58 16N 29 35 01E
Description: This is one of the most substantial sites along the northern shore of the lake. It is a tell that is referred to by the locals as Al-Gamal. It takes the form of a promontory that extends for c. 250m N-S, 200m E-W and 13m high. The tell contains many archaeological remains and evidence for occupation; however, an area on the north-west side has been destroyed and levelled to make a football pitch.

The tell is almost entirely covered in building material such as limestone blocks and red bricks, as well as a num-

Fig. 6.54. Site 204-205.

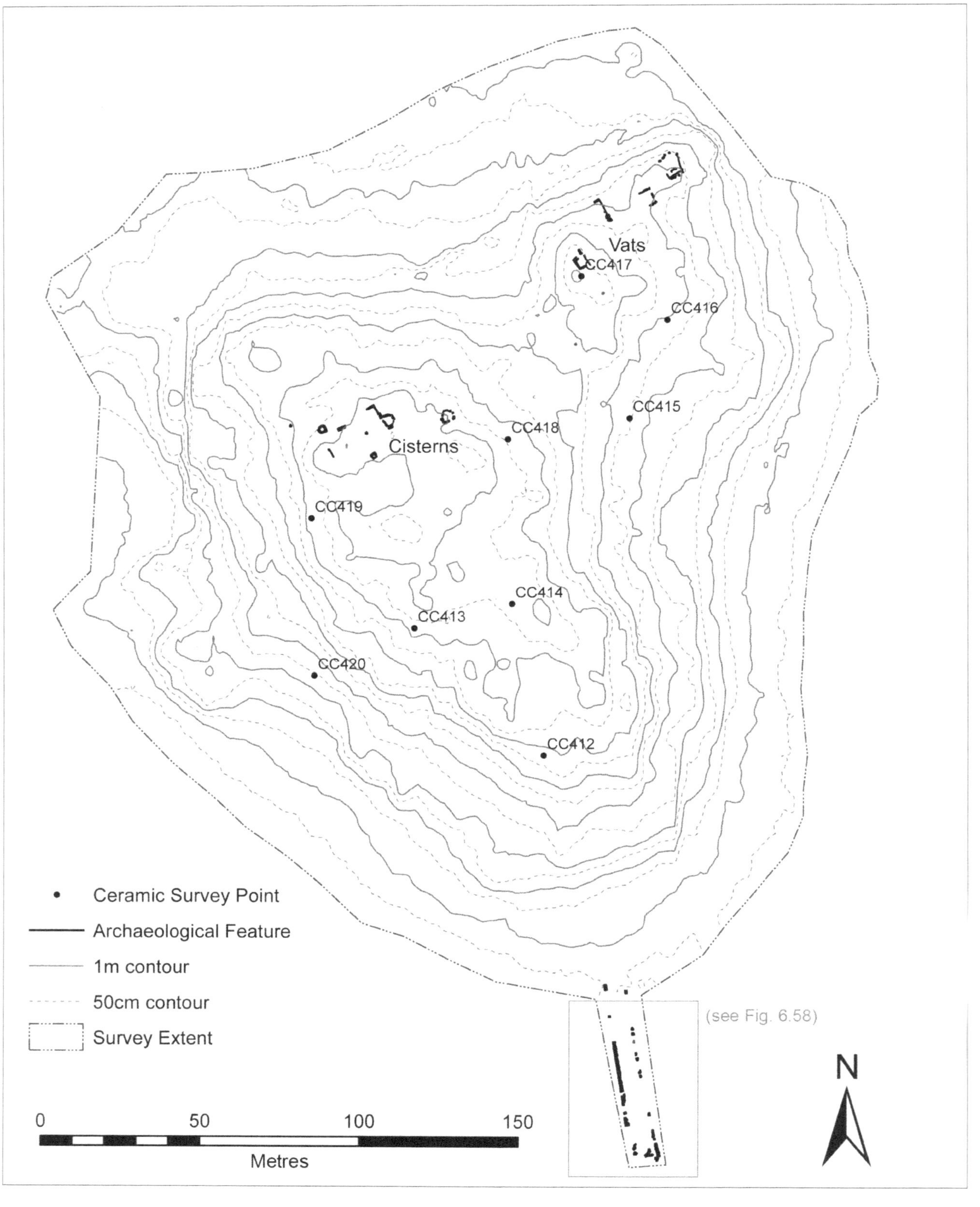

Fig. 6.55. Site 204-205 general view from Mareotis Island.

Fig. 6.56. (above) Late-Roman cistern at Site 204-205.

Fig. 6.57. (right) Monolith at Site 204-205.

ber of clearly aligned wall remains. There are also a number of features that appear to be associated with the storage and use of water. A significant archaeological feature on this site is a Late Roman cistern located to the west of the site (Fig. 6.56). It was not possible to enter the cistern and plan it from the inside; however, by looking from its opening it was realized that the cistern is at least 3m deep and it consists of more than one chamber with a vaulted entrance, which was decorated with an incised seashell – a common motif in the Roman period (Kadous 2001: 385). It seems that the cistern was largely rock-cut; however, and limestone blocks were used to build and reinforce the upper parts of its walls. The cistern was plastered with several layers of red mortar (*opus signinum*). An open channel connects the entrance of the cistern with a circular structure some 3m in diameter, observed to the west. This could also be interpreted as the top of a cistern. Further evidence for disturbed cisterns and channels was noted in the ploughed fields to the north of the site.

The tell also contains the remains of at least three square basins made of fired bricks and lined with red mortar (*opus signinum*), possibly part of a bath complex. The basins were located to the east of the site at a distance of about 140m from the large Late Roman cistern. To the east of the basins, on the side of the tell above the easterly football pitch, a large retaining wall built of large stone blocks was observed.

It is worth mentioning that all the wall remains that were recorded on the tell are located in between the basins to the east and the cistern in the west. Also fragments of glass, marble, porphyry, a monolith (Fig. 6.57), as well as iron slag and pottery sherds, were located on the tell. Site 204-205 has a sample of 351 indicator sherds. Sparse Ptolemaic pottery is present, potentially as early as the late 4th century BC but more likely from the late 3rd through 1st centuries BC with a small number of Early Roman sherds. The main occupation got underway during the late 4th and particularly the 5th century AD with the largest peak during the 7th century. Late Roman material covered

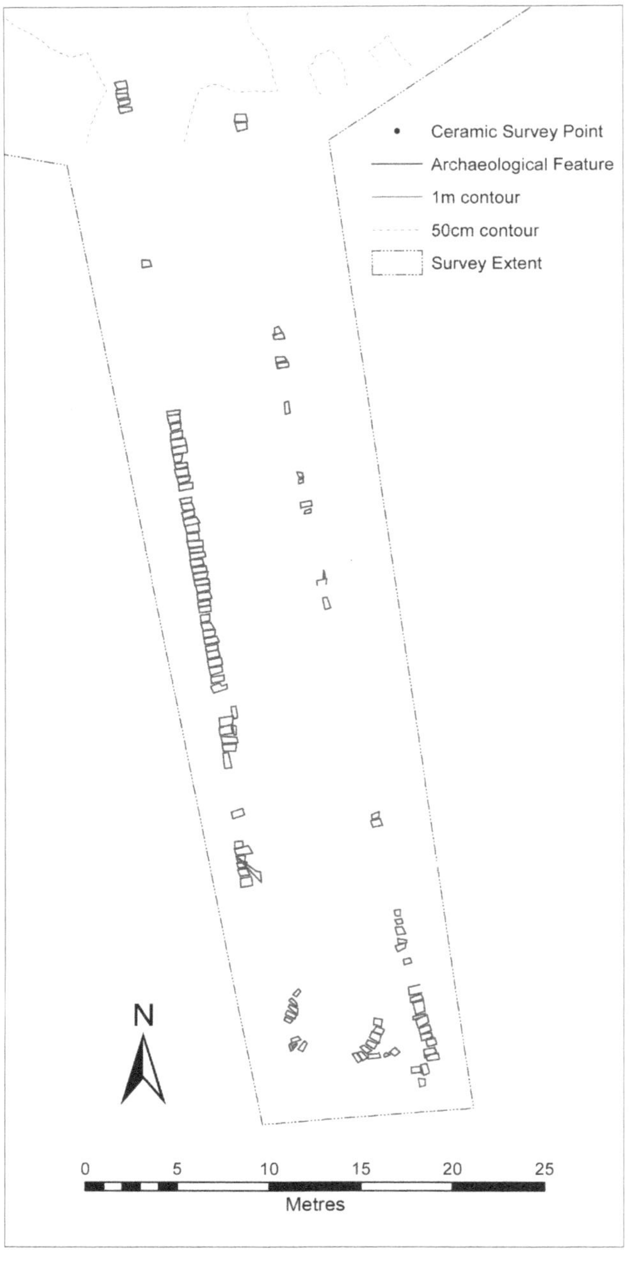

Fig. 6.58. (right) Site 204-205 plan of the jetty.

Fig. 6.59. (below) Site 204-205 jetty - looking south.

Fig. 6.60. (below, right) Site 204-205 jetty - looking north.

Graph 6.13. Bar graph showing the breakdown of form types by period Site 204-205.

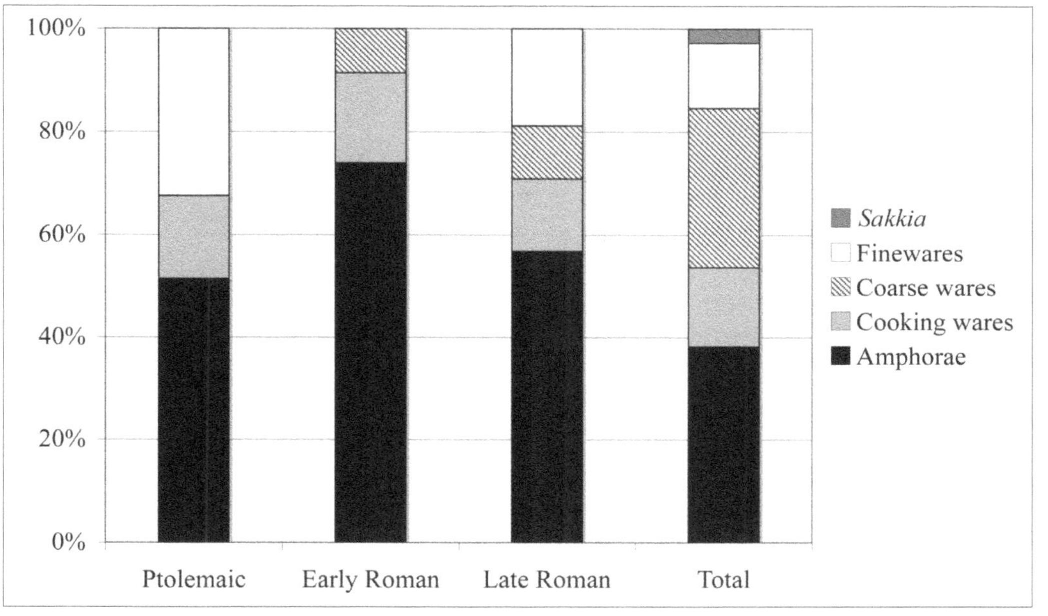

the whole of Site 204, whilst Ptolemaic and Early Roman pottery was concentrated at the west of the site (CC412, CC419, CC420) with rare Ptolemaic sherds distributed across the entire site. Amphorae, comprising almost half of the assemblage, were concentrated to the south of the site (CC412); elsewhere assemblages were mixed domestic wares. *Sakkia* pot sherds (10) clustered next to a rectangular structure, suggest there may have been a *sakkia* (water-wheel) nearby.

Among the main features associated with the site is a jetty that extends into the water at the foot of the promontory (Figs 6.58, 6.59 & 6.60). The jetty is 60m long and 6m wide and constructed of regular limestone blocks c. 0.7m x 0.35m x 0.40m. The longitudinal sides of the jetty are constructed of blocks arranged in headers and filled with rubble. In some parts of the jetty there is evidence that there was another upper course of curved limestone blocks along the edges. At the foot of the tell, particularly to the east of the jetty further, waterfront blocks were noted; however, it was not possible to record them in detail due to the rising lake levels.

It is noticeable that the site is directly opposite to Sites 23 and 40 on the northern shore of Mareotis Island. Also from the study of the large ceramic samples collected from Site 40 it is evident that both Site 204-205 and Site 40 were active during the same period i.e. during the Late Roman period between the 5th to 7th centuries AD.

About 600m to the west of Site 204-205, there is a second tell, smaller in size, c. 100m x 50m and 4m high. It is known locally as Abu Halis. The tell contains plenty of remains including limestone blocks, pottery and fired bricks; however, it is badly disturbed and therefore no walls or structures could be recorded.

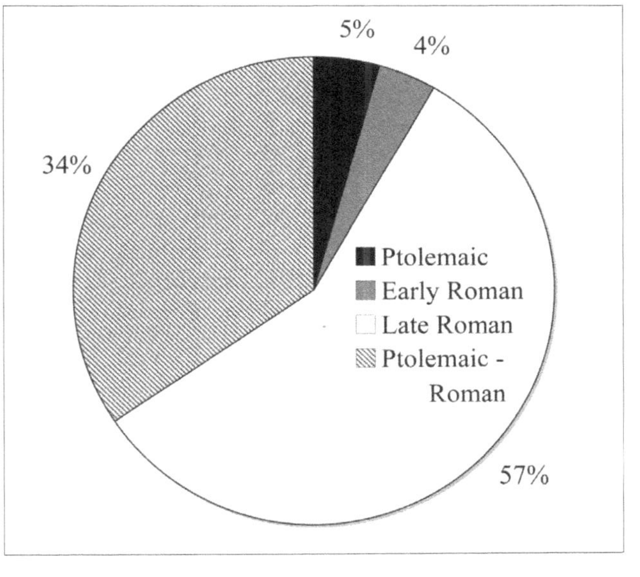

Graph 6.14. Pie graph showing the chronological breakdown of pottery from Site 204-205.

Table 6.16. Quantity of pottery types for Site 204-205.

Type	**No.**	**%**
Finewares		
African Red Slip ware (ARS) 104 (no. 101)	1	0.3
African Red Slip ware (ARS) 104-6 (no. 102)	1	0.3
Cypriot Red Slip ware (CRS)	1	0.3
Cypriot Red Slip ware (CRS) 2 (nos 103-4)	3	0.9
Cypriot Red Slip ware (CRS) 9 (nos 105-6)	7	2.0
Egyptian black slip dish (no. 56)	1	0.3
Egyptian black slip fish dish (nos 54-5)	1	0.3
Egyptian Red Slip ware bowl (no. 60)	2	0.6
Egyptian Red Slip ware A (ERSA)	1	0.3
Egyptian Red Slip ware A (ERSA) bowl (no. 73)	1	0.3
Egyptian Red Slip ware A (ERSA) bowl (nos 74-5)	2	0.6
Egyptian Red Slip ware A (ERSA) copy of ARS 75 (no. 64)	1	0.3
Egyptian Red Slip ware A (ERSA) copy of ARS 91D (no. 68)	1	0.3
Egyptian Red Slip ware A (ERSA) copy of CRS 9 (no. 76)	2	0.6
Egyptian Red Slip ware B (ERSB) copy of ARS 104C (nos 70-1)	5	1.4
Egyptian Red Slip ware B (ERSB) copy of ARS 67	1	0.3
Egyptian Red Slip ware B (ERSB) copy of ARS 84 (nos 65-6)	1	0.3
Egyptian Red Slip ware B (ERSB) copy of ARS 91A (no. 67)	1	0.3
Egyptian Red Slip ware B/C (ERSB/C) copy of ARS 104B (no. 69)	1	0.3
Egyptian Red Slip ware C (ERSC) copy of CRS 9 (no. 76)	2	0.6
Egyptian silt red slip fish dish (nos 54-5)	2	0.6
Imported Late Roman Red Slip ware bowl	2	0.6
Coarse wares		
Abu Mena basin (nos 79-80)	21	6.0
?Abu Mena basin (no. 81)	5	1.4
Abu Mena jug	(1)	0.0
Aswan jug	1	0.3
Egyptian basin	12	3.4
Egyptian bowl	5	1.4
Egyptian casserole	1	0.3
Egyptian jar	2	0.6
Egyptian marl *sakkia* pot (nos 35-41)	1	0.3
Egyptian miscellaneous coarse ware	26	7.4
Egyptian silt bowl/dish	6	1.7
Egyptian silt casserole (no. 48)	2	0.6
Egyptian silt casserole (nos 49-51)	20	5.7
Egyptian silt casserole lid (no. 53)	7	2.0
Egyptian silt cooking pot	10	2.8
Egyptian silt cooking pot (no. 44)	2	0.6
Egyptian silt dolium	2	0.6
Egyptian silt funnel strainer (no. 33)	1	0.3
Egyptian silt jug	14	4.0
Egyptian silt lid	10	2.8
Egyptian silt *sakkia* pot (nos 35-41)	9	2.6
Egyptian small coarse ware handle	14	4.0
Egyptian? skillet handle (no. 52)	3	0.9
Mareotic jug	1	0.3
Amphorae		
Abu Mena LR Amphora 5 (nos 87-9)	65	18.5
Aegean LR Amphora 2	2	0.6
Campanian 3rd century amphora (no. 137)	1	0.3
Campanian Dressel 2-4 (no. 136)	1	0.3
Cilician/Cypriot LR Amphora 1 (nos 146-9)	32	9.1
Egyptian silt AE3	3	0.9
Egyptian LR Amphora 7	2	0.6
Gaza LR Amphora 4 Majcherek Forms 2-4 (nos 154-7)	8	2.3
Knidian handle	2	0.6
Koan (nos 126-30)	5	1.4
Mareotic AE1/2 base (no. 7)	1	0.3
Mareotic unidentified type	1	0.3
Tunisian Africana III (no. 151)	1	0.3
Palestine LR Amphora 5 (no. 158)	8	2.3
Rhodian IE2/IF (nos 121-6)	4	1.1
Total	351 (1)	100%

Site 207-208 (including Sites 206 & 209) (Al-Quseir, SCA No. 110313) (Figs 6.1 & 6.61; Graphs 6.15 & 6.16; Table 6.17)
Location: 30 57 49N 29 33 56E to 30 57 37N 29 33 50E
Description: This site was investigated in 2004, 2006 and 2007 and it is of considerable size consisting of two tells separated by orchards and a football pitch. The western tell (Site 208) extends for c. 300m E-W and c. 350m N-S (Fig. 6.62), while the eastern tell (Site 207) extends for c. 350m E-W and c. 270m N-S (Fig. 6.63). They are both c. 12m high and were most probably once a single, large tell that has been artificially destroyed and flattened in the middle. In total the tell would have extended from east to west for c. 650m and from north to south for c. 300m.

Both tells are covered with large quantities of limestone blocks and ceramics, which indicate extensive occupation in antiquity. Moreover, a number of significant archaeological features were recorded, including the remains of the lower courses of a number of walls made of limestone blocks. One of the walls recorded on the western tell was more than 20m long which indicates that it belonged to a substantial building seen in the centre of image Fig. 6.64.

The site contains the remains of at least three wells and cisterns, one of which is still in use (well associated with Site 207; Fig. 6.65). The entrance of the wells are made of limestone blocks of various sizes; however, there is no evidence for the use of lime mortar or *opus singninum*. The entrances to the wells are generally square or rectangular in shape and they range in size from c. 0.5m x 1m to c. 1m x 1m. The western tell (Site 208) for example, contains a well with a rectangular entrance c. 0.80m x1.2m, which has evidence for what appears to be a water collection basin next to the entrance. The water lifted from the well was poured into the basin possibly for watering animals.

A substantial archaeological feature at the site is a 55m long x 10m wide jetty that extends into the lake from the foot of the western tell (Site 208; Figs 6.62, 6.66 & 6.67). At least three courses of limestone bocks are visible in the construction of the jetty. The upper level of the longitudinal sides of the jetty are made of rows of limestone blocks (c. 0.5m x 0.2m) arranged in headers (see Fig. 6.66). A second row of limestone blocks that are curved on their outside edge, extended along the edge of the jetty on top of the header blocks (Figs 6.68 & 6.69), in a similar fashion to the jetty at Site 204 (see above). However, unlike the jetty at Site 204, the sides of this jetty were built with more than one abutting row of blocks, so that in some places each side was up to 2m wide. The gap between the two sides was filled with small irregular stones and rubble imbedded in lime mortar. Moreover, it seems that this jetty has gone through different phases of building since some sections, particularly the end of the jetty that extends into the water, seem to have been rebuilt and extended using limestone blocks of different sizes and shapes.

There is another feature regarding this jetty that was not observed anywhere else in the lake. On the upper course of stones at the leeside of the jetty, there are at least three blocks carved in the form of short columns c. 0.25m in diameter and c. 0.15cm in height (Fig. 6.70). Those were probably used as mooring posts for tying up ships anchored to the jetty.

Fig. 6.61. Site 207-208 view from island.

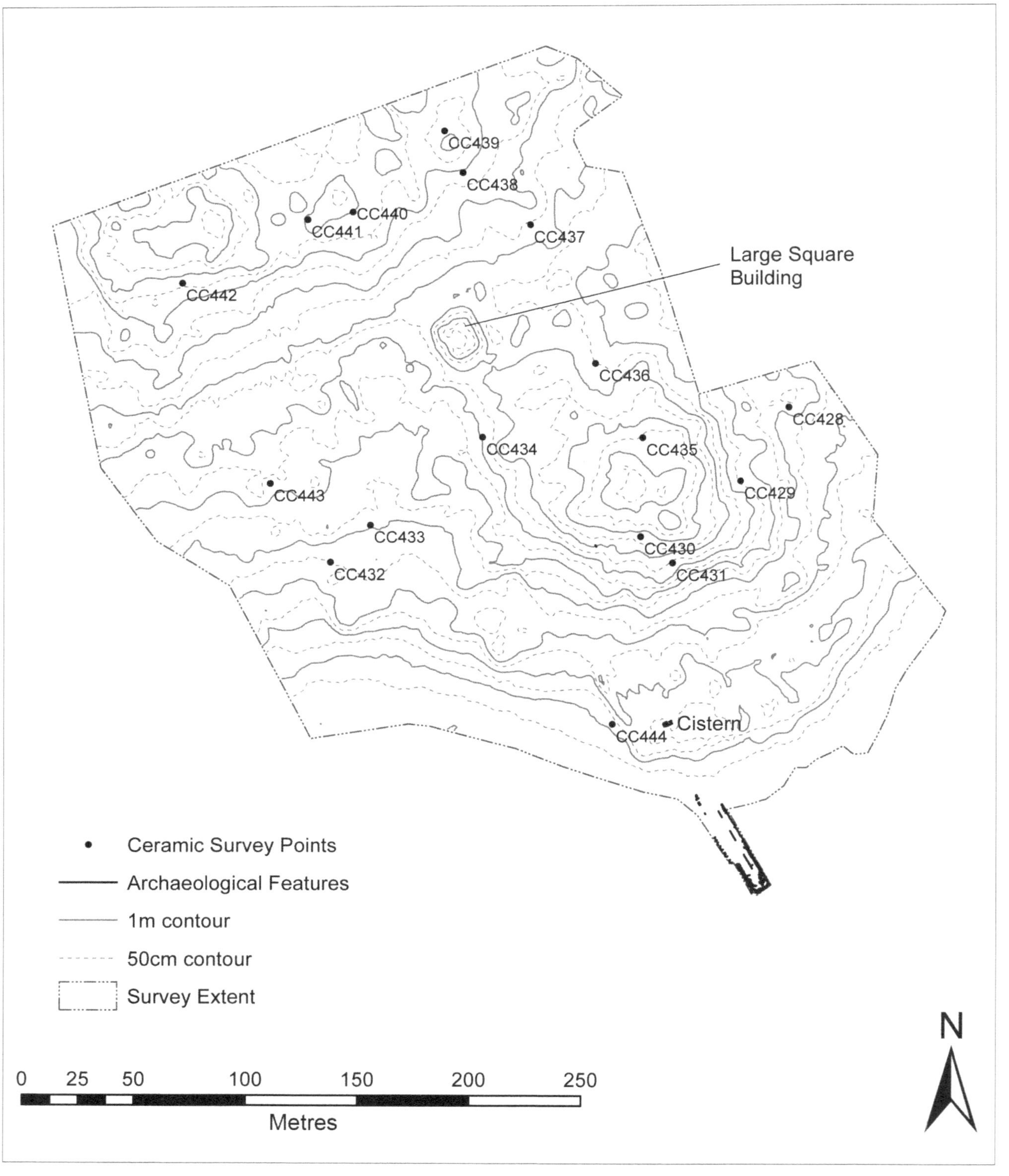

Fig. 6.62. Site 208 (western tell).

About 200m to the west of this jetty there are some badly preserved traces of a possible quay made of limestone blocks; unfortunately most of the blocks are lost beneath the lake surface.

Site 207-208 has a sample of 821 indicator sherds which chronologically compare to Site 204 (see above). In the eastern half of the site all ceramic circles possessed a range of domestic wares. Late Roman (5th – 7th century AD) material was well represented in every area mixed with rare Early Roman sherds. Ptolemaic pottery was concentrated in ceramic circle CC426, at the centre of the eastern side of the site. The site's western area can be roughly divided into two domestic sectors: a hill to the south and a ridge to

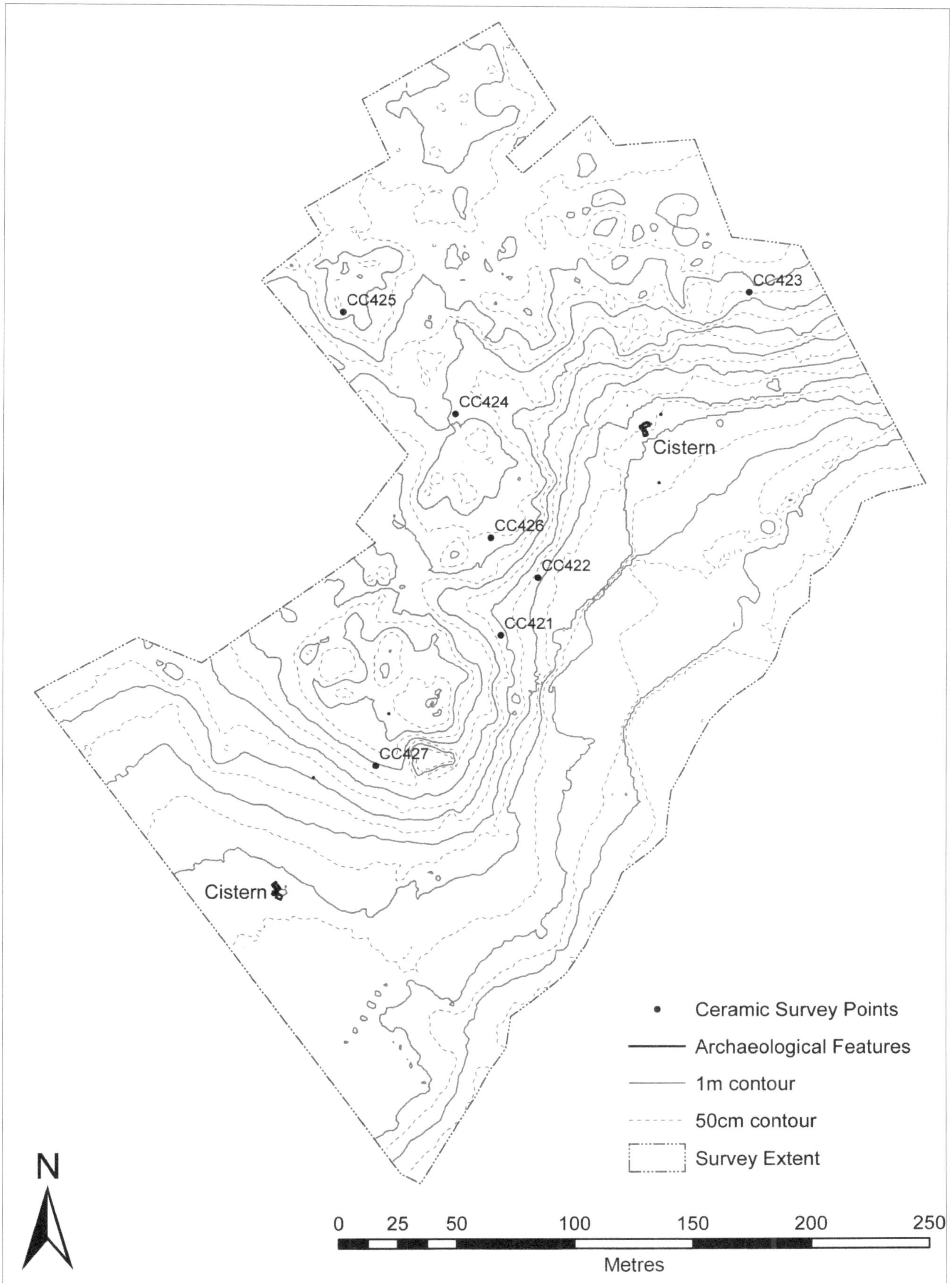

Fig. 6.63. Site 207 (eastern tell).

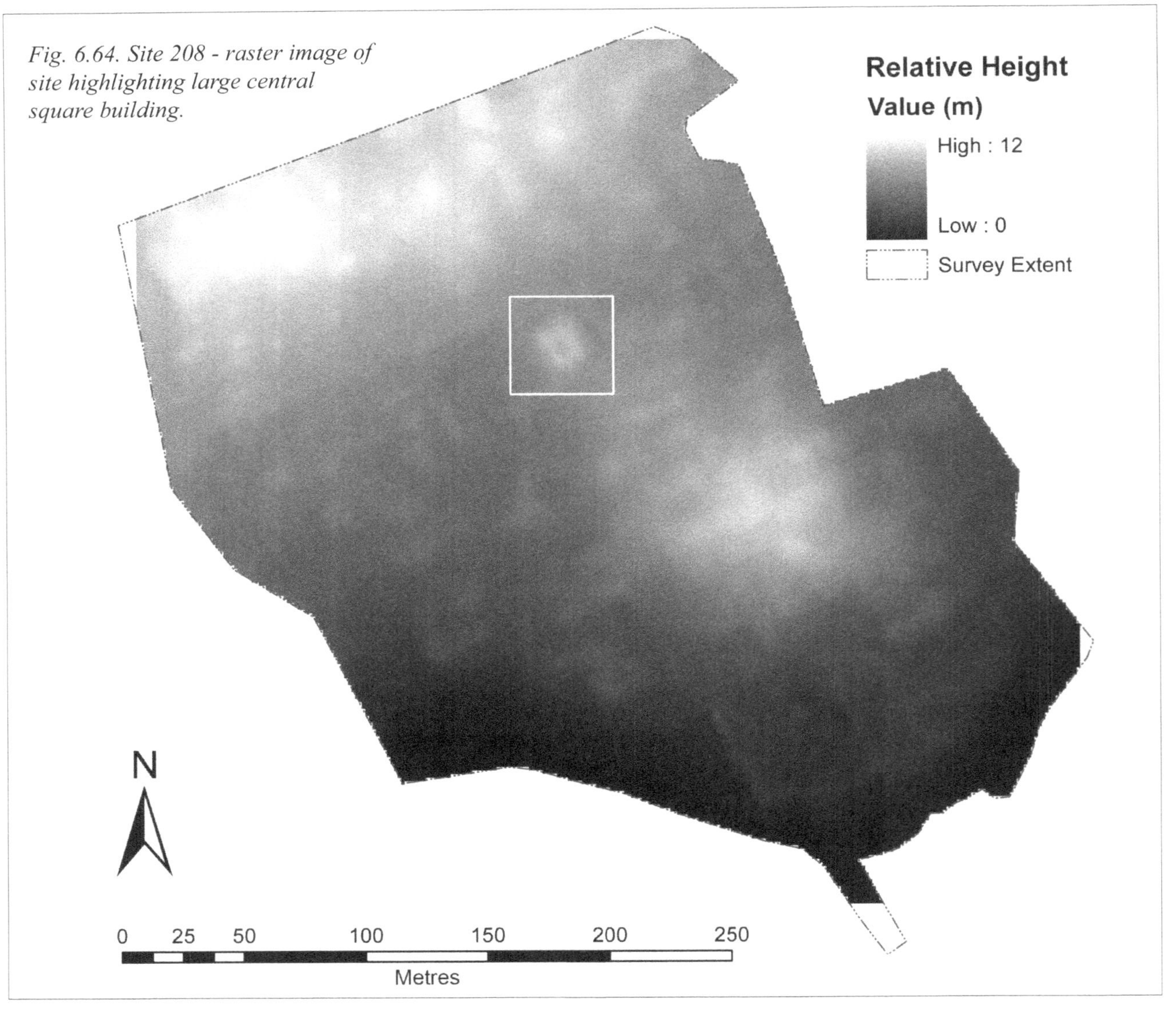

Fig. 6.64. Site 208 - raster image of site highlighting large central square building.

Fig. 6.65. Cistern/wall associated with Site 207.

Fig. 6.66. Jetty Site 208 - header blocks.

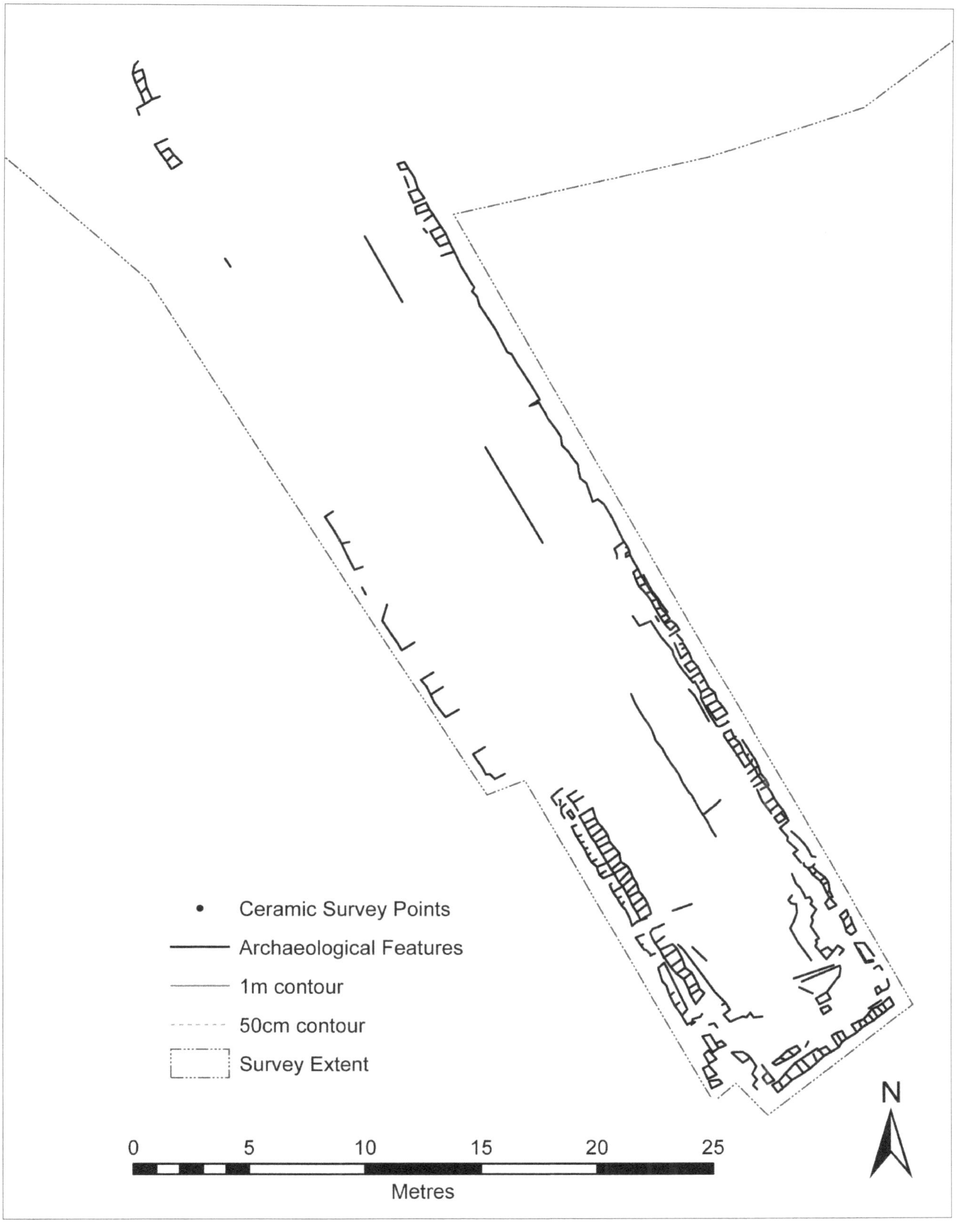

Fig. 6.67. Site 208 plan of jetty.

the north. Ptolemaic material was concentrated around the base of the southern hill (CC428, CC429, CC430, CC431, CC434). Elsewhere there was a concentration of Late Roman pottery, with transport amphorae especially common near the jetty (C44). The northern ridge was almost entirely Late Roman in date (CC437-CC442), as was a small rise to the west of the southern hill (CC432, CC433, CC443).

Fig. 6.68. Jetty Site 208 - curved blocks.

Fig. 6.69. Jetty Site 208 - header blocks.

Fig. 6.70. Mooring post on jetty Site 208.

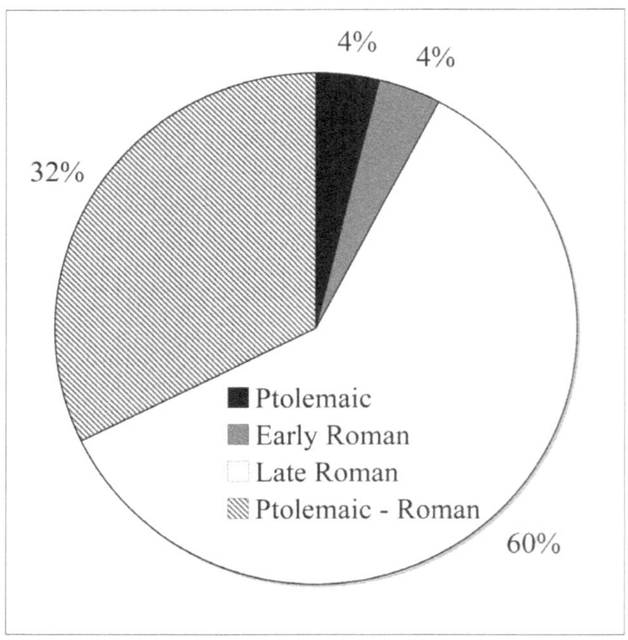

Graph 6.15. Pie graph showing the chronological breakdown of pottery from Site 207-208.

Graph 6.16. Bar graph showing the breakdown of form types by period Site 207-208.

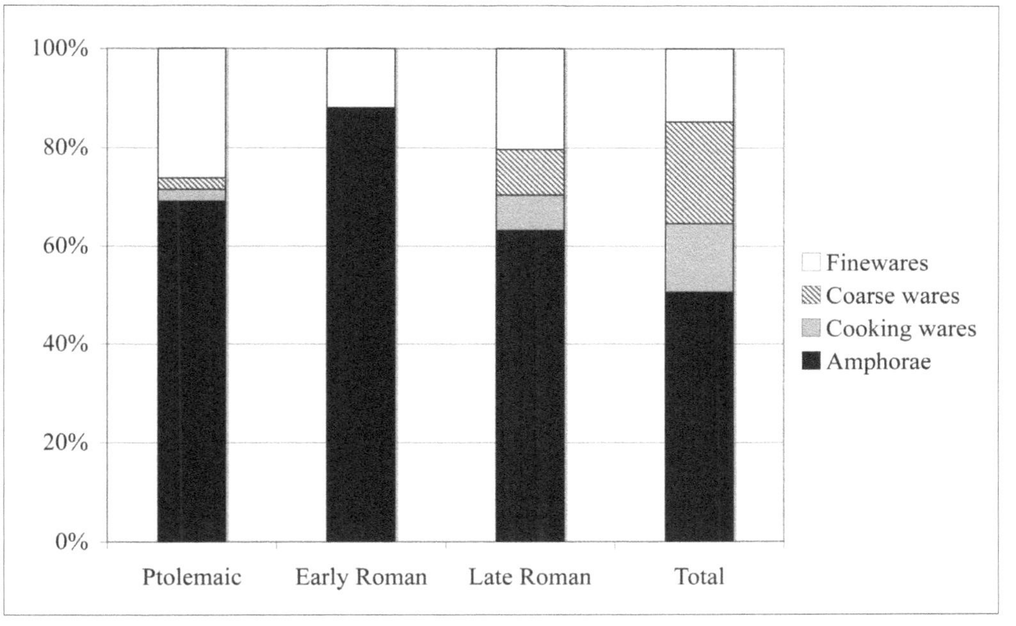

Table 6.17. (below) Quantity of pottery types for Site 207-208 (continued on the next page).

Type	No.	%
Finewares		
African Red Slip ware (ARS) 103	1	0.1
African Red Slip ware (ARS) 104 (no. 101)	5	0.6
African Red Slip ware (ARS) 104-6 (no. 102)	3	0.4
African Red Slip ware (ARS) 105	3	0.4
African Red Slip ware (ARS) 107	1	0.1
African Red Slip ware (ARS) 108	1	0.1
African Red Slip ware (ARS) 32/58	1	0.1
African Red Slip ware (ARS) 67 (no. 99)	1	0.1
African Red Slip ware (ARS) 99 (no. 100)	3	0.4
Cypriot Red Slip ware (CRS)	7	0.9
Cypriot Red Slip ware (CRS) 2 (nos 103-4)	13	1.6
Cypriot Red Slip ware (CRS) 5	1	0.1
Cypriot Red Slip ware (CRS) 8	1	0.1
Cypriot Red Slip ware (CRS) 9 (nos 105-6)	37	4.5
Eastern Sigillata A (ESA)	1	0.1
Egyptian black slip bowl (nos 57-9)	1	0.1
Egyptian black slip bowl footring base	8	1.0
Egyptian Ptolemaic/Early Roman red slip bowl/dish	24	2.9
Egyptian Red Slip ware A (ERSA)	6	0.7
Egyptian Red Slip ware A (ERSA) copy of ARS 84 (nos 65-6)	1	0.1
Egyptian Red Slip ware A (ERSA) copy of ARS 99	2	0.2
Egyptian Red Slip ware A (ERSA) copy of CRS 9 (no. 76)	1	0.1
Egyptian Red Slip ware B (ERSB) copy of ARS 84 (nos 65-6)	3	0.4
Egyptian Red Slip ware B (ERSB) copy of ARS 91A (no. 67)	2	0.2
Egyptian Red Slip ware B (ERSB) copy of ARS 96	4	0.5
Egyptian Red Slip ware B/C (ERSB/C) copy of ARS 104 base (no. 72)	2	0.2
Egyptian Red Slip ware B/C (ERSB/C) copy of ARS 104B (no. 69)	1	0.1
Painted unidentified	1	0.1
Phocaean Red Slip ware (PRS) 3 (nos 108-9)	2	0.2
Coarse wares		
Abu Mena basin (nos 79-80)	29	3.5
Abu Mena miscellaneous coarse wares	11	1.3

Egyptian basin	24	2.9
Egyptian bowl	15	1.8
Egyptian jug	3	0.4
Egyptian marl jug	2	0.2
Egyptian marl juglet (no. 21)	5	0.6
Egyptian silt bowl/dish	2	0.2
Egyptian silt casserole	4	0.5
Egyptian silt casserole (nos 49-51)	50	6.1
Egyptian silt cooking pot	50	6.1
Egyptian silt cooking pot (no. 47)	1	0.1
Egyptian silt dolium	3	0.4
Egyptian silt jar/jug with twisted handle (no. 27)	1	0.1
Egyptian silt jug	12	1.5
Egyptian silt lid	13	1.6
Egyptian silt miscellaneous coarse wares	8	1.0
Egyptian silt *sakkia* pot (nos 35-41)	3	0.4
Egyptian small coarse ware handle	26	3.2
Amphorae		
Abu Mena LR Amphora 5 (nos 87-9)	134	16.3
Aegean hollow foot	1	0.1
Cilician Dressel 30 (nos 143-4)	3	0.4
Cilician/Cypriot Agora G199 (no. 142)	4	0.5
Cilician/Cypriot Egloff 169 (no. 145)	6	0.7
Cilician/Cypriot LR Amphora 1 (nos 146-9)	132	16.1
Egyptian LR Amphora 7	14	1.7
ER silt ribbed amphora	4	0.5
Gaza LR Amphora 4 Majcherek Forms 2-4 (nos 154-7)	22	2.7
Imported unidentified type	22	2.7
Knidian handle	5	0.6
Knidian IIB/IIC (nos 113-18)	1	0.1
Koan (nos 126-30)	11	1.3
Mareotic AE1/2 base (no. 7)	5	0.6
Mareotic AE1/2 long handle (nos 4-5)	1	0.1
Mareotic AE4 (nos 13-17)	8	1.0
Mareotic Mons Claudianus Type 22/3 (nos 9-12)	3	0.4
Mareotic unidentified type	21	2.6
Palestine LR Amphora 5 (no. 158)	11	1.3
Rhodian IE2/IF (nos 121-6)	9	1.1
Tunisian Africana IID (no. 152)	2	0.2
Unsourced imported type (no. 169)	1	0.1
Western Asia Minor LR Amphora 3	2	0.2
Total	821	100.0%

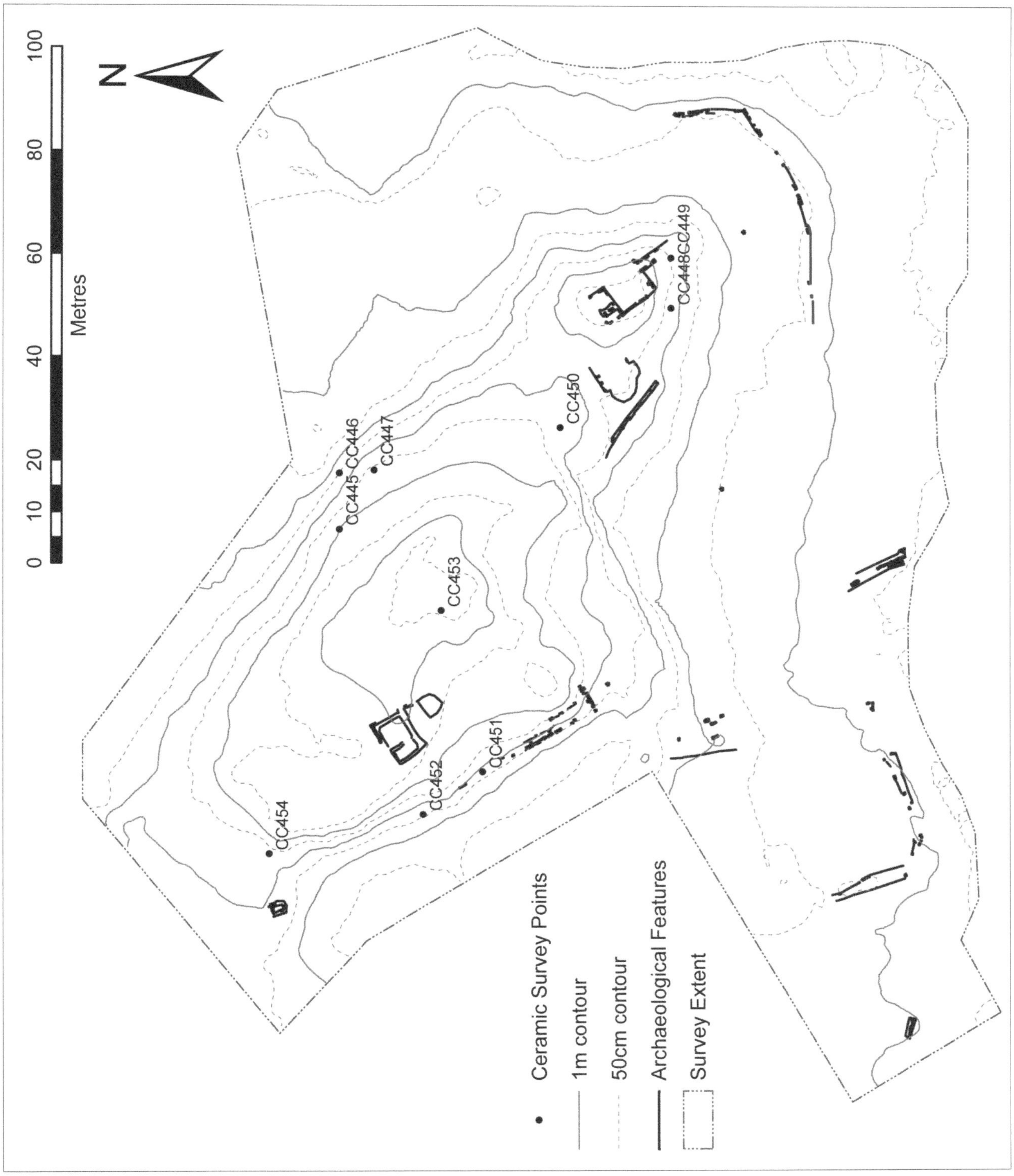

Fig. 6.71. Site 210-211.

Site 210-211 (Nakhel) (Figs 6.71 & 6.72; Graph 6.17; Table 6.18)
Location: 30 57 22N 29 33 23E to 30 57 20N 29 33 21E
Description: This site is less than 1km west of Site 207. It is an elongated promontory that extends for 150m N-S and 70m E-W and it is c. 6m high. The site consists of two mounds about 20m apart. The southern mound is 120m N-S by 50m E-W and the northern mound is 30m N-S by 20m E-W. The tell contains plenty of evidence for occupation from the 4th or 3rd century BC to the 7th century AD, in addition to a number of waterfront installations. Accordingly, the features recorded at this site can be divided into two groups: structures recorded on the tell and those recorded close to the waterline.

To the northwest of the site a well was recorded. The entrance of the well is 2m x 1m and is made of limestone blocks. About 35m south of the well, the remains of a 9m x

Fig. 6.72. General view of Site 210-211.

6m building were recorded on top of the southern mound. However, it is noticeable that the floor of the recorded building was made of burned bricks and *opus signinum*. This could be an indication for the existence of a bath complex or a building such as a house or a villa with a basin or *natatio* located within it (Fig. 6.73). A 30m long wall made of limestone blocks extended in a N-S direction only 9m west of the burnt brick building. At the southern end of this wall an 8m long section was recorded as the wall turned to the east.

Another building of similar dimensions to the first one (6m x 9m) was recorded on top of the small mound c. 100m southeast of the first building. Unlike most other sites where limestone had been the main building material used, at this site fired bricks were also extensively used in construction. However, there are some features that were recorded which were exclusively built of limestone blocks. Those are largely waterfront structures such as a 60m long waterside wall that was recorded at the foot of the northern mound. At least two courses of limestone blocks (0.5m x 0.25m x 0.25m) were visible in the waterside wall. It would appear that this wall surrounded the southern side of the foot of the hill and possibly functioned as a protection against potential sedimentation. The position and shape of this structure has proven to be quite unique at sites located on the northern shore of the lake.

About 60m west of the last visible part of the waterside wall exists another limestone structure although mostly destroyed. It is the remains of a jetty-like feature that extends in a N-S direction for c. 12m. The structure is totally landlocked as a result of sediment accumulation. About 40m west of this feature, another section of the waterside wall was recorded. The section is 50m long and it is made of limestone blocks arranged in two rows. Therefore, it is possible that the quay was linked to the waterside structure and that together they formed the main maritime feature at this site.

To the north of the maritime structures and west of the main tell site, a limestone block structure was recorded. The structure took the form of a large platform that follows the topography of the western slopes of the tell. It is almost 2m in height and extends for a distance of some 25m and is orientated perpendicular to the shoreline, constructed of cut limestone blocks (Fig. 6.74).

Site 210 has a sample of 271 indicator sherds potentially spanning from the late 4th century BC to the 7th century AD, with peaks during the late 3rd to 1st centuries BC, and the 5th to 6th centuries AD. Thirty-four *sakkia* pot sherds were concentrated next to a rectangular structure (CC448, CC449) as well as on a slope by the main hill (CC445), suggesting there was a *sakkia* (water-wheel) nearby. Amphorae comprised less than half of the assemblage (126) and all areas had a good range of domestic pottery of all dates, apart from a complex of structures associated with ceramic circles CC448 and CC449, which were Late Roman in date.

Fig. 6.73. Bath complex at Site 210-211.

Fig. 6.74. Platform structure extending south towards the shore at Site 210-211.

Graph 6.17. Pie graph showing the chronological breakdown of pottery from Site 210-211.

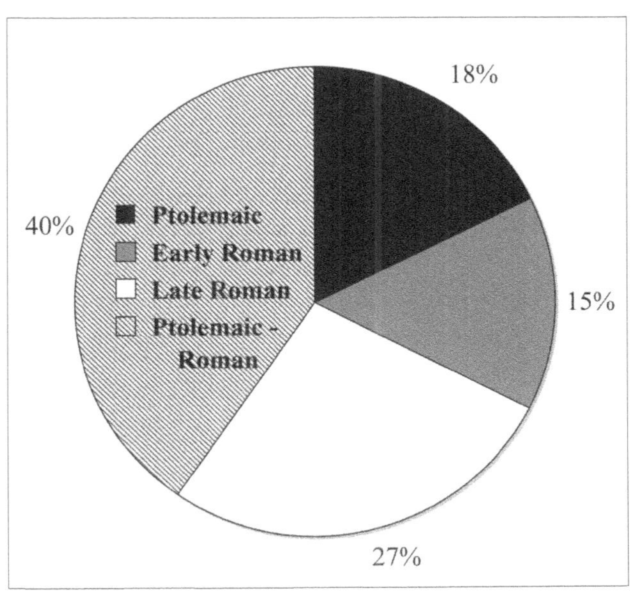

Table 6.18. Quantity of pottery types for Site 210-211.

Type	**No.**	**%**
Finewares		
African Red Slip ware (ARS)	1	0.4
African Red Slip ware (ARS) 104 (no. 101)	1	0.4
Cypriot Red Slip ware (CRS) 2 (nos 103-4)	4	1.5
Cypriot Red Slip ware (CRS) 9 (nos 105-6)	9	3.3
Eastern Sigillata A (ESA)	3	1.1
Eastern Sigillata A (ESA) 45 (no. 96)	1	0.4
Egyptian black slip bowl footring base	3	1.1
Egyptian Ptolemaic/Early Roman red slip bowl/dish	4	1.5
Egyptian Red Slip ware B/C (ERSB/C) copy of ARS 104B (no. 69)	1	0.4
Egyptian silt painted	(1)	0.0
Imported Late Roman Red Slip ware bowl	5	1.8
Italian Sigillata (ITS)	1	0.4
Megarian bowl	(1)	0.0
Phocaean Red Slip ware (PRS) 3C (nos 108)	5	1.8
Coarse wares		
Abu Mena basin (nos 79-80)	2	0.7
Egyptian casserole	6	2.2
Egyptian cup	1	0.4
Egyptian jug (no. 20)	2	0.7
Egyptian marl miscellaneous coarse ware	2	0.7
Egyptian silt cooking pot	28	10.3
Egyptian silt cooking pot (no. 45)	9	3.3
Egyptian silt dolium	6	2.2
Egyptian silt jar (no. 43)	1	0.4
Egyptian silt jar/jug with twisted handle (no. 27)	2	0.7
Egyptian silt jug	4	1.5
Egyptian silt lid	6	2.2
Egyptian silt miscellaneous coarse ware	2	0.7
Egyptian silt *sakkia* pot (nos 35-41)	34	12.5
Egyptian small coarse ware handle	2	0.7
Amphorae		
Abu Mena LR Amphora 5 (nos 87-9)	2	0.7
Campanian 3rd century amphora (no. 137)	1	0.4
Campanian Dressel 2-4 (no. 136)	4	1.5
Cilician Dressel 30 (nos 143-4)	5	1.8
Cilician Pompeii V (no. 141)	1	0.4
Cilician/Cypriot Agora G199 (no. 142)	3	1.1
Cilician/Cypriot Egloff 169 (no. 145)	7	2.6
Cilician/Cypriot LR Amphora 1 (nos 146-9)	28	10.3
Egyptian LR Amphora 7	(1)	0.0
Gaza LR Amphora 4 Majcherek Forms 2-4 (nos 154-7)	6	2.2
Imported unidentified type	8	3.0
Knidian handle	10	3.7
Koan (nos 126-30)	13	4.8
Mareotic AE1/2 base (no. 7)	4	1.5
Mareotic AE4 (nos 13-17)	10	3.7
Mareotic Mons Claudianus Type 22/3 (nos 9-12)	5	1.8
Mareotic unidentified type	6	2.2
Rhodian IE2/IF (nos 121-6)	9	3.3
Tunisian Africana IID (no. 152)	2	0.7
Western Asia Minor LR Amphora 3	2	0.7
Total	271 (3)	100%

Site 255 (Tell Samir) (Figs 6.1, 6.75)
Location: 30 57 14N 29 32 54E
Description: This is a small isolated site distinguished by two rectangular red brick, plaster-lined basins surrounded by scattered pottery and fired bricks. They were aligned at right angles next to each other and measured approximately 4 x 1m. Limited information was compiled on this site and no ceramics were collected. However, the nature of the fired bricks indicates that it was Roman in date.

Fig. 6.75. Site 255 basin.

Site 253 (Fig. 6.76; Graph 6.18; Table 6.19)
Location: 30 57 15N 29 32 44E
Description: This was originally an inland site that is located c. 1km west of Site 210-211 and some 300m from the lake's present shoreline. The site is a relatively small tell 50m N-S x 60m E-W and it is 6m high. It is believed to have been much larger in antiquity having been flattened to create orchards and fields which surround the site on all sides. Moreover, the shoreline to the south of the site has been artificially excavated to create fish farms and irrigation canals. Accordingly, the site is badly destroyed and the remains of many buildings only partially visible. However, the most visible building is located at the highest point on the tell. It is a roughly square building that measures c. 6.8m x 7.8m (Fig. 6.77). The building has a double wall and the walls are built of limestone blocks. Each wall is c. 0.6m thick and between the two walls there is a layer of red mortar *opus signinum*, probably of a Late Roman date. The interior of the walls are lined with a layer of *opus signinum*. The use of red mortar in the walls implies that the building was associated with liquid, perhaps water or wine. Therefore, it could be associated with a winery or more likely a treading platform of a wine press. It was not possible to locate any waterfront installation associated with this structure as the shoreline has been subject to much destruction.

Site 253 has a sample of 37 indicator sherds ranging between the late 4th or 3rd centuries BC and the Late Roman period, which is the most common. The absence of Abu Mena amphorae may suggest the site was not occupied during the 7th century AD. Seventy-eight percent of the ceramic assemblage is amphorae, broken down by sherd numbers as Ptolemaic (11), Early Roman (3) and Late Roman (15).

Fig. 6.76. Site 253.

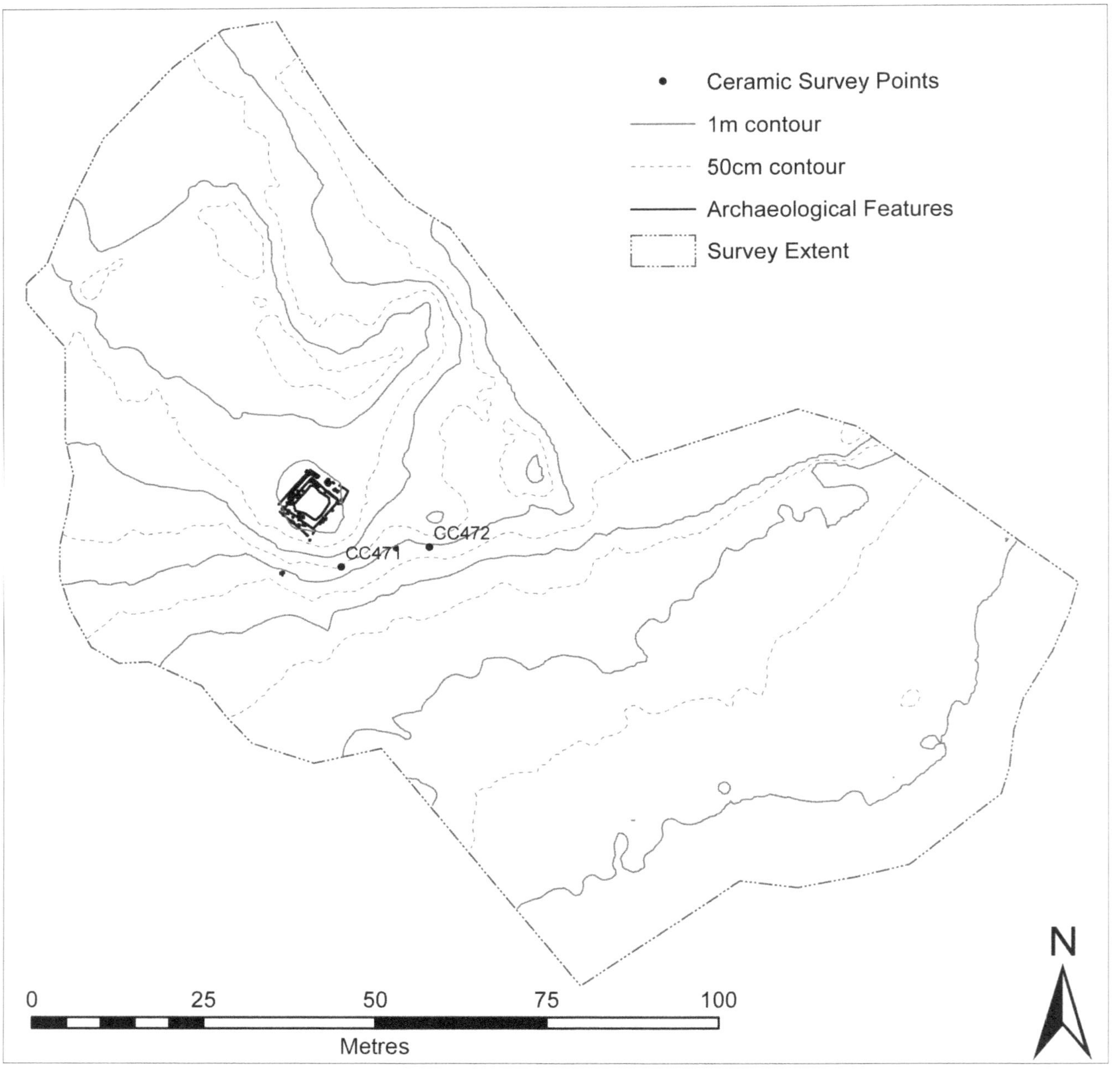

Fig. 6.77. Square building at Site 253 looking south-west.

Table 6.19. (left) Quantity of pottery types for Site 253.

Type	No.	%
Finewares		
African Red Slip ware (ARS) 103	2	5.4
Egyptian Ptolemaic/Early Roman red slip bowl/dish	3	8.1
Coarse wares		
Egyptian miscellaneous coarse ware	1	2.7
Egyptian silt basin (no. 82)	1	2.7
Egyptian silt jug	1	2.7
Amphorae		
Cilician Agora M54 (no. 140)	1	2.7
Cilician/Cypriot Egloff 169 (no. 145)	1	2.7
Cilician/Cypriot LR Amphora 1 (nos 146-9)	8	21.6
Egyptian LR Amphora 7	1	2.7
Gaza LR Amphora 4 Majcherek Forms 2-4 (nos 154-7)	5	13.5
Knidian handle	2	5.4
Knidian IIB (no. 110)	2	5.4
Koan (nos 126-30)	1	2.7
Mareotic AE1/2 base (no. 7)	2	5.4
Mareotic AE1/2 long handle (nos 4-5)	2	5.4
Mareotic AE4 (nos 13-17)	1	2.7
Mareotic Mons Claudianus Type 22/3 (nos 9-12)	1	2.7
Rhodian IE2/IF (nos 121-6)	2	5.4
Total	37	100%

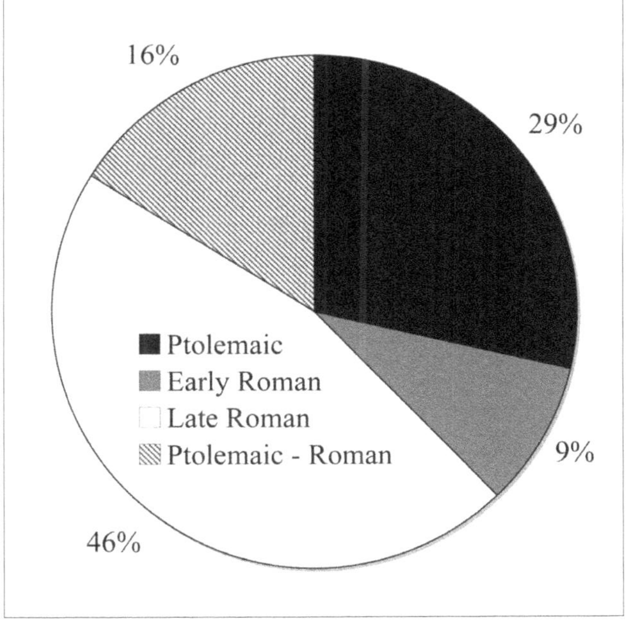

Graph 6.18. Pie graph showing the chronological breakdown of pottery from Site 253.

Site 252 (Table 6.20)
Location: 30 57 02N 29 32 29E
Description: This site is located c. 500m west of Site 252. It is located on a small promontory, about 60m N-S x 30m E-W and 4m high, and it is c. 100m from the present shoreline of the lake. The area is used as a rubbish dump and it is badly disturbed. However, there are some remains of limestone building blocks and few pieces of ceramics in addition to traces of wall outlines. Some 200m to the west of the site extending over the flat land between the road and the lake shore, further ceramics were collected indicating that the site was perhaps more extensive than presently indicated in antiquity. Site 252 has a sample of 17 indicator sherds, showing no clear patterning, potentially from the late 3rd or 2nd century BC through the Late Roman period with no exclusively 7th century material present.

Type	**No.**
Aegean hollow foot amphora	1
Campanian Dressel 2-4 (no. 136)	1
Cilician/Cypriot LR Amphora 1 (nos 146-9)	1
Cypriot Red Slip ware (CRS) 2 (nos 103-4)	1
Eastern Sigillata A (ESA)	(1)
Egyptian silt cooking pot	1
Egyptian silt jug	2
Egyptian silt lamp	(1)
Egyptian silt lid	1
Gaza LR Amphora 4 Majcherek Forms 2-4 (nos 154-7)	1
Glazed (?modern)	(2)
Knidian handle	1
Koan (nos 126-30)	1
Mareotic AE1/2 base (no. 7)	1
Mareotic Mons Claudianus Amphora Type 22/3 (nos 9-12)	(1)
Mareotic unidentified amphora	3
Rhodian IE2/IF (nos 121-6)	2
Total	17 (5)

Table 6.20. Quantity of pottery types for Site 252.

Site 212-213 (Sidi Shanawir) (Figs 6.78 & 6.79; Table 6.21)
Location: 30 54 46N 29 27 40E to 30 54 48N 29 27 28E
Description: This site is about 7.5km west of Taposiris Magna and in contrast to sites east of Taposiris Magna, Site 212-213 is much flatter with a more uniform topography. The surveyed area measures 650m E-W, 250m N-S and is generally some 1-2m above the lake's level with the exception of a small tell, c. 40m x c. 20m, located to the north of the site. The tell is c. 8m high and 300m from the present shoreline. The north-western area of the tell is occupied by a modern Islamic cemetery. The archaeological remains recorded at this site overlook the present shoreline and could have been even closer to the waterline in antiquity.

This site contains the remains of a substantial series of multi-room buildings close to the edge of the water, all constructed of limestone blocks and lime mortar (Fig. 6.78). The lower courses of four central buildings were recorded. Their dimensions from east to west are 20m x 15m, 40m x 20m, 30m x 7m and 13m x 8m, and they are about 150m north of the present shoreline. By looking at these buildings, it becomes evident that they have gone through different phases of construction. It is noticeable that the walls are relatively thick (c. 1m) and that they are made of blocks of different sizes. Also there is no evidence for the use of red mortar *opus signinum* in the buildings. Considering the fact that there appears to have been sedimentation along the lake edge, it is possible that the buildings closest to the shoreline could have been used as a quay for mooring vessels in antiquity. What appears to be a mound of ballast stone was recorded south of these buildings, together with evidence of burning. The construction of the waterfront buildings suggests that they could have been used as storage facilities for different commodities transported around the lake.

The site has a sample of 18 indicator sherds. Of those that were dateable all were Late Roman, of late 4th or 5th to 7th centuries AD.

It is noticeable that Site 212-213 is located immediately opposite Site 44 on the southern shore of the lake, therefore contact between the two sites was possible by water in antiquity.

Type	No.
Abu Mena LR Amphora 5 (nos 87-9)	5
Egyptian Red Slip ware B/C (ERSB/C) copy of ARS 104C (nos 70-1)	2
Egyptian silt base	1
Egyptian silt casserole (nos 49-51)	6
Egyptian silt casserole lid (no. 53)	1
Egyptian LR Amphora 7	1
Mareotic unidentified amphora	1
Unidentified imported amphora	1
Total	18

Table 6.21. Quantity of pottery types for Site 212-213.

Fig. 6.78. Buildings close to the water at Site 212-213.

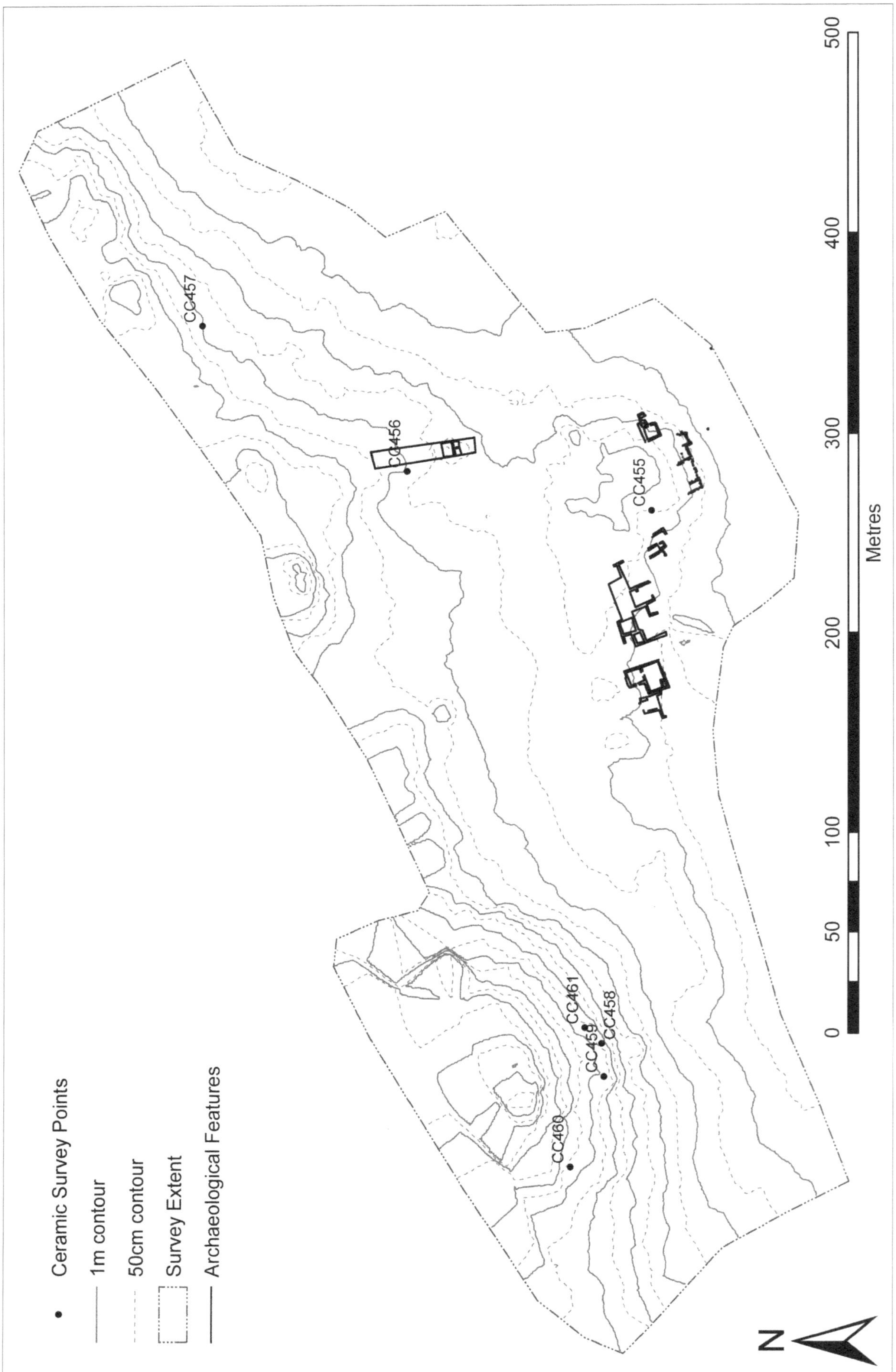

Fig. 6.79. Site 212-213.

Site 214-215 (Fig. 6.80; Graph 6.19; Table 6.22)
Location: 30 53 30N 29 25 32E to 30 53 36N 29 25 22E
Description: This site is located about 4.5km west of Site 212-213 and it is the most westerly archaeological site recorded along the northern shore of the lake within the current survey area. Like Site 212-213 it is relatively flat and its topography is quite uniform. The site covers an area of c. 350m NW-SE and 650m SW-NE and is made up of a series of small mounds, c. 4m in height, which are aligned NW-SE for a distance of about 350m.

Fig. 6.80. Site 214-215.

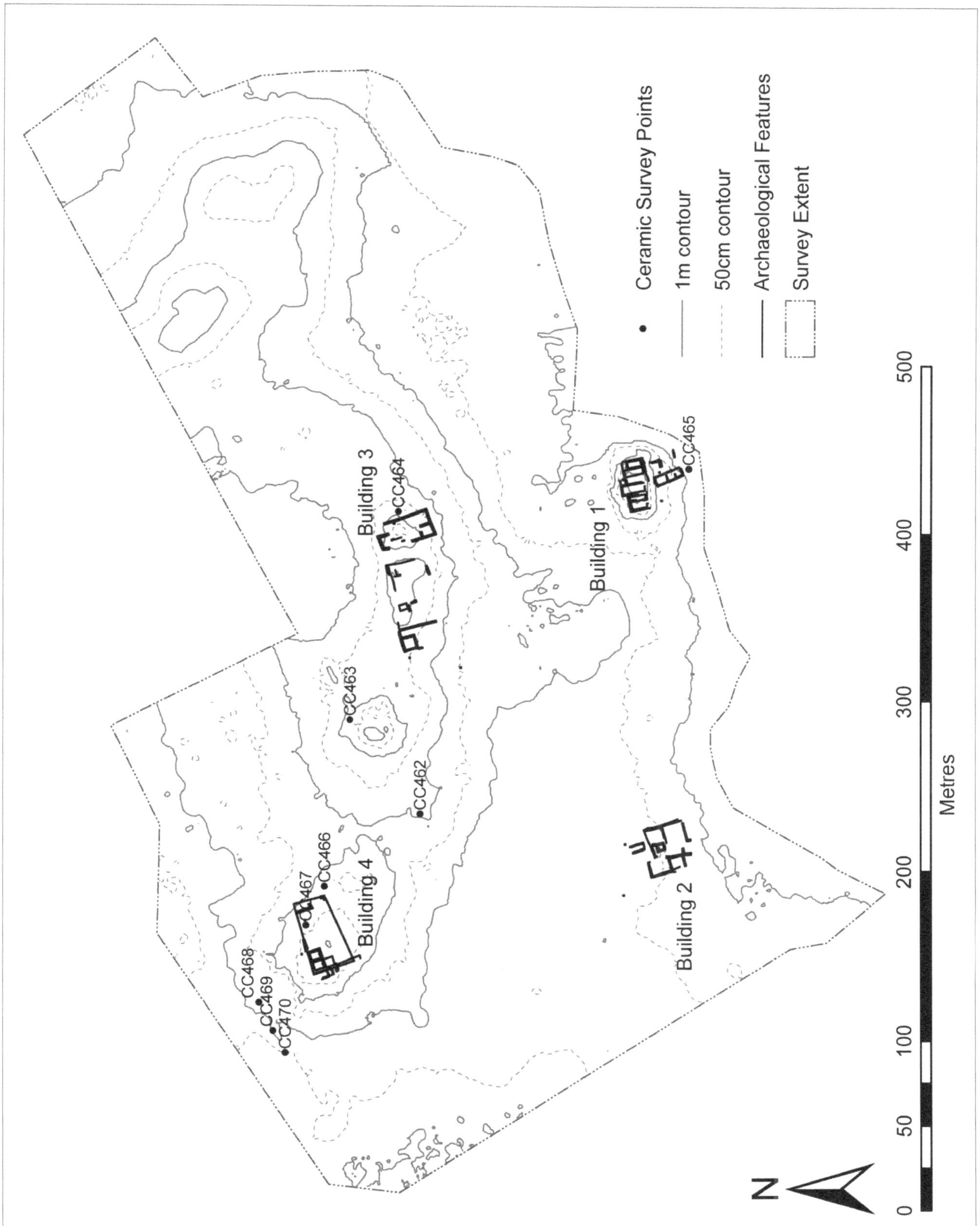

Fig. 6.81. Building 1 Site 214-215, looking south.

Fig. 6.82. Building 1 plaster walls Site 214-215.

Fig. 6.83. Building 1 tiled floor Site 214-215.

Fig. 6.84. Structure to the south of Building 1 Site 214-215.

Fig. 6.85. Building 4 wine vats Site 214-215.

The remains of four areas of activity were recorded at the site. Three of them, those areas closest to the shore, take the form of multi-room buildings, while the fourth building located at a distance of c. 200m inland is a large winery complex.

Building 1 is constructed on a small tell at the waterline and had been partially excavated revealing clear wall outlines and structural features (Fig. 6.81). The tell measures c. 45m E-W and 20m N-S and is 1-2m high. The partially excavated building is rectangular in shape and measures c. 30m E-W x 12m N-S, and is divided internally by a number of walls which extend in a N-S direction. The walls, which are quite thick (c. 0.7-1m), are made of rough limestone blocks of various sizes and are constructed in a mixture of building styles (ashlar, *opus incertum*). Also there is evidence for plaster on the interior of some of the walls (Fig. 6.82) and red mortar on the exterior. The remains of the building's wall are 0.5-0.8m high.

The floor of Building 1 was paved with rectangular limestone tiles, each measuring c. 0.4m x 0.8m x 0.1m (Fig. 6.83). This is an unusual feature which has not been noticed in any other building throughout the survey area. About 6m south of the main Building 1 there is another structure that measures c. 6m x 16m and extends almost to the present water's edge (Fig. 6.84). It is situated c. 2m below the elevation of the main building. Moreover, as a result of sediment accumulation the structure is mostly buried with only its outline visible. In antiquity this could have been a jetty that served as a maritime installation for the main building. This building and the associated maritime installation appear to be of significant importance; however, its exact function has yet to be determined.

Building 2 was recorded c. 200m west of Building 1. It is located on the shoreline, and therefore its walls are mostly buried under the sediments and only 0.05-0.1m of the

Fig. 6.86. Building 4 wine vats Site 214-215.

height of walls are visible. The building is almost square in shape (c. 25m x 25m) and it is divided internally into four smaller rooms. Its wall arrangement is similar to that of Building 1; however, evidence of plaster was not noticeable.

The third building is located inland c. 140m north of Building 1 and measures c. 70m E-W and 30m N-S. However, it is unclear if it is one building divided into at least three longitudinal rooms or if the rooms are unconnected. The walls of the building(s) are similar in structure and dimension to the other two buildings which suggest they are contemporary. However, it is worth mentioning that very few ceramic sherds were found in the vicinity of Buildings 1, 2 and 3 which made dating them through ceramic samples problematic.

The fourth building on this site is located inland c. 200m north of the present shoreline. It is a partially excavated winery complex, considered to be one of the largest in the Mareotic region (Rodziewicz 1998b). Moreover, it is the only winery recorded on the northern shore of the lake. The complex measures c. 40m E-W and 20m N-S and contains two treading vats, each measuring 5m x 5m (Figs 6.85 & 6.86). The vats are made of limestone and red bricks and are lined on the inside with several layers of *opus signinum*. The vats open onto a collection basin that is almost completely buried under sediment. The outer walls that surround the complex are similar in structure to the walls of Buildings 1, 2 and 3, made of limestone in *opus incertum*. To the west of the vats the remains of another structure were recorded, the floor of which consists of square red bricks with evidence of burning and pottery sherds in the vicinity. It is evident that that this was a large scale wine production centre which could have been associated with the other buildings recorded in the area.

Therefore, Buildings 1 and 2 which were constructed close to the ancient shoreline of the lake could have been used as warehouses and storage facilities in association with the inland wine production centre.

It is worth mentioning that one of the main distinctive features of the area west of Taposiris Magna is the absence of high mounds and tells close to the shoreline. Extensive flat areas up to 700m wide separate the shoreline from the coastal ridges. These flat stretches would have been suitable for the cultivation of vines and hence this would explain the existence of a winery complex in this area.

Moreover, it is noticeable that Site 214-215 is located opposite to Site 108-109 on the southern shore of the lake.

The distance between the two sites is c. 1.5km indicating relatively easy contact across the lake between the two sites, thus reinforcing the idea that the two sites were linked in antiquity.

Site 214 has a sample of 113 indicator sherds, mostly of Ptolemaic date, followed by Late Roman. The Ptolemaic material dates from the late 3rd to 1st centuries BC. The Late Roman pottery is 5th to 7th centuries AD, although the small quantity of Abu Mena amphorae may suggest that it was also sparsely occupied during the 7th century. Over half the sherds belonged to transport amphorae (66). The site is divided into two distinct areas. In the northwest the wine vat of Building 4 is associated with Ptolemaic and Early Roman amphorae and some domestic pottery (C466-CC470), whereas the southeast of the site was entirely Late Roman in date and domestic in nature. Though local amphorae were common, Rhodian imports were more frequently found and their association with the wine vat suggests they may have been reused there for bottling wine. The fact that imported amphorae are dominant is intriguing, as even in this relatively early period local amphora production was developed enough to cater to the Mareotic wine industry

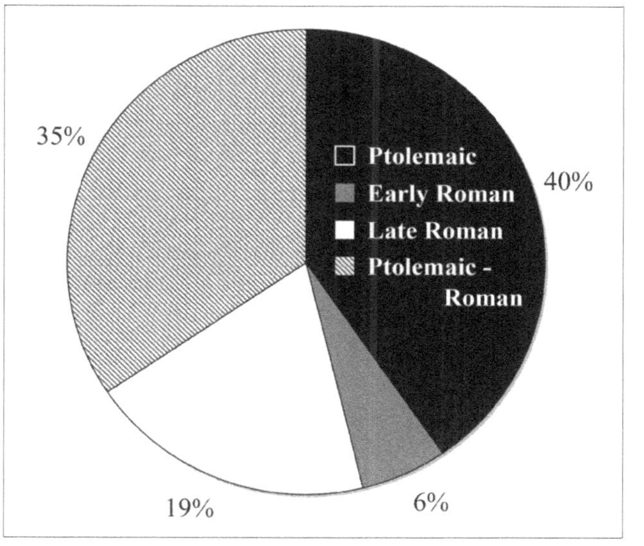

Graph 6.19. Pie graph showing the chronological breakdown of pottery from Site 214-215.

Table 6.22. Quantity of pottery types for Site 214-215.

Type	No.	%
Finewares		
Cypriot Red Slip ware (CRS) 9 (nos 105-6)	2	1.8
Eastern Sigillata A (ESA) dish	1	0.9
Egyptian Ptolemaic/Early Roman red slip bowl/dish	1	0.9
Egyptian Red Slip ware B/C (ERSB/C) copy of ARS 104B (no. 69)	1	0.9
Egyptian silt red slip fish dish (nos 54-5)	1	0.9
Imported Late Roman Red Slip ware bowl	(1)	0.0
Coarse wares		
Egyptian bowl	3	2.7
Egyptian casserole	5	4.4
Egyptian silt bowl/dish	2	1.8
Egyptian silt casserole (no. 48)	1	0.9
Egyptian silt casserole (nos 49-51)	1	0.9
Egyptian silt cooking pot	20	17.7
Egyptian silt cooking pot (no. 45)	2	1.8
Egyptian silt jug	2	1.8
Egyptian silt miscellaneous coarse ware	1	0.9
Egyptian silt *sakkia* pot (nos 35-41)	1	0.9
Egyptian small coarse ware handle	3	2.7
Amphorae		
Abu Mena LR Amphora 5 (nos 87-9)	2	1.8
Aegean LR Amphora 2	1	0.9
Cilician/Cypriot LR Amphora 1 (nos 146-9)	12	10.6
Gaza LR Amphora 4 Majcherek Forms 2-4 (nos 154-7)	2	1.8
Knidian handle	2	1.8
Koan (nos 126-30)	4	3.5
Mareotic AE1/2 base (no. 7)	2	1.8
Mareotic AE1/2 long handle (nos 4-5)	4	3.5
Mareotic AE1/2 short handle (no. 6)	1	0.9
Mareotic AE4 (nos 13-17)	3	2.7
Mareotic unidentified type	1	0.9
Palestine LR Amphora 5 (no. 158)	1	0.9
Rhodian IE2/IF (nos 121-6)	31	27.4
Total	113 (1)	100%

6.4 Sites located on Mareotis Island. SCA No. 110323 (Fig. 6.1)

Mareotis Island is one of the most distinctive geomorphological and archaeological features in the western Mareotic Arm. The island is located c. 3.5km west of the Sidi Kerir road and it extends for c. 3.7km in a NE-SW direction. It is located c. 580m from the southern shoreline of the lake and c. 1.4km from the northern shoreline and it reaches its maximum width of c. 680m at its eastern end. The island consists of a series of limestone mounds supporting aeolian soils, while marshland extends along its shores.

Geomorphological investigation in the region indicates that Mareotis Island is part of a calcareous ridge that extends west from Marea Peninsula. The ridge runs parallel to the lake's southern shoreline, and in antiquity, the depression between the ridge and the southern shore of the lake was water-logged to a greater or lesser degree. In other words, Mareotis Island was an island in antiquity (see Chapter 5, this volume).

Archaeological investigation of Mareotis Island has revealed that the majority of archaeological material is concentrated on the eastern and western ends of the island where the remains of two substantial urban centres exist. The central section of the island ridge, which extends for c. 1.5km, contains considerably less urban archaeological remains and more evidence for industrial and rural activities, particularly amphora production.

It is also noticeable that the cluster of archaeological sites at the eastern end of the island face Site 202-203 on the northern shore of the lake, while the cluster of sites at the western end of the island face Site 204-205. Interestingly, no sites were recorded between Site 202-203 and Site 204-205 on the northern shore of the lake, and no coastal sites were recorded along the opposite shore of the central section of the island. Therefore, it is possible that the development of human activities on Mareotis Island in antiquity was supported by the establishment of contacts between the island and the northern shore of the lake.

6.4.1 Sites located on the eastern end of the island (Fig. 6.87)

The eastern end of the island covers an area that measures c. 1km NE-SW and c. 680m NW-SE at its widest. The area comprises a limestone ridge that measures c. 800m x 300m and is over 6m high. The foot of the ridge is located c. 50m from the northern shore of the island and c. 200m from the southern shore of the island.

Archaeological remains at the eastern end of the island are generally concentrated on the ridge and along the northern shoreline.

From the initial survey in 2004 it was apparent that a number of the sites, particularly those located on the ridge, had already been partially investigated. In addition, the detailed investigation of Mareotis Island that was conducted in 2007, not only revealed that some of the sites initially recorded in 2004 are more extensive than originally believed, but that many are connected to each other and can thus be discussed as a unit. Thus, in many cases the division of sites is somewhat arbitrary as in effect, the archaeology is almost continuous across the extent of the eastern end of the island. Therefore, in the following section sites will be grouped according to their spatial, chronological or functional characteristics. Interpretation of the chronology and morphology of the eastern end of the island is supplemented by ceramic and sedimentological survey (Fig. 6.88).

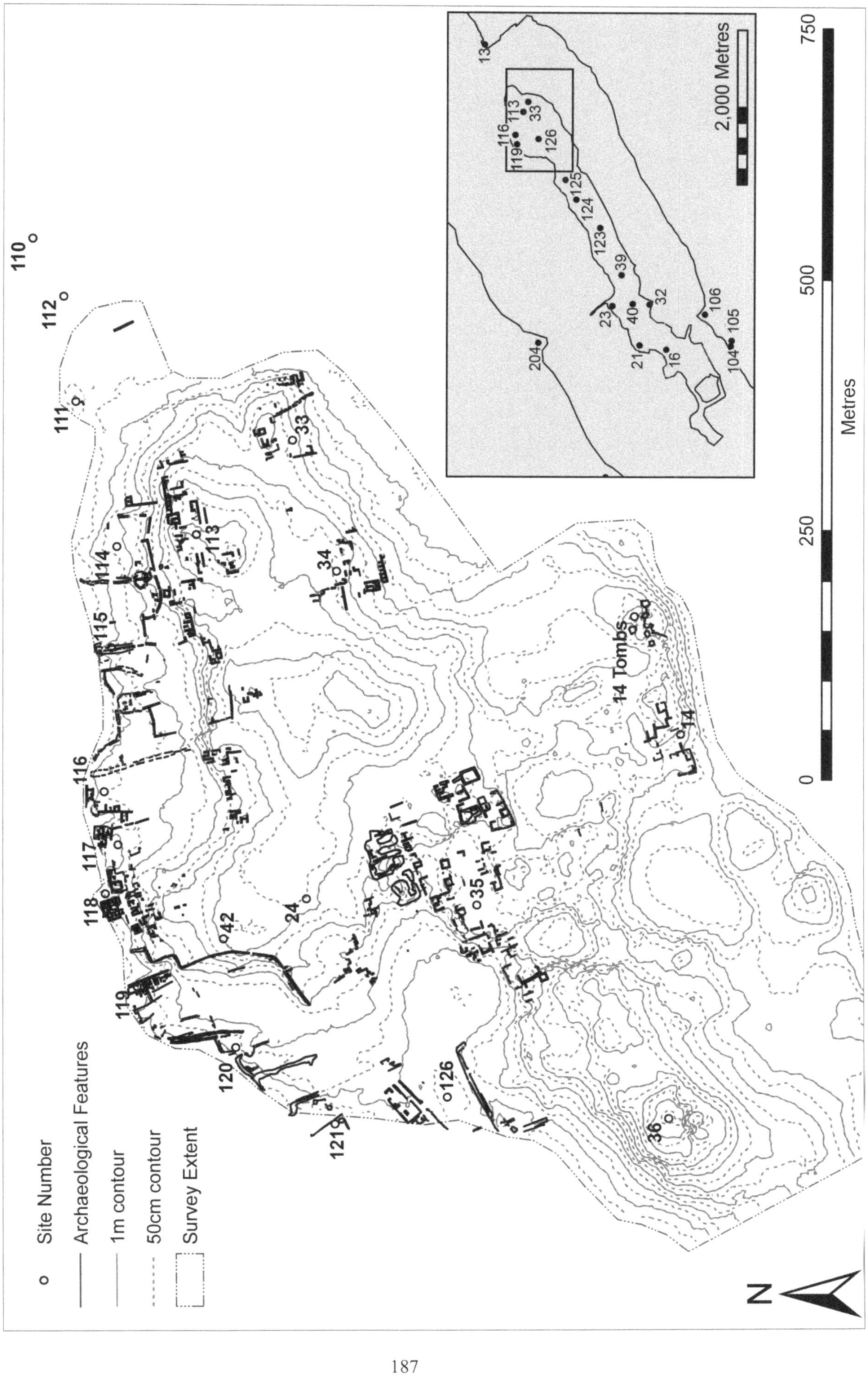

Fig. 6.87. Overview of eastern end of island and principal sites.

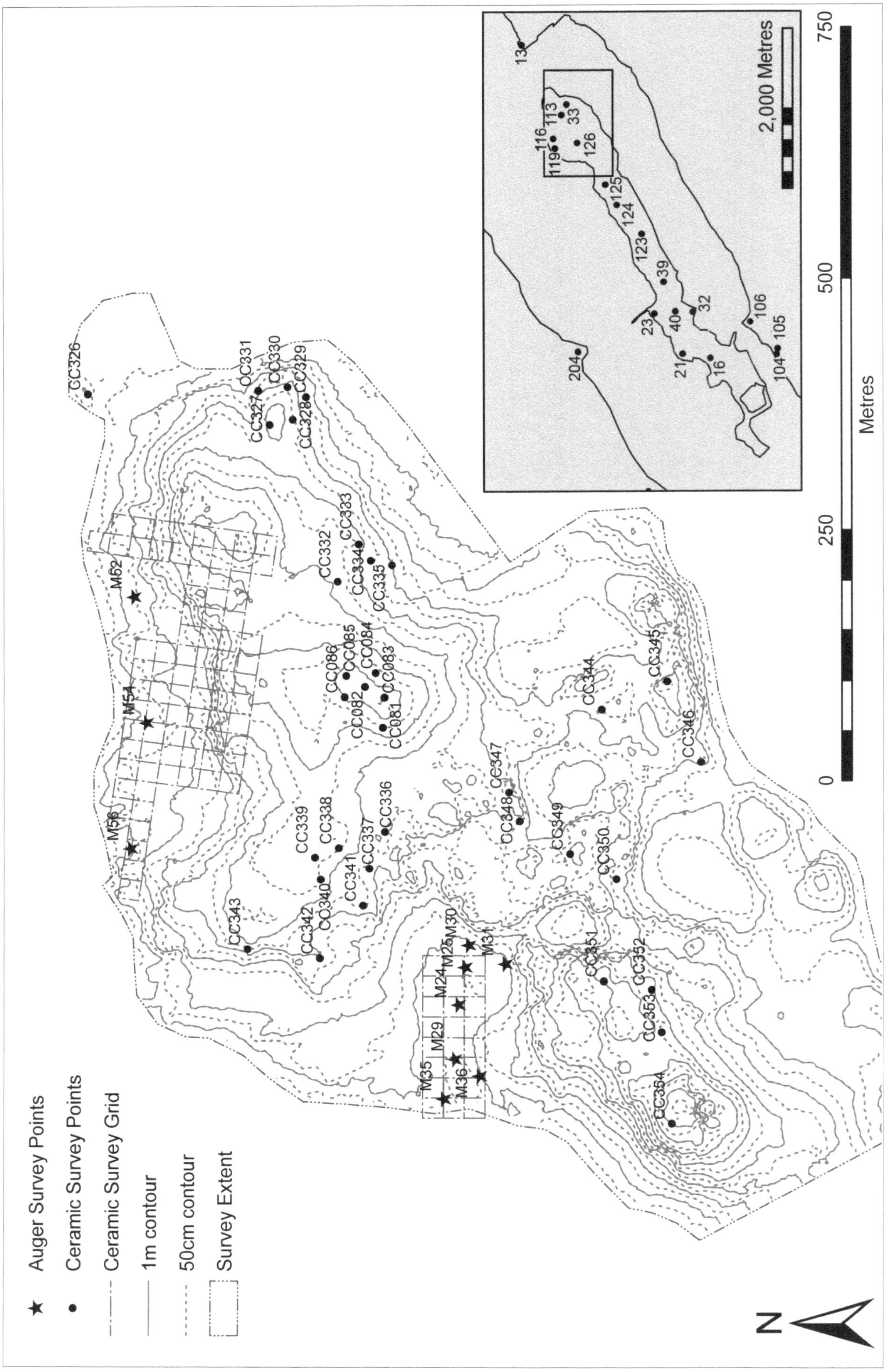

Fig. 6.88. Eastern island ceramic and augur survey.

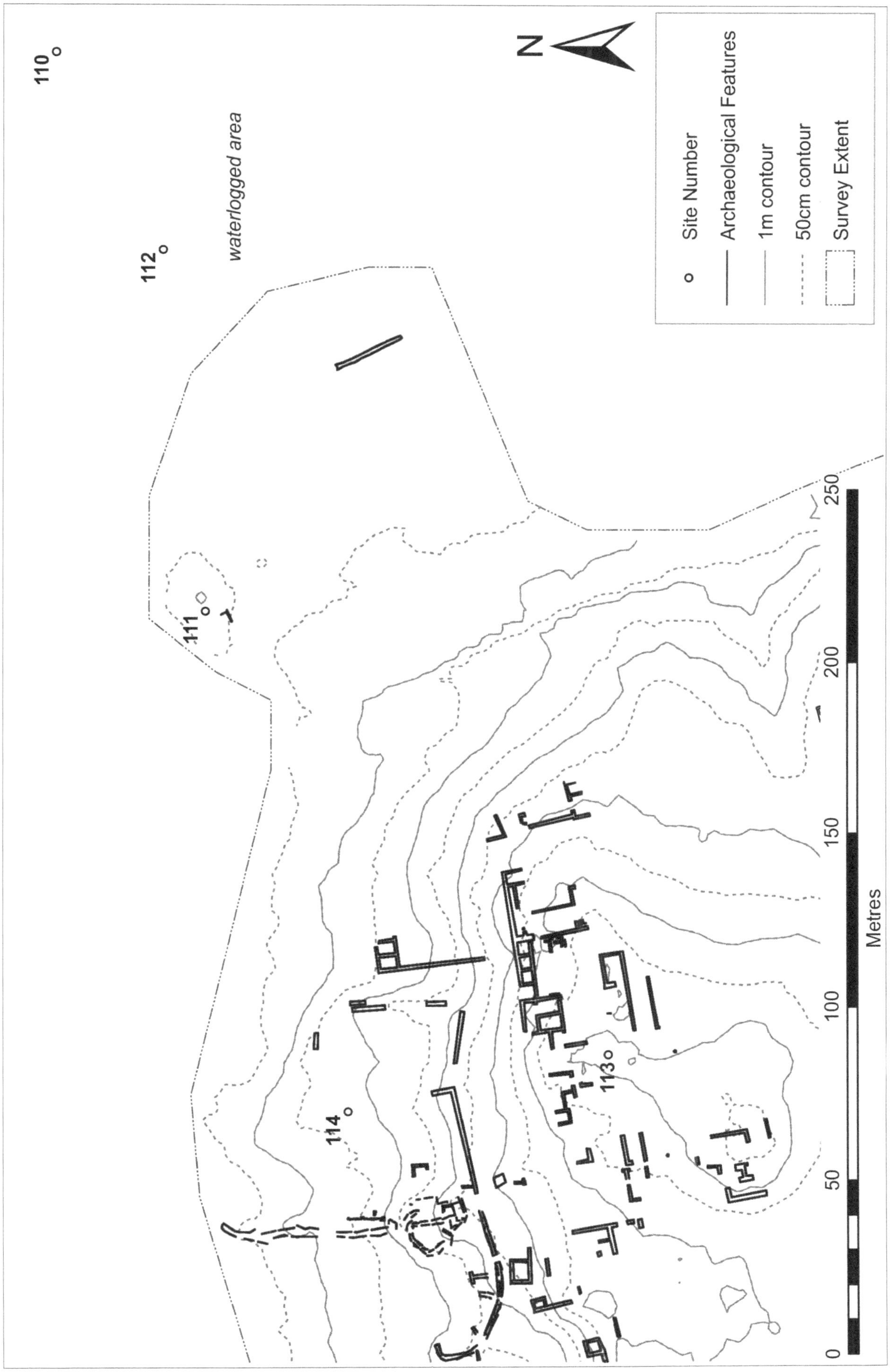

Fig. 6.89. Location of Sites 110-112 relative to associated sites on the island.

Sites 110, 111 & 112 (Fig. 6.89; Table 6.23)
Location: 30 58 27N 29 37 04E to 30 58 28N 29 36 58E
Description: Sites 110, 111, and 112 are located at the very eastern end of Mareotis Island. The area is low-lying and marshy, lying close to the current water level and is constantly subject to the effects of the changing water level of the lake. In 2004, when this area was first recorded, the site was located almost at the water level; however, at present this area is mostly inundated, or *sabkha* and marshland as a result of the rise of the water level.

To the east the remains of a mole made of irregular limestone blocks which vary in size are visible (Site 110). The mole is located at the end of a modern causeway and it appears to have been subject to much reuse. The remaining part of the mole is c. 26m long and 4m wide and the blocks that were used to build the mole are severely eroded.

Fig. 6.90. View from Site 111 to northerly offshore islet.

About 70m west of the mole (Site 110) are what appear to be the remains of a former coastal structure (Site 112). Stones and blocks are scattered in an area about 50m long and 15m wide; however, it is not possible to determine the actual dimensions of the structure. Ceramics were absent from this site therefore, dating was not possible.

About 85m to the west of the area of the scattered blocks (Site 112) traces of a large rectangular building were noted on the shoreline (Site 111). This building included the remains of two perpendicular walls c. 40m E-W and 30m N-S made of irregular limestone blocks which were badly eroded. The site contained a great deal of ceramics, also badly eroded. About 250m north of the rectangular building there is a small islet (c. 12m x 15m) that was visible in the lake when the site was first recorded in 2004. The N-S wall of the rectangular building disappeared under water in the direction of the island, therefore it is possible that when the water level was lower in antiquity there could have been a link between the building and the island (Fig. 6.90). To the west of Site 111 there is a small north-facing bay c. 130m wide.

Few datable pottery sherds were collected from Site 111, totalling a sample of six indicator sherds potentially spanning between the late 3rd and the 1st centuries BC, although largely dating to the 2nd and 1st centuries BC.

Type	**No.**
Egyptian silt casserole (no. 48)	1
Knidian IIG (no. 119)	1
Rhodian IE2/IF (nos 121-6)	1
Mareotic AE1/2 short handle (no. 6)	3
Total	6

Table 6.23. Quantity of pottery types for Site 111.

Site 33 (Fig. 6.91; Graph 6.20; Table 6.24)
Location: 30 58 19N 29 36 58E
Description: This is a small site located to the south of Site 113 overlooking the south-eastern corner of the island. It lies on an elevated area and slopes down towards the south-eastern shoreline of the island until it is cut by a modern canal that borders the whole southern shore of the island. The site covers an area of c. 50m N-S and 80m E-S; however, it probably extended further eastwards in antiquity but has since been subject to destruction as a result of the construction of the canal.

The site contains at least three groups of buildings. The main group is located on the higher ground to the north and includes the remains of two rooms 4m x 4m in dimension, in addition to a number of other walls made of limestone blocks. The association between the walls is difficult to determine.

The second group is located c. 12m southwest of the first. It includes a 22m long wall that runs N-S, in addition to a second row of buildings located to the east of the long wall that appear to have been divided into small units.

The final group of building remains is located c. 50m to the east and consists of an elongated pile of rubble c. 20m N-S and 2m E-W. Again associated with this rubble wall and to the east of it, a further cluster of small regular unit structures were apparent.

Site 33 has a sample of 112 indicator sherds. The majority date to the 2nd to 1st centuries BC and the mid 1st to mid 3rd centuries AD. Only a very small amount of Late Roman pottery (5th to 7th centuries) was present. Half of the assemblage was amphorae with Mareotic types, particularly AE4 being the most common.

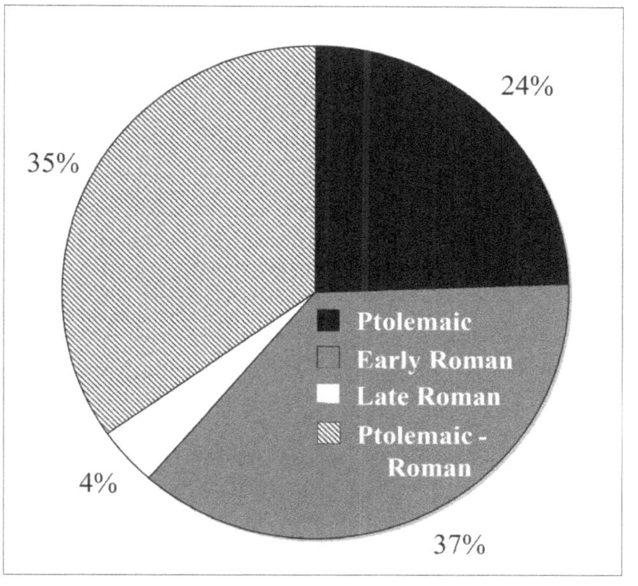

Graph 6.20. Pie graph showing the chronological breakdown of pottery from Site 33.

Table 6.24. Quantity of pottery types for Site 33.

Type	No.	%
Finewares		
Eastern Sigillata A (ESA)	(1)	0.0
Egyptian black slip bowl/ dish footring base	1	0.9
Egyptian silt copy of Cypriot Sigillata P40/1 (no. 61)	1	0.9
Imported Late Roman Red Slip ware bowl	1	0.9
Coarse wares		
Egyptian basin	2	1.8
Egyptian bowl	2	1.8
Egyptian bread mould (no. 83)	5	4.5
Egyptian casserole	2	1.8
Egyptian silt bowl/dish	2	1.8
Egyptian silt casserole (no. 48)	8	7.1
Egyptian silt casserole (cf. Hayes & Harlaut 2002: fig. 29)	4	3.6
Egyptian silt cooking pot	3	2.7
Egyptian silt cooking pot (no. 45)	3	2.7
Egyptian silt lid	5	4.5
Egyptian small coarse ware handle	3	2.7
Mareotic jug	4	3.6
Mareotic/silt miscellaneous coarse ware	9	8.0
Amphorae		
Abu Mena LR Amphora 5 (nos 87-9)	1	0.9
Cilician Dressel 30 (nos 143-4)	1	0.9
Cilician/Cypriot LR Amphora 1 (nos 146-9)	2	1.8
Egyptian LR Amphora 7	(1)	0.0
Imported unidentified type	1	0.9
Koan (nos 126-30)	2	1.8
Mareotic AE1/2 (nos 1-3)	6	5.4
Mareotic AE1/2 short handle (no. 6)	10	8.9
Mareotic AE4 (nos 13-17)	21	18.8
Mareotic Mons Claudianus Type 22/3 (nos 9-12)	8	7.1
Mareotic unidentified type	1	0.9
Tunisian unidentified type	4	3.6
Total	112 (2)	100%

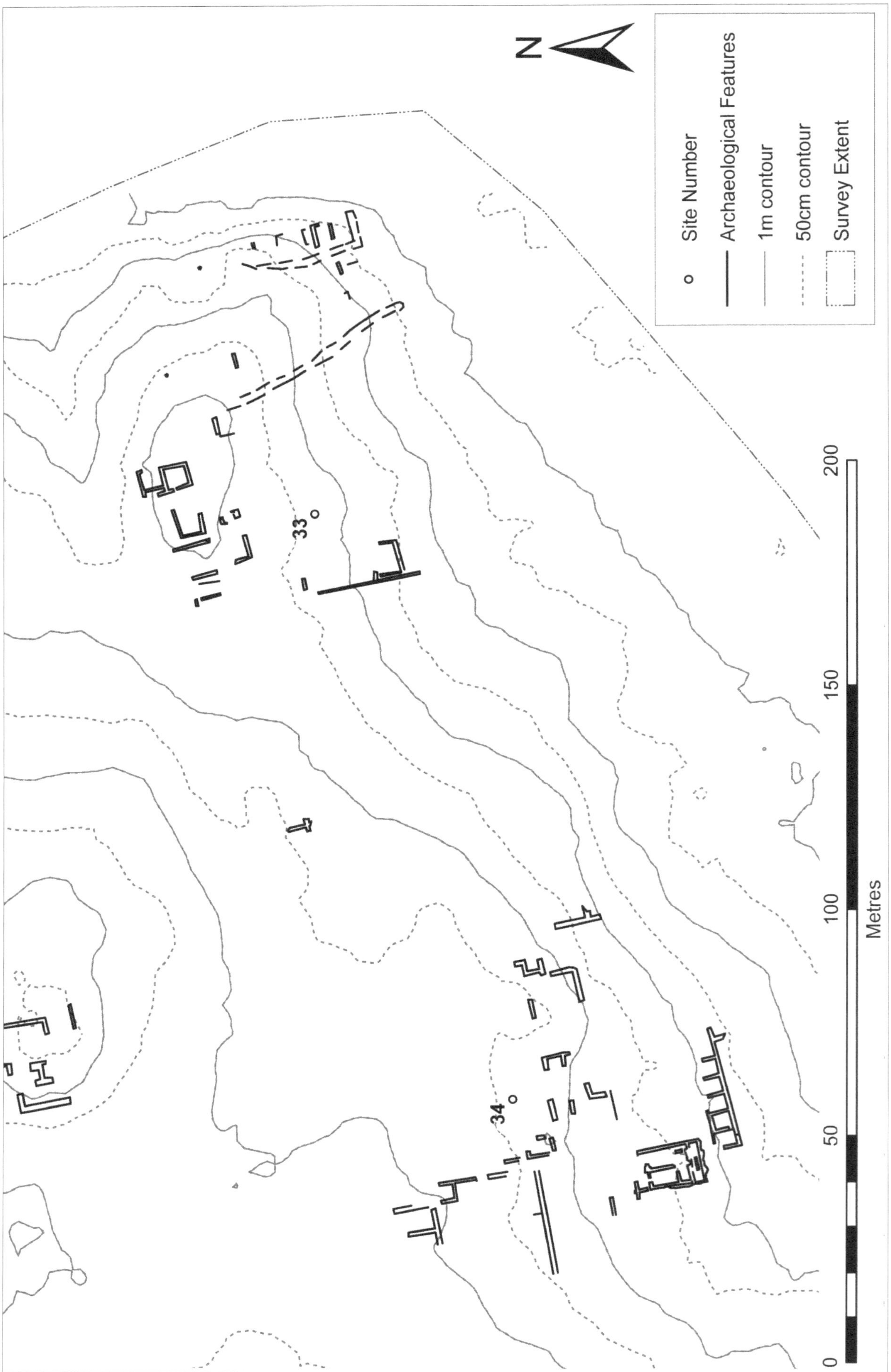

Fig. 6.91. Site 33 and Site 34.

Site 34 (Fig. 6.91; Graph 6.21; Table 6.25)
Location: 30 58 16N 29 36 53E
Description: Some 150m west of Site 33 a further cluster of buildings was observed. The buildings were constructed of modest stone blocks and had been exposed as a result of previous excavation. The buildings were planned but no further study was undertaken of these structures.

Site 34 has a sample of 72 indicator sherds dating from the late 3rd century BC, but mostly 2nd/1st centuries BC. Early Roman sherds are rare and most of the 17% shown on Graph 6.21 are probably Ptolemaic in date.

Table 6.25. (right) Quantity of pottery types for Site 34.

Graph 6.21. (below) Pie graph showing the chronological breakdown of pottery from Site 34.

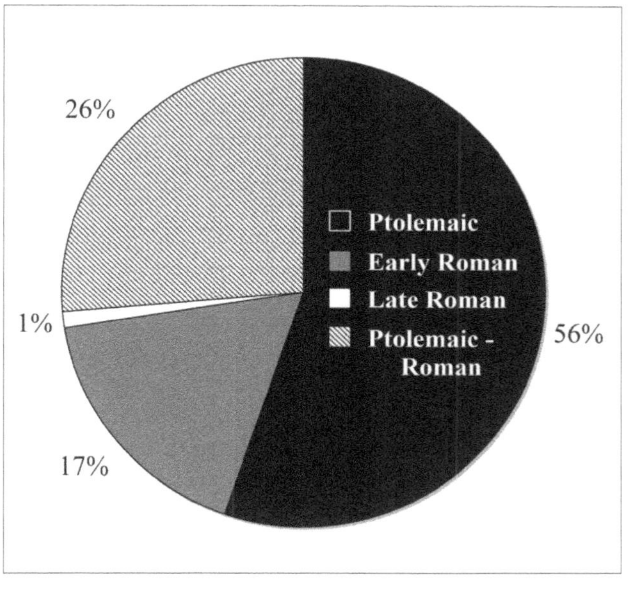

Type	No.	%
Finewares		
Eastern Sigillata A (ESA)	1	1.4
Egyptian silt black slip fish dish (nos 54-5)	1	1.4
Egyptian silt red slip fish dish (nos 54-5)	1	1.4
Megarian bowl	1	1.4
Coarse wares		
Egyptian casserole	4	5.6
Egyptian silt casserole (no. 48)	6	8.3
Egyptian silt cooking pot (no.45)	2	2.8
Egyptian silt dolium	2	2.8
Egyptian silt jar/jug with twisted handle (no. 27)	1	1.4
Egyptian silt juglet (no. 22)	1	1.4
Egyptian silt *sakkia* pot (nos 35-41)	1	1.4
Egyptian small coarse ware handle	1	1.4
Mareotic/Egyptian silt unidentified type	8	11.1
Amphorae		
Knidian handle	1	1.4
Koan (nos 126-30)	13	18.1
Mareotic AE1/2 (nos 1-3)	5	6.9
Mareotic AE1/2 base (no. 7)	6	8.3
Mareotic AE1/2 short handle (no. 6)	8	11.1
Rhodian IE2/IF (nos 121-6)	7	9.7
Tunisian unidentified type	2	2.8
Total	72	100%

Sites 113, 114 & 115 (Figs 6.87, 6.89, 6.92 & 6.93)
Location: 30 58 25N 29 36 52E to 30 58 22N 29 36 54E & 30 58 20N 29 36 46E to 30 58 24N 29 36 45E
Description: This group of sites is located to the west of Site 111 and extends for a distance of c. 400m E-W along the main ridge at the eastern end of the island and for c. 200m N-S from the top of the ridge to the northern shoreline of the island.

Site 113 (Figs 6.93 & 6.94; Graphs 6.22 & 6.23; Table 6.26)
Description: Site 113 is the main site that extends along the top of the ridge at the eastern end of the island. It stretches c. 370m E-W in direction and it extends northwards into the coastal plain for c. 80m.

This site is mainly covered with extensive remains of walls and buildings of various sizes and differing construction techniques. It is evident that the site has been subject to previous limited excavation by the local authorities; however, the overwhelming majority of the site has yet to be investigated in detail. Those remains that have been exposed are largely in a good state of preservation; however, the majority of structures remain buried.

One of the distinctive features of this site is the difference in construction techniques observed between certain buildings. A 12m x 7m previously excavated section of a particularly significant building on this site (30 58 21N 29 36 49E), revealed that the walls were made of sharply cut, large, dressed, ashlar limestone blocks (1m x 0.6m x 0.3m) arranged in headers without the use of mortar (Fig. 6.95). The building was monumental in nature and Hellenistic in style and no comparable structures were recorded anywhere else in the survey region. Hellenistic ceramics were found in association with this structure. In nearby buildings the walls were made of small irregular limestone blocks arranged in *opus incertum*.

The first major structure recorded at the eastern end of the ridge is a large complex that covers an area of c. 47m E-W and 20m N-S. The complex previously subject to limited excavation, contains a series of at least ten rooms of various sizes arranged in two lines extending east to west. Some of the rooms are relatively small, measuring c. 3m x 3m, while others are larger measuring 6m x 11m. Moreover, in the middle of the complex there is a drainage system and the remains of a small basin lined with *opus signinum* (Fig. 6.96). This complex could very well be a house or a residential area associated with pebble lined floors and baths. In addition to these significant features there are numerous walls and linear features. The alignment of these walls along an E-W axis could imply the existence of a street or a pathway located to the north of the buildings. The partially excavated nature of this area and the extensive building remains that continue down onto the plain to the north reveal the rich and densely occupied character of the ridge.

Site 113 has a sample of 3,362 indicator sherds belonging to mid 4th BC to 7th centuries AD, although most are 2nd to 1st centuries BC. Ptolemaic occupation was concentrated along the coast, also seen at the nearby Sites 111, 115-120 and 126, that represent the coastal boundary of the same settlement. During the Early Roman period the site contracted away from the shore over a significantly smaller area, which was maintained during the 5th to 7th centuries AD when there was a limited revival of the site. Concentrations of Late Roman pottery were found in quantity only in ceramic grids 02, 41, 48, 49, 53, 55, 56, 60 and 71. The relatively small amount of Abu Mena amphorae may reflect a lack of 7th century AD occupation. A good mixture of imported and local wares was present. As elsewhere, the material consisted mostly of amphorae, but during the Late Roman period the number of finewares increased.

Fig. 6.92. General view of Sites 113-115 looking north.

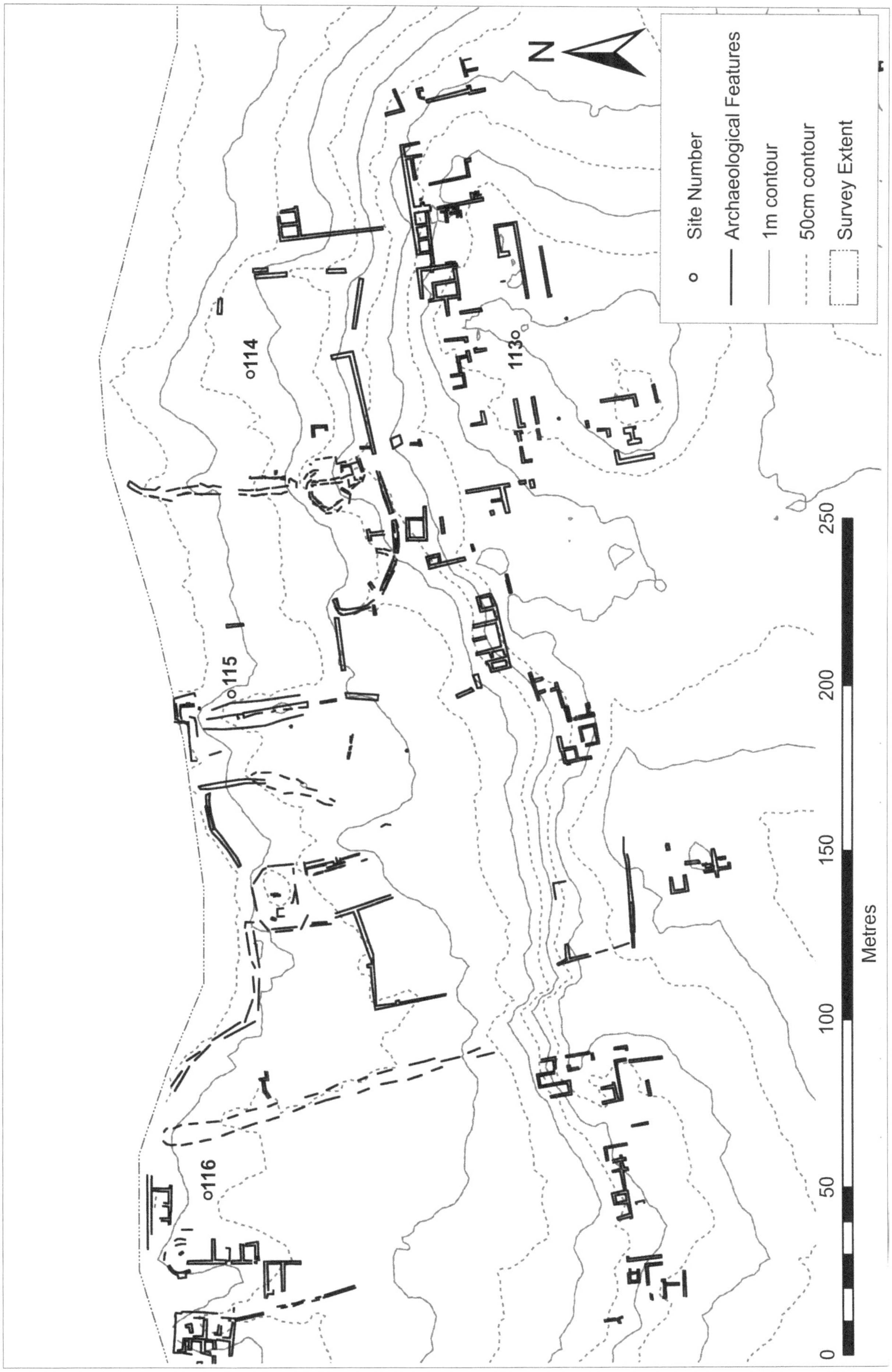

Fig. 6.93. General view of Site 113.

Fig. 6.94. Site 113 general view looking south.

Fig. 6.95. Hellenistic building Site 113, partially exposed.

Fig. 6.96. (left) Lined drain Site 113.

Graph 6.22. (below) Pie graph showing the chronological breakdown of pottery from Site 113.

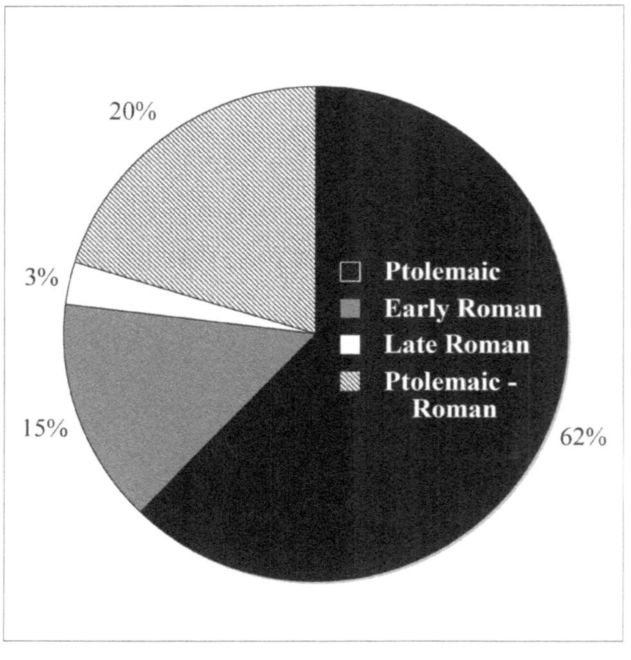

Graph 6.23. Bar graph showing the breakdown of form types by period Site 113.

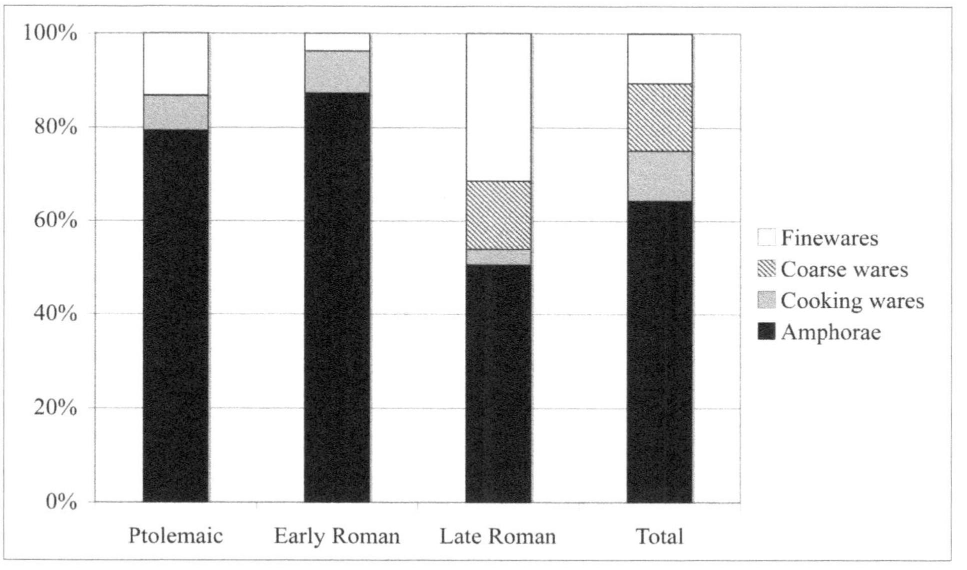

Table 6.26. (below) Quantity of pottery types for Site 113 (continued on the next page).

Type	**No.**	**%**
Finewares		
African Red Slip ware (ARS) 104-6 (no. 102)	3	0.1
African Red Slip ware (ARS) 67 (no. 99)	1	0.0
Cypriot Red Slip ware (CRS)	3	0.1
Cypriot Red Slip ware (CRS) 2 (nos 103-4)	2	0.1
Cypriot Red Slip ware (CRS) 9 (nos 105-6)	8	0.2
Eastern Sigillata A (ESA) 22 (no. 95)	5	0.1
Egyptian black slip bowl (nos 57-9)	22	0.7
Egyptian black slip bowl/dish footring base	45	1.3
Egyptian Ptolemaic/Early Roman red slip bowl/dish	165	4.9
Egyptian red slip bowl (no. 60)	98	2.9
Egyptian Red Slip ware B (ERSB) copy of ARS 84 (nos 65-6)	1	0.0
Egyptian Red Slip ware B/C (ERSB/C)	1	0.0
Egyptian Red Slip ware C (ERSC)	6	0.2
Egyptian silt black slip fish dish (nos 54-5)	12	0.4
Egyptian silt red slip fish dish (nos 54-5)	24	0.7
Glazed (?modern)	(2)	0.0
?Imported black slip bowl/dish footring base (no. 94)	2	0.1
Imported Late Roman Red Slip ware bowl	1	0.0
Phocaean Red Slip ware (PRS) 3 (nos 108-9)	2	0.1
Coarse wares		
Abu Mena miscellaneous coarse ware	4	0.1
Abu Mena basin (nos 79-80)	8	0.2
Egypt silt pedestal base (no. 85)	5	0.1
Egyptian basin	26	0.8
Egyptian bowl	24	0.7
Egyptian casserole	11	0.3
Egyptian marl jug	1	0.0
Egyptian marl jug (no. 55)	1	0.0
Egyptian marl juglet (no. 21)	1	0.0
Egyptian marl juglet base (no. 28)	2	0.1
Egyptian marl miscellaneous coarse ware	1	0.0
Egyptian marl *sakkia* pot (nos 35-41)	2	0.1
Egyptian silt bowl/dish	7	0.2
Egyptian silt casserole (no. 48)	107	3.2
Egyptian silt casserole (nos 49-51)	3	0.1
Egyptian silt casserole cf. (Hayes & Harlaut 2002: fig. 29)	20	0.6
Egyptian silt casserole cf. (Hayes & Harlaut 2002: fig. 55)	11	0.3
Egyptian silt cooking pot	103	3.1
Egyptian silt cooking pot (no. 44)	5	0.1

Egyptian silt cooking pot (no. 45)	46	1.4
Egyptian silt cooking pot (no. 47)	3	0.1
Egyptian silt cooking pot/jar (no. 42)	1	0.0
Egyptian silt dolium	42	1.2
Egyptian silt funnel strainer (no. 33)	2	0.1
Egyptian silt jar/jug with twisted handle (no. 27)	6	0.2
Egyptian silt jug	25	0.7
Egyptian silt lid	49	1.5
Egyptian silt mortarium	6	0.2
Egyptian skillet handle (no. 52)	2	0.1
Egyptian small coarse ware handle	134	4.0
Mareotic/silt miscellaneous coarse ware	139	4.1
Amphorae		
Abu Mena LR Amphora 5 (nos 87-9)	4	0.1
Campanian Dressel 1A (no. 135)	4	0.1
Campanian Dressel 2-4 (no. 136)	2	0.1
Campanian Greco-Italic (no. 134)	11	0.3
Cilician Dressel 4 (nos 138-9)	1	0.0
Cilician Pompeii V (no. 141)	2	0.1
Cilician/Cypriot LR Amphora 1 (nos 146-9)	33	1.0
Egyptian silt AE3	3	0.1
Egyptian LR Amphora 7	3	0.1
Egyptian silt Mons Claudianus Type 1	2	0.1
Gaza LR Amphora 4 Majcherek Forms 2-4 (nos 154-7)	4	0.1
Imported amphora (no. 171)	1	0.0
Imported unsourced whole-mouth amphora (no. 159)	5	0.1
Knidian handle	164	4.9
Knidian I (no. 111)	5	0.1
Knidian IIB/IIC (nos 113-18)	4	0.1
Knidian IIB (no. 110)	11	0.3
Knidian IIG (no. 119)	14	0.4
Koan (no. 131)	1	0.0
Koan (nos 126-30)	412	12.3
Mareotic AE1/2 (nos 1-3)	331	9.8
Mareotic AE1/2 base (no. 7)	577	17.2
Mareotic AE1/2 long handle (nos 4-5)	55	1.6
Mareotic AE1/2 short handle (no. 6)	190	5.7
?Mareotic AE1/2 variant (no. 165)	1	0.0
Mareotic AE4 (nos 13-17)	19	0.6
Mareotic Mons Claudianus Type 22/3 (nos 9-12)	12	0.4
Mareotic tall pot stand (no. 8)	7	0.2
Mareotic tubular hollow base (no. 19)	1	0.0
Mareotic unidentified type	28	0.8
Rhodian IB (no. 120)	10	0.3
Rhodian IE2/IF (nos 121-6)	198	5.9
Thasos (nos 132-3)	2	0.1
Tripolitanian ?I or II (no. 150)	3	0.1
Tunisian Africana III (no. 151)	1	0.0
Tunisian unidentified type	6	0.2
Unsourced imported amphora	30	0.9
Unsourced imported amphora (no. 161)	1	0.0
Unsourced imported amphora (no. 164)	2	0.1
Unsourced imported amphora (no. 166)	1	0.0
Unsourced imported amphora (no. 167)	1	0.0
Unsourced imported amphora (no. 168)	1	0.0
Western Asia Minor LR Amphora 3	1	0.0
Total	3362 (2)	100%

Site 114-115 (Figs 6.97, 6.98 & 6.101; Table 6.27) (see above for location)
Description: Site 114 and 115 merge together and occupy the northern foot of the ridge and the plain that extends from the ridge to the shoreline to the north. At the foot of the ridge there is a series of buildings that extends in a N-S direction until they reach the shoreline. The eastern-most of these buildings measures 30m N-S and 10m E-W and

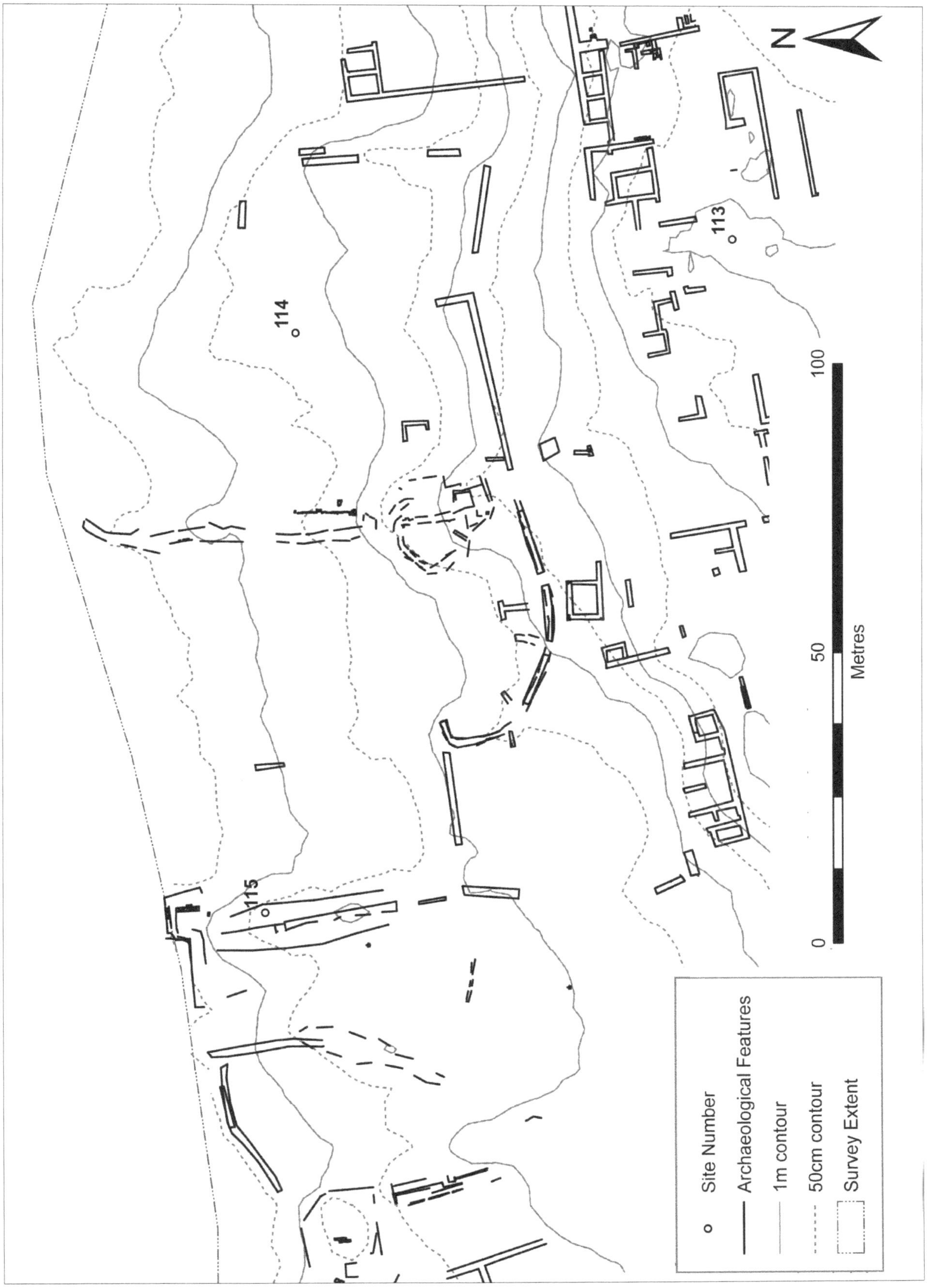

Fig. 6.97. Site 114-115.

Fig. 6.98. General view of Site 114-115 looking northeast.

Fig. 6.99. Platform at Site 115.

includes at its northern end two small rooms each measuring c. 4.5m x 3m (Site 114). The walls of this structure are c. 1m wide and are made of small irregular limestone blocks. Less than 10m to the west of this building exists an enclosure that measures c. 40m N-S and c. 60m E-W. The enclosure contains evidence for a number of walls and smaller rooms; however, the building has been subject to the accumulation of sediment and hence many of the walls are buried.

To the west of this group of buildings, a series of longitudinal platform or jetty-like linear features extend perpendicular to the shoreline that terminate at the present water's edge. At least four similar linear structures could be identified between Sites 114 and 116. This first one extends for 70m along its length N-S and is 2m wide. It is made of semi-regular limestone blocks arranged in stretchers; however, the majority of its preserved length has been weathered by erosion.

About 60m to the west exists another linear feature that stretches from N-S for c. 60m to terminate at the waterline (Site 115). At the northern end of this linear, jetty-like feature, there is a platform that measures c. 20m E-W and 7m N-S and it is made of limestone ashlar blocks (Fig. 6.99). The platform delimits the northern end of this linear, jetty-like structure although it is partly buried under lake sediments. About 25m to the west of this second linear feature, a third linear feature was observed; however, it is in a poor state of preservation. The visible remains of the third linear feature are c. 17m long N-S and at its northern end exists a platform that measures 17m x 12m. From the platform to the west extends a quay-like or lake wall structure made of rubble that is some 130m

Fig. 6.100. Lake wall at Site 115 looking west.

in length (Fig. 6.100). This feature extends west as far as Site 116. This feature is interrupted more than once along its length, while some sections are buried under lake sediments; however, it could have delineated the shoreline at this part of the island functioning as a quay or lake wall.

The dating of Site 114-115 relied mainly on the limited datable ceramic samples collected, which decreased in number closer to the shoreline as a result of the accumulation of lake sediments. Therefore, along the shoreline only 10 sherds were collected; all were imported amphorae, covering the period between the late 4th or 3rd and the 1st centuries BC and the 3rd and 4th centuries AD.

Type	**No.**
Koan (nos 126-30)	1
Knidian handle	3
Tunisian Africana IID (no. 152)	1
Rhodian IE2/IF	5
Total	10

Table 6.27. Quantity of pottery types for Site 114-115.

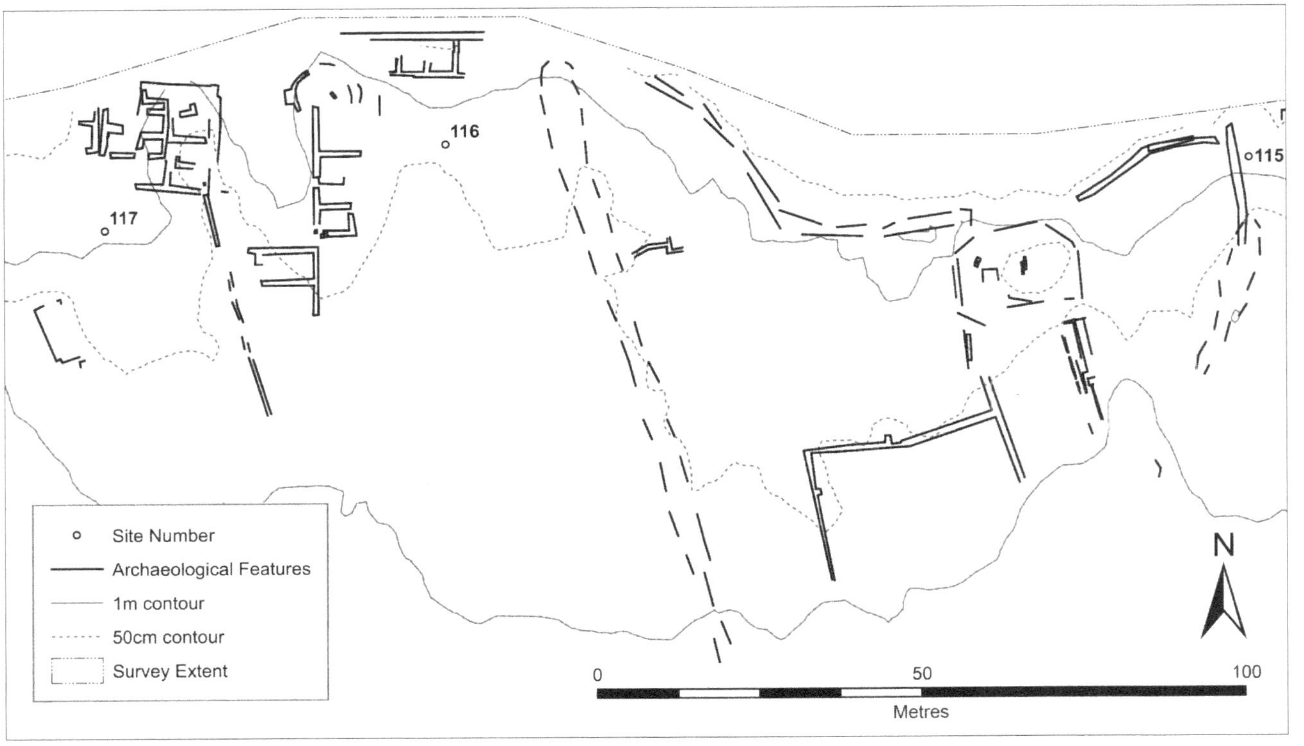

Fig. 6.101. Sites 116-117.

Sites 116-119 (Fig. 6.87)
Location: 30 58 25N 29 36 44E to 30 58 22N 29 36 45E 30 58 18N 29 36 33E to 30 58 21N 29 36 34E
Description: The main characteristic feature of this area is that it contains waterfront sites located along the north-eastern shore of Mareotis Island. This group of sites covers an area of approximately 220m E-W and c. 60m N-S.[5] They extend across a flat area to the north of the ridge. This area has been subject to heavy siltation that has resulted in some of the archaeological remains, particularly close to the waterline, being buried under lake sediments. Therefore, cleaning and limited excavation were carried out in this area to be able to record the archaeological remains at the waterfront.

5. The location for this group of sites is given above, and the accompanying figures confirm their relative locations.

Site 116 (Fig. 6.101; Graph 6.24; Table 6.28)
Site 116 is defined to the east by a linear feature made of rubble and small irregular blocks (Fig. 6.102). It is 100m long and 4m wide and extends perpendicular to the shoreline from the ridge at Site 113 to the edge of the lake. About 12m to the west of the northern end of this linear feature exist the remains of an 11m long wall that extends parallel to the shoreline. The wall encloses to the south at least four adjacent small rooms (Fig. 6.103). The internal dimensions of these rooms are c. 3-4m x 3.5m and they probably belonged to a maritime structure of some sort – perhaps a storage facility.

About 5m to the west of these rooms another coastal structure exists. It is a wall that stretches N-S perpendicular to the shoreline, for c. 33m. There are indications of rooms butting against the wall on both sides to the east and to the west (Fig. 6.104). The internal dimensions of these rooms are between 7.8m and 4.3m E-W and approximately 3.5m N-S. The northern end of the longitudinal wall ends in what appears to be a round structure that measures 10m in external diameter and 8m in internal diameter. The layout and location of these buildings imply that they were maritime in nature.

Site 116 has a sample of 25 indicator sherds. Rhodian sherds may represent occupation from the late 3rd century BC, but it is more likely that the Ptolemaic occupation spans the 2nd and 1st centuries BC. A small amount of Roman material was also present. The Early Roman sherds represent Late Ptolemaic/Early Roman occupation and exclusively Early Roman pottery is absent.

Fig. 6.102. Linear feature at Site 116.

Fig. 6.103. (below) Parallel lake wall and adjacent rooms at Site 116.

Fig. 6.104. (above) Rooms to the west of the lake wall Site 116.

Table 6.28. (left) Quantity of pottery types for Site 116.

Type	**No.**	**%**
Finewares		
Cypriot Red Slip ware (CRS) 9 (nos 105-6)	1	4.0
Egyptian bowl/dish footring base	1	4.0
Egyptian red slip bowl (no. 60)	1	4.0
Coarse wares		
Egyptian casserole	1	4.0
Egyptian marl jug	1	4.0
Egyptian silt casserole (cf. Hayes & Harlaut 2002: fig. 29)	2	8.0
Egyptian silt miscellaneous coarse ware	2	8.0
Amphorae		
Cilician/Cypriot LR Amphora 1 (nos 146-9)	1	4.0
Koan (nos 126-30)	2	8.0
Mareotic AE1/2 (nos 1-3)	6	24.0
Mareotic AE1/2 base (no. 7)	1	4.0
Mareotic AE1/2 short handle (no. 6)	1	4.0
Rhodian IE2/IF (nos 121-6)	4	16.0
Western Asia Minor LR Amphora 3	1	4.0
Total	25	100%

Graph 6.24. (below) Pie graph showing the chronological breakdown of pottery from Site 116.

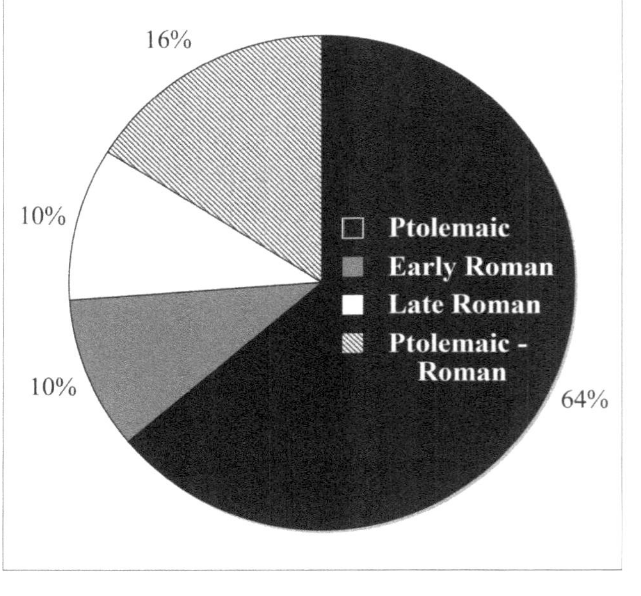

Fig. 6.105. Site 117 blocks.

Site 117 (Fig. 6.101; Table 6.29)
Description: Site 117 is located c.10m west of Site 116 and extends in a N-S direction perpendicular to the shoreline.

In 2004 when this site was first recorded, a series of large limestone blocks, each measuring c.1m x 0.6m x 0.4m, were found lying along the shore for c. 13m. However, the blocks showed some indications of having been disturbed and probably transported from another site and reused. Also their size and shape were unlike any of the blocks used in the adjacent sites. Due to a rise in water levels the blocks were not visible for recording in the 2007 season (Fig. 6.105).

However, the main archaeological feature on this site is located c. 37m to the south of the limestone blocks. It is a multi-room building that covers an area of c.18m x 12m at the shoreline with a 0.7m wide linear feature extending from its south-east corner for 35m to the south. There are at least two adjacent rooms within the building complex each measuring c. 7m x 5m. However, there are more remains of walls further to the west which could be associated with the building. In this case the total E-W dimension of the building would be c. 20m.

Considering the layout of the archaeological features at Site 117, it is possible that the buildings here have gone through different phases of construction as a result of changes in water level and sedimentation. Site 117 has a sample of 12 indicator sherds. Those that could be dated belong to Ptolemaic period, mostly of the 2nd and 1st centuries BC although the Knidian handle could potentially be earlier. The assemblage can be viewed as a continuation of Site 113 that was essentially of this same date.

Type	**No.**
Egyptian basin	1
Egyptian cooking pot	1
Egyptian marl jug	1
Egyptian red slip bowl/dish footring base	2
Egyptian silt cooking pot (no. 45)	1
Knidian handle	1
Mareotic AE1/2 (nos 1-3)	5
Total	12

Table 6.29. Quantity of pottery types for Site 117.

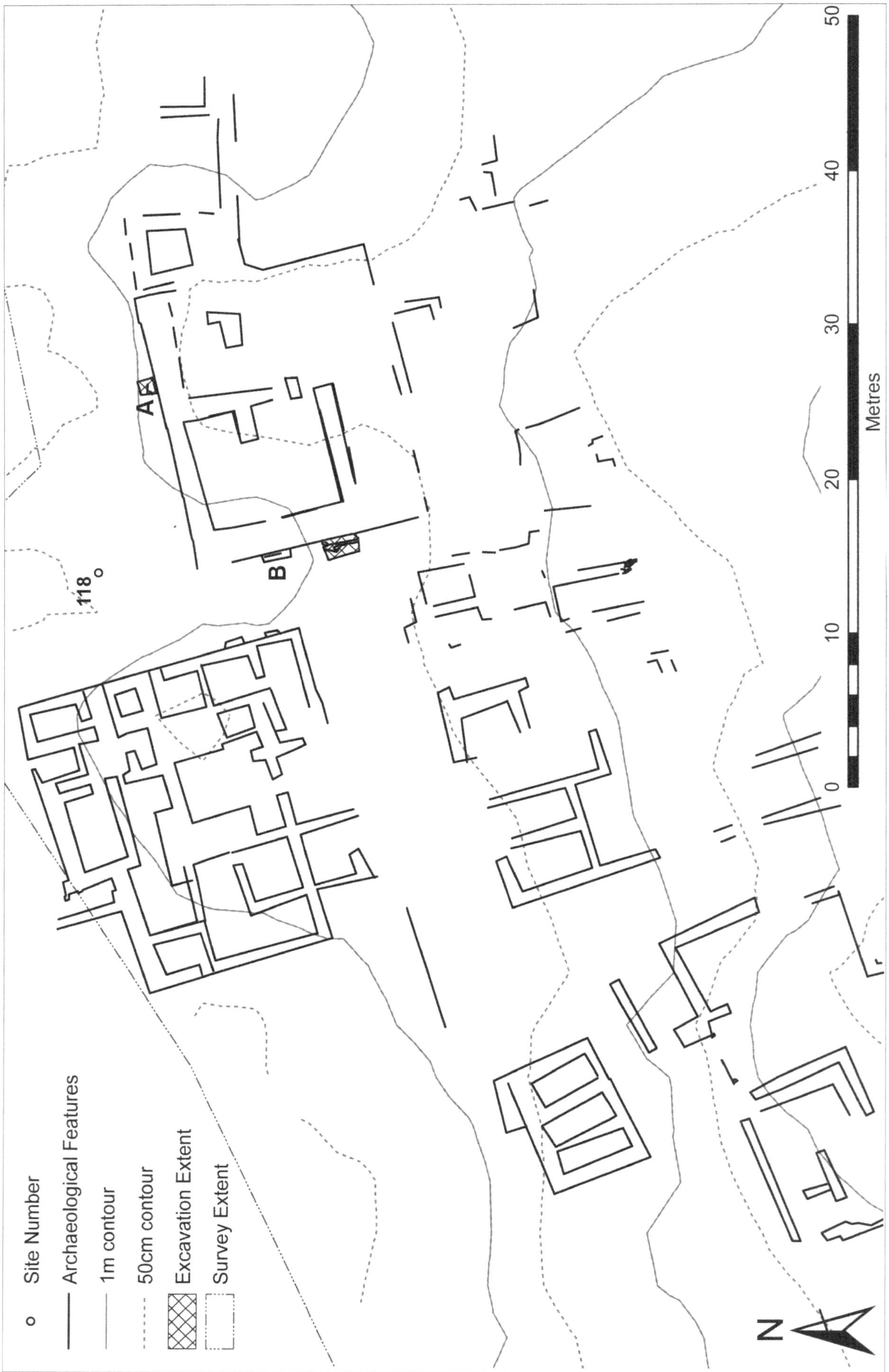

Fig. 6.106. Site 118. (A) denotes the excavation in Fig. 6.109; (B) denotes the excavation in Fig. 6.110.

Fig. 6.107. General view of Eastern Building Site 118.

Site 118 (Figs 6.87, 6.106; Graph 6.25; Table 6.30)
Description: Site 118 is located c. 20m west of Site 117 and covers and area of c. 120m E-W and 60m N-S. The area between Site 117 and Site 118 is a depression filled in with lake sediments and dense vegetation.

Site 118 contains the remains of at least three multi-roomed coastal structures in different states of preservation. The first most easterly building measures 18m E-W x 15m N-S and it is located less than 3m from the waterline (Fig. 6.107). The remains of the external walls of the building rise to c. 0.4m in height (Fig. 6.108). They are 1-2m thick and are mostly made of medium size, irregular limestone blocks; however, limited excavation at the site revealed that the foundation of the building was made of smaller stones arranged in at least three courses c. 0.3m in height. On top of the lower courses, a second later phase of construction was noted that consisted of walls made of courses of limestone blocks of which three courses were recorded (Figs 6.109 & 6.110). Inside the building there is evidence for at least two rooms each measuring c. 8m N-S and 7m E-W, and other additional walls, although it was difficult to determine their relative association.

About 5m to the west of and 13m in front of this building, another multi-roomed structure of similar construction was recorded. The building, which measures c. 20m x 20m, appears to have been built on a raised platform that overlooks the shoreline boarded to the east and west by small bays (Fig. 6.111). The remains of numerous walls exist inside the building, creating a number of internal rooms of different shapes and sizes. Limited excavation was undertaken of this building during the 2008 season which enabled the clear delineation of the walls and internal rooms (Figs 6.112 & 6.113). Again it is possible that this building consisted of multiple phases of use although further excavation is needed to confirm this hypothesis. There is evidence for water erosion along the northern shoreline walls of the building. To the south and west of the building there are several walls that belong to at least four other smaller buildings. However, these buildings are located in a heavily silted area, so further excavation is required to reveal their relationship to each other and their association with the other buildings at the site.

Fig. 6.108. External walls of the Eastern Building Site 118.

Fig. 6.109. Excavated section of wall Site 118. (A) in Fig. 6.106.

Fig. 6.110. Excavated section of wall Site 118. (B) in Fig. 6.106.

Fig. 6.111. (below) General view of Western Building Site 118.

Fig. 6.112. Internal rooms revealed as part of excavation of Western Building Site 118.

Finally, it is worth mentioning that in the 2004 season, a potential mole or jetty was noted between Site 117 and Site 118, located some distance offshore. A pile of rubble and limestone blocks extended into the water for c. 20m and it is thought that it may have extended to a small islet located 125m offshore. However, this feature was not visible during later seasons due to the recent rise of water level.

Site 118 has a sample of 186 indicator sherds from the excavation. The pottery is dominated by Ptolemaic material with types classified as Ptolemaic/Early Roman more likely to be Ptolemaic. Pottery from the mid 4th to 3rd centuries is present, but the 2nd to 1st centuries BC are more substantial. The earliest excavated levels contained Knidian amphorae Types I and IIB, a Rhodian amphora of Type IB and a whole-mouth amphora (no. 159), reinforcing the importance of this site for mid 4th to 3rd centuries occupation. In contrast to most survey collections, finewares were the most common group (66), followed by amphorae (50), cooking wares (45) and other coarse wares (25).

Fig. 6.113. Internal rooms revealed as part of excavation of Western Building Site 118.

Table 6.30. Quantity of pottery types for Site 118.

Type	No.	%
Finewares		
African Red Slip ware (ARS)	2	1.1
Egyptian black slip bowl (nos 57-9)	5	2.7
Egyptian black slip bowl/dish footring base	4	2.2
Egyptian Ptolemaic/Early Roman red slip bowl/dish	21	11.3
Egyptian red slip bowl (no. 60)	28	15.1
Egyptian silt red slip fish dish (nos 54-5)	5	2.7
?Italian Sigillata (ITS)	1	0.5
Coarse wares		
Abu Mena basin (nos 79-80)	1	0.5
Egyptian bowl	1	0.5
Egyptian marl jug	7	3.8
Egyptian marl juglet or unguentarium base (no. 29)	1	0.5
Egyptian miscellaneous coarse ware	2	1.1
Egyptian silt casserole (no. 48)	2	1.1
Egyptian silt casserole (cf. Hayes & Harlaut 2002: fig. 29)	1	0.5
Egyptian silt casserole (cf. Hayes & Harlaut 2002: fig. 55)	5	2.7
Egyptian silt cooking pot	7	3.8
Egyptian silt cooking pot (no. 45)	7	3.8
Egyptian silt dolium	4	2.2
Egyptian silt juglet or unguentarium (no. 25)	2	1.1
Egyptian silt juglet or unguentarium base (no.31)	1	0.5
Egyptian silt jug	5	2.7
Egyptian silt lid	3	1.6
Egyptian silt miscellaneous coarse ware	1	0.5
Egyptian small coarse ware handle	20	10.8
Amphorae		
Abu Mena LR Amphora 5 (nos 87-9)	1	0.5
Imported unidentified type	3	1.6
Imported unsourced whole-mouth amphora (no. 159)	1	0.5
Knidian handle	15	8.1
Knidian I (no. 111)	1	0.5
Knidian IIB/IIC (nos 113-18)	1	0.5
Knidian IIB (no. 110)	3	1.6
Koan (nos 126-30)	2	1.1
Mareotic AE1/2 (nos 1-3)	11	5.9
Mareotic AE1/2 base (no. 7)	5	2.7
Mareotic Mons Claudianus Type 22/3 (nos 9-12)	1	0.5
Mareotic tall pot stand (no. 8)	1	0.5
Rhodian IB (no. 120)	2	1.1
Rhodian IE2/IF (nos 121-6)	3	1.6
Total	186	100%

Graph 6.25. Pie graph showing the chronological breakdown of pottery from Site 118.

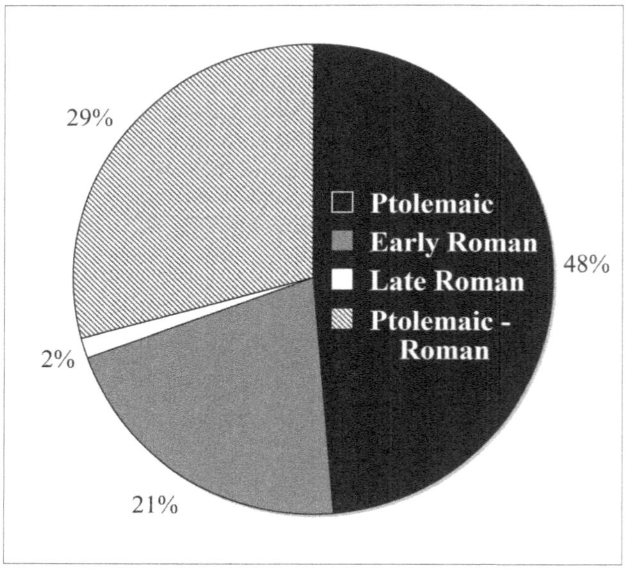

Site 119 (Figs 6.87, 6.114, 6.115 & 6.119; Graph 6.26; Tables 6.31 & 6.32)
Description: Site 119 is located on an elevated platform c. 40m west of Site 118, in an area where the coastline of the eastern end of the island turns towards the south. The site extends for c. 50m from N-S and 60m E-W; however, the main archaeological remains occupy an area that measures 40m N-S and 25m E-W. The main feature is a struc-

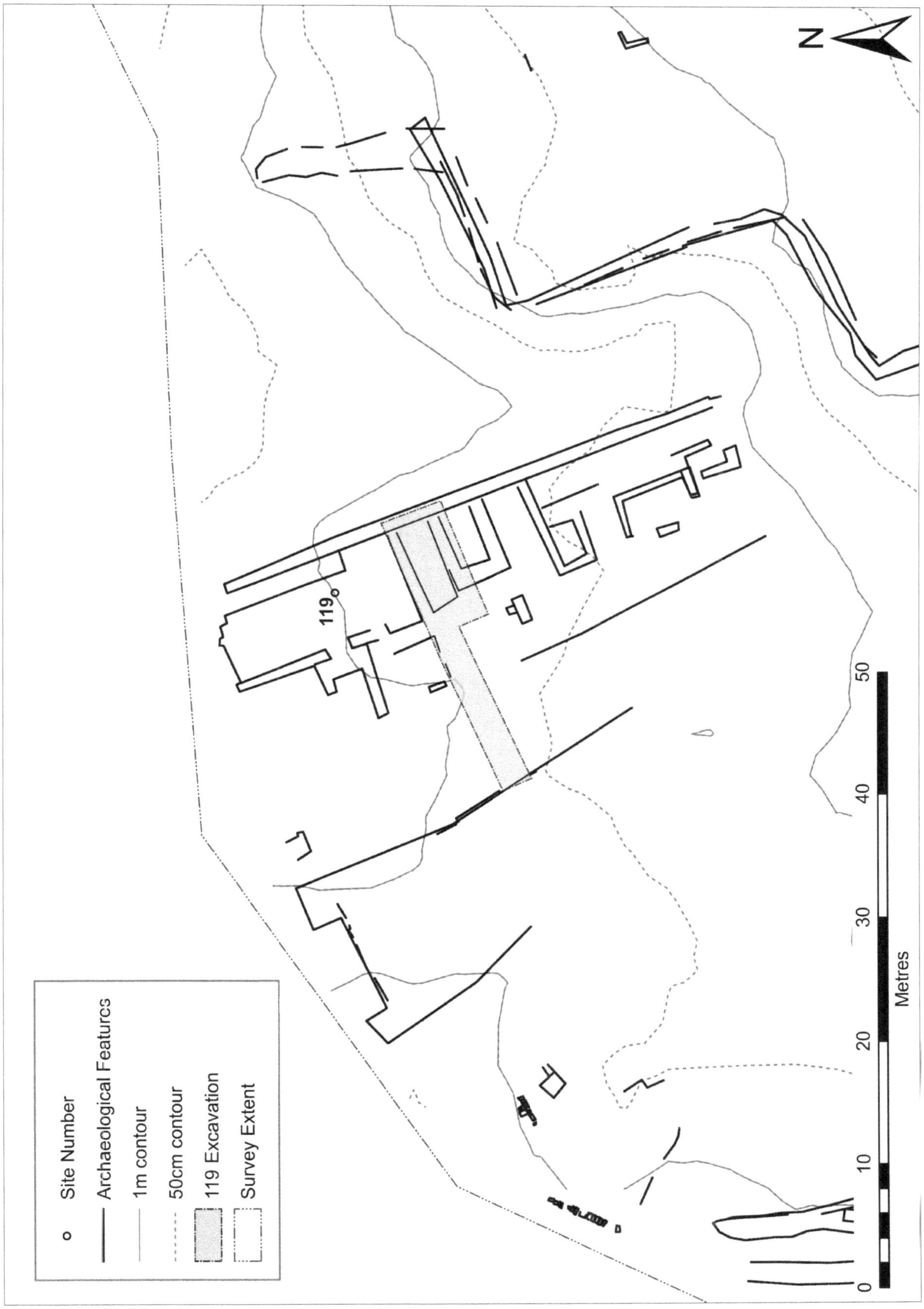

Fig. 6.114. Topography and plan of excavated area Site 119.

Fig. 6.115. General view of Site 119 looking east.

ture that extends from the shoreline southwards, aligned consistently with the majority of linear features along the northern coast of the eastern end of the island.

Limited excavation was carried out at this site to ascertain the nature of the platform-like structure. Partial cleaning along the eastern external wall of this structure revealed that the foundation of the wall was made of regular limestone blocks arranged in stretchers; however, the upper courses, of which two remain, were made of irregular and various sized limestone block. A number of internal walls were recorded and their different alignments, shapes and sizes indicate several phases of construction (Fig. 6.116).

Thorough cleaning of what is referred to as Building 1 within this structure (Fig. 6.116) revealed the remains of two areas, one to the north and one to the south. The first and most southerly area is a rectangular enclosure that measures c. 9m x 4.5m and contains two rooms. Both rooms have almost the same dimensions, c. 3m E-W x 2.70m N-S, and their walls are made of irregular limestone blocks, some with lime mortar. It was noticeable that the walls of these two rooms are relatively thick as they reach up to 0.6m wide. In the middle of the most westerly of the two rooms a uniform, solid block of stones equating to a paved area or foundation of irregular limestone blocks was noted, leaving only a narrow open passage around the edge of the room (Fig. 6.117). Traces of burning were clearly noted around this central paved area. Accordingly, the thick walls and the paved areas could have functioned as the foundation for an upper structure such as a second floor. In the eastern room there were further traces of burning along the northern wall. The foundation of both rooms in Building 1 sit on lake sediments and date from the early Ptolemaic era. Later deposits date the main activities in this building to the late Ptolemaic period to the 1st century BC. This building was robbed out during the Late Roman era.

A second building referred to as Building 2 (Fig. 6.116) was added to the west of Building 1 in the Ptolemaic period. Some time after the 3rd century BC, a third building, Building 3, was added to the west of Building 2. All three buildings had been abandoned by the late 2nd to possibly early 1st century BC. Building 2 was constructed on the same alignment as Building 1 and is also rectangular in shape measuring c. 2.5m N-S and at least 5m E-W. The building is paved with large limestone blocks; however, along its southern wall there are a series of at least four 0.85m x 0.75m pits that were excavated to a depth of 0.25m (Fig. 6.118). Two of the pits contained the remains of imported Rhodian amphorae dating to the mid to late 2nd centuries BC. Accordingly, it is believed that the structure was used as a storage facility.

Building 3 contains the remains of an oven. To the west of this area there are several scattered sections of walls and paved floors that have been subject to heavy siltation but may represent the eastern wall of a fourth building. These remains appear to be Late Roman in date.

About 27m to the west of the main building are the remains of what appears to be an elevated circular structure. The structure was made of a discontinuous line of limestone blocks arranged in headers that extends for some 11m along the edge of the water.

Only eight indicator sherds were collected from the surface of Site 119. This included sherds that ranged from the 2nd century BC to the 1st BC/AD and the mid 5th through mid 6th centuries AD.[6] Two hundred and seventy-three indicator sherds were excavated from Site 119. This assemblage is dominated by Ptolemaic amphorae from the mid-late 4th to the 1st centuries BC, although the Early and Late Roman periods are also represented. Most of the Early Roman pottery could also be Ptolemaic in date. Amphorae account for over 50% of the assemblage.

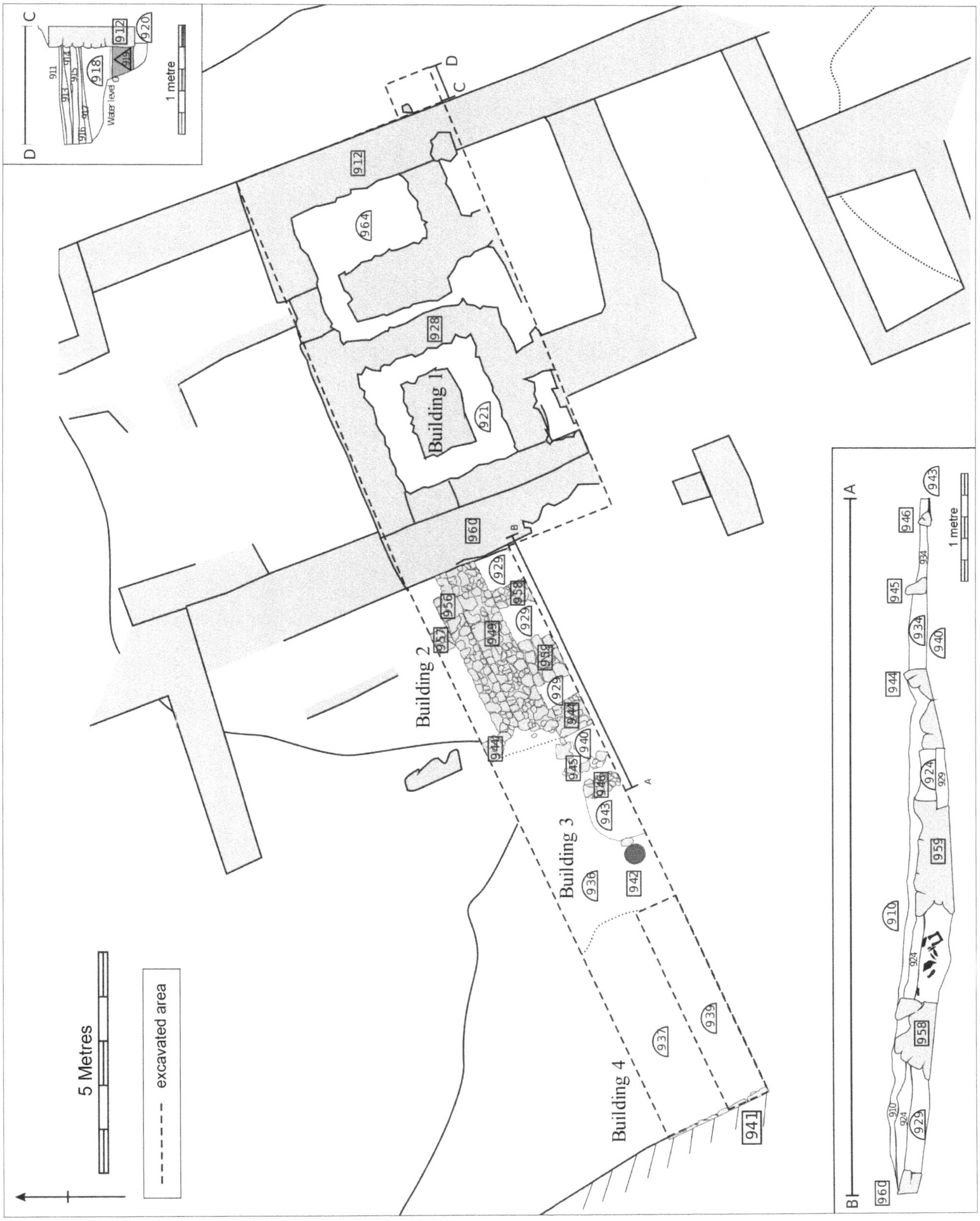

Fig. 6.116. Plan of Site 119 excavation.

6. Because the total survey assemblage was so small the surface finds were considered with the excavation material.

Fig. 6.117. Building 1 west room excavated at Site 119.

Fig. 6.118. Building 2 south pits excavated at Site 119 looking ENE.

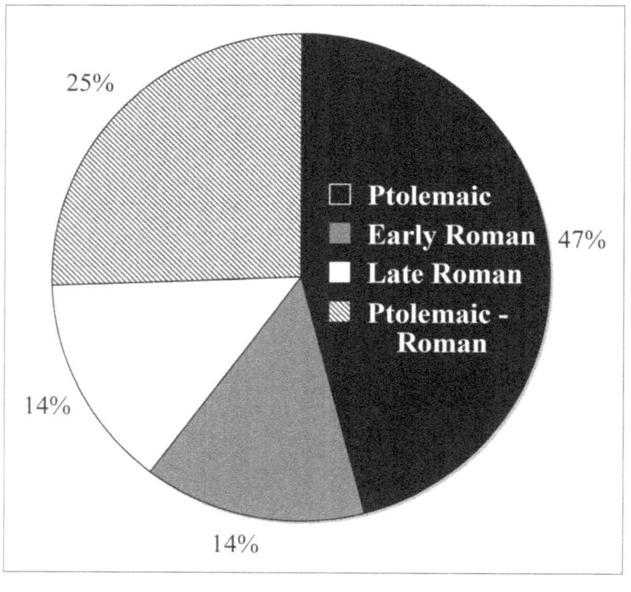

Graph 6.26. (left) Pie graph showing the chronological breakdown of pottery from Site 119.

Table 6.31. Quantity of pottery types for Site 119 survey.

Type	No.
Cypriot Red Slip ware (CRS) 2 (nos 103-4)	1
Egyptian miscellaneous cook ware	1
Egyptian Ptolemaic/Early Roman red slip bowl/dish	1
Egyptian small coarse ware handle	1
Koan (nos 126-30)	2
Mareotic AE1/2 base (no. 7)	1
Tunisian unidentified type	1
Total	8

Table 6.32. Quantity of pottery types for Site 119 excavation.

Type	**No.**	**%**
Finewares		
African Red Slip ware (ARS)	1	0.4
Cypriot Red Slip ware (CRS)	4	1.5
Cypriot Red Slip ware (CRS) 2 (nos 103-4)	1	0.4
Cypriot Red Slip ware (CRS) 9 (nos 105-6)	3	1.1
Egyptian black slip bowl (nos 57-9)	1	0.4
Egyptian black slip bowl/dish footring base	3	1.1
Egyptian black slip cup	2	0.7
Egyptian Ptolemaic/Early Roman red slip bowl/dish	8	3.0
Egyptian red slip bowl (no. 60)	22	8.1
Egyptian Red Slip ware A (ERSA)	1	0.4
Egyptian Red Slip ware B/C (ERSB/C)	2	0.7
Egyptian silt black slip fish dish (nos 54-5)	1	0.4
Imported red slip ?crater (no. 93)	1	0.4
Painted unidentified	(1)	0.0
Coarse wares		
Abu Mena basin (nos 79-80)	2	0.7
Egyptian basin	2	0.7
Egyptian bowl	3	1.1
Egyptian goblet/cup	3	1.1
Egyptian marl jug	16	5.9
Egyptian marl juglet (no. 24)	3	1.1
Egyptian miscellaneous cook ware	5	1.8
Egyptian silt casserole (no. 48)	4	1.5
Egyptian silt casserole (cf. Hayes & Harlaut 2002: fig. 29)	4	1.5
Egyptian silt cooking pot	12	4.4
Egyptian silt dolium	8	2.9
Egyptian silt jug	2	0.7
Egyptian silt lid	1	0.4
Egyptian silt *sakkia* pot (nos 35-41)	2	0.7
Egyptian small coarse ware handle	10	3.7
Amphorae		
Abu Mena LR Amphora 5 (nos 87-9)	6	2.2
Campanian Dressel 1A (no. 135)	1	0.4
Campanian Greco-Italic (no. 134)	2	0.7
Cilician Dressel 30 (nos 143-4)	1	0.4
Cilician Pompeii V (no. 141)	1	0.4
Cilician/Cypriot Egloff 169 (no. 145)	1	0.4
Cilician/Cypriot LR Amphora 1 (nos 146-9)	4	1.5
Egyptian LR Amphora 7	2	0.7
Gaza LR Amphora 4 Majcherek Forms 2-4 (nos 154-7)	7	2.6
Gaza/Palestine LR Amphora 4/5 handle	2	0.7
Imported unidentified type	2	0.7
Imported unsourced whole-mouth amphora (no. 159)	1	0.4
Knidian handle	16	5.9
Knidian I (no. 111)	2	0.7
Knidian IIB (no. 110)	9	3.3
Koan (nos 126-30)	12	4.4
Mareotic AE1/2 base (no. 7)	21	7.7
Mareotic AE1/2 long handle (nos 4-5)	1	0.4
Mareotic AE1/2 short handle (no. 6)	2	0.7
Mareotic AE4 (nos 13-17)	5	1.8
Mareotic Mons Claudianus Type 22/3 (nos 9-12)	1	0.4
Mareotic unidentified type	2	0.7
Rhodian IB (no. 120)	1	0.4
Rhodian IE2/IF (nos 121-6)	35	12.8
Tripolitanian II (no. 150)	4	1.5
Tunisian unidentified type	3	1.1
Tunsian Africana IID (no. 152)	1	0.4
Unsourced amphora (no. 162)	1	0.4
Total	273 (1)	100%

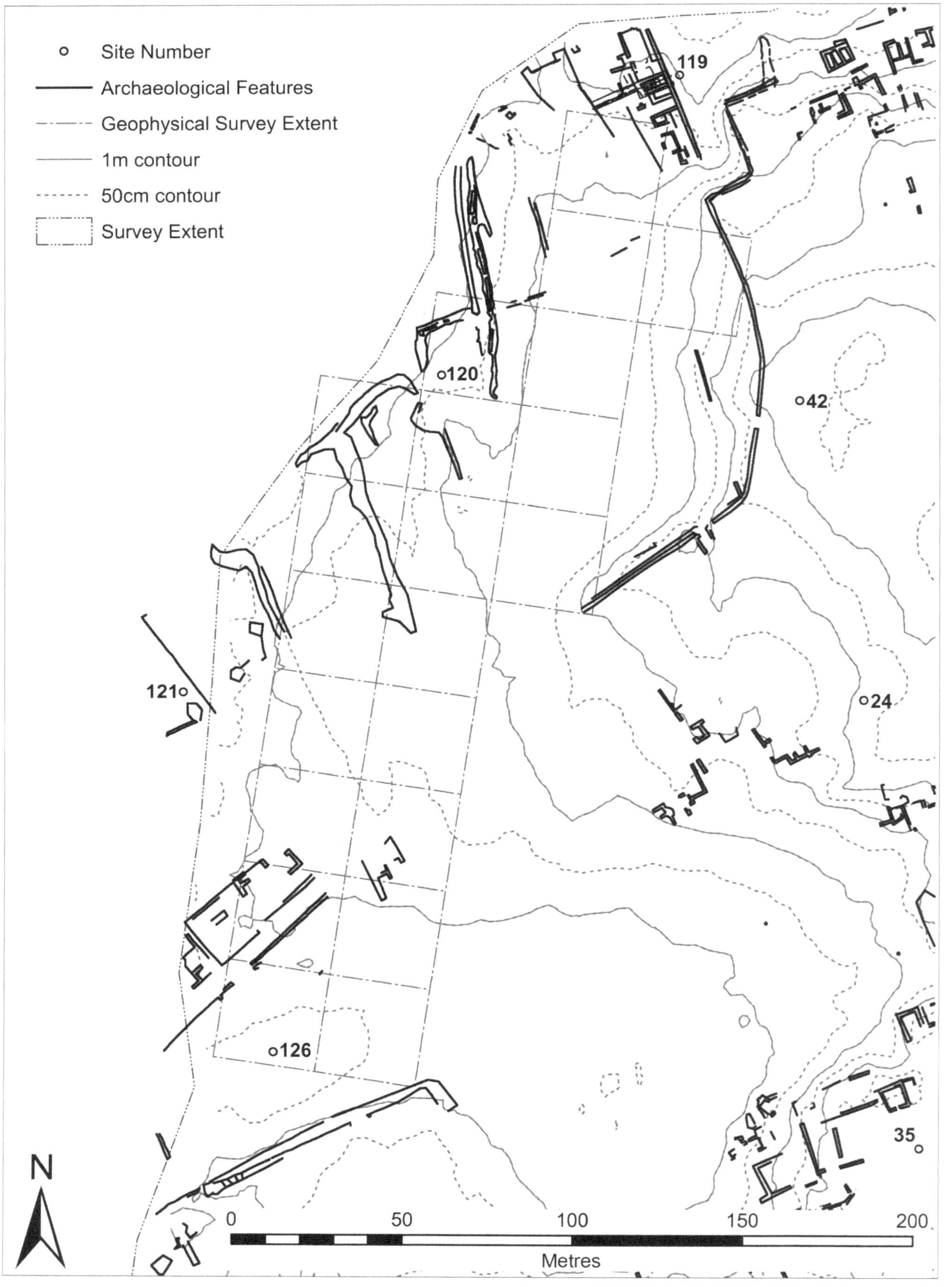

Fig. 6.119. Site 120 topographic survey and location of geophysics grids.

Site 120 (Fig. 6.119; Graph 6.27; Table 6.33)
Location: 30 58 20 N 29 36 33E to 30 58 15N 29 36 32E
Description: The alignment of Site 120 is not so dissimilar from the previous Sites 116-119. Site 120 is located directly to the southwest of Site 119 and it extends southwards along the shore for c.180m and eastwards for c. 100m toward the western end of the ridge. However, the nature of these structures appears to differ from previous structures although this is difficult to determine in detail as they were largely distinguished through geophysical survey and observations of wall alignments on the ground (Fig. 6.120).

Fig. 6.120. Site 120 results of geophysical survey.

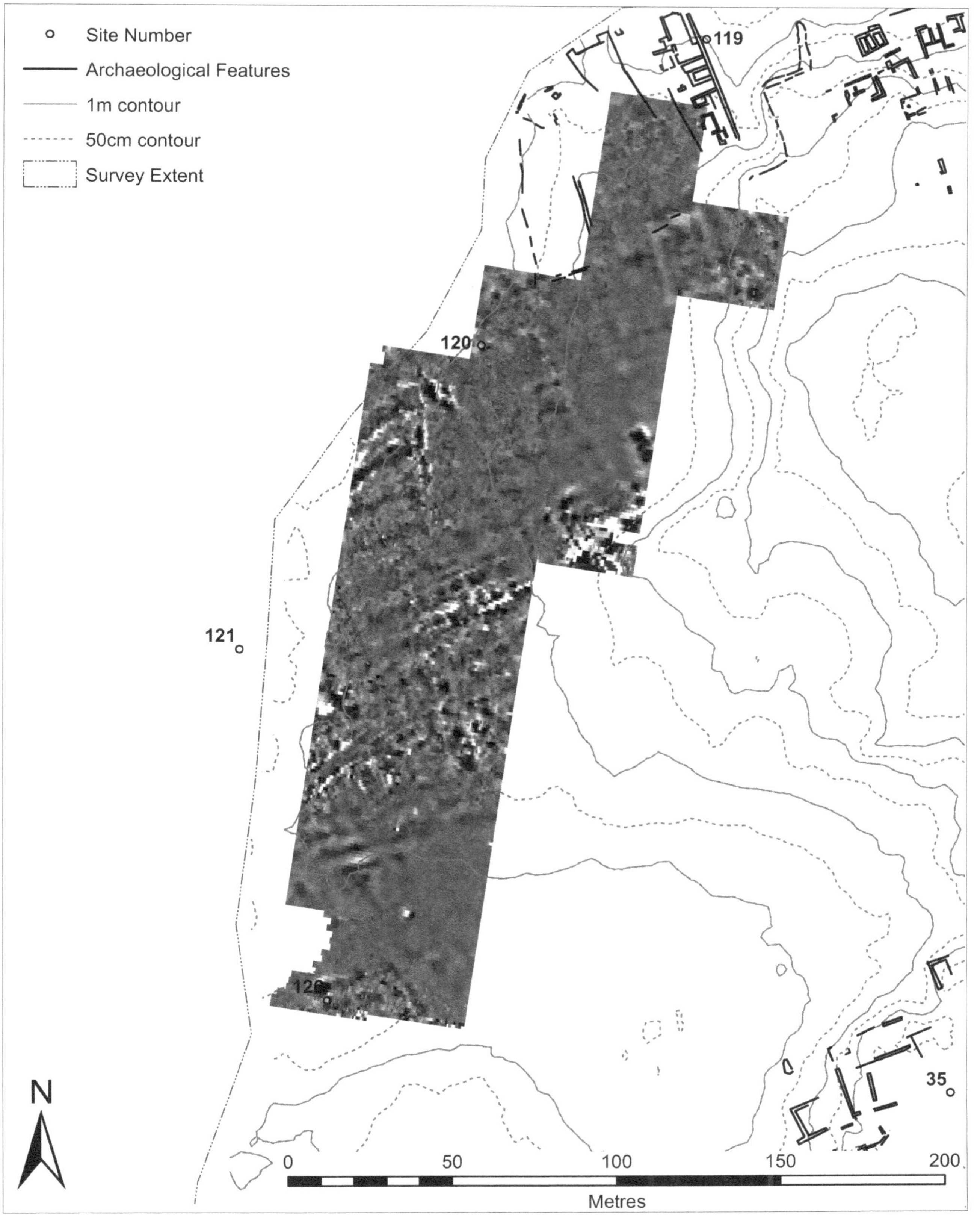

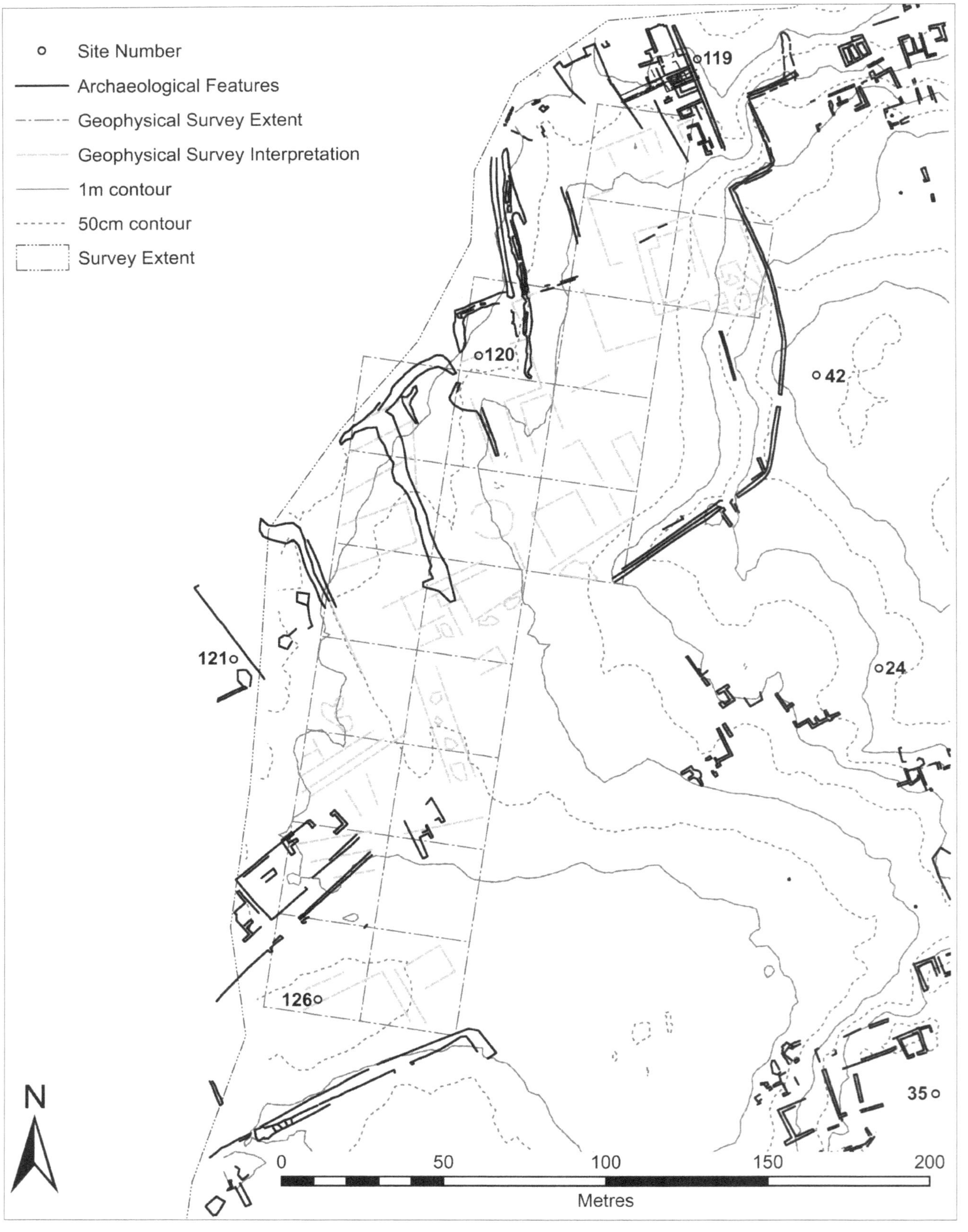

Fig. 6.121. Site 120 interpretation of geophysical survey.

The site is located on a rocky lowland and is associated with scattered limestone boulders and rubble. It is generally lower in level than the elevated platforms to the north-east (Sites 119-114). Towards the east along the shoreline the remains of a series of walls and linear features were noticed; however, they were difficult to identify amongst the rubble. These linear features were observed as low rubble walls 0.5m thick; their northern lake-side ends are close to the current waterline and appear to extend inland for distances of between 25 to 60m. None of these walls reached the foot of the limestone ridge and in most cases extended less than half way across the plain. Three of these walls were spaced approximately 35m apart with a further group 30m to the east that was composed of three roughly parallel walls in very close proximity. The site has been subject to sedimentation and thus geophysical survey conducted in the area was able to reveal more detail in relation to these linear N-S features

At the shoreline of the south-western end of Site 120 there is a rectangular building that measures c. 48m NE-SW x 18m NW-SE. The building is aligned NE-SW and its south-western end almost extends into the present water level. In the northern part of Site 120, a wall extends in a northerly direction from the site for c. 50m along the shoreline. In the north this wall turns eastwards and terminates to the west of the circular structure associated with Site 119 (Fig. 6.121).

Site 120 has a sample of 36 indicator sherds that date to between the late 3rd or 2nd centuries BC through the Late Roman period. Most of the well-dated material is from the Ptolemaic period and the lack of exclusively Early Roman types indicates that most sherds in this category are probably Ptolemaic. Two-thirds of the pottery is amphorae (24) and the absence of the usually common Abu Mena LR Amphora 5 and LR Amphora 1 suggests that the site was not occupied during the 7th century AD.

Table 6.33. (right) Quantity of pottery types for Site 120.

Type	No.	%
Finewares		
Cypriot Red Slip ware (CRS) 9 (nos 105-6)	1	2.8
Egyptian Ptolemaic/Early Roman red slip bowl/dish	1	2.8
Coarse wares		
Abu Mena *sakkia* pot (nos 35-41)	1	2.8
Egyptian silt casserole (no. 48)	4	11.1
Egyptian silt casserole (cf. Hayes & Harlaut 2002: fig. 55)	2	5.6
Egyptian silt cooking pot	2	5.6
Egyptian small handle from coarse ware	1	2.8
Amphorae		
Campanian Dressel 1A (no. 135)	1	2.8
Egyptian LR Amphora 7	1	2.8
Gaza LR Amphora 4 Majcherek Forms 2-4 (nos 154-7)	2	5.6
Imported unidentified type	2	5.6
Koan (nos 126-30)	4	11.1
Mareotic AE1/2 base (no. 7)	6	16.7
Mareotic AE1/2 short handle (no. 6)	2	5.6
Mareotic unidentified type	2	5.6
Rhodian IE2/IF (nos 121-6)	2	5.6
Tunisian unidentified type	2	5.6
Total	36	100%

Graph 6.27. Pie graph showing the chronological breakdown of pottery from Site 120.

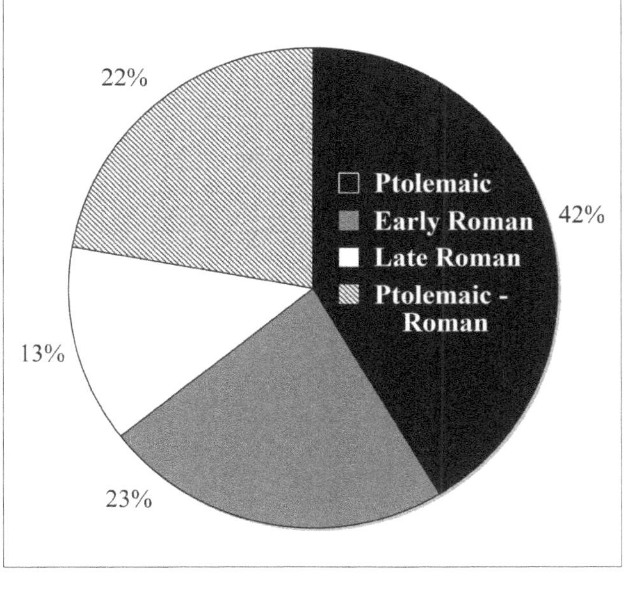

It is noticeable that Sites 116-120 have several features in common. The main archaeological features are located along the shoreline of the lake on elevated platforms that are boarded from the east and west by low depressions.

The archaeological remains mostly represent linear features perpendicular to the shore and multi-roomed structures that could have been subject to several phases of building and reuse. The location of these buildings at the shoreline means that they were probably subject to continuous silting in antiquity, which may explain the different building phases.

Unlike Site 113 on the top of the ridge that was probably associated with civic and residential activities, the sites along the north-western shores of the island were probably maritime and commercial in nature. They could represent the main warehouses and maritime facilities on Mareotis Island.

Site 121 (Figs 6.119, 6.122)
Location: 30 58 17N 29 36 32E
Description: Located between Site 120 and Site 126 along the western shoreline of the northeast of the island, some isolated features were recorded in the 2004 field season. The main feature was an oven-like circular structure that measures 2.7m internal diameter while its external diameter is 4.7m. The main structure was made of fired brick and was surrounded by brick. The structure contained a stone flue that measured c. 0.8m in diameter at its southern end. To the southeast of the oven there was a patch of well preserved stone floor that was located c. 12m from the waterline in 2004.

The location of the oven in a low area close to the shoreline is not clearly understood. Even the type of oven and its exact function is not clear. Moreover, when this site was revisited in 2007, the archaeological features were submerged under the lake waters and thus could not be recorded in detail.

Fig. 6.122. Site 121 oven.

Site 126 (Figs 6. 119, 6.123 & 6.124; Table 6.34)
Location: 30 58 13N 29 36 32E to 30 58 14N 29 36 38E
Description: This site is located to the south of Site 120. It is characterised by a marshland depression that extends from the shore inland in an E-W direction for c. 180m, and its maximum N-S extent is c.100m. Sedimentological analysis that was carried out at this depression revealed that it was filled with lake water in antiquity (see Chapter

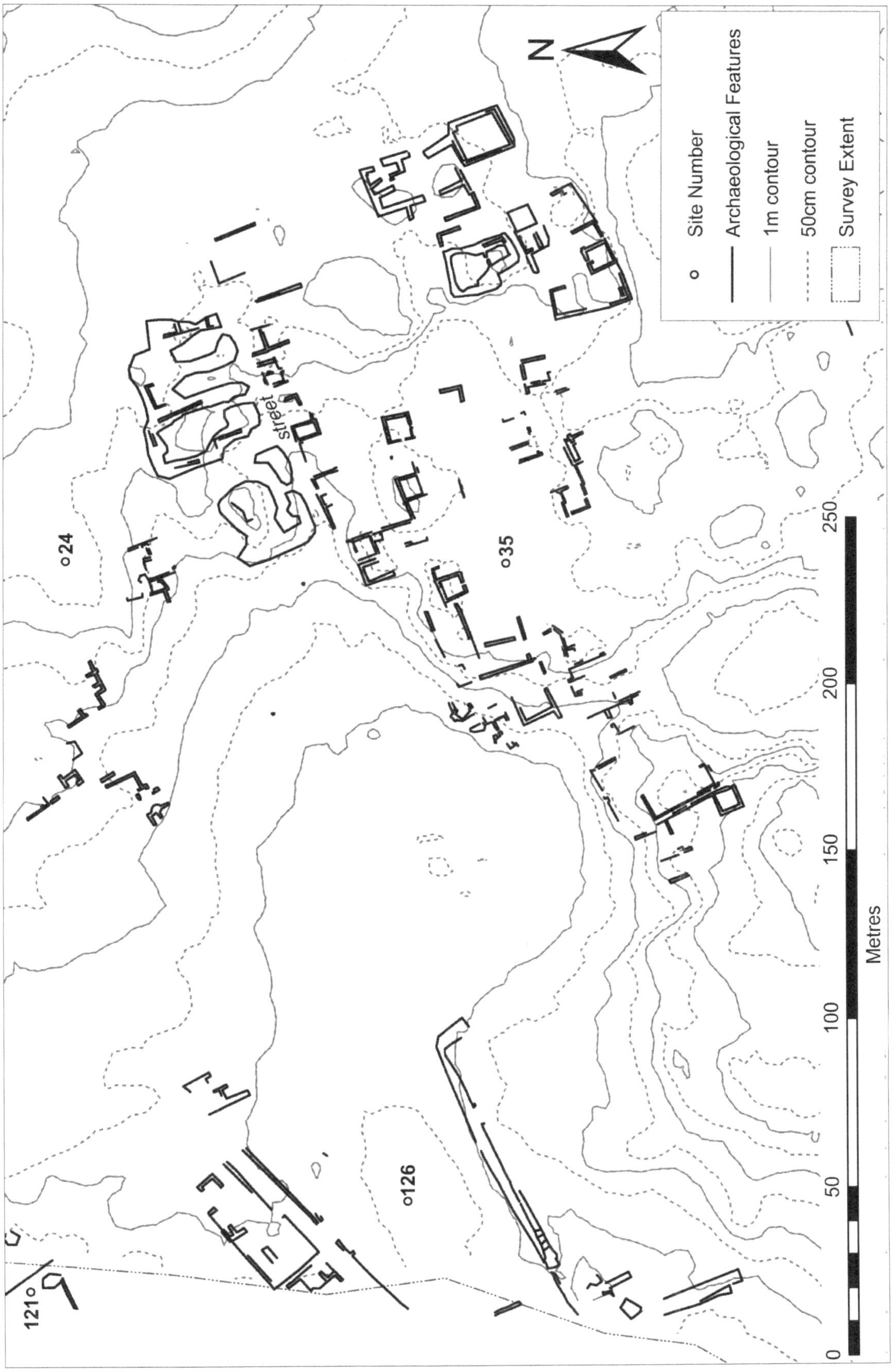

Fig. 6.123. Site 126 and Site 35.

Fig. 6.124. General view of inlet Site 126 looking west.

5); accordingly, the depression took the form of a sheltered embayment and could have been used as a natural harbour. The entrance for the embayment took the form of a channel. The surface remains indicate a channel width of c. 45m wide (N-S) and 90m long (E-W). This channel led to the main body of the depression that extended to the foot of the ridge occupied by Site 35.

The archaeological remains at Site 126 delimit the northern and southern edges of the entrance to the embayment and extend beyond its shores to the east, south and north. Immediately to the north and south of the embayment entrance a series of limestone linear, quay-like features determine the edges of the entrance. To the south the wall extends some 90m and is c. 4m wide (Fig. 6.125) before turning to the south at its south-western end and continuing for some 40m to the south. It is constructed of large, limestone ashlar blocks. At the north-east end of the wall there is a gap along the edge that measures c. 6m and faces the northern edge of the channel entrance.

On the northern side of the channel entrance there is a well preserved building and a wall that extends in a NE-SW direction almost parallel to the wall on the southern side of the channel (Fig. 6.123). The wall is made of irregular limestone blocks and large ashlar blocks. It is c. 65m long also with a gap that mirrors the opening identified in the wall to the south of the entrance. The building runs north of the wall and parallel to it at a distance of c. 7m. The building measures c. 35m x 13m and it has an opening that measures c. 4m halfway along its southern side. This building could have been part of a cluster of buildings that extended over Site 120, essentially linking Sites 126 with the northern Site 120 (Fig. 6.121). The northern and southern walls of the embayment entrance could have been utilised as harbour quays. However, the geophysical survey (see Fig. 6.121) indicated that in fact the channel was narrower than the impression the two channel walls gave on the ground, with a further wall within the entrance making it c. 20m wide.

On top of the ridge at the south-eastern end of the depression there are the remains of a series of partially excavated buildings (Fig. 6.123). The buildings are arranged along what appears to be a street front aligned ENE-WSW that extends from the embayment Site 126 up the ridge (Fig. 6.126), adjacent to Site 35 to the south and Site 24 and Site 42 to the east. The buildings are partially excavated and of fairly uniform layout, some of which appear to be linked to channels (Figs 6.127 & 6.128). On the ridge above the street and buildings to the south, further building outlines were identified. Thus, it is probably safe to say that Site 126 and Site 35 were functionally connected. While Site 126 represented the maritime facade where boats entered, Site 35 could have been urban in nature.

Despite extensive gridding the environmental conditions meant that few ceramic samples were collected from Site 126. It has in total a sample of only 13 indicator sherds and one body sherd that mostly date to the 2nd and 1st centuries BC with a body sherd from a 4th to 7th centuries AD casserole.

Fig. 6.125. Southern entrance wall Site 126 looking east.

Fig. 6.126. Street front to east of Site 126 above inlet, looking east.

Fig. 6.127. Buildings associated with the street front above Site 126.

Fig. 6.128. (left) Channels within the buildings to the south of the street of Site 126.

Table 6.34. Quantity of pottery types for Site 126.

Type	**No.**
Egyptian black slip bowl (nos 57-9)	1
Egyptian silt casserole (nos 49-51)	(1)
Egyptian silt casserole (cf. Hayes & Harlaut 2002: fig. 29)	1
Egyptian silt cooking pot (no. 44)	1
Egyptian silt miscellaneous coarse ware	2
Koan (nos 126-30)	1
Mareotic AE1/2 base (no. 7)	4
Mareotic AE1/2 long handle (nos 4-5)	3
Total	13 (1)

Site 24 (Figs 6.87, 6.123, 6.129; Graph 6.28; Table 6.35)
Location: 30 58 18N 29 36 39E
Description: This site occupies the top of the ridge to the east above Site 126. It is a relatively flat open area with very few visible remains and as such no features were recorded in the area. Ceramic survey revealed a sample of 82 indicator sherds, primarily Ptolemaic in date, including pottery from the late 3rd century BC but mostly from the 2nd and 1st centuries. At the site there are only sparse exclusively Early Roman sherds (1st/2nd centuries AD); equally there are only sparse 7th century AD types. Half of the assemblage is amphorae and includes a single example from Chios.

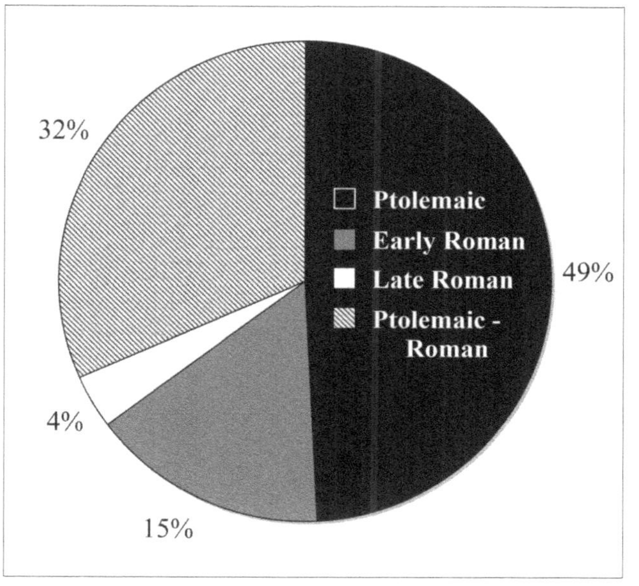

Graph 6.28. (right) Pie graph showing the chronological breakdown of pottery from Site 24.

Table 6.35. (below) Quantity of pottery types for Site 24.

Type	**No.**	**%**
Finewares		
Eastern Sigillata A (ESA)	1	1.2
Egyptian black slip bowl/dish footring base	3	3.7
Egyptian Ptolemaic/Early Roman red slip bowl/dish	5	6.1
Egyptian silt black slip fish dish (nos 54-5)	1	1.2
Egyptian silt red slip fish dish (nos 54-5)	6	7.3
Coarse wares		
Egyptian bowl	1	1.2
Egyptian miscellaneous coarse ware	8	9.8
Egyptian silt casserole (no. 48)	4	4.8
Egyptian silt casserole (cf. Hayes & Harlaut 2002: fig. 29)	2	2.4
Egyptian silt cooking pot (no. 45)	2	2.4
Egyptian silt cooking pot (no. 47)	1	1.2
Egyptian silt dolium	3	3.7
Egyptian silt jar/jug with twisted handle (no. 27)	1	1.2
Egyptian small handle from coarse ware	2	2.4
Amphorae		
Abu Mena LR Amphora 5 (nos 87-9)	3	3.7
Chian	1	1.2
Imported unidentified type	1	1.2
Koan (nos 126-30)	9	10.9
Mareotic AE1/2 (nos 1-3)	13	15.9
Mareotic AE1/2 base (no. 7)	2	2.4
Mareotic AE1/2 short handle (no. 6)	4	4.9
Mareotic Mons Claudianus Type 22/3 (nos 9-12)	1	1.2
Mareotic unidentified type	2	2.4
Rhodian IE2/IF (nos 121-6)	5	6.1
Unsourced amphora (no. 162)	1	1.2
Total	82	100%

Site 42 (Figs 6.87, 6.129; Graph 6.29; Table 6.36)
Location: 30 58 21N 29 36 39E
Description: To the north of Site 24 and defining the western edge of the ridge to the east of Site 120, Site 42 occupies an elevated area of open ground that extends to the plain on the north shore towards Site 118 and Site 119. Site 42 reveals the remains of numerous walls particularly along the northern edge and down to the plain, and forms a westerly extension of the main urban settlement (Site 113) at the east end of the island.

Fig. 6.129. Site 42 so-called "city wall".

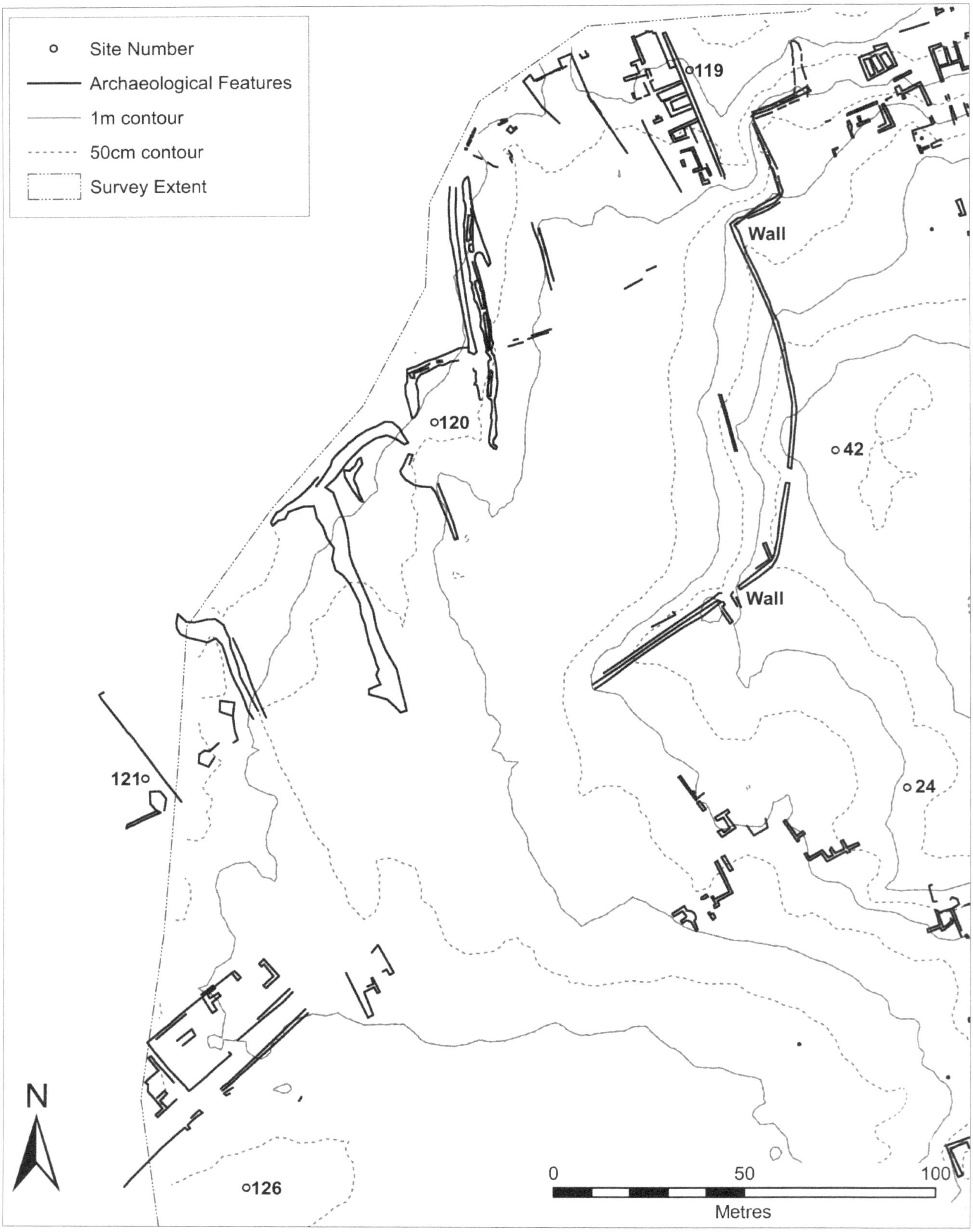

Table 6.36. Quantity of pottery types for Site 42.

Type	**No.**	**%**
Finewares		
African Red Slip ware (ARS) 104 (no. 101)	1	2.0
Eastern Sigillata A (ESA)	(5)	0.0
Egyptian black slip cup	1	2.0
Egyptian painted cup	2	4.0
Egyptian Ptolemaic/Early Roman red slip bowl/dish	4	8.0
Egyptian silt black slip fish dish (nos 54-5)	1	2.0
Glazed (?modern)	(2)	0.0
Coarse wares		
Egyptian basin	2	4.0
Egyptian casserole	3	6.0
Egyptian miscellaneous coarse ware	4	8.0
Egyptian silt casserole	1	2.0
Egyptian silt casserole (no. 48)	5	10.0
Egyptian silt cooking pot	2	4.0
Egyptian silt dolium	1	2.0
Egyptian silt jug	1	2.0
Egyptian silt lid	1	2.0
Egyptian small handle from coarse ware	1	2.0
Amphorae		
Abu Mena LR Amphora 5 (nos 87-9)	1	2.0
Cilician/Cypriot LR Amphora 1 (nos 146-9)	(1)	0.0
Knidian handle	2	4.0
Knidian ID (no. 112)	1	2.0
Knidian IIG (no. 119)	1	2.0
Koan (nos 126-30)	9	18.0
Mareotic AE1/2 (nos 1-3)	2	4.0
Mareotic Mons Claudianus Type 22/3 (nos 9-12)	1	2.0
Rhodian IE2/IF (nos 121-6)	2	4.0
Unsourced amphora	1	2.0
Total	50 (8)	100%

The most substantial structure at Site 42 is a continuous wall made of rubble and piled limestone blocks with a number of openings that measures 240m in length and up to 2m wide and c. 1m in height. The wall follows the contour of the western limit of the ridge and determines the sites westward extent (Fig. 6.129). The wall meanders southwards from the shoreline west of Site 118 and 30m east of Site 119 towards the foot of the ridge and then turns westwards following the contours of the ridge to the west and south of Site 119. It continues to the south and southwest winding along the top of the ridge and following the contour of the edge of the ridge, terminating in the south, northeast of Site 126. Despite the fact that the wall has fallen in places, other sections that are extant reveal its substantial construction of limestone blocks. The wall may have served as a boundary wall or had some defensive function protecting the settlement from the west. It appears to divide the upper town on the ridge from the lower plain and maritime installations to the north and west and as such is referred to as the "wall" possibly a "city wall" (Fig. 6.129).

Site 42 has a sample of 50 indicator and eight body sherds. The pottery represents activity in this area from the mid 4th century BC to the 7th century AD, especially the 2nd/1st centuries BC; in this respect the assemblage resembles the material connected with the more elevated areas of Site 113. None of the Early Roman pottery shown in Graph 6.29 belongs exclusively to the Early Roman period and in this context is more likely to be Ptolemaic in date.

Graph 6.29. Pie graph showing the chronological breakdown of pottery from Site 42.

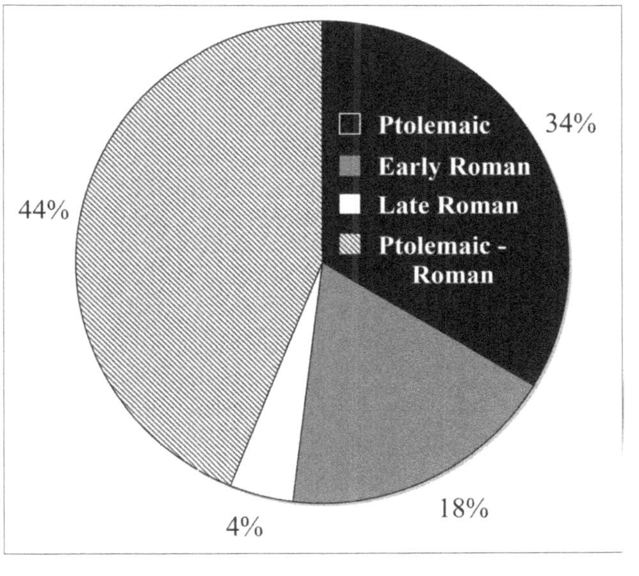

Site 35 (Figs 6.123, 6.130; Graphs 6.30 & 6.31; Table 6.37)
Location: 30 58 10N 29 36 37E to 30 58 14N 29 36 44E
Description: To the south and southeast of Site 126, extending almost east to Site 113, the top of the ridge is covered in extensive and densely packed buildings, building remains and materials. The layout and construction styles of the visible remains indicate some degree of social organisation, such as possible administrative and commercial areas. Some of the buildings are substantial in construction and many are grouped around what appear to be large, open, generally low-lying areas at a number of locations on top of the ridge. Ceramics and building remains continue to the north across the top of the ridge to the east of the "city wall" but here they are less substantial.

A sample of 372 indicator sherds dating potentially between the late 3rd century BC and the 7th century AD were collected. Most of the pottery is 5th to 7th centuries AD with the 7th century particularly well represented in the sample, although there is also a small peak during the 2nd and 1st centuries BC. The ware types are well distributed, with approximately half belonging to amphorae (mostly accounted for by LR Amphora 1 and Abu Mena LR Amphora 5); the rest are domestic wares.

Fig. 6.130. General view of Site 35, looking E-S-E.

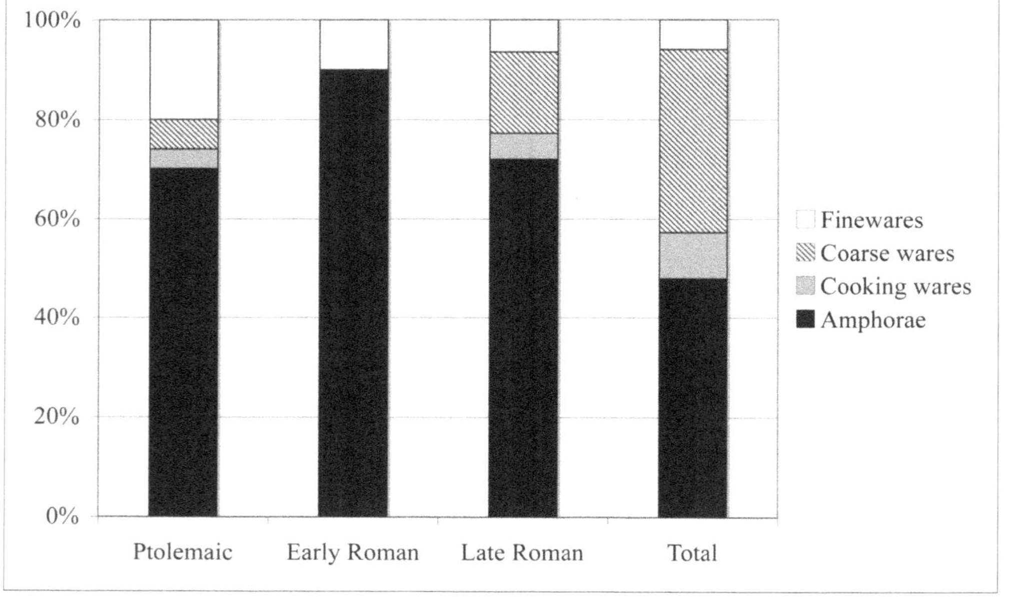

Graph 6.30. Bar graph showing the breakdown of form types by period Site 35.

Table 6.37. Quantity of pottery types for Site 35.

Type	No.	%
Finewares		
African Red Slip ware (ARS) 107	1	0.3
Cypriot Red Slip ware (CRS) 2 (nos 103-4)	1	0.3
Cypriot Red Slip ware (CRS) 9 (nos 105-6)	3	0.8
Eastern Sigillata A (ESA)	1	0.3
Egyptian black slip bowl/ dish footring base	2	0.5
Egyptian Ptolemaic/Early Roman red slip bowl/dish	10	2.7
Egyptian Red Slip ware A (ERSA) copy of ARS 84 (nos 65-6)	1	0.3
Egyptian Red Slip ware A (ERSA) copy of ARS 99	1	0.3
Egyptian Red Slip ware A (ERSA) copy of CRS 9 (no. 76)	2	0.5
Egyptian Red Slip ware C (ERSC) misc	2	0.5
Coarse wares		
Abu Mena basin (nos 79-80)	27	7.3
Egyptian basin	18	4.8
Egyptian basin	1	0.3
Egyptian casserole	3	0.8
Egyptian miscellaneous coarse ware	22	5.9
Egyptian silt bowl/dish	2	0.5
Egyptian silt casserole (nos 49-51)	6	1.6
Egyptian silt casserole lid (no. 53)	3	0.8
Egyptian silt cooking pot	12	3.2
Egyptian silt cooking pot (no. 45)	2	0.5
Egyptian silt dolium	3	0.8
Egyptian silt funnel strainer (no. 33)	1	0.3
Egyptian silt jar/jug with twisted handle (no. 27)	3	0.8
Egyptian silt jug	5	1.4
Egyptian silt lid	9	2.4
Egyptian small handle from coarse ware	53	14.2
Amphorae		
Abu Mena LR Amphora 5 (nos 87-9)	77	20.7
Cilician/Cypriot Egloff 169 (no. 145)	1	0.3
Cilician/Cypriot LR Amphora 1 (nos 146-9)	38	10.2
Egyptian LR Amphora 7	(1)	0.0
Gaza LR Amphora 4 Majcherek Forms 2-4 (nos 154-7)	1	0.3
Imported unidentified type	5	1.3
Koan (nos 126-30)	11	3.0
Mareotic AE1/2 (nos 1-3)	3	0.8
Mareotic AE1/2 base (no. 7)	3	0.8
Mareotic AE1/2 short handle (no. 6)	14	3.8
Mareotic AE4 (nos 13-17)	2	0.5
Mareotic Mons Claudianus Type 22/3 (nos 9-12)	5	1.3
Mareotic unidentified type	9	2.4
Palestine LR Amphora 5 (no. 158)	6	1.6
Rhodian IE2/IF (nos 121-6)	1	0.3
Tripolitanian II (no. 150)	1	0.3
Tunisian Africana IID (no. 152)	1	0.3
Total	372 (1)	100%

Graph 6.31. Pie graph showing the chronological breakdown of pottery from Site 35.

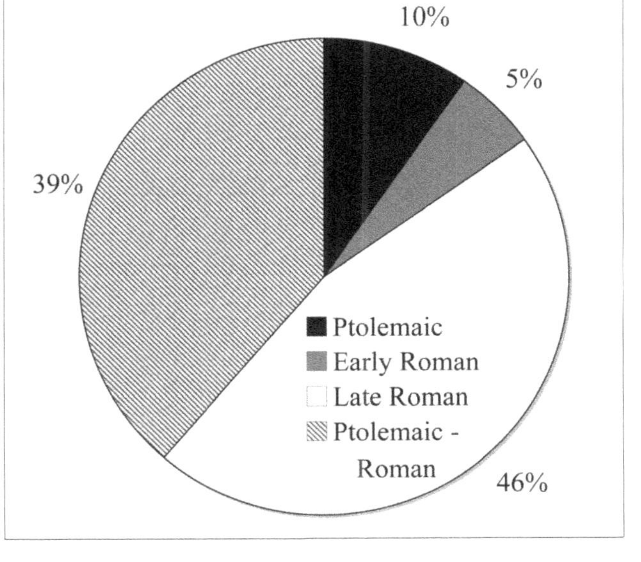

Site 14 (Figs 6.87, 6.131 & 6.132; Graph 6.32; Table 6.38)
Location: 30 58 08N 29 36 50E to 30 58 07N 29 36 46E
Description: Site 14 is made up of two sections, one to the east and one to the west. To the east, at least five groups of rock-cut tombs and quarries with square entrances have been identified. One of the rock-cut tombs had a number of loculi or chambers leading off the main shaft (Figs 6.133 & 6.134). To the west aligned along the edge of a ridge that currently defines the southern shoreline of the island, were a series of buildings of fairly uniform structure that looked south over the low-lying marshy land. The buildings were constructed of limestone blocks and were generally square in shape with smaller internal rooms.

To the west of the site the land falls away to a marshy channel leading to a shallow depression. To the north are a series of buildings, the exact layout of which was difficult to determine due to their disturbed nature. Further north still below the central ridge, a number of small stone quarry sites were identified. Site 14 represents the most substantial remains visible on the south-east end of the island.

Site 14 has a sample of 79 indicator sherds spread between the 2nd century BC and the 7th century AD. The 2nd and 1st centuries BC are the best represented with another small peak between the late 4th and 7th centuries AD. Amphorae account for approximately half the assemblage, with local and Koan types the most common.

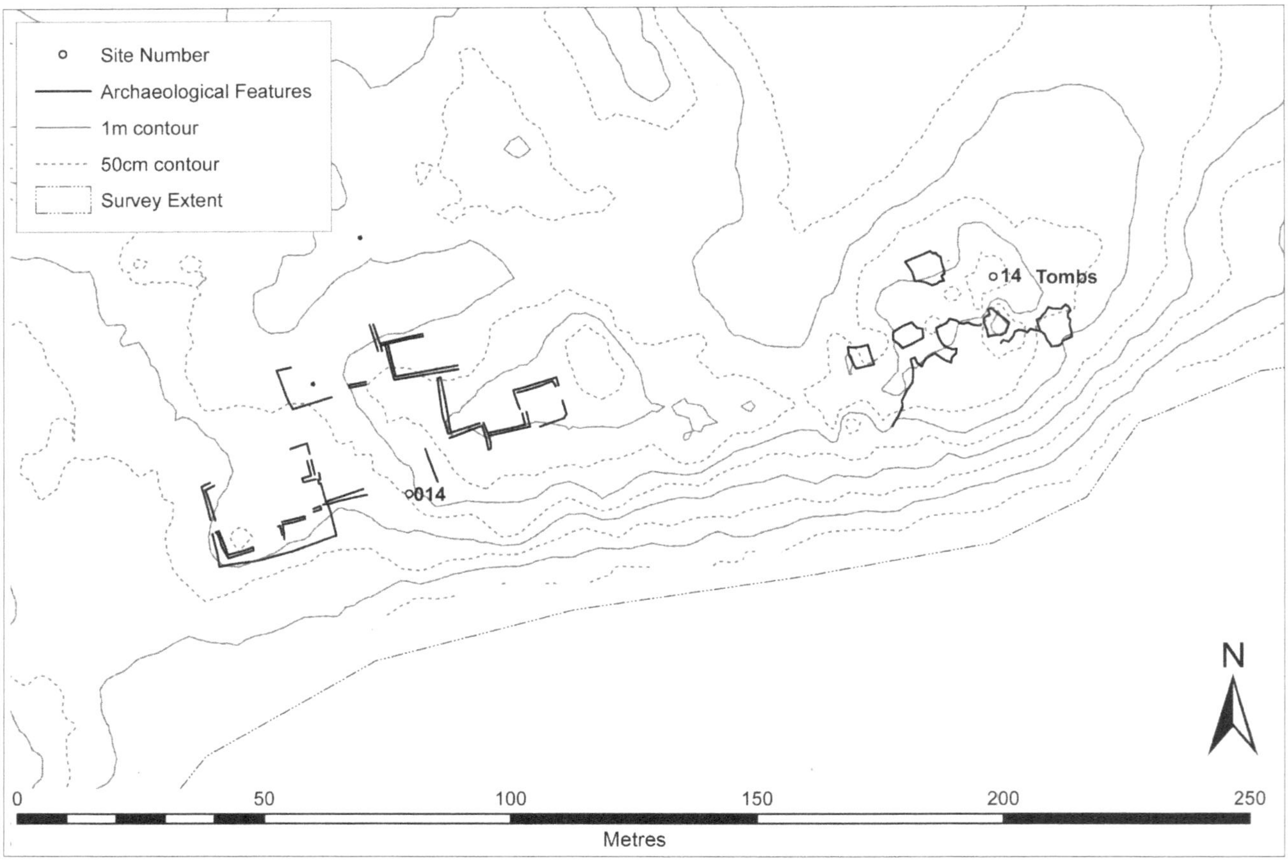

Fig. 6.131. (above) Site 14.

Fig. 6.132. General view of Site 14 looking east.

Fig. 6.133. Tombs Site 14.

Fig. 6.134. Internal rooms of tombs at Site 14.

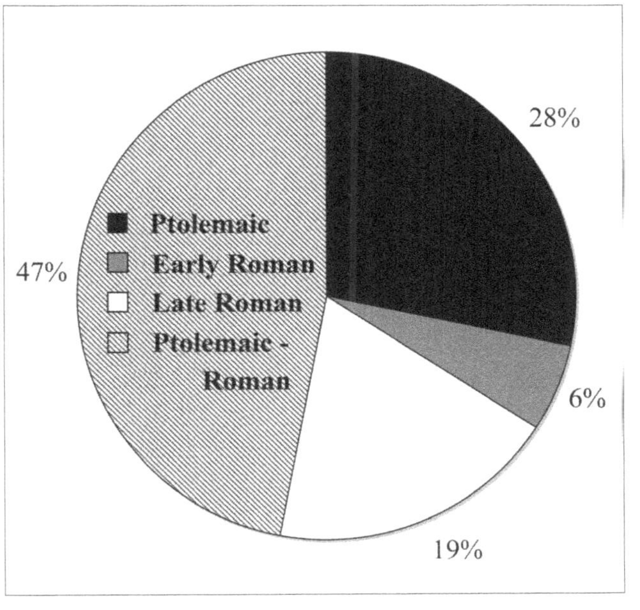

Graph 6.32. Pie graph showing the chronological breakdown of pottery from Site 14.

Table 6.38. Quantity of pottery types for Site 14.

Type	**No.**	**%**
Finewares		
Cypriot Red Slip ware (CRS) 2 (nos 103-4)	2	2.5
Egyptian black slip bowl (nos 57-9)	1	1.3
Egyptian Ptolemaic/ Early Roman red slip bowl/dish	4	5.1
Phocaean Red Slip ware (PRS) 3 (nos 108-9)	1	1.3
Coarse wares		
Abu Mena basin (nos 79-80)	1	1.3
Egyptian basin	1	1.3
Egyptian miscellaneous coarse ware	5	6.3
Egyptian silt casserole (no. 48)	2	2.5
Egyptian silt cooking pot	2	2.5
Egyptian silt dolium	9	11.4
Egyptian silt jar/jug with twisted handle (no. 27)	1	1.3
Egyptian silt lid	4	5.1
Egyptian silt *sakkia* pot (nos 35-41)	1	1.3
Egyptian small handle from coarse ware	9	11.4
Mareotic jug	1	1.3
Amphorae		
Abu Mena LR Amphora 5 (nos 87-9)	2	2.5
Cilician/Cypriot Egloff 169 (no. 145)	1	1.3
Cilician/Cypriot LR Amphora 1 (nos 146-9)	7	8.9
Gaza LR Amphora 4 Majcherek Forms 2-4 (nos 154-7)	1	1.3
Koan (nos 126-30)	4	5.1
Mareotic AE1/2 short handle (no. 6)	19	24.1
Mareotic AE4 (nos 13-17)	1	1.3
Total	79	100%

Fig. 6.135. Quarrying associated with Site 36.

Site 36 (Fig. 6.87; Graph 6.33; Table 6.39)
Location: 30 58 07N 29 36 31E to 30 58 10N 29 36 37E
Description: This site is located at the western-most limit of sites that were recorded at the eastern end of the island. It is a limestone hill c. 250m NE-SW and 100m NW-SE and its maximum height is 8m. The central island ridge extends southwest of Site 126 and narrows to the west delimited by two embayments, one on the northern shore of the lake and the other to the south. Site 36 is located on top of the ridge sandwiched between the two embayments, the width of the island at this point being c. 300m. The main archaeological features at Site 36 are the remains of small quarrying areas and a few poorly preserved walls (Fig. 6.135).

Site 36 has a sample of 56 indicator sherds, most probably belonging to the 2nd to 1st centuries BC but with a discontinuous span between the late 4th or 3rd centuries BC to the 7th century AD. Only the Egyptian silt casserole (Hayes & Harlaut 2002: fig. 55) belongs exclusively to the Early Roman period; all other sherds assigned to this time frame could equally be Ptolemaic. The site is unusual in having more finewares (29) than amphorae (20), suggesting domestic occupation.

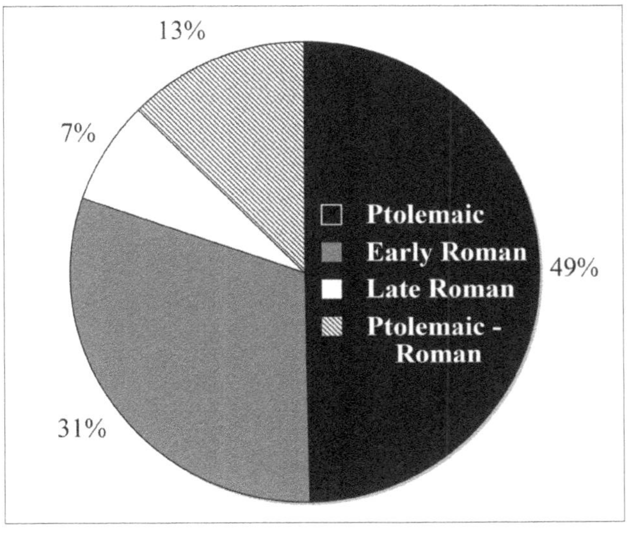

Graph 6.33. (left) Pie graph showing the chronological breakdown of pottery from Site 36.

Type	No.	%
Finewares		
Egyptian black slip bowl (nos 57-9)	1	1.8
Egyptian black slip bowl/dish footring base	4	7.1
Egyptian Ptolemaic/Early Roman red slip bowl/dish	15	26.8
Egyptian red slip bowl (no. 60)	5	8.9
Egyptian black slip fish dish (nos 54-5)	1	1.8
Egyptian silt red slip fish dish (nos 54-5)	3	5.4
Coarse wares		
Egyptian miscellaneous coarse ware	1	1.8
Egyptian silt casserole (cf. Hayes & Harlaut 2002: fig. 55)	1	1.8
Egyptian silt cooking pot	4	7.1
Egyptian silt lid	1	1.8
Amphorae		
Abu Mena LR Amphora 5 (nos 87-9)	3	5.4
Cilician/Cypriot LR Amphora 1 (nos 146-9)	1	1.8
Knidian handle	2	3.6
Knidian IIB/IIC (nos 113-18)	2	3.6
Mareotic AE1/2 (nos 1-3)	9	16.1
Rhodian IE2/IF (nos 121-6)	2	3.6
Unsourced imported amphora	1	1.8
Total	56	100%

Table 6.39. (above) Quantity of pottery types for Site 36.

6.4.2 Sites located in the middle section of the island
(Fig. 6.136)

To the west of Site 36, the middle section of the island extends for c. 1800m westwards until Site 39. This section of the island has an average width of c. 300m and it consists of a series of high limestone mounds that extend along the central ridge of the island. The lowland areas between the mounds are covered with aeolian soils and small rocks, while along the shoreline extend marshland and lake sediments. This middle section of Mareotis Island contains, from east to west, Sites 125, 124, 37, 38, 123, 43 and 39. The seven sites are, for the most part, fairly discrete units. Many of them, as described below, are associated with pottery production.

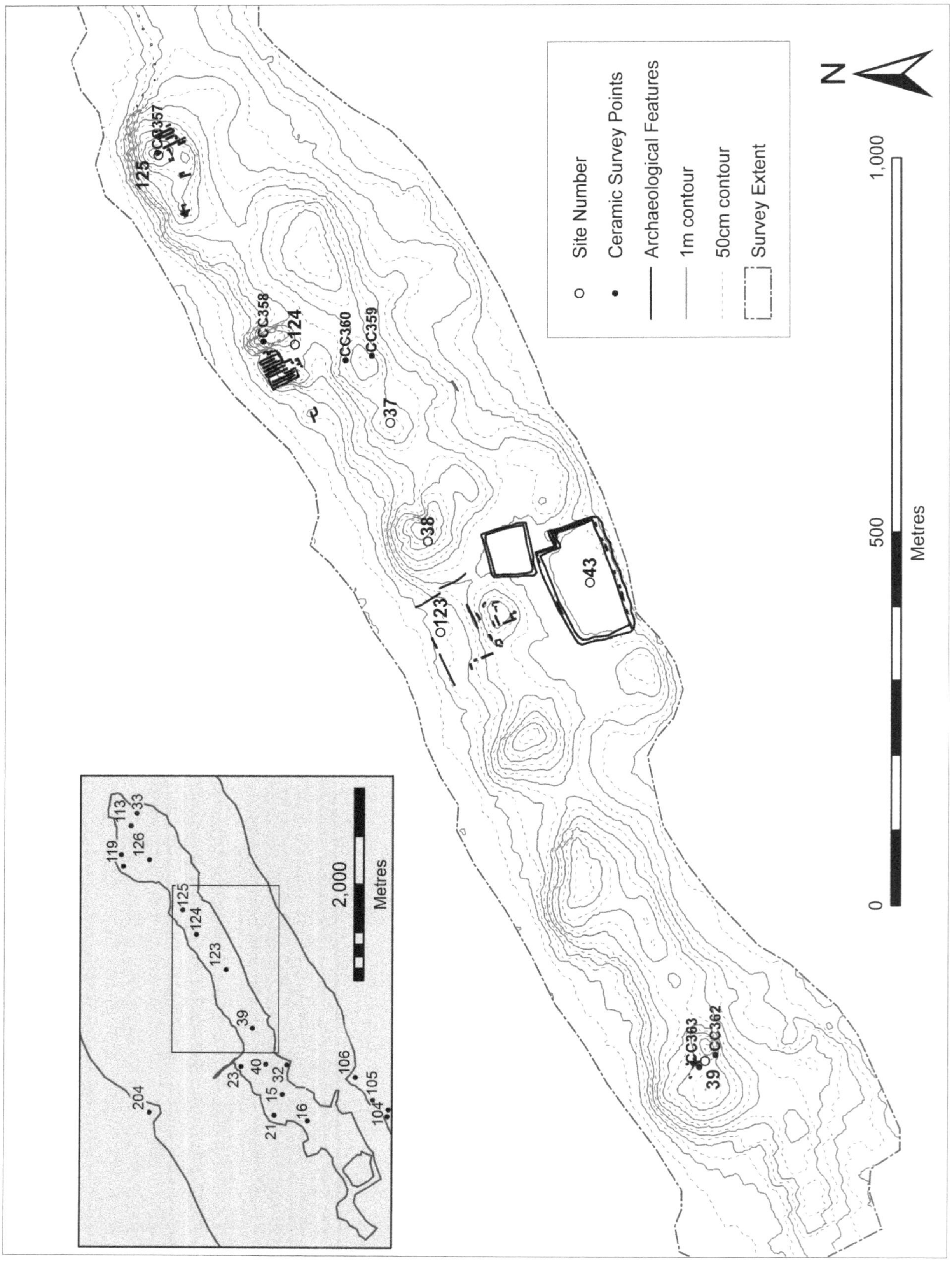

Fig. 6.136. Overview of middle section of island with site location, topography, features and ceramic circles noted.

Site 125 (Figs 6.136, 6.137 & 6.138; Graph 6.34; Table 6.40)
Location: 30 58 04N 29 36 20E
Description: This site is located to the west of a northern embayment on top of the limestone ridge. It extends over an area of c. 170m E-W and c. 90m N-S and is 8m high. The site overlooks the northern shore of the island and drops steeply down towards it, while the distance between the foot of the ridge and the current northern shore of the island is c. 130m.

Large quantities of pottery sherds on top of the mound were noticed which represents evidence for pottery production (Fig. 6.139). To the east of the pottery dumps there are the

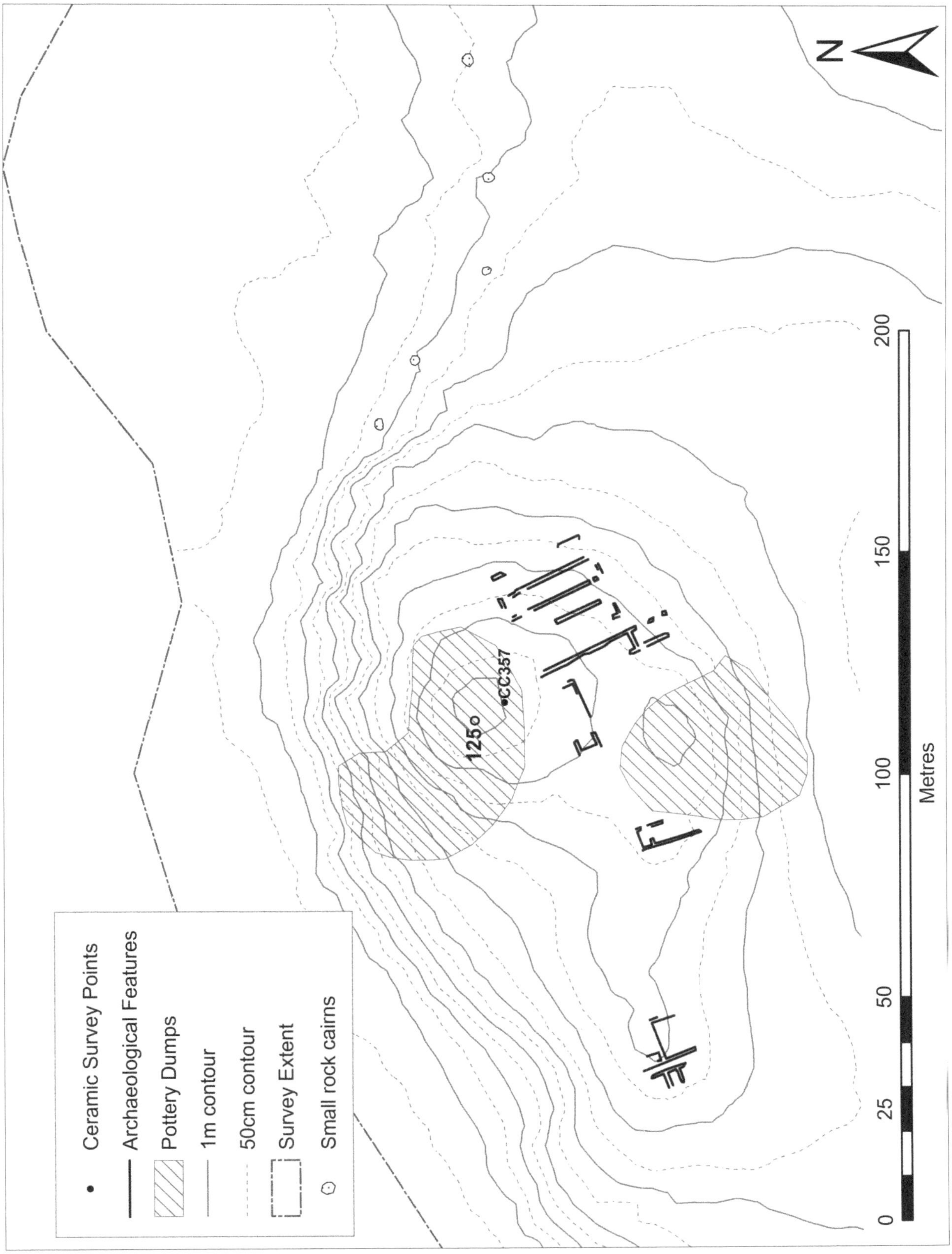

Fig. 6.137. Site 125.

remains of a number of walls that are aligned in an E-W direction. The walls are c. 0.8m thick and represent the remains of at least two partially preserved rooms with plaster lined walls, each measuring c. 30m x 6m (Fig. 6.140). These could have been storerooms for the pottery.

Site 125 is a kiln site with a sample of 160 locally produced amphorae and related sherds. The pottery represents activity in this area restricted to the 2nd and 1st centuries BC. Some are clearly over-fired kiln wasters.

Fig. 6.138. General view of Site 125 looking east.

Fig. 6.139. Site 125 pottery pile.

Fig. 6.140. Site 125 wall.

Table 6.40. Quantity of pottery types for Site 125.

Type	No.	%
Mareotic AE1/2 short handle (no. 6)	1	0.6
Mareotic AE1/2 base (no. 7)	8	5.0
Mareotic AE1/2 (nos 1-3)	147	91.9
Mareotic AE1/2 long handle (nos 4-5)	1	0.6
Mareotic tall pot stand (no. 8)	3	1.9
Total	160	100%

Graph 6.34. Pie graph showing the chronological break-down of pottery from Site 125.

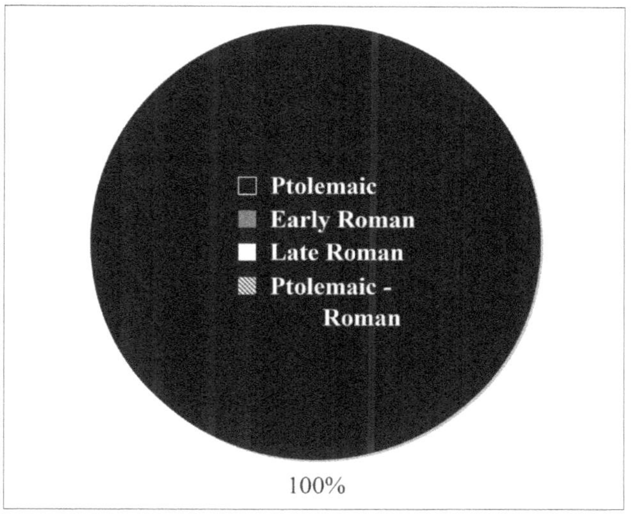

Site 124 (Figs 6.136, 6.141 & 6.142; Graph 6.35; Table 6.41)
Location: 30 57 55N 29 36 09E to 30 57 59N 29 36 10E
Description: This site is located c. 300m to the southwest of Site 125. The site consists of two mounds that reveal extensive evidence for pottery production, particularly amphora. The first mound overlooks the northern shore of the island. It measures c. 70m NW-SE by c. 30m SW-NE and is c. 4m high. About 100m S-SW of it, there is another mound that measures c. 70m E-W, 5m N-S and is

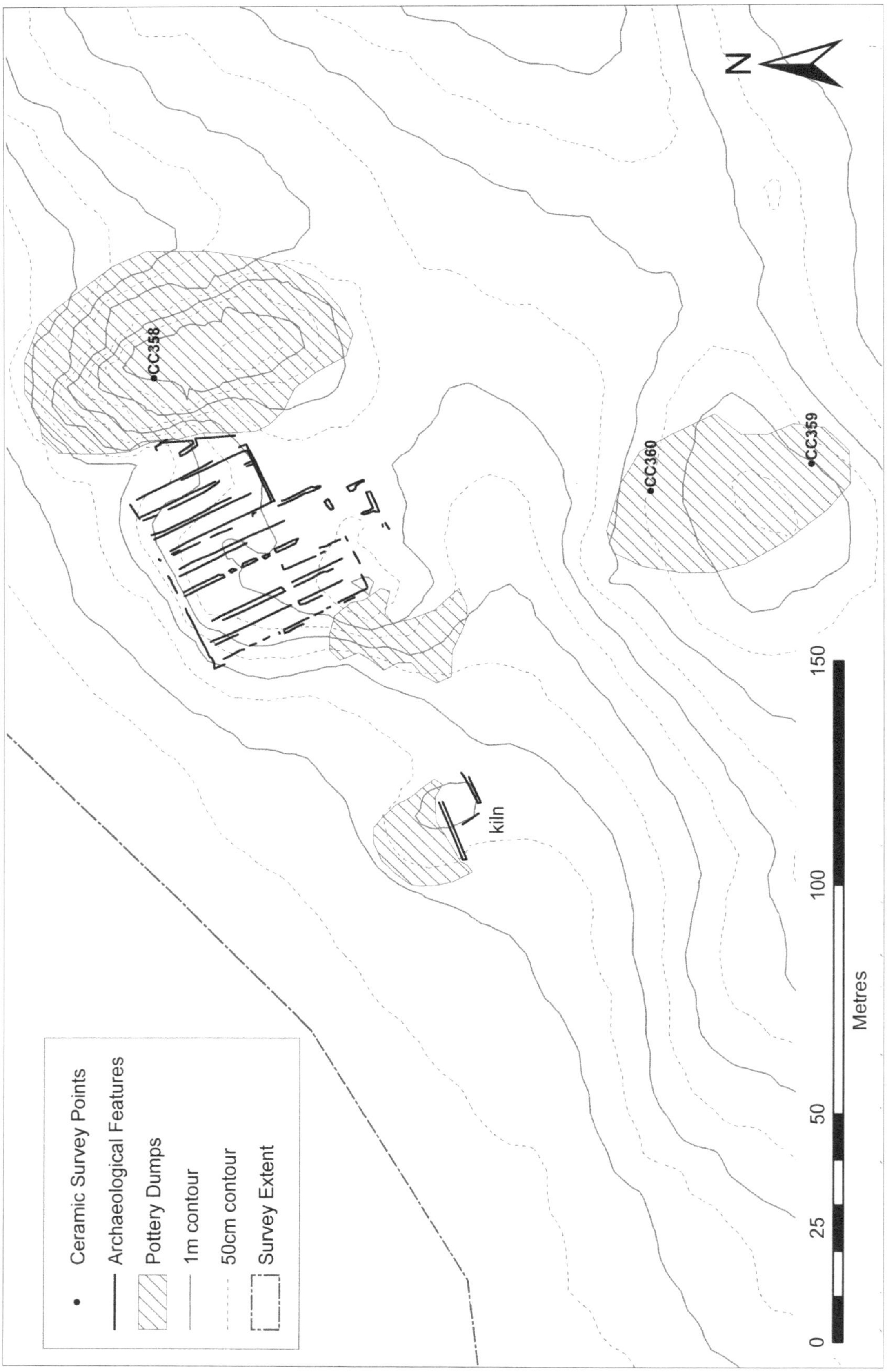

Fig. 6.141. Site 124.

Fig. 6.142. General view of Site 124 looking towards the storeroom.

Fig. 6.143. Site 124 pile of sherds, looking north.

c. 4m high. Both mounds and the areas in between them are covered with large quantities of pottery sherds (Fig. 6.143). To the southwest of the first mound there are the remains of a kiln that has burnt out; the kiln structure itself had a diameter of about 8m. Large quantities of pottery wasters cover the area around the remains of the kiln.

At the centre of the site, on the lower ground to the west of the principal pottery mound, there are a series of at least eight linear walls made of irregular limestone blocks. The walls are c. 25m long and 1m thick, while the distance between them is 3-5m (Fig. 6.144). These are probably the remains of storerooms or magazines that were used for storing the amphorae produced on this site. It is noticeable; however, that there was no broken pottery in the storerooms but that the floors of the warehouses were covered with large amounts of broken shells that had been brought from the lake and used to create a floor surface (Fig. 6.145).

Site 124 is an early Roman amphora kiln site, where a sample of 159 sherds (mostly local amphorae) was collected. Apart from one Ptolemaic sherd, the dated pottery belongs to the mid 1st to the mid 3rd centuries AD.

Fig. 6.144. Site 124 Storeroom wall, looking north.

Fig. 6.145. Site 124 warehouse floor lined with shell.

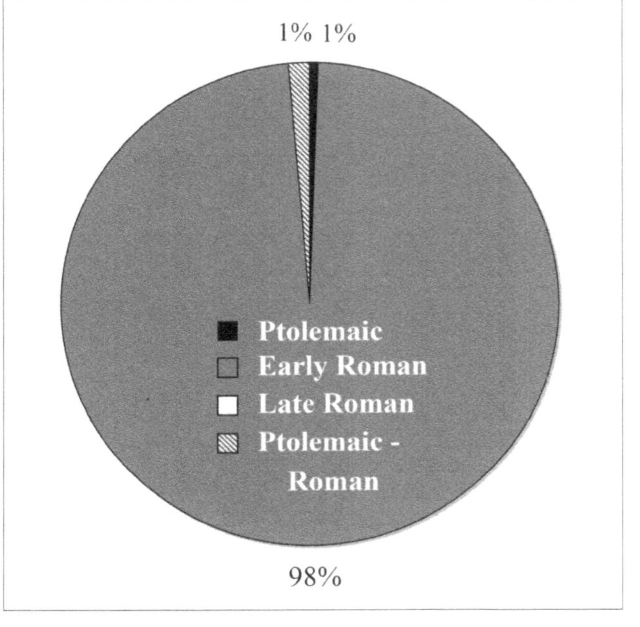

Graph 6.35. (above) Pie graph showing the chronological breakdown of pottery from Site 124.

Type	No.	%
Egyptian silt casserole (cf. Hayes & Harlaut 2002: fig. 55)	1	0.6
Egyptian silt dolium	2	1.3
Imported unsourced whole-mouth amphora (no. 159)	1	0.6
Mareotic Mons Claudianus Amphora Type 22/3 (nos 9-12)	38	23.9
Mareotic AE4 (nos 13-17)	117	73.6
Total	159	100%

Table 6.41. Quantity of pottery types for Site 124.

Site 37 (Fig. 6.136; Graph 6.36; Table 6.42)
Location: 30 57 52N 29 36 07E
Description: This site is located approximately at the centre of the island, at a distance c. 100m west of Site 124. It is located on the extension of the limestone ridge of the island and measures c. 75m E-W and c. 75m N-S and it is 7m high.

The site contains two quarries: one on the northern side, which measures 12m by 20m, and the other is located c. 30m to the east and measures 30m by 25m. Also there is some evidence of structures in the area; however, they are poorly preserved.

Site 37 has a sample of 120 indicator sherds dating potentially from the late 4th or more likely late 3rd century BC and the mid 3rd century AD. Most of the assemblage dates to the 2nd to 1st centuries BC with a single Late Roman sherd. The dominance of Mareotic AE1/2 amphorae (57%) may suggest a nearby kiln, but imported Hellenistic amphorae were also fairly well represented.

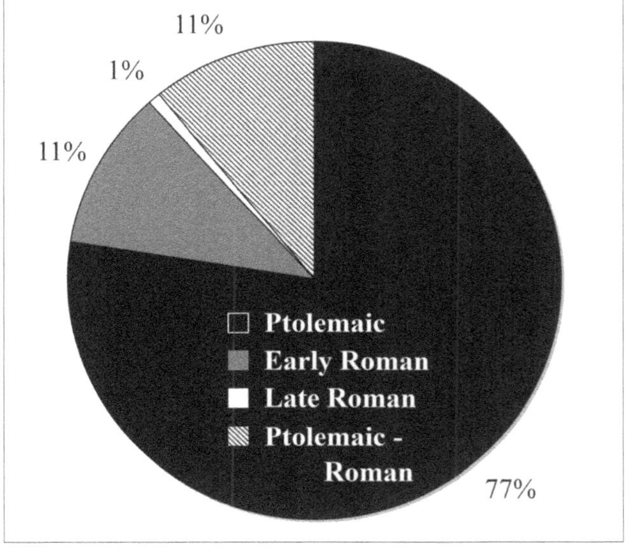

Type	No.	%
Finewares		
Egyptian black slip bowl/ dish footring base	5	4.2
Egyptian Ptolemaic/Early Roman red slip bowl/dish	1	0.8
Coarse wares		
Egyptian basin	4	3.3
Egyptian bowl/dish footring base	2	1.7
Egyptian small handle from coarse ware	6	5.0
Amphorae		
Koan (nos 126-30)	4	3.3
Knidian handle	5	4.2
Mareotic AE4 (nos 13-17)	9	7.5
Rhodian IE2/IF (nos 121-6)	14	11.7
Cilician/Cypriot LR Amphora 1 (nos 146-9)	1	0.8
Mareotic AE1/2 short handle (no. 6)	6	5.0
Mareotic AE1/2 base (no. 7)	28	23.3
Mareotic AE1/2 (nos 1-3)	34	28.3
Mareotic AE1/2 long handle (nos 4-5)	1	0.8
Total	120	100%

Table 6.42. (above) Quantity of pottery types for Site 37.

Graph 6.36. Pie graph showing the chronological breakdown of pottery from Site 37.

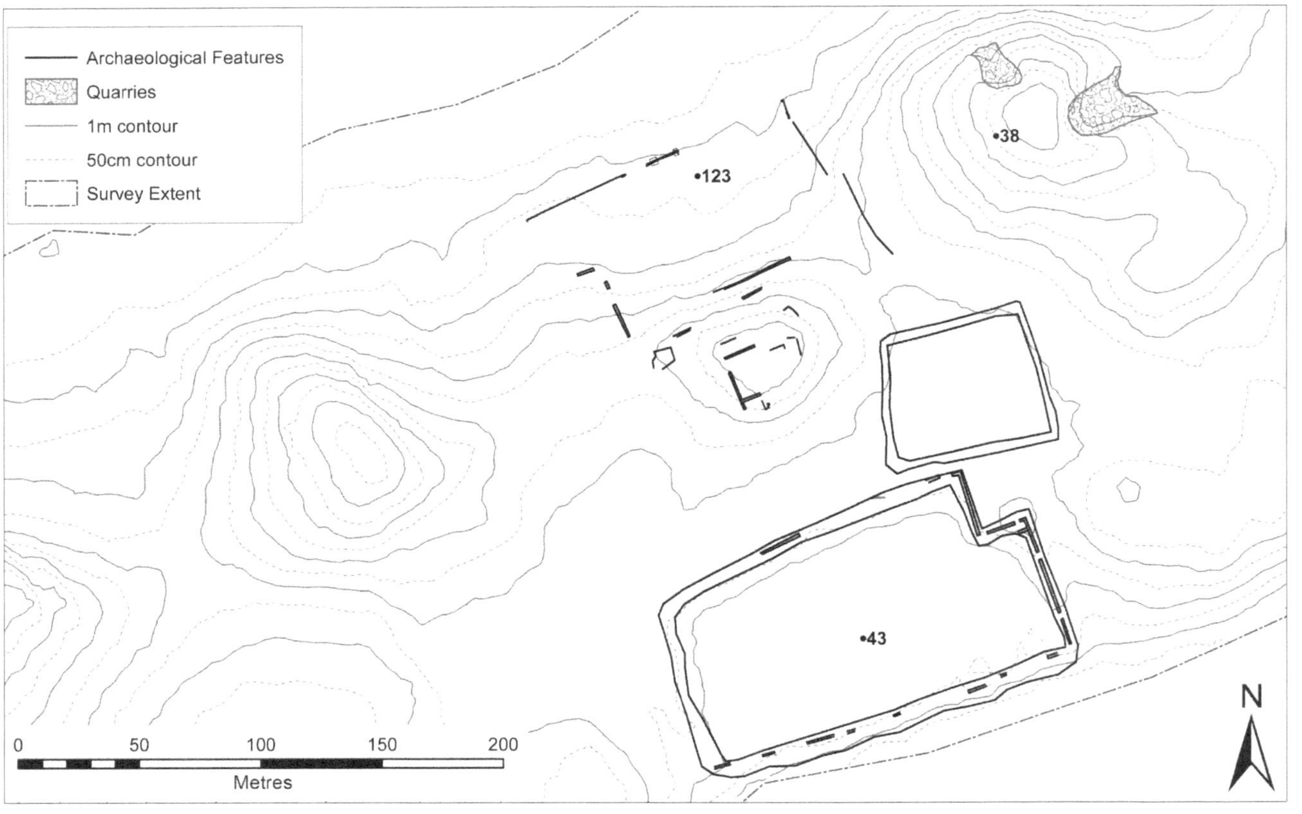

Fig. 6.146. Location of Sites 38, 43 & 123.

Site 38 (Fig. 6.136 & 6.146; Graph 6.37; Table 6.43)
Location: 30 57 49N 29 35 57E
Description: This site is located to the east of Site 123. It is a small hill that measures 60m N-S and 80m E-W and is c. 7m high. The site contains evidence of quarrying activity (Fig. 6.147) as well as the remains of a plaster lined channel that runs for 27m along the ridge (not planned). This channel could have been functionally associated with the water retaining system present at Site 123 to the west (see below).

Site 38 has a sample of 34 indicator sherds representing discontinuous activity from the 2nd/1st centuries BC to the 7th century AD. Most of the indicators, c. 59%, belong to Mareotic amphorae.

Fig. 6.147. Quarries at Site 38.

Type	No.	%
Finewares		
Cypriot Red Slip ware (CRS) 2 (nos 103-4)	3	8.8
Coarse wares		
Egyptian silt casserole (nos 49-51)	1	2.9
Egyptian silt lid	1	2.9
Egyptian silt miscellaneous coarse ware	4	11.8
Egyptian small handle from coarse ware	1	2.9
Mareotic/silt jug	1	2.9
Amphorae		
Abu Mena LR Amphora 5 (nos 87-9)	3	8.8
Imported unidentified type	1	2.9
Mareotic AE1/2 base (no. 7)	8	23.5
Mareotic AE4 (nos 13-17)	5	14.7
Mareotic Mons Claudianus Type 22/3 (nos 9-12)	2	5.9
Mareotic unidentified type	4	11.8
Total	34	100

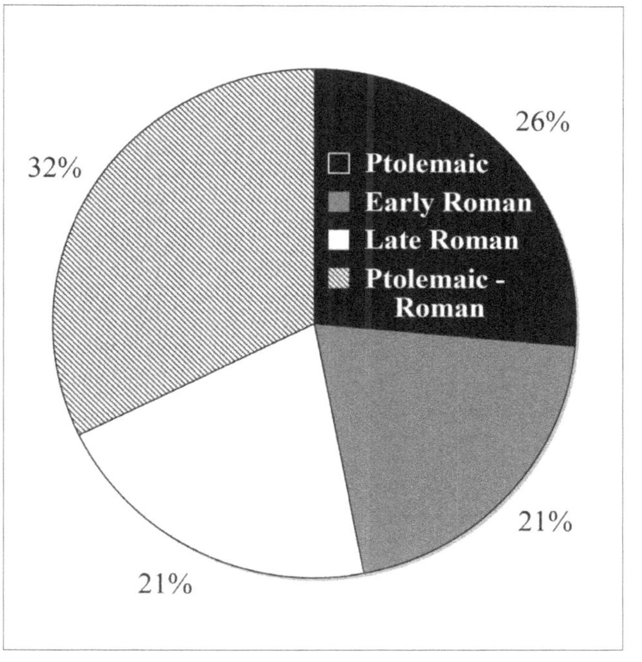

Graph 6.37. (above) Pie graph showing the chronological breakdown of pottery from Site 38.

Table 6.43. Quantity of pottery types for Site 38.

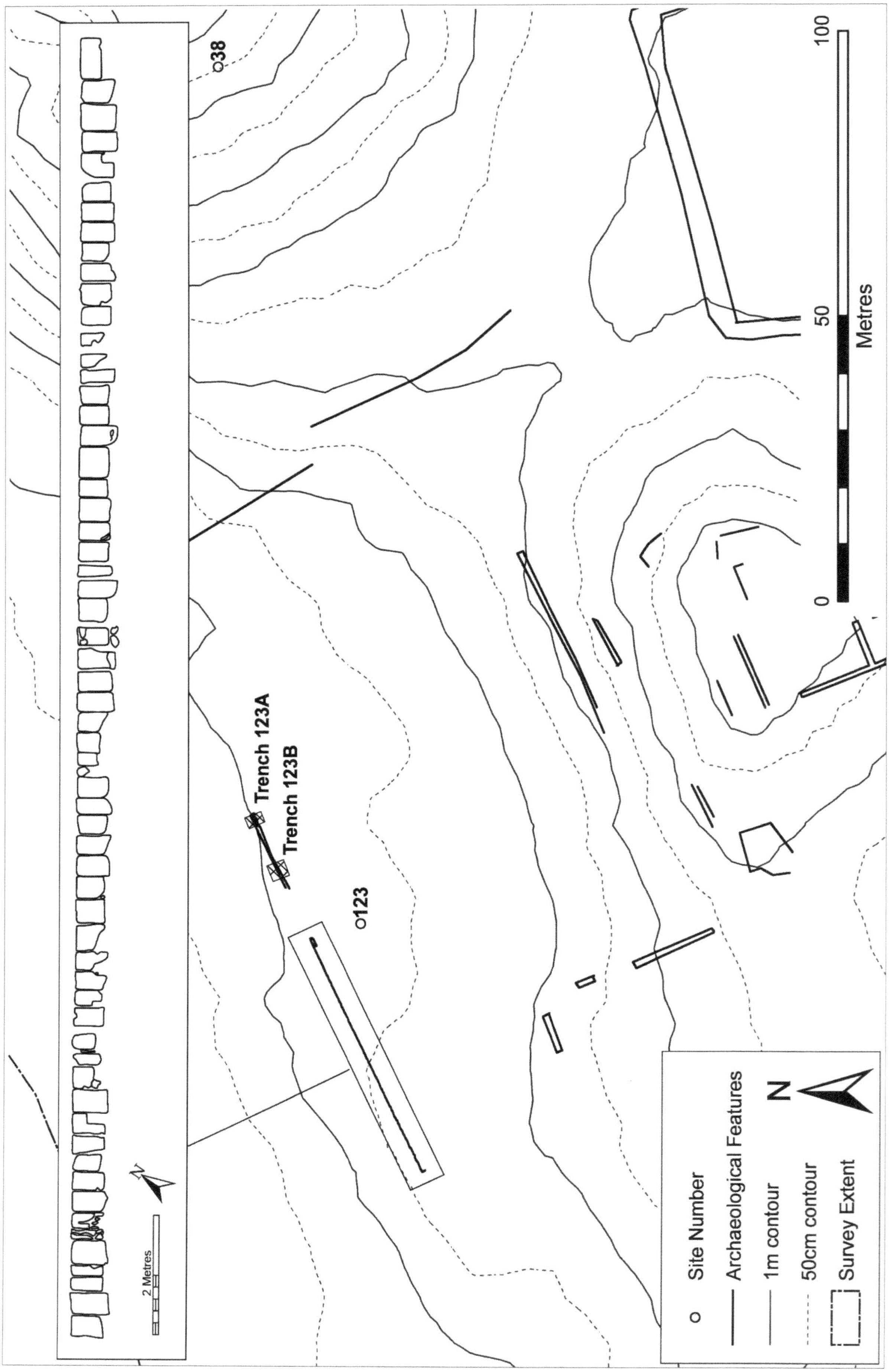

Fig. 6.148. Plan of long wall in context Site 123.

Site 123 (Figs 6.136, 6.146 & 6.148; Graphs 6.38 & 6.39; Tables 6.44 & 6.45)
Location: 30 57 51N 29 35 52E
Description: This site essentially consists of a long stretch of wall that extends along the northern shore of the island on a flat area of aeolian silts and includes a scatter of buildings and channels on the ridge to the south (Fig. 6.148). The lake side wall runs parallel to the shoreline for c. 70m at a distance of c. 40m from the present waterline; however, when this site was first recorded in 2004, it was more than 90m from the waterline (Fig. 6.149). The wall is made of one course of large limestone blocks that measure 0.6m x 0.3m x 0.25m, and that are arranged in headers facing the shoreline. There is a gap towards the eastern end of the wall (Figs 6.150 & 6.151).

Two trenches towards the eastern end of this wall were excavated in order to determine the depth and extant courses of the wall, the nature of sediments either side of this wall and its relationship with the lake. Both trenches (Trenches 123A & 123B; Fig. 6.151) were abutted by 4th to 7th century ceramics. The wall in Trench 123B to the west appears to have been robbed in sections in the Late Roman period [952]. The date of its foundation was not determined. In the trench to the east Trench 123A, the wall appears to have been established on a 3rd to 1st centuries BC horizon [908]. However, this deposit was cut [907] in the Late Roman period. Therefore, the actual date of construction of the wall is ambiguous; however, the later Roman activity could also relate to robbing out or maintenance of the walls

Fig. 6.149. (above) Site 123 wall extent.

Fig. 6.150. (below) Excavation of long wall Site 123. Trench 123B looking east towards Trench 123A.

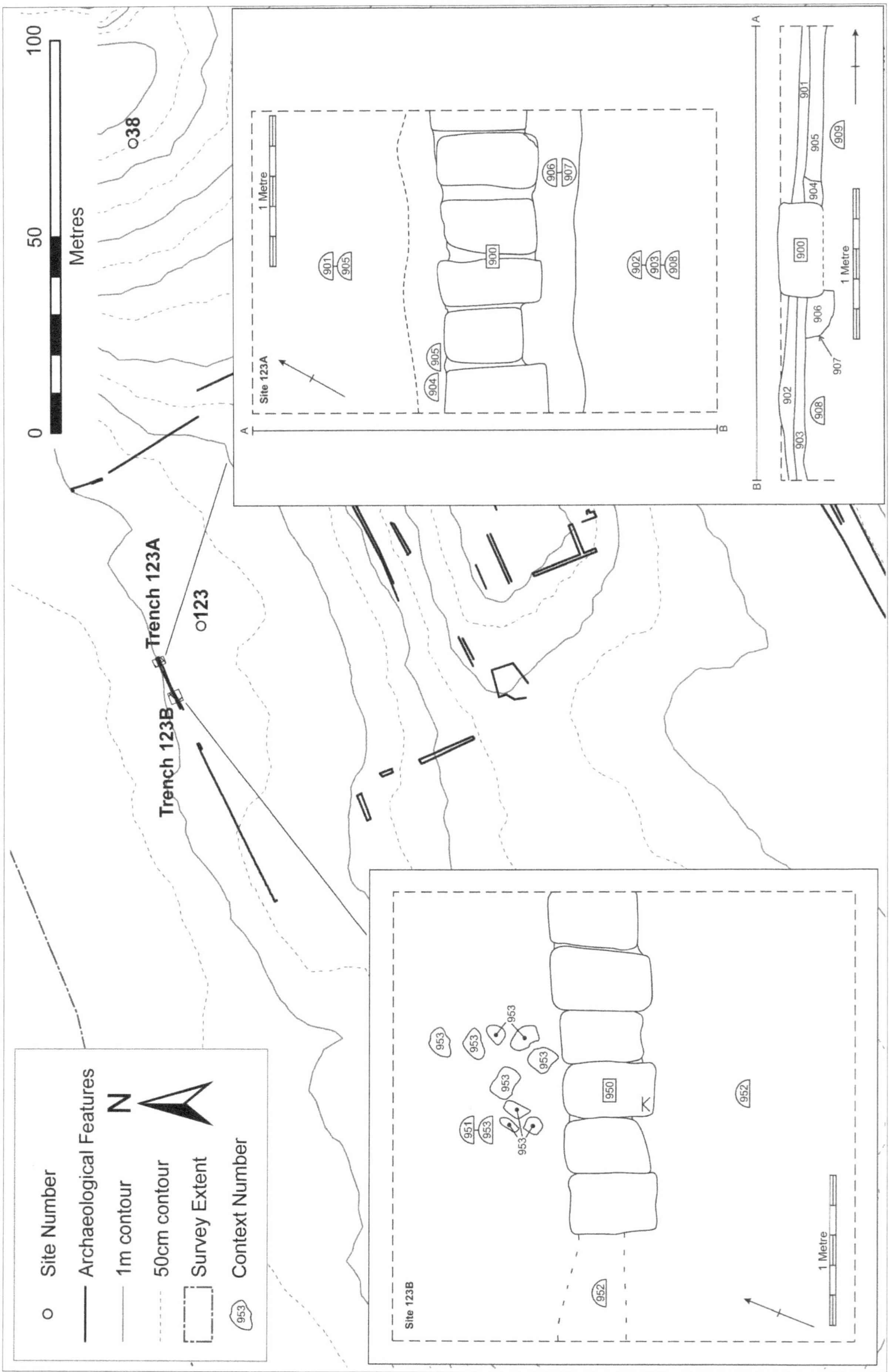

Fig. 6.151. Site 123 plan of excavation Trench 123A to the east and Site 123B to the west, set within topographic context.

as identified in Trench 123B. The wall is only one course deep in both trenches and thus is assumed to have been the base of what was formerly a more vertically extensive wall (represented by wall tumble [953] in Trench 123B). The sediment matrices in both trenches on both sides of and beneath the wall were similar, indicating that the wall had no direct relation to the lake edge in antiquity.

At a distance of c. 32m north of the eastern end of this wall, a second 27m long wall extends perpendicular to the shoreline; unfortunately, it is in a poor state of preservation and was not visible at the time of survey (not planned). A third smaller linear feature is located roughly c. 47m east of the eastern end of the first wall and runs in a N-S direction to the south for 8m. The wall is made of large limestone blocks, similar to the ones used in the first wall. The three walls identified at Site 123 could have been part of the same structure.

On the ridge above the walls to the south, slag, fired brick and limestone plaster were identified, together with a series of channels, one of which was plaster-lined and extended for over 6m in length. A series of associated room units were also noted (Fig. 6.148).

Site 123 has a surface collection sample of 60 indicator sherds which, apart from three sherds from a Knidian amphora of the late 4th or 3rd century BC, belong to the Early and Late Roman periods to the 7th century AD. The mid 1st to mid 3rd centuries AD Mareotic AE4 is the single most common type (29) and may come from the nearby kiln Site 124. In contrast, the 189 indicator sherds from the excavation at Site 123 are biased toward Late Roman with some Ptolemaic and Early Roman sherds. The assemblage is fairly evenly distributed between finewares, coarse wares and amphorae.

Type	**No.**	**%**
Finewares		
African Red slip ware (ARS)	1	1.7
Cypriot Red Slip ware (CRS)	1	1.7
Cypriot Red Slip ware (CRS) 9 (nos 105-6)	2	3.3
Egtypian Red Slip ware B (ERSB) copy of ARS 84 (nos 65-6)	1	1.7
Coarse wares		
Egyptian bowl	1	1.7
Egyptian silt cooking pot	2	3.3
Egyptian silt lid	1	1.7
Egyptian small handle from coarse ware	3	5.0
Amphorae		
Abu Mena LR Amphora 5 (nos 87-9)	4	6.7
Cilician/Cypriot LR Amphora 1 (nos 146-9)	6	10.0
Gaza LR Amphora 4 (nos 154-7)	2	3.3
Knidian IIB (no. 110)	3	5.0
Mareotic AE4 (nos 13-17)	29	48.3
Mareotic Mons Claudianus Type 22/3 (nos 9-12)	4	6.7
Total	60	100%

Table 6.44. (above) Quantity of pottery types for Site 123 surface collection.

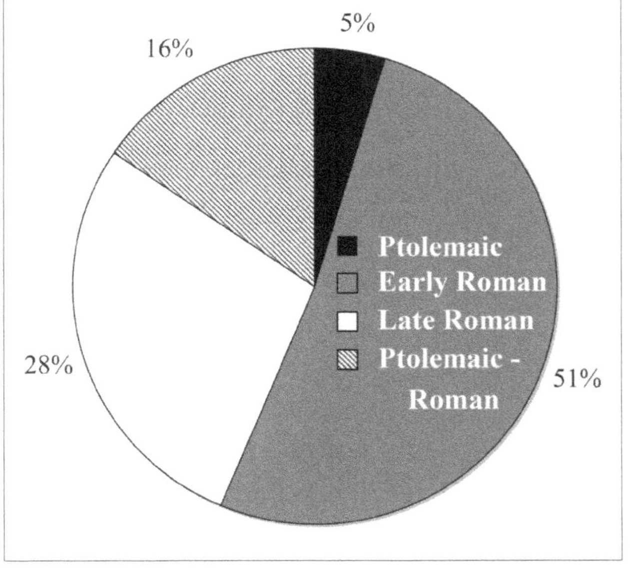

Graph 6.38. Pie graph showing the chronological breakdown of pottery from Site 123 surface collection.

Table 6.45. Quantity of pottery types for Site 123 excavation.

Type	**No.**	**%**
Finewares		
African Red Slip ware (ARS) 67	6	3.2
African Red Slip ware (ARS) 99	2	1.1
Cypriot Red Slip ware (CRS)	1	0.5
Cypriot Red Slip ware (CRS) 2 (nos 103-4))	5	2.6
Cypriot Red Slip ware (CRS) 7	1	0.5
Cypriot Red Slip ware (CRS) 8	1	0.5
Cypriot Red Slip ware (CRS) 9 (nos 105-6)	6	3.2
Egyptian painted	1	0.5
Egyptian Ptolemaic/Early Roman red slip bowl/dish	7	3.7
Egyptian Red Slip ware A (ERSA) copy of ARS 91A (no. 67)	2	1.1
Egyptian Red Slip ware B (ERSB) copy of ARS 84 (nos 65-6)	9	4.7
Egyptian Red Slip ware B (ERSB) copy of ARS 99	3	1.6
Egyptian Red Slip ware B/C (ERSB/C) (no. 77)	1	0.5
Egyptian Red Slip ware B/C (ERSB/C) bowl	7	3.7
Egyptian Red Slip ware B/C (ERSB/C) copy of CRS 9B/C (no. 76)	2	1.1
Egyptian silt red slip fish dish (nos 54-5)	1	0.5
Phocaean Red Slip ware (PRS) 3	2	1.1
Coarse wares		
Egyptian basin	4	2.1
Egyptian bowl	1	0.5
Egyptian marl juglet (no. 24)	7	3.7
Egyptian marl juglet base	1	0.5
Egyptian silt bowl/dish	1	0.5
Egyptian silt cooking pot	7	3.7
Egyptian silt dolium	2	1.1
Egyptian silt jug	20	10.6
Egyptian silt lid	3	1.6
Egyptian silt *sakkia* pot (nos 35-41)	4	2.1
Egyptian small handle from coarse ware	9	4.8
Mareotic jug	2	1.1
Amphorae		
Abu Mena LR Amphora 5 (nos 87-9)	9	4.8
Cilician/Cypriot LR Amphora 1 (nos 146-9)	17	9.0
Gaza LR Amphora 4 (nos 154-7)	7	3.7
Imported unidentified type (no. 174)	1	0.5
Imported unsourced whole-mouth amphora	1	0.5
Knidian handle	2	1.1
Koan (nos 126-30)	2	1.1
Mareotic AE 1/2 base (no. 7)	3	1.6
Mareotic AE 1/2 long handle (nos 4-5)	2	1.1
Mareotic AE4 (nos 13-17)	16	8.5
Mareotic Mons Claudianus Type 22/3 (nos 9-12)	1	0.5
Mareotic unidentified type	8	4.2
Palestine LR Amphora 5 (no. 158)	1	0.5
Rhodian IE2/IF (nos 121-6)	1	0.5
Total	189	100%

Graph 6.39. Pie graph showing the chronological breakdown of pottery from Site 123 excavation.

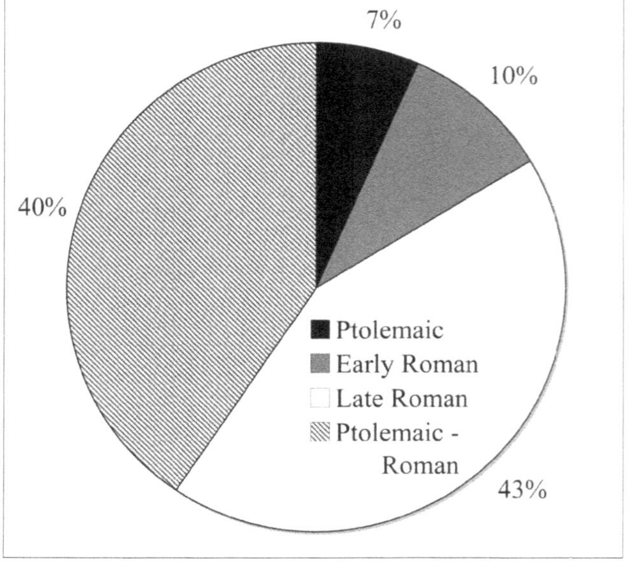

Site 43 (Fig. 6.146)
Location: 30 57 45 N 29 36 01E
Description: This site is located to the south of Site 123 on a flat area at the southern shore of the island. The site includes the remains of a terraced enclosure surrounded by straight walls made of rubble and small irregular limestone blocks (Fig. 6.152). The enclosure measures c. 150m E-W and 100m N-S and is aligned with the southern shore of the lake. It is possible that the enclosure was used for cultivation. Near the centre of the terrace are the remains of a structure that measures c. 20m x 30m and was composed of rubble walls and a stony platform. No ceramic samples were collected from this site.

Fig. 6.152. Structural remains Site 43.

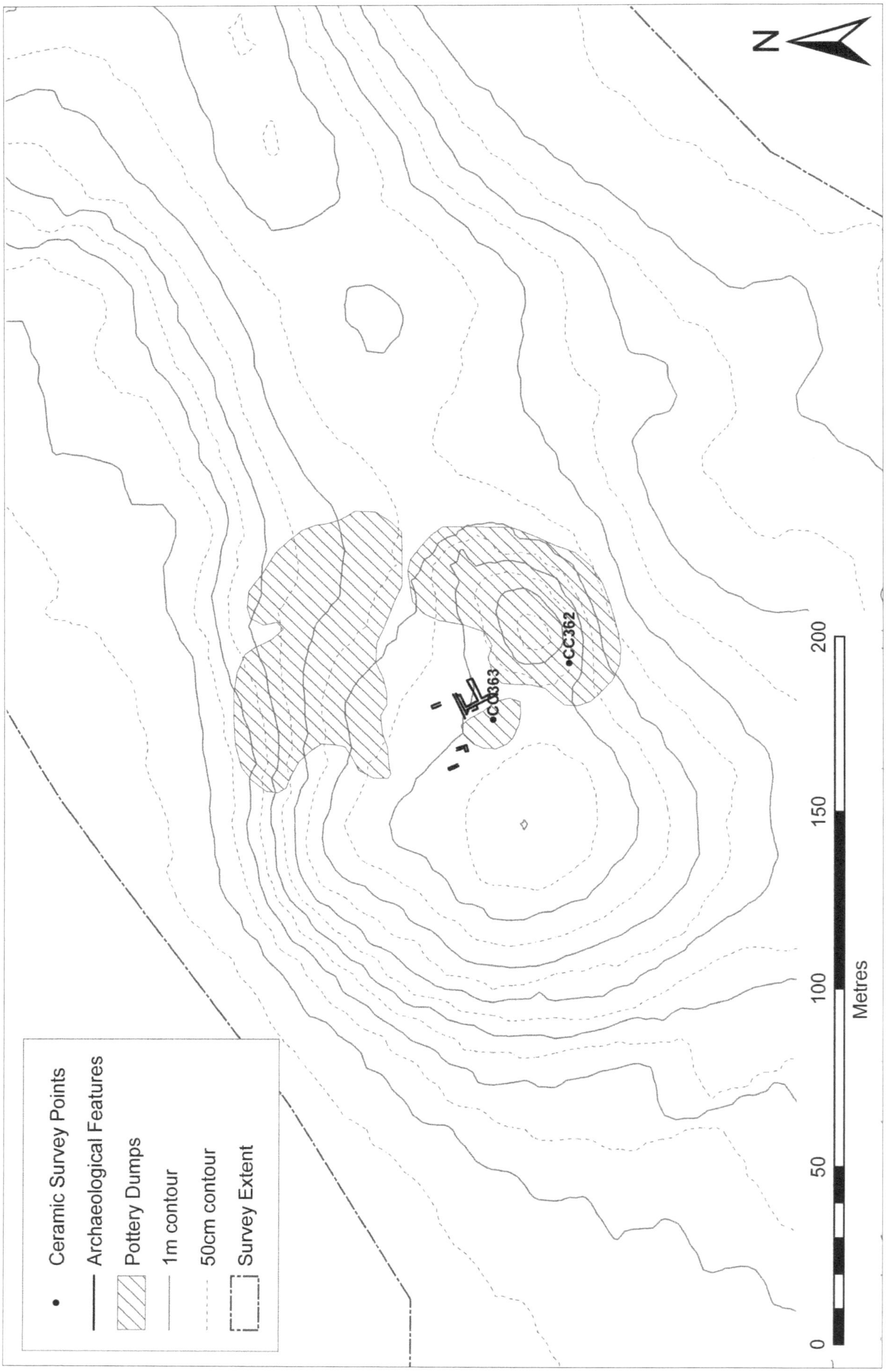

Fig. 6.153. Site 39.

Fig. 6.154. (above) General view of Site 39.

Site 39 (Figs 6.153, 6.163 & 6.154; Graph 6.40; Table 6.46)
Location: 30 57 40N 29 35 35E
Description: The site is located on the central ridge on top of a small hill overlooking the northern shore of the island (Fig. 6.136). The hill measures c. 125m x 120m and the site covers an area of 100m N-S and 80m E-W and extends over part of the hill top and down to the northern foot of the hill.

The site contains large quantities of pottery wasters and broken amphorae fragments forming two large concentrations, one on top of the hill and the other extends down from the top of the hill towards the coastal lowland plain. Moreover, there are the remains of a kiln structure on the lower land north of the hill. The features at Site 39 all indicate that it was involved in amphorae production in antiquity.

Between the two concentrations of pottery fragments towards the north of the hill there are the remains of a number of stone walls that measure c. 1m thick and extend for c. 30m N-S (Fig. 6.155). These walls form what appear to be a large elongated building that could have been utilised as a warehouse or storage facility for the pottery produced at this site.

Site 39 has a sample of 178 indicator sherds spanning potentially from the 2nd/1st centuries BC through the mid 3rd century AD, but most of the sherds belong to the 2nd and 1st centuries BC. The material consisted mostly of amphorae (174), almost exclusively wasters of AE1/2 from the nearby kiln. There are no sherds of exclusively Late Roman date.

Fig. 6.155. Stone wall Site 39.

Type	No.	%
Finewares		
Egyptian red slip bowl (no. 60)	1	0.6
Egyptian red slip bowl/dish footring base	1	0.6
Egyptian silt red slip fish dish (nos 54-5)	1	0.6
Coarse wares		
Egyptian bowl/dish footring base	1	0.6
Amphorae		
Knidian handle	2	1.1
Koan (nos 126-30)	1	0.6
Mareotic AE1/2 (nos 1-3)	55	30.8
Mareotic AE1/2 base (no. 7)	103	57.8
Mareotic AE1/2 long handle (nos 4-5)	1	0.6
Mareotic AE1/2 short handle (no. 6)	1	0.6
Mareotic AE4 (nos 13-17)	1	0.6
Mareotic tall pot stand (no. 8)	8	4.4
Mareotic unidentified type	1	0.6
Unidentified imported (no. 172)	1	0.6
Total	178	100%

Table 6.46. (left) Quantity of pottery types for Site 39.

Graph 6.40. Pie graph showing the chronological breakdown of pottery from Site 39.

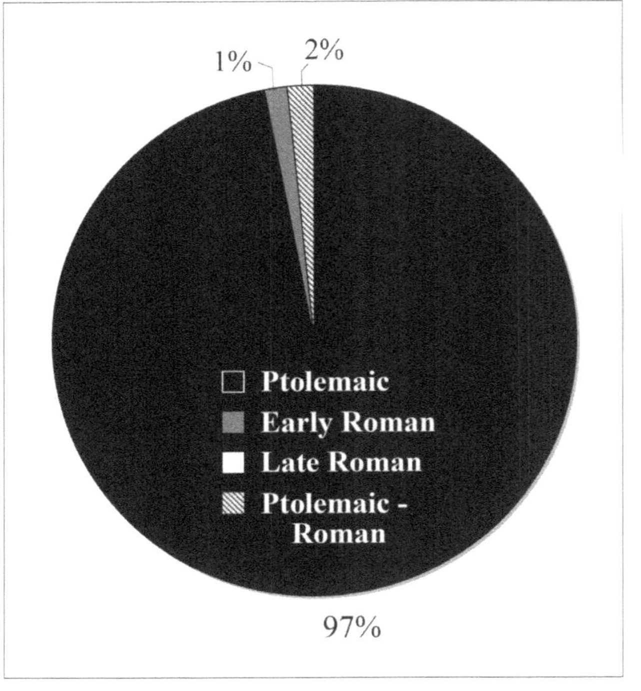

6.4.3 Sites located at the western section of the island

(Figs 6.156-6.158)

The western settlement occupies a similar location to the eastern settlement, situated on the high ground of the limestone ridge which measures 830m x 200m. The area exhibits the remains of various types of buildings with a mixed function suggested by the construction materials and surface finds. Overall the preservation of these structures is not good; a large area in the extreme west has been heavily damaged by earthmoving machines, and in other instances only patchy areas of recent construction and dislocated wall lines survive. However, those buildings that are still extant on the top of the ridge are fairly extensive and further buildings extend north onto the plain and towards the shore of the lake below. A number of linear features also associated with waterfront structures are noted on the low-lying plain.

Fig. 6.156. Topgraphical overview of the western end of the island and the locations of the principal sites.

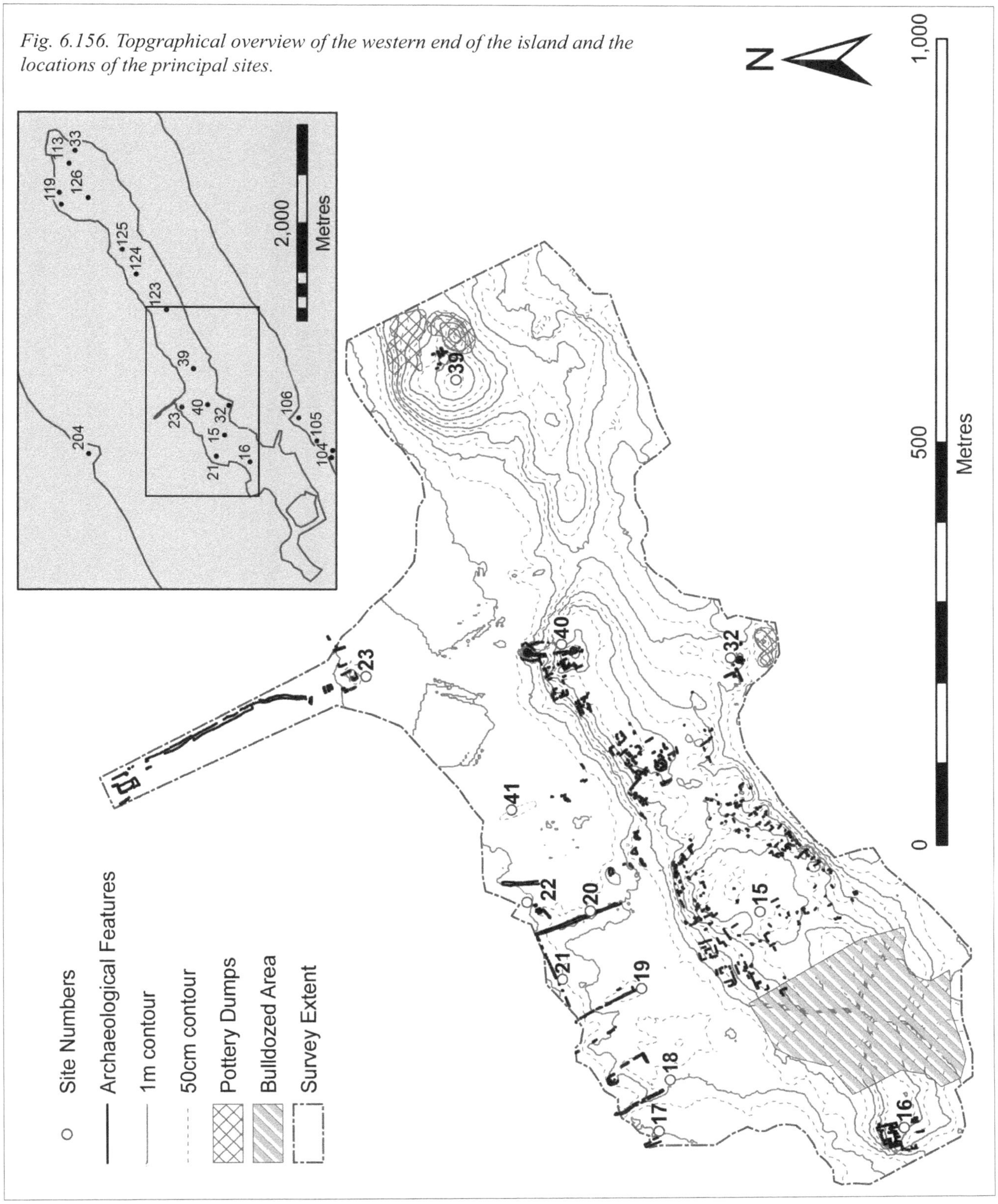

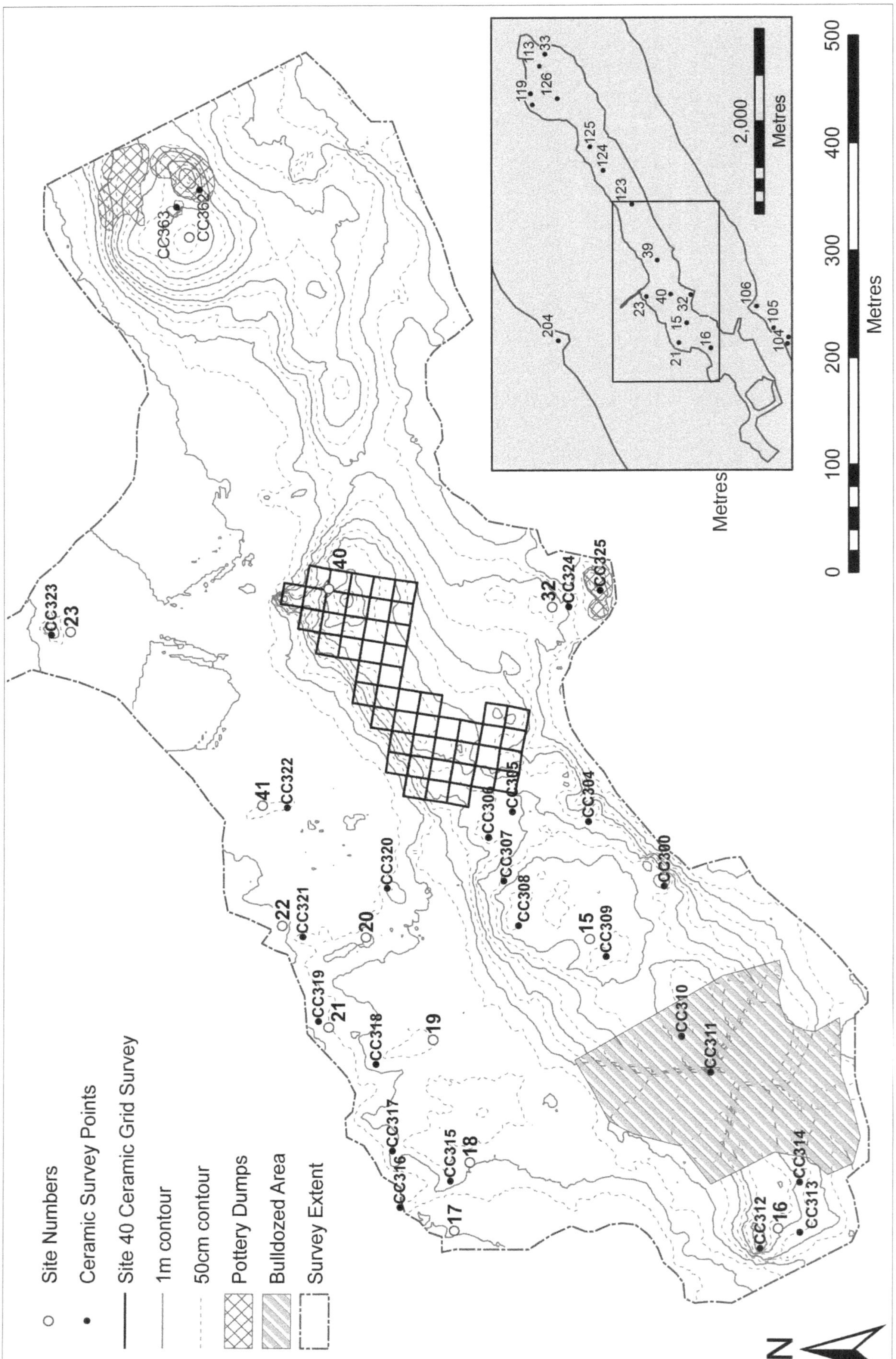

Fig. 6.157. Western island ceramic survey details.

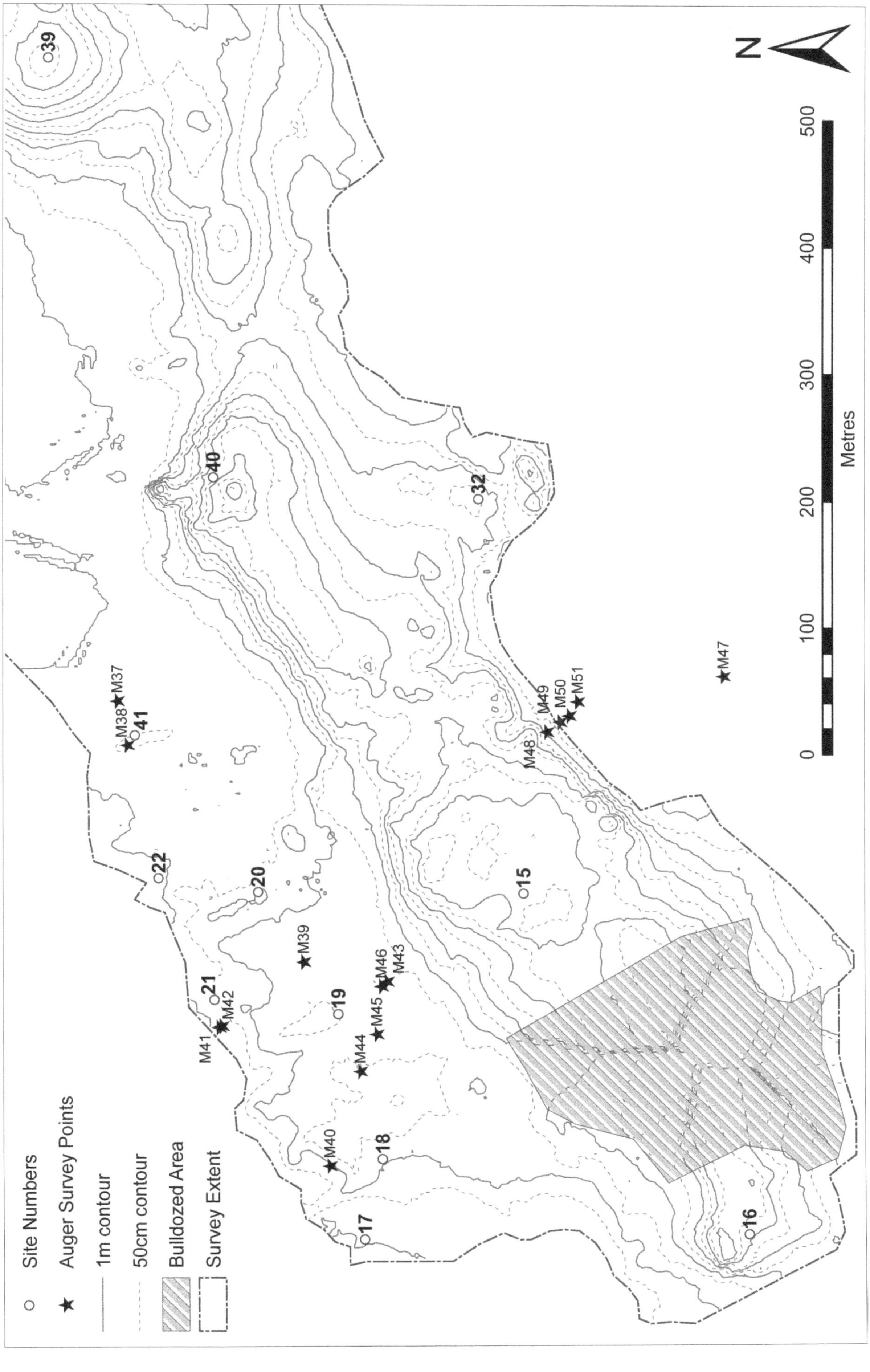

Fig. 6.158. Western island augur survey details.

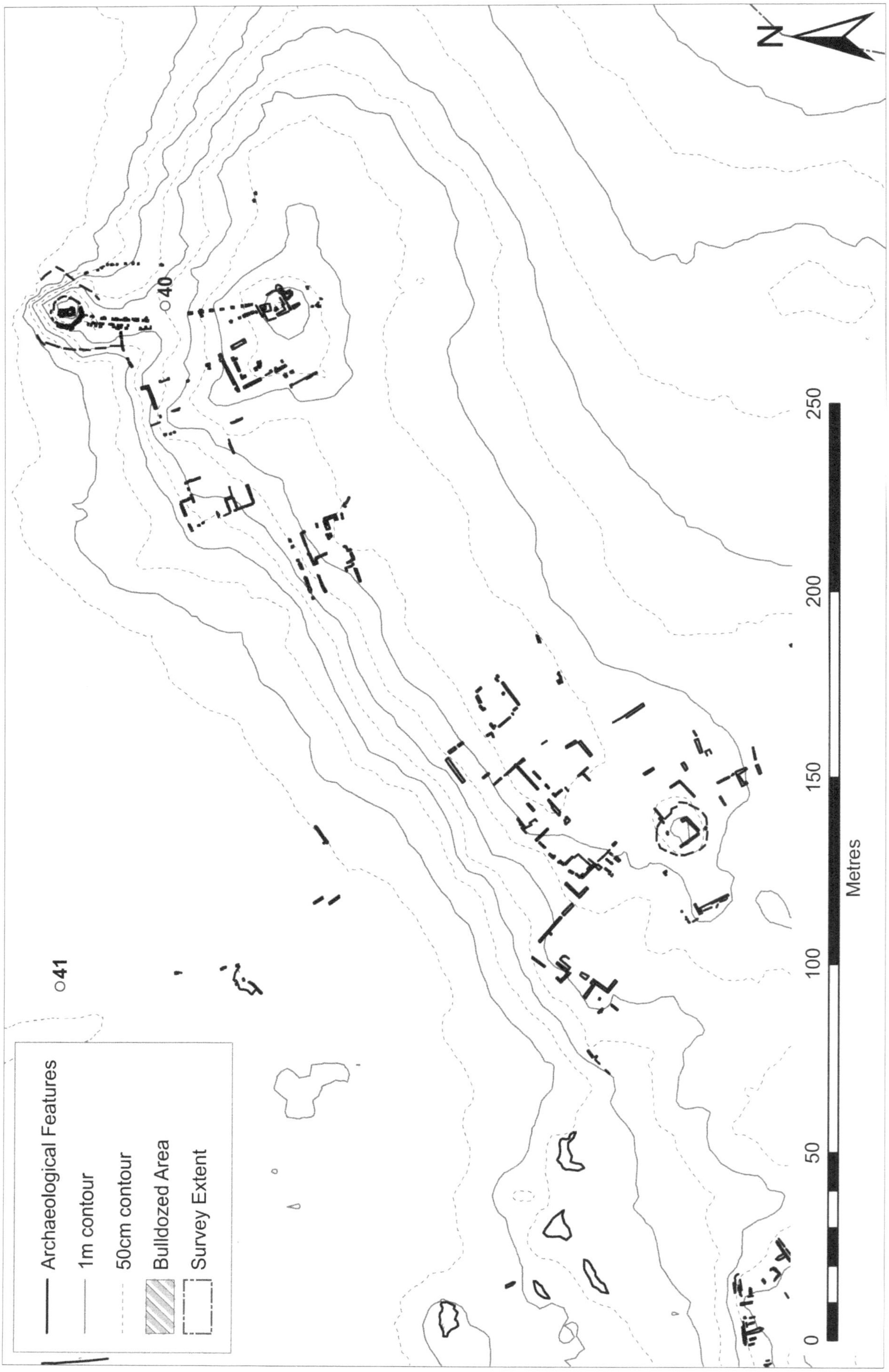

Fig. 6.159. General plan of Site 40.

Fig. 6.160. General view of Site 40 looking north.

Site 40 (Fig. 6.159; Graphs 6.41 & 6.42; Table 6.47)
Location: 30 57 37N 29 35 20E to 30 57 31N 29 35 15E
Description: Site 40 and Site 15 are the principal sites that occupy the top of the central, western island ridge. Site 40 covers an area that measures c. 230 m NE-SW x 80m N-S and is c. 7m high. This is one of the most significant sites on the western section of the island. It merges with Site 15 to the west, making the division between the two quite arbitrary.

The north-eastern-most part of the site is a headland that projects from the ridge and slopes steeply down to the marshland which occupies the area between the ridge and the northern shore of the island (Figs 6.160 & 6.161).

Fig. 6.161. Site 40 view of headland from northwest.

Fig. 6.162. Detail of Site 40.

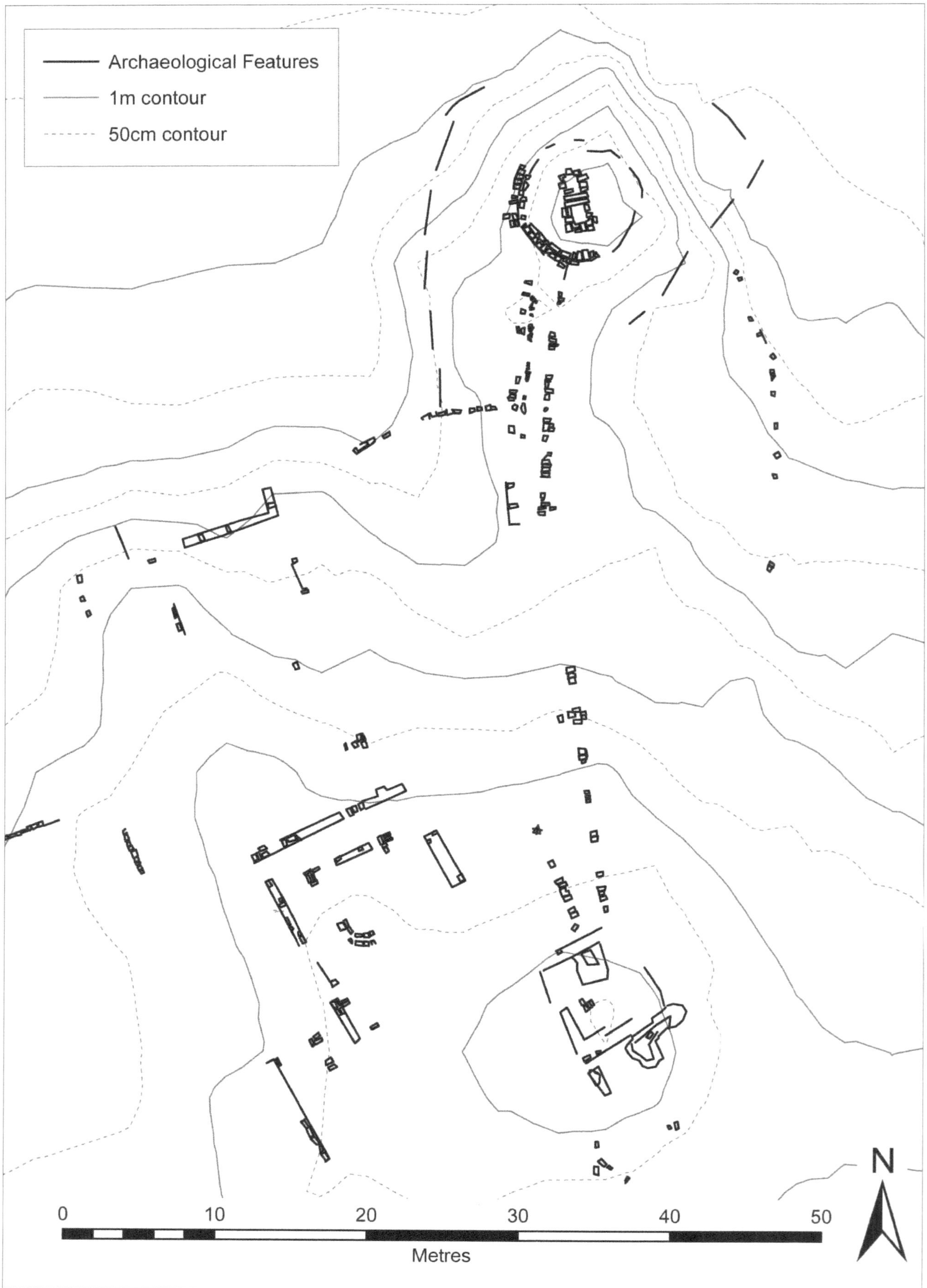

At the foot of the headland there is a stone-lined well which could have been part of the water management system associated with this site (see Chapter 5).

On top of the headland are the remains of a circular structure that measures c. 8m in diameter that is believed to be a *sakkia* (Figs 6.162 & 6.163). The *sakkia* is delineated by a double circular outside wall that measures c. 0.9m thick and is made of limestone blocks. In the centre of the circular structure are the remains of a platform 1.9m wide and 4.3m long. Inside this structure are two stone-lined pits now filled with rubble that measure 0.9m wide and 1.3m long. These holes would have housed the wooden wheel of the *sakkia* (Fig. 6.164).

Directly to the south of the *sakkia* is a bridge or a pathway c. 2m wide and c. 45m long delineated by two walls, one on either side (Fig. 6.165). The bridge leads to the entrance of a water tank which measures 7.20m x 6.30m and is lined with red mortar (*opus signinum*). The water tank is probably part of a cistern complex that extends underground; accordingly, both the *sakkia* and the tank could be functionally linked as the *sakkia* could have been used for lifting water which was then transported in channels across the bridge to be stored in the cistern.

To the west of the bridge and the water tank there are the remains of a number of walls which belong to at least three buildings (Fig. 6.162). The first building is located 12m to the west of the water tank. Its external dimensions are c. 11m NE-SW x 14m NW-SE and its walls are c. 0.6m thick. Fragments of internal walls suggest a central room and a 2m wide corridor along its northern and eastern edges.

To the northwest of these walls, at the northern edge of the ridge, c. 50m west of the *sakkia* complex, exist the remains of a building that extends over an area c.7m NE-SW & 17m NW-SE (Fig. 6.159). About 16m to the southwest of these walls there are some scattered sections of walls which probably belonged to a single building. The walls extend across an area that measures 19m NE-SW x 10m NW-SE; however, several sections are missing.

All the buildings that were recorded in this area have a similar orientation NE-SW and are aligned with the ridge. The site seems to be urban in nature with medium sized

Fig. 6.163. Site 40 sakkia *top of platform looking north.*

Fig. 6.164. Detail of sakkia *top Site 40.*

Fig. 6.165. Site 40 channel link between sakkia *and bridge to the south.*

Graph 6.41. Pie graph showing the chronological breakdown of pottery from Site 40.

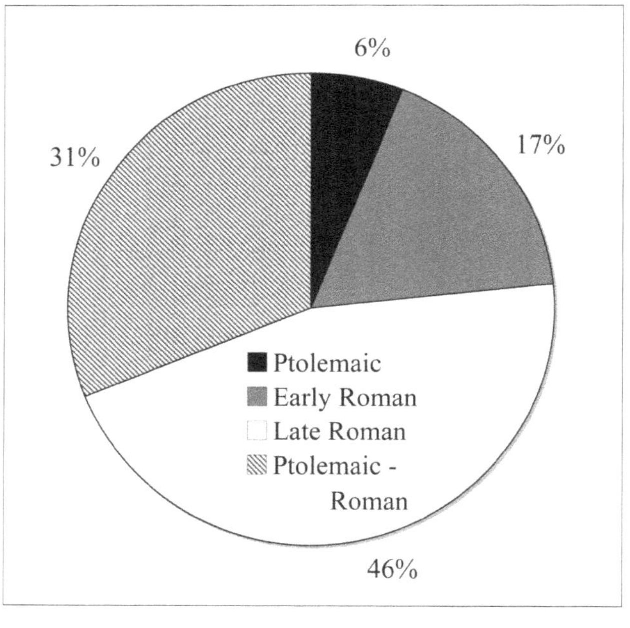

buildings. About 40m to the west of this cluster of buildings there is another cluster on top of the ridge that slopes down towards the northern plain (Fig. 6.159). This area is c. 85m NE-SW x 75m NW-SE and it contains the remains of numerous walls. The general alignment of the walls is NE-SW and NW-SE; however, with the exception of what appears to be the remains of a 9m x 8m room at the eastern end of the site, the association of the other walls with specific buildings is difficult to determine. Nevertheless, the density of wall remains in this area suggest another urban centre, quite similar in extent to the rest of Site 40.

Site 40 has a sample of 2,344 indicator sherds. Although the sequence spans between the mid 4th century BC to the 7th century AD, the best represented period is the 5th to 7th centuries AD, followed by the mid 1st to mid 3rd centuries AD. The bar graph shows the distribution of the main ware groups over time. *Sakkia* pot sherds were particularly well represented, concentrated in the north-east corner of the site, and associated with a structure that may be a *sakkia* (water-wheel). Amphorae dominated the assemblage both locally and regionally produced for all periods, together with LR Amphora 1 during the Late Roman period.

Table 6.47. Quantity of pottery types for Site 40 (continued on the next page).

Type	**No.**	**%**
Finewares		
African Red Slip ware (ARS)	3	0.1
African Red Slip ware (ARS) 104 (no. 101)	2	0.1
African Red Slip ware (ARS) 104-6 (no. 102)	1	0.0
African Red Slip ware (ARS) 105	1	0.0
African Red Slip ware (ARS) 67 (no. 99)	1	0.0
African Red Slip ware (ARS) 99 (no. 100)	2	0.1
Cypriot Red Slip ware (CRS)	9	0.4
Cypriot Red Slip ware (CRS) 2 (nos 103-4)	44	1.9
Cypriot Red Slip ware (CRS) 9 (nos 105-6)	33	1.4
Egyptian black slip bowl	1	0.0
Egyptian black slip bowl (nos 57-9)	1	0.0
Egyptian Ptolemaic/Early Roman red slip bowl/dish	28	1.2
Egyptian red slip bowl (no. 60)	8	0.3
Egyptian Red Slip ware B (ERSB) copy of ARS 84 (nos 65-6)	1	0.0
Egyptian Red Slip ware B/C (ERSB/C)	8	0.3
Egyptian Red Slip ware B/C (ERSB/C) bowl	5	0.2
Egyptian Red Slip ware C (ERSC)	6	0.3
Egyptian Red Slip ware C (ERSC) copy of ARS 84 (nos 65-6)	5	0.2
Egyptian Red Slip ware C (ERSC) copy of CRS 9 (no. 76)	2	0.1
Imported Late Roman Red Slip ware bowl	2	0.1
Phocaean Red Slip ware (PRS) 3 (nos 108-9)	3	0.1
Coarse wares		
Abu Mena miscellaneous coarse ware	83	3.5
Abu Mena basin (nos 79-80)	23	1.0
Abu Mena *sakkia* pot (nos 35-41)	8	0.3
Egyptian basin	23	1.0
Egyptian bowl	47	2.0
Egyptian marl jug (no. 23)	1	0.0
Egyptian marl juglet (no. 21)	2	0.1
Egyptian marl juglet base (no. 30)	1	0.0
Egyptian marl miscellaneous coarse ware	2	0.1
Egyptian marl *sakkia* pot (nos 35-41)	2	0.1
Egyptian marl strainer	1	0.0
Egyptian marl/Aswan strainer (no. 32)	1	0.0
Egyptian silt bowl/dish	17	0.7
Egyptian silt casserole	23	1.0
Egyptian silt casserole (nos 49-51)	8	0.3
Egyptian silt casserole (cf. Hayes & Harlaut 2002: fig. 29)	1	0.0
Egyptian silt casserole (cf. Hayes & Harlaut 2002: fig. 55)	2	0.1
Egyptian silt casserole lid (no. 53)	4	0.2
Egyptian silt cooking pot	52	2.2
Egyptian silt cooking pot (no. 45)	6	0.3
Egyptian silt cooking pot (no. 47)	1	0.0
Egyptian silt dolium	68	2.9
Egyptian silt funnel strainer (no. 33)	7	0.3
Egyptian silt jar/jug with twisted handle (no. 27)	1	0.0
Egyptian silt juglet (no. 22)	7	0.3
Egyptian silt lid	29	1.2

Egyptian silt miscellaneous coarse ware	35	1.5
Egyptian silt *sakkia* pot (nos 35-41)	49	2.1
Egyptian small handle from coarse ware	154	6.6
Amphorae		
Abu Mena LR Amphora 5 (nos 87-9)	206	8.8
Aegean hollow foot	2	0.1
Campanian 3rd century amphora (no. 137)	2	0.1
Chian	1	0.0
Cilician Dressel 30 (nos 143-4)	3	0.1
Cilician/Cypriot Egloff 169 (no. 145)	7	0.3
Cilician/Cypriot LR Amphora 1 (nos 146-9)	573	24.4
Egyptian LR Amphora 7	6	0.3
Egyptian silt Mons Claudianus Type 1	1	0.0
Gaza LR Amphora 4 Majcherek Forms 2-4 (nos 154-7)	90	3.8
Imported unidentified type	22	0.9
Knidian handle	8	0.3
Knidian ID (no. 112)	2	0.1
Koan (nos 126-30)	6	0.3
Kom Abou Billou LR Amphora 5 (no. 90)	7	0.3
Mareotic AE1/2 (nos 1-3)	12	0.5
Mareotic AE1/2 base (no. 7)	47	2.0
Mareotic AE1/2 long handle (nos 4-5)	2	0.1
Mareotic AE1/2 short handle (no. 6)	49	2.1
Mareotic AE4 (nos 13-17)	237	10.1
Mareotic Mons Claudianus Type 22/3 (nos 9-12)	141	6.0
Mareotic unidentified type	64	2.7
Palestine LR Amphora 5 (no. 158)	7	0.3
Rhodian IB (no. 102)	1	0.0
Rhodian IE2/IF (nos 121-6)	7	0.3
Tripolitanian II (no. 150)	1	0.0
Tunisian Africana IID (no. 152)	2	0.1
Tunisian Africana III (no. 151)	1	0.0
Tunisian unidentified type	10	0.4
Western Asia Minor LR Amphora 3	3	0.1
Total	2344	100%

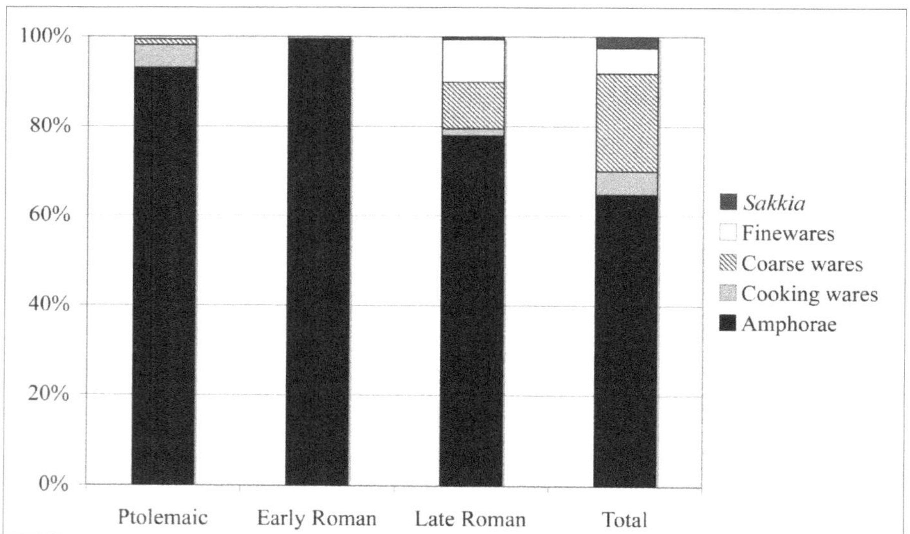

Graph 6.42. Bar graph showing the breakdown of form types by period Site 40.

Site 15 (Figs 6.156 & 6.166; Graphs 6.43 & 6.44; Table 6.48)
Location: 30 57 28N 29 35 14E to 30 57 31N 29 35 11E 30 57 29N 29 35 05E to 30 57 24N 29 35 10E
Description: This large site occupies the central ridge at the western end of Mareotis Island. The area of the site measures 200m NW-SE x 280m NE-SE and is c. 7m high. It is separated from Site 40 by a 50m-wide depression. The western side of the site, an area roughly 200m x 200m, shows clear evidence of extensive recent bulldozer disturbance; accordingly, the archaeological remains probably once extended further to the west of its present extent.

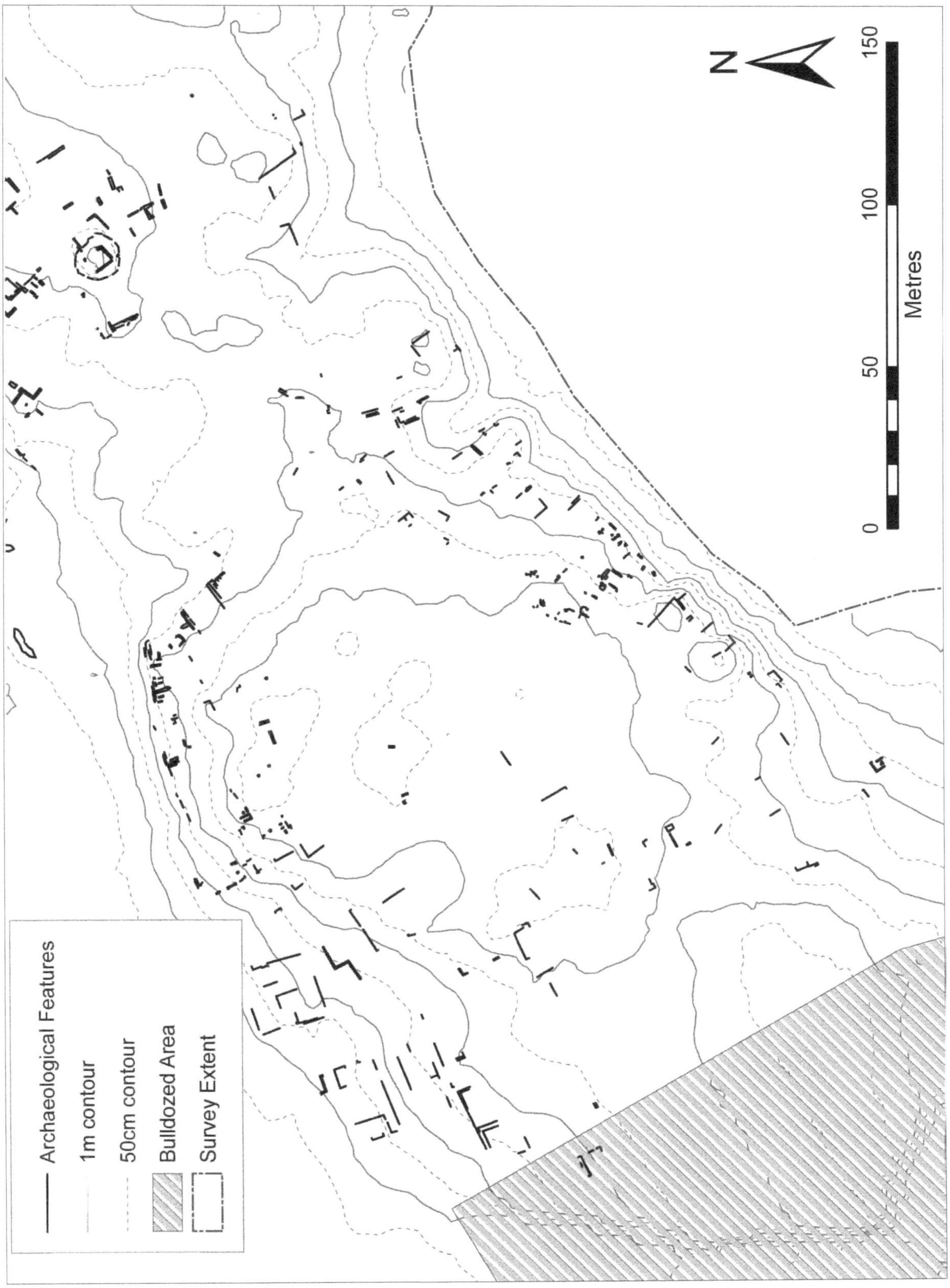

Fig. 6.166. Site 15.

Fig. 6.167. Site 15 detail of wall remains.

Archaeological remains on this site consist of numerous fragmentary structures that cover almost the entire area and continue down the ridge's northern slope towards the lowland plain. However, more visible remains were recorded along the edges and sides of the mound than in the central region. The recorded structures are generally in a poor state of preservation and are very difficult to associate with specific building layouts. Nevertheless, along the northern side of the ridge the remains of larger and more coherent wall alignments were recorded. At least two concentrations of walls could be recognised; the first, to the east, measures 80m x 40m and the second, to the west, measures 80m x 50m. Both are aligned NE-SW. These buildings overlooked the northern shore of the island where a number of waterfront structures were recorded (Sites 17-22). Moreover, some concentrations of pottery wasters and kiln debris were noticed; however, no building could be identified as being associated with industrial activities.

On the southern side of the central ridge of the island, a number of buildings were recorded that were located on the edge of the ridge, overlooking the southern shore (Fig. 6.167). Each building or complex of buildings, determined a specific unit and in many cases its construction was relatively clear, forming a row of buildings along the southern edge of Site 15. There are some comparisons between these buildings at Site 15 and those recorded at Site 14 at the south-eastern end of the island (see above).

Site 15 has a sample of 314 indicator sherds representing activity potentially from the late 3rd century BC into the Late Roman period, particularly the 7th century AD. LR Amphora 1 and Abu Mena LR Amphora 5 were the most common amphorae.

Considering their location and type of recorded remains, it seems reasonable to suggest that both Site 15 and Site 40 could be associated with the waterfront structures located to the north, as was the case with the relationship between Site 113 and the buildings on the northern plain at the eastern end of the island.

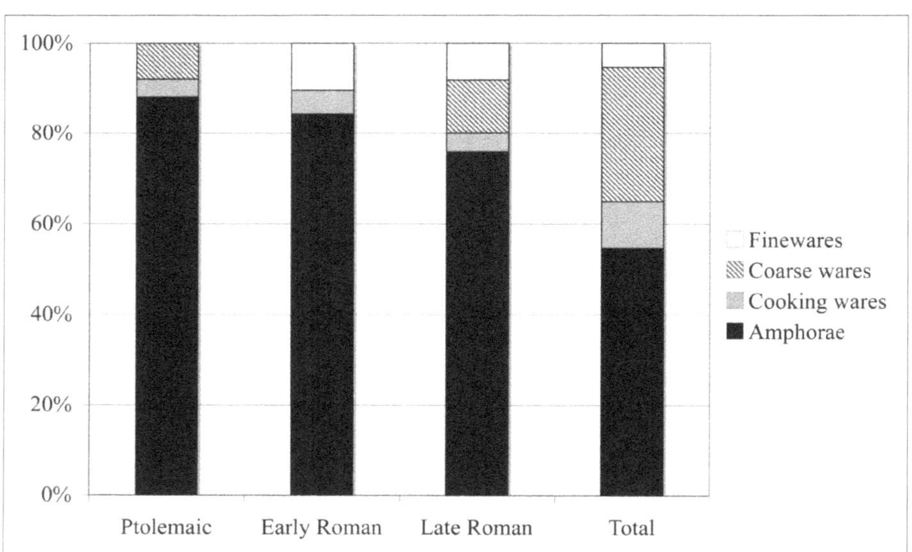

Graph 6.43. Bar graph showing the breakdown of form types by period Site 15.

Table 6.48. Quantity of pottery types for Site 15.

Type	No.	%
Finewares		
Cypriot Red Slip ware (CRS) 2 (nos 103-4)	1	0.3
Cypriot Red Slip ware (CRS) 9 (nos 105-6)	4	1.3
Eastern Sigillata A (ESA)	1	0.3
Egyptian Ptolemaic/Early Roman red slip bowl/dish	3	1.0
Egyptian Red Slip ware A (ERSA) copy of ARS 99	1	0.3
Egyptian Red Slip ware B/C (ERSB/C)	6	1.9
Egyptian Red Slip ware C (ERSC) copy of CRS 9 (no. 76)	1	0.3
Imported Late Roman Red Slip ware bowl	1	0.3
Italian Sigillata (ITS)	1	0.3
Coarse wares		
Abu Mena basin (nos 79-80)	15	4.8
?Abu Mena brazier (no. 84)	1	0.3
Egyptian basin	10	3.2
Egyptian goblet/cup	2	0.6
Egyptian marl miscellaneous coarse ware	4	1.3
Egyptian marl strainer (no. 34)	2	0.6
Egyptian silt bowl/dish	1	0.3
Egyptian silt casserole (nos 49-51)	3	1.0
Egyptian silt casserole (cf. Hayes & Harlaut 2002: fig. 55)	1	0.3
Egyptian silt casserole lid (no. 53)	3	1.0
Egyptian silt cooking pot	8	2.5
Egyptian silt cooking pot (no. 47)	1	0.3
Egyptian silt dolium	5	1.6
Egyptian silt funnel strainer (no. 33)	1	0.3
Egyptian silt jar/jug with twisted handle (no. 27)	2	0.6
Egyptian silt lid	15	4.8
Egyptian silt miscellaneous coarse ware	9	2.9
Egyptian silt *sakkia* pot (nos 35-41)	1	0.3
Egyptian skillet handle (no. 52)	1	0.3
Egyptian small handle from coarse ware	33	10.5
Mareotic jug	2	0.6
Amphorae		
Abu Mena LR Amphora 5 (nos 87-9)	73	23.2
Cilician/Cypriot LR Amphora 1 (nos 146-9)	43	13.7
Egyptian LR Amphora 7	(1)	0.0
Gaza LR Amphora 4 Majcherek Forms 2-4 (nos 154-7)	12	3.8
Imported unidentified type	1	0.3
Koan (nos 126-30)	2	0.6
Mareotic AE1/2 (nos 1-3)	2	0.6
Mareotic AE1/2 short handle (no. 6)	14	4.5
Mareotic AE4 (nos 13-17)	11	3.5
Mareotic Mons Claudianus Type 22/3 (nos 9-12)	4	1.3
Mareotic tall pot stand (no. 8)	1	0.3
Mareotic unidentified type	4	1.3
Palestine LR Amphora 5 (no. 158)	1	0.3
Rhodian IE2/IF (nos 121-6)	3	1.0
Tunisian Africana III (no. 151)	1	0.3
Other		
Egyptian marl lamp (no. 91)	3	1.0
Total	314 (1)	100%

Graph 6.44. Pie graph showing the chronological breakdown of pottery from Site 15.

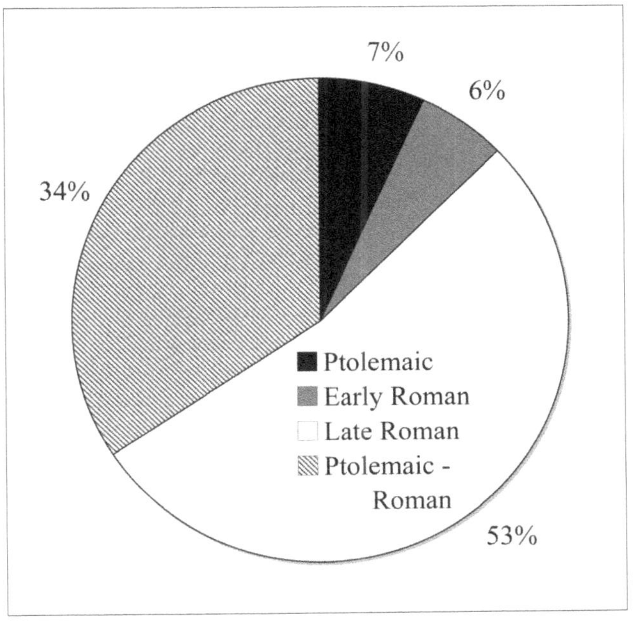

Site 32 (Figs 6.156, 6.168; Graph 6.45; Table 6.49)
Location: 30 57 28N 29 35 20E
Description: This site is an amphora kiln complex that is located on the lowland at the southern shore of the island c. 200m south of the ridge of Site 40, in the eastern part of the west end of the island. The site is characterised by the existence of a mound of amphora wasters, measuring 40m x 20m and is at least c. 2m in height, that is located at the most southerly point of the site (Fig. 6.169). About 20m to the north of the pottery mound, the remains of a large kiln were discovered and recorded (Fig. 6.170). The internal diameter of the kiln is c. 8m, while the 2.3m thick external

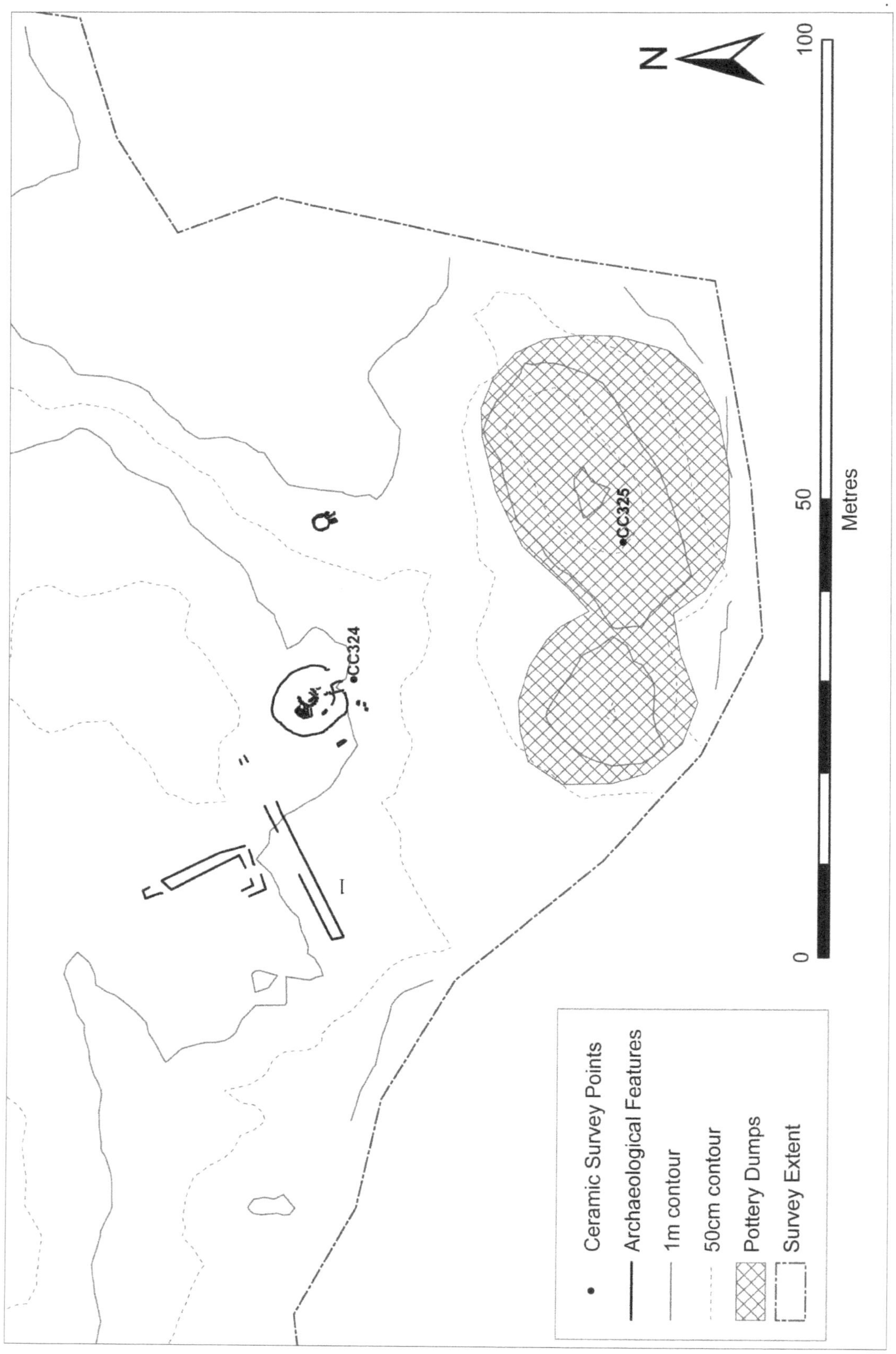

Fig. 6.168. Site 32.

Fig. 6.169. Site 32 pottery mound.

walls give an external diameter of c. 12m, which makes this one of the largest kilns recorded in Egypt (Empereur & Picon 1992: 146; Empereur 1993: 41). At ground level the firing plate was visible, as well as some of the perforations that allowed hot air from the firing chamber below to access the main chamber of the kiln. The lower entrance to the firing chamber was recorded at the southern side of the kiln (Fig. 6.171). However, none of the superstructure of the kiln has survived.

About 15m to the east of the kiln, a small round structure was recorded. It has an external diameter of 1.7m and is constructed of 0.1m thick fired bricks (Fig. 6.172), yet its function and association with the kiln is unclear. Less than 10m to the northwest of the large kiln, some walls that appear to be associated with the kiln complex were recorded. The walls extended over an area some 17m NW-SE and 22m NE-SW and could be the remains of associated storage facilities and warehouses.

Site 32 has a sample of 112 indicator sherds. Apart from two imported sherds, the material was exclusively kiln products of c. mid 1st through mid 3rd centuries AD.

Fig. 6.170. Site 32 kiln, looking south towards pottery dumps.

Fig. 6.171. (above) Site 32 kiln and entrance to firing chamber.

Fig. 6.172. (right) Site 32 circular feature to east of kiln.

Graph 6.45. (below) Pie graph showing the chronological breakdown of pottery from Site 32.

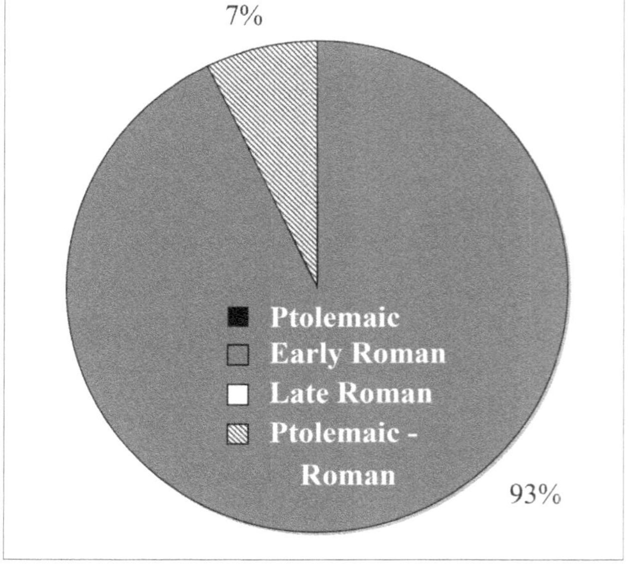

Table 6.49. (below) Quantity of pottery types for Site 32.

Type	**No.**	**%**
Koan (nos 126-30)	1	0.9
Mareotic AE4 (nos 13-17)	88	78.6
Mareotic Mons Claudianus Type 22/3 (nos 9-12)	12	10.7
Mareotic short pot stand (no. 18)	2	1.8
Mareotic unidentified amphora	8	7.1
Tunisian unidentified amphora	1	0.9
Total	112	100%

Site 41 (Fig. 6.174)
Location: 30 57 34N 29 35 15E to 30 57 38N 29 35 12E
Description: This site is located in the lowland to the north of the island ridge and Site 40. The site contains a poorly defined linear feature that extends for c. 90m in a N-S direction. The feature is made of limestone blocks and is c. 15m wide (Fig. 6.173); however, several parts of the feature have been eroded and sedimentation in the area is extensive. This feature could possibly be a jetty that extended into the water perpendicular to the shoreline just at the foot of the ridge. Site 41 has a single undated rim from an unidentified Mareotic amphora. The dating of this site therefore is assumed to mirror that of Site 40 to the north (see above).

Fig. 6.173. Wall at Site 41 and general view of area.

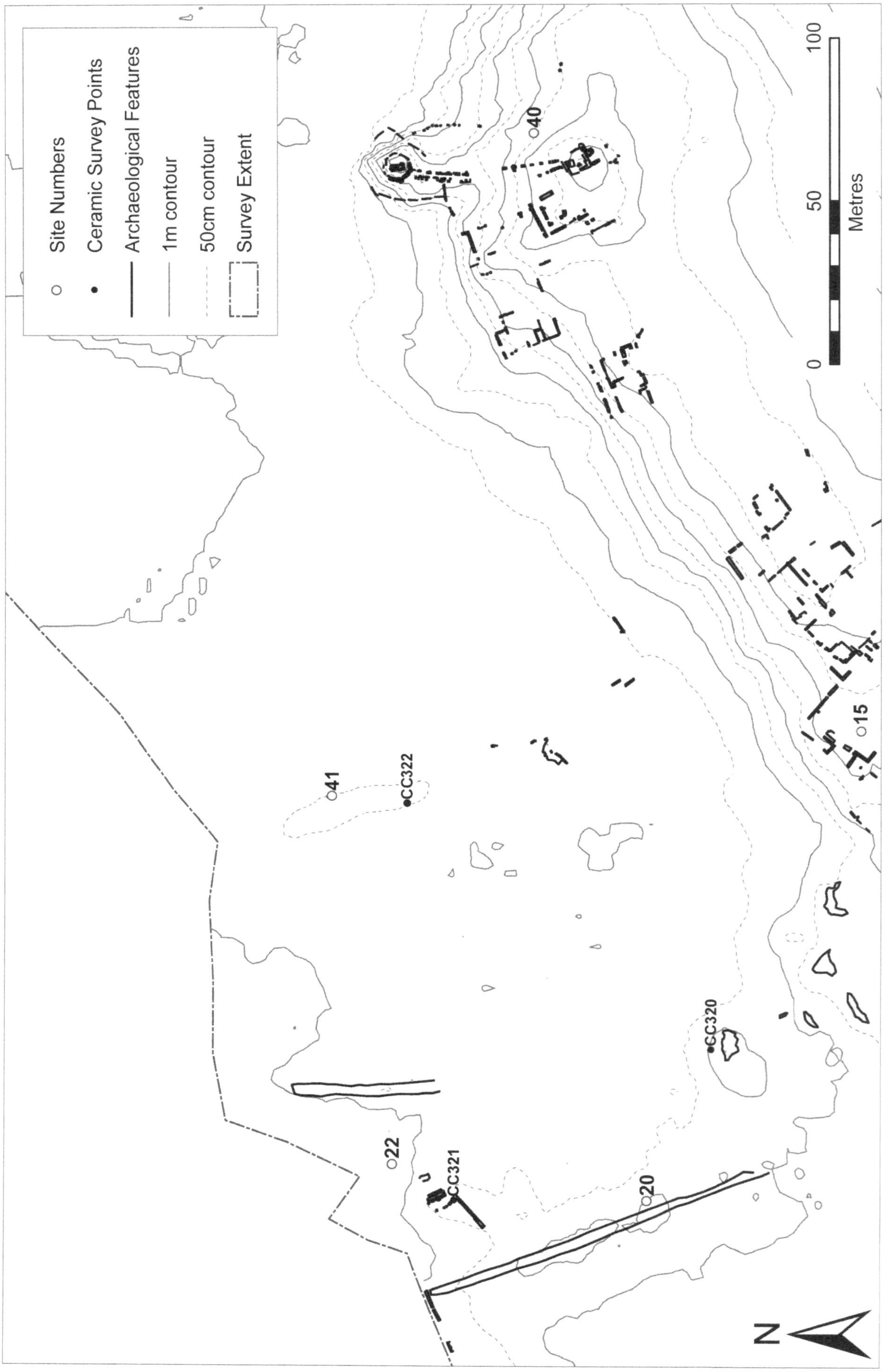

Fig. 6.174. Site 41.

Site 23 (Figs 6.157, 6.175 & 6.176; Table 6.50)
Location: 30 57 43N 29 35 19E to 30 57 52N 29 35 13E
Description: This site is located on the northern shore of the island at the north-eastern limit of the western section of the island. The site consists of a small mound that measures 23m E-W x 20m N-S and rises c. 3m above the lake level (Fig. 6.177). Since the site was first recorded in 2004 the lake level has risen, isolating the mound from the main body of the island to the south. On the mound there are limestone blocks that equate to a building that

Fig. 6.175. Site 23.

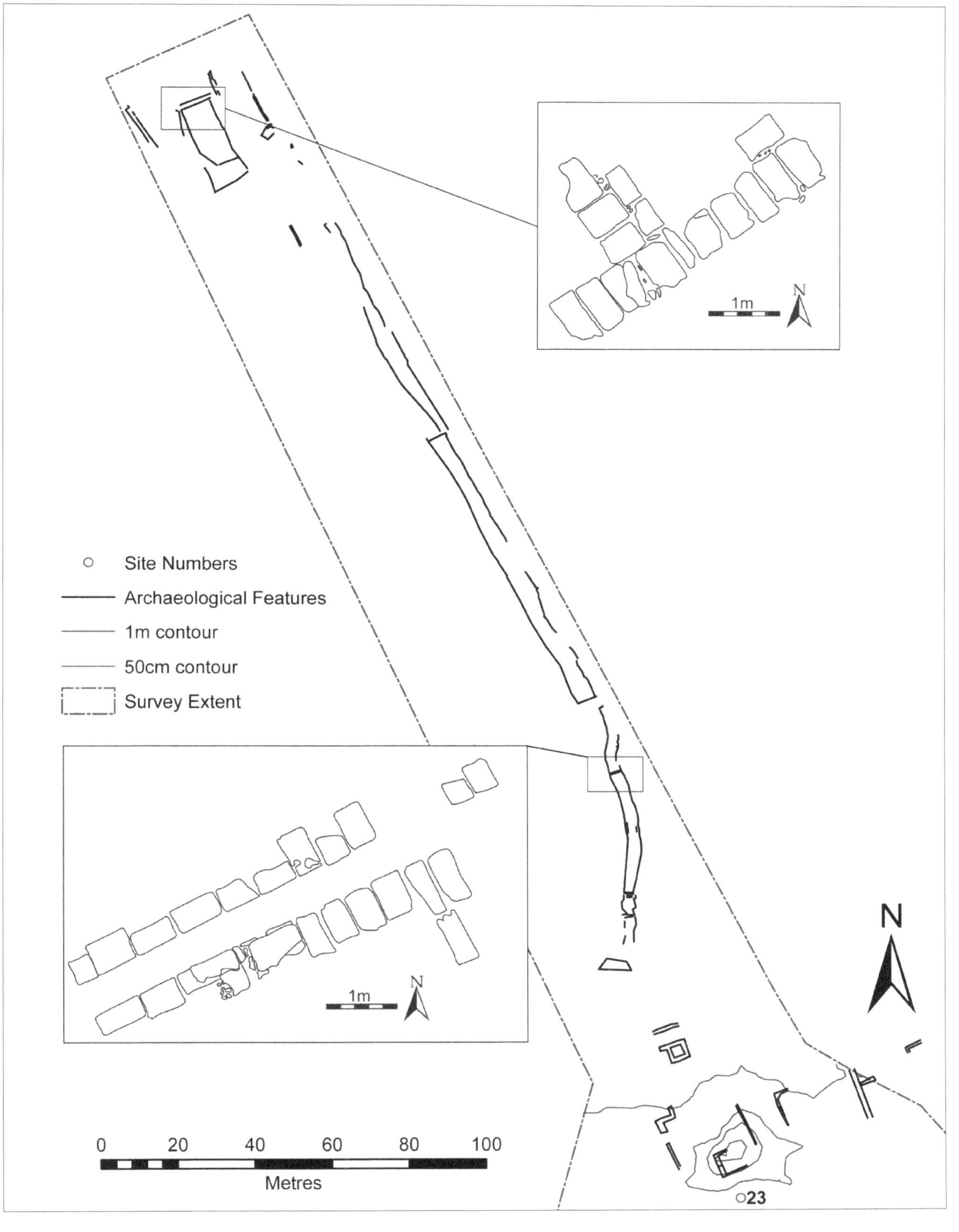

Fig. 6.176. View of Site 23 from Site 40 with Site 204 on the north shore in background.

Fig. 6.177. Site 23 view of mound from west.

Fig. 6.178. View from Site 23 mound, north along jetty.

measures c. 15m N-S x 12m E-W, in addition to plenty of pottery sherds that cover the mound. Moreover, on the low land that surrounds the mound, there are more remains of structures.

The most significant of the remains at Site 23 is a jetty-like feature that extends northwards into the water for c. 300m. The feature connects with a small island in the middle of the lake (Fig. 6.178). The island measures c. 30m x 30m and on it there are the remains of a 20m x 10m rectangular building which was built using large regular limestone blocks arranged in several courses. At present at least three courses are visible. From the square building on the island three jetties extended further north into the lake. They were made of limestone blocks and they measure in length, from east to west, 15m, 7m and 15m, respectively.

The feature probably functioned as a jetty. It was eroded at several locations along its length; however, there was evidence for the use of two rows of large regular limestone blocks arranged in headers filled in between with boulders and small stones. Close to the shore the feature was curved in shape (Fig. 6.179), as the structure extended into the lake it became straighter in section. At intervals along the length of the jetty there were a series of channels that allowed the water to flow across the jetty to prevent sediments building up against the side of the structure (Fig. 6.180).

Fig. 6.179. (above) Site 23 near shore: curved section of jetty.

Fig. 6.180. (below) Site 23 detail of jetty.

Site 23 has a sample of 15 indicator sherds ranging between the late 2nd century BC and the 7th century AD. Mid 1st through mid 3rd centuries AD is best represented, based on the Mareotic AE4.

It is worth mentioning that this site is located directly opposite Site 204 on the northern shore of the lake and that the distance between the small island at the end of the jetty and the jetty associated with Site 204 is only c. 550m, which is the shortest distance at any point in the lake between the northern shore of the island and the northern shore of the lake (Fig. 6.176).

Table 6.50. Quantity of pottery types for Site 23.

Type	**No.**
Abu Mena LR Amphora 5 (nos 87-9)	3
Egyptian Ptolemaic/Early Roman red slip bowl/dish	1
Egyptian silt casserole (nos 49-51)	1
Egyptian silt casserole (cf. Hayes & Harlaut 2002: fig. 29)	2
Egyptian small handle from coarse ware	1
Mareotic AE4 (nos 13-17)	7
Total	15

Sites 17-22 (Fig. 6.181)
Location: 30 57 36N 29 35 08E to 30 57 33N 29 34 59E
Description: This group of coastal sites occupies the north-eastern shore of the island north of Site 15. The area is characterised by heavy siltation and vegetation growth which made detailed recording of the remains quite problematic, and required the use of magnetic survey to be able to detect buildings that lay beneath the sediments (Figs 6.182-6.184).

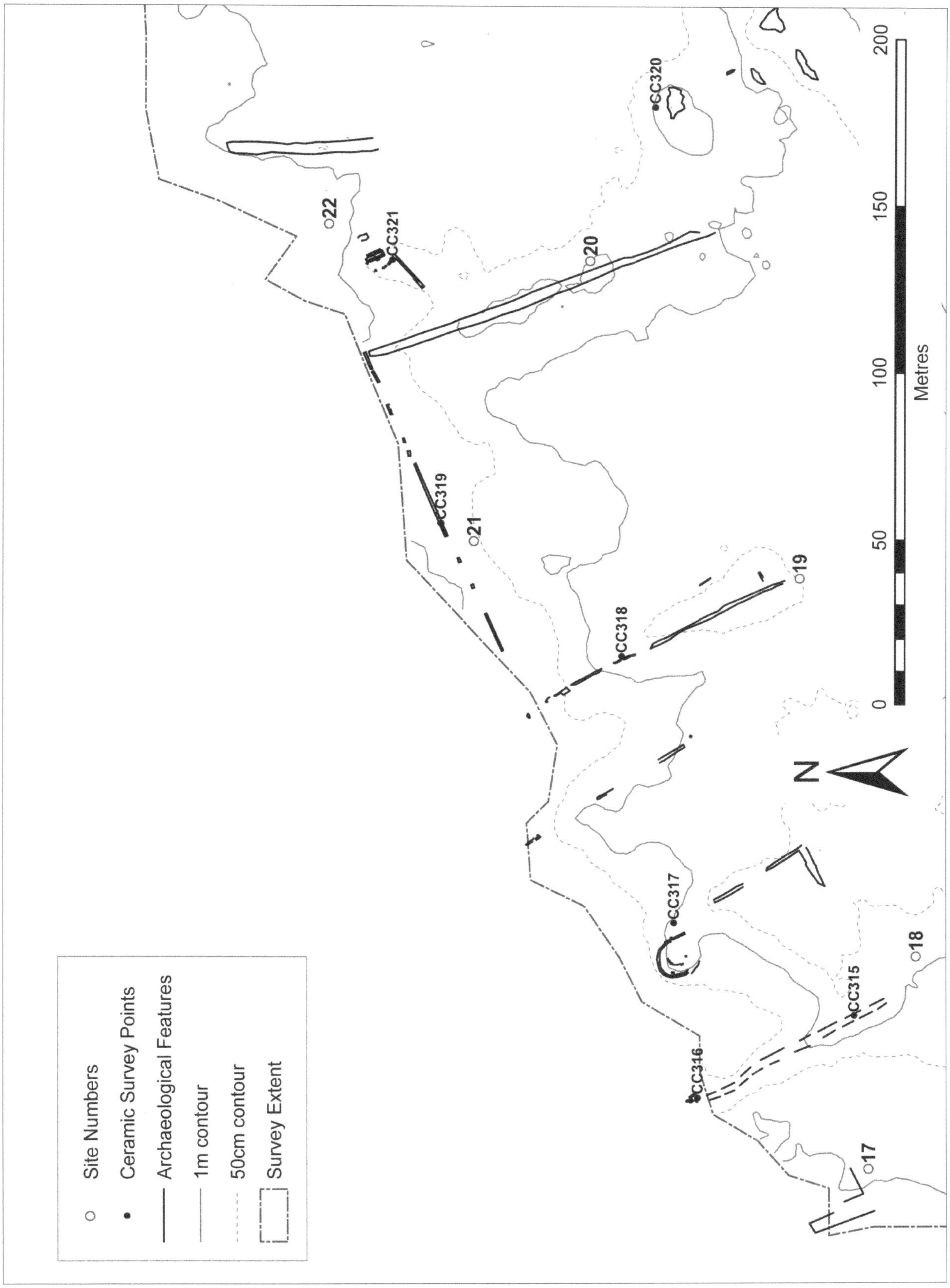

Fig. 6.181. Site 17 to Site 22.

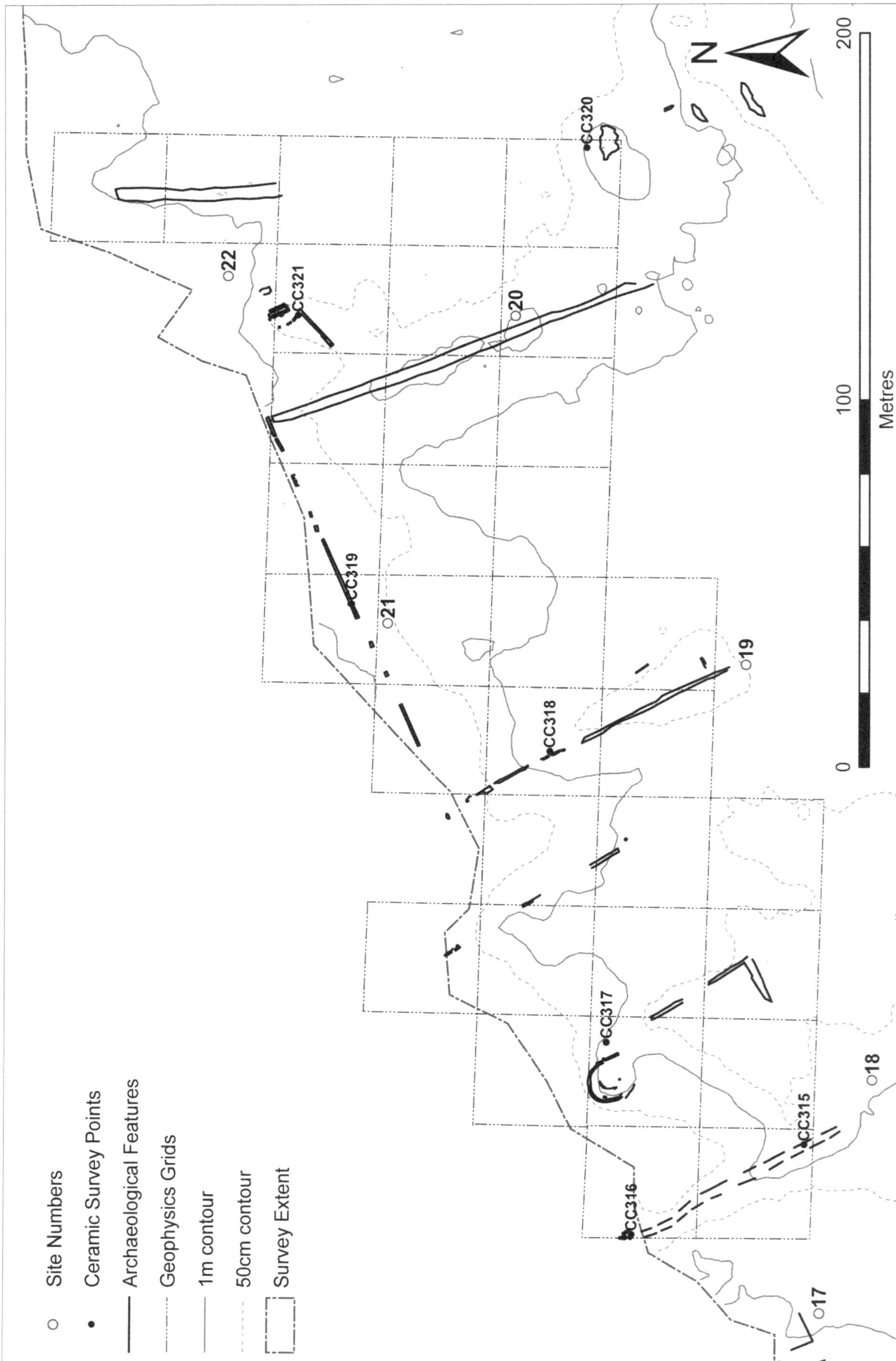

Fig. 6.182. Geophysics grids for Site 17 to Site 22.

Fig. 6.183. Geophysics results for Site 17 to Site 22.

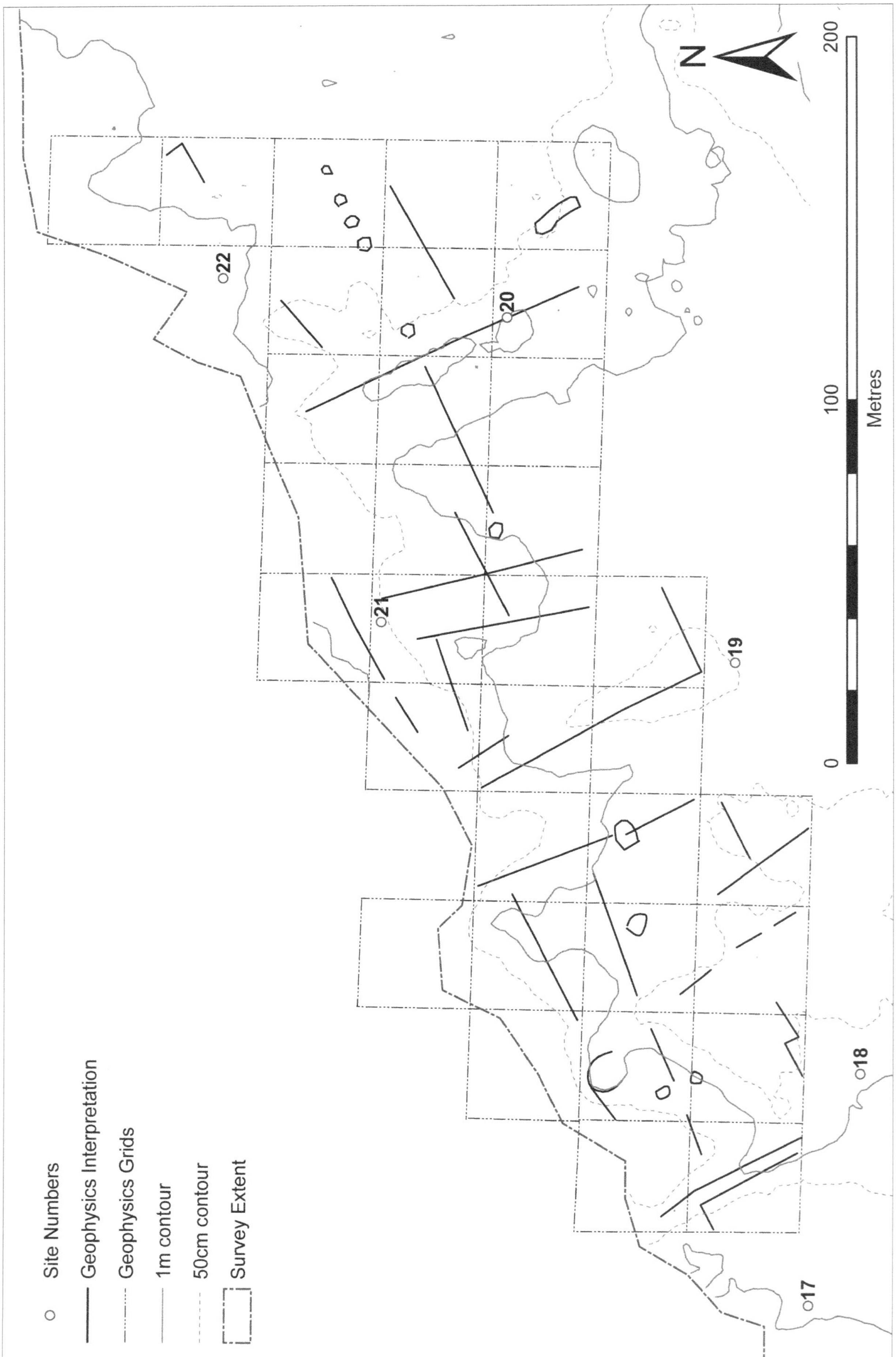

Fig. 6.184. Geophysics interpretation Site 17 to Site 22.

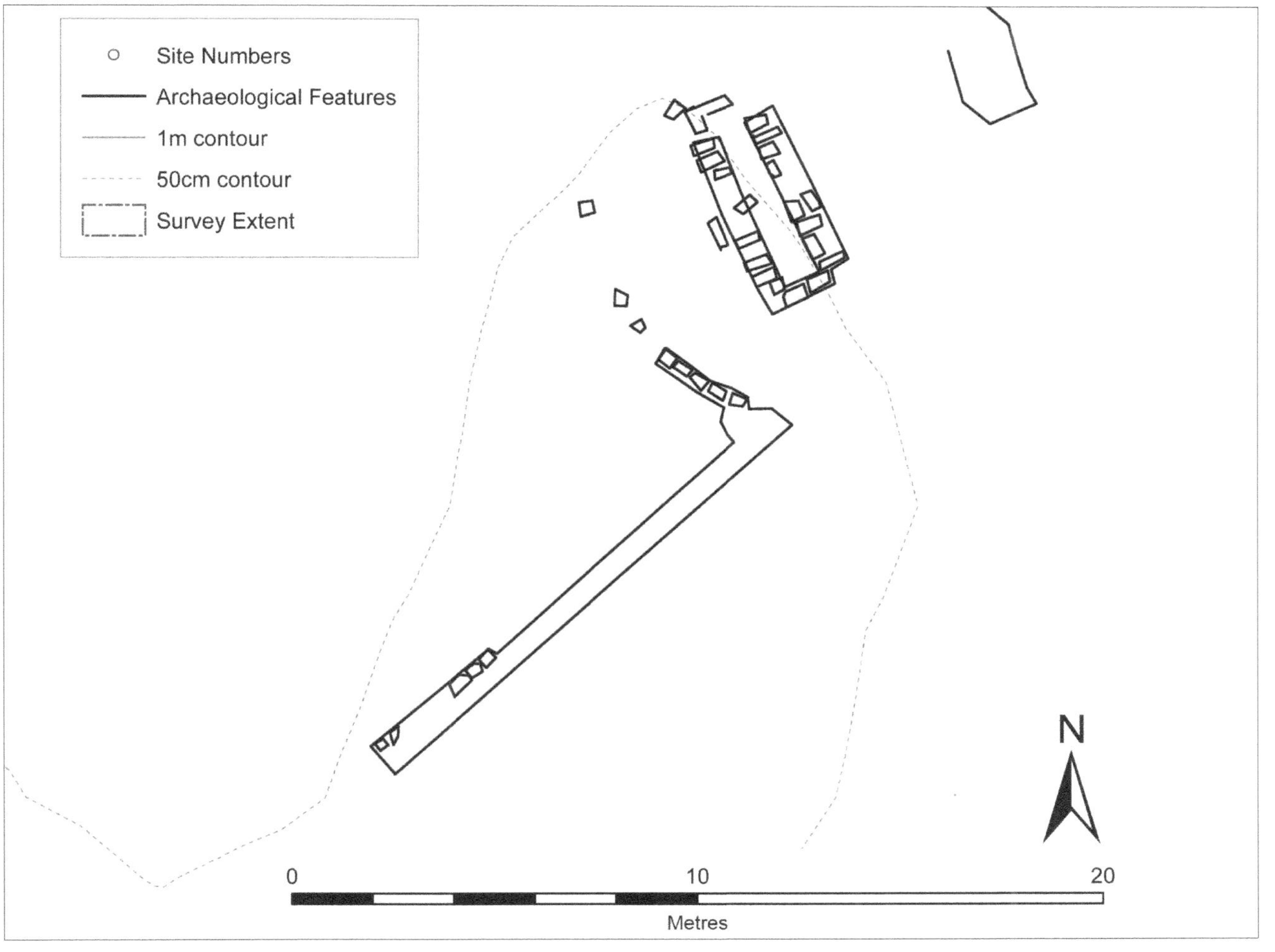

Fig. 6.185. Site 22.

Site 22 (Figs 6.181 & 6.185)
Location: 30 57 36N 29 35 09E
Description: Site 22 contained one distinctive archaeological feature. It appears to be a section of the external wall of a *sakkia* (Fig. 6.186). Judging from the measurements of the surviving section of wall, the *sakkia's* diameter could have been c. 8m diameter, similar to the one recorded at Site 40. The wall is c. 0.5m thick and it is made of regular limestone blocks. At the centre of the outer wall there are the remains of a rectangular structure that measures 5m x

Fig. 6.186. Site 22 sakkia.

Fig. 6.187. Wall associated with Site 22.

2m made of large limestone blocks. The structure seems to be hollow in the middle and filled by sediments, therefore this was probably the area where the wooden wheel of the *sakkia* was located. Linked to the southern side of the *sakkia*'s external wall extends a linear feature made of limestone blocks and measuring 13m long NW-SW and up to 1m wide (Fig. 6.187). The function of this wall is uncertain.

The ceramic assemblage associated with Site 22 was collected together with Site 20 (see below, Table 6.51).

Site 21 (Figs 6.181 & 6.188)
Location: 30 57 35N 29 35 05E
Description: Site 21 is a linear feature that stretches for a distance of c. 245m along the northern shoreline of the island. Its eastern end was recorded c. 20m from Site 22 and it is made of limestone blocks measuring roughly 0.4m by 0.3m and laid as stretchers facing the water. The size, nature and arrangement of this structure imply that it had a maritime function, possibly a lake wall or a quay, or was linked with agricultural practices (see Chapter 5, this volume).

Site 21 has a sample of just one indicator and three body sherds. The dateable sherds belong only to the Late Roman period (5th to 7th centuries AD).

Fig. 6.188. General view of lake wall Site 21.

Site 20 (Figs 6.181, 6.183; Graph 6.46; Table 6.51)
Location: 30 57 33N 29 35 08E
Description: Site 20 is a N-S aligned 2m wide linear feature which extends from the foot of the mound at Site 15 some c. 135m north to the lake edge. Along the length of the feature there is some evidence of building blocks which have been buried by aeolian sediments. At the northern end of the linear feature to the west there is a curved wall made of limestone blocks. The exact function of the curved wall is unclear since it has been subject to heavy siltation and erosion.

The ceramic assemblage at Site 20 was considered together with the ceramics collected from Site 22 and collectively has a sample of 50 indicator sherds. Although potentially dating from the late 4th century BC the spread is between the late 3rd and the 1st centuries BC, with later periods to the 7th century AD poorly represented. Most of the assemblage comprises amphorae, particularly local or regional types, although Rhodian is also common.

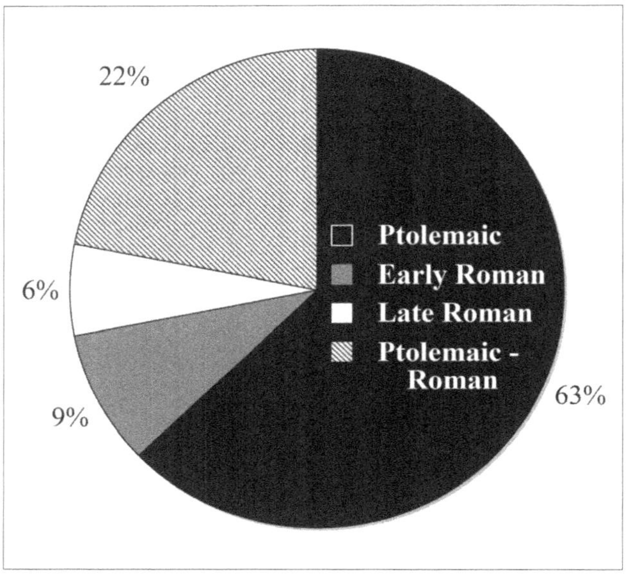

Type	No.	%
Finewares		
Egyptian Ptolemaic/Early Roman red slip bowl/dish	1	2.0
Painted unidentified	(1)	0.0
Coarse wares		
Egyptian silt basin	1	2.0
Egyptian silt bowl	5	10.2
Egyptian silt miscellaneous coarse ware	1	2.0
Egyptian small handle from coarse ware	1	2.0
Amphorae		
Abu Mena LR Amphora 5 (nos 87-9)	2	4.1
Cilician/Cypriot LR Amphora 1 (nos 146-9)	1	2.0
Knidian handle	5	10.2
Knidian IIG (no. 119)	1	2.0
Koan (nos 126-30)	2	4.1
Mareotic AE1/2 base (no. 7)	13	26.5
Mareotic AE4 (nos 13-17)	3	6.1
Mareotic unidentified type	2	4.1
Rhodian IE2/IF (nos 121-6)	11	22.4
Total	50	100%

Table 6.51. (above) Quantity of pottery types for Site 20.

Graph 6.46. Pie graph showing the chronological breakdown of pottery from Site 20.

Site 19 (Fig. 6.181; Table 6.52)
Location: 30 57 33N 29 35 04E
Description: Site 19 is located c. 110m west of Site 20. The site comprises another linear feature that extends for c. 60m back from the shoreline on a N-S alignment. Several sections of this feature are not visible along its length as a result of erosion and siltation; however, there is clear evidence for the use of regular limestone blocks in the construction arranged in single and double rows, up to 1m wide.

Site 19 has a sample of just 10 sherds, but the main periods are all represented from the $2^{nd}/1^{st}$ centuries BC.

In 2004 it was noticed that the lake wall at Site 21 extended westward until it intersected with the northern ends of the linear features associated with Sites 20 and 19. However, the exact functional relationship between the lake wall in Site 21 and the features of Sites 20 and 19 is difficult to determine as a result of dense siltation. On the other hand, it is possible that the linear features at Site 20 and 19 could have functioned as causeways linking the lake-side sites with the ridge at Site 15.

Type	**No.**
Cilician/Cypriot LR Amphora 1 (nos 146-9)	(1)
Egyptian silt basin	4
Egyptian silt lid	2
Mareotic AE1/2	2
Mareotic AE4 (nos 13-17)	1
Total	9 (1)

Table 6.52. Quantity of pottery types for Site 19.

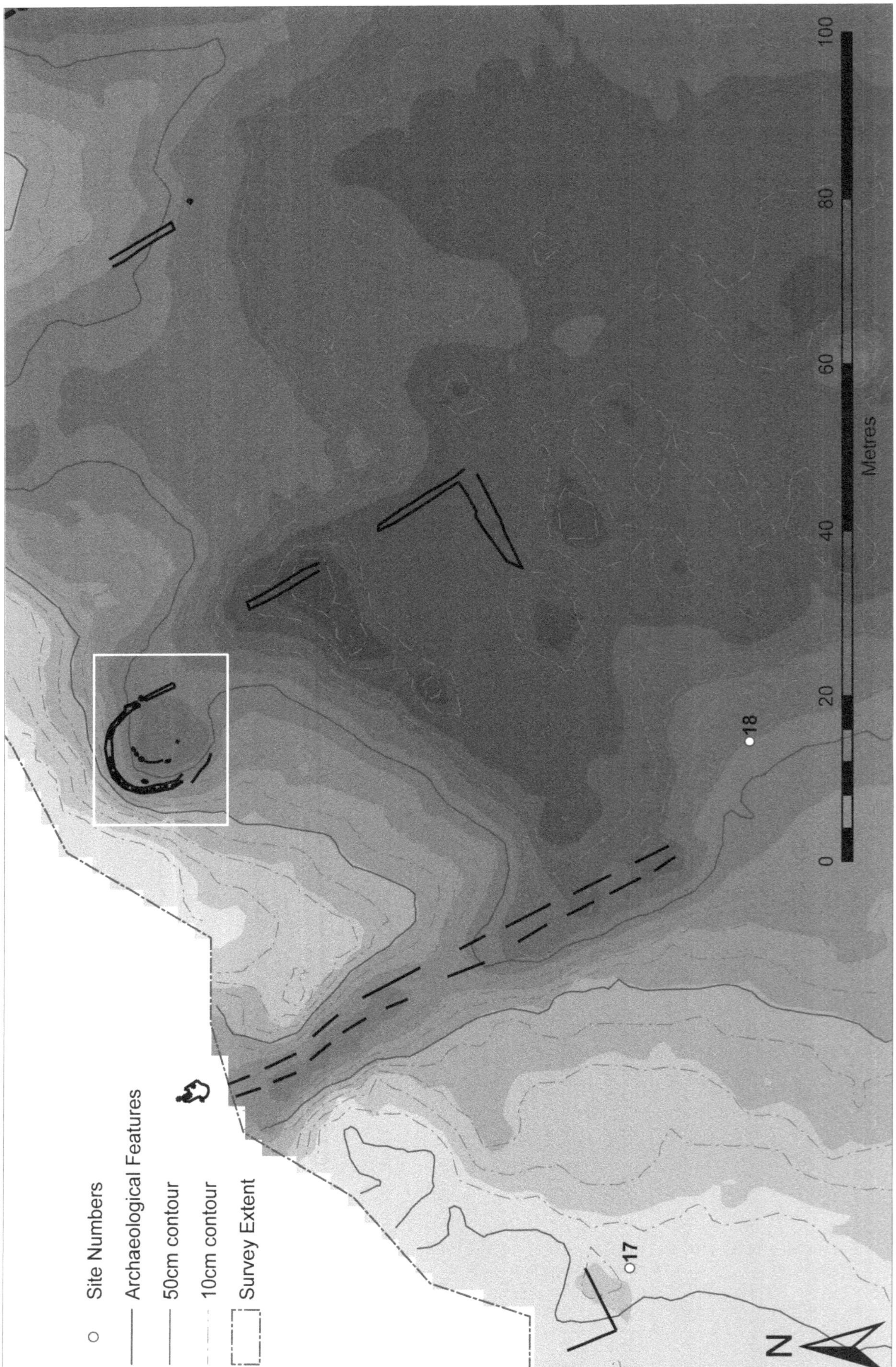

Fig. 6.189. Enhanced topographic view of Site 18. Dark grey is high ground and light grey is lower ground. The white rectangle denotes the sakkia detailed in Fig. 6.190.

Site 18 (Figs 6.181 & 6.189; Graph 6.47; Table 6.53)
Location: 30 57 33N 29 35 00E
Description: Site 18 is located c. 50m west of the linear feature of Site 19. The site contains evidence for at least two linear features, between 1.5-3m wide, one of which extends perpendicular to the shoreline in a N-W direction, and the other in a E-W direction from the southern end of the first linear feature. The features are quite disturbed; however, they seem to have been made of irregular limestone blocks. The E-W aligned feature measures c. 50m, while the N-S features measures c. 40m and they enclose a large space. At the northern end of the N-S wall there is a circular building that measures c. 10m in external diameter (Figs 6.190 & 6.191). The wall of the circular structure is made of limestone blocks, c. 0.6m x 0.3m and is arranged mostly in headers. It was evident that the circular structure has been disturbed; therefore it was not possible to determine its exact function, but the possibility of it being another *sakkia* can not be dismissed.

Site 18 has a sample of 38 indicator sherds potentially dating from the late 4th century BC, but more likely the 2nd/1st centuries BC and the 7th century AD. The periods best represented were the 2nd/1st centuries BC followed by the 5th to 7th centuries AD. Twenty-six indicators are amphorae.

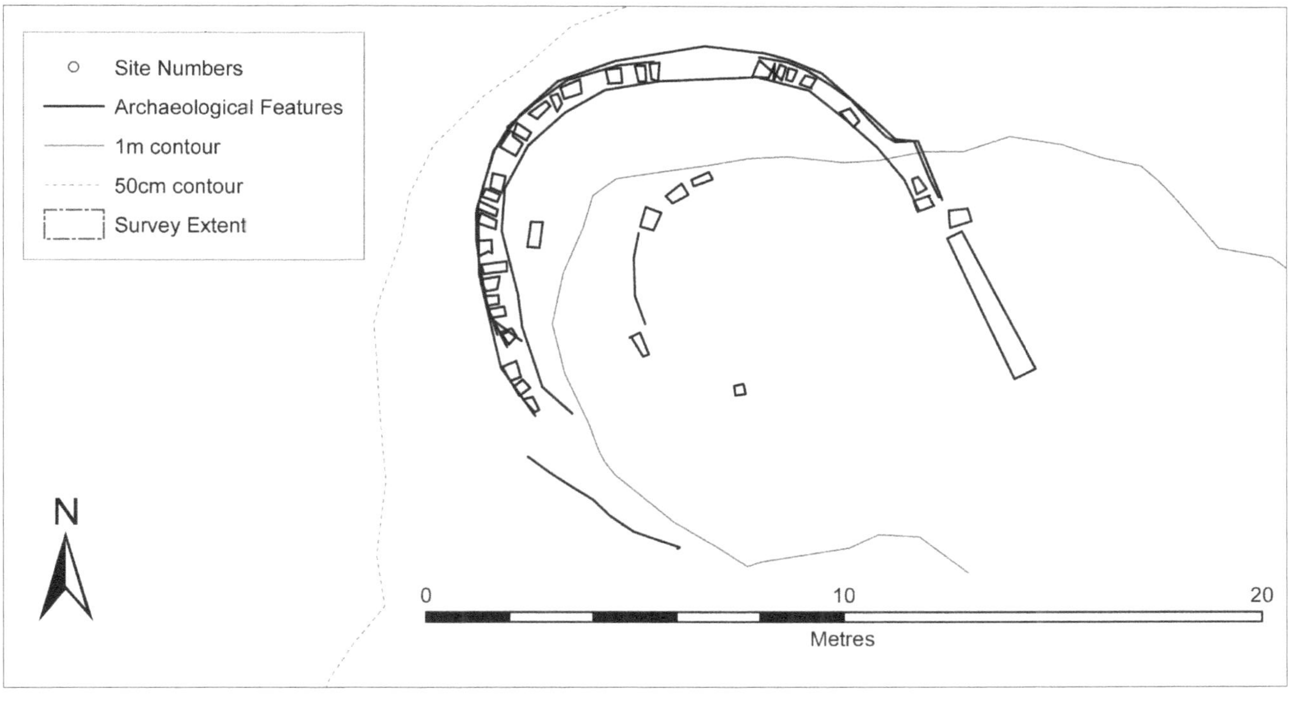

Fig. 6.190. (above) Site 18 detail of sakkia *and topography.*

Fig. 6.191. One side of Site 18 sakkia.

Table 6.53. Quantity of pottery types for Site 18.

Type	No.	%
Finewares		
Cypriot Red Slip ware (CRS) 9 (nos 105-6)	1	2.6
Egyptian silt red slip fish dish (nos 54-5)	2	5.3
Coarse wares		
Egyptian basin	4	10.5
Egyptian bowl	1	2.6
Egyptian marl strainer (no. 34)	1	2.6
Egyptian silt cooking pot	1	2.6
Egyptian silt miscelleaneous coarse ware	1	2.6
Egyptian small handle from coarse ware	1	2.6
Amphorae		
Abu Mena LR Amphora 5 (nos 87-9)	(1)	0.0
Cilician/Cypriot LR Amphora 1 (nos 146-9)	4	10.5
Gaza LR Amphora 4 Majcherek Forms 2-4 (nos 154-7)	4	10.5
Knidian handle	5	13.2
Mareotic AE1/2 (nos 1-3)	2	5.3
Mareotic AE1/2 short handle (no. 6)	6	15.8
Mareotic AE4 (nos 13-17)	2	5.3
Mareotic Mons Claudianus Amphora Type 22/3 (nos 9-12)	3	7.9
Total	38 (1)	100%

Graph 6.47. Pie graph showing the chronological breakdown of pottery from Site 18.

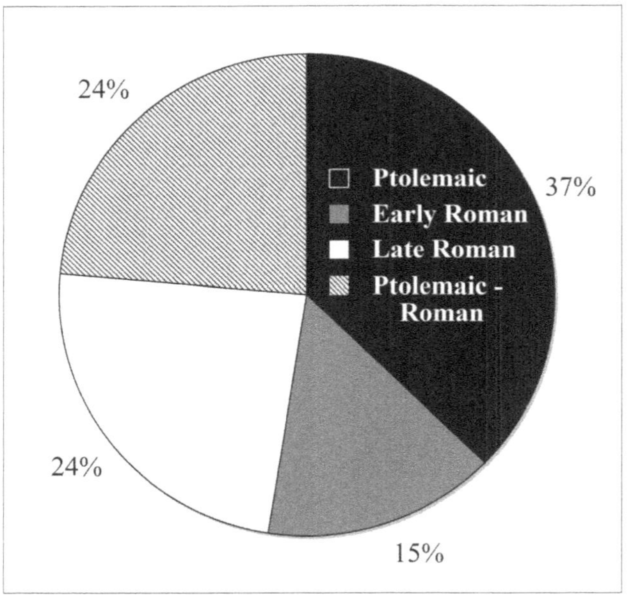

Site 17 (Figs 6.181, 6.192; Table 6.54)
Location: 30 57 31N 29 34 57E
Description: Site 17 is the western-most of this group of lake-side sites. It is located c. 40m west of the circular structure (*sakkia*) of Site 18 and it contains a 60m long and 4m wide linear feature that extends in a N-W direction perpendicular to the shoreline almost into the water. The linear feature is an elongated mound made of limestone blocks and rubble; however, it is interrupted in several sections. At the northern end of this mound, there is a limestone platform that measures c.3m N-S x 1.7m E-W. The platform is made of blocks of limestone arranged in headers and probably marked the northern end of a quay-like structure.

Very limited (five) pottery samples were collected from this site; however, they represent activity from the late 1st to 2nd centuries AD.

Type	**No.**
Egyptian small handle from coarse ware	2
Mareotic unidentified amphora	1
Mareotic Mons Claudianus Amphora Type 22/3 (nos 9-12)	2
Total	5

Table 6.54. Quantity of pottery types for Site 17.

Fig. 6.192. Site 17 looking north.

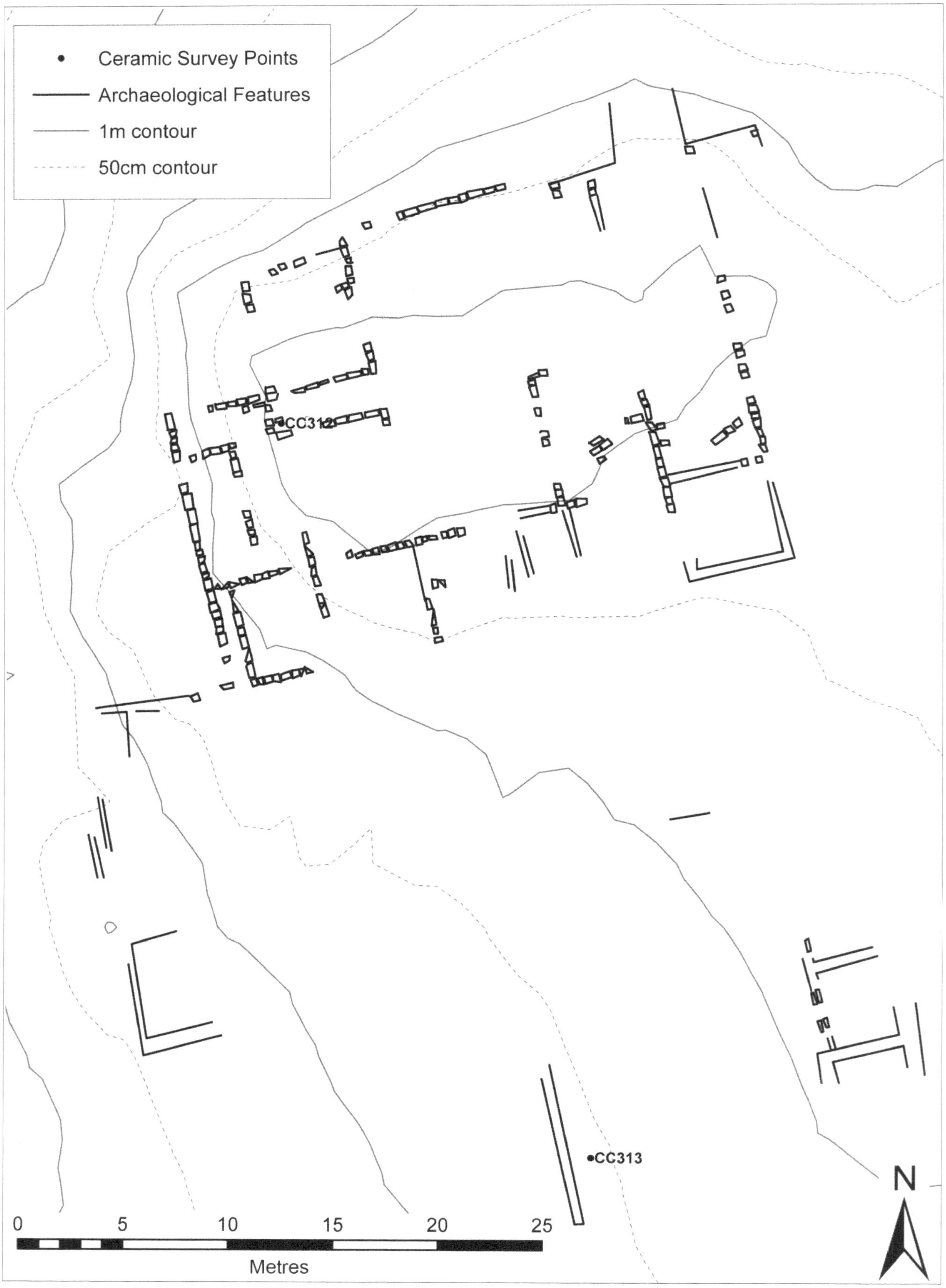

Fig. 6.193. Site 16.

Site 16 (Figs 6.156, 6.181, 6.193 & 6.194; Graph 6.48; Table 6.55)
Location: 30 57 22N 29 34 57E
Description: This is the western-most site that was recorded on Mareotis Island. It occupies the western tip of a hill that measures 80m E-W x 60m N-S and c. 6m in height. The eastern part of the hill has been subject to intense bulldozing; therefore, the western end of the central ridge probably extended further than it does currently. Additionally, the bulldozer damage to the east obscures the relationship between this main site and the hill at Site 15 (Fig. 6.195). The archaeological remains on Site 16 consist mainly of a large square, multi-roomed building that occupies the top of the tell and measures 30m E-W x 20m N-S (Fig. 6.196). At the northern and western sides of the building the hill slopes down steeply towards the shoreline. The external walls of the building are abutted with a series of small rooms of different sizes. The central section of the building consists of a rectangular courtyard that measures c. 12m x 7m.

Fig. 6.194. Site 16 general view.

Fig. 6.195. (below) Bulldozing associated with Site 16.

Fig. 6.196. Rooms recorded at Site 16.

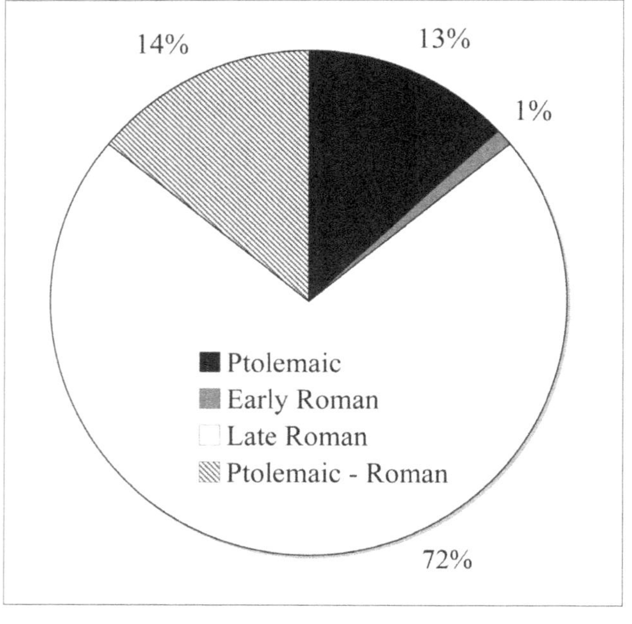

About 15m to the south of the building there are some poorly preserved walls that could have belonged to another building, possibly also associated with Site 16.

Site 16 has a sample of 35 indicator sherds mostly belonging 5th to 7th centuries AD with a small amount of Ptolemaic pottery dating between the mid 4th and 2nd/1st centuries BC. There is an absence of pottery of the Early Roman period and nearly half the assemblage consists of LR Amphora 1.

Type	**No.**	**%**
Finewares		
Cypriot Red Slip ware (CRS)	1	2.9
Cypriot Red Slip ware (CRS) 9 (nos 105-6)	1	2.9
Egyptian Red Slip ware B/C (ERSB/C)	1	2.9
Coarse wares		
Egyptian silt dolium	1	2.9
Egyptian silt lid	1	2.9
Egyptian silt miscellaneous coarse ware	2	5.7
Egyptian small handle from coarse ware	1	2.9
Amphorae		
Abu Mena LR Amphora 5 (nos 87-9)	2	5.7
Aegean LR Amphora 2	1	2.9
Cilician/Cypriot LR Amphora 1 (nos 146-9)	17	48.6
Gaza LR Amphora 4 Majcherek Forms 2-4 (nos 154-7)	2	5.7
Knidian I (no. 111)	1	2.9
Koan (nos 126-30)	1	2.9
Mareotic AE1/2 (nos 1-3)	3	8.6
Total	35	100%

Table 6.55. (above) Quantity of pottery types for Site 16.

Graph 6.48. Pie graph showing the chronological breakdown of pottery from Site 16.

Chapter 7. Conclusions

7.1 Introduction

Unlike previous research conducted in the Mareotic region that was until recently restricted to site or function specific investigation (see Chapter 2), the Lake Mareotis Research Project has, for the first time, systematically identified, investigated and surveyed comprehensively and inclusively all extant remains of over 70 sites along the western Mareotic Arm of Lake Mareotis. This is an area of approximately 40km E-W by 3km N-S from Sidi Kerir to El-Hammam, equating to 350 hectares of topographic data (see Fig. 1.5). The sites recorded date from the Hellenistic period through to the 7th century, and vary extensively in nature, size and function. Yet collectively, their number, variety of function and scale, all serve to demonstrate the importance of this area particularly in relation to Alexandria and the mechanisms by which Mareotic products were produced and transported to the city.

The nature and size of the sites identified vary from rural small-holdings to substantial urban settlements, many with associated production sites, water storage facilities and agricultural and industrial complexes. Local pottery production is indicated by numerous kiln sites discovered in the region, particularly on Mareotis Island. The study of ceramic assemblages collected from the surveyed sites indicates that the amphora production centres were active from the Ptolemaic to the mid 3rd century AD. There is also considerable evidence for imported pottery from as early as the mid 4th century BC, although not gaining in quantity until the late 4th or the second quarter of the 3rd centuries BC, and extending through to the mid 7th century. In addition to ceramic production and importation (discussed below), there are remains of wineries and numerous features associated with agriculture and water management.

Through examination of the archaeological sites that were recorded along the shores of the western Mareotic Arm and on Mareotis Island, it can be inferred that there are two groups of sites that were associated with the utilisation and management of water in Lake Mareotis in antiquity. The first group of sites are the maritime and waterfront installations that were involved in navigation and shipping across the lake, and the second group of sites display evidence for water management, for both domestic and agricultural purposes.

7.2 Waterfront installations

7.2.1 Harbours

The first category of waterfront installations constitutes substantial harbour complexes. Only two sites in the region fit this description but were not studied as part of the Lake Mareotis Research Project: Marea/Philoxenité and Taposiris Magna. The complexity and magnitude of these waterfront structures are not represented or certainly no longer visible elsewhere in the entire Mareotic region (see Chapter 2). The two harbours however, date to quite different periods; Taposiris Magna is essentially Hellenistic in date, while Marea mostly dates to the Late Roman period. They are both also associated with relatively large towns and much historical and archaeological evidence indicates that these two towns were probably amongst the largest and most active along the shores of Lake Mareotis in antiquity.

7.2.2 Jetties

The second type of waterfront site that was recorded along the shores of the western Mareotic Arm consists of different types of anchorage facilities such as quays and jetties, which form the majority of maritime installations in the region. More than ten, and possibly as many as 20, different anchorage facilities were recorded on the northern and southern shores of the lake and on the northern shore of Mareotis Island (Fig. 7.1). Possibly the most substantial of them is a *kibotos* or box-shaped harbour (Site 09) (see Chapter 6). With the exception of this square harbour on the southern shore of the lake, all the other anchorage facilities along the shores of the lake take the form of jetties that extend into the water perpendicular to the shore. The technique used in the construction of most of the jetties was to build two parallel single or double breadth piers of limestone and fill the space between them with rubble. With the exception of the significant harbour structures at Marea and Taposiris Magna, the three sites with the most substantial jetty structures are located on the northern shore of the lake opposite Mareotis Island, Sites 204-205 (Al-Gamal) and 207-208 (Al-Quseir), and on the northern shore of the island Site 23. A number of other jetties, although not as substantial and in some cases not securely dated (see Chapter 6), are recorded along the southern shore of the lake and the northern shore of Mareotis Island. It is assumed that these jetties were also used to help facilitate the shipment of Mareotic products and transport of people around the lake. During the course of the Lake Mareotis Research Project survey, it became apparent that the anchorage facilities along the northern shore of the lake, particularly east of Taposiris Magna, were largely associated with civic and residential sites, which showed little evidence for economic activities, while those along the southern shore of the lake and on Mareotis Island also have association with commercial and industrial activities.

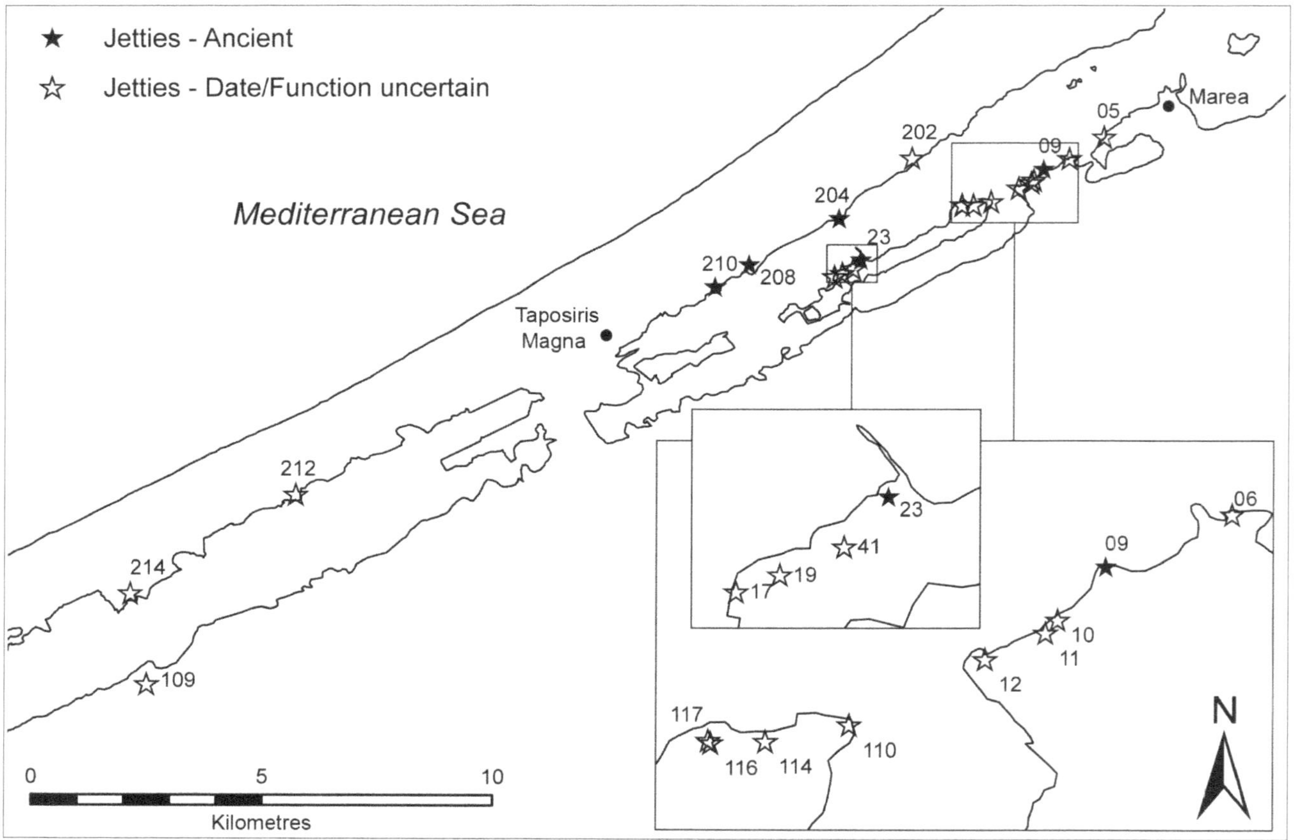

Fig. 7.1. Location of sites with jetties around the shores of Lake Mareotis.

Fig. 7.2. Location of sites with lake walls around the shores of Lake Mareotis.

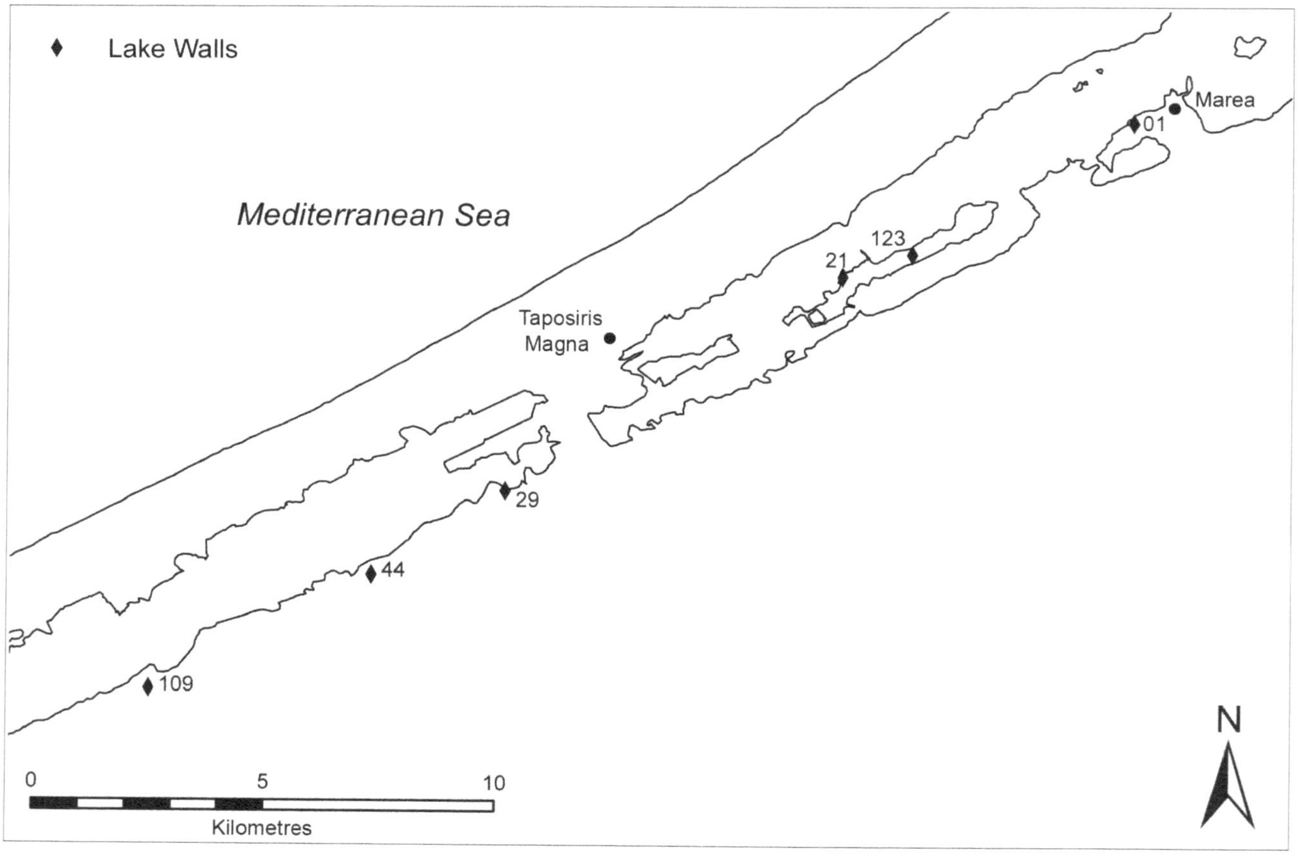

7.2.3 Lake walls

The third type of maritime installation that was found in the region can be described as a sea or, more accurately, a lake wall. Unlike the jetties that extend perpendicular to the shore, lake walls are invariably constructed parallel to the shore and were presumably intended, at least in one capacity, to define the shores and protect them from the effects of silting and sedimentation. Possibly as many as six lake walls were discovered in the survey region (Fig. 7.2). These kinds of structures are mainly found along the southern shore of the lake and the northern shore of Mareotis Island, whose shorelines are more vulnerable to silting and the deposition of sediments as a result of the prevailing north-westerly winds that carry sediment from the coastal ridges across and into the lake. Besides acting as a form of protection against silting, the lake walls could also have been utilised as docking facilities or quays for merchant vessels. Another possible function for such structures was to retain rainwater in their lee for agricultural purposes, perhaps the cultivation of reeds as is still witnessed in the region and elsewhere in North Africa today (Bonvallot 1986; Schiettecatte, *et al.* 2005; see Chapter 5). The longest of these lake walls, some 250m in length, is located at Site 21 on the northern shore at the western end of Mareotis Island.

7.2.4 Shoreline structures

The fourth and final type of coastal structures are multi-roomed buildings that are located at the present waterline and, in some cases, platform-like structures that appear to extend into the water. Examples of this type of structure are found at Sites 117, 118 and 119 all located at the north-eastern shore of the island. These buildings probably functioned as storage facilities and warehouses for different commodities that were traded across the lake, either local products or imports. By examining the remains of these structures, particularly on Maerotis Island, it is evident that they had undergone different phases of construction. Moreover, it seems that the sections of the structures closest to the waterline were subject to the effect of accumulated sediments, and hence had to be rebuilt. In other words, the different phases of building and modification of these structures could be the result of adapting to physical changes to the waterline over time (e.g. Site 118).

7.3 Water management systems

The second group of sites is associated with water management and the utilisation of the lake for domestic and agricultural purposes. These sites included a range of different structures including evidence for *sakkias* (water-wheels) and *sakkia* pots for lifting water (Fig. 7.3), cisterns for storing water and wells for accessing ground water (Fig. 7.4). However, such sites varied in their nature and location along the shores of the lake. For example, the sites that contained evidence for *sakkias* include Site 02 where the *sakkia* was used for lifting water from a well into a large basin that probably belonged to a bath complex. Sites 106, 104-105, 44 and 22 also contain evidence for *sakkias*,

Fig. 7.3. Location of sites with sakkias *around the shores of Lake Mareotis.*

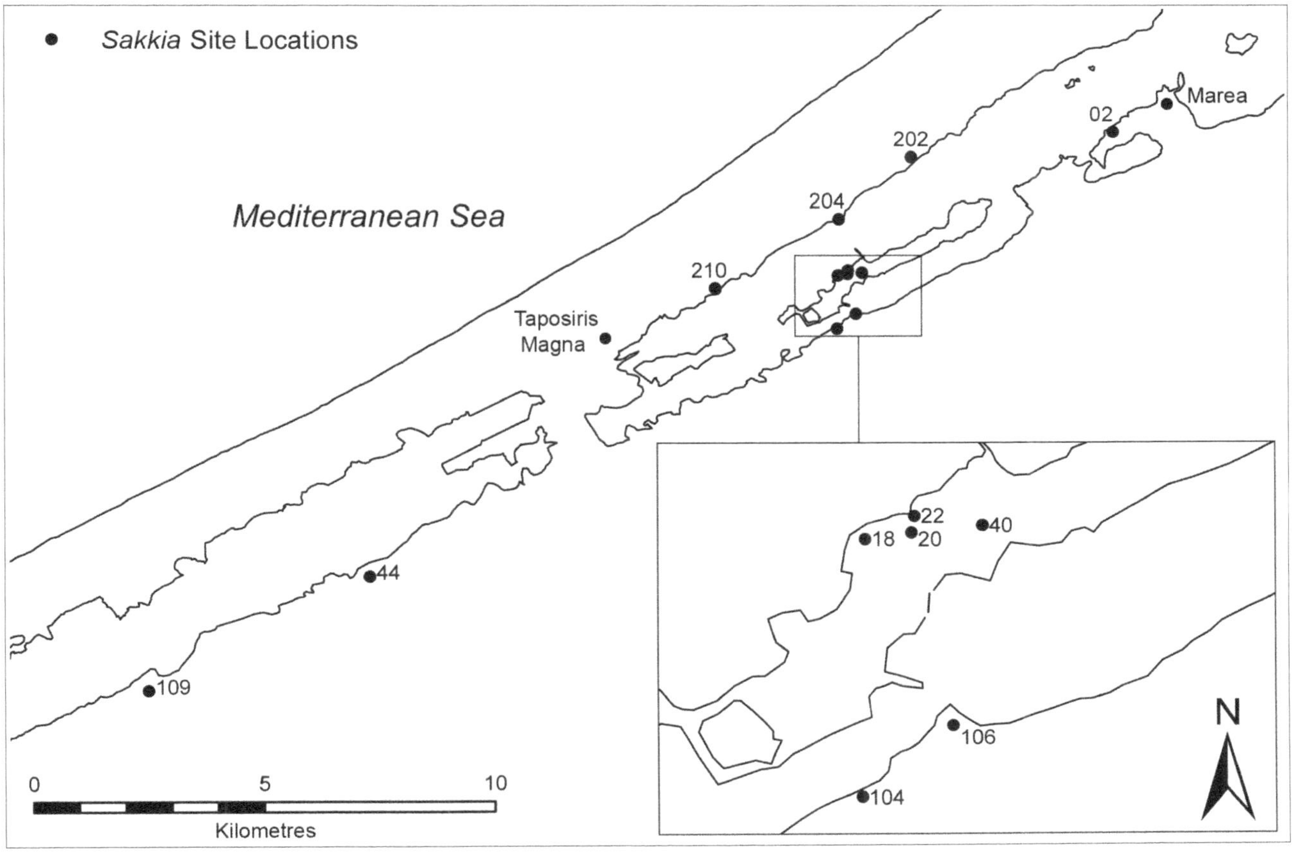

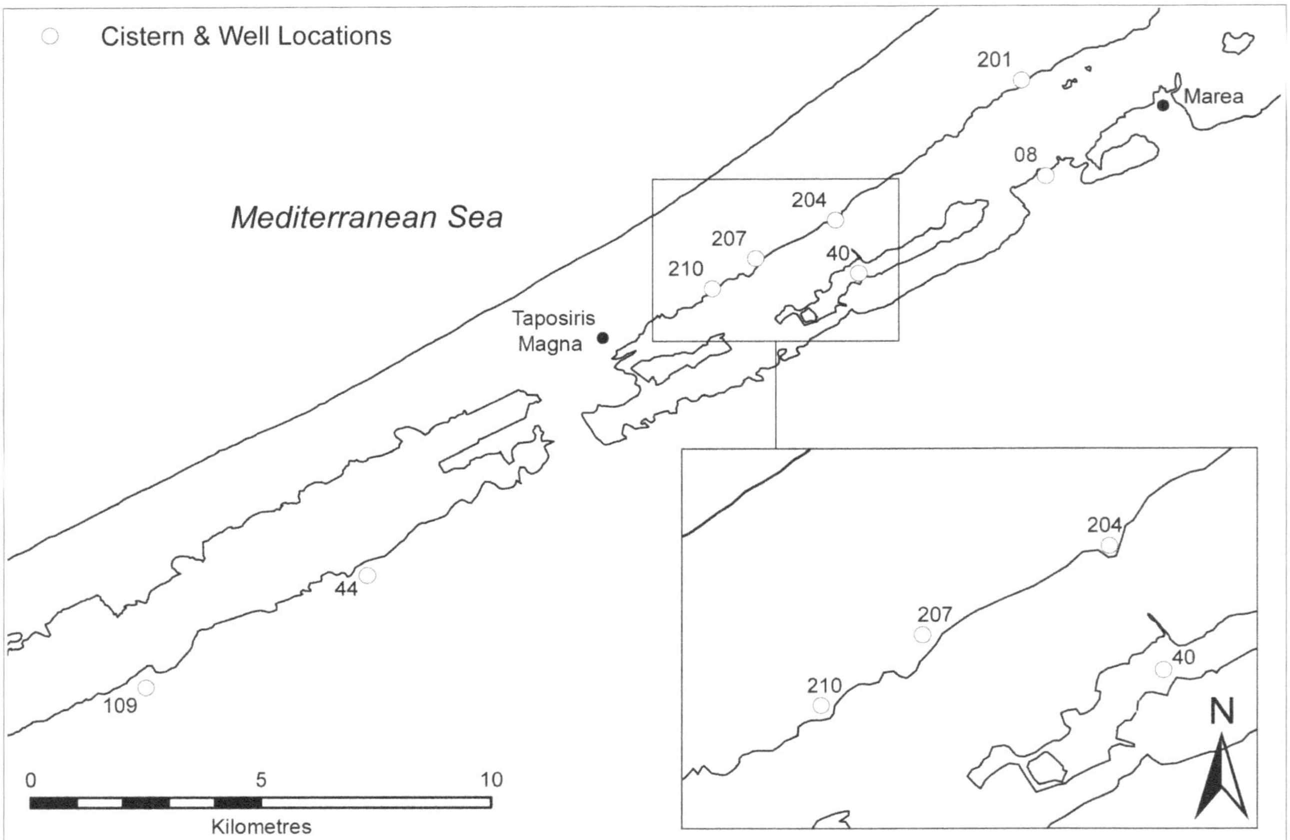

Fig. 7.4. Location of sites with cisterns and wells around the shores of Lake Mareotis.

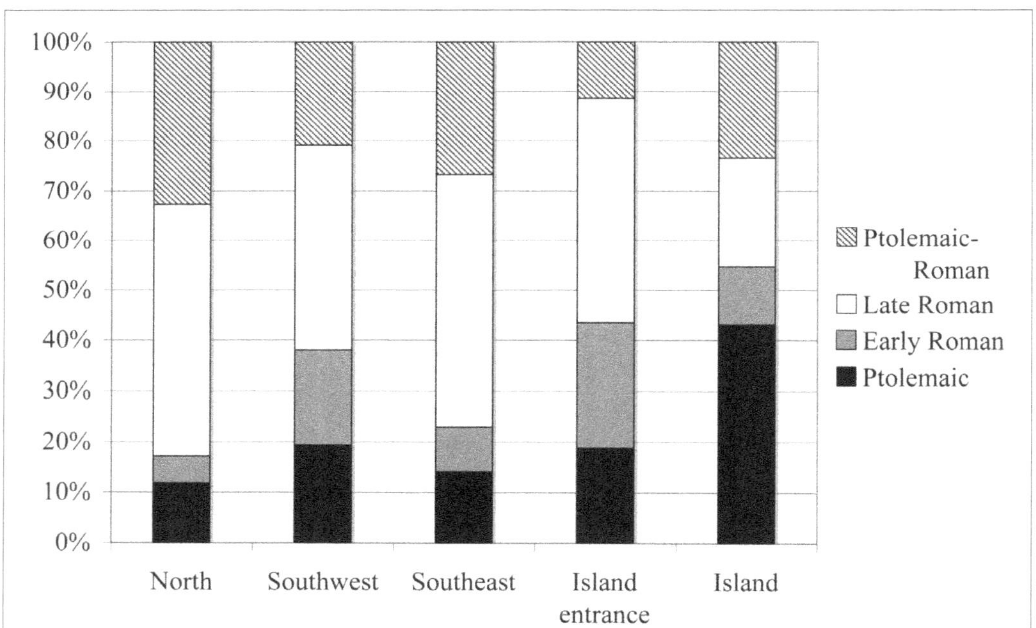

Fig. 7.5. Dated distribution of ceramics by period across the Lake Mareotis survey region.

however, in these cases they were probably used for lifting water for irrigation. On the other hand, the *sakkia* at Site 40 is quite unique in its location as well as its use. Its location on top of a headland more than 7m above the present lake level, is unparalleled in the region. The *sakkia* is connected to a channel that leads to what appears to be a bath complex (see Chapter 6). It should be noted that the majority of *sakkia* were located either on the southern shore of the lake or on the northern shore of Mareotis Island. Significantly, the presence of identifiable *sakkia* features and *sakkia* pots is only correlated in some, and not all, instances.

In addition to the *sakkia* found at a number of sites, cisterns and wells were identified on both shores of the lake, such as at Sites 08, 109, 201, 210, 44, 204 and 40 (see Fig. 7.4). However, it must be noted that cisterns and wells have different functions. Cisterns are used for storing water obtained from another source, such as rain water, or lake water lifted by *sakkias*, which is usually carried into the cistern through stone water channels. Wells, on the other hand, are dug in order to access ground water in areas where other sources of water are not accessible or not suitable for the specific required use. In antiquity, as today due to its proximity to the sea, water in the western Mareotis Arm was affected by saltwater seepage and hence was brackish and possibly undrinkable, which explains the existence of numerous wells as a means of obtaining fresh ground water for domestic purposes. According to De Cosson (1935: 100-5) wells and cisterns were prolific here in antiquity and they were found spread throughout the Mareotis region.

7.4 General observations

(with assistance from R. Tomber & R. Thomas)

The observations made above demonstrate the potential for the region to illuminate more detailed interpretation of the settlements and activities around the shores of Lake Mareotis in antiquity. They also highlight how much more fine-grained insight could be acquired with further investigation. This is beyond the reach of this enquiry; as the project's primary focus was afterall survey not excavation, which would clearly afford a more nuanced appreciation of past activities. However, by looking at the distribution of archaeological sites in general and those associated with activities relating to the lake in particular, a number of observations can be made.

There appears to be a concentration of sites in the area between Marea and Taposiris Magna, a distance of some 15km, while only a few sites, although quite substantial in size, were recorded at the far western end of the lake. It is also noticeable that there is a distinction in function, size, and to a certain extent, date, between sites located on the northern shores of the western Mareotic Arm of the lake and those to the south. To understand better the chronological distribution of the sites, the ceramics relating to the main areas are displayed both by period (Fig. 7.5) and by date (Fig. 7.6).

The region is broadly divided into the northern and southern lake shores. The southern shore is divided into four distinct units: settlements to the east are believed to have been associated with Marea (this is partly based on their physical location (see Chapter 5 and below) and their ceramic assemblage (see Chapter 4 and Fig. 7.5); Mareotis Island has a substantial number of sites and appears to have operated somewhat independently to the rest of the southern shore settlements; although sites located on the approaches to the island were associated with the island; and finally, sites to the west were geographically distinct from others along the south shore (see below).

Those sites identified on the northern shore date from the Hellenistic to Late Roman periods with a concentration of activity in the Late Roman period (Figs 7.5 & 7.6). They were primarily tell sites and their size ranged from c. 7,000 to 180,000 sqm. The ceramic assemblages at these sites included a mixture of amphorae, finewares, table wares and cooking wares, with less amphorae than is seen elsewhere in the survey region (Fig. 7.7). Finewares and amphorae include imports, with the earlier material originating largely from the Aegean region and later material from the eastern Mediterranean (Fig. 7.8) (see Chapter 4).The Lake Mareotis Research Project did not identify any amphora production sites on the north coast (Fig. 7.9).

As noted, many of the sites located on the northern shore contained wells and cisterns as well as evidence for mor-

Fig. 7.6. Distribution of ceramics through time across the Lake Mareotis survey region.

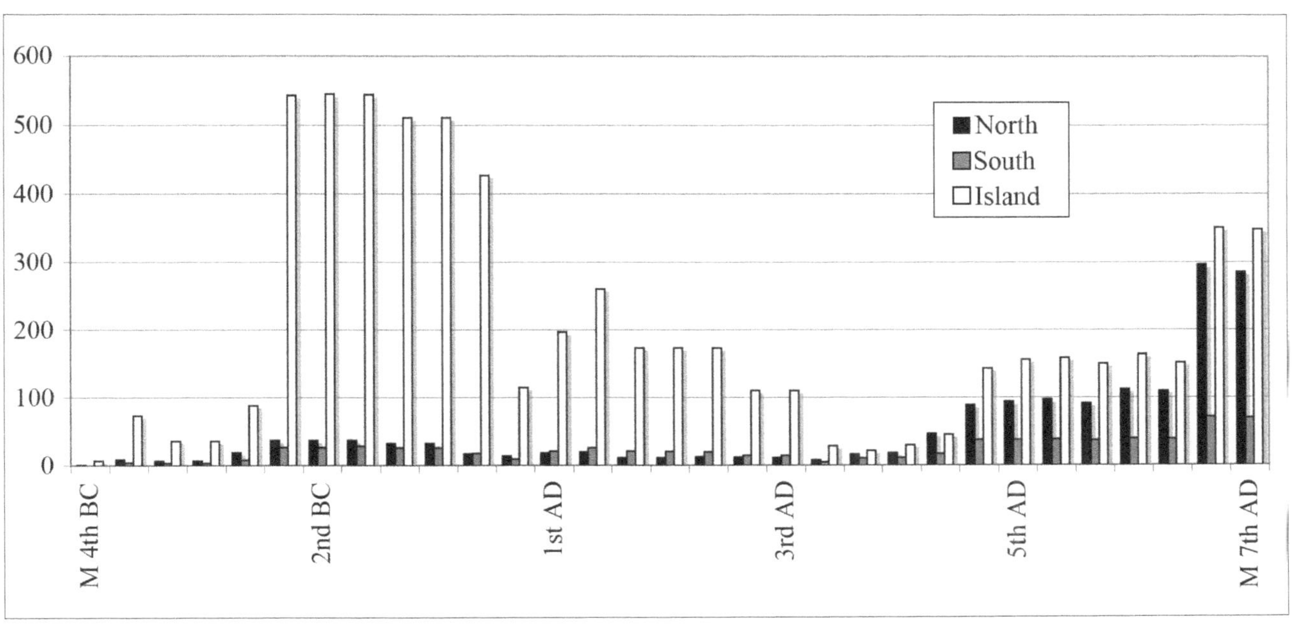

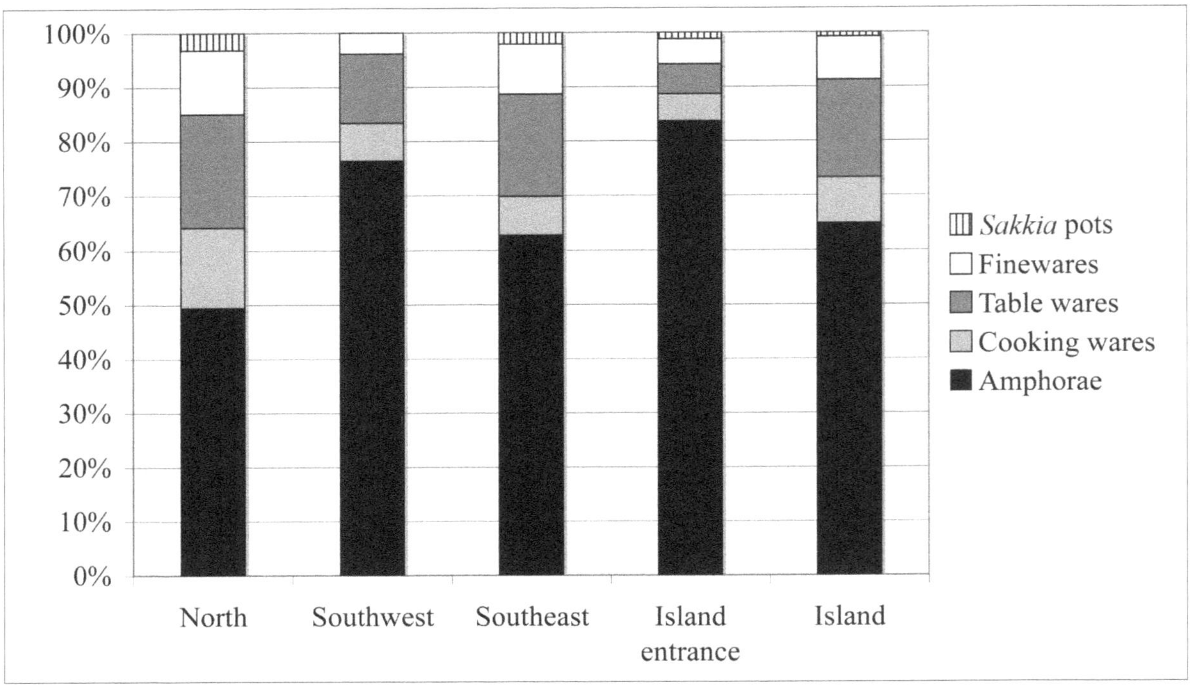

Fig. 7.7. Distribution of ceramic form types across the Lake Mareotis survey region.

Fig. 7.8. Distribution of imported ceramic source regions across the Lake Mareotis survey region.

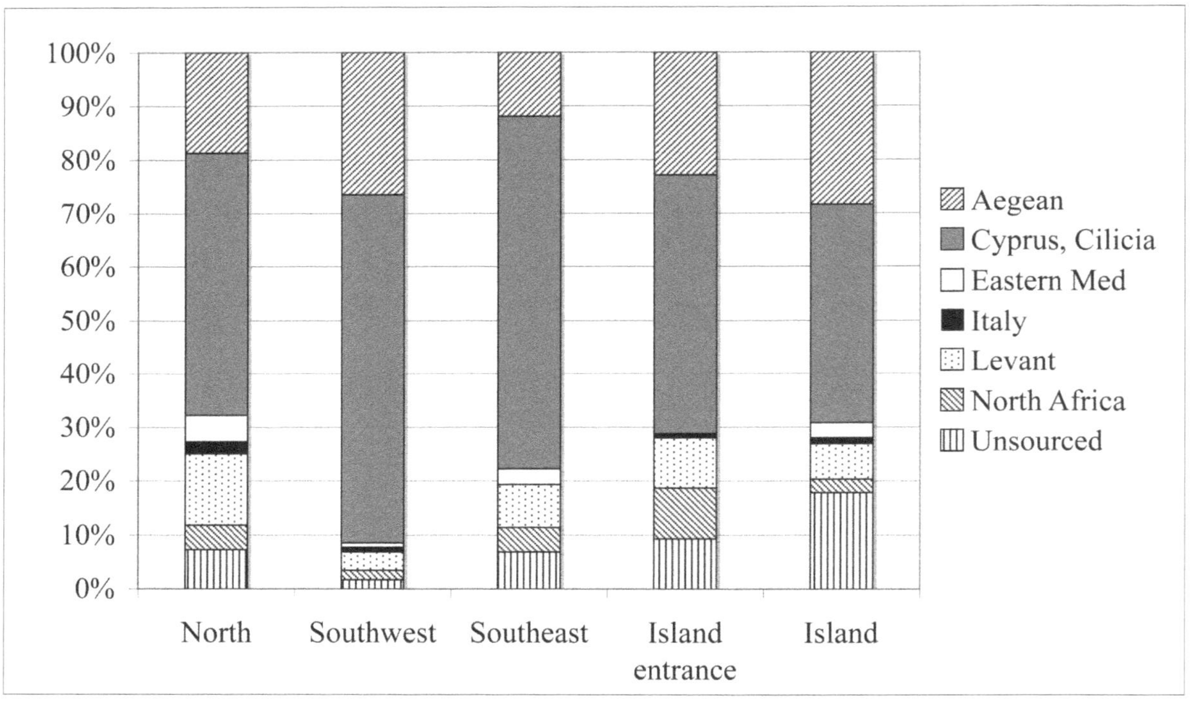

tar-lined basins, probably from bath complexes (Figs 7.10, 7.4). However, there is limited evidence for irrigation in the form of *sakkias* or water-wheels, thus suggesting that these sites did not require large volumes of water for irrigation as due to their location on the coastal ridge, a short distance from the sea to the north and the lake to the south, they lacked space for extensive arable land (see Fig. 7.3; see also Fig. 7.7 although it shows a larger proportion of *sakkia* pots in the north relative to the other areas in the survey region, it actually represents a smaller number of *sakkia* pots when compared to the total assemblages in the other areas. This could reflect sample size, sample strategy or site date (see Chapters 4 and 6). Each site was a contained and distinct unit, often densely occupied. The north shore sites are believed to be civic and residential in nature, as supported by their functionally diverse ceramic assemblages (Fig. 7.7). Many sites had direct association with the waterfront, and a number supported jetties (see Fig.

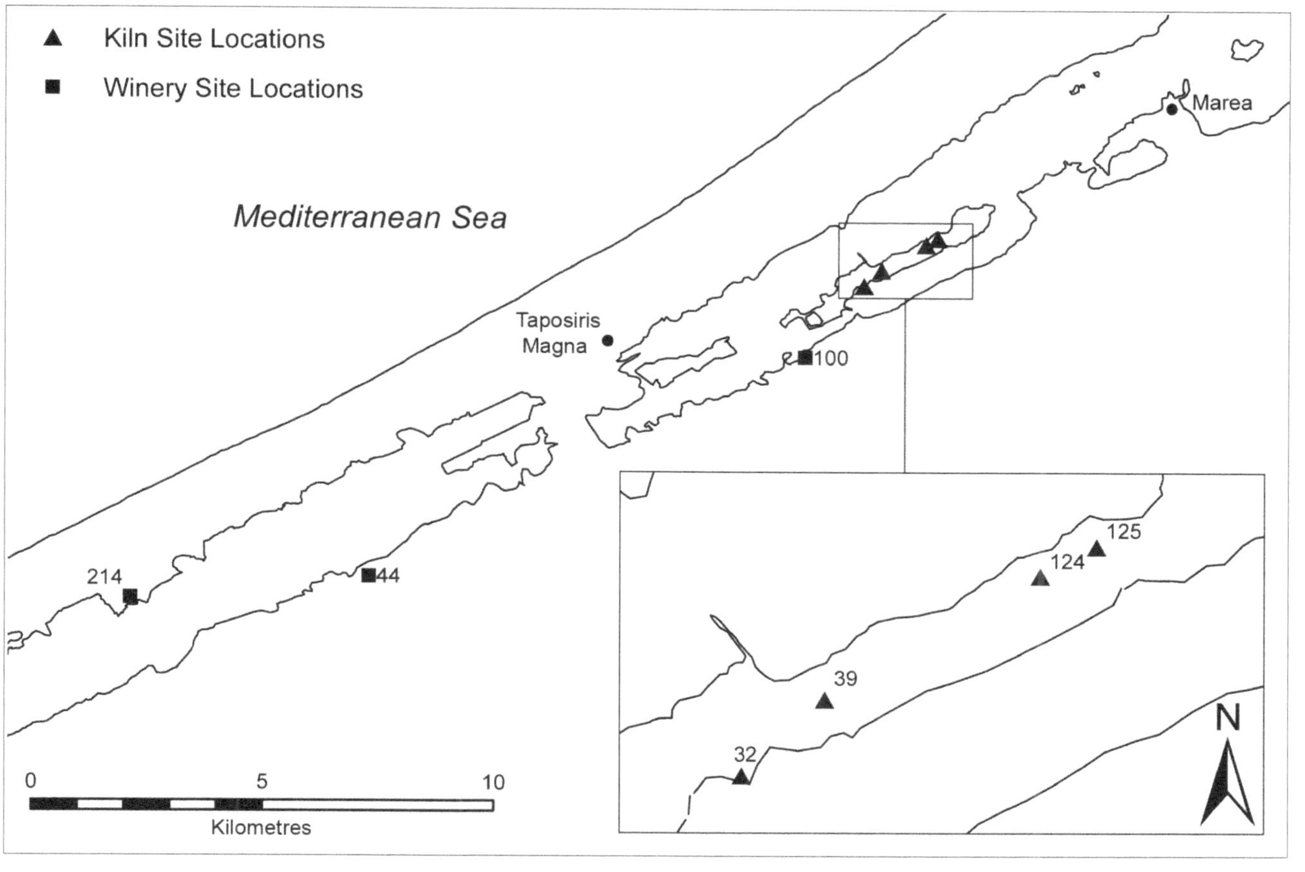

Fig. 7.9. Location of sites with kilns and/or wineries around the shores of Lake Mareotis.

Fig. 7.10. Location of sites with lined basins around the shores of Lake Mareotis.

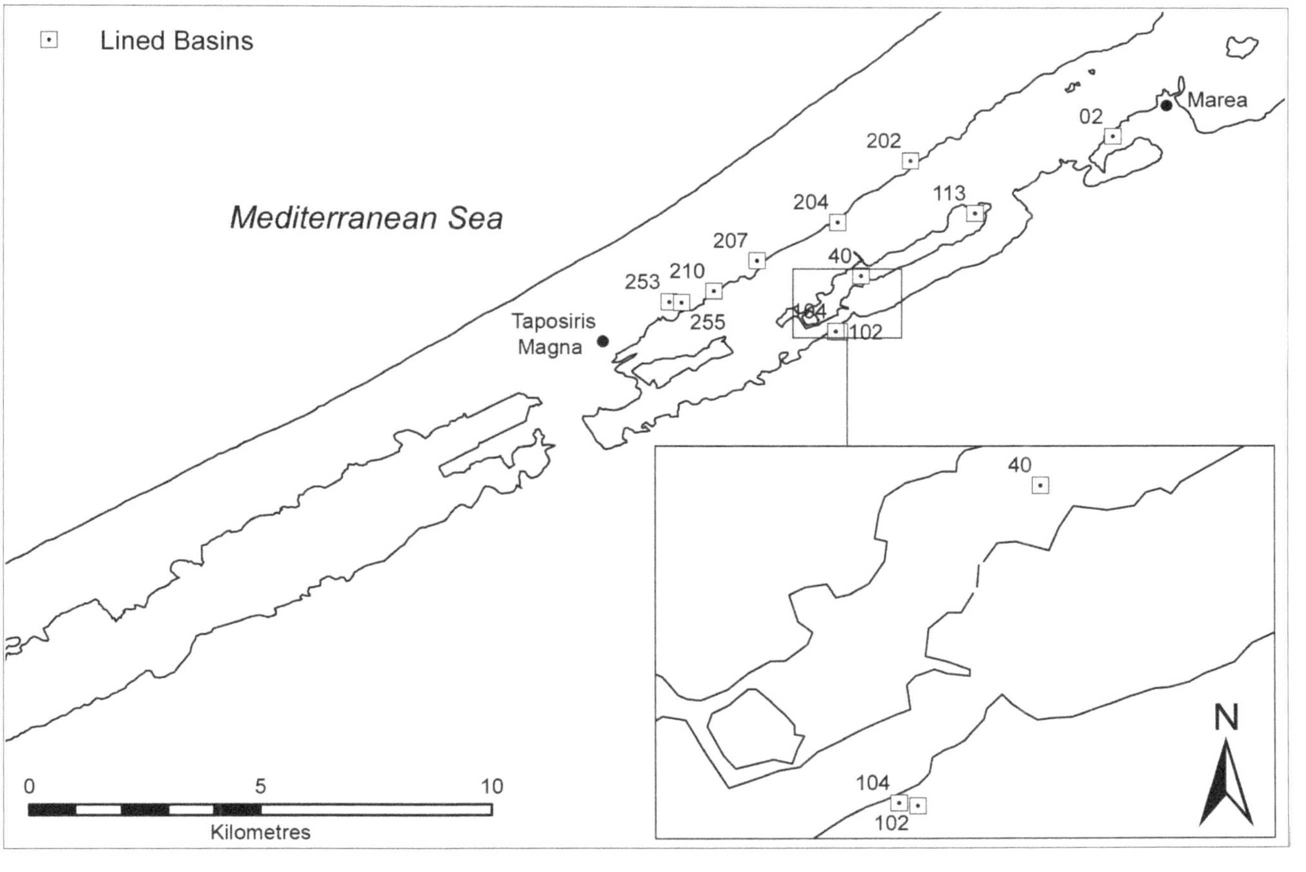

7.1). Spatial and functional relationships between specific sites on the northern shore and sites on the island and the southern shore were also observed. For example, one of the largest sites on the northern shore of the lake (Site 204-205) is situated immediately opposite a settlement located at the western end of the island (Site 23), with jetties extending from both sites across the lake towards each other. The distance between the two sites represents the narrowest gap between the north and south shores anywhere along the western Mareotic Arm, extending some 550m distance (see Chapter 6 for details). In addition, the two sites would appear to date to approximately a similar period, both being Late Roman in date, although the assemblage at Site 23 is very small. The apparent connection between these sites may be associated with controlling vessel movement across the lake.

On the southern shore, sites located to the west formed distinct, and in some cases (Site 44 and Site 109), quite substantial units, and are spaced well apart. To the east, sites were located on a limestone ridge that effectively forms an extension of the ridge upon which both Mareotis Island and the site of Marea are situated. This ridge extends for approximately 9km E-W and is located at a distance of c. 800m from the present southern shoreline of the lake. Arguably, these sites, although less substantial in scale, reflect similar dates and activities to Marea (see Chapter 2), perhaps suggesting a possible extension of the site of Marea along the ridge to the west. Those sites closest to Marea (Sites 01-05), which lies just a short distance to the east, contained wine production facilities and/or *sakkias*.

Two sites, both located on the southern shore, stand out as exceptions to the others noted along the southern shores; the *kibotos* (the square-shaped harbour) (Site 09), and the 'complex building' (Site 13). It has been proposed that both these buildings date to the Pharaonic period (Haggag 1984: 277-80). With the exception of a few ceramics previously identified in the region by El-Fakharani (El-Fakharani 1983: 176-8), no Pharaonic material has been identified at any of the sites recorded in the survey area. However, these buildings might help resolve the mystery of the so far elusive harbour of Marea which was known to have been an important town in Pharaonic times (Fraser 1972: 146; El-Fakharani 1983: 176).

Essentially, sites on the southern shore, although also exhibiting urban concentrations, were more commonly associated with industrial, commercial and agricultural activities than those sites located on the north shore.

Sites located on Mareotis Island were largely concentrated on the limestone ridge particularly at the western and eastern extremes of the island. Fig. 7.5 indicates that the island had more Hellenistic material than any other area particularly towards the eastern end. This is mirrored in Fig. 7.6, which also shows an additional, but less substantial, double peak of activity in the Early and Late Roman periods; Late Roman material is particularly notable towards the western end of the island. The ceramic assemblages indicate some imported material (Fig. 7.11), but in general the ceramic assemblage was locally produced, particularly the amphorae. The nature of the structures, with the exception of the centrally located industrial-scale Ptolemaic and Early Roman amphora kiln sites, which follow a practice of locating industrial activities outside the main settlements (Rodziewicz 1988, 1990, 1995), is essentially urban in character. The scale of the buildings, particular-

Fig. 7.11. Distribution of ceramic fabric types across the Lake Mareotis survey region.

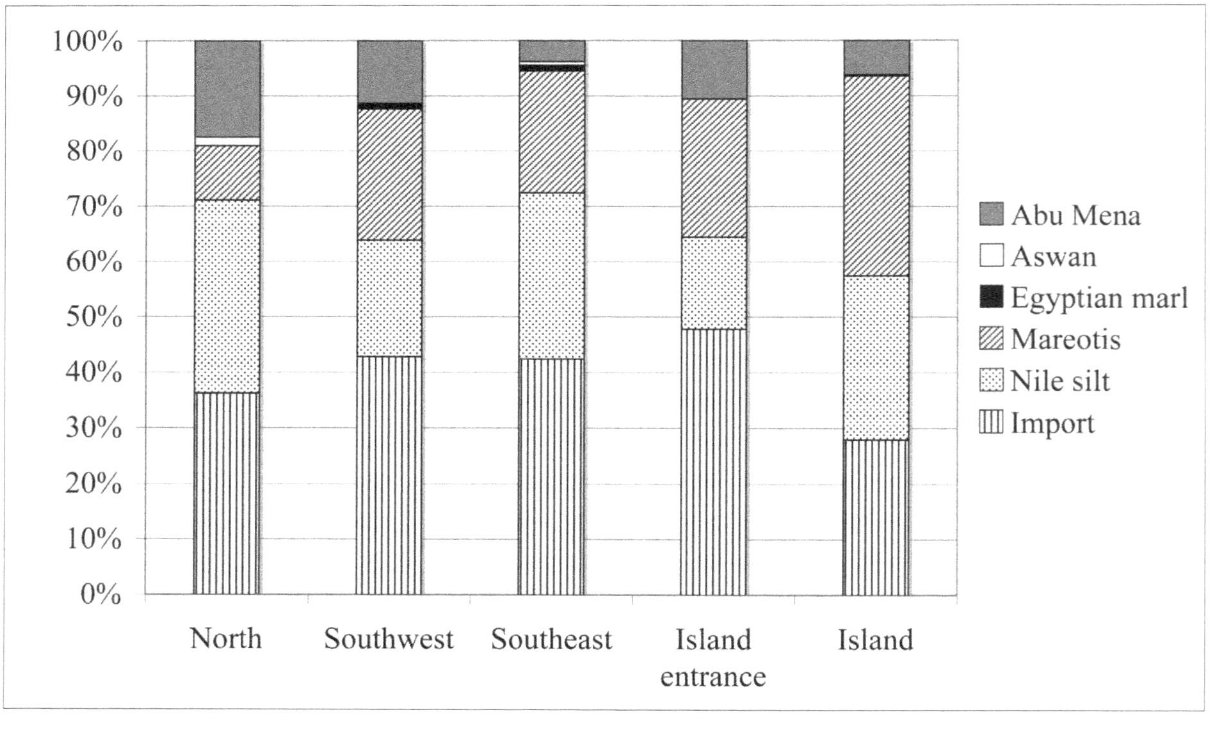

ly those located on the ridge to the east, is extensive and often densely packed, and many are associated with numerous waterfront structures, including a series of jetties and platforms (see Fig. 7.1), possible warehouses and a small inlet embayment, that are all located along the plain on the north-eastern shore. Besides Taposiris Magna, the eastern end of the island appears to have been one of the most densely occupied areas of the western Mareotic Arm during the Hellenistic period. At the western end of the island, the settlement extends north from the ridge over a flat plain. Whereas the ridge supports further urban structures, the plain to the north appears to be more agriculturally orientated, with features that include possible lake walls and *sakkias* (see Figs 7.2 & 7.3). As noted in Chapter 5, the area between the southern shore of the lake and the island ridge that extends as far east as the Marea Peninsula, was a low, marshy area in antiquity and as such, access between the southern shore of the lake and the island, was considerably restricted, possibly explaining why very few sites were located there.

Overall, the settlements on the southern shores including the island were occupied during similar periods to the sites located on the northern shore, however, with more extensive Ptolemaic and Early Roman material present in the south (Figs 7.5 & 7.6). In the early period, pottery forms are represented by domestic and industrial wares, particularly as a result of amphora production on the island, which dominate the combined assemblages (Fig. 7.7). In the Early Roman period amphora production continues but domestic material is less prolific. The production of amphorae appears to have halted after the 3rd century AD whilst there is an increase in wares representative of domestic activities, which includes a high proportion of Late Roman imports from Cyprus/Cilicia, especially finewares (Fig. 7.8). In addition, it was noted that imported material from throughout the entire survey region was evident during the Hellenistic period, largely amphorae from the south-eastern Aegean region, particularly the Dodecanese Islands of Kos and Rhodes and Knidos on the Datça Peninsula. Likewise, the Late Roman period assemblages contained large quantities of imported pottery from around the eastern Mediterranean, but mostly from Cyprus/Cilicia.

Finally, it is interesting to note that almost all the amphora and wine production sites in the region, as well as the ancient *sakkia* installations (De Cosson 1935; Empereur & Picon 1998; Rodziewicz 1998b), were located on the southern shore of the lake or on Mareotis Island, the focus of agricultural and industrial activities in the region (see Figs 7.3 & 7.9). The reason that agricultural and industrial activities were concentrated on the southern shores of the Mareotic Arm is mainly due to the character of this fertile plain that comprised stretches of flat arable land. In antiquity this area would have supported and enabled agricultural activities to flourish and as such was known for the quality of its vines, olives and fruits, as well as for the cultivation of flax and papyrus (Athenaeus 1.33.d-e; Pliny 13.22.71; Strabo 17.1.14; Empereur & Picon 1998; Horden & Purcell 2002: 353; McGovern 2003: 121-3). Yet despite the enhanced appreciation of the archaeology of the region that the Lake Mareotis Research Project has provided, it is still unclear as to the actual scale of agricultural activities in the area. Was the agricultural hinterland along the shores of the western Mareotic Arm large enough to meet the demands of Alexandria? Do our sites represent large villas with agricultural land or fully functioning estates that were established as part of the Romanisation of economic practice? The spatial and temporal relationship between the sites would infer the latter but without further more in depth investigation of the sites, these questions remain unanswered. What is evident however, is that the abundance of calcareous clay, particularly suitable for amphora production, resulted in a thriving large-scale amphora industry along the southern shore of the lake (Empereur & Picon 1986: 103-9; Empereur & Picon 1992; Empereur & Picon 1998; Rodziewicz 1998b).

7.5 Pottery kilns and amphora production

(with assistance R. Tomber)

For supplying a large city like Alexandria with its needs of wine, beer and oil, great quantities of amphorae must have been produced in the Mareotic region. Thus, as was the case in other places in the Greco-Roman world, wine-producing estates in the Mareotic region were also involved in large-scale amphora production – a fact that has left plenty of evidence in the archaeological record (Rathbone 1991: 304; Empereur & Picon 1992: 147; Wendrich, *et al.* 2003: 72). Several examples of kiln sites from the Hellenistic and Roman periods have been identified in the Mareotic region, although they surely represent a small fraction of the many that once existed. Most kiln sites are identified by mounds of amphora refuse that were rejected due to misfiring or other defects that occurred during the manufacturing process; however, on rare occasions, the actual kilns survive. The recent discovery of a kiln beneath the basilica at Marea would be once such example (Szymań-ska & Babraj 2004).

During the 1970s and 1980s Empereur and Picon (1986: 103-9, 1992, 1998) identified a series of 28 amphora production sites in an area of about 30km in extent, from Al-Amreya, c. 20km southwest of Alexandria, to Taposiris Magna. Most of the amphora kiln sites were located east of Marea, while only three sites were reported in the area from Marea to Taposiris Magna. The recorded sites were in the form of hills comprised mainly of layers of broken amphorae, in some cases as large as 50m across and 20m high, many associated with extensive traces of burning. The sites ranged in date from the 2nd century BC to the 6th century AD; however, the majority of them, about 17 sites, were producing amphorae between the 1st and 3rd centuries AD (Empereur & Picon 1998).

The remains of two excavated amphora kilns were both associated with large amounts of refuse. The first one is at Al-Amreya (Abd El-Fattah 1998), while the other one was excavated at Taposiris Magna (El-Ashmawi 1998). In both cases, the structure of the kilns was similar. They were round structures made of burned bricks, and each kiln consisted of two chambers, the lower one being the firing chamber and the upper one the pottery chamber; the two chambers being separated from each other by a gridded floor. The holes in the floor enabled hot air to pass from the lower chamber, where the fuel was burned, to the upper chamber where the amphorae were stacked to be fired; therefore, the upper chamber was probably roofed to trap the heat, however, no traces of the roofs were visible (Peacock & Williams 1991: 47-8; Sciallano & Sibella 1994: 13; Abd El-Fattah 1998: 43-6; El-Ashmawi 1998: 58). The first kiln, at Al-Amreya, dates to the 2nd – 3rd centuries AD and it measures c. 6m in diameter, whereas the kiln at Taposiris Magna dates to the 1st – 3rd centuries and measures c. 10m in diameter with its fire chamber about 2m high (Empereur & Picon 1992: 145-6; Empereur 1993: 41).

The recent survey conducted by the Lake Mareotis Research Project has added to the work conducted by Empereur and Picon (1986, 1992, 1998) and has recorded evidence for at least four large amphora production sites on Mareotis Island (Sites 125, 124, 39, 32), including evidence of at least three kilns (Sites 124, 39, 32) (see Fig. 7.9). The kiln identified at Site 32 was in particularly good condition and comparable to the one that was recorded at Taposiris Magna. With a diameter of just over 12m, it is considered to be one of the largest amphora kilns that survives from antiquity in the Mediterranean (Empereur & Picon 1992: 146; Empereur 1993: 41)

It is worth mentioning that the study of the amphora production sites revealed that some sites were active during the Hellenistic period (Sites 125, 39), while others were mainly active in the Early Roman period (Sites 124, 32). It was also noticeable that all the kilns and the amphora production sites recorded in the region, either by Empereur and Picon or by the Lake Mareotis Research Project, including the one associated with Taposiris Magna, were located along the southern shore of the Mareotic Arm or on Mareotis Island. The main reason for this is the availability of clay that was used for the manufacture of the amphorae, while clay beds seem completely absent from the northern shore of the lake due to the proximity to the coastal ridge. Conversely, the kiln sites were generally located very close to the lake's shore which would have helped facilitate the transport of their products to Alexandria and beyond. Thus, as mentioned previously, the production of amphorae in the Mareotic region was linked to the production of wine, which predominantly took place also along the southern shores of the lake, where flat, fertile land was located (Rodziewicz 1998b) (see Fig. 7.9).

The abundance of wine and amphora production in the Mareotic region demonstrates that the shores of Lake Mareotis were important industrial centres in Hellenistic and Roman Egypt, at least in the service of Alexandria. The results from the Lake Mareotis Research Project further highlight how significant a production centre this area was, perhaps more so than previously realised, and that a substantial investment was made into the infrastructure of the region. It also indicates what an important contribution this region made to the industrial life of Egypt, and at the same time raises questions as to the scale of production, the distribution mechanisms, and the markets operating in the region. A comparison between ceramic finds in the Lake Mareotis region with material recovered from and imported to Alexandria, serves to highlight the nature of the relationship between the two areas and the broader region.

7.6 Comparison of Lake Mareotis and Alexandrian ceramic assemblages (R. Tomber)

Here the amphora assemblages, which reflect on local agricultural activity, consumption and importation from Alexandria and Mareotis, are compared. Syntheses of the Alexandrian patterns are best laid out by Senol (2007) and Majcherek (2004). Future analysis of this material would also benefit from comparisons with material from the broader Western Delta region.

The Lake Mareotis Research Project Ptolemaic pottery assemblage is similar to assemblages from Alexandria in terms of imports, with Aegean examples dominating. At Alexandria imports occur in decreasing quantity as Rhodian, Knidian and to a lesser extent Koan. These three main types occur in the same order of frequency in Lake Mareotis, occurring as 5.7% Rhodian, 4.9% Knidian and 2.5% Koan fabric of the total amphora assemblage. They follow the same pattern when calculated as a percentage of the Ptolemaic amphora assemblage, respectively 12%, 10.5% and 5.3%. In excavated deposits from Alexandria, Rhodian vessels are concentrated in deposits between the 4th – 1st centuries BC; Knidian between the late 4th to the first half of the 3rd centuries BC, and Koan after the second half of the 2nd century BC (Senol 2007: 62-3). The Alexandrian deposits clearly provide tighter dating than those from the Lake Mareotis Research Project surface collections, and indicate an earlier wave of Rhodian material than the Lake Mareotis material, which seems to commence during the late 3rd century BC. This difference however, may result from the greater control of the Alexandrian excavated contexts, ours being mostly represented by handles that are less chronologically sensitive than more complete vessels. (please see the introduction to Chapter 6).

Overall there is a notable lack of AE2, AE4 and especially AE1 in Alexandrian contexts (Senol 2007: 61, diagram 2). It was not possible to positively identify AE1 from the Mareotis sites but AE1/2 (27.6% of all amphorae and 58.7% of all Ptolemaic amphorae) and AE4 were common not only at the production sites but also at associated sites. AE4 accounts for 9.5% of all amphorae and 44.9% of Early Roman amphorae. This raises the question of a market for these vessels. Mareotis products can be identified elsewhere in Egypt, particularly AE4 which have a wide, but thin distribution both to the West, exported via Alexandria, and from the Red Sea East as far as India and south to Kushite Sudan.

Apart from AE4, and in smaller quantities, AE3, Early Roman amphora types are not common in the Mareotis survey material and it is difficult to generalise about them.

Cilician types are reported from both Mareotis and Alexandria, including Pompeii V, Agora M 54 and Dressel 2-4; equally Campanian Dressel 2-4 vessels are rare in both areas. The biggest difference seems to be the popularity of Cretan amphora forms in Alexandria (Senol 2007: 63-4) which appear to be absent from the Lake Mareotis region.

A series of excavated Late Roman ceramic horizons from Alexandria that date between the mid 5th and the late 7th centuries AD each contain predominantly LR Amphora 4 from Gaza, and in lesser quantities, the Cilician/Cypriot LR Amphora 1 (Majcherek 2004). This is in contrast to the Lake Mareotis assemblages, where as a proportion of the total amphora assemblage LR Amphora 1 (17.9%) is the most common, followed by LR Amphora 5 from Abu Menas (10.6%), with LR Amphora 4 (3.1%) a poor third (similarly as a proportion of the Late Roman amphora assemblage they rank in the same order at 53%, 31.6% and 9.3%). The small numbers of the Abu Mena LR Amphora 5 from Alexandria is analogous to the situation with Mareotic products during the Early Roman period.

Preliminary information on pottery from Schedia promises some parallels with the Mareotis material, for example during the early period AE4 is well represented, with LR Amphora 1 and LR Amphora 4 notable during the late period (Martin 2008).

Imported pottery is sometimes used as a measure to gauge economic activity or prosperity. In Fig. 7.11 imports comprise between c. 28% and 48% of the Mareotic assemblages from different locations, with the smallest quantity from the island, where kiln sites are identified, and the largest from the island entrance. It therefore seems that here local production and perhaps more importantly site function, has the largest effect on the quantity of imports.

However, the question still remains: to which destinations were the large numbers of ceramics, clearly being produced in the Lake Mareotis region, being transported? The evidence suggests that while there are comparisons with Alexandrian patterns, the majority of material is not ending up in Alexandria, and although we have evidence for its wider distribution throughout Egypt, the quantities are small in comparison to the scale of production. Schedia provides an exception and it would appear that much of the Mareotic material is being shipped through here to the rest of Egypt (Martin 2008). The ceramic data collected from the Lake Mareotis Research Project have begun to raise such questions, while further quantified data from the region should begin to elucidate some answers, and also allow for a more informed understanding of the mechanisms of transportation of their products and their containers.

7.7 Lake Mareotis transportation systems in the service of Alexandria

When Strabo (17.1.7) speaks about the water supply for Lake Mareotis, he mentions that it is "...filled by many canals from the Nile, both from above and on the sides, and through these canals the imports are much larger than those from the sea, so that the harbour on the lake was in fact richer than that on the sea". On the basis of this and a number of other accounts (Strabo 17.1.22), we have an impression of intense maritime traffic crossing the length and breadth of the lake carrying various products and cargoes to Alexandria. Merchandise which would have been transported to Alexandria for local consumption and for transhipment to other Mediterranean harbours, and would have included Egyptian products (Rickman 1971: 300-6; Rickman 1980: 231-5; Lewis 1983: 165-7; Peacock 1992: 5-7; Peacock 2002: 426-7), as well as products imported via the Red Sea from India, Arabia and East Africa (Strabo 2.5.12; Casson 1991: 200-12; Peacock 2002: 432-3). At the same time, Alexandria was receiving a variety of imports from the Mediterranean, for local consumption and for transhipment south. Yet, as noted, the role that Lake Mareotis played in this internal transport system has traditionally been somewhat unclear and there is still a considerable degree of ambiguity concerning the exact number, location and the routes of the numerous canals that served the lake and the nature of the transportation systems that operated across its waters.

The most important canal was the Schedia Canal (see Chapter 2.3.5). Schedia was, particularly during the Ptolemaic period, the main Nile emporium, customs harbour and checkpoint east of Alexandria, where custom duties were imposed on imported and exported goods (Empereur 1998a: 225; Bergmann & Heinzelmann 2003). As it approached Alexandria, the Schedia Canal bifurcated into two branches in the Alexandrian suburb of Eleusis (El-Nozha). The southerly branch continued parallel to the lake's northern shore, until it debouched into Lake Mareotis southeast of Alexandria, close to the eastern or Canopic Gate of Alexandria (Strabo 17.1.16). According to Strabo (17.1.7), boats also sailed from the Nile to the Canopic Branch and through the network of canals that fed Lake Mareotis from the south and east, then across the lake northwards to Alexandria. This indicates that navigation on Lake Mareotis was intense and multi-directional. It also raises a point about the practicalities of sailing in Lake Mareotis, particularly from south to north against prevailing winds.

The predominant winds along the north coast of Egypt are north-westerly and they prevail more than 40% of the time throughout the year and more than 70% of the time during the summer sailing season (El-Zouka 1979: 125-7; El-Gindy 1999: 17). Thus, merchant vessels sailing in Lake Mareotis from south to north would have faced a direct headwind, which meant that the boats had to tack in order to reach Alexandria. Tacking in Lake Mareotis was possible considering the large area of the water body; however, tacking from the southern limits of the lake to Alexandria would have meant that boats would have to travel several times the direct distance across a water body full of shallows and marshlands and against prevailing winds. There is no doubt that it would have been less challenging in the flood season when the lake waters would have been both vertically and laterally more extensive, however, the prevailing winds were inevitably a critical factor that impacted on the speed of the crossing. In the 5th century St. Palladius (7.1) mentioned that he sailed across Lake Mareotis from north to south, from Alexandria to the monastic settlement of Mount Nitria, a distance of about 50km, in a day and a half. However, sailing across the lake in the opposite direction would have taken much longer, possibly as long as four to five days.

Such an extended period of travel across the lake would have laid boats vulnerable to another challenge that prevailed on Lake Mareotis in antiquity. Achilles Tatius (4.12) in the 2nd century and Heliodorus (1:14) in the 3rd century spoke of piracy and bandits on Lake Mareotis. The marshes and islands of the lake provided excellent hideouts for groups of bandits and their vessels. Also, the large size of the lake made it quite difficult to guard and control, therefore, it is possible that sailing across the lake with valuable commodities potentially incurred considerable risk.

Moreover, settlements located on the southern and eastern shores of Lake Mareotis were far more susceptible to sedimentation from silts deposited via the nearby Canopic Branch of the Nile, particularly during the flood season, as well as sediment which had been carried by the prevailing winds across the lake from the N-W to the S-E. The build-up of sediments and thus the unstable nature of the southern and eastern shores of the lake, would have made them unsuitable for the construction of substantial waterfront structures. Whilst southern and eastern shore settlements were undoubtedly actively engaged in agricultural and industrial production mainly in the service of Alexandria, it could be suggested that the more stable western Mareotic Arm was more proactive in supplying and supporting the waterborne transportation of goods across the lake. This hypothesis is partially supported by the numerous waterfront facilities recorded in this region as part of the Lake Mareotis Research Project (see Chapter 6 and Chapter 7.2). To date no waterfront installations have been noted in the Western Delta Survey (Wilson 2007, 2010; Wilson & Grigoropolous 2009; see Chapter 2), perhaps having been long abandoned, silted beneath the southern and eastern shores of the lake.

There were two ways for river vessels to travel to and from Alexandria, either across the lake, or along the Canopic Branch of the Nile via the Schedia Canal. Considering the arguments outlined above, particularly in relation to prevailing winds, it seems reasonable to suggest that the majority of north-bound traffic probably went via the Canopic Branch and the Schedia Canal, rather than across the lake. Sailing south across the lake could have been conducted with greater ease. Along those stretches of the canal where boats had to manoeuvre against the wind, they could have been towed along from the shore, a standard procedure for moving boats in rivers and canals.

Thus, Strabo's statement (17.1.7) about the lake harbour south of Alexandria, being richer than the seaport of Alexandria is verified. At the time of Strabo, the Schedia Canal debouched into Lake Mareotis, so all the canal traffic had to pass through the lake. Moreover, boats coming from the western arm of the lake also arrived at the lake harbour. Therefore, it is possible that the lake harbour was in fact very busy receiving and dispatching river vessels from the Nile as well as from the western arm of the lake. Likewise, it is not unreasonable to suggest that E-W commercial traffic along the western Mareotic Arm was probably more intense and more regular than the N-S traffic that passed through the main body of the lake. Archaeological investigation in the Mareotic region has revealed that the number, nature and extent of archaeological sites along the shores of the Mareotic Arm are significant when compared to anywhere else in the Western Deltaic region (Blue & Ramses 2005; Blue 2010a, 2010b; Wilson 2007, 2010). This is not surprising considering that settlements in this region were located far from the silting effects of Nile sediments, the coastline was more stable, prevailing winds were more favourable for E-W movement, and settlements were in close proximity to Alexandria. Thus, the contribution of the western Mareotic Arm to the economy of ancient Alexandria and hence of Egypt as a whole, was probably far more significant than previously suspected; in fact it would appear that this was one of the most active areas of economic activity in the Lake Mareotis region during the Hellenistic, Roman and Byzantine eras.

7.8 In conclusion

Despite being essentially a survey project with very limited excavation, the research conducted along the western arm of Lake Mareotis by the Lake Mareotis Research Project clearly makes a significant contribution to our understanding of the archaeology of the region. However, it also reminds us how thin the archaeological record still is and how little we still know, and yet how very important it is, particularly in an area where textual evidence is limited. The work substantiates the rural character of this region, with its food production and processing installations, kiln sites producing amphorae from local clay, and numerous storage facilities. But it still leaves open questions relating to population density, and whether or not sites were continuously occupied. The relationships between sites, between the smaller sites and the apparently more important settlement complexes such as Marea, Taposiris Magna and Abu Mena, are still open to debate. Questions such as, which were the main administrative units, where they all part of the same administrative units, and what was their relative contribution to the economy of the region, have yet to be answered. Lake Mareotis, and the western arm in particular, was clearly instrumental in transporting goods across the lake, and yet, we still have very limited insight into exactly how goods were transported, within what transportation systems, along what supply lines, and to where.

Despite these uncertainties, a number of observations regarding the Lake Mareotis region in antiquity emerge. Alexandria was neither an agricultural nor an industrial city; its economy was primarily based on commerce, administration and the services that the city and its harbours provided for internal and overseas transport (Lukaszewicz 1998: 109). However, it is increasingly evident that the Mareotic region in general and the western Mareotic Arm in particular, played a critical role in the economy of ancient Alexandria. Commercial activities in Alexandria were directly related to agricultural and industrial activities that took place around the shores of Lake Mareotis. The continuous supply of staples, raw materials and manufactured products from the Mareotic region to Alexandria was thus vital for the survival of the city itself, as well as for its commercial role as an entrepôt of trade for the Hellenistic and Roman world (Bowman & Rathbone 1992: 125).

Bibliography

Abd El-Fattah, A. 1998. Recent Discoveries in Alexandria and the Chora. In J.-Y. Empereur (ed.), *Commerce et Artisanat dans l'Alexandrie Hellénistique et Romaine.* Bulletin de Correspondance Hellénique, Supplément 33: 37-53.

Administration égyptienne de topographie. 1931. *Description des repères de niveau de l'ouest Delta (ouest de la Branche Rosette), département de Behera – Province de Mariout,* 1.1 (Cairo: Ministère des Finances).

Akamatis, I. 2000. *Ενσφράγιστες αμφορέων Πέλλας, Ανασκαφή 1980-1987. Πι ομάδες Παρμενίσκυ και Ρόδου* [*Stamped Amphora Handles from theAgora at Pella. Excavations 1980-1987. Groups of Parmeniskos and Rhodes*] (Athens: ΒΙΒΛΙΟΘΗΚΗ ΕΝ ΑΘΗΝΑΙΣ ΑΡΧΑΙΟΛΟΓΙΚΗΣ ΕΤΑΙΡΕΙΑΣ).

ALAMIM project. 2007. *Alexandria Lake Maryut Integrated Management, Alexandria, Egypt.* Stocktaking analysis (a), background material, third draft, workshop report (Alexandria) (http://www.medcities.org/docs/1-ALAMIMproject2date-Maha.pdf; Accessed 14.08.2011).

Arthur, P. & Williams, D. 1992. Campanian wine, Roman Britain and the third century A.D. *The Journal of Roman Archaeology* 5: 250-260.

El-Ashmawi, F. 1998. Pottery Kiln and Wine Factory at Burg El-Arab. In J.-Y. Empereur (ed.), *Commerce et Artisanat dans l'Alexandrie Hellénistique et Romaine.* Bulletin de Correspondance Hellénique, Supplément 33: 55-64.

El-Asmar, H.M. 1994. Aeolianite sedimentation along the northwestern coast of Egypt: evidence for middle to late quaternary aridity. *Quaternary Science Reviews* 16: 699-708.

El-Asmar, H.M. & Wood, P. 2000. Quaternary shoreline development: the northwestern coast of Egypt. *Quaternary Science Reviews* 19: 1137-1149.

Awad, I. 2009. Lac Mariout: L'eau dans tous ses états car tographiques. In I. Hairy (ed.), *Du Nil à Alexandrie: Histoire d'eaux* (Alexandria: Éditions Harpocrates): 190-205.

Babraj, K. & Szymańska, H. 2010. Marea or Philoxenite? Polish Excavations in the Mareotic Region 2000-2007. In L. Blue (ed.), *Lake Mareotis: Reconstructing the Past. Proceedings of the International Conference on the Archaeology of the Mareotic Region Held at Alexandria University, Egypt, 5th-6th April 2008* (Oxford: BAR Publishing): 75-85.

Bagnall, R. 1993. *Egypt in Late Antiquity* (Princeton, N.J.: Princeton University Press).

Bailey, D.M. 1975. *A Catalogue of the Lamps in the British Museum.* 1: *Greek, Hellenistic and Early Roman Pottery Lamps* (London: British Museum).

Bailey, D.M. 1980. *A Catalogue of the Lamps in the British Museum.* 2: *Roman Lamps made in Italy* (London: British Museum).

Bailey, D.M. 1998. *British Museum Expedition to Middle Egypt. Excavations at el-Ashmunein, V. Pottery, Lamps and Glass of the Late Roman and Early Arab Periods* (London: British Museum).

Ballet, P. 1997. Péluse. Le théâtre romain. *Cahiers de la Céramique Égyptienne* 5: 109-121.

Ballet, P. 2003. La céramique, contextes et classification. In P. Ballet, N. Bosson & M. Rassart-Debergh, *Kellia* II. *L'hermitage copte QR 195. 2. Céramique, inscriptions, décors* (Cairo: Institut Français d'Archéologie Orientale): 3-207.

Ballet, P. 2007. Un atelier d'amphores LRA 5/6 à pâte alluviale dans le Delta occidental. Kom Abou Billou/Térénouthis. In S. Marchand & A. Marangou (eds.), *Amphores d'Egypte de la basse époque à l'époque Arabe,* I (*Cahiers de la Céramique Égyptienne* 8): 157-160.

Ballet, P. & Picon, M. 1987. Recherches préliminaires sur les origines de la céramique des Kellia (Egypte). Importations et productions égyptiennes. *Cahiers de la Céramique Égyptienne* 1: 17-48.

Bergmann, M. & Heinzelmann, M. 2003. *Schedia (Kom El-Giza and Kom El-Hamam, Department of Beheira): Report on the Documentation and Excavation Season 18th March-18th April 2003* (http//www.schedia.de/schedia_2003.pdf; Accessed 14.08.2011).

Bergmann, M. & Heinzelmann, M. 2004. *Schedia, Alexandria's Harbour on the Canopic Nile (Kom El-Giza/ Department of Beheira). Preliminary Report on the Second Season 2004* (http//www.schedia.de/schedia_ 2004.pdf; Accessed 14.08.2011).

Bergmann, M. & Heinzelmann, M. 2005. *Schedia, Alexandria's harbour on the Canopic Nile. Interim report on a German mission at Kom el Gizah / Beheira (2003-2005)* (http//www.schedia.de/schedia_2003_2005.pdf; Accessed 14.08.2011).

Bergmann, M., Heinzelmann, M. & Martin, A. 2010. Schedia, Alexandria's Harbour on the Canopic Nile. Interim Report on the German Mission at Kom el Giza/Beheira (2003-2008). In L. Blue (ed.), *Lake Mareotis: Reconstructing the Past. Proceedings of the International Conference on the Archaeology of the Mareotic Region Held at Alexandria University, Egypt, 5th-6th April 2008* (Oxford: BAR Publishing): 107-117.

Bernasconi, M.P, Stanley, D.J & Di Geronimo, I. 1991. Molluscan faunas and paleobathymetry of Holocene sequences in the northeastern Nile delta, Egypt. *Marine Geology* 99: 29-43.

Bezeczky, T. 2005. Late Roman amphorae from the Tetragonos-Agora in Ephesus. In S. Ladstätter & A. Hofeneder (eds.), *Spätantike und mittelalterliche Keramik aus Ephesos*. Archäologische Forschungen 13 (Wein: Verlag der Österreichischen Akademie der Wissenschaften): 203-247.

Blue, L. 2010a. Lake Mareotis Research Project. In L. Blue (ed.), *Lake Mareotis: Reconstructing the Past. Proceedings of the International Conference on the Archaeology of the Mareotic Region Held at Alexandria University, Egypt 5th-6th April 2008* (Oxford: BAR Publishing): 25-33.

Blue, L. (ed.) 2010b. *Lake Mareotis: Reconstructing the Past. Proceedings of the International Conference on the Archaeology of the Mareotic Region Held at Alexandria University, Egypt 5th-6th April 2008* (Oxford: BAR Publishing).

Blue, L. & Ramses, S. 2005. *Lake Mareotis Research Project*. Unpublished Survey Report, University of Southampton, Southampton.

Bonifay, M. 2004. *Études sur la céramique romaine tardive d'Afrique* (Oxford: BAR Publishing).

Bonvallot, J. 1986. Tabias et Jessour du sud Tunisien. Agriculture dans les zones marginales et parade à l'érosion. *Cahiers Orstom Pédol* 22.2: 163-172.

Börker, Chr. & Burow, J. 1998. *Die hellenistischen Amphorenstempel aus Pergamon* (Berlin, New York: Walter de Gruyter).

Boussac, M.-F. & El Amouri, A. 2010. The Lake Structures at Taposiris. In L. Blue (ed.), *Lake Mareotis: Reconstructing the Past. Proceedings of the International Conference on the Archaeology of the Mareotic Region Held at Alexandria University, Egypt, 5th-6th April 2008* (Oxford: BAR Publishing): 87-105.

Bowman, A. & Rathbone, D. 1992. Cities and Administration in Roman Egypt. *The Journal of Roman Studies* 82: 107-127.

Buchi, E. 1973. Banchi di anfore romane a Verona. Note sui commerci cisalpini. *Il Territorio veronese in età romana. Atti del convegno tenuto a Verona, 22-24 ott. 1971* (Verona: Accademia di agricoltura, scienze e lettrere di Verona): 531-637.

Butzer, K.W. 1962. Pleistocene stratigraphy and prehistory in Egypt. *Quaternaria* 6: 451-477.

Casson, L. 1991. *The Ancient Mariners* (Princeton, N.J.: Princeton University Press).

Charvet, P. (trans.) 1997. *Strabon, le voyage en Egypte, un regard romain* (Paris: Nil éditions).

Chen, Z., Warne, A.G. & Stanley, J.D. 1992. Late quaternary evolution of the northwestern Nile Delta between the Rosetta promontory and Alexandria, Egypt. *Journal of Coastal Research* 8.3: 527-561.

De Cosson, A. 1935. *Mareotis, being a short account of the history and ancient monuments of the north-western desert of Egypt and of lake Mareotis* (London: Country Life Ltd.).

Demesticha, S. & Michaelides, D. 2001. The excavation of a Late Roman 1 amphora kiln in Paphos. In E. Villeneuve & P.M. Watson (eds.), *La céramique byzantine et proto-Islamic en Syrie-Jordanie (IVe – VIIIe siècles apr. J.C.) Actes du colloque tenu à Amman les 3, 4 et 5 décembre 1994* (Beyrouth: IFAPO): 289-296.

Dzierzbicka, D. 2005. Wineries in Graeco-Roman Egypt. *Journal of Juristic Papyrology* 35: 9-89.

Dzierzbicka, D. 2010. Wineries of the Mareotic Region. In L. Blue (ed.), *Lake Mareotis: Reconstructing the Past. Proceedings of the International Conference on the Archaeology of the Mareotic Region Held at Alexandria University, Egypt, 5th-6th April 2008* (Oxford: BAR Publishing): 127-133.

Egloff, M. 1977. *Kellia: La poterie copte. Quatre siècles d'artisanat et d'échanges en Basse-Egypte*. Recherches suisses d'archéologie copte 3 (Geneva: Georg, Librairie de l'Université).

Élaigne, S. 1998. Alexandrie – Etude préliminaire d'un contexte céramique du Haut-Empire. *Etudes alexandrines* 1: 75-113.

Élaigne, S. 2000a. Fine ware from late Hellenistic (second half of the first century BC), Augustan and Tiberian deposits of the French excavations in Alexandria (Egypt). *RCRF Acta* 36: 19-30.

Élaigne, S. 2000b. Imitations locales de céramiques fines importées: le cas des *colour-coated ware* dans les contexts hellénistiques d'Alexandrie. *Cahiers de la Céramique Égyptienne* 6: 99-112.

Empereur, J.-Y. 1986. Un atelier de Dressel 2-4 en Egypte au IIIe siècle de notre ère. In J.-Y. Empereur & Y. Garlan (eds.), *Recherches sur les amphores grecques.* Bulletin de Correspondance Hellénique, Supplément 13: 599-608.

Empereur, J.-Y. 1993. La Production Viticole dans l'Égypte Ptolémaïque et Romaine. In M.C. Amouretti & J.P. Brun (eds.), *La production du vin et de l'huile en Méediterranée.* Bulletin de Correspondance Hellénique, Supplément 26: 39-47.

Empereur, J.-Y. 1998a. *Alexandria Rediscovered* (New York, Paris: George Braziller).

Empereur, J.-Y. 1998b. Les Amphores Complètes du Musée d'Alexandrie: Importations et Productions Locales. In J.-Y. Empereur (ed.), *Commerce et Artisanat dans l'Alexandrie Hellénistique et Romaine.* Bulletin de Correspondance Hellénique, Supplément 33: 393-399.

Empereur, J.-Y. (ed.) 1998c. *Commerce et Artisanat dans l'Alexandrie Hellénistique et Romaine.* Bulletin de Correspondance Hellénique, Supplément 33.

Empereur, J.-Y. 2002. *Alexandria: Past, Present and Future* (London: Thames & Hudson).

Empereur, J.-Y. (ed.) 2006. *Description de l'Égypte Coll. les grandes expéditions scientifiques du 19e siècle*, I (Paris: Éditions Harpocrate [DVD]).

Empereur, J.-Y. & Picon, M. 1986. Á la recherche des fours d'amphores. In J-Y. Empereur & Y. Garlan (eds.), *Recherches sur les amphores grecques.* Bulletin de Correspondance Hellénique, Supplément 13: 103-126.

Empereur, J.-Y. & Picon, M. 1989. Les régions de production d'amphores Impériales en Méditerranée orientale. *Amphores Romaines et Histoire Économique: Dix Ans de Recherche.* Collection de l'École français de Rome 114 (Rome: L'École français de Rome): 223-248.

Empereur, J.-Y. & Picon, M. 1992. La reconnaissance des productions des ateliers céramiques: l'exemple de la Maréotide. *Ateliers de potiers: productions céramiques en Égypte (Cahiers de la Céramique Égyptienne* 3): 145-152.

Empereur, J.-Y. & Picon, M. 1998. Les Atelier d'Amphores du Lac Mariout. In J.-Y. Empereur (ed.), *Commerce et Artisanat dans l'Alexandrie Hellénistique et Romaine.* Bulletin de Correspondance Hellénique, Supplément 33: 75-91.

Engemann, J. 1992. A propos des amphores d'Abou Mina. *Ateliers de potiers: productions céramiques en Égypte (Cahiers de la Céramique Égyptienne* 3): 153-159.

Ettlinger, E., Hedinger, B., Hoffmann, B., Kenrick, P.M., Pucci, G., Roth-Rubi, K., Schneider, G., Von Schnurbein, S., Wells, C.M. & Zabehlicky-Scheffenegger, S. 1990. *Conspectus formarum terrae sigillatae Italico modo confectae* (Bonn: Dr. Rudolf Habelt GMBH).

El-Fakharani, F. 1974. The Lighthouse of Abusir in Egypt. *Harvard Studies in Classical Philology* 78: 257-272.

El-Fakharani, F. 1983. Recent Excavations at Marea in Egypt. *Das Römisch-Byzantinische Ägypten* II. *Aegyptiaca Treverensia: Trierer Studien zum griechisch-römischen Ägypten* (Mainz: Verlag Philipp Von Zebren): 175-186.

El-Fakharani, F. 1984. The Kibotos of Alexandria. In S. Stucchi & M. Aravantinos (eds.), *Giornate di Studio in Onore di Achille Adriani* (*Studi Miscellanei* 28): 23-28.

Al-Falaki, M.S. (trans.) 1966. رسالة عن الإسكندرية القديمة M.B. Astronome, *Mémoire sur l'antique Alexandrie,* 1872] (Alexandria: Dar Nashr Al-Thaquafa).

Finkielsztejn, G. 2001. *Chronologie détaillée et révisée des éponymes amphoriques rhodiens, de 270 à 108 av. J.-C. environ. Premier bilan* (Oxford: BAR Publishing).

Flaux, C. forthcoming. *Geomorphological investigations in Maryut Lake, north-west Nile delta. Enviromental evolution and interactions with land occupation since 8000 years.* PhD thesis, Aix-Marseille I University, CEREGE (UMR 6635) & CEAlex (USR 3134).

Flaux, C., Morhange, C., Marriner, N. & Rouchy, J-M. in press. Bilan hydrologique et biosédimentaire de la lagune du Maryût (delta du Nil, Egypte) entre 8000 et 3200 ans cal. B.P. *Géomorphologie, relief, processus et environnement.*

Fraser, P.M. 1972. *Ptolemaic Alexandria* (Oxford: Clarendon Press).

Frihy, O.E. 1996. Some Proposals for Coastal Management of the Nile Delta Coast. *Ocean and Coastal Management* 30.1: 43-59.

Frihy, O.E., Dewidar, Kh.M. & El-Raey, M.M. 1996. Evaluation of Coastal Problems at Alexandria, Egypt. *Ocean and Coastal Management* 30.2-3: 281-295.

Gabel, C. & Petruso, K. 1980. *An Environmental and Cultural Study at Lake Maryut, Lower Egypt.* African Studies Center Working Papers No. 25. Boston University, Massachusetts.

Gempeler, R.D., 1992. *Elephantine* X. *Die Keramik römischer bis früharabischer zeit.* Archäologische Veröffentliclhlungen 43 (Cairo: Deutsches Archäologisches Institut Abteilung).

El-Gindy, A. 1999. Meteorological and Hydrodynamic Conditions in the Eastern Harbour of Alexandria and its Vicinity. In Y. Halim (ed.), *Proceedings of the Workshop on the Status of Pilot Project for the Sustainable Development of the Submarine Archaeological Sites at Qayetbey Citadel and Eastern Harbour of Alexandria, 20-21 November 1999.* Reports on Hydrodynamics, Geophysics, Morphology and Geology II (Alexandria): 1-82.

Goddio, F., Bernand, A., Bernand, E., Darwish, I., Dunand, F., de Graaw, A., Kiss, Z. & Yoyotte, J. 1998 (eds.), *Alexandria: The Submerged Royal Quarters* (London: Periplus).

Goiran, J.P., Marriner N., Morhange, C., Abd el-Maguib, M., Espic, K., Bourcier, M. & Carbonel, P. 2005. Evolution géomorphologique de la façade maritime d'Alexandrie (Egypte) au cours des six derniers millénaires. *Méditerranée* 1.2: 61-64.

Goodfriend, G.A. & Stanley, D.J. 1996. Reworking and discontinuities in Holocene sedimentation in the Nile Delta: documentation from amino acid racemization and stables isotopes in mollusks shells. *Marine Geology* 129: 271-283.

Gouda, G.H. 1994. جيومورفولوجية مصر [*Geomorphology of Egypt*]. In Y. Ibrahim & B. Ibrahim (eds.), جغرافية مصر. [*Geography of Egypt*] (Cairo: Hai'a Al Kitab): 45-90.

Grace, V.R. 1949. Standard pottery containers of the ancient Greek world. *Hesperia, Supplement* 8: 175-189.

Grace, V.R. 1953. The eponyms names on Rhodian amphora stamps. *Hesperia* 22: 116-128.

Grace, V.R. 1985. The middle stoa dated by amphora stamps. *Hesperia* 54: 1-54.

Guelorget, O. & Perthuisot, J.P. 1983. Le domaine paralique. Expressions géologiques, biologiques et économiques du confinement. *Travaux du laboratoire de Géologie, Ecole Normale Supérieure Paris* 16: 1-136.

Haas, C. 1997. *Alexandria in Late Antiquity: Topography and Social Conflict* (Baltimore: The John Hopkins University Press).

Haggag, M. 1984. *Ports in Ancient Egypt till the Arab Conquest.* MA thesis, Alexandria University.

Haggag, M. 2010a. Fawzi El-Fakharani: Pioneer Excavator at Mareotis. In L. Blue (ed.), *Lake Mareotis: Reconstructing the Past. Proceedings of the International Conference on the Archaeology of the Mareotic Region Held at Alexandria University, Egypt, 5th-6th April 2008* (Oxford: BAR Publishing): 1-2.

Haggag, M. 2010b. The City of Marea/Philoxenité. Reflections on the Alexandria University Excavations, 1977-1981. In L. Blue (ed.), *Lake Mareotis: Reconstructing the Past. Proceedings of the International Conference on the Archaeology of the Mareotic Region Held at Alexandria University, Egypt, 5th-6th April 2008* (Oxford: BAR Publishing): 47-56.

Hairy, I. & Sennoune, O. 2006. Géographie historique du canal d'Alexandrie. *Annales islamologiques* 40: 247-278.

Hamdan, G. 1980. شخصية مصر: دراسة في عبقرية المكان, I [*Egypt's Identity: A Study of the Genius of the Place*, I] (Cairo: Alam Al-Kutub).

Hassouba, A.M.H 1995. Quaternary sediments from the coastal plain of northwestern Egypt (from Alexandria to El Omayid). *Carbonates and Evaporites* 10.1: 8-44.

Hassouba, H. & Shaw, H.F. 1980. The occurrence of palygorskite in quaternary sediments of the coastal plain of north-west Egypt. *Clay Minerals* 15: 77.

Hayes, J.W. 1972. *Late Roman Pottery* (London: British School at Rome).

Hayes, J.W. 1985. Sigillate orientali. *Enciclopedia dell'Arte Antica, Atlante delle Forme Ceramiche* II, *Ceramica Fine Romana nel Bacino Mediterraneo (Taro Ellenismo e Primo Impero)* (Rome: Istituto della Enciclopedia Italiana): 1-96.

Hayes, J.W. & Harlaut, C. 2002. Ptolemaic and Roman pottery deposits from Alexandria. In J.-Y. Empereur (ed.), *Alexandrina* 2 (*Études alexandrines* 6) (Cairo: Institut Français d'Archéologie Orientale): 99-138.

Hein, A., Georgopoulou, V., Nodarou, E. & Kilikoglou, V. 2008. Koan amphorae from Halasarna – investigations in a Hellenistic amphora production centre. *Journal of Archaeological Science* 35: 1049-1061.

Heinzelmann, M. 2005. *Schedia, Alexandria's River Harbour on the Canopic Nile: Evidence from Geophysical and Archaeological Investigations 2003/2004.* Paper presented at the conference: 'City and Harbour: The Archaeology of Ancient Alexandria'. University of Oxford, St. Hugh's College, 18-19 December 2004.

Hopkinson, D.J. 2007. *An Assessment of Graeco-Roman Lakeside Agriculture and Trade in the Mareotic Region of Egypt.* MA thesis, University of Southampton.

Horden, P. & Purcell, N. 2002. *The Corrupting Sea* (Oxford: Blackwell).

Hume, W.F. & Hughes, F. 1921. *The soils and water supply of the Maryut district, west of Alexandria.* Egyptian Survey Dept. Pub. 37 (Cairo: Ministry of Finance).

Humphrey, J., Oleson, J. & Sherwood, A. 1999. *Greek and Roman Technology – A Sourcebook* (London: Routledge).

Jöhrens, G. 1999. *Amphorenstempel im Nationalmuseum von Athen zu den von H.G. Lolling aufgenommenen "unedierten Henkelinschriften."* (Mainz: Deutsches archälogisches Institut, Abteilung Athen).

Jöhrens, G. 2001. Amphorenstempel hellenistischer Zeit aus Tanais. *Eurasia Antiqua* 7: 367-479.

Jondet, G. 1921. *Atlas historique de la ville et des ports d'Alexandrie* (Cairo: Mèmoires Presentes a la Sociètè Sultanieh de Gèographie).

Kadous, E. 2001. آثار الإسكندرية القديمة [*Monuments of Ancient Alexandria*] (Alexandria: El-Hadary Press).

Karagiorgou, O. 2001. LR2: a Container for the Military Annona on the Danubian Border? In S. Kingsley & M. Decker (eds.), *Economy and Exchange in the East Mediterranean during Late Antiquity: Proceedings of a Conference at Somerville College, Oxford, 29th May, 1999* (Oxford: Oxbow): 129-166.

Keay, S.J. 1984. *Late Roman Amphorae in the Western Mediterranean. A Typology and Economic Study: the Catalan Evidence* (Oxford: BAR Publishing).

Keay, S.J. & Williams, D.F. 2005. *Amphora: a Digital Resource* (http://ads.ahds.ac.uk/catalogue/archive/amphora_ahrb_2005/; Accessed 27.02.2011).

Khalil, E.K.H. 2005. *Egypt and the Roman maritime trade: a focus on Alexandria.* PhD thesis, University of Southampton.

Koehler, C.G. 1979. *Corinthian A and B transport amphoras.* PhD thesis, Princeton University.

Kotb, T.H.S., Watanabe, T., Ogino, Y. & Tanji, K.K. 1999. Soil salinization in the Nile delta and related policy issues in Egypt. *Agricultural Water Management* 43: 329-261.

Lewis, N. 1983. *Life in Egypt under Roman Rule* (Oxford: Clarendon Press).

Lukaszewicz, A. 1998. Les Activités Commerciales et Artisanales dans Alexandrie Romaine à La Lumière des Papyrus. In J.-Y. Empereur (ed.), *Commerce et Artisanat dans l'Alexandrie Hellénistique et Romaine.* Bulletin de Correspondance Hellénique, Supplément 33: 107-133.

Majcherek, G. 1992. The late Roman ceramics from sector "G" (Alexandria 1986–1987). *Etudes et Travaux* 16: 82-117.

Majcherek, G., 1995. Gazan Amphorae: Typology Reconsidered. In H. Meyza & J. Młynarczyk (eds.), *Hellenistic and Roman Pottery in the Eastern Mediterranean – Advances in Scientific Studies. Acts of the II Nieborów Pottery Workshop* (Warsaw: Research Centre for Mediterranean Archaeology, Polish Academy of Sciences): 163-178.

Majcherek, G. 2004. Alexandria's long-distance trade in late Antiquity – the amphora evidence. In J. Eiring & J. Lund (eds.), *Transport Amphorae and Trade in the Eastern Mediterranean. Acts of the International Colloquium at the Danish Institute at Athens, September 26–29, 2002* (Athens: Monographs of the Danish Institute at Athens 5): 229-237.

Majcherek, G. & El-Shennawi, A. 1992. Research on amphora production on the northwestern Coast of Egypt. *Ateliers de potiers: productions céramiques en Égypte (Cahiers de la Céramique Égyptienne* 3): 129-136.

Manacorda, D. 2001. Le fornaci di Giancola (Brindisi): archeologia, epigrafia, archeometria. In F. Laubenheimer (ed.), *20 ans de recherches à Sallèles d'Aude* (Paris: Presses Universitaires Franc-Comtoises).

Martin, A. 2008. Pottery from Schedia near Alexandria (Egypt). *RCRF Acta* 40: 263-269.

McGovern, P.E. 2003. *Ancient Wine: The Search for the Origins of Viniculture* (Princeton, N.J.: Princeton University Press).

Meteorological Atlas of Egypt. 1931. Prepared by the Physical Department, Ministry of Public Works. Presented to the International Geographical Congress at Paris, 1931 by command of His Majesty King Fouad I (Giza: Survey of Egypt).

Meulien, C. 1999. *Le G.P.S au service de l'archéologie* (Paris: Travaux de fin d'étude, Ecole Supérieure des Géomètres et Topographes).

Meyza, H. 2007. *Cypriot Red Slip Ware: Studies on a Late Roman Levantine Fine Ware* (Warsaw: Centre d'Archéologie Méditerranéenne de l'Académie Polonaise des Sciences).

Monachov, S.Iu. 1999. K tipologii knidskikh amfor IV-II vv. do n.e. [Towards a typology of Knidian amphoras of 4th-2nd c BC]. *Боспорский феноменон: зреческая культура на периферий античнозо мира* [*The Bosporan phenomenon: Greek Culture on the Periphery of the Ancient World*] (St. Petersburg: Insti tute of the History of Material Culture of the Russian Academy of Sciences): 161-172. (http://www.chass.utoronto.ca/amphoras/trans/sym-t99.htm; Accessed 27.02.2011).

Monachov, S.Iu. 2005. Rhodian amphoras: developments in form and measurements. In V. Stolba & L. Hannestad (eds.), *Chronologies of the Black Sea area in the period c. 400–100 B.C.* Black Sea Studies 3 (Aarhus: Aarhus University Press): 69-95.

Morhange C., Laborel, J. & Hesnard, A. 2001. Changes of relative sea level during the past 5000 years in the ancient harbour of Marseilles, Southern France. *Palaeogeography, Palaeoclimatology, Palaeooecology* 166: 319-329.

Nenna, M.-D. & Seif el-din, M. 2000. *La vaiselle en faïence d'époque gréco-romaine.* Études alexandrines 4 (Cairo: Institut Français d'Archéologie Orientale).

Néret, G. 1997. *Description de l'Égypte* (Köln: Taschen).

Nicolaou, I. & Empereur, J.-Y. 1986. Amphores Rhodiennes de Musée de Nicosie. In J.-Y. Empereur & Y. Garlan (eds.), *Recherches sur les amphores grecques.* Bulletin de Correspondance Hellénique, Supplément 13: 515-533.

Nilsson, M.P. 1909. *Timbre amphoriques de Lindos* (Copenhagen: Exploration archéologique de Rhodes V).

Peacock, D. 1992. *Rome in the Desert: A Symbol of Power.* An Inaugural Lecture delivered at the University of Southampton.

Peacock, D. 2002. The Roman Period. In I. Shaw (ed.), *The Oxford History of Ancient Egypt* (Oxford: Oxford University Press): 422-445.

Peacock, D.P.S. & Williams, D.F. 1986. *Amphorae and the Roman Economy. An Introductory Guide* (New York, London: Longman).

Peacock, D.P.S. & Williams, D.F. 1991. *Amphorae and the Roman Economy* (New York, London: Longman).

Petruso, K. & Gabel, C. 1982. *Marea: A Byzantine Port in Northern Egypt.* African Studies Center Working Papers No. 62. Boston University, Massachusetts.

Pichot, V. 2010. Marea Peninsula: Occupation and Workshop Activities on the Shores of Lake Mariout in the Work of the Center d'Études Alexandrines (CEAlex, CNRS USR 3134). In L. Blue (ed.), *Lake Mareotis: Reconstructing the Past. Proceedings of the International Conference on the Archaeology of the Mareotic Region Held at Alexandria University, Egypt, 5th-6th April 2008* (Oxford: BAR Publishing): 57-66.

Plaziat, J.-C. & Younis, W.R. 2005. The modern environments of Molluscs in southern Mesopotamia, Iraq: A guide to paleogeographical reconstructions of Quaternary fluvial, palustrine and marine deposits. *Carnets de Géologie / Notebooks on Geology* - Article 2005/01 (CG2005_A01)(http://paleopolis.rediris.es/cg/CG2005_A01/CG2005_A01.pdf; Accessed 14.08.2011).

El-Raey, M., Nassr, S., Frihy, O., El Desouki, S. & Dewidar, Kh. 1995. Potential impact of accelerated sea-level rise on Alexandria Governorate, Egypt. *Journal of Coastal Research,* SI 14: 190-204.

Rathbone, D. 1991. *Economic Rationalism and Rural Society in Third Century A.D. Egypt* (Cambridge: Cambridge University Press).

Reinhardt, E.G, Stanley, D.J & Schwarcz, P. 2001. Human-induced desalinization of Manzala lagoon, Nile Delta, Egypt: evidence from isotopic analysis of benthic invertebrates. *Journal of Coastal Research* 17.2: 431-442.

Reynolds, P. 2003. Pottery and the economy in eighth century Beirut: an Umayyad assemblage from the Roman Imperial baths (BEY 045). *VIIe Congrès International sur la Céramique Médiévale en Méditerranée* (Athens: Minisère de al Culture Caisse des Recettes Archéologiques): 725-734.

Reynolds, P. 2005. Levantine amphorae from Cilicia to Gaza: a typology and analysis of regional production trends from the 1st to 6th centuries. In J.Mª. Gurt i Esparraguera, J. Buxeda i Garrigós & M.A. Cau Ontiveros (eds.), *LRCW I. Late Roman Coarse Wares, Cooking Wares and Amphorae in the Mediterranean. Archaeology and Archaeometry* (Oxford: BAR Publishing): 563-611.

Rickman, G. 1971. *Roman Granaries and Store Buildings* (Cambridge: Cambridge University Press).

Rickman, G. 1980. The Grain Trade under the Roman Empire. In J.H. D'Arms & E.C. Kopff (eds.), *The Seaborne Commerce of Ancient Rome: Studies in Archaeology and History*. Memoirs of the American A cademy in Rome 36 (Rome: American Academy in Rome): 261-275.

Riley, J.A. 1979. The coarse pottery from Benghazi. In J.A. Lloyd (ed.), *Sidi Khrebish Exavations, Benghazi (Berenice)*, II (Tripoli: Dept. of Antiquities, Ministry of Teaching and Education, People's Socialist Libyan Arab Jamahiriya): 91-497.

Rodziewicz, M. 1976. *Alexandrie*, I. *La céramique romain tardive d'Alexandrie* (Warsaw: Éditions Scientifique de Pologne).

Rodziewicz, M. 1983. Alexandria and District of Mareotis. *Graeco-Arabica* 2: 199-216.

Rodziewicz, M. 1984. *Alexandrie* III. *Les habitations romaines tardives d'Alexandrie á la lumiere des fouilles polonaise a Kom el-Dikka* (Warsaw: Éditions scientifiques de Pologne).

Rodziewicz, M., 1986. Mareotic incised pottery of Coptic period. In P. Bridell (ed.), *Le site monastique Copte des Kellia. Actes du Colloque de Genève 13 au 15 août 1984* (Geneva: Mission Suisse d'Archéologie Copte de l'Université de Genève): 311-322.

Rodziewicz, M. 1988. Remarks on the Domestic and Monastic Architecture in Alexandria and Surroundings. In E.C.M. van den Brink (ed.), *The Archaeology of the Nile Delta, Proceedings of the Seminar held in Cairo, 19-22 October 1986* (Amsterdam: Netherlands Institute of Archaeology and Arabic Studies in Cairo): 267-276.

Rodziewicz, M. 1990. Taenia and Mareotis: Archaeological Research West of Alexandria. *Acta of the First International Colloquium of the Egyptian Society of Greek and Roman Studies*, I (Cairo): 62-80.

Rodziewicz, M. 1995. Eco-Archaeology of Ancient Alexandria and Mareotis. In A.A. Hussein, M. Miele & S. Riad (eds.), *Proceedings of the Egyptian-Italian Seminar on Geosciences and Archaeology in Mediterranean Countries, Cairo, November 28-30, 1993* (Cairo: The Geological Survey of Egypt): 127-139.

Rodziewicz, M. 1998a. From Alexandria to the West by Land and by Waterways. In J.-Y. Empereur (ed.), *Commerce et Artisanat dans l'Alexandrie Hellénistique et Romaine*. Bulletin de Correspondance Hellénique, Supplément 33: 93-103.

Rodziewicz, M. 1998b. Classification of Wineries from Mareotis. In J.-Y. Empereur (ed.), *Commerce et Artisanat dans l'Alexandrie Hellénistique et Romaine.* Bulletin de Correspondance Hellénique, Supplément 33: 27-36.

Rodziewicz, M. 1998c. Experimental identification of local and imported pottery from Mareotis. In J.-Y. Empereur (ed.), *Commerce et Artisanat dans l'Alexandrie Hellénistique et Romaine*. Bulletin de Correspondance Hellénique, Supplément 33: 245-260.

Rodziewicz, M. 2002. Mareotic Harbours. In C. Décobert (ed.), *Alexandrie Médiévale* 2. Études Alexandrines 8 (Cairo: Institut Français d'Archéologie Orientale): 1-22.

Rodziewicz, M. 2003. Philoxenité, Pilgrimage Harbour of Abu Mina. *Bulletin de la Société Archéologique d'Alexandrie* 47: 27-47.

Rodziewicz, M.D. 2010. On Interpretations of Archaeological Evidence Concerning Marea and Philoxenite. In L. Blue (ed.), *Lake Mareotis: Reconstructing the Past. Proceedings of the International Conference on the Archaeology of the Mareotic Region Held at Alexandria University, Egypt, 5th-6th April 2008* (Oxford: BAR Publishing): 67-74.

Said, R. 1981. *The Geological Evolution of the River Nile* (New York: Springer-Verlag).

Said, R. 1990. Quaternary. In R. Said (ed.), *The Geology of Egypt* (Rotterdam: A.A. Balkema): 487-507.

Said, R. 1993. نهر النيل ، نشأته واستخدم مياهه في الماضي والمستقبل *[The River Nile: Its Origin and Utilization in the Past and Future]* (Cairo: Dar Al-Helal).

Said, R. 2002. Did Nile Flooding Sink Two Ancient Cities? *Nature* 415: 37-38.

SCA GIS Unit & CULTNAT. 2002. *Archaeological Geographical Information System Project: No.4. The Rest of Lower Egypt Governorates* (Cairo: CULTNAT Press).

El-Sayed, M.K. & Khadr, A. 1999. Report on Geological Aspects of the Eastern Harbour and its Surroundings. In Y. Halim (ed.), *Proceedings of the Workshop on the Status of Pilot Project for the Sustainable Development of the Submarine Archaeological Sites at Qayet bey Citadel and Eastern Harbour of Alexandria, 20-21 November 1999*. Reports on Hydrodynamics, Geophysics, Morphology and Geology II (Alexandria): 191-251.

Schiettecatte, W., Ouessar, M., Gabriels, D., Tanghe, S., Heirman, S. & Abdelli, F. 2005. Impact of water harvesting techniques on soil and water conservation: a case study on a micro catchment in southeastern Tunisia. *Journal of Arid Environments* 61: 291-313.

Sciallano, M. & Sibella, P. 1994. *Amphores, comment les identifier?* (Edisud: Aix-en-Provence).

Sennoune, O. 2008. *Alexandrie et les récits de voyageurs du VIème siècle à 1798*. PhD thesis, Université Lumière Lyon 2.

Senol, A.K. 2007. A statistical essay on the distribution of imported amphora finds of the CEAlex salvage excavations. In S. Marchand & A. Marangou (eds.), *Amphores d'Egypte de la basse époque à l'époque Arabe,* I (*Cahiers de la Céramique Égyptienne* 8): 57-75.

Shahin, A.A. 1965. ملاحظات علي جيومورفولوجية المنطقة الشرقية من إقليم مريوط [Remarks on the Geomorphology of the Eastern Area of the Mariut Region]. *Bulletin of the Faculty of Arts* 19: 193-214.

Al-Shayeb, Z. (trans.) 2002. وصف مصر (الجزء الثالث): دراسة للمدن والأقاليم المصرية. *Description of Egypt III: A Study of the Egyptian Towns and Regions*] (Cairo: Institut d'Égypte).

Sivan, D., Wdowinski, S., Lambeck, K., Galili, E. & Raban, A. 2001. Holocene sea-level changes along the Mediterranean coast of Israel, based on archaeological observations and numerical model. *Palaeogeography, Palaeoclimatology, Palaeoecology* 167: 101-117.

Snape, S. 1997. Pelusium (South). *Cahiers de la Céramique Égyptienne* 5: 103-108.

Stanley, J.D. 2005a. Growth faults, a distinct carbonate-siliciclastic interface and recent coastal evolution, NW Nile Delta, Egypt. *Journal of Coastal Research*, SI 42: 309-318.

Stanley, J.D. 2005b. Submergence and burial of ancient coastal sites on the subsiding Nile delta margin, Egypt. *Méditerranée* 1.2: 65-73.

Stanley, J.D. & Toscano, M.A. 2009. Ancient archaeological sites buried and submerged along Egypt's Nile delta coast: gauges of Holocene delta margin subsidence. *Journal of Coastal Research* 25.1: 158-170.

Stanley, J.D. & Warne, A.G. 1993. Nile delta: recent geological evolution and human impact. *Science* 260: 630-634.

Starr, C.G. 1941. The Roman Imperial Navy 31 B.C. – A.D. 324 (New York: Cornell University Press).

Szentléleky, T. 1969. *Ancient Lamps* (Amsterdam: Adolf M. Hakkert).

Sztetyllo, Z. 1991. *Nea Paphos IV: Pottery Stamps (1975-1989)* (Warsaw: Centre d'Archéologie Méditerranéenne de l'Académie Polonaise des Sciences et Centre Kazimierz Michałowski d'Archéologie Méditerranéenne de l'Université de Varsovie).

Szymańska, H. & Babraj, K. 2008. *Marea* V.1: *Byzantine Marea – Excavations in 2000-2003 and 2006* (Krakow: Muzeum Archeologiczne W Krakowie).

Tomber, R. 2006. The pottery. In D.P.S. Peacock & V.A. Maxfield (eds.), *Mons Claudianus survey and excavation,* III: *Ceramic vessels and related objects* (Cairo: Institut Français d'Archéologie Orientale): 3-238.

Tomber, R. 2007. Early Roman Egyptian amphorae from the Eastern Desert of Egypt: a chronological sequence. In S. Marchand & A. Marangou (eds.), *Amphores d'Egypte de la basse époque à l'époque Arabe,* II (*Cahiers de la Céramique Égyptienne* 8): 525-536.

Tomber, R. 2009. Imitation and diffusion: the case of Dressel 30 in Egypt. In J.H. Humphrey (ed.), *Studies on Roman Pottery of the Provinces of Africa Proconsularis and Byzacena (Tunisia). Hommage à Michel Bonifay.* Journal of Roman Archaeology, Supplement 76: 151-156.

Touchart, L. 2000. *Les lacs, origine et morphologie* (Paris: Harmattan).

Vörös, G. 2001. *Taposiris Magna: Port of Isis* (Budapest: Egypt Excavation Society).

Warne, A.G. & Stanley, D.J. 1993. Late Quaternary Evolution of the Northwest Nile Delta and Adjacent Coast in the Alexandria Region, Egypt. *Journal of Coastal Research* 9.1: 26-64.

Weheba, A.M. 1989. الجغرافيا التاريخية [*Historical Geography*] (Alexandria: Monshaa Al- Macaref).

Wendrich, W., Tomber, R., Sidebotham, S., Harrell, J., Cappers, R. & Bagnall, R. 2003. Berenike Crossroads: The Integration of Information. *Journal of Economic and Social History of the Orient* 46.1: 46-87.

Whitbread, I.K. 1995. *Greek Transport Amphorae: a Petrological and Archaeological Study* (London: British School at Athens).

Will, E.L. 1987. The Roman amphoras. In M.A. McCann, J. Bourgeois, E.K. Gazda, J.P. Oleson & E.L. Will, *The Roman Port and Fishery of Cosa: A Center of Ancient Trade* (Princeton, N.J.: Princeton University Press): 171-220.

Williams, D.F. 2005. An integrated archaeometric approach to ceramic fabric recognition: a study case on late Roman Amphora 1 from the eastern Mediterranean. In J.Mª. Gurt i Esparraguera, J. Buxeda i Garrigós & M.A. Cau Ontiveros (eds.), *LRCW I. Late Roman Coarse Wares, Cooking Wares and Amphorae in the Mediterranean. Archaeology and Archaeometry* (Oxford: BAR Publishing): 613-624.

Wilson, P. 2007. *Western Delta Regional Survey, Abu Matamir*. (http://www/dur.ac.uk/penelope.wilson/Delta/Abu-Matamir.html; Accessed 14.08.2011).

Wilson, P. 2010. Recent Survey Work in the Southern Mareotis Area. In L. Blue (ed.), *Lake Mareotis: Reconstructing the Past. Proceedings of the International Conference on the Archaeology of the Mareotic Region Held at Alexandria University, Egypt, 5th-6th April 2008* (Oxford: BAR Publishing): 119-125.

Wilson, P. & Grigoropolous, D. 2009. *The West Nile Delta Regional Survey, Beheira and Kafresh-Sheikh Provinces*. D.M. Bailey, J.R. Dickinson & A.J. Spencer (eds.), Excavation Memoir 86 (London: Egypt Exploration Society).

Wilson, R.J.A. 1990. *Sicily under the Roman Empire: the archaeology of a Roman Province, 36BC – AD 535* (Warminster: Aris & Phillips).

De Wit, H.E. 1993. The evolution of the early Nile delta as a factor in the development of human culture. In L. Krzyzaniak, M. Kobusiewicz & J. Alexander (eds.), *Environmental Change and Human Culture in the Nile Basin and Northern Africa until the Second Millenium B.C.* Studies in African Archaeology 4 (Poznan: Poznan Archaeological Museum): 305-320.

El-Zouka, M.K. 1979.:مناطق الاستصلاح الزراعي في غرب دلتا النيل دراسة جغرافية [*Irrigation Areas in the Western Delta: A Geographical Study*] (Alexandria: Dar Al-Gameat Al- Mesria).

www.ingramcontent.com/pod-product-compliance
Ingram Content Group UK Ltd.
Pitfield, Milton Keynes, MK11 3LW, UK
UKHW061845041026
15591UKWH00015B/913

9 781407 308623